# Revolutionaries for the Right

**The New Cold War History**
Odd Arne Westad, editor

This series focuses on new interpretations of the Cold War era made possible by the opening of Soviet, East European, Chinese, and other archives. Books in the series based on multilingual and multiarchival research incorporate interdisciplinary insights and new conceptual frameworks that place historical scholarship in a broad, international context.

A complete list of books published in The New Cold War History is available at www.uncpress.unc.edu.

# Revolutionaries for the Right

Anticommunist Internationalism and Paramilitary Warfare in the Cold War

**Kyle Burke**

The University of North Carolina Press  Chapel Hill

This book was published with the assistance of the Authors Fund of the University of North Carolina Press.

© 2018 The University of North Carolina Press
All rights reserved

Designed and set in Arno Pro and Klavika types by Rebecca Evans
Manufactured in the United States of America

The University of North Carolina Press has been a member of the Green Press Initiative since 2003.

Jacket illustrations: Kalashnikov rifles © iStockphoto.com/by_nicholas.

Library of Congress Cataloging-in-Publication Data
Names: Burke, Kyle (Historian), author.
Title: Revolutionaries for the right : anticommunist internationalism and paramilitary warfare in the Cold War / Kyle Burke.
Other titles: New Cold War history.
Description: Chapel Hill : University of North Carolina Press, [2018] | Series: The new Cold War history | Includes bibliographical references and index.
Identifiers: LCCN 2017053872 | ISBN 9781469640730 (cloth : alk. paper) | ISBN 9781469640747 (ebook)
Subjects: LCSH: Anti-communist movements—History—20th century. | Anti-communist movements—International cooperation. | Conservatism—History—20th century. | Revolutions—History—20th century. | Paramilitary forces—History—20th century. | Cold War.
Classification: LCC HX44 .B773 2018 | DDC 324.1/309045—dc23 LC record available at https://lccn.loc.gov/2017053872

Portions of chapter 2 appeared in "Radio Free Enterprise: The *Manion Forum* and the Making of the Transnational Right in the 1960s," *Diplomatic History* 40, no. 1 (January 2016): 111–39.

For Nina and Norah

Contents

Abbreviations ix

**Introduction** 1

1 **The Flames of Anticommunist Revolution** 12

2 **Crossroads of Conservatism** 28

3 **Revolution and Counterrevolution** 55

4 **Covert Warriors for Hire** 86

5 **Private Wars in Central America** 118

6 **Rebels for the Cause** 155

**Conclusion. The Twilight of the Anticommunist International** 197

Acknowledgments 219

Note on Sources 225

Notes 229

Bibliography 317

Index 339

# Abbreviations

The following abbreviations are used throughout the text.

| | |
|---:|---|
| ABN | Anti-Bolshevik Bloc of Nations |
| ACAKFF | American Committee to Aid Katanga Freedom Fighters |
| ACC | American-Chilean Council |
| ACWF | American Council for World Freedom |
| AFIO | Association of Former Intelligence Officers |
| APACL | Asian Peoples' Anti-Communist League |
| ARENA | Alianza Republicana Nacional (El Salvador) |
| ARCI | Aide Refugee Chinese Intellectuals |
| ASC | American Security Council |
| CACC | Christian Anti-Communist Crusade |
| CAL | Confederación Anticomunista Latinoamericana |
| CCNA | Consejo Chileno de Norte América |
| CFA | Committee for a Free Afghanistan |
| CMA | Civilian Military Assistance |
| COINTELPRO | Counter Intelligence Program (FBI) |
| CORU | Coordination of United Revolutionary Organizations |
| DINA | Dirección de Inteligencia Nacional (Chile) |
| FDN | Fuerza Democrática Nicaragüense |
| FEMACO | Federación Anticomunista Mexicana |
| FMLN | Farabundo Martí Liberación Nacional (El Salvador) |

| | |
|---|---|
| **FNLA** | Frente Nacional de Libertação de Angola |
| **FORI** | Friends of Rhodesian Independence |
| **FSLN** | Frente Sandinista Liberación Nacional (Nicaragua) |
| **GMD** | Guomindang |
| **HOP** | Hrvatski oslobodilački pokret (Croatian Liberation Movement) |
| **IACDC** | Inter-American Confederation for the Defense of the Continent |
| **ISI** | Inter-Services Intelligence (Pakistan) |
| **JCR** | Junta Coordinadora Revolucionaria |
| **KPNLF** | Khmer Peoples' National Liberation Front (Cambodia) |
| **MLN** | Movimiento de Liberación Nacional (Guatemala) |
| **MPLA** | Movimento Popular de Libertação de Angola |
| **OSS** | Office of Strategic Services |
| **OUN** | Organization of Ukrainian Nationalists |
| **SOG** | U.S. Army Studies and Observation Group/Special Operations Group |
| **UNITA** | União Nacional para a Independência Total de Angola |
| **USCWF** | United States Council for World Freedom |
| **WACL** | World Anti-Communist League |
| **WYCF** | World Youth Crusade for Freedom |
| **YAF** | Young Americans for Freedom |
| **ZANU** | Zimbabwe African National Union |
| **ZAPU** | Zimbabwe African People's Union |

Revolutionaries for the Right

# Introduction

On September 5, 1985, retired U.S. Army general John K. Singlaub, a thirty-year veteran of special operations, took the stage at an upscale hotel in Dallas, Texas. In the glow of crystal chandeliers and television camera lights, Singlaub straightened his back and surveyed the crowd.[1] Seated behind him were the leaders of anticommunist paramilitary groups from Afghanistan, Angola, Ethiopia, Cambodia, Laos, Vietnam, and Nicaragua, surrounded by the flags of two dozen nations that had fallen under communist rule in the previous forty years. The auditorium was filled with business owners, wealthy socialites, former military and intelligence officers, aspiring mercenaries, and a legion of activists from the United States, Asia, Latin America, Africa, and Europe.[2] They had gathered for the annual conference of the World Anti-Communist League (WACL), which drew its members from more than one hundred countries spread across five continents. Singlaub, who had recently secured the chairmanship of the league, saw the conference as a way to unite the struggles of disparate movements and, in time, foment a global anticommunist revolution.[3] "Now is the time to go on the offensive," he proclaimed, to the audience's delight.[4]

Giving voice to an old idea that had circulated throughout anticommunist circles in the United States and abroad for decades, Singlaub firmly believed that armed civilians in communist countries were the key to winning the Cold War. By 1985, the Reagan administration had embraced that vision, enacting a plan to roll back communism through foreign paramilitaries in half a dozen countries in Asia, Africa, and Latin America. However, even though the administration had thrown its support behind these scattered movements, Singlaub was convinced that real change would only come from outside the state. Many Americans opposed their country's involvement in far-flung conflicts, prompting Congress to pass laws constraining the administration's covert wars in Angola and Nicaragua. Legislators were threatening to do the same in other wars. Thus, Singlaub proclaimed that the WACL and its affiliated organizations would coordinate private aid for anticommunist guerrillas while U.S. congressmen vacillated. He told one reporter, "We are trying to organize programs of support to anti-Communist resistance movements to fill in the gaps left by the idiocies of Congress."[5] Singlaub hoped to reverse the presumably rising tide of communism by linking, as one commentator put it, "those who are willing to lose their lives with those who are willing to risk at least a part of their fortune."[6]

Using private funds to wage covert wars, Singlaub and others hoped to avoid the partisan and bureaucratic struggles of government and circumvent popular debate about American foreign policy. To that end, international groups such as the WACL would be tools for creating a form of combat that depended not upon the state but rather sympathetic donors who financed paramilitary undertakings. One journalist who covered the proceedings noted that this was to be a "new factor in Third World politics," a "ready-made, fundraising network for rightists."[7]

To most Americans, this network seemed to appear overnight. But in fact it was the culmination of decades of alliance-building between conservatives in the United States and kindred movements in Europe, Latin America, Asia, and Africa—what I call the anticommunist international. *Revolutionaries for the Right* tells the story of how the anticommunist international came into being and what its proponents hoped to achieve. It explains their successes, their failures, and the consequences of their actions. Tacking between the United States and many other countries, it offers a new history of the anticommunist Right in the Cold War.

---

This story begins in the late 1940s and early 1950s. In the wake of the Second World War, anticommunist groups from Eastern Europe and Asia began working together in the hope of launching guerrilla wars in the Soviet Bloc and China. By the end of the 1950s, they had drawn actors from the Americas into their work. From the United States came leading figures in the emerging conservative movement, such as William F. Buckley, Clarence Manion, and Marvin Liebman, who hoped to expand upon their domestic activities and initiate a "worldwide anticommunist revolution," as Liebman put it.[8] From Latin America came right-wing civilians, state officials, and paramilitaries who believed the region was under assault from the Soviet Union and its puppet in Cuba, Fidel Castro. From southern Africa came the citizens of white-dominated states and a smattering of homegrown anticommunist groups. Their forays into international activism—embodied in conferences, lecture tours, rallies, training academies, and propaganda campaigns—fashioned an imagined community, a global anticommunist brotherhood.

Despite those successes, the dream of a worldwide anticommunist revolution remained out of reach through the 1970s, mostly because the proliferating connections between rightists in different parts of the world proved difficult to manage. Actors and organizations competed with one another over means and about what their revolution truly meant. Most agreed that communism had to be defeated, but there was little consensus about what should take its place. Those tensions were exacerbated by the practical difficulties of fomenting armed uprisings in communist countries. Private groups had far fewer resources than governments and consistently struggled to send arms, supplies, and funds to paramilitary groups behind the Iron and Bamboo Curtains. Moreover, U.S. failure in Vietnam indicated to many anticommunists that the United States could no longer be counted upon to stand up to the Soviet Union and its allies.

Some settled for acts of terror, hoping to draw international attention to the plight of their subjugated nations. Others cast their lot with murderous right-wing regimes in Latin America. Believing they were taking over for a faltering United States, they helped intimidate, disappear, and kill civilians on three continents. Their extralegal violence triggered investigations from U.S. and international policing agencies, which began to chip away at the foundations of the anticommunist international. Disillusioned by years of failure and frustration, and confronted with a growing radicalism amongst their allies abroad, many leading U.S. conservatives ceded ground within the movement in the late 1970s.

Meanwhile, after a wave of revelations about the United States clandestine services' activities reached the public in the wake of the Vietnam debacle, Congress passed new laws limiting the ability of the executive branch and the military to wage covert war. Following lawmakers' lead, Presidents Gerald Ford and Jimmy Carter forced more than a thousand clandestine warriors from their jobs in the CIA and the U.S. military. Many more, such as John Singlaub, left voluntarily, embittered by the new constraints on U.S. foreign policy. Politicized by their experiences on—or rather behind—the front lines of the Cold War, these men had managed covert actions from gunrunning and sabotage to the creation of thousands-strong paramilitary armies. For them, this kind of combat was the most viable weapon in the global struggle against communism. It was heroic and individualistic, and it took place with little scrutiny from the outside. Moreover, it did not require the sacrifice of American lives or large amounts of treasure. When properly motivated and armed, foreign paramilitaries could do the dirty work of fighting communism in the global South.

As ex-soldiers and spies filtered into the conservative movement in the late 1970s and early 1980s, they revitalized the anticommunist international, drawing closer to the many of the same forces that a previous generation of American activists had found so distasteful. They traveled the world to build alliances with right-wing leaders and guerrilla movements, generating many of the ideas and impulses that came to be known as the Reagan Doctrine—a global offensive of anticommunist guerrillas in Nicaragua, Angola, Mozambique, Ethiopia, Laos, Cambodia, Vietnam, and Afghanistan. Speaking in a language of masculinity and brotherhood, they linked these disparate conflicts into a joint struggle, aimed not only at rolling back communism but spreading religious values and free markets.

When parts of that program ran into trouble, ex-soldiers and spies used their connections with overseas groups to solicit private donations, purchase weapons and supplies, and send them to embattled guerrillas. Some even joined the guerrillas in the field as military advisors or mercenaries. They did so because they favored privatization and free-market mechanisms, and because they clung to gendered assumptions about the kind of action needed to win the Cold War—hard men fighting secret wars with little government involvement. Simply put, their paramilitary campaigns offered both profits and power outside of the state.

It all fell apart in the late 1980s. The Iran-Contra scandal put an end to much of this paramilitary activity, while the collapse of the Soviet Union made the anticommunist international obsolete. Nevertheless, the paramilitary endeavors of the Reagan era provided the institutional and ideological foundations for the rise of private military companies in subsequent years. They also lent legitimacy to a growing right-wing militia movement whose violent campaigns against the U.S. government and other enemies at home escalated as the Cold War came to an end.

---

For most U.S. historians, the rise of the Right is a domestic story. For some, it is a tale about how integration in schools, neighborhoods, and workplaces generated white racial backlash and refashioned rights-based political discourse.[9] For others, it is a story of rich conservative businessmen using their wealth to oppose organized labor while championing the virtues of limited government and the free market.[10] For labor historians, the key narrative is how the decline of American industry reoriented national politics during the protracted period of economic turmoil that began in the early 1970s.[11] And for historians attuned to fears and panics about crime, it's a story about how conservatives gained power by harnessing law-and-order rhetoric to sway white voters troubled by civil unrest in the late 1960s and afterward.[12]

Taken as a whole, this scholarship shows how modern American conservatism took root in the racialized landscape of the postwar era and grew during periods of wrenching social, political, economic, and cultural change. Conservatives challenged the power of the federal government, countered New Deal liberalism, and constrained the civil rights, labor, and feminist movements. They generated newfound support for free-market policies among working- and middle-class Americans that dismantled large parts of the New Deal state. In short, according to the prevailing scholarship, the conservative movement, and the broader rightward political trajectory that it inspired, has been the most important force in U.S. politics since the late 1960s.

That story is convincing but it is not complete. The majority of historians who write about modern American conservatism portray it as a reactionary force that was mostly concerned with domestic issues. And even those historians who have examined U.S. conservatives within an international context have done so by focusing on a particular region or country, especially Latin America, China, and Vietnam.[13] Only a handful or works have tackled the rise of the Right on the world stage—and many of those have offered descriptions of, rather than explanations for, the bonds that U.S. conservatives formed with like-minded individuals, movements, and states overseas.[14] Without an international framing, we are unable to see the rise of American conservatism in the global context that its proponents understood themselves to be working in. That is what *Revolutionaries for the Right* offers.

Starting in the early Cold War, the same years in which the modern conservative movement exploded in the United States, right-leaning Americans began working to build a genuinely international movement stretching across Asia, Africa, Europe, and Latin America. In so doing, they renounced much of the isolationism that had dominated their foreign policy approaches since the early twentieth century. Rather than withdraw from the world, they sought a more active engagement with it. From the 1950s onward, they demonstrated a deep interest in, and commitment to, the global South. Yet many remained skeptical that the U.S. government, including the military, should or could vanquish Marxism in Asia, Africa, and Latin America. Instead, they pinned their hopes to homegrown forces that could root out communist subversion or destabilize communist nations from within.

The rise of the Right was therefore not simply a domestic phenomenon but a transnational one. For the political, intellectual, cultural, religious, and financial bonds that linked American conservatives to anticommunist forces abroad also transformed the tenor and trajectory of the U.S. Right. Throughout the Cold War, conservative Americans viewed domestic crises through the lens of overseas developments, and vice versa. Their understandings of many things—the beneficence of white supremacy in Rhodesia, the unwavering anticommunist stance of Taiwan, the free-market revolution of Pinochet's Chile, and the unrealized potential of anticommunist guerrillas in Nicaragua and Afghanistan—often shaped their aspirations at home. Searching abroad for parables and solutions, they sought to curb the civil rights movement, to make the United States a truly anticommunist state, to privatize industry and deregulate capital, and to make armed citizens agents of meaningful change.

Like U.S. diplomats and military leaders, missionaries and development theorists, conservative activists from the United States discovered places and people that proved beyond their mastery. Most of their frustrations stemmed from their inability to command their foreign allies, to harness their movements for American ends, and to uproot deep-seeded strains of radicalism. In other words, they discovered that the international Right was much older, larger, and more complex than they had assumed. Indeed, during the 1920s and 1930s, a variety of far-right groups in Europe and the Americas had started to see one another as potential allies. Yet they fell short of creating a viable international movement.[15]

However, the emergence of the Cold War gave new form and substance to these attempts to build an anticommunist international. A growing wave of communist triumphs—Soviet expansion in Eastern Europe, the victory of Mao Zedong's forces in China, and the spread of revolutionary movements in Asia, Africa, and Latin America—drew rightists from different parts of the globe together. What began in the late 1940s as a set of diffuse connections flourished in the following decades into a mosaic of individuals and movements that took anticommunism as their central organizing principle and saw themselves as *the* defenders of national traditions and established hierarchies, harkening back to an imagined past of simpler times. Those shared assumptions and aspirations notwithstanding, U.S. conservatives and their allies abroad often advocated competing political, economic, and cultural visions. Making "revolution against revolution—not just a revolution but revolution as such," as political scientist Corey Robin has described this project, was a formidable task.[16]

Nevertheless, the task of building an anticommunist international was made easier by the global growth of U.S. power after the Second World War, embodied in a constellation of military bases and alliances, economic relationships, development projects, cultural exchanges, and migration patterns.[17] And so when conservative Americans traveled abroad in search of allies, they benefitted immensely from the institutions that undergirded U.S. power on the world stage—none more so than the Central Intelligence Agency, which supported an array of anticommunist organizations around the world. Indeed, many of the individuals and groups that conservative Americans encountered in their quest for a global movement had, at some point, worked with the CIA. In some cases, those links were fleeting and inconsequential. In others, they were powerful and enduring.

Despite the myriad ways in which U.S. power supported their efforts, U.S. conservatives still struggled mightily to lead the anticommunist revolution they so desired. In part, that was because many of them doubted their government could be trusted to carry out the right kind of revolution in the global South. They often worked outside of the state rather than in conjunction with it. But their struggles also stemmed from the fact that the Cold War, a truly global conflict, produced complex and changing connections between rightists in Asia, Africa, Latin America, and Europe.[18] Put another way, while conservatives from the United States sought to enlist various states, movements, and individuals for their own purposes, their foreign allies proved equally adept at cultivating relationships amongst each other, often with little or no involvement from Americans.

These patterns of collaboration and conflict made the Cold War's anticommunist underground a contentious world in which Americans and others jockeyed for power. Nevertheless, Americans believed that their substantial coffers and extensive political connections bestowed them a leadership position. To that end, they raised millions of dollars from citizens and corporations, drawing upon the very same financial networks that propelled the rise of the Right at home. They also raised funds outside of the United States, assembling a sizeable war chest that was subject to very little scrutiny.

This money supported initiatives that mirrored the covert actions of the CIA, the U.S. military, and other nations' clandestine services. U.S. conservatives funded radio schools for peasants in Latin America and a private volunteer program modeled upon the Peace Corps. They supported exiled partisan warriors from the Soviet Bloc, smuggled Bibles into Eastern Europe, and assisted a breakaway regime in the Congo. They organized tours for foreign anticommunists to politick in cities, towns, and colleges across the United States. They managed propaganda agencies for Taiwan, Rhodesia, Chile, and many other right-wing regimes. They hosted and traveled to international conclaves that drew activists from across the globe. And, most importantly, they backed a series of anticommunist guerrilla movements in Latin America, Asia, and Africa.

It is tempting to see this anticommunist underground as simply an outgrowth of U.S. covert actions in the Cold War. It is better understood, however, in the context of similar networks of concerned citizens and non-governmental organizations (NGOs) that transformed geopolitics in the second half of twentieth century. Starting in the late 1940s and accelerating in the 1970s, groups of activists from Europe, the United States, and elsewhere forged alliances with one another to pressure states into protecting human rights, freezing their nuclear arsenals, and negotiating peace—efforts that hastened major shifts in the Cold War and eventually contributed to its end.[19] The figures who populate *Revolutionaries for the Right* had much in common with those people. They, too, contemplated the links between local, national, and international developments, and cultivated relationships across borders. They also used similar modes of activism, forging a complex web of private groups to pressure governments while also fashioning programs that functioned independently of states and, sometimes, against their laws.

Nowhere was that more clear than in the anticommunist international's embrace of paramilitary violence. From the late 1950s onward, many on the right—both in the United States and abroad—believed that ordinary people fighting guerrilla wars were *the* key to defeating Marxism. Their heroes were men with guns, paramilitaries whom they called "freedom fighters." Despite differences in the scale and nature of conflicts from China to Cuba to the Congo, they tended to see these forces as brothers-in-arms, the vanguard of a global revolution in which communism would vanish from the face of the Earth.

That conviction is jarring. Most historians do not think of conservatives and rightists—whether in the Americas, Asia, Africa, or Europe—as internationalists, let alone revolutionaries fighting wars of national liberation. Instead, historians tend to see them as parochialists, reactionaries, or counterrevolutionaries.[20] But as the story that follows will show, many of those who populated the Cold War's right-wing underground also saw themselves as internationalists *and* as revolutionaries. That seemingly paradoxical stance derived from their belief that anticommunism was itself a revolutionary creed that promised to liberate the world's peoples from a future of totalitarianism.

Over time, these dreams of anticommunist revolution caused Americans to launch paramilitary actions overseas. A generation of U.S. special-operations soldiers and intelligence officers who left their jobs to become anticommunist activists in the Reagan era made that possible. Convinced that defeat in Vietnam and new intelligence reforms had crippled the U.S. government's ability to fight communism, these men launched private military assistance efforts in a half-dozen nations—Nicaragua, El Salvador, Afghanistan, Angola, Cambodia, Laos, and Vietnam. Spearheaded by retired U.S. Army General John K. Singlaub, who had run paramilitary armies in France, Manchuria, and Vietnam, these campaigns used donations from wealthy Americans to pay for supplies, weapons, recruitment drives, and training programs.

In doing so, Singlaub and other activists worked in the shadow of the state to spur anticommunist guerrillas to victory on the battlefield. Yet their aspirations extended far beyond that. For they wished to transform these disparate movements into an international force that would ultimately end the Cold War by making the Soviet Union and its allies fight several unwinnable wars on three continents at the same time. As Singlaub summed it up, "The process of liberation behind the Iron and Bamboo Curtains must be encouraged, supported, coordinated, and sustained as much as possible." Only this "global strategy" could guarantee "peace and security" for future generations.[21]

Harsher realities often overshadowed such fantasies of international anticommunist revolution, especially in countries that had already gone communist. Therefore, many of the leaders and movements with whom Americans sought common cause saw wars of liberation in their home countries as their central project. Whether that translated into a sustained international revolutionary project afterward was, for them, far less important. Even so, their armed campaigns produced a combustible mix of violence, nationalism, and revolution that wreaked havoc in many parts of the globe.

As conservative Americans embraced armed anticommunists in the global South, they struggled to balance their revolutionary aspirations with complicated and often conflicting racial priorities. By and large, they trafficked in the same racial tropes that guided much of U.S. foreign policy in the Cold War—that white, European-descended peoples were more advanced and therefore obligated to lead nonwhite peoples into a capitalist modernity.[22] However, they also placed a great deal of faith in nonwhites whom they believed could and should lead their own countrymen into the future. This conviction undergirded their support for the Nicaraguan Contras, the Afghan *mujahedin*, Angola's Jonas Savimbi, and many other armed movements. By cloaking themselves in the garb of anticommunist guerrillas in the global South—sometimes quite literally—conservative Americans were making the case that they, not leftists or liberals, were in fact the real revolutionaries, the true warriors for democracy for all. That vision was strained, convoluted, contradictory, and often backwards looking. Nevertheless, it held great power for many on the right.

U.S. conservatives' affinity for anticommunist guerrillas in the global South also stemmed from and reinforced gendered assumptions about the kind of action needed to win the Cold War.[23] They tended to believe that the struggle against communism could only be won through a style of combat that prioritized manly virtues such as courage, strength, and derring-do.[24] For them, paramilitary or guerrilla warfare was the ideal mode of action not just because it destabilized communist nations from within, but also because it embodied and enhanced the gendered notions they held dear. Simply put, these were hard men doing the hard work of fighting subversives and building strong societies.

At the same time, visions of a global anticommunist revolution blurred the line between state-sanctioned and vigilante violence at home and abroad. In the United States, the Right's veneration of foreign anticommunist guerrillas, especially in the Reagan era, catalyzed and legitimized a growing paramilitary subculture. Through training camps, gun shows, movies, and magazines, many American men, often disgruntled Vietnam veterans, came to see armed action as the best way to reclaim the economic and political power they believed they had lost at home, while also combatting their perceived enemies abroad.[25] This led some to seek work as mercenaries in Africa, Latin America, and Asia. Many more just dreamt of doing so.

In either case, the circulation of violence—both actual and imagined—between the United States and overseas battlegrounds caused these men to think they were rekindling the masculine virtues that had once propelled the United States' rise to global power and that were presumably extinguished during the post-Vietnam period of self-doubt and retreat from war. Filling out that worldview was the belief that the federal government had fallen under the control of weak liberals and career bureaucrats who talked too much and accomplished too little. And so they hoped to shift war-making into an extralegal realm that was free from both.

During the Reagan era, then, conservative activists, retired covert warriors, aspiring mercenaries, and anticommunist guerrillas all shared the belief that they could not only fill in for the state, but do a better job for less money. Yet their activities held within them the seeds of their undoing. Private paramilitary campaigns skirted U.S. laws—particularly the Neutrality Act and the Foreign Agents Registration Act—and therefore opened their participants to prosecution or other legal actions.[26] Beyond that, these campaigns were often overawed by the activities of states, especially the U.S. government, which had far greater access to weapons, supplies, and all the other things needed to fight a guerrilla war. That presented a formidable challenge to private paramilitary campaigns even as governments lost their monopoly over the global arms trade in the later years of the Cold War.

Nevertheless, the anticommunist international did reshape the world, just not as it intended. When the Cold War ended, newly created private military corporations refashioned the paramilitary schemes of the 1980s into money-making ventures in southern Africa, Eastern Europe, and the Islamic world. By crystallizing their relationships with states through contracts, they resolved some of the problems that had doomed previous efforts while creating new dilemmas in their place. Meanwhile, the revolutionary war that U.S. conservatives had tried to enact abroad turned inwards. In the late 1980s and early 1990s, armed right-wing groups in the United States began preparing for guerrilla war against an array of domestic enemies, above all the federal government.

Anticommunist internationalists had once dreamed of revolutionaries for the Right. Instead, they created mercenaries and terrorists.

# 1 | The Flames of Anticommunist Revolution

In March of 1957, conservative organizer Marvin Liebman embarked on a two-week mission to forge bonds with anticommunist groups in Japan, South Korea, Taiwan, the Philippines, and Hong Kong. His ultimate purpose, he later recalled, was to initiate a "worldwide anticommunist revolution by establishing an organization to coordinate and mobilize international activity that would combat the Moscow-based International." It was to be a kind of "anti-Comintern" with Liebman pulling the strings.[1] The Asian Peoples' Anti-Communist League (APACL) sponsored his trip, paying for his airfare, lodging, and meals, and introducing him to state officials and activists. From Tokyo, Liebman traveled to Taipei, Hong Kong, Seoul, Bangkok, and finally, to Saigon, where he attended the third annual meeting of the APACL.[2] There he met more than a hundred delegates from across East and Southeast Asia, as well as a few exiled anticommunists from Eastern Europe, particularly Ukraine and Hungary.[3]

Presiding over the conference in Saigon was South Vietnam's Ngo Dinh Diem, the U.S.-backed dictator who rose to power in the wake of the French withdrawal from Indochina. In his keynote speech, Diem explained that anticommunists in different parts of the world were actually fighting the same struggle, despite the distances and circumstances separating them. He asserted that "if communist expansion is conceived on a world scale," then the "free nations of the world should act under the sign of close cooperation. It is through common action that we can keep a tenacious and unscrupulous enemy in check." Speaking of the "brotherly cooperation" that bonded the assembled delegates, Diem urged them toward the "victorious outcome of the struggle which we are all carrying out for a just and noble cause."[4]

Despite the presence of Diem and many other important officials from South Vietnam, Taiwan, and South Korea, some of Liebman's new contacts came from organizations that even he admitted "were little more than letterheads." Still he remained optimistic that this rag-tag collection of anticommunists could be turned into a formidable geopolitical force.[5] So did his hosts. The world was ripe for anticommunist armed struggle, they said. The failed Hungarian Revolution of 1956 indicated that ordinary people across Eastern Europe were now ready to pick up arms and liberate their nations from Soviet rule.[6] Others speculated that widespread suffering in communist China, particularly among peasants, would soon provide the spark for an insurgency of millions that would drive Mao Zedong from power.[7] The only thing these people needed was help from their friends abroad. As one delegate summed it up, "We must feed the flames of anticommunist revolution everywhere."[8]

Many anticommunists saw themselves as brothers-in-arms leading a global revolution in the late 1950s. For them, anticommunism was an inherently international endeavor, one that hinged on the efforts of kindred movements working against the same enemy in different contexts. It depended not so much on external military might, like that of the United States, but the will of peoples *within* communist countries. These men were the key to defeating the Soviet Union and its allies because they could unravel communist states from the inside out. In other words, only they could make victory permanent. More than anything else, that conviction was what linked anticommunist internationalists to one another in the early Cold War. In their minds, freeing the world from communism, and thereby laying the foundations for a new age in human history, required, above all, cooperation.

---

Landing in Saigon in 1957, Marvin Liebman was stepping into a torrent of American political activism that had been flowing in Asia for at least a decade. In the wake of the Second World War, as the Nationalist forces of Jiang Jieshi retreated to the island of Taiwan, off the southeastern coast of mainland China, Jiang's supporters in the United States quickly began working to legitimize his regime and shift international opinion, particularly that of U.S. policymakers, away from communist China. This was a difficult task, despite most Americans' disdain for Mao Zedong and the Communist Party of China. During the Chinese Civil War, Jiang had earned a reputation for brutality, duplicity, and mismanagement, all of which became even clearer after his forces, known as the Guomindang (GMD), forced the Japanese from the island of Taiwan in 1945. As the GMD took over, food shortages and runaway inflation led to mounting frustration among workers and farmers.[9] On February 28, 1947, this anger exploded, as thousands of people took the streets of Taipei in protest.

The GMD responded with mass arrests and the murder of more than 10,000 civilians—actions that established a pattern of rule for the following years.[10]

When Jiang reassembled his armies on Taiwan in December 1949 to establish the Republic of China, he had few champions in the United States. Even though his diehard supporters did not command broad influence, they did manage to keep U.S. military and economic aid flowing to his regime in 1949 and 1950.[11] As Taiwan stabilized under the authoritarian rule of Jiang, the Guomindang carried out reforms that laid the foundations for a robust economy based upon manufacturing and agriculture. Yet in the 1950s, Taiwan's potential for economic progress and political stability was hardly certain. Jiang's regime faced serious challenges—both on the island and from communist China.

Americans' passion for Jiang Jieshi and his regime on Taiwan stemmed from long-held beliefs that China was the key to U.S. economic and political power in Asia. From the mid-nineteenth century onwards, many U.S. politicians, businessmen, and labor leaders, especially those who supported the Republican Party, had talked of "opening" China to American capitalism, a project that would uplift the Chinese and the American people at once by making them partners—albeit unequal ones—in international trade.[12] At the same time, a close economic relationship between the two countries promised religious deliverance. Christian missionaries from the United States used the bonds of trade to convert millions, including most of the Guomindang's leadership, to their faith.[13] Americans insisted that such a project separated the United States from its rival imperial powers. While other nations sought colonial dominion, Americans only wanted collaborative enterprise and Christian salvation. Those sentiments, which reaffirmed Americans' self-understandings as democratic liberators, also legitimized a dual portrait of China in American minds, blending tradition and capitalism, Confucianism and Christianity, past and future.[14]

Yet this does not fully explain why U.S. conservatives devoted so much attention to Taiwan during the 1950s. The onset of the Cold War does. For in the wake of the Chinese Communist Party's victory in 1949 and its surprise entry into the Korean War, U.S. conservatives found in Jiang Jieshi's Taiwan an opportunity to build a new internationalist vision that countered the containment policies of the Truman and Eisenhower administrations. Rather than cede China to the communists and hope to contain any further advances, as most U.S. policymakers sought, conservative Republicans in Congress believed that Jiang Jieshi and his military could overthrow Mao's China, thereby removing a crucial pillar of support from other communist forces elsewhere in Asia.[15] In their view, Taiwan would fulfill vital foreign policy goals without having to expend American lives abroad. Moreover, if Jiang's soldiers were successful, mainland China would once again be open to American businesses and missionaries.[16]

To make that dream into a reality, Americans with economic or religious stakes in China formed a series of private lobbying groups in the late 1940s and early 1950s. The most influential was Alfred Kohlberg's American China Policy Association, founded in 1946. Kohlberg had made a fortune importing textiles from China, and his organization relied mostly on his private coffers to publish opinion pieces in major newspapers and send letters to members of Congress and the State Department. Within a few years, the American China Policy Association had provided the template for the "loose coalition of former military officers, Christian missionaries, members of Congress, academics, and independent anticommunist leaders who militantly opposed communism in Asia" that soon became known as the China Lobby.[17] Although the China Lobby was largely unsuccessful in persuading the U.S. government that Jiang's regime could spearhead a military offensive to retake the mainland, it was a persistent thorn in the side of the State Department and the Truman and Eisenhower administrations, effectively red-baiting officials who suggested accommodation with communist China.[18]

Building upon the China Lobby's efforts, Marvin Liebman became perhaps the most important American civilian working on behalf of Jiang Jieshi and the Guomindang in the 1950s. But he was, in many ways, an unlikely candidate to lead a crusade against communism in China. Unlike Kohlberg and most other members of the China Lobby, Liebman had never lived in China, nor did he have business interests there. Instead, his activism in Asia emanated from his peculiar journey from socialism to anticommunism. Born in 1923 to Jewish immigrants from Galicia, in western Ukraine, Liebman grew up in a Brooklyn neighborhood that was, in his recollection, a "polyglot community of middle-class families." Like many other young people in New York during the Depression, Liebman was enthralled by leftist politics, joining the Young Communist League in 1937 and volunteering at radical publications such as *New Masses* magazine. It was around this time, too, that Liebman discovered his homosexuality, which he would struggle to keep secret until very late in his life.[19]

Serving in the Army during World War II, Liebman was, by his own admission, hardly a competent soldier. Assigned first as a cook and then as a journalist, he managed to avoid combat while deployed in Italy and North Africa. Nevertheless, his experiences overseas resembled that of many American soldiers who found the military to be, in historian Allan Bérubé's formulation, a "national coming out experience."[20] In Naples and Casablanca, Liebman found other gay men, easing his feelings of abnormality and shame. It did not last. While stationed in Cairo, Army authorities discovered a series of love letters that he had penned to a companion on a troop ship. Accused by his commanding officers of being a "cocksucker" and a "faggot," Liebman was sent back to New York with a "blue discharge"—the Army's preferred method for dealing with suspected homosexuals, forcing them from the service and barring them from receiving veterans' benefits.[21]

For the next few years, Liebman drifted through New York's bohemian subculture, working the occasional odd job with little sense of direction or purpose. He married a woman briefly, but they divorced after six months. He maintained his affinity for socialism, though more out of habit than conviction. After working for a few months in the mail room of New York's Liberal Party, he took a job with the International Rescue Committee, an anti-Stalinist group that was helping refugees flee Eastern Europe for West Germany, Austria, France, and Britain.[22]

While on a fundraising trip to Los Angeles in 1951, Liebman experienced a political conversion. At the behest of his employer, he met Elinor Lipper, a Russian exile who had just published a book documenting the eleven years she spent in the Gulag camp of Kolyma.[23] Her tales of suffering and despair shattered his illusions of the Soviet Union and socialism. She revealed that much of the Soviet economy was based on slave labor extracted from people who had been arbitrarily arrested and then sent to Siberia. He later recalled, "Her story overwhelmed me. I felt totally betrayed. What was worse, because I had believed in the Soviet Union, I felt personally responsible for what had happened to her. The change seemed quick, but it was really the culmination of five years of internal intellectual conflict that I had hidden from myself. This catharsis . . . was a turning point in my life."[24]

Almost overnight, Liebman transformed into a fervent anticommunist. In January of 1952, pulling on a few connections from the International Rescue Committee, he helped found the awkwardly named Aide Refugee Chinese Intellectuals (ARCI), which sought to resettle 25,000 Chinese intellectuals from the mainland, first in Taiwan and then, hopefully, in the United States.[25] It was in this role that Liebman found his talent for political organizing. Based on his "knowledge of how the left organized," he established the template that would guide his and others' international work in the following years. The plan was simple: create a mailing list of prominent figures; invite these people to serve as sponsors or advisory-board members; print letterhead with their names; appoint a well-known businessman to serve as treasurer and corporate fundraiser; appoint or elect a chairman; and, most importantly, set up an executive committee to "really do the work or rubber stamp what you are doing."[26] This strategy allowed for the rapid organization of political action groups that could boast impressive membership lists, prestigious sponsors, and deep pockets, all under the control of a few dedicated activists.

Liebman's plan brought quick success. He soon enlisted Walter H. Judd, a Republican Congressman from Minnesota, to be the key spokesman and fundraiser for the ARCI. Judd had served as a Protestant medical missionary in China during the 1920s and 1930s, where he witnessed firsthand the brutality and deprivation that accompanied communist rule. That led him to lobby on behalf of Jiang's forces during and after the Japanese invasion of the mainland. Elected to Congress in 1942, Judd became renowned for his expertise in foreign affairs and his eloquent opposition to American rapprochement with communist China.[27] With Judd as a public face, the ARCI quickly garnered funds from the Ford and Rockefeller foundations. More money came from the State Department and the CIA, which sought to use Liebman's group, in his estimation, "to expand their intelligence network in Hong Kong," a city where many American, British, Soviet, and Chinese spies operated. After an initial survey mission in February, ARCI set up an office in Hong Kong, which received thousands of resettlement applications from exiled doctors, scholars, scientists, lawyers, and other professionals.[28]

By the summer of 1952, Liebman had come to believe that his organization should initiate a propaganda campaign on behalf of Taiwan. This shift into political activism distanced Liebman from other members of the ARCI, and drew him closer to the Committee for a Free Asia, a CIA front that managed a radio and print campaign denouncing communism from Japan to Pakistan.[29] Eager for CIA funds, and titillated by the thought of being a spy, Liebman agreed to carry a briefcase with $25,000 in cash to help Chinese refugees in Hong Kong publish anticommunist literature.[30]

Liebman branched out on his own in 1953, founding an organization to protest the admission of China to the United Nations. Known as the Committee of One Million, it featured many of the same people with whom Liebman had worked over the previous years, especially Walter Judd. But while the ARCI had largely avoided political advocacy, the Committee of One Million dove headlong into it. By mid-decade it had become the premier organization advocating on behalf of Jiang's regime in Taiwan. Yet most of its rhetoric and literature was devoted to denouncing Communist China rather than explaining precisely what the United States had to gain in an alliance with Taiwan beyond the murky notion that Jiang and the Guomindang could someday retake the mainland.[31] And, despite its name, the Committee of One Million was in reality a letterhead organization whose "one million" members were little more than signatures on a 1954 petition sponsored by Judd, Liebman, and a few others.[32]

Still, Liebman's work with the Committee of One Million attracted the attention of anticommunist groups and statesmen across East and Southeast Asia. They invited him to tour Southeast Asia and participate in the third Asian Peoples' Anti-Communist League conference in Saigon in May of 1957. Liebman was thrilled, even though he knew very little about the group. In public, it appeared as a private organization of anticommunist civilian leaders who aspired to build a mass movement across national borders. In fact, the APACL stemmed from a meeting in June 1954 in Chinhae, South Korea, in which state officials from Taiwan, South Korea, and the Philippines, eager to create an international organization to counter the influence of the Soviet Union and communist China, laid out the initial charter and elected members.[33] The CIA possibly provided some of the start-up funds for the APACL, as some journalists later alleged, though definitive proof of this has not yet emerged.[34] In any case, many at the time understood the APACL to be an instrument of U.S. policymaking—the "lackeys of the imperialists," as the North Vietnamese communist radio station, Voice of Vietnam, put it.[35]

The leaders of the APACL wanted to create a "united anti-Communist front for Asian peoples."[36] They hoped to do that by coordinating the activities of local and national anticommunist groups and by waging "psychological and political warfare" through propaganda campaigns, mass rallies, conferences, and radio and television broadcasts—sometimes in collaboration with U.S. intelligence units.[37] These efforts, they said, would foment a broad-based anticommunist movement in Asia, stretching from Taiwan to China to Pakistan and everywhere in between. And so, throughout the late 1950s, APACL leaders led rallies in a dozen cities in Taiwan, South Korea, South Vietnam, and the Philippines. They created auxiliary organizations for students and women, and put on traveling exhibits that displayed photos of life and death under communism.[38] They also made plans to smuggle pamphlets into communist countries and help refugees return to their homelands, while publishing a multi-language library that dealt with everything from agriculture to industrial development to guerrilla war.[39]

As a result, the APACL evolved into a key conduit through which anticommunist leaders and civilians across the region developed closer ties to each other. It also provided a platform for Asian leaders, like South Korea's Syngman Rhee, to transmute the Domino Theory. American officials had often warned their allies in Asia that communism would fell one country after another, spreading outwards from China. But Rhee reversed that notion, explaining that communism was equally poised to conquer the United States without quick action. "I've been telling Americans," Rhee said, "that first you'll give up Southern California, then Northern California, and then the White House." Other nations, such as France and England, he said, would follow suit.[40]

Although the APACL strove toward a broad-based grassroots movement, its most active members were state officials and military officers from Taiwan, Korea, the Philippines, Thailand, and South Vietnam.[41] Its long-serving chairman, Taiwan's Dr. Ku Chen Kang, had been a member of the Guomindang's Supreme National Defense Council during World War II. He later served as a senior advisor to Jiang Jieshi as well as a member of the GMD's Central Standing Committee.[42] Another leader, Ramon Bagatsing, head of the Philippines chapter, was elected to the Filipino congress in 1957 and maintained close relationships with major political figures such as Ferdinand Marcos, Cornelio Villarreal, and Ramon Magsaysay, all of whom would appear at APACL conferences in the late 1950s.[43] Almost all of the APACL's South Korean delegates were drawn from the Korean military and, later, the Korean Central Intelligence Agency (KCIA). The same went for the group's South Vietnamese branch, since most of its members were military or intelligence officers.[44] Therefore, while nominally a private entity, the APACL had strong ties to the governments of Taiwan, South Korea, the Philippines, and South Vietnam—part of their attempts to build a regional program of cooperation to confront communist insurgencies in Southeast Asia as well as subvert communist states such as China from within.[45]

The key to that cooperation was covert warfare. APACL leaders said they were ready to use the same kinds of tactics the communists did: "infiltration, instigation, economic manipulation, public demonstrations, terrorism, subversion, guerrilla warfare, and assassination."[46] In so doing, they offered public assurances that Asian anticommunists were doing everything in their power to combat their enemies. Indeed, since the mid-1950s, military and intelligence officers from Taiwan, South Korea, the Philippines, and South Vietnam had been working in concert with the United States to exchange intelligence on suspected subversives, disseminate propaganda, and run secret military operations in mainland China and Southeast Asia.[47] In Taiwan, Jiang Jieshi and his son colluded with the CIA to turn the island into the principal base for waging clandestine warfare against mainland China.[48] In the Philippines, American intelligence officers helped the Filipino government wage a brutal war against a popular resistance movement known as the Huks. Overseen by U.S. Air Force officer Edward Lansdale, Filipino paramilitaries and police units disseminated disinformation, tortured suspected enemies, and employed "hunter-killer teams" to murder Huk leaders and sympathizers[49]—efforts that APACL leaders saw as a model for other conflicts.[50] In South Korea, a similar story unfolded. There the CIA and the State Department bankrolled paramilitary programs designed to wipe out guerrilla forces that remained after the end of the Korean War in 1953.[51] These counterrevolutionary efforts radiated across Asia in the late 1950s, appearing in Thailand, Vietnam, Laos, and elsewhere.[52]

Beyond covert action, APACL leaders also saw themselves as offering an alternative to the non-aligned movement that formed in the wake of the Bandung Conference of 1955. Whereas the Bandung Conference sought an independent path for Asian countries, aligned with neither the United States or the Soviet Union, APACL leaders argued that militant anticommunism was the only legitimate path for Asian nationalism in the region—a position that placed them firmly on the side of the United States.[53] Still, they wanted more latitude than U.S. policy allowed. Throughout the late 1950s and early 1960s, they often called for the creation of a mutual defense pact along the lines of the American-designed Southeast Asia Treaty Organization, which excluded most Asian countries. Their hopes for a unified military defense were matched by their persistent belief that mainland China was seething with resentment against the communists and that it could be turned into a popular revolt—but only with sufficient aid from other Asian countries.[54]

Thus, while the APACL's psychological and political warfare campaigns intersected with those of the CIA and other instruments of U.S. power, the group's increasingly shrill calls for greater autonomy distanced it from the Eisenhower administration, the CIA, and the U.S. military. APACL leaders would seek new allies and new sources of funding to carry out their work. Soon enough, they would embrace visions of anticommunist guerrilla warfare.

---

The leaders of the Asian Peoples' Anti-Communist League first turned their attention to Europe. In the late 1950s, they began working with exiled anticommunists from the Soviet Bloc, united under the banner of the Anti-Bolshevik Bloc of Nations (ABN). Key to this group was Yaroslav Stetsko of the Organization of Ukrainian Nationalists (OUN), a secretive paramilitary organization that sought to overturn Soviet rule through guerrilla warfare.[55] A fierce nationalist who wanted to liberate—and purify—Ukraine, Stetsko had spent most his adult life fighting the Russians. By the 1930s, he had joined the radical faction of the OUN led by Stepan Bandera, helping to build a close relationship between anti-Soviet partisans in the province of Galicia and members of the Nazi high command.[56]

When the Nazis invaded western Ukraine in June 1941, Stetsko and other nationalists seized the opportunity to drive out the Soviets. Behind Nazi lines, OUN units carried out their own campaign of ethnic cleansing and murder against Jews, traitors, and Soviet officials and sympathizers. After that, Stetsko called a national assembly in the western city of L'viv and installed himself as prime minister of an independent Ukraine.[57] Yet his tenure lasted only a month. While the Nazi leadership had played to the yearnings of Ukrainian nationalists for years, they had little use for an independent Ukraine, as its territory was to be colonized by victorious Germans.[58] In July, the Nazis arrested Stetsko and Stepan Bandera, and sent them to the Sachsenhausen concentration camp, where they lived in relative comfort as political prisoners.[59]

Meanwhile, their followers created a new guerrilla organization under the name of the Ukrainian Insurgent Army (UIA) and began killing thousands of German soldiers, forcing many units to retreat.[60] As the Nazis withdrew from much of Ukraine, the UIA leadership returned to the old enemy, the Soviet Union. They began making plans to share weapons and information with nationalist guerrillas from Belorussia, Croatia, Romania, Hungary, and other "subjugated nations." In late November 1943, as the Soviet Union regained control over eastern Ukraine, representatives from twelve different nations and ethnic groups convened in the Ukrainian city of Zhitomir to set up an "Anti-Bolshevik Front." The war still raging in Eastern Europe, however, made collaboration between underground forces separated by hundreds of miles and hundreds of thousands of enemy troops—German and Soviet—practically impossible, at least for the moment.[61]

This notion of a joint revolutionary struggle persisted in the minds of anti-Soviet partisans as they fled to West Germany after the war. Having evaded the reach of Soviet authorities, Stetsko and other exiled members of the OUN reconvened in Munich, a city rife with disgruntled nationalist and fascist leaders from Croatia, Romania, Belorussia, Georgia, Hungary, and elsewhere. Stetsko reached out to these men to form a common front and secure backing from western governments. The result was the Anti-Bolshevik Bloc of Nations.[62] Conceived as a means to continue armed struggles in the Soviet bloc, the ABN soon began broadcasting anticommunist propaganda and smuggling arms and supplies to embattled anti-Soviet forces behind the Iron Curtain. Their efforts, especially those of the Ukrainians, received some support from the British intelligence service MI6 and, to a lesser extent, the CIA, since both agencies were willing to overlook abundant evidence of past war crimes.[63]

But as the Soviet Union tightened its grip over Eastern Europe in the late 1940s, it quickly dismantled the ABN's armed campaign, using well-placed informants to sabotage partisan units and massacre sympathizers. By 1948, only a few small pockets of resistance in the Carpathian and Crimean Mountains remained. No longer able to trust the secrecy of the ABN, British and American intelligence agencies distanced themselves from its leaders.[64] With these defeats, the ABN turned to publishing anti-Soviet propaganda, organizing mass rallies, demonstrations, press conferences, and international conventions, and politicking in displaced persons camps in West Germany.[65]

In his public appearances and writings, Stetsko maintained that the only way to counter Soviet power was to wage a "coordinated and systematic freedom campaign" across Eastern Europe.[66] Drawing on his time as partisan, Stetsko insisted the greatest weapon in the struggle against communism was the will of those peoples straining under the yoke of Soviet rule. By taking up arms, ordinary men, motivated by God and nationalism, could dissolve the Soviet empire from within.[67] Stetsko's faith in wars of national liberation hinged on his conviction that the Soviet Union's expansion into Eastern Europe could only be understood as part of the long history of Russian imperialism stretching back to the conquests of Tsar Peter the Great. To reverse centuries of Russian domination, Stetsko and others called for the realization of nations based upon strict ethnic identities. According to historian Anna Holian, the ABN leadership "foresaw a great unmixing of populations, as each national group 'returned' to its rightful homeland."[68] In the words of a British diplomat, this was "an attempt to turn back the clock 400 years."[69] But for Stetsko and other ABN leaders, the creation of ethno-national states would help each people achieve "social justice," a vision of political and economic organization that can best be described as "national socialist, stressing the equality for the nation rather than the working class."[70] That led rival émigré groups to denounce the ABN's brand of ethnic nationalism as Nazism reborn.[71]

Unable to return home, ABN leaders worked instead among exile communities spread across four continents, forming chapters in Berlin, Paris, London, Toronto, New York, Chicago, Detroit, Sydney, and Buenos Aires. Headquartered in Munich, the ABN consisted of five sections—military, diplomatic, youth, counter-espionage, and propaganda—each operating as independent cells.[72] Its monthly newsletter, *ABN Correspondence*, published in English, German, French, and Spanish, had a small but dedicated readership in Western Europe, North America, and, after 1955, in Asia, as the APACL began to republish articles.[73]

In exile, Stetsko maintained a life on the move, traveling to meet foreign dignitaries and anticommunist activists in dozens of nations. Generally accompanied by his wife, Slava, a fierce activist in her own right, he spent many hours with Spain's General Francisco Franco, as well as Jiang Jieshi and Walter Judd.[74] In Britain, he formed friendships with John Finlay Stewart, founder of the Scottish League for European Freedom, which often lobbied on behalf of Eastern European exiles, and retired British Army General John Frederick Charles Fuller, a prominent military strategist who had been a high-ranking member of Sir Oswald Mosley's defunct British Union of Fascists.[75] Like Stetsko, both Stewart and Fuller believed that national liberation movements in Eastern Europe were the key to rolling back the Soviets' postwar gains.[76] Their argument rested on two presumptions. First, that ordinary people were so dissatisfied with communist rule that they would take up arms against it; and second, that these people, when properly armed, could take on the Red Army and, if not defeat it outright, at least create enough havoc and kill enough soldiers to force the Soviets to withdraw.[77]

Although these connections broadened the ABN's influence, they also pushed the organization to the right of American and British intelligence agencies, which came to see it as out of touch with the reality on the ground in the Soviet Bloc.[78] The ABN exaggerated "the strength of the resistance movement behind the Iron Curtain," concluded one British diplomat.[79] Another said the ABN's support for the "near-apocryphal resistance movements behind the Iron Curtain" was a "poor guide to the formulation of a rational foreign policy."[80] Strategically and symbolically, the ABN was too risky. In secret communiqués, U.S. policymakers denounced Stetsko and those around him for having "totalitarian tendencies," not least of which was a penchant for killing rivals.[81]

Although U.S. officials believed the ABN's guerrilla war in Eastern Europe had little potential, they did toy with the idea of arming exiles along conventional lines. In the late 1940s and early 1950s, members of the State Department and the Defense Department talked of creating the Volunteer Freedom Corps, which would organize thousands of exiles, including many still living in displaced persons' camps, into a battalion under the command of U.S. and NATO officers. The Volunteer Freedom Corps, Americans hoped, would prevent exiles from sliding into radical groups like the ABN.[82] The proposal met stiff resistance in Congress and from U.S. allies in Europe who thought European civilians would regard a U.S.-backed exile army as a "burdensome and dangerous mercenary force." U.S. statesmen also feared that "armed camps of expatriates would become breeding grounds for destabilizing revolutionary movements"—much like the Anti-Bolshevik Bloc of Nations. In 1954, President Dwight Eisenhower pulled the plug.[83]

ABN leaders also glimpsed American weakness in the United States' response to the Hungarian Revolution of 1956. When the Hungarian government tried to create a multiparty democracy and withdraw from Moscow's Warsaw Pact, Soviet premier Nikita Khrushchev sent in the Red Army to quell the uprising. Hungarians formed guerrilla units to defend their country, believing that the United States would come to their aid. For years, Eisenhower and Secretary of State John Foster Dulles had suggested that, stoking anti-Soviet sentiment in Hungary through broadcasts from Radio Free Europe. At the crucial moment, however, they decided against supporting the Hungarians. Outmanned and outgunned by 60,000 Soviet soldiers, the rebels died in droves. To Stetsko and other ABN leaders, this was clear proof that the United States had given up on liberating Eastern Europe through force of arms. Indeed, Dulles said as much behind closed doors. "We have always been against violent revolution," he explained to Eisenhower.[84]

In the wake of the failed Hungarian Uprising, British and American support for the ABN evaporated. Yaroslav Stetsko now looked for aid from the Asian People's Anti-Communist League, whose members also dreamt of liberating their homelands from communist rule. By 1957, the two groups had started to work together to create an international movement. As Stetsko and his cohort of ex-partisans moved into new circles, they carried with them their dreams of guerrilla warfare. Those ideas would circulate throughout the anticommunist underground over the following decades, drawing ever more adherents who saw in paramilitarism the path to power.

---

Anticommunists from Latin America also joined this growing international movement. Since the early 1940s, if not earlier, a world of homegrown right-wingers in the Caribbean basin had been working together across national borders to prevent communist forces from gaining ground in their countries, paving the way for CIA interventions in Guatemala and elsewhere in the 1950s. Unfolding in a loose network of private citizens, statesmen, and military leaders, their collaboration stemmed from a few shared convictions—that communists had infiltrated many sectors of public life, that they were controlled by outsiders, and that their talk of reform or revolution meant little more than the imposition of totalitarian regimes that would seize land, factories, and capital, overturn established hierarchies and patterns of deference, and dissolve the Catholic church. Painting in broad strokes, they portrayed trade unionists, students, peasants, and anyone else who mobilized against inequality as communists.[85]

That was the line taken by the Inter-American Confederation for the Defense of the Continent (IACDC), founded in Mexico City in 1953 by Jorge Prieto Laurens. A politician from San Luis Potosí who financed several right-wing groups at Mexican universities, Prieto Laurens believed that his country's elected leaders were blind to the spread of international communism to the Americas.[86] Without any real backing from the Mexican state, Prieto Laurens sent his deputies to El Salvador to meet the exiled Guatemalan Generals Castillo Armas and Miguel Ydígoras Fuentes, promising them financial and material aid to overthrow the democratically elected government of socialist Jacobo Arbenz.[87]

While Prieto Laurens was offering his support to the generals plotting the Guatemalan coup, he organized a series of international conferences to build closer relationships with rightist political and military leaders from across Latin America.[88] The CIA kept its distance at first, convinced that Prieto Laurens and his deputies were "highly unreliable and unpredictable."[89] However, after Prieto Laurens had secured some financial backing from private citizens and businesses in Mexico, El Salvador, and Honduras, the agency threw its support behind him.[90] At the behest of CIA officer E. Howard Hunt, it pledged $25,000 to "underwrite the full expenses" of the first conference, held in Mexico City in 1954, thereby providing Prieto Laurens and those around him with a platform from which they could denounce Arbenz's government.[91]

When the coup in the Guatemala succeeded in June 1954, however, the CIA turned its back on Prieto Laurens. Without funds from the U.S. government, he looked to Brazil, forming a close friendship with Admiral Carlos Penna Botto, a retired officer who had supported the fascist powers during World War II, and who now believed, implausibly, that the Brazilian government had become a proxy of the Soviet Union.[92] Together Prieto Laurens and Botto began searching abroad for allies with whom they could share ideas and resources. By 1957, the pair had cultivated relationships with leaders from the APACL and the ABN, traveling to their conferences in Taipei and Munich, and publishing articles in their publications. That is how Marvin Liebman came to know them.[93]

Hoping to lead this coalescing movement, Liebman started raising money for a new organization that would bring them all together.[94] After several months of planning, in March of 1958, members of the Committee of One Million, the APACL, the ABN, and the IACDC gathered in Mexico City to form the World Anti-Communist Congress for Liberation and Freedom.[95] Its official proclamation illustrated the global ambitions of those who attended. They pledged to bring people from all "races, nationalities, countries, and creeds" together to "unify our programs, coordinate our work, and take progressive actions directed against our communist enemy." Through common action, the Congress said, anticommunists could reverse patterns of racism and imperialism that began during the European conquests of the sixteenth century and now continued under the Soviet Union and its proxies. For the delegates who met in Mexico City, the Soviets had cynically manipulated national liberation movements in the global South to build their own imperial project. Homegrown leftist "revolutionaries" were thus little more than tools with which the Soviets hoped to conquer all the world's peoples.[96]

In pledging to unite all "races, nationalities, countries, and creeds," anticommunists were fashioning a worldview that harnessed anticolonial discourses to promote the transnational revolutionary violence of the Right. By cooperating, the Congress declared, disparate groups would be able to render the "moral and material support to forces behind the Iron Curtain in Europe and Asia" and thus achieve the "ultimate objective of liberating and restoring national independence, freedom and liberty to all the enslaved peoples on their ethnic territories."[97] In Liebman's estimation, this was the first time that "independent anticommunist organizations jointly approved and, indeed, sponsored a workable plan leading toward coordinated international action."[98]

Despite or perhaps because of its bold pledges, the World Anti-Communist Congress for Freedom and Liberation lasted for less than a year. By July 1958, just four months after its first meeting, Liebman and the other Americans had soured on the idea, pulling the Committee of One Million—and its financial resources—from the Congress. Publicly, Liebman said the lack of cohesion amongst different groups with disparate visions had killed the Congress. In his resignation letter, he explained it was too hard to "coordinate the activities of organizations and movements, representing different points of view, which sometimes run counter to each other, without careful and time consuming groundwork." Absent a firm foundation, this version of the anticommunist international was "destined for failure."[99]

What frustrated Liebman most was his inability to control the organization once foreign actors got involved. Years later he claimed that the problems had been manifest at the outset, when he paid Prieto Laurens to host the conference. "The moment Laurens got the money, he started to take over," he recalled. "I discovered too late that his international anticommunist connections were with the most extreme right-wing organizations, many anti-Semitic." He was especially troubled when he learned that Yaroslav Stetsko and other members of the ABN had collaborated with the Nazis in western Ukraine, where many of his Jewish relatives were murdered during the war. Liebman later lamented that he "had lost control to a bunch of jerks."[100]

The remaining members of the Congress were confused and angered by the departure of the Americans.[101] Liebman started to receive phone calls that he assumed were from Stetsko's people calling him a "Jew Bolshevik" and threatening his life. He considered buying a sawed-off shotgun for protection.[102] The threats proved hollow, and soon more quotidian tasks took the place of mortal danger. Since Liebman had been in charge of the group's finances, his final task was to return the remaining funds to the Congress.[103] His resignation proved prophetic. In his absence, the Congress was unable to decide on a suitable leader as regional factions pressed their own candidate forward.[104] When no one took charge, the Congress disbanded.

---

The failure of the World Anti-Communist Congress for Freedom and Liberation should have spoiled American conservatives' dreams of an anticommunist international, but it did not. For years afterward they kept up their work with the APACL and, to a lesser extent, the ABN, traveling abroad to their conferences, publishing each other's propaganda, issuing joint statements, collaborating on projects, and raising funds together.[105] Drawing closer to kindred forces abroad, Liebman and other Americans sharpened their conviction that communism was a global problem that required a global solution. Meanwhile, their overseas allies worked on their own, often without any involvement from Americans.

Yet making an anticommunist international was a difficult task. U.S. conservatives and their allies abroad disagreed about exactly who should lead this coalition and whose interests it should represent. Adding to that challenge, Americans were increasingly unsure about how their work fit with U.S. official policy, especially covert actions mounted by the CIA. After all, the state could invest far greater resources into anticommunist initiatives, especially weapons and soldiers, than private groups could muster on their own. However, in the 1960s, as many of the CIA's covert actions in Cuba, the Congo, and Vietnam failed—or at least did not live up to expectations—U.S. conservatives and their allies abroad grew convinced that they could do better. That belief propelled a slew of new groups into the anticommunist international.

## 2 | Crossroads of Conservatism

If the late 1950s were years of hope for anticommunist internationalists, then the early 1960s were years of panic and desperation. Three unfolding struggles drove those fears. The first was the Cuban Revolution of 1959, and the inability of the U.S. government, Cuban exiles, and their allies in the Caribbean basin to unseat Fidel Castro's regime. The second was the mounting armed conflict in Southeast Asia, above all the war in Vietnam. And the third was the decolonization crisis in the Congo and its reverberations across southern Africa. Each of these events, in its own way, signaled to anticommunist internationalists that the forces of totalitarianism were marching roughshod across the globe, and that the U.S. government, for whatever reason, had failed to stop them. As Clarence Manion, a leading light in the American Right, summed it up, the "bloody troubles" in Latin America, Asia, and Africa were just "well planned skirmishes in the big world-wide conflict that is being directed from the communist control tower in the Kremlin." But many Americans—especially U.S. policymakers—were "fat, soft, and tired." They failed to realize that "we are at war." The question, then, was a simple one: "Will we fight, or will we surrender?"[1]

Anticommunist internationalists redoubled their efforts. They drew strength not only from each other but also from a growing conservative mobilization in the United States. Through myriad local struggles about churches and schools, segregation and taxation, right-leaning Americans coalesced into a broad-based national movement that was especially potent in the suburbs of Sunbelt cities like Los Angeles, Phoenix, and Atlanta. That movement laid the groundwork for Arizona senator Barry Goldwater's 1964 presidential campaign, which unfolded as an assault against moderates within the Republican Party, and then against liberals and leftists on the national stage. Although Goldwater went down in one of the worst electoral defeats in U.S. history, and many contemporaries wrote off the "radical Right" as hopelessly out of touch with the mainstream currents of U.S. history, the movement he helped inspire continued to grow throughout the decade.²

Flush with funds and capable of reaching ever larger numbers of Americans through an expanding network of independent, conservative media outlets, internationally minded Americans such as Marvin Liebman and William F. Buckley found many new resources to aid their friends abroad. In the Caribbean basin, they allied themselves with authoritarian right-wing regimes in Nicaragua and Guatemala, and lent support to Cuban exiles bent on retaking their homeland from Fidel Castro. In Southeast Asia, they joined leaders from Taiwan, South Korea, and South Vietnam in calling for greater Asian involvement in the Vietnam War. They also collaborated on psychological warfare campaigns to sway the hearts and minds of ordinary people in Vietnam and other zones of conflict. In Africa, conservative Americans worked on behalf of Moïse Tshombe's breakaway regime in the Congo, before shifting their efforts to the newly independent, white-supremacist state of Rhodesia. Moving in ever wider arcs abroad, U.S. conservatives brought home parables about the kinds of action needed to purge the United States of any vestige of communism.

All of this created an international crossroads that linked conservative activists, students, businessmen, politicians, and media figures from the United States to like-minded people in Asia, Latin America, and Africa. Theirs was a world set apart from the grassroots organizing that propelled the Goldwater campaign in cities and towns across the United States. International activism was nothing if not expensive and time-consuming. It required significant financial resources and a work life that allowed one to spend weeks or months abroad. As a result, the vast majority of U.S. conservatives who toiled overseas in these years came from an insular group of wealthy leaders who were also spending millions of dollars to combat organized labor and the civil rights movement. Their international activism was, in many ways, an extension of their work at home, particularly the notion that private money was the key to dismantling the Left.³

The infusion of large sums of American cash into the anticommunist international opened up new possibilities in the 1960s. It also strengthened the conviction—widely shared by many rightists in the United States and abroad—that the U.S. military and the CIA could not keep the world safe from communism. Only homegrown anticommunist forces, whether in Cuba, China, or the Congo, could do that. They were to be the vanguard in the unfolding struggle for the fate of the world.

The ubiquitous anticommunist organizer Marvin Liebman first met William F. Buckley in 1955. They soon became close friends. Liebman was enthralled by Buckley, and it is not hard to imagine why.[4] While Liebman was a late convert to conservatism, finding his place on the right after spending years working for socialist groups in New York City, Buckley had been literally born into it. The son of an affluent lawyer and oil baron, Buckley grew up on his family's sprawling estates in Connecticut and Mexico before attending a series of elite boarding schools in preparation for Yale University, from which he graduated in 1950. His early life offered the "ideal training for a young conservative raised in the shadow of revolution," as historian Kim Philips-Fein put it.[5] Fighting communism became a lifelong pursuit. With his family connections and Ivy League education, a career in the United States' clandestine services seemed likely. He worked for the CIA for a brief time in Mexico City after finishing college—translating books for his handler, E. Howard Hunt—but decided his talents were better suited to building a political movement in the United States.[6]

A devout Catholic, Buckley became a darling of the Right after publishing his first two books, the first a critique of Yale University's declining religious and moral instruction and the second a screed defending Senator Joseph McCarthy's communist witch hunt.[7] The success that followed helped Buckley generate the necessary capital to start his magazine, the *National Review*, which depended heavily on the patronage of publisher William Rusher and a circle of conservative businessmen who advertised in its pages. Targeted at "thoughtful people" and "opinion makers," the *National Review* was instrumental in linking the abstract principles of disparate conservative thinkers from Edmund Burke through Russell Kirk with a variety of contemporary issues, such as labor-management relations, the promises of the free market, desegregation of schools and workplaces, and atomic warfare.[8]

Insofar as the magazine advocated a consistent position on foreign affairs, it came from political philosopher and former Trotskyist James Burnham. His monthly column, titled the "Third World War," often urged the United States to roll back communism by fomenting armed uprisings in the Soviet Union, communist China, and their proxies.[9] As such, the *National Review*'s worldview tended to dovetail with that of militant anticommunists in Latin America, Asia, Africa, and Europe who made similar calls for wars of national liberation in their homelands. It made sense, then, for Buckley to use his magazine as a conduit for them to make their calls directly to American audiences.

As Buckley moved into the anticommunist international, others followed. One was Clarence Manion, an influential conservative-radio-show host from Indiana. Rising from a Kentucky family of modest means, Manion had worked as a lawyer for several years before becoming Dean of the University of Notre Dame Law School, where he honed an antifederal government philosophy in his books and lectures.[10] By 1940 he was a leading member of the America First Committee, a coalition of intellectuals, politicians, students, and activists that opposed U.S. entry into World War II and, at times, sided with the fascist powers in Europe.[11] After the war, he helped organize Republican senator Robert Taft's successive bids for the presidency before taking a blue-ribbon post in the Eisenhower administration. However, Manion's ardent defense of the Bricker Amendment, which sought to cripple the president's abilities to negotiate and sign treaties, ended his formal political career just as it began.[12] President Dwight Eisenhower dismissed Manion in February 1954.[13]

Disillusioned with the mainstream Republican Party and its embodiment in the Eisenhower administration, Manion retired to his home in South Bend, Indiana. There, he devoted himself to finding a way to carve out a space for "true conservatives" in the U.S. political scene.[14] He decided to create a radio show and, in October 1954, the *Manion Forum of Opinion* burst across the airwaves. It quickly grew into one of the largest political programs of its time, broadcast on nearly three hundred stations in forty-four states, garnering a peak listenership of more than four million. Despite its popularity and mounting operational costs, Manion rarely solicited advertising money. Rather, his show was financed almost entirely by donations from businesses of every size.[15] That nationwide fundraising network made Manion an important behind-the-scenes player in the burgeoning conservative movement. Corresponding frequently with William F. Buckley, he financed the publication of Barry Goldwater's *Conscience of a Conservative*, which made the Arizona senator the national standard bearer for the conservative movement in the early 1960s.[16]

Like Buckley, Manion initially concerned himself with matters of domestic politics and political economy.[17] But foreign policy issues began to filter into the show in the late 1950s, as Manion offered a series of programs denouncing U.S. aid to the Soviet Union while agonizing over the plight of Eastern Europe's "captive nations."[18] Still, Manion, like Buckley, was mostly aloof from the kinds of international work that Marvin Liebman had been doing. He cared deeply about events abroad, but felt little compulsion to change them directly. Communist conquest in Europe and Asia was alarming yet relatively remote.

The Cuban Revolution of 1959 changed all of that. Within little more than a year, Fidel Castro and his lieutenants had solidified a military and economic alliance with the Soviet Union, setting Cuba on the path to its own brand of socialism. To many Americans, including President John F. Kennedy and his key advisors, that meant not only the loss of a key ally in the Caribbean basin, but, more importantly, the establishment of a base from which the Soviet Union could launch assaults elsewhere in the American hemisphere. As relations between Washington and Havana deteriorated, the Kennedy administration initiated a CIA-sponsored invasion plan first drafted under Eisenhower. Armed Cuban exiles would retake the island and then launch a popular uprising to oust Castro. It was a disaster. After training on a CIA base in Guatemala for a few weeks, the paramilitaries, operating under the name Brigade 2506, arrived at Cuba's Bay of Pigs on April 16, 1961. But Fidel Castro's army was prepared, and Kennedy withdrew U.S. air support just as the exiles reached Cuban shores. Equipped with tanks and jets, Castro's soldiers routed the invasion force, killing many and imprisoning those who did not escape. In the following weeks, Castro used the invasion as a unifying symbol to rally Cubans in support of his socialist state, while building a closer relationship with Moscow.[19]

For Buckley and Manion, the Bay of Pigs fiasco was instantly familiar. It was like the failed Hungarian Revolution of 1956 all over again, only this time much closer to home. As in Hungary, they said, the U.S. government, particularly the CIA, had failed to adequately support a popular uprising against a communist regime, and thereby condemned those brave souls to certain death. Their views on the matter were sharpened by Cuban paramilitaries who had survived the invasion and then returned home to castigate the Kennedy administration for not giving them sufficient help. Manion, for one, featured Bay of Pigs veterans on his programs several times a year, where they described how the Kennedy administration had forsaken them by not providing enough supplies, weapons, and air cover and then refusing to mount subsequent actions to liberate imprisoned "freedom fighters."[20] These narratives about the Bay of Pigs, wherein plucky freedom fighters died because weak-willed politicians failed them at the crucial moment, spread across conservative outlets in the United States in the early 1960s. As one exile summed it up, "The Cuban exiles, who trusted the USA, our faithful and powerful long time friend, were distraught and convinced that they had been betrayed."[21] These ideas merged with contemporary narratives about how the U.S. government had abandoned other "freedom fighters"—particularly in China and Hungary—thereby giving up on its avowed mission to help free peoples resist the onslaught of totalitarian forces.

Bay of Pigs veterans were a small if vocal slice of a larger movement of Cuban exiles who dreamt of returning home, and who found themselves drawn into anticommunist circles in the United States. In the aftermath of the 1959 revolution, tens of thousands of Cubans, including not a few supporters of the deposed dictator Fulgencio Batista, had fled the island. They arrived in Miami, Tampa, and New York City, where the U.S. government welcomed them with open arms, offering unprecedented access to housing and business loans, English-language courses, job training, and an easy path to citizenship. As they settled in the United States, many of these exiles filtered into the ranks of the nascent conservative movement. It was not particularly surprising given that many of those who comprised Cuba's ruling classes before the revolution—and thus the first stream of exiles to the United States—had become wealthy and powerful by working with the same American businessmen who were financing the rise of the Right in the United States. Important differences notwithstanding, many Cuban exiles' worldview—fear of communism matched with faith in private enterprise and Christianity—often overlapped with that of right-leaning Americans.[22]

One of these exiles-turned-activists was Luis V. Manrara, a public accountant who escaped from Cuba to Miami in 1960. He hadn't been a strong Batista supporter, but Castro and his band of revolutionaries appalled him.[23] Shortly after his arrival, Manrara and ten other exiles founded the Truth about Cuba Committee to publish propaganda in English and Spanish, raise awareness about the plight of Cubans, and pressure officials to take actions against Castro.[24] Funded by donations from thousands of individuals, as well as the Bacardi Corporation and other Cuban-owned businesses, it was first and foremost an "educational, non-profit organization" disseminating "factual information" about what "has happened and is happening in Cuba under the communist regime."[25] In so doing, Manrara and other leaders hoped their activism would prompt American citizens and Cuban exiles to help the island's people foment an uprising from below. For Manrara, it was clear that the Cuban people were losing their faith in the revolution but did not yet have the means to retake the island since "the small minority backing Castro has the arms and is completely ruthless." It was "impossible to organize a well-coordinated revolt that could overthrow the Communist regime without outside help." Americans had the "right and the duty to promote the liberation of Cuba."[26]

Manrara also insisted that U.S. and Latin American civilians had to take armed action in their own countries against the "avalanche of professional revolutionaries" cascading across the hemisphere. The communists' strategy of guerrilla warfare offered "little, if any, opportunity for the military might of the United States to fight a conventional war." And so "it was imperative that citizens of every country be organized to fight and defeat the socialist/communist conspiracy in their home front." They "would be wise to follow" Lenin's revolutionary tactics, "but in reverse."[27]

By mid-decade, Manrara's organization was working alongside a slew of Cuban-American groups, including the CIA-backed Cuban Freedom Committee, to promote the liberation of the island.[28] Many received significant resources from the U.S. government, but Luis Manrara and other Cuban leaders nevertheless insisted liberal diplomats had betrayed their cause. And after 1964, as the Johnson administration and the CIA started to pull support from Cuban exile groups bent on retaking the island, the exiles increasingly turned to private sources of funding to maintain their war. Yet they insisted that this shift was of their own volition rather than an imposed necessity. In their telling, they solicited private funds to break free of the U.S. government, which sought to use their war for its own goals. As one militant exile put it in 1964, "We welcome the aid of those individual Americans who wish to help in our struggle. But, in the view of the experience at the Bay of Pigs, we can never again accept aid as subordinates of U.S. policy." Loosed from the state, Cubans now took it upon themselves to "spark the coming revolt and to support it with our funds, our faith, and if necessary, our lives."[29]

Several paramilitary organizations, with names such as Alpha 66 and the Insurrectional Movement for the Recovery of the Revolution, led the way. Shortly after the Bay of Pigs fiasco, they began soliciting funds from businesses and individuals in Miami and other U.S. cities.[30] They trained guerrilla armies deep in the Florida Everglades, and managed secret arsenals and fleets of small motorboats. They detonated bombs, launched nighttime raids, and carried out acts of sabotage in Cuba. Then they hailed these clandestine acts as proof that ordinary Cubans on the island were taking up arms against Castro.[31] Most of their resources came directly from Cuban communities, rather than deep-pocketed conservative donors or from leading figures like Manion or Buckley. Instead, conservative media networks served to popularize the exiles' struggle and to win new converts—in other words, to legitimize their extralegal war. Yet their campaigns failed to bring the desired results. If anything, they generated more support for Castro's regime, proving that the Cuban Revolution was indeed under attack. They also provoked responses from domestic policing agencies. For instance, former pediatrician Orlando Bosch, who commanded the Insurrectional Movement for the Recovery of the Revolution, was arrested several times in the 1960s for orchestrating bombings in Cuba, Puerto Rico, and the United States, eventually receiving a ten-year prison sentence.[32] Dissatisfied with the U.S. government's waning support for their paramilitary campaigns, Cuban exiles began looking further afield for new backers in Mexico and Central America.[33]

As Cuban exiles broadened their horizons in the Americas, so did Clarence Manion, William F. Buckley, and other conservative leaders from the United States. They did so for personal as much as ideological reasons. Buckley's family had investments throughout the Caribbean basin, while Manion's show received generous funding from a number of U.S. companies with interests in Central America, Cuba, and Mexico. Those financial stakes allied Manion and Buckley with others who stood to lose money if and when communist governments took power elsewhere in Latin America and nationalized U.S.-owned property and enterprises. Manion formed a close bond with Spruille Braden, a businessman and former ambassador to Cuba, Colombia, and Argentina, who had also helped conceive and execute the 1954 coup that ousted Guatemala's Jacobo Arbenz from power.[34] A member of the John Birch Society, Braden had earned a reputation as a hardline anticommunist with the overseas experience and connections to back it up. Because of that, he became one of Manion's most valued guests, appearing several times a year in the early 1960s to warn listeners about the spread of communism throughout Latin America.[35]

Braden convinced Manion that his show could aid embattled anticommunist regimes in Guatemala and Nicaragua. And so, in 1961, Manion sent his daughter Marilyn to Guatemala City to meet President Miguel Ydígoras Fuentes, then to Managua to interview Nicaraguan President Luis Somoza Debayle.[36] Both leaders had risen to power in the bloody, volatile world of Central American politics, and each of their countries were key nodes in the informal empire erected by U.S. businesses in the region. In Guatemala, the United Fruit Company had dominated the nation's economy and politics since the late nineteenth century, subverting democracy by propping up a series of authoritarian governments.[37] Miguel Ydígoras Fuentes, a right-wing general who had conspired with Castillo Armas to overthrow Jacobo Arbenz in 1954, became president when an assassin killed Armas in 1958.[38] In Nicaragua, the story was roughly the same. Since the 1930s, U.S. policymakers had supported the dictatorial regime of Anastasio Somoza, who nurtured close ties with American corporations, accumulating in the process millions of acres of land and a fortune close to $600 million. When an assassin murdered the elder Somoza in 1956, his son Luis Somoza Debayle took the reins of power.[39]

Both Ydígoras and Somoza served as reliable allies to U.S. politicians and capital, crushing internal enemies with state security forces, death squads, and rural paramilitary organizations.[40] They also supported armed initiatives against Castro's Cuba. When the CIA needed somewhere to train its paramilitary force for the Bay of Pigs invasion, both Ydígoras and Somoza had happily offered their countries as staging grounds.[41] In short, these were men who, unlike the Kennedy administration, could be counted on. Convinced that the Bay of Pigs debacle underscored just how uncommitted Kennedy was to fighting communism, Clarence Manion, Spruille Braden, and others commended the methods used by Somoza and Ydígoras to stamp out any spark of revolution in their own countries.[42] In a characteristic remark, Manion praised the Guatemalan military coup—and its subsequent purge of leftists, socialists, union leaders, and dissenters—as a "spirited and singularly successful resistance" against the "terrible disease of communism."[43] Meanwhile, Somoza and Ydígoras used their connections with U.S. conservatives to reach ordinary Americans and urge them to join the hemispheric fight. Transmitted via taped interviews in heavily accented English, their liturgies about the communist threat could have been ripped from the pages of any conservative periodical, though sometimes they made pointed pleas to U.S. investors.[44]

Drawing closer to right-wing regimes in Nicaragua and Guatemala, Americans organized several lobbying groups to pressure Congress into sending them larger sums of military and economic aid. William F. Buckley and Marvin Liebman ran the Committee for the Monroe Doctrine, which sponsored letter-writing campaigns, published newspaper columns, and sent thousands of pieces of literature to Guatemala and Nicaragua, as well as Mexico, Colombia, Venezuela, and El Salvador. It was in many ways a right-wing version of the United States Information Service, minus the federal funds.[45] Another group organized by Buckley and Liebman, the Inter-American Literacy Foundation, constructed a network of "radio schools" where peasants in Colombia listened to broadcast sermons about the benefits of the free enterprise system and the need for inter-American cooperation in the anticommunist struggle.[46]

Those Americans who devoted their time and energy to anticommunist initiatives in Latin America saw in the region parables for the possible outcomes of domestic conflicts—especially the growing civil rights and student protest movements. For example, on a series of *Manion Forum* programs in 1962 and 1963, Ydígoras had fumed about the young men whisked away to Mexico City, Havana, Prague, and Moscow to be "trained, indoctrinated, brainwashed—and then sent back to their respective schools."[47] Somoza echoed that Nicaraguan students "were being trained in Moscow to spread the disease of Communism in Central America."[48]

Americans charged that the same tactics were at play on college campuses in the United States.[49] Much like their counterparts in Latin America, student radicals at home praised Fidel Castro and "proceeded under the expert direction" of the Communist Party, as Manion put it.[50] To those on the U.S. Right, groups with vastly dissimilar politics—the National Students Association, the Students for a Democratic Society, the Americans for Democratic Action, the Young People's Socialist League, the Student Non-Violent Coordinating Committee—were all little more than communist fronts. Thus, many in the U.S.

Right argued that the repressive methods employed in Central America were the best way to stem the tide of student radicalism in the United States.[51] Their affinity for right-wing, authoritarian governments in Latin America would only grow.

---

As several wars in Southeast Asia escalated in the early 1960s, U.S. conservatives directed more time and energy to their allies there. Taiwan continued to serve as a kind of lodestar, pointing the way forward. By 1961, William F. Buckley was using the *National Review* to promote the successes of Jiang's regime, touting its importance to the global anticommunist struggle.[52] In June of that year, the magazine featured an interview between Marvin Liebman and Jiang in which the general insisted that the mainland was still ripe for a "full-scale anticommunist revolution." Confident that ordinary Chinese were ready to pick up arms, Jiang argued that the real question was what kind of assistance they could count on from the outside world. As usual, he likened the situation to that of Hungary in 1956. If only there had been a "free Hungarian government" in exile when the "freedom fighters" struck, they would have had enough arms and supplies to combat communist troops. The failure of Hungarian Revolution served as an allegory about a potential uprising in China. Jiang noted that Taiwan would certainly aid an uprising on the mainland—but he maintained that more assistance from the United States would be needed if such a revolt were to be successful.[53]

Jiang's enduring belief that his countrymen, like the Hungarians, could be transformed into guerrillas spurred the Asian Peoples' Anti-Communist League to call for a contingent of "Asian volunteers" for war against communist China. This army would retake the Chinese mainland, distribute weapons and supplies, instruct peasants in guerrilla warfare, and, ultimately, drive a wedge between communist China and its allies in Southeast Asia.[54] Dubbed the Free Asian Brigade or, alternatively, the Asian Freedom Legion, APACL leaders envisioned that it would eventually march into Laos, Cambodia, and Vietnam to wipe out homegrown communist cadres.[55] According to Filipino congressman Ramón Bagatsing, the force would shift the burden of fighting communism from American soldiers to Asian civilians, which was necessary since Indochina had "been too long under the colonial domination of France" and the presence of white U.S. troops there "may still create suspicion." In contrast, he argued, the people would see a contingent of volunteer Asian soldiers and paramilitaries as a legitimate expression of Asian self-determination. It would also be "more adapted to the tropical jungle warfare," since the Chinese, Filipinos, and Japanese were "similar in ethnological distinction and cultural development." If successful, the force would allow Asian peoples to retain control over the anticommunist revolution and thus shape the postwar landscape.[56]

APACL leaders had some reason to think that might happen. Remnants of the Guomindang armies remained in parts of southern China, particularly along its borders with Burma and Laos. If they could arm the local populations in these areas, APACL leaders believed, peasants would join the leftover GMD troops in guerrilla assaults against the communists.[57] Yet the CIA had attempted to carry out a similar operation in the early 1950s, with dreadful results. It spent more than $100 million dropping agents and weapons into Burma and southern China, only to watch them disappear. The GMD armies on the mainland were generally less interested in fighting Mao's communists than they were in harvesting and selling opium.[58] Few outside of the CIA were aware of that failure, however. And so the APACL's plan to raise a contingent of volunteers for a guerrilla war in China received warm support from conservative luminaries in the United States.[59]

Although flawed in so many ways, that faith continued to guide conservative Americans' work in Vietnam in the 1960s.[60] A former French colony, Vietnam had gained independence under the leadership of Ho Chi Minh, a nationalist and a communist who guided Vietnamese soldiers and civilians to victory over the course of a brutal war that stretched from 1946 through 1954. Fearful of communist expansion in Asia, U.S. leaders had thrown their support behind the embattled French colonial regime, eventually subsidizing the bulk of the war's costs. When the French surrendered in 1954, U.S. leaders tried to make the newly created South Vietnam into a permanent anticommunist state, run by the corrupt American-educated, Catholic "mandarin" Ngo Dinh Diem. Committed to a unified and independent Vietnam, the communists in the North sought to overthrow the U.S.-backed regime in Saigon. As an insurgency known as the National Liberation Front (NLF), or Viet Cong, spread throughout the South after 1959, the U.S. government channeled massive amounts of funds and weapons to Diem's regime, while also committing larger and larger amounts of U.S. troops. By 1965, U.S. soldiers in South Vietnam numbered roughly 180,000, and were engaged in combat in many parts of the country. All of that only galvanized the NLF, which rallied hundreds of thousands to its cause.[61]

As U.S. combat soldiers arrived in greater numbers, leaders from the APACL grew wary. While praising the resolve of the Johnson administration and its generals, many insisted that Taiwan and other states were better positioned to root out the communists—not only in Vietnam but also in China, from where they believed the insurgency really emanated. They made that point at international conferences that attracted a growing number of Americans, including former Vice President Richard Nixon, who spoke at the organization's tenth conference in Taipei in November 1964.[62]

While Nixon's involvement was passing, it still lent legitimacy to Asian anticommunists who called for greater autonomy in fighting wars in their part of the world. By 1965, several American groups had cast their lot with the APACL and its plan for a Taiwanese-led invasion of the mainland. One was the Free Pacific Association, an anticommunist news agency founded by a Belgian-born Catholic priest named Raymond De Jaegher, who had spent two decades as a missionary in Vietnam. Serving as a special advisor to Ngo Dinh Diem, De Jaegher turned his group into a propaganda agency for Diem's regime, publishing materials for audiences in the United States and Southeast Asia.[63] De Jaegher's main partner was another Catholic clergyman, Reverend Daniel Lyons, a Jesuit priest and professor of economics at Gonzaga University. A rising star in the burgeoning Catholic conservative movement, Lyons had spent two decades proselytizing in Southeast Asia, and styled himself as an unparalleled expert on Vietnam.[64]

Like other Catholics who joined the conservative movement, Lyons and De Jaegher saw the Cold War as not just a political or military conflict, but a struggle between atheism and Christianity. They supported firm U.S. action in Southeast Asia, but were still convinced that American intervention in Vietnam was bound to fail unless Taiwan and other anticommunist states led military operations within and against communist China. "We cannot solve the Asian problem merely by trying to solve the problem in Vietnam," Daniel Lyons explained, because the "head of the snake is in China." Put another way, Americans could not hope to contain communism in Vietnam without eradicating its roots in China, and the best way to do that was to let Asians take up arms against Mao's regime. In his estimation, all that was needed was for Taiwan to "establish a beachhead of 50 or 100 miles," and then people from across China would "come to them" to join the war as volunteers or paramilitaries.[65] That plan, as Clarence Manion noted, would obviate the need for a large-scale U.S. military intervention. The United States, he said, would be wise to not overcommit its troops to a single theater of combat, especially one as murky and volatile as Southeast Asia.[66]

Ideas about race figured heavily into Americans' calls for a greater Asian role in Vietnam. In 1964, retired U.S. Army general Bonner Fellers, a specialist on psychological warfare who had played a leading role in the U.S. occupation of Japan after World War II, appeared on the *Manion Forum* to explain why Americans shouldn't fight in Vietnam. "It would be grievous mistake to commit American troops to full-scale combat," he said, because of the "peculiar racial characteristics of Asiatic peoples who stand by idly and see the white man—giant that he may be—failing in South Vietnam." Americans in Vietnam had inherited the "oriental hatred" for French and British imperialism, and therefore the Vietnamese would "resent the white man killing other Vietnamese, even though those killed may be communist enemies." Instead, Fellers recommended his experience waging counterinsurgency campaigns in the Philippines where the "Filipinos faced the Communist threat with their own people," not U.S. troops. "Gradually our oriental friends off the Asiatic coast could and would replace the white man in South Vietnam," Fellers predicted. Only "they could make a victory permanent."[67]

Although that conviction was at odds with U.S. conservatives' growing calls for a decisive American military campaign in Vietnam, it nevertheless guided several U.S.-based groups. In 1965, De Jaegher and Lyons founded the National Committee for the Liberation of China to promote the mainland invasion scheme.[68] At the same time, they ran the Asian Speakers Bureau, which brought politicians, academics, businessmen, and journalists from Taiwan, South Korea, the Philippines, Thailand, and South Vietnam to the United States for national speaking tours. Hailed as the "foremost experts on Vietnam and Southeast Asia," they visited college campuses, conservative fundraisers, and meetings of the John Birch Society, making the same basic pitch. U.S. military intervention—while a noble endeavor—was ultimately misguided, they said. The war was best left to Asian anticommunists.[69]

American military intervention in Vietnam had yet another drawback. As early as 1965, many U.S. conservatives began to worry about the antiwar protests spreading across the country. Though Americans from all walks of life denounced the war, U.S. conservatives were most troubled by young, radical students who appeared to flaunt conventional codes of morality, and who employed vitriolic language like the common refrain "One, two, three, four, we don't want your fucking war."[70] A small but vocal minority of protestors had gone so far as to declare their support for the National Liberation Front and North Vietnam. At rallies on U.S. college campuses, some students brandished North Vietnamese flags and shouted "Ho, Ho, Ho Chi Minh, the NLF is gonna win!"[71]

The apparently treasonous activities of American students certainly worried Buckley, Liebman, and Manion, all the more so when they compared American youths to their counterparts in Taiwan, South Korea, and South

Vietnam. There was a solution, however. If young Americans had the opportunity to meet their cohorts in Asia and learn of their struggles, then perhaps that would quell some of the antiwar fervor on U.S. college campuses. The Young Americans for Freedom (YAF) was the obvious choice to carry out such a mission. Since its founding in 1960, the group had fanned across the country, claiming nearly fifty thousand members by 1964. Financed with hundreds of thousands of dollars from small businesses and major corporations, the organization carved out a premier position within the conservative movement, forging a new generation of activists and politicians.[72] By 1965, a few YAF leaders had begun branching out overseas, attending conferences of the APACL and networking with young people from Taiwan, Thailand, the Philippines, Japan, Korea, Australia, and South Vietnam.[73]

That led YAF leaders to launch what they called the World Youth Crusade for Freedom (WYCF) in the summer of 1965.[74] Its main purpose was "to meet with as many young people as possible; to let them know that the majority of American youth were anti-Communist; to learn as much as possible about the true situation in these areas so that we could report back to young Americans throughout the country; to lay the organizational groundwork for effective local anti-Communist youth action and . . . provide the basis for coordinated anti-Communist youth action throughout the world."[75] Within a few months, they had secured nearly $55,000 in funds, much of which came from Walter Judd, William F. Buckley, William Rusher, and other luminaries associated with the *National Review*.[76] The omnipresent Marvin Liebman stepped in as the treasurer and administrator of the WYCF's fundraising campaigns.[77]

The YAF used its substantial war chest to publish multi-language propaganda and stage a series of rallies in American, Asian, and European cities.[78] These demonstrations garnered ecstatic praise from anticommunist youth groups in South Vietnam that flooded Huston's office with gratifying messages.[79] The success of the assemblies, Huston declared, was the "first step towards molding together a permanent anti-Communist international apparatus."[80] For Liebman, this "marked this first time that youth groups from many nations participated in a *coordinated* joint anticommunist venture."[81]

Inspired by the rallies, YAF leaders hatched a plan to send conservative college students from the United States to Asia, where they could help locals in towns, villages, and rural areas organize new anticommunist programs. Named the Freedom Corps and sponsored by YAF's corporate backers, it was to be a "private volunteer anti-Communist Peace Corps" made up of students from top-tier American universities. After training at Yale University, the Freedom Corps members would travel to South Vietnam, India, Singapore, the Philippines, and Australia. Their goal was to establish a "program of work and cooperation to meet the Communists on their own ground... working among young people all around the world."[82]

Believing they were "mobilizing armies for the revolutionary struggle" which had "too long been the undisputed monopoly of the Communists," the Freedom Corps operatives deployed across Southeast Asia, each assigned to work under the aegis of a different national APACL chapter.[83] Trouble was apparent from the start. In Taiwan, Freedom Corps workers clashed with the Peace Corps, whose volunteers denounced the young conservatives as "fascists." Meanwhile, the volunteer who went to Saigon discovered, much to his dismay, that the Vietnamese students, like many of their American counterparts, did everything they could to avoid military service and were generally apathetic, if not outright hostile, to the anticommunist cause. Yet other Freedom Corps workers believed they had made a difference. An operative assigned to rural villages in South Vietnam found the peasants there dedicated to fighting communism and therefore grateful for his work.[84] Returning home, Freedom Corps envoys traveled across the country to share their experiences with other students in the College Republicans, the Intercollegiate Society for Individualists, and the College Conservative Council.[85]

But the Freedom Corps project was an expensive charade. Only a handful of volunteers ever made it to Southeast Asia and most of them just visited Taiwan. By 1968, it was finished. Marvin Liebman regretted his participation. "Despite our great hopes and rhetoric... I considered it fruitless," he later wrote. Recalling the disaster of the World Anti-Communist Congress for Liberation and Freedom in 1958, Liebman did not want to be "involved in building another façade, especially one that could be exposed as such." Ironically, the failure of the Freedom Corps affirmed Liebman's "sneaking admiration" for those young men and women who opposed the war in Vietnam. Filled with "frustration and rage, they took to the streets and campuses to fight for something they believed with all their hearts." He could "never find that passion in the activities of the conservative youth."[86]

Despite the dissolution of the Freedom Corps, its corporate backers thought it a worthy effort, and remained committed to molding a cadre of anticommunist youth in the United States. In 1966, members of the American Security Council, a consortium of defense industry lobbyists and hawkish policymakers that maintained files on thousands of Americans it suspected were subversives, broke ground on a private anticommunist training academy known as the Freedom Studies Center. Modeled on a similar school run by the APACL in South Korea, and housed in a Tudor-style mansion on a 700-acre property in the rural hamlet of Boston, Virginia, the center was supposed to "turn out professionals in psychological warfare."[87]

The idea for the academy came from retired CIA officer Edward Lansdale and John M. Fisher, a former FBI agent and Sears executive who was then chairing the American Security Council.[88] Both men sensed a massive gap in how the Soviets and Americans approached the world. The Soviets, Fisher said, had some "6,000 political warfare schools." The United States, on the other hand, did not have a single place "where we teach how to fight what we call the Cold War"—although the CIA, the FBI, the U.S. military, and many major universities did precisely that.[89] After soliciting donations, Fisher and Lansdale hired a group of retired intelligence officers to serve as instructors.[90] By 1969, the school had set up a dormitory so students could immerse themselves in the study of "psycho-political warfare" under the tutelage of Lansdale, CIA Director William Colby, U.S. Army General Lyman Lemnitzer, Representative Richard Ichord, chair of the House Un-American Activities Committee, and a network of "overseas affiliates."[91] Lansdale warned that the academy was not to be a "private intelligence organization," but he still insisted that it should be capable of "sending small teams to foreign countries, upon request," to "resolve problems of concern to freedom"—places like the Congo and Vietnam.[92]

However, the Freedom Studies Center never launched any overseas programs, preferring instead to train people to carry out their missions within international businesses or government agencies. A decade after its founding, "hundreds of congressional aides, retired military officers, and corporate executives" had moved through its programs.[93] One graduate, the YAF's Tom Charles Huston, became President Richard Nixon's internal security advisor, authoring an abortive plan to spy on those American citizens whom Nixon feared would harm the United States and its image abroad—mostly antiwar and civil rights activists.[94] Others used their training to lay siege to the U.S. foreign policy establishment from within. By the mid-1970s, the Freedom Studies Center housed a team of hardline anticommunists who sought new paths to victory in the Cold War. From the richly manicured grounds of what one journalist called the West Point of the Cold War, they would help make anticommunist internationalism into state policy during the Reagan era.[95]

---

Alongside their projects in Latin America and Asia, U.S. conservatives turned their efforts to Africa. A few right-leaning Christian groups had been working in Africa for decades, but it was the Congo's decolonization crisis that galvanized the U.S. Right. Soon after Belgium granted independence to the Congo on June 30, 1960, the new nation exploded into civil war. As factions battled for control, a black, Christian-educated businessman named Moïse Tshombe led a secession movement in the southeastern province of Katanga, the richest region in the Congo. In Katanga, several Belgian companies, most notably the conglomerate known as Union Minière, had generated enormous profits from copper, cobalt, and uranium mines.[96] The region was also home to most of the Congo's white settlers, who believed they shared a common historical lineage and destiny with whites in South Africa and Rhodesia.[97]

In seceding, Tshombe had the full support of the Belgian government and the mining firms, which sent white soldiers and mercenaries to train his gendarmerie and protect Belgian investments.[98] Amidst the chaos, Patrice Lumumba, the Congo's first prime minister, struggled to maintain control. He petitioned the United Nations to send troops to put down the secessionist revolt and oust Belgian forces from the country. However, when the U.N. troops arrived, they were mostly interested in safeguarding white colonists.[99] Seeing the United Nations as little more than a front for Belgian and U.S. interests, Lumumba turned to the Soviet Union. The CIA began plotting against Lumumba, while the Eisenhower administration publicly shifted its support to his rivals. As these hostile forces mounted, Lumumba remained a genuine nationalist, deeply opposed to foreign control of his country. His dedication ended up costing him his life. On January 17, 1961, soldiers commanded by Joseph Mobutu, Army Chief of Staff, arrested Lumumba and flew him to Katanga. Under the supervision of Belgian military officers, Tshombe's soldiers tortured and then executed him.[100]

Lumumba's murder and the subsequent election of a U.S.-backed leader did not resolve the secession crisis. The continued support of Belgian financiers allowed Tshombe to maintain tenuous control over Katanga and a state apparatus that was "designed mainly for the protection of European lives and property," as one diplomat later put it.[101] His grasp on power, however, was starting to slip. His use of mercenaries, his ties to Belgian companies, and the brutal execution of Lumumba by his forces dissolved whatever support he might have had in the United Nations. After diplomatic initiatives stalled in late 1961, U.N. troops began military operations against Tshombe's rump state, carried out with the agreement of the Kennedy administration, which provided planes, weapons, and a small amount of military advisors.[102]

When the United States joined the offensive against Tshombe, conservative Americans banded together in support of his cause. In December of 1961, Marvin Liebman organized the American Committee for Aid to Katangan Freedom Fighters (ACAKFF) to raise funds, spread propaganda, and lobby Congress.

As he did with many of his other groups, Liebman recruited several of his pals from the *National Review* to serve on the advisory board.[103] But for the position of executive director, Liebman reached out to Max Yergan, a prominent African-American activist who had taken a hard turn toward the right in the early 1950s. Before his conversion to conservatism, Yergan had spent decades spearheading anticolonial efforts in Africa, working alongside Paul Robeson and W. E. B. Du Bois in the Council on African Affairs.[104] By 1955, he was speaking on behalf of the white-supremacist state of South Africa, as well as the Portuguese colonial regime in Angola.[105] By selecting an African-American who had renounced his ties to the Left to lead the committee, Liebman was attempting to undercut critics who charged, rightly, that it supported European colonialism over the nationalist aspirations of Africans. The pair reached out to Tshombe in a flurry of telegrams and letters, promising to support his cause in any way they could.[106]

The pro-Tshombe campaign clashed with the CIA and the State Department, which had thrown their support behind Mobutu, his army, and the U.N. forces. And members of the ACAKFF were keen to highlight this disparity. Tshombe's forces were "not fighting for freedom against the conventional totalitarian powers," but instead an "organization that has the backing of the free world and is utilizing American arms, equipment, and personnel."[107] Those charges tapped into U.S. conservatives' profound hatred for the United Nations and its complicated bureaucratic system, perceiving the organization as an impediment to the global anticommunist struggle.[108]

The committee soon sought to intervene directly in the conflict. In the final weeks of 1961, it called for Americans to "contribute funds which will be used to help supply the freedom fighters in Katanga with arms and other material to carry on their fight."[109] Comparing the Katangans' plight to that of Yugoslavians and Indonesians, who had also fallen under "communist rule," Max Yergan explained that ordinary Katangan men would use these weapons to defend "themselves, their wives and children and homes and places of work."[110] But it's doubtful that the arms the committee hoped to provide would have gone to Katangan soldiers—let alone ordinary people. More likely, they would have gone to the white mercenaries that Tshombe used to buttress his rule. Hailing from Belgium, Britain, France, Rhodesia, and South Africa, they were motivated by a deep sense of anticommunism and a lust for adventure. Earning the nickname *les affreux*, the "frightful ones," they battled U.N. forces while also terrorizing and plundering those Katangans who opposed Tshombe and the Belgians.[111] Perhaps the most well-known was "Mad" Mike Hoare, a Dublin-born soldier who had fought for the British Army in India and Burma during World War II before embarking on a career as a soldier-for-hire in Africa. Leading an outfit of a few hundred men, Hoare relished the freedom and pugnacity of mercenary life, explaining that "you can't win a war with choir boys."[112]

The committee was better suited to shape ideas about Tshombe than supply weapons to his soldiers or mercenaries. In early 1962, it sent Professor Ernest van den Haag, a Dutch-American sociologist and *National Review* contributor who had testified before the United Nations in support of South African apartheid, to Katanga on a "fact finding" mission.[113] Van den Haag already sympathized with the Belgians, since according to him the Congolese were "neither educated nor experienced enough to administer a vast country."[114] Of course, Tshombe was the exception to the rule—a fiercely anticommunist African who could overcome tribal divisions and who understood the importance of white-led capitalism to improving the lives of his people.[115] Van den Haag also sought to diminish concerns about Tshombe's mercenaries.[116] "Far from constituting a threat of civil war or disorder, these 'mercenaries' helped avoid it," van den Haag wrote. "They kept the Katanga army disciplined; it never degenerated into a murderous rabble, as did other sectors of the Congo army."[117]

Although the Committee was never able to send any weapons to Tshombe—for legal and logistical reasons—it did help sway policymakers in support of Tshombe. After a brief exile in 1963, Tshombe returned to the Congo at the request of the Johnson administration to serve as the new prime minister.[118] Resuming power with U.S. support, Tshombe oversaw a massive paramilitary operation that employed mercenaries from South Africa, Rhodesia, Belgium and France, CIA-trained Cuban exiles, and African gendarmes to crush a revolt of Lumumba's followers in the northeastern part of the country.[119] The U.S. government supported his mercenary forces with weapons and planes for a few months, but soon grew concerned that Tshombe's efforts to recruit more white South Africans would damage his standing with other African leaders.[120]

The tables turned on Tshombe again. In 1964, a rival, the Congo's president Joseph Kasavubu, charged him with treason, forcing him to flee to Spain.[121] In exile, Tshombe maintained his relationships with Belgian and Portuguese financiers, as well as the governments of South Africa and Rhodesia, talking openly and often about his plans to retake his country with an army of hired guns.[122] By the end of 1966, he and his backers had mercenaries training in camps in France, Belgium, and Angola.[123] A few had even led a brief revolt in the city of Stanleyville.[124] Back in the Congo, General Joseph Mobutu staged a coup and, after taking power, tried Tshombe *in absentia* for treason and sentenced him to death. What happened next is still shrouded in some mystery, but the outlines are fairly well known. On July 2, 1967, Tshombe boarded a private plane in Ibiza, Spain, bound for Africa, probably the Congo or a neighboring country. After taking off, someone hijacked the plane and forced its pilots to land in Algeria.[125] When it touched down, Algerian authorities arrested Tshombe, claiming that the plane was loaded with weapons, threw him in a cramped, windowless cell, and told the world that he would soon be extradited to the Congo for his execution.[126]

Tshombe's allies in the United States were appalled. In the span of a few days, Marvin Liebman, William F. Buckley, and a few others devised the Tshombe Emergency Committee to press for his release from prison and safe passage to Spain.[127] Over the next three months, they launched a series of "overt and covert efforts" to secure his release. On the overt front, they published editorials in leading newspapers across the country and spoke on television and radio about how Tshombe was a committed anticommunist and ally of capitalism. They condemned the kidnapping as a violation of international law, particularly the right of asylum.[128] They also began working with a Chicago-based lawyer, Luis Kutner, petitioning the United Nations for a writ of habeas corpus that would allow Tshombe to face his accusers in court.[129] Meanwhile, the committee lobbied state officials from Israel, Tunisia, Senegal, Liberia, and Spain.[130] In the U.S. Senate, Strom Thurmond and Thomas Dodd castigated their colleagues for not doing enough to save a stalwart anticommunist ally.[131]

In secret, Liebman worked on a plan to secure Tshombe's release without the involvement of the United Nations, the U.S. government, or any other states. In late July, Liebman and Kutner received a series of letters from a mysterious source claiming that they could get Tshombe out of prison and deliver him to Switzerland, but only for the right price. They weighed the scheme for a few weeks before giving up on it.[132] By October 1967, Liebman was willing to concede that their "overt and covert efforts" had "not been very effective."[133] Tshombe languished in prison in Algeria for more than two years. He died there in June 1969 from what his captors said was heart failure. In the United States, his allies mourned the passing of yet another anticommunist warrior on whom the U.S. government had turned its back. That was why, they said, Tshombe died with a "broken heart."[134]

Nevertheless, the campaign to put Tshombe in power—and keep him there—had sharpened the conviction that U.S. conservatives were on the right side of national liberation in Africa, and that they could channel significant resources, including weapons, to their allies abroad. To them, Tshombe represented a comfortable kind of decolonization, in which elite black Africans would manage the transition from colony to nation without altering the existing racial, political, and economic order, thereby ensuring that communists would not gain a foothold in these new countries. Tshombe's failure, when viewed against the backdrop of the Congo's independence struggles, reinforced the belief that decolonizing countries would be inexorably drawn into the Soviet empire if they jettisoned the institutions white colonizers had built. "Independence for the Congo was pushed ahead of schedule with a resultant chaos," said one pro-Tshombe U.S. writer. "Agitators for racial equality set off an orgy of rape, mutilation, and murder."[135] Moreover, Joseph Mobutu's regime had destroyed the racial harmony that had supposedly existed in the era of Belgian rule, and which Tshombe had tried preserve by seceding from the Congo. What had once been a "peaceful and prosperous" country was now governed by "black racist rule," as Mobutu "waged a violent anti-white campaign."[136]

If Tshombe represented an acceptable path for African nations, then Rhodesia was the ideal. Perhaps the most peculiar of all decolonization stories, Rhodesia had been colonized by the British in the late nineteenth century. A few hundred thousand settlers arrived over the following decades, and Rhodesia moved through a series of imperial classifications as the British government tweaked its colonial system in Africa.[137] Throughout those changes, three elements of Rhodesian society persisted. First, white settlers always represented a tiny fraction of the overall population. Second, despite their numbers, whites controlled most of the country's land and capital. And third, whites maintained their economic domination through a complex system that excluded most blacks from the voter rolls and sharply limited the power of the small number that did qualify.

As African nationalists pressed for independence in the 1950s and the 1960s white Rhodesians concluded that their privileged position was under attack. The Congo crisis magnified those fears, as violence and upheaval there had caused many white colonists to flee. Migrating into and through Rhodesia, they carried tales of what independence under African leadership had meant for them. Meanwhile, whites in Rhodesia grew increasingly dissatisfied with the British government, which was swiftly dissolving its African colonies in favor of independent states based on majority rule. For that meant, in most places, that blacks would dominate these new countries.[138] After all, even at its peak in 1961, Rhodesia's white population only numbered some 277,000, compared to more than four million Africans as well as smaller numbers of Indians and others. By 1965, the white population was rapidly shrinking—the result of a "white flight" that resembled the mass migration of whites from U.S. cities, but on a national rather than municipal scale.[139]

Rather than cede to demands for majority rule, the governing Rhodesian

Front party and its supporters opted to leave the British Empire altogether. In November 1965, Rhodesian Prime Minister Ian Smith issued a Unilateral Declaration of Independence from Britain, proclaiming "We have struck a blow for the preservation of justice, civilization, and Christianity." Smith called his government "the ultimate bastion against communism on the African continent," and explained that there would be "no African rule in my lifetime... The white man is master of Rhodesia. He has built it, and he intends to keep it."[140] Many in Africa, Western Europe, and the United States condemned Rhodesia, and no nation recognized the newly independent state. The British government quickly imposed economic sanctions that targeted Rhodesia's major exports—chrome, steel, tobacco, and manufactured goods—and forbade the sale of petroleum to Smith's regime. In 1968, the United Nations enacted an almost total embargo on trade with and investment in Rhodesia.[141]

Rhodesia's only real ally was the apartheid government of neighboring South Africa, with which white Rhodesians shared many ideas and assumptions. Since the late nineteenth century, when the British and Dutch colonized the region, white settlers had excluded blacks from political participation and installed coercive labor regimes.[142] After the Second World War, under pressure from African nationalists, the South African legislature created the apartheid system, which classified black citizens into distinct racial groups with prescribed rights. By 1961, as South Africa gained formal independence from Great Britain, the apartheid system had made it a pariah, denounced by the United Nations, scores of African leaders, and even a growing number of U.S. politicians—although most U.S. leaders still preferred apartheid to African nationalism in the early 1960s.[143] As rogue states of sorts, Rhodesia and South Africa found much common ground. By the end of the decade, South Africa had sent troops to Rhodesia to help defend Ian Smith's government from internal and external challenges.[144]

Nevertheless, Rhodesia faced many obstacles: the demographic collapse of its white population, a pair of African nationalist movements with armed wings, and a nearly complete lack of legitimacy in Africa and on the broader international stage. Sensing that, U.S. conservatives established an overlapping network of private groups through which Americans could learn about Rhodesia firsthand and then share their knowledge with friends, coworkers, and elected officials when they arrived back in the United States. Their experiences of Rhodesia ended up shaping not only how they understood decolonization in Africa, but also how they viewed racial problems at home.[145]

At the center of that network was the Friends of Rhodesian Independence (FORI). Founded by Marvin Liebman in 1966, the FORI used funds from the

Rhodesian government and U.S. businesses to publish a newsletter and brochures, and to subsidize trips to Salisbury and other cities. Those Americans who supported the FORI believed it was fulfilling a vital service since "the field of African affairs is largely in the hands of organizations and individuals irrevocably committed to the very kind of 'liberal' dogmas which weakened and ultimately destroyed the cause of freedom in postwar China."[146]

By 1966, the organization boasted 180 chapters across the United States, attracting members of the John Birch Society, the Liberty Lobby, and other right-wing groups. The FORI paid for Max Yergan and George Schuyler—the leading African Americans in the conservative movement—to trek across Rhodesia. It did the same for Ohio Congressman John Ashbrook and several professors from Georgetown University's Center for Strategic and International Studies, a foreign-policy think tank with connections to the CIA.[147] At the same time, Max Yergan's group, the American African Affairs Association, published its own studies about communist subversion in southern Africa and financed Rhodesian excursions for James Kilpatrick, the staunch segregationist editor of the *Richmond New Leader*, and other conservatives from the U.S. South.[148] Likewise, Clarence Manion enlisted his show as a propaganda machine for both the Rhodesian and South African governments, which paid for him to visit the region in 1968.[149] Others in Manion's orbit, such as Cuban exile Luis Manrara and Catholic priest Daniel Lyons, also traveled to South Africa where they met members of the right-wing National Council to Combat Communism, as well as journalists, professors, government officials, and military leaders.[150]

Through these connections, Rhodesians and South Africans explained to American audiences how their societies depended upon the achievements of white settlers rather than the exploited labor of oppressed indigenous peoples. One member of the Rhodesian government put it this way: "It is the enterprise of the European population" that had "been responsible for developing the country's natural resources, building its towns and factories, communications systems, and various institutions that provide employment."[151] Americans parroted those narratives. On the *Manion Forum*, Anthony Harrigan, a veteran journalist and member of the American Security Council, gave a history lesson to justify white rule. Before whites came to Rhodesia, he explained, "It was a completely undeveloped land." However, once whites had subdued the black populations, the country became "a classic example of Western Enterprise. Had white Westerners not settled there, one can be sure that the land would still be in the Stone Age."[152]

Tales of white-led development bolstered Americans' belief that whites in

Rhodesia and South Africa shared a common past with white settlers in the United States. In each case, Americans said, whites had carved out civilization in a harsh terrain populated by backwards, racially inferior, and hostile peoples.[153] That helped Americans argue that the British government's actions in the United Nations were hypocritical. One cartoon in the *Dan Smoot Report*, a weekly newsletter, joked that if the United Nations had been around in 1776, then angry British officials would have showed up demanding "sanctions against this rebel who has set up an all-white rule in a nation of Redskins!"[154]

Meanwhile, Rhodesians and South Africans told Americans that white leadership in Africa held out the promise for black development.[155] A representative from the Parliament of South Africa explained how apartheid was distinct from segregation in the United States. While segregation "amounted to discrimination," apartheid "embarked upon a policy of developing the separate homelands, the historic homelands of all the black people." In this view, apartheid "would allow blacks to have self-determination and, eventually, if they wished to, sovereignty."[156] In a similar vein, white Rhodesians explained how their system of government allowed blacks to benefit from a "wide variety of public and private programs to raise their standards," including education, medicine, and agriculture.[157] One activist summed it up in a letter to President Richard Nixon: "Rhodesia and South Africa are performing the noblest and most practical service possible to the Negro—helping him to help himself."[158]

For their part, right-leaning white Americans insisted that the United States could learn much from white regimes in southern Africa. Journalist Ralph de Toledano, for one, believed that if "the Rhodesian system been employed in the United States after the War between the States, the advance of the Negro would have been accelerated and our present convulsions avoided," referring obliquely to the civil rights movement.[159] To some Americans, Rhodesia appeared as a superior society in which racial conflict had been all but eliminated. After visiting the country in 1967, one writer described what he saw as "an evolving multiracial society in which both races increasingly will share in the political, economic, and social development of their pioneer land." It was refreshing. An "American visitor, familiar with the uneasy vibrations of our own urban life, knows that racial tensions can be sensed" at home. But in Rhodesia, he "senses none of these tensions."[160]

All this talk about black development and racial harmony belied white Americans' real interest in Rhodesia and South Africa. For as millions of African Americans across the United States mobilized against injustice and inequality in the 1960s, many in the U.S. Right looked to Rhodesia and South Africa to help them make sense of a growing radicalism within the civil rights movement. Starting in 1964, black frustrations had exploded in hundreds of rebellions in Los Angeles, Detroit, Newark, Chicago, and many other major cities. As activists inspired by Malcolm X and Robert F. Williams moved from peaceful resistance to armed defense, many whites concluded that such hostility could only be the work of communist agents.[161] Clarence Manion summed it up in 1967: the U.S. "race riots" were just "one front in a worldwide war" waged by communists.[162] Others made the same basic point, warning that Robert F. Williams was a "Cuban-style revolutionary intent on the violent overthrow of the United States," and predicting that "unlimited colored immigration" from Africa would only bring more black revolutionaries into the United States.[163]

Denouncing civil rights advocates as communists was nothing new, of course, but the ways in which white conservatives made those links in the 1960s hinged on their understandings of what was taking place in Africa and other parts of the decolonizing world. As African Americans talked of black liberation in the United States in the same terms used by armed anticolonial movements in Africa and elsewhere, U.S. conservatives surmised that a race war at home was imminent, and that the Soviet Union was behind it all.[164] Thus, they flattened an old and complex set of ideas that had animated pan-African movements since the 1920s into a global communist conspiracy in which blacks—whether in the United States or Africa—were nothing more than pawns of Soviet conquest. Such a framing allowed whites to ignore the central claims of most civil rights and Black Power activists—access to housing, jobs, and political power, and an end to racist practices in policing, courts, and other public arenas—in favor of images of armed black revolutionaries stalking the streets of American cities. Summing up that view, a reporter for the Christian Anti-Communist Crusade asserted, "Racial revolution has replaced 'workers revolution' as the course of the communist plot to conquer the United States."[165]

Fears of racial revolution in the United States legitimized vigilante violence against African Americans and others. In the early 1960s, membership in the Ku Klux Klan—in reality a series of competing Klan groups—skyrocketed, surpassing 50,000 by 1965. Across the South and in many other parts of the country, Klansmen intimidated African Americans, bombed churches, and murdered scores of civil rights activists and leaders. They hoped to forestall change by turning back the clock to a time when blacks knew their place.[166] For that reason, South Africa and Rhodesia had an obvious appeal. Analogizing circumstances, Klansmen and like-minded members of White Citizens' Councils believed that their counterparts in Africa had taken admirable measures to stamp out challenges from blacks—not only legal discrimination and state repression but also vigilante violence.[167] The admiration flowed in the opposite direction too. Some white South Africans studied the "methods of the Ku Klux Klan" and donned its trademark white hoods and gowns. One group hoped to intimidate members of the African National Congress by scrawling "Ku Klux Klan Africa" on the walls of its office in Cape Town.[168] Realizing the Klan's popularity overseas, Terry Venable, who ran the Imperial Knights of the Ku Klux Klan, tried to establish a branch at Rhodes University in South Africa.[169]

For those right-leaning Americans who saw black freedom struggles in the United States and Africa as two sides of the same coin—and who saw Africans and African Americans as essentially the same people—the spread of leftist national liberation movements in Africa was profoundly disturbing. By the late 1960s, many nationalist movements in South Africa, Rhodesia, Mozambique, Angola, and elsewhere had taken up the Marxist cause and allied themselves with Cuba and the Soviet Union, which offered funds, weapons, advisers, and soldiers. Unfolding on a massive scale, these movements mobilized large swaths of the black population against racial inequality, political disfranchisement, and economic injustice.[170] The proliferation of popular revolutions in southern Africa confirmed conservatives' greatest fears about racial subversion in the United States. In their eyes, black freedom, whether at home or abroad, threatened nothing less than a return to barbarism. As one commentator reckoned, "Where the 'Winds of Change' have blown" and "civilized men have bowed to them, civilization has disappeared."[171]

That fear, above all, was what drew U.S. conservatives to southern Africa. For in Rhodesia they found parables for—and solutions to—domestic racial crises. At the same time, the heroic myths that white Rhodesians built around their nation and its peculiar rebellion helped conservative Americans maintain their self-image as anticolonial liberators, even as they supported the remnants of violent colonial regimes. In their eyes, Rhodesia had cast off the chains of British imperialism and forestalled communist conquest in Africa. By helping Rhodesia's cause, Americans joined that struggle.

---

In the 1960s, conservative Americans took a more active role in the anticommunist international. Using a vast fundraising network, they helped expand its size and scope, drawing more people and groups into the movement. They also established many of the core convictions—and contradictions—that would guide it in later years. Talking in the language of national liberation and revolution, they argued that anticommunist guerrillas, supported by right-wing states and private groups, should be the vanguard in the global struggle against communism. But in supporting undemocratic regimes in Latin America, Asia, and Africa, they undercut their claims to revolution.

And so, despite major investments of money, time, and other resources, Americans still struggled to build the anticommunist international. In part, that was because the funds they raised through private channels often paled in comparison to those generated by the state. At a deeper level, it was because the disparate causes to which U.S. conservatives dedicated themselves had little in common except a vague notion of fighting communism. Simply put, Cuba, Vietnam, and the Congo were very different places with very different wars. Moreover, those struggles often had less to do with the Cold War than they did with the growing conflict between the industrialized global North and the decolonizing yet dependent global South.[172]

Still, their efforts had lasting effects. In the following years, many U.S. conservatives used the connections forged during the 1960s to mobilize a transnational movement that renounced the *realpolitik* of cooperation and negotiation.[173] Rather than fueling détente, they continued to work toward a world in which communism had vanished from the face of the earth. The vehicle for this campaign, many hoped, would be the newly formed World Anti-Communist League.

# 3 | Revolution and Counterrevolution

In September 1967, as the number of U.S. troops in Vietnam approached 500,000, a small band of Americans arrived at a mountainside palace just outside of Taipei, Taiwan.[1] Led by organizer Marvin Liebman, former U.S. Congressman Walter Judd, and Catholic Reverend Daniel Lyons, they had traveled to Taiwan for the first meeting of the World Anti-Communist League (WACL). Meeting hundreds of activists from Asia, Africa, Latin America, and Eastern Europe, they spent a week electing officers and hammering out a constitution.[2] The Americans and the other delegates hoped the new group would expand the Right's global reach, forming the basis for a "strong anti-Communist united front" across the world.[3] As they met, accolades flooded in from right-wing authoritarians such as South Korea's Park Chung Hee, South Vietnam's Nguyen Van Thieu, and Paraguay's Alfredo Stroessner.[4]

Connecting anticommunist groups from five continents, the WACL aimed to fight communism by lending what it called "spiritual and material support" to the "liberation movements in captive nations under communist rule."[5] To the Americans who witnessed the birth of the WACL, it offered fresh hope after years of frustration. Since the 1950s, they had been working to build the anticommunist international, but they didn't have much to show for it.[6] It seemed as if the communists had gained ground everywhere—Vietnam, Cuba, the Congo, even the United States. But the WACL, with its broad geographic base and deep connections to right-wing governments, suggested that the Right's kind of revolution might yet be realized.

It took less than a decade for most Americans to sour on the WACL and its affiliates. The group was too radical and too uncontrollable, they said. Moreover, the Americans' vision of the anticommunist international—centered on propaganda campaigns, training academies, and conferences—clashed with the violent actions of their overseas allies. Talking about wars of national liberation was one thing. Making them was another.

When Americans began to cede ground within the movement, their allies in Latin America took over. Convinced that the United States was failing in its mission to fight communism, right-wing civilians and state officials from Chile, Argentina, Paraguay, and other nations drew closer to kindred movements in Asia and Europe. Hoping to lead a new charge against the global Left, they mobilized their own network of state security forces, private groups, mercenaries, and paramilitaries to purge their societies of suspected subversives and eliminate their opponents abroad. Thus, as left-wing revolutionaries fashioned a global offensive through transnational violence in the 1970s, their opponents followed suit.[7] They would make the anticommunist international more lethal.

---

Arriving in Taiwan in the fall of 1967, the Americans found a legion of right-wing activists who hoped the WACL could become the nerve center of global anticommunist revolution, a means to coordinate armed movements spread across Eastern Europe, Asia, Africa, and Latin America. That was mostly bluster. Instead of sponsoring uprisings in communist countries, the WACL leadership contented themselves with hosting semi-annual meetings and public rallies, sponsoring letter-writing campaigns, channeling funds to new anticommunist groups, and publishing a library of books and pamphlets on subjects ranging from economic development, transnational political organizing, communist drug-smuggling plots, and guerrilla warfare. Nevertheless, it was the only collection of anticommunist groups with a truly global reach.[8]

Since most Americans came as observers to WACL conferences in these years, few had any direct role in shaping its early activities. Of those, Catholic priests Raymond De Jaegher and Daniel Lyons, who had formed several groups in the mid-1960s to liberate mainland China from communist rule, were the most active. They gave speeches, wrote articles for WACL publications, and led courses at the group's "political warfare" academy in South Korea, known as the Freedom Center.[9] Others did much of the same, presenting papers and authoring pamphlets, often parroting the party line of the Guomindang, which dominated the WACL in its early years.[10]

Fearing that they were losing ground in the movement to Taiwan, leading activists and intellectuals in the United States decided they had to find new ways to coordinate their overseas work. In February of 1970, Lee Edwards—a former member of the Young Americans for Freedom who had attended several conferences in Asia—asked a few dozen conservative luminaries to come to

Washington, D.C., for a "private, off-the-record meeting" to determine a course of action "to be taken by individuals and organizations determined to combat tyranny around the world."[11]

A few weeks later, twenty men convened at the luxurious Mayflower Hotel in Washington, D.C., for a weekend summit. Most had been involved in international work for years. U.S. Senator Walter Judd was there, and so was *National Review* publisher William Rusher.[12] Fred Schwarz, an Australian physician-turned-firebrand who led the Christian Anti-Communist Crusade, also turned up, much to the delight of the others. Schwarz was renowned for his popular line of "anticommunist schools" which drew adherents from California to Connecticut, and which produced a steady stream of revenue, more than million dollars a year.[13] With such a robust financial base, Schwarz had expanded his group overseas, sponsoring schools and publishing propaganda in India, Taiwan, Mexico, Brazil, and South Africa.[14] In British Guiana, his agents had gotten involved in local politics by shuffling thousands of dollars to anticommunist officials there, acts that led to the Crusade's expulsion.[15]

Although these men were among the wealthiest and most powerful figures in the growing conservative movement in the United States, they felt impotent on the world stage. Fearing that leftists were advancing everywhere, they decided to form an overarching group to provide new direction for Americans' international anticommunist endeavors.[16] The result was the American Council for World Freedom (ACWF), a coalition of U.S. groups working to build closer bonds with kindred movements in Asia, Africa, Europe, and Latin America. To lead the group, they elected John Fisher, head of the hawkish group of defense industry lobbyists known as the American Security Council.[17] Anticommunists in Asia and elsewhere cheered the creation of the ACWF—a "solid unity of all the leading U.S. anti-communist groups," said one. They were particularly excited about the involvement of the Christian Anti-Communist Crusade and the American Security Council both of which boasted broad financial bases and advisory committees of bankers, businessmen, and retired military leaders. In other words, these were men who had access to money and power, and who could therefore channel substantial resources into the anticommunist international, something that seemed all the more important as the U.S. military struggled in Southeast Asia.[18]

Indeed, the formation of the ACWF came at a crucial moment in the Vietnam War. In the United States, the antiwar movement had reached a new peak, drawing support from a broad swath of Americans and putting serious pressure on the Nixon administration to cease hostilities. Meanwhile, in Vietnam, communist forces continued to gain ground. The U.S. military's counterinsurgency strategy was always one step behind the guerrillas. American-led forces failed to stop the flow of soldiers and supplies along the Ho Chi Minh Trail and struggled to win the hearts and minds of the Vietnamese people, mostly because American firepower was often brought to bear on those civilians whom the U.S. military was supposed to be defending.[19] President Richard Nixon's buildup of the South Vietnamese Army after 1969, known as Vietnamization, had not brought victory any closer.[20]

Across the United States, indeed across the world, many observers proclaimed what Nixon administration officials whispered in private—the United States was retreating from the war. Beyond that, the massive opposition that the war generated in the United States, particularly among countercultural elements, indicated to conservatives that the United States was abandoning its mission as world leader, retreating into a morass of immorality and cowardice. Combined, the drugs, demonstrations, riots, and the collapse of the American military effort in Vietnam suggested that the United States was faltering.[21]

Asian anticommunists saw the same picture and hoped the ACWF, with its deep pockets and high-profile leaders, would reverse the drift of U.S. politics toward peace in Vietnam and coexistence with communism. They denounced those "liberal elements" who were trying to "force their government to withdraw the U.S. forces from South Vietnam by resorting to teach-ins, demonstrations, and parades."[22] "In a country where the air of appeasement is very strong," said one, the "ACWF's birth as a new united front against Communism carries tremendous political significance."[23] In turn, the Americans hoped that greater investment in the anticommunist international would improve their image as lily-white conservatives at home. "No one will be able to accuse us of racism now," one foolishly cheered. Beyond that, the group's endeavors would show the world that many Americans, despite the growth of the antiwar movement, remained resolutely anticommunist.[24]

Such optimistic rhetoric masked the quotidian problems of organizational work. From the start it wasn't entirely clear what the ACWF was to supposed do.[25] Its member groups—the Committee of One Million, the American Security Council, the Christian Anti-Communist Crusade, and others—all had their own sources of funding and their own pet projects at home and abroad. In its first few years, then, the ACWF served merely as a clearinghouse for different pieces of literature. The handful of original pamphlets and broadsides produced by the group mostly concerned events in Southeast Asia, as ACWF leaders chastised the Nixon administration's handling of the war in Vietnam, particularly its refusal to allow Taiwan and other Asian anticommunist states to take over for U.S. forces—again echoing views long put forward by Jiang

Jieshi and the Guomindang.[26] The group also helped stage demonstrations in New York, Washington, D.C., and elsewhere protesting American overtures toward communist China. But those rallies were always dwarfed by the antiwar demonstrations, which could attract hundreds of thousands.[27] The Right may have been on the rise in the United States in the early 1970s—best evidenced by Nixon's landslide victory in the 1972 presidential election—but that did not always translate into much grassroots activity for the broader cause of the anticommunist international.

In late 1971, conservative leaders decided to cast their lot with the World Anti-Communist League.[28] Most believed that a truly powerful international movement was still within reach and that Americans might yet lead it to victory.[29] With more than 100 chapters spread across five continents, the WACL was without rival the largest international anticommunist group. Over the next few years, Americans took a more active role within the group, chairing committees, planning conferences, and corresponding with overseas affiliates. But, as in previous years, they started to worry that some of their allies abroad were liabilities. In the 1973, the annual WACL conference in London was canceled when the British government refused to grant visas to many of its members, citing their reputations for violence and radicalism.[30]

The apparent disarray within the movement presented an opportunity for the Americans to seize control.[31] In early 1974, lawyer and activist Fred Schlafly secured the chairmanship of the WACL, causing his friends to toast him as the "top anticommunist in the world."[32] Husband of Phyllis Schlafly, the conservative movement's most influential female voice, Fred had helped his wife manage a series of political organizations, efforts that introduced him to like-minded activists from across the country and across the world.[33] Drawing on his extensive personal and political connections, he believed American leadership would revitalize the WACL, marginalizing its radical elements, removing ineffective chapters, and building stronger bonds between those individuals and groups that he deemed worthy.[34] He also planned to use the new technology of computerized direct-mailing lists, pioneered by conservative activist Richard Viguerie, to create a broad base of grassroots activists and deep-pocketed financiers in the United States—a technique that had already raised millions of dollars for domestic groups.[35]

Heading the WACL would be a difficult task. In the early 1970s, the WACL's leaders, mostly a core of old-guard anticommunists from Taiwan, South Korea, South Vietnam, and the Philippines, had incorporated dozens of new chapters.[36] Some, like the Japanese chapter Kokusai Shokyo Rengo (the International Federation for Victory over Communism), had all of the trappings of a mass movement. Founded in the late 1950s by two former members of the Japanese High Command imprisoned as Class-A war criminals, it staged rallies of thousands and intimidated labor unions and other left-leaning groups.[37] But most of the new WACL chapters, especially those from Africa and the Middle East, were not much more than letterhead organizations with a handful of members, tiny budgets, and no real influence in their home countries. Others, like the Anti-Bolshevik Bloc of Nations, had earned a reputation for violence and extremism.[38] Too many of the WACL's chapters drew their members from "neo-Nazi, ex-Nazi, fascist, neo-fascist" circles, said one concerned party.[39]

As Schlafly and other Americans struggled to manage their overseas allies, they also fretted about the direction of conservatism at home and its embodiment in the Nixon administration. While they had been stalwart supporters of Nixon's presidency in its early years, they soon grew disillusioned with his handling of the war in Vietnam, not to mention many of his domestic policies. Although his program of Vietnamization—the gradual replacement of U.S. soldiers with South Vietnamese ones—pleased many who had long called for more Asian involvement in fighting the war, they were frustrated by the lack of results.[40] As the war continued to flounder, many conservatives found Nixon's talk about détente, about cooperation and negotiation, and about normalizing relations with communist China reprehensible.[41] Their allies in Asia and Europe felt the same way.[42] Nixon had once talked of winning the Cold War. Now he was seeking stability by making it permanent. Fearing U.S. decline on the international stage, Nixon was, in his words, settling for a world that would "remain half-Communist rather than becoming entirely Communist."[43]

Unlike Nixon, Schlafly desired not stability but victory.[44] To make that point, he spent some $200,000 to host the WACL's 1974 conference at the luxurious Mayflower Hotel in Washington, D.C.[45] The stars of the conservative movement filled the program. William F. Buckley gave the keynote address.[46] U.S. Senators Strom Thurmond and Jesse Helms, both arch-segregationists and vehement anticommunists, served as co-chairmen, lending the proceedings their official blessing.[47] Conference literature made it clear that Thurmond and Helms, unlike the architects of détente, sought "freedom and justice for all." Accommodation and negotiation with the Soviet Union and China would only make life harder for the true "allies of the Free World"—those men and women who were "fighting the common enemy" of "communist tyranny."[48] This was more of a symbolic stance than a strategic one, a way to shore up U.S. conservatives' anticommunist credentials as the Nixon administration maneuvered for "peace with honor" in Vietnam and détente with the Soviet Union and China[49]

In Washington, anticommunists from Asia, Latin America, Africa, and Europe rebuked détente, calling instead for renewed armed struggles in those nations controlled by the Soviet Union, Red China, and their allies. Many insisted that "wars of national liberation" were still the best path forward. Ukrainian Yaroslav Stetsko, the former Nazi collaborator who ran the group of exiled partisans known as the Anti-Bolshevik Bloc of Nations, presented the clearest articulation of that idea. He asserted that "simultaneous and not separate, isolated revolutionary uprisings of the subjugated peoples are the surest road to liberation." Real and lasting change could only come through "armed people" practicing the "primitive method" of guerrilla warfare. As usual, he held up the anti-Soviet partisan wars that raged in Eastern Europe during and after World War II as the ideal model for national liberation movements elsewhere.[50] Others made calls to wage guerrilla wars across the globe, from Cuba to Croatia to China, pleas that fused nationalism and internationalism. While these guerrilla wars were fundamentally national projects—aimed at freeing one people or another—the imagined bonds of fraternity between armed anticommunists offered a vision of joint struggle. By waging simultaneous wars of national liberation against communist proxy states, they hoped to defeat not just the Soviet Union, but to eradicate communism itself, thereby transforming the entire world.

However, the WACL conference in Washington served primarily as an instrument of propaganda. Bringing hundreds of anticommunists to one place and then having them expound about the need for greater cooperation in "wars of national liberation" was, in many ways, the goal itself. To those Americans who staged the conference, image trumped reality. What mattered was creating the impression that anticommunist groups from five continents were working together to roll back communism. They were less concerned about whether those connections were put to any use on the ground. In place of works and wars, words and wishes would suffice.

In this sense, the 1974 conference represented the high-water mark for the kind of anticommunist international that Americans had been trying to build since the late 1950s. Soon the tide began to recede. In the weeks after the summit, major rifts began to divide the Americans from their overseas allies. Some of these tensions had already appeared the previous year, when members of the British WACL chapter contacted their American counterparts about the unsavory characters who made up the WACL.[51] After conducting their own investigation, Fred Schlafly and other Americans began to see their allies for who they really were. Most of the leaders in the Anti-Bolshevik Bloc of Nations, like Yaroslav Stetsko, had fought with the Nazis and continued to drape their "national liberation" movements in the vestiges of World War II–era fascism. Even worse, the ABN's Croatian members had been bombing buildings, hijacking planes, and killing their foes and rivals for years.[52] Americans laid the blame for much of this at the feet of Taiwanese and South Korean leaders who lacked "sophistication and sensitivity in making judgments about Western 'anticommunists.'" The Asian chapters had also exercised poor acumen by recruiting a cabal of financiers from the Saudi royal family whose motives were not entirely clear.[53]

Over the course of 1975, Fred Schlafly and other Americans began to disentangle themselves from the WACL. Schlafly resigned his position as chair, and his chapter resolved to stop paying its dues and participating in future meetings.[54] In response, some alleged that Schlafly was part of a "Zionist front," working to "prevent the expansion of the WACL" by "sabotaging" its activities.[55] Others blamed Marvin Liebman, denouncing him as a "Jew who sold out the WACL" in the late 1960s.[56] At their meetings and in their publications, a score of WACL leaders condemned the departing Americans as communist stooges.[57] In private correspondence to one another, the Americans struggled to explain how things had gotten so bad so quickly.[58] Their sense of despair only grew over the next two years. The Watergate scandal had unraveled the Nixon presidency. His successor, Gerald Ford, offered little hope to anticommunist internationalists since he was also committed to détente. The 1976 election of Jimmy Carter was harder to accept. Promising a new path in U.S. foreign relations, based on restraint, circumspection, and negotiation, Carter signaled to anticommunists—in the United States and the wider world—that the U.S. government had quit the Cold War.

---

The Americans were right to worry about their overseas allies' growing capacity for violence. Leading the way was a network of right-wing civilians, political leaders, and paramilitary groups in Latin America. As Cuban-inspired guerrilla movements started appearing in a handful of Latin American countries in the mid-1960s, their opponents on the Far Right responded with covert campaigns of their own.[59]

Some of the first moves came from Mexico. In 1967, Raimundo Guerrero, a right-wing professor at the Universidad Autónoma de Guadalajara, the only private university established during the Mexican Revolution, founded the Federación Mexicana Anticomunista (FEMACO). In public, Guerrero described it as a coalition of business and student groups from twenty-four Mexican states.[60] In reality, FEMACO was a front organization for an ultra-right-wing movement called the Tecos. Developing out of the Cristeros, a Catholic paramilitary army that battled the Mexican government in the 1920s, the Tecos remained armed as the Mexican state consolidated its power. During the Second World War, the Nazis recruited several Tecos leaders, urging them to attack the U.S. border.[61] The Tecos never did that, and instead targeted their adversaries in Mexico.[62]

After the war, Guerrero took the reins, rebuilding the Tecos at the Universidad Autónoma de Guadalajara. Using funds from the U.S. government and the Ford and Rockefeller Foundations, he built an educational program that rejected state intervention in the economy, exalting individualism within a militant and conservative Catholic framework.[63] Marginalized from the secular, populist, and socialist mainstream of Mexican politics, the Tecos plotted their assault on the Mexican establishment and its perceived connections to Castro's Cuba. On campus, they "were the ones who dictated the rules about what to think, what was permitted to say, how to dress, which films were not to be watched, and who may attend a function."[64] All of this ensured that, in the words of a Mexican journalist who spent a decade researching Latin America's extreme Right, the university became "one of the major fascist centers of Latin America and perhaps the world."[65] In the group's magazine *Replica* and other publications, Guerrero vilified leftists and Jews, asserted that communism had infiltrated schools, unions, and government, and talked of purging Mexican society of its subversive elements.[66] Soon Guerrero began reaching out to right-wing groups at other major Mexican universities. His networking helped the Tecos expand their financial base and political connections, transforming the Mexican extreme Right from a constellation of small groups into a complex network of interdependent organizations with common funding and a shared set of convictions. Within a few years, hundreds of industrialists, bankers, and college professors had joined the group as members or sponsors.[67]

Beyond building a political movement, Guerrero sought a more direct engagement with suspected subversives. In the mid-1960s, the Tecos began forming armed bands to terrorize their opponents. They also started working with Cuban exiles in Mexico and Miami, who provided funds, weapons, and tactical training.[68] Collaborating with anti-Castro paramilitaries such as Alpha 66 helped the Tecos carry out many "assassinations, bombings, kidnappings, intimidation, and other forms of terrorism" over the following years.[69] Although Mexican intelligence services routinely monitored the Tecos, they did very little to stop the group's extralegal activities.[70]

By the late 1960s, as the Mexican government confronted an armed insurgency in its rural southern states, Raimundo Guerrero believed that his group needed more support from abroad to truly counter the threat of communism in the Americas. The World Anti-Communist League seemed the most appropriate avenue for that. Guerrero's FEMACO—essentially the Tecos—joined in 1968. Over the next few years, they labored quietly, helping to plan conferences, raise money, and bring more Latin Americans into the fold. It paid off. In 1972, Guerrero secured election as WACL chairman, bringing the group's annual conclave to Mexico City in August of that year.

At that summit, he proposed the creation of the Confederación Anticomunista Latinoamericana (CAL), a coalition of right-wing organizations from Central and South America. An international body in the Americas was only proper, he said, since communism "fights to conquer and enslave all the peoples of the free world." Moreover, since the communists used "secret international guerrilla organizations and covert agents" to infiltrate "schools, churches, businesses, civic associations, and the state," Latin American anticommunists had to create their own clandestine network to counter the moves of the subversives.[71]

The CAL was a response to growing connections, both real and imagined, between leftists in the Americas and elsewhere in the world. That alliance was most clearly embodied in the Organization of Solidarity with the People of Asia, Africa and Latin America, founded in 1966 in Cuba to unite leftist and anti-imperial movements across three continents.[72] In the eyes of Guerrero and his acolytes, the communists were now on the offensive, as evidenced by the success of the National Liberation Front in Vietnam, the election of socialist Salvador Allende in Chile, and the apparent union of radical leftist groups throughout the developed and developing world.[73] To counter that, Guerrero said the CAL would take shape as a broad front of political parties, labor unions, agrarian syndicates, intellectual groups, clergy, radio and television stations, journalists, lawyers, and other professionals. Funding would come from "philanthropists" willing to support the CAL with a "minimum donation of $1,000."[74] Others agreed, calling for a "regional financing secretariat" composed of "private companies, banking institutions, industrialists, businessmen, (and) professionals," supplemented by whatever funds that friendly governments—especially ones run by military juntas—could provide.[75] The executive committee of the WACL accepted Guerrero's proposal, giving him sixth months to assemble an executive board and secure financial backers.

Guerrero spent the next year building the infrastructure of the CAL.[76] In Mexico, he recruited members of the Tecos to help, relying heavily on Rafael Rodriguez, a young journalist and part-time lecturer at the Universidad Autónoma de Guadalajara who, like Guerrero, believed that international communism was a Jewish plot for world domination.[77] After a few months of correspondence, in July of 1973, a dozen delegates from Mexico, Brazil, Chile, Guatemala, El Salvador, and Paraguay arrived for a secret meeting in Alto Paraná, a remote, rural province of Paraguay. There, far away from the eyes of the world, they laid out the basic structure of the CAL.[78]

The most important branch was to be the Political Parties and Military Organizations section, which recruited members of the armed forces and rightist political parties into the CAL and coordinated activities between groups in different countries. They also drew up plans for an educational institute, based in Guadalajara, and an international news agency to "counter campaigns against the governments, political parties, and anticommunist organizations" of Latin America.[79] By 1974, the group boasted more than a thousand members.[80] Although Guerrero had envisioned the CAL as a coalition of political parties, unions, clerics, and professionals, its most active members came, unsurprisingly, from the military and police forces of Central and South America. Inclined to see any challenge to oligarchy and inequality as a communist assault, most had received instruction at some point from the United States, either at the School of the Americas in Panama or through in-country training programs sponsored by the U.S. military or the State Department's Office of Public of Safety.[81]

The CAL chapter in Paraguay was led by Dr. Antonio Campos Alum, head of the secret police known as La Técnica.[82] A close friend of Paraguay's right-wing dictator, Alfredo Stroessner, Campos Alum had been fighting leftist subversion for most of his life. In 1955, he had traveled to Washington, D.C., to learn interrogation and torture methods from the CIA and the FBI. The following year, he returned to Paraguay with a U.S. Army officer who, under the cover of a USAID development program, helped Campos Alum establish La Técnica.[83] It soon became Stroessner's primary instrument of "political intelligence and repression," maintaining a huge network of informants and spies and a database of suspicious persons.[84] For decades, Campos Alum's men arrested and tortured thousands of civilians, claiming that they were part of a Marxist insurgency threatening to overthrow the country, though most were simply dissidents who challenged Stroessner's rule.[85] Like Campos Alum, many other CAL leaders were active or retired military and intelligence officers from Chile, Argentina, Brazil, Bolivia, and a half-dozen other countries.[86] The rest were right-leaning civilians from the professional classes, mostly doctors, lawyers, and businessmen.[87]

Drawn from the conservative ruling circles of their nations, they were deeply troubled by the changing currents of Latin American politics in the early 1970s. Across the continent, "radical social revolution was a real possibility for millions of people, coloring everyday life with hope or dread depending on the circumstances and political views of each individual," as journalist John Dinges once put it.[88] For those on the left, there was much to celebrate. The Cuban Revolution had already shown that Latin Americans could cast off the chains of U.S. imperialism through armed action. Now, the 1970 election of President Salvador Allende in Chile demonstrated that socialism could be achieved through peaceful, democratic means. Throughout Latin America, young people, workers, and peasants took to the streets, demanding social justice and an end to oligarchic rule and foreign exploitation. A small number of them sought more radical change. In the early 1970s, Marxist guerrillas initiated or stepped up campaigns of kidnapping, assassination, and bombings in Argentina, Brazil, Uruguay, Paraguay, Bolivia, Mexico, and several other countries.[89] Although inspired by the Cuban Revolution, most did not receive much in the way of material and financial support from Fidel Castro's government, which took a cautious approach in the hemisphere from the mid-1960s onward.[90]

Latin American rightists, however, understood these upheavals in terms of an international communist assault on democracy, Christianity, and the free market system. In their view, Cuba and the Soviet Union were set on conquering the entire hemisphere through terrorism and subversion. The election of socialist Salvador Allende, who was committed to nationalizing Chile's raw materials, countering U.S. economic and political dominance, and empowering workers and poor people, was a harbinger of a frightening future. Allende had knitted together a powerful coalition of moderates and leftists that included a few former guerrillas.[91] Should communists and their allies follow this same path in other countries, civilization would be swept away. Yet there was hope. When Chilean soldiers commanded by General Augusto Pinochet overthrew Allende on September 11, 1973, conservatives across Latin America rejoiced. The Chilean Right had defeated a major enemy and was now transforming the country to prevent leftists from ever gaining power again. While Marxist movements still existed across Latin America, Pinochet's coup suggested their days were numbered.

That spirit of promise and peril hovered over the public debut of the CAL. Held in Rio de Janeiro in January of 1974, four months after Pinochet's coup, it attracted some 200 delegates from nearly every Latin American country.[92] The Brazilian military government did not officially sanction the proceedings, but it did send several of its highest ranking officers to attend panels and give speeches.[93] The conference took place in an "atmosphere of secrecy," as an armed guard closely monitored the activities of journalists.[94]

The secrecy was not without reason. Over the course of a week, CAL leaders laid out their "plans of action" to deal with a host of enemies. They told journalists about their schemes to "combat and exterminate Red subversion in schools and universities," and to counter "communist propaganda in all of its aspects." They discussed strategies to expose and arrest communists who had infiltrated labor unions and peasant collectives. And they condemned the Catholic doctrine of Liberation Theology, in which priests identified themselves with the struggles of the poor, as another form of "communist subversion."[95]

Chile's coup lit the way forward. General Pinochet sent several members of his junta to deliver a personal message. In it, he presented his takeover and the purge of Chilean society that followed as a model for other countries to follow. Chile was the "best example of the reaction of a democratic country to the totalitarian attacks of international communism." The Chilean people, now in their "right mind," were "moving towards progress."[96] All of that suggested to a Soviet correspondent who covered the proceedings that the men who assembled in Rio de Janeiro were part of a "profascist" movement that had gained "shameful notoriety in their own countries through their foul activities."[97]

While the Chilean delegation celebrated the 1973 coup, they said little about how the Pinochet regime was dealing with its enemies. Nevertheless, many knew the score. Since taking power, Pinochet had erected a vast apparatus of terror. In the chaos that followed the coup, soldiers and paramilitaries began rounding up suspected subversives, arresting more than 13,000 teachers, journalists, students, union members, clergy, land-reform activists, and artists.[98] Some had been supporters of the Allende regime, others members of the Socialist and Communist Parties. Many had no deep affiliation with the Left but simply knew someone that the security forces did not trust. In the basements of the city's soccer stadiums and in police stations across the city, intelligence officers and counterinsurgency specialists tortured and executed their prisoners. They pulled their captives' fingernails and beat them with their fists. They raped women and attached electrodes to men's genitals. In the countryside, mobile bands of soldiers and paramilitaries purged towns, villages, and prisons of suspected subversives in what became known as the Caravan of Death.[99] The terror was not really about procuring information. Rather, it was meant to liquidate the Left and crush any resistance to the new regime by filling the population with fear. It soon took on an evangelical dimension. Chile was being cleansed before its rebirth.[100] Within a few years, some 3,200 Chileans had been "disappeared" or executed, and another 30,000 imprisoned. Eventually, nearly 200,000 would flee the country.[101]

The Pinochet regime's purge of Chilean society, which fused the power of the state with vigilante violence, served as a clarion call for those who met in Rio de Janeiro. CAL leaders started to see their organization as an instrument of political terror—capable of working in conjunction with, but independent from, state agencies. In one meeting, CAL leaders announced that they would help "all countries" in Latin America create "paramilitary groups" composed of "former members of the armed forces to confront the Marxist guerrillas in defense of their nations."[102] Simply put, CAL leaders saw it as their task to help create death squads in every nation. They also aimed to supply state agencies with information gathered by private groups. As Mexico's Rafael Rodriquez told the press, the conference had "technical papers about how to combat terrorism, kidnappings, and the urban and rural guerrillas" and planned to "put them at the disposal governments and armed forces."[103] And finally, CAL leaders hoped to pressure their governments to "adopt measures" against "priests and superiors of the Catholic Church who had committed themselves to communism."[104]

By January of 1974, then, the CAL had facilitated connections between military and police leaders and rightist civilians in several key Latin American countries. A few months later, at the 1974 WACL conference in Washington, D.C., members of the CAL and their allies in the military and police forces of Chile, Argentina, and Paraguay held another secret meeting. Behind closed doors, they pledged to exchange intelligence and, in time, collaborate on counterinsurgency operations. That formed the foundation for the transnational program of intelligence sharing, torture, disappearance, and murder known as Operation Condor.[105]

Operation Condor signaled a major shift toward the right in Latin America's Southern Cone. In Argentina, the military ousted centrist president Isabel Perón in 1976 and installed a ruling junta under the command of General Jorge Rafael Videla, initiating a Dirty War that killed some 30,000 civilians—surpassing the number of dead in Chile by a factor of ten. In neighboring Uruguay, the military also seized power in a slow-motion coup over the course of several years. In Brazil and Paraguay, long-running military dictatorships expanded their programs of state terror, ruthlessly suppressing any political challenges. Like Pinochet's Chile, these regimes were a conservative response to the political and economic upheavals that had wracked the continent for more than a decade. They shared a deep suspicion of leftist politics in particular and democracy in general. Most military leaders and economic elites loathed the wave of radicalism that swept across Latin America in the wake of the Cuban Revolution. And they had little patience for governments that dealt with popular frustrations by nationalizing industries, asserting workers' rights, attempting land reform, implementing price controls, and placing restrictions on foreign companies. To reverse those trends, they advocated, in varying degrees, free-market reforms that generated new wealth for professionals and landed elites while undercutting the economic security and political power of the landless and the working classes.[106]

Often styling themselves as successors to interwar fascism, the Southern Cone dictatorships embraced a number of far-right figures and ex-Nazis who moved through a transatlantic underground of political parties, religious organizations, and masonic lodges. Setting up shop in Buenos Aires, Asunción, Santiago, and other cities, they republished Nazi tracts, talked of Jewish plots for world domination, and urged the dictatorships to seek common cause with armed right-wing groups in Italy, Germany, and Spain. Some, such as former Gestapo chief Klaus Barbie, the notorious Butcher of Lyon, lent their expertise to the dictatorships' security services, helping smuggle weapons and eliminate targets across national borders.[107]

The Southern Cone dictatorships and their supporters on both sides of the Atlantic believed they were fighting a Third World War, a framework that encompassed old threats as well as new ones. For instance, when leftist guerrillas from Argentina, Chile, Uruguay, and Bolivia formed an alliance, known as the Junta Coordinadora Revolucionaria (JCR), military leaders and economic elites realized that Marxist insurgencies had entered a more dangerous, more transnational phase. They said that "subversion . . . recognizes no borders or countries, and the infiltration penetrates all levels of national life."[108] In the eyes of the military and its civilian supporters, the Soviet Union and its proxies had turned to "new and radical means to overthrow free societies and impose Marxism." But armed revolutionaries were only one part of the problem. There was also, as historian Jerry Dávila argues, a "cultural, or more precisely, counter-cultural" danger, a broad range of "subversives" that included rock musicians, young people, journalists, teachers, and "anyone who advocated for social justice."[109]

The notion of a Third World War hinged on the perception, shared by many military leaders and rightist civilians in Latin America, that the United States had abandoned the fight against communism. By late 1976, the decline and fall of South Vietnam, the Watergate scandal, the realpolitik of détente, and the human rights–oriented policies of the incoming Carter administration all signaled to South American military leaders that the United States was no longer willing to do what was needed to stop socialist revolutionaries.[110] As one Argentine death squad commander declared at a CAL meeting, the "peoples and countries of Latin America" had to "make a unified front against the menace of communism" since the United States did "not seem to understand their situation." In other words, Latin Americans had to realize that "we are alone and released to our own strength."[111]

Operation Condor was therefore a potent weapon in the global struggle against communism and subversion—a transnational response to a transnational threat. Much more than an intelligence sharing operation, it facilitated the seizure, torture, and murder of thousands of suspected subversives across state borders. Operating largely under the direction of the dictatorships' secret intelligence branches, state officials were able to deny Operation Condor's existence even as many citizens were aware of its activities. Drawing upon U.S. technology and counterinsurgency techniques, Operation Condor united military and police units with right-wing paramilitaries and mercenaries from Central and South America, Western Europe, and, in a few cases, the United States. At the start, the Chilean intelligence service, DINA (Dirección de Inteligencia Nacional), was the most active branch. However, by early 1976, the secret intelligence services of Argentina, Uruguay, Paraguay, and Brazil were all working in concert with one another. Bolivia and Peru joined a few years later.[112]

The murder of exiled Chilean general Carlos Prats demonstrated Operation Condor's fearsome power. Prats had been an important part of Allende's government and fled the country in the weeks after Pinochet took power. From his residence in Buenos Aires, he remained a vocal critic of the Chilean regime, writing a memoir and passing information to international human rights groups. In September 1974, the head of Chilean intelligence, Manuel Contreras, decided to kill the exiled general, possibly with direct authorization from Pinochet. Contreras set about recruiting a hit team, hiring an American civilian named Michael Townley, who had been living in Chile for decades. Townley had freelanced for the CIA in the months leading up to the coup and now sought steady employment from DINA. Armed with explosives and detonators from the Chilean intelligence service, Townley and his wife traveled to Buenos Aires, using fake passports supplied by the Argentine embassy. When they arrived they began stalking Prats' every move, sometimes relying upon Argentine police informants. After a few days of surveillance, they planted a bomb underneath his car. Late one night, as Prats and his wife returned to their flat, Townley was waiting down the street. He hit the detonator as Prats exited his car. The massive explosion killed Prats and his wife instantly. Pieces of the incinerated vehicle were found on the roof of a nearby building.[113]

This extralegal assassination established a model for future actions in which state security agencies contracted private citizens and vigilante groups to spy on, intimidate, and murder their political opponents.[114] As a U.S. diplomatic cable reported in 1976, Operation Condor utilized "special teams from member countries who are to travel anywhere in the world" to kill suspected subversives.[115] U.S. authorities were well aware of the assassinations, and indeed had facilitated them by setting up Operation Condor's secret communication network, by training many of its members, and by providing Southern Cone security services with intelligence dispatches from the FBI, the CIA, and the Department of Defense.[116]

High-profile assassinations were only the tip of the iceberg. Right-wing military leaders, intelligence officers, and civilians also worked together to shuttle detainees between countries for torture and execution, thereby preventing leftists from seeking refuge in one country or another. By 1976, the entire Southern Cone was no longer safe for anyone who opposed the dictatorships, especially those engaged in revolutionary activity.

Operation Condor was everywhere and yet nowhere. It was terrifying precisely because it rarely left a trace—either of its existence or of the fate of its victims. In March 1980, for instance, Argentine intelligence officers received permission from their counterparts in Brazil to capture two members of the Argentine guerrilla group called the Montoneros who were visiting Rio de Janeiro. Horacio Campiglia and Susana Binstock had flown from Mexico City to Rio to meet a comrade who, unbeknownst to them, had already been captured and tortured into revealing their upcoming rendezvous. With that information, the Argentines nabbed the pair as they got off the plane, confiscated their travel documents, and then flew them back to Argentina on U.S.-supplied C-130 military aircraft. Back in Rio, two Argentine agents posed as Campiglia and Binstock and pretended to check into a hotel, creating a paper trail that indicated the pair was still alive somewhere. In reality, the captured Montoneros were in Buenos Aires, imprisoned in the Campo de Mayo, one of the city's many secret detention and torture facilities. They were never seen again, alive or dead, just two among the thousands "disappeared" by Operation Condor.[117]

The Confederación Anticomunista Latinoamericana functioned as a central part of the Operation Condor network in several ways. First, it provided a forum in which military officers from right-wing regimes coordinated counterinsurgency strategy and exchanged intelligence.[118] From 1974 onward, semi-annual meetings of the CAL and its secret coordinating committee allowed military and paramilitary leaders to strengthen their bonds and explore new threats.[119] Beyond greasing the wheels of the Operation Condor death machine, the CAL also served as a potent ideological weapon, a way for right-wing regimes to display their commitment to anticommunism to their people, to each other, and to the rest of the world.

In many ways, the CAL was the public face of the secret Condor program. Its conferences were staged with the full cooperation of military governments in Argentina, Paraguay, and Brazil, whose leaders provided security, arranged safe travel, financed the proceedings, gave speeches, and sent warm messages of support.[120] On several occasions, military dictators attended conferences, where they praised the group's activities to the press. Moreover, heads of state security forces such as Antonio Campos Alum, chief of Paraguay's secret police, and Guillermo Suarez Mason, commander of the Argentine intelligence service known as Batallón de Inteligencia 601, occupied key administrative posts within the organization.[121] CAL leaders also made inroads into the civilian world by reaching out to wealthy citizens who supported the dictatorships' radical economic programs. For instance, the Uruguayan chapter sponsored an "Enterprise Forum" in 1974, where "more than 300 businessmen from Uruguay, Argentina, Chile and Paraguay" gathered to exchange ideas and promote "free enterprise" policies.[122]

Beyond propaganda and public spectacle, the CAL also served as a link between state officials, civilians, and right-wing vigilante groups in Central America. The group already included members of Nicaraguan dictator Anastasio Somoza's inner circle, who regularly applauded his rule at conferences throughout the 1970s.[123] By mid-decade, the CAL had incorporated paramilitary leaders and security officers from Guatemala and El Salvador as well. In 1974, Mario Sandoval Alarcón, a Guatemalan politician responsible for thousands of murders and disappearances, brought his political party, the Movimiento de Liberación Nacional (MLN), into the CAL fold.[124] Like many Latin American rightists, he, too, had a long history with the CIA, having participated in the 1954 overthrow of Guatemala's socialist president, Jacobo Arbenz.[125] In 1960, Sandoval formed the MLN to purge Guatemalan society, including moderate elements of the military, of any vestiges of communism. He often referred to the MLN as the "party of organized violence."[126] Over the next few years, Sandoval and his lieutenants eschewed state-led modernization and development in favor of racial nationalism, vehement anticommunism, and free-market ideology.[127] At the same time, he oversaw much of Guatemala's counterinsurgency operations, which targeted a small Marxist guerrilla movement but mostly killed students, labor leaders, and, especially, Indian peasants, whom Guatemala's ruling classes saw as backward and racially inferior.[128]

Both a political party and a paramilitary organization, the MLN became the preferred political institution for Guatemala's military officers and wealthy landowners who wished to maintain their power over working-class Guatemalans and the largely Mayan peasantry.[129] In the late 1960s, the MLN's leadership formed several death squads, including the band known as La Mano Blanco (The White Hand) which claimed responsibility for the deaths of hundreds of "subversives" every year.[130] As Sandoval once boasted to one American journalist, "We of the Liberación were the vanguard group that got this started... The terrorism of the guerrillas, which has resulted in the death of many of our [MLN] people, has forced the government to adopt a plan of complete illegality, but this has brought results."[131] In parts of the countryside, in historian Greg Grandin's words, the MLN's "rural vigilante structure became the state."[132] Sandoval was never shy about what this meant for the Guatemalan people. His forces were "wiping out the opposition."[133]

In the mid-1970s, while Sandoval served as Guatemala's vice president, he worked to internationalize his movement by reaching out to other right-wing groups in Latin America and Asia.[134] He and his lieutenants became regular features at CAL and WACL conferences, and some occupied important administrative posts.[135] These public summits granted them an international platform to denounce U.S. policies toward Guatemala and Central America, which they saw as favoring human rights over decisive action against subversives. Above all, Sandoval and his allies despised President Jimmy Carter's insistence that U.S. military and economic aid to the Guatemalan government would only continue if the regime reigned in the death squads, stopped the disappearances and murders, held free elections, and respected human rights.[136]

Public condemnations of Carter and détente were only part of Sandoval's strategy. Like members of the Chilean and Argentine juntas and their civilian supporters, Sandoval also sought closer cooperation with kindred movements abroad to maintain his war against domestic enemies as U.S. military aid evaporated in the late 1970s.[137] He sent his subordinates to Buenos Aires to receive instruction in counter-insurgency and interrogation techniques from Argentine military and intelligence officers.[138] During that same time, he also made several trips to Taiwan, using his WACL connections get funds from the Guomindang government and secure training in psychological and political warfare for his men at Taiwan's military academy.[139]

Meanwhile, Sandoval and other CAL leaders lent support to right-wing paramilitaries in neighboring El Salvador, where several armed leftist movements were challenging the corrupt, oligarchic government.[140] Sandoval formed a close relationship with Major Roberto D'Aubuisson of the Salvadoran army's intelligence branch.[141] In 1978 and 1979, Sandoval helped D'Aubuisson create a paramilitary political party, which D'Aubuisson later christened the Alianza Republicana Nacional, known by its acronym, ARENA.[142] Inspired by Sandoval's movement, D'Aubuisson built ARENA by fusing nationalism, anticommunism, and free-market ideology with the counterinsurgency techniques he had learned at the Political Warfare Cadres Academy in Taiwan and the U.S. military's School of the Americas.[143]

Nicknamed "Blowtorch Bob" for his sadistic interrogation methods, D'Aubuisson had created several death squads in the late 1960s and early 1970s which he then absorbed into ARENA's party structure.[144] A combination of active-duty soldiers and right-wing vigilantes who were funded by wealthy Salvadorans, including exiles in the United States, these death squads formed the core of D'Aubuisson's political program. They murdered thousands of peasants, laborers, union officials, political figures, and religious leaders—most notably Archbishop Oscar Romero, gunned down in 1980 by D'Aubuisson's men while celebrating mass—in the hope of destroying poor peoples' will to resist.[145]

Like Sandoval, D'Aubuisson used his international connections for more than propaganda. In the late 1970s, he, too, traveled to Taiwan several times, securing weapons and "political warfare" training for high-ranking military officers.[146] Through this training program, he was able to harness greater control over his nation's security apparatus, creating a staff of officers whose first loyalty was to him, even after he retired. When a military coup forced D'Aubuisson from the armed forces in 1979, he again turned to the CAL/Operation Condor network for support. In 1980, he attended the annual CAL conference in Buenos Aires to obtain funds, weapons, and advisers for El Salvador's security forces and death squads. Through Sandoval, D'Aubuisson met several members of the Argentine military command who agreed to help. A few months later, fifty Argentine military advisers arrived in El Salvador, where they trained the Salvadorans in the methods they had perfected in Argentina's Dirty War—torture, assassination, disappearances, and the like. By doing so, the Argentine military junta was not just helping out a kindred movement in El Salvador. Much more than that, the Argentines were taking over for a beleaguered U.S. government that was giving up on its anticommunist mission.[147]

The CAL also attracted Cuban exiles. Since the late 1960s, several Cuban groups had escalated their covert war against Castro's government, using donations to purchase weapons in the United States as well as a hemispheric black market. Alpha 66 and other paramilitary groups seized Cuban vessels at sea, raided the island's coastline, committed acts of sabotage, skirmished with Cuban troops in remote areas, hijacked planes, and assassinated enemies. Soon they started to see the United States as a battleground too, carrying out high-profile kidnappings and bombings in New York, Miami, and other major American cities.[148] In so doing, they contributed to a wave of domestic terrorism—both leftist and rightist—that swept across the United States in the late 1960s and early 1970s. In an eighteen-month period in 1971 and 1972 alone, radicals of one stripe or another detonated some 2,500 bombs across the country.[149]

For the exiles, paramilitary action was the last best option. As an Alpha 66 spokesman explained, "Limited or guerrilla warfare is the only solution of overthrowing Castro and communism. It is suicide and stupid to attempt to do it in any other way."[150] Most U.S. policymakers felt otherwise. The FBI and the U.S. Coast Guard tried to shut down Alpha 66 and other exile groups in the early 1970s, seizing files from their headquarters in Miami, capturing their boats, and prosecuting several leaders for violating arms-smuggling and neutrality statutes. But these actions only succeeded in distancing militant Cubans from the Nixon and Ford administrations, as many became bitter at what they saw as the selective enforcement of U.S. law.[151]

No longer able to count on the massive U.S. aid that sustained their campaigns under the Kennedy and Johnson administrations, Cuban exiles looked toward Latin America's right-wing regimes and their civilian supporters. In March 1975, leaders from several Cuban exile groups went to Santiago to meet Augusto Pinochet. The dictator promised arms and supplies but only if the Cubans united their many factions into one umbrella organization.[152] A few months later, members of the five largest exile groups formed a coalition known as CORU (Coordination of United Revolutionary Organizations), possibly with the approval of the CIA.[153] Within a year, CORU agents had carried out a string of bombings in the United States and the Caribbean. They also became assets for the Chilean intelligence service DINA, gathering information and participating in several high-profile assassinations.[154]

Members of Alpha 66 and other exile groups sought further political and financial support by sending delegations to the annual WACL conferences, where the Cubans offered the old invectives against Castro and communism, and networked with members of rightist groups abroad.[155] In turn, members of the CAL's Mexican chapter, such as Rafael Rodriguez, participated in Alpha 66 gatherings in New York and Los Angeles, discussing plans to retake the island with "hundreds of leaders from more than forty Cuban organizations."[156] Meanwhile, Cuban exiles traveled to Taiwan and other countries, hoping to build an "international fund" that would finance an "anti-communist army of occupation, composed of free men and women of all the world."[157]

Operation Condor extended into Europe as well. Chilean officials worried that South American revolutionaries were working with the German Red Army faction, a left-wing terrorist group that carried out bombings and assassinations in West Germany and allied itself with other armed groups such as the Palestine Liberation Organization.[158] Fearing Latin American leftists would share weapons and resources with kindred movements in Europe and the Middle East, Chile's DINA exchanged lists of subversives with the West German intelligence service, the Bundesnachrichtendienst. Meanwhile, contract-killer Michael Townley "established contact with two unidentified right-wing groups in Germany" to incorporate them into Chile's intelligence network.[159]

Despite that collaboration between Chilean and West German intelligence, Operation Condor could pose a serious problem for the West German government. Since 1945, many former Nazis and Nazi collaborators had fled to Argentina and other Southern Cone countries. While most lived quiet lives, hoping to evade Nazi hunters, a small but dedicated set threw themselves into political action, believing they could use transnational violence to oust the communist regimes back home. Chief among them was the Croatian Liberation Movement. Also known by its acronym in Serbo-Croatian, HOP, short for Hrvatski oslobodilački pokret, it was one of the many émigré groups that comprised the Anti-Bolshevik Bloc of Nations. And like the other members of the ABN, the HOP dated back to the Second World War. An heir to the genocidal regime of Nazi puppet Ante Pavelić, which collapsed in 1945, it had chapters in Croatian communities spread across Western Europe, North America, and Australia. Using funds from those enclaves, it launched a series of clandestine operations to destabilize communist rule back home. HOP leaders hoped to create a new, independent Croatia by arming insurgent forces in Yugoslavia. Struggling mightily to get weapons and supplies behind the Iron Curtain, they settled for acts of terrorism instead.[160]

Starting in the early 1960s, members of the HOP carried out dozens of bombings and plane hijackings in West Germany and other European countries. While their main goal was to use these sensational acts of violence to draw international attention of the plight of their people, they also hoped to eliminate as many communist officials as possible.[161] In public, they claimed legitimacy through spectacular violence, painting their movement as the true national government of Croatia.[162] They excoriated the Yugoslavian government for suppressing Croatian nationalism and religious identity, and for forcing Croats to share a nation with Serbs. Although this talk pleased exiles hoping to return to their homeland, no states or foreign leaders recognized the HOP as a government-in-exile.[163]

As the group emerged as a transnational terrorist force, it fused with the Operation Condor network. In Argentina and Paraguay, a few Croatian exiles worked in tandem with state officials and right-wing militias, exchanging intelligence and coordinating counter-subversion operations.[164] At the same time, state security forces used the Croatians' paramilitary network in Western Europe to plot assassinations in Germany, Italy, and other countries, although most were never carried out.[165]

Sometimes this cooperation backfired. Such was the case of Jozo Damjanovic, a zealous Croatian nationalist who had been imprisoned in West Germany for several acts of terrorism, including attempted assassination.[166] After a few years on the run in Europe, he settled in Paraguay. He maintained connections with Croatian exile groups, receiving funds from chapters in North America and Western Europe.[167] In June 1976, he got word that a Yugoslavian ambassador was planning to visit Asunción. He seized the opportunity to kill a communist official. But on the day, he got confused, mistaking the Uruguayan ambassador for his Yugoslavian counterpart. Damjanovic emptied his pistol into the Uruguayan and then fled the scene. His error created a minor scandal for Stroessner's government, which soon arrested him. Officials from Uruguay demanded his extradition to Montevideo to face trial for the murder, while West German authorities insisted that he should return to Europe to answer for his crimes there.[168] In the end, neither was successful, and Damjanovic spent the next sixteen years in a Paraguayan prison.[169]

Damjanovic's story was exceptional, but also illustrative. For it laid bare the possibilities and problems of the anticommunist international in the 1970s, particularly its paramilitary dimensions. Simply put, it demonstrated how armed right-wingers working across national borders were often allies of state security services, sometimes enemies, and occasionally both.

As the Confederación Anticomunista Latinoamericana and the World Anti-Communist League grew more radical in the mid-1970s, so did its allies in the United States. After Fred Schlafly and his colleagues left the WACL in 1975, a new chapter under the leadership of a British anthropologist named Roger Pearson took their place. Known as the Council on American Affairs, it mixed anticommunism with unbridled anti-Semitism, drawing on Pearson's lifelong advocacy for white racial purity.[170] After migrating to the United States in 1965, Pearson began working with Willis Carto, a California businessman who ran the Liberty Lobby, a right-wing group that also trafficked in white supremacy.[171] In the United States, Pearson taught at several universities while publishing a series of books expounding his views on the Nordic race.[172] By the mid-1970s, he had softened his rhetoric a bit, which helped him secure positions on the advisory boards of the American Security Council and the Heritage Foundation.[173]

Pearson soon recruited Senator Jesse Helms of North Carolina, the loudest anticommunist voice in the Republican Party, who had long defended white supremacy in the United States.[174] In 1975, Pearson brought Helms and several members of his staff to a CAL meeting in Rio de Janeiro. With typical vitriol, the senator from North Carolina upbraided the "U.S. political system" for having "grown sick." He talked of how "our leaders had failed us"—especially President Nixon and Secretary of State Henry Kissinger, whose policies of détente "conceded Communist strength and organization" and "demoralized and disrupted free nations." In contrast, Latin America's military governments and their civilian supporters had succeeded where Americans had foundered. For Helms, it was "encouraging that the people themselves, when faced directly with Communism as a life-or-death threat, have the power of rousing themselves to save their nation." Perhaps Americans could follow a similar path, to "take direct action ourselves to support and nourish the growth of honest nationalism in every country, including the United States." To that end, he called for Americans to build "a program of training in organizational techniques and counter-Communist action," modeled upon those of the Southern Cone.[175]

Despite his friendships with major political figures like Jesse Helms, Pearson struggled with his group's image. When he brought the annual WACL meeting to Washington, D.C., in 1978, some eight hundred delegates arrived, many from the European and Latin American extreme Right.[176] This proved to be a public relations disaster. In Washington, Latin American military leaders discussed counter-subversion with Italian neo-fascist paramilitaries who had carried out several recent bombings and murders.[177] A contingent of French right-wingers met with William Pierce, a former member of the American Nazi Party who authored *The Turner Diaries*, an apocalyptic novel in which white Americans wage guerrilla warfare against a dictatorial government controlled by Jews. A delegate from Mexico called a recent Holocaust documentary "another gigantic campaign of Jewish propaganda to conceal their plot for world domination." Some South Africans passed out literature celebrating apartheid. A few Americans hawked Klan T-shirts, "swastika marked German coins, and cassette tapes of Nazi marching songs."[178] Seeing this, Soviet officials protested the meeting to the State Department, claiming it violated U.S. statutes forbidding hostile demonstrations in close proximity to their embassy.[179]

For many Americans, this was all too much. Even members of the John Birch Society, long the standard-bearer for the Far Right in the United States, began to see the WACL as too radical. "When you get some clown who comes along and wants to 'purify' everything," one Bircher noted, "that's when the really ugly stuff starts." Journalists who covered the conference described how the "forces of authoritarianism, neo-fascism, racial hierarchy, and anti-Semitism" had taken over a once-respectable organization.[180] Rather than deal with the fallout, Pearson closed his chapter.[181] His exit, however, did little to change the World Anti-Communist League, which retained many of its extremist and paramilitary elements after his departure.

---

Even as U.S. conservatives tried to withdraw from the anticommunist international in the mid-1970s, Operation Condor brought them back in. Their most obvious collaboration came through the American-Chilean Council (ACC), which lobbied on behalf of the Chilean military regime and its allies in the Southern Cone. Since 1973, reports about human rights violations in Chile and the death machine of Operation Condor had flooded across international media outlets. Exiles told about the disappearances and torture, about the terror of the police and the military. Although the full extent of the repression would not be known for decades, these accounts turned many Americans away from Pinochet's regime, which emerged in the mid-1970s as the most menacing face of the Southern Cone dictatorships, even though the Argentine junta killed more of its own citizens.

In the United States, widespread antipathy to a right-wing regime that murdered civilians, including a few American citizens, finally propelled congressional action.[182] In December 1975, Congress moved to suspend all U.S. arms sales to Chile, while setting a low ceiling for economic aid. Meanwhile, U.S.-backed financial institutions such as the World Bank curtailed loans to the Chilean government. The Ford administration publicly distanced itself from Pinochet, although Secretary of State Henry Kissinger continued to offer modest assurances of U.S. support in private. As Jimmy Carter took office in 1977, his emphasis on protecting human rights widened the gulf between the U.S. government and the Southern Cone states—although many U.S. intelligence officials in South America continued to sanction Operation Condor behind closed doors.[183]

The founders of the ACC believed they could reverse this river of anti-Pinochet sentiment. The group took shape in early 1974, shortly after Pinochet's coup, when the Chilean ambassador in Washington, D.C., reached out to William F. Buckley to create a propaganda campaign to counter negative images of Chile in the United States. He asked for the name of a "public relations firm that might help them out," and Buckley recommended his good friend Marvin Liebman, who had just recently returned from London penniless, having lost all of his money in a failed attempt as a theater producer. Despite the fact that Liebman did not have an office or a staff, he accepted the offer, eager to get back into his old line of work.[184]

After a preliminary meeting, Liebman proposed a plan for action. The ACC was to be financed by "American firms doing business in Chile so that the council would be completely independent of the Chilean government."[185] Yet that was never the case. Early on, Liebman's contacts from the Chilean embassy agreed to bring their own front organization, known as Consejo Chileno de Norte America (CCNA), into the mix. Funded almost entirely by the Chilean junta, the CCNA was run by Mario Arnello, a lawyer who would later become Pinochet's ambassador to the United Nations, and Nena Ossa, a journalist and government attaché who had penned several anti-Allende articles in the *National Review*.[186] As he had done with so many other organizations, Liebman recruited his influential friends, with whom he had partnered on previous projects in Asia and southern Africa, to serve as the council's advisory board.[187]

Since the ACC's credibility depended upon its image as an independent entity free from state involvement, Liebman registered the group with the Justice Department as an agent of the CCNA rather than the Chilean government.[188] That diversion hid its links to Pinochet's regime, but the ACC was, in reality, just another arm of Chile's formidable security apparatus. The military junta would give money to major U.S. businesses with investments in Chile, such as "Dow Chemical, General Tire, Continental Copper and Steel, Esso Standard Oil, and ITT."[189] These firms would then "funnel contributions" to the American Chilean Council, supplemented with any additional funds they chose to give.[190] By 1976, the ACC had an annual operating budget of about $200,000, of which $150,000 went to publishing articles, books, and pamphlets, financing trips to Chile, and purchasing ad space in newspapers.[191] To add to the difficulties of laundering money, Liebman also had to deal with brash members of the Chilean military and intelligence services, whose public involvement would spoil everything. When several of them visited New York in April 1975 to help coordinate the ACC's operations, Liebman worried the visits might generate too much attention. A Chilean colleague put Liebman's fears to rest, assuring him that only "four Army men" knew about their plans and that they had been "highly discreet."[192] Indeed, the nexus remained secret for years. As the money poured in, Liebman and those around him considered putting the ACC to work for embattled Nicaraguan dictator Anastasio Somoza and other right-wing regimes in the Americas.[193]

ACC propaganda made simplistic arguments about Soviet and Cuban subversion in Latin America. It portrayed Salvador Allende and his government as communist puppets bent on destroying capitalism and paving the way for Marxist conquests elsewhere in the hemisphere. The 1973 coup was thus necessary to prevent a "bloody civil war or a communist takeover."[194] But ACC leaders generally worried less about Chile's dead socialist leader than they did about the "hostile treatment" that Pinochet's "firm and staunch anticommunist" regime was now receiving from the U.S. government. In direct-mail fundraising letters, the ACC chalked up the U.S. arms embargo, the reduction of economic aid, and diminishing foreign investments in Chile not to well-placed human rights concerns, but instead to a "communist propaganda campaign" that caused Americans to forget how the previous government "violated almost every Chilean law in its desperate attempt to create a socialist state."[195] Even Secretary of State Henry Kissinger—Pinochet's greatest defender in the Ford administration and a supporter of Operation Condor—had been duped. According to the ACC, Kissinger, the architect of détente, was presiding over a "foreign policy of punishing our friends and rewarding our enemies."[196]

Beyond castigating Allende and his alleged supporters in the United States, the ACC worked to portray Pinochet as a true free-marketer whose policies were laying the foundations for Chile's economic future. Guided by a group of Chilean economists who had studied the theories of Milton Friedman at the University of Chicago, the junta tried to rid the country of economic planning.[197] It privatized most of the nation's state-owned companies and banks, embraced new forms of speculative finance, removed tariffs, and cut government spending for all branches except the military. These changes were so wrenching that they created a recession overnight—a necessary process, according the free-marketers. The recession was tearing up the old economic base and building a new one in its place, another facet of Chile's rebirth.[198] After visiting the country on an ACC-sponsored trip in 1978, one *National Review* writer proclaimed that Pinochet had cultivated a "Chilean Spring," ushering in a new era of prosperity. "The Chilean economy is taking a cold shower," he wrote. "Tariff barriers have come down; foreign imports are soaring." Competition was the order of the day. Uncompetitive enterprises that were kept alive by political patronage in the Allende era were now being "forced to the wall," a metaphor that unwittingly evoked the image of a firing line.[199]

The regime's economic policies could only be sustained by continued political terror and the complete absence of democratic institutions. And so on the rare occasions when Pinochet's supporters acknowledged the terror, they dismissed it as a brief if unpleasant interregnum. While this adjustment took place, the military regime's repression was simply installing a "period of civil calm" in which "economic and political reconstruction" could go forward.[200] After visiting Chile in 1978, the *National Review*'s William Rusher claimed he "was unable to find a single opponent of the regime in Chile (as distinguished from New York) who believes the Chilean government engages" in torture.

As for "political prisoners," Rusher noted that although "about four thousand Allende sympathizers were prosecuted and convicted of specified crimes after the 1973 coup," all but a "dozen or so were sent into exile abroad or were jailed." Rusher also dispelled rumors about the "disappeared," conjecturing that they were "mostly just leftists who died right after the coup or fled the country since they had been posing as rightists and now they feared being discovered." And even if Pinochet had taken illegal or excessive actions, it hardly mattered, Rusher explained, since his regime was creating a "truly powerful and sinewy Chilean economy," and "sacrifices to this end are very much worth making."[201]

Others made similar points. Republican Congressman Larry McDonald went to Chile in 1978 and returned home to argue that political repression in Chile only occurred because of time constraints. The military had to "restore order and deal with 30,000 guerrillas"—a hugely exaggerated figure—with only a "few days of preparation" before the coup. The regime did not engage in systematic repression but simply used its constitutional authority to "detain suspected terrorists without pressing charges." While McDonald conceded that a few "isolated instances" of torture took place, he pointed out that they were "not the results of government policy" and that "the guilty parties were being punished."[202] Both claims were false. But McDonald's logic, which undergirded the ACC's entire propaganda campaign, generated a positive feedback loop for political repression. Since Chile was under assault by communists, the military had to deal with them by any means. Charges that these measures violated human rights were dismissed as communist disinformation, which then required ever harsher methods to stamp out. This was the same kind of thinking the junta employed as it purged Chilean society.

The ACC also cast doubt about growing evidence of Operation Condor's secret transnational assassination plots in the United States and elsewhere. In 1976, DINA chief Manuel Contreras recruited the American contract killer Michael Townley to murder exiled diplomat Orlando Letelier, a former member of the Allende regime and one of Pinochet's fiercest opponents abroad. Townley assembled a team of right-wing Cubans who helped him place a bomb underneath Letelier's car. They pressed the detonator as Letelier traveled down a busy street in downtown Washington, D.C., in the middle of morning rush hour. He and his passenger, Ronni Moffitt, a young woman who had been working as his assistant, died instantly. When evidence of the plot began to surface, the ACC published a series of reports claiming left-wing Cuban terrorists had in fact killed Letelier.[203] It was yet another line of disinformation pressed by Pinochet's regime, part of a ruse to hide its involvement in a brazen murder on U.S. soil. Shortly after the assassination, Liebman met with the head of DINA, Manuel Contreras, who was illegally visiting the United States, to discuss the ACC's work. During this meeting, Contreras spoke in hushed tones about the Letelier murder, indicating to Liebman that Chile's top intelligence officer "probably did have a lot to do with the assassination."[204] Despite that awareness, the ACC continued to insist that Pinochet's regime had no part in the murder.[205]

Americans managed their mixed feelings about Pinochet's terror by celebrating his free-market program. Indeed, the economic reforms undertaken by the military government had long been advocated by hardline conservatives in the United States who despised any form of state economic planning or market intervention. They, too, hoped to enact massive tax cuts, privatize services, deregulate industries and financial markets, and cut social spending.[206] But since they were unable to undertake such sweeping changes in the United States, many on the right looked with awe toward Chile. They came to see the political repression as instrumental to Chile's transformation. It might not have been pretty, but perhaps it was necessary.

Since Pinochet's supporters were so dazzled by his free-market program, they sometimes invoked the metaphor of revolution to describe his regime.[207] Yet others said Pinochet had in fact enacted a counterrevolution, and that was why his regime mattered to the cause of anticommunist internationalism. As Marvin Liebman explained, "Chile is one of the few nations—if not the only one—which has achieved a successful counter-revolution against a Marxist and Soviet-oriented regime. Hopefully, we may see other equally successful efforts around the world such as which were tried and failed in Hungary and Czechoslovakia. Chile may well be establishing a pattern for such counter-revolutionary societies."[208]

His words illustrated the uncertainty that surrounded the anticommunist international in the era of the Southern Cone dictatorships. Since the late 1950s, many on the U.S. Right, especially Liebman, had talked of fomenting a "worldwide anticommunist revolution."[209] But how did Chile fit into that project if Pinochet—and by extension the other Southern Cone military regimes—had in fact led a counterrevolution? It was a muddy issue, and nobody in the United States or elsewhere made much of an attempt to make it any clearer. The dictatorships were killing subversives. In the final analysis, that was what really mattered.

Ideological imprecision was the least of Liebman's worries. By 1978, the U.S. Department of Justice had launched an investigation of the ACC and its ties to the Chilean government. In December, prosecutors charged that the ACC had been engaged in a "secret and illegal propaganda campaign" at the behest of

Pinochet's regime. Seizing the ACC's records, they discovered that the Chilean government had provided most of the funds for the group, setting up a covert network that shipped money through fronts and businesses. According to the suit, Liebman's outfit violated the Foreign Agents Registration Act of 1938, which stipulated that any individual or organization that represented a foreign government in the United States must register as such with the Justice Department. Since Liebman had registered only as an agent of the CCNA and not of the Chilean government, his funding scheme broke the law.[210]

Liebman feigned ignorance about the role of Pinochet's regime in financing the ACC, still hoping to maintain the illusion that it was simply a collection of concerned citizens and businesses. He understood that if "we were registered as an agent of the Chilean government, whatever effect we had would be lost." At his deposition in Washington, D.C., he attempted to limit the damage by pleading the Fifth Amendment to nearly every question the prosecuting attorney asked.[211] Still, the image of the ACC had been irreparably tarnished. The investigation had revealed it as a front for a murderous dictatorship and there was little its backers could do to salvage its reputation.[212]

The most lasting effects of the American Chilean Council's work were within conservative circles in the United States and the Southern Cone countries, gratifying Pinochet's diehard supporters but producing few converts. More importantly, the Justice Department's investigation deepened their suspicion that the U.S. government could not be trusted to lead the global crusade against Marxism. Violence in service of anticommunism was of little concern. The real problem, they said, was that the United States had given up on the Cold War.

---

By projecting violence across national borders, the Southern Cone dictatorships benefitted from—and contributed to—the broader transformation of geopolitics known as globalization. They harnessed new technologies and transnational flows of people, ideas, capital, and weapons to eliminate enemies on three continents. In so doing, they disrupted the balance of power within the anticommunist international. At the start of the 1970s, the Americans thought they were poised to lead the movement. By the end of the decade, they found themselves bound up in a world of violence beyond their control. Sometimes troubled by the bloodshed, they more often found hope. In their eyes, the Southern Cone dictatorships had taken over for the United States during its moment of weakness. U.S. leaders, for whatever reason, had appeared to surrender in the wake of the Vietnam War. That belief, in turn, reinforced the recurring conviction that foreign forces should lead the charge against communism.

The murderous Operation Condor network made it clear that anticommunists could achieve gruesome results by working together across national borders. Yet even when absorbed into the bloody machinery of Operation Condor, Americans' visions of the anticommunist international, centered on conferences, propaganda campaigns, and lobbying efforts, could only achieve so much. The dissolution of the ACC showed that. U.S. conservatives needed more like-minded Americans who intimately understood covert action—how to make it work and how to avoid being caught. Fortunately for them, a generation of high-ranking military and intelligence officers were on their way out of the United States' clandestine services. Having managed an array of covert actions since the earliest days of the Cold War, they would launch a new bid to lead the anticommunist international.

# 4 | Covert Warriors for Hire

In the summer of 1978, retired U.S. Army General John K. Singlaub, a thirty-year veteran of special operations, joined the American Security Council as a paid lecturer.[1] As he traveled the country, he spoke to conservative groups about the need for a renewed anticommunist offensive, both at home and abroad. He told audiences that liberals in Congress had gutted the United States' clandestine forces by organizing new intelligence oversight committees and passing new laws forbidding U.S. covert operations. He also talked of how President Jimmy Carter had purged the highest ranks of the CIA and the military, removing hundreds of soldiers and spies who had done the United States' dirty work since the end of World War II. In his eyes, the United States was no longer able to wage the kind of war needed to defeat the communists—covert, unconventional, paramilitary combat.[2]

Singlaub was part of a wave of ex-CIA and -military men who flooded into the conservative movement in the late 1970s. They brought with them ideas, skills, and contacts from decades of service behind the frontlines of the Cold War. Since many Americans abhorred the use of U.S. troops abroad after the debacle in Vietnam, retired covert warriors concluded that paramilitary groups were the ideal, indeed the only, forces that could roll back communist gains in the global South. Playing upon fears of American national decline and military impotence, Singlaub and others argued that the state's deteriorating covert war-making abilities signaled its larger failures on the world stage. To remedy that, ex-soldiers and spies joined lobbying groups and think tanks, hoping to educate Americans and pressure politicians. At the same time, they formed private companies that could fill in for the state, enterprises that promised steady profits and policymaking power in retirement. Loosed from the state, they took the central idea that had animated U.S. conservatives' overseas work in previous years—that private money could succeed where the state failed—and pushed it further into the realms of paramilitary warfare.

The conviction that the U.S. government—particularly the CIA and the military—was failing to fight communism also spurred hundreds of American men to seek new lives as mercenaries, first in Southeast Asia and then in southern Africa. They, too, believed they were filling in for a liberal-hampered U.S. government, carrying forward the mission that they had been given in the Vietnam War and other Cold War contests. If the state would not fight communism, they argued, then private citizens must lead the way.

In the late 1970s, then, these two camps of revanchist Americans—retired covert warriors and aspiring mercenaries—shared many of the same ideas and impulses. Their simultaneous groping toward a form of warfare that united concerned American citizens with overseas anticommunist paramilitaries helped revitalize the international crusade launched by an earlier generation of U.S. conservatives and their allies abroad. That campaign would be most fully realized in the Reagan era. For now, newfound scrutiny of the CIA and the U.S. military convinced many Americans that they would need to do better.

---

When John Singlaub retired in 1978, the clandestine branches of the U.S. government seemed to be in crisis. For more than a decade, public scrutiny of U.S. covert actions had been growing in fits and starts. Journalists uncovered a string of operations that tarnished the image of the CIA and the clandestine branches of the U.S. military—secret bombing campaigns, coups, assassination plots, and so on.[3] In the words of William Colby, a thirty-year veteran of the CIA whom President Richard Nixon appointed as director in 1973, these news stories "triggered a firestorm" that confirmed Americans' greatest "fears and suspicions" about the CIA.[4]

As anti–Vietnam War activism moved from the streets and into the halls of government, legislators clamored for serious inquiry into the U.S. intelligence community's past crimes. President Gerald Ford appointed a blue-ribbon commission of national security stalwarts to probe the CIA, but few in Congress or the media had faith in the White House after the Watergate scandal. In early 1975, Senate and House leaders responded by mounting their own investigation that undertook a much deeper analysis of the CIA's activities and abuses.[5] It became known as the Church Committee, after Senator Frank Church, a Democrat from Idaho, who served as its public face and presented many of its most penetrating questions about the legality and morality of CIA actions. Church had already made a name for himself as a staunch critic of the Vietnam

War, and took a decidedly dim view of American covert actions.[6] In a session about the CIA's deeds in Chile, Church scolded National Security Advisor Henry Kissinger, telling him the agency had carried out "appalling" and "utterly unprincipled" acts. Having conspired to overthrow a democratically elected government, Church said, the CIA had abandoned its "traditional expression of the right of self-determination."[7]

The results of the Church Committee's two-year inquiry were stunning. Americans discovered that the CIA's covert actions far exceeded anything most imagined. The committee uncovered evidence of CIA assassination plots and coup attempts against Fidel Castro of Cuba, Rafael Trujillo of the Dominican Republic, Patrice Lumumba of the Democratic Republic of the Congo, Ngo Dinh Diem of South Vietnam, Salvador Allende of Chile, and a bevy of other foreign leaders. It documented the CIA's paramilitary activities in Laos and Cambodia during the Vietnam War, its efforts to recruit mercenaries for the Congo in the mid-1960s, and a litany of illegal operations that targeted U.S. citizens at home, a direct violation of the CIA's official mandate. It became clear that the CIA, in the supposed interests of the United States, had subverted popular sovereignty across the globe, not only through high-profile assassinations and paramilitary schemes but also a perpetual pattern of bugging, disinformation, and propaganda.[8] These revelations underscored the terrifying power of the United States' clandestine agencies, while also shedding light onto many of the unsavory forces that American officials collaborated with—death squads, mercenaries, paramilitaries, vigilantes, and the like. But legislators quickly lost control of the narrative. The hearings unwittingly lent credence to swelling conspiracy theories in which the CIA was an omnipotent and malevolent force that controlled world affairs from the shadows.[9]

Learning the long and sordid history of the CIA caused Church and other lawmakers to question the morality of overthrowing foreign governments and supporting right-wing dictators in the name of anticommunism—a central tenet of U.S. foreign policy since the start of the Cold War.[10] The Ford administration sought to limit the damage, saying that their probe was hurting the CIA's ability to conduct espionage while also damaging United States' image abroad. There were other consequences, Ford said. Public revelations about the CIA would put the lives of American agents at risk.[11] Church countered that the committee's investigation was necessary to recover the United States' moral standing in the world. On the television program *Face the Nation*, he asserted that people in other countries "admire us more for standing up to our democratic ideals than they have ever loathed us for whatever mistakes we've made."[12]

For Church and his colleagues, misguided CIA activities struck at the United States' core principles. "The most important costs, even of covert actions which remain secret, are those to American ideals of relations among nations and of constitutional government," the committee stated in its report about the coup in Chile. "Given the costs of covert action, it should be resorted to only to counter severe threats to the national security of the United States."[13] The committee called for better statutory guidelines and greater congressional control over the intelligence community. Still, the committee recognized covert actions were necessary parts of U.S. foreign policy, but "only when no other means will suffice to meet extraordinary circumstances involving grave threats."[14]

Americans learned about the CIA's sordid history in other ways. While the Church Committee made headlines, former CIA officers published exposés about their time in the agency. The most important was Philip Agee, whose book, *Inside the Company*, chronicled his years managing bribery schemes, bugging operations, and disinformation campaigns across Latin America. In his narrative, Agee named hundreds of former and current CIA officers, agents, and assets.[15] This infuriated the CIA leadership. In their eyes, Agee had threatened the security of hundreds of field operatives. When questioned by *Newsweek* magazine about Agee's book, Director of Central Intelligence William Colby answered, "I think it's terrible, frankly, because this puts people's reputations in bad shape, it puts people in physical danger."[16] Agee's book, along with a few other tell-all memoirs from ex-CIA men, gave rise to a new vein of muckraking journalism that targeted the United States' intelligence underground.[17] Magazines such as *Counterspy* and the *Covert Action Information Bulletin*, the latter founded with Agee's help, revealed the identities of agents in Europe, Asia, Africa, and the Middle East, and worked to sabotage the CIA's activities.[18]

The election of Jimmy Carter to the presidency in 1976 expanded executive and congressional oversight of the CIA and the covert branches of the U.S. military. As the first post–Vietnam War president, Carter had a considerable opportunity to redefine American foreign policy, to reject the maxims of the Cold War.[19] For Carter, that meant shifting the United States away from military intervention and covert action in favor of policies that protected human rights. In recognizing that there were limits on what the United States could achieve through military means, Carter favored negotiation over confrontation, giving greater weight to the policy of détente established by his predecessors, at least in his first years in the White House.[20]

Changes would have to be made in the CIA. Shortly after taking office in January of 1977, Carter appointed Navy Admiral Stansfield Turner as Director of Central Intelligence. No dove, Turner was a career officer who had attended the U.S. Naval Academy at the same time as Carter, and had risen to the position of commander of NATO forces in southern Europe in 1975.[21] Still, within a few months of his appointment, Turner decided to remove many of the agency's top officers. In what he referred to as a "straightforward management decision," his office issued pink slips to 198 officers in the CIA's covert-action branch, the Directorate of Operations, in October 1977. More than 600 firings followed over the next twelve months.[22]

Most of those removed from the agency were not lowly field agents but high-ranking station chiefs who oversaw all of the CIA's activities in a particular country. As journalists were quick to point out, many were members of the CIA's old guard who had served in the Office of Strategic Services, a forerunner to the CIA that conducted espionage and paramilitary activities behind enemy lines during World War II.[23] Over the course of the three decades since the CIA's founding, they had amassed great power within the agency, shifting its activities from the collection of information to the waging of covert warfare. But to some of the CIA's younger members, these experienced operators were little more than "deadwood left over from the Cold War" that needed chopping.[24]

Turner had several reasons for removing the agents. The first was that, with the end of the Vietnam War, the CIA had far less of a need for clandestine operations, especially the kinds of paramilitary and assassination programs that the agency had been running in Southeast Asia. At the same time, he argued, advances in electronic surveillance made some covert agents in the field obsolete.[25] Financial restrictions from the White House's Office of Management and Budget also played a role, though Turner halved the number of agents that the office had originally asked him to remove.[26] Above all, Turner's dismissal of the agents was part of an overarching effort to reshape the fundamental mission of the CIA and the rest of the intelligence community. If the guiding principles of Carter's foreign policy were human rights and non-intervention, Turner argued, then covert actions should take a backseat to more traditional forms of espionage.[27]

Many in the agency were predictably irate. They called it the Halloween Massacre. Anti-Turner placards filled the hallways of the CIA's headquarters in Langley, Virginia, while disgruntled agents aired their grievances to the press in an unprecedented fashion. Some told reporters that Turner was "fragmenting" the agency, that he had "demoralized" most of its senior and mid-level officers.[28] More troubling were allegations that Turner, and by extension Carter, had reduced the agency's prestige and operational capabilities. "The CIA is being turned into just another bunch of bureaucrats," chided one commentator. In a different vein, General Vernon Walters, a former Deputy Director of Intelligence, argued that even though clandestine operations gathered only ten percent of the CIA's information total, this was the most important kind of intelligence. Reducing the number of spies in the field and hampering their ability to conduct covert actions, he claimed, would inevitably mean a decline in the quality of American intelligence.[29]

Conservative activists and politicians echoed these concerns. Former Nixon aide Patrick Buchanan bemoaned that the purges of high-ranking officers removed from the agency "thousands of man-hours of invaluable intelligence experience and irreplaceable contacts and confidences built up over long careers."[30] Another charged that the Church Committee had created "serious problems for the intelligence community" because "foreign governments are reluctant to provide sensitive information to our intelligence services," fearing leaks and reprisals against their operatives.[31] To Francis J. McNamara, a former research director for the House Un-American Activities Committee, this all amounted to a "super assault on America's intelligence-gathering agencies" that "undermined the very foundation of United States' and free-world security at a time when not only this country but the very concept of democracy has more active, organized, and bitter enemies than ever—and when Soviet military might is greater and more Communist agents are placed in a larger number of nations than in any previous period."[32]

U.S. conservatives also pressed these points on the international stage. In December 1975, evangelical preacher Billy James Hargis addressed the WACL conference in Rio de Janeiro. Speaking to intelligence offices and military leaders from the Southern Cone dictatorships—then engaged in the transnational campaign of disappearance and murder called Operation Condor—Hargis argued that "these congressional investigations into the CIA and FBI must be stopped because they are left-wing inspired. And the left will be content with nothing less than stripping America naked before domestic and foreign enemies alike."[33] Many military and intelligence officers from Latin America's Southern Cone agreed, believing that the Church Committee had sapped the power of the United States to fight communist subversion in the Americas and elsewhere.[34] So did erstwhile clients of the CIA, such as Cuban exiles and the Angolan paramilitary group UNITA, whose leaders lamented how the U.S. "government was paralyzed by Watergate and the investigations of the CIA."[35]

Despite the impassioned rhetoric of angry agents and conservative critics, the Church Committee hearings and Carter's reforms did not dramatically alter the CIA's operational capabilities. The agency still maintained a massive network of intelligence officers, agents, and assets around the world. Nor did the reforms signal an unwillingness of liberals to use covert action as, by 1979, Carter had authorized the CIA to arm and supply rebel groups in Afghanistan. Instead, the most important consequence of the Church Committee hearings registered outside of the state. The personnel cuts created a pool of politicized covert warriors with no place to go.[36] Free from their jobs in the U.S. government, embittered by the firings, and eager to reclaim power, many turned to the private sector and the world of conservative activism for employment.

---

John Singlaub had spent much of his thirty years in the U.S. Army and the CIA waging unconventional warfare, training paramilitary groups, and running sabotage and psychological warfare campaigns. He developed a network of contacts that spanned the globe and was especially strong in Western Europe and Southeast Asia—foreign government officials, military leaders, guerrilla commanders, and arms traffickers. He also cultivated modes of combat that left few traces of American involvement. His was an insular and secretive world populated by men who prioritized courage, hardness, self-reliance, and derring-do. In their view, real American leadership in the Cold War did not require high-tech weaponry or large-scale armies so much as it did the physical and mental toughness to help other people fight their own wars. For them, paramilitary, guerrilla, and counterinsurgency campaigns offered a more muscular vision of what Americans should be doing to help their allies than the United States' diplomats and foreign aid workers could provide. Sacrificing comfort and family lives, they sought to beat the communists at their own game.[37]

Singlaub joined the Army at the start of the Second World War.[38] In 1942, he was ready to ship out to Europe as a platoon leader. But just before departing, he accepted an invitation to join the Office of Strategic Services (OSS), the nascent clandestine service of the U.S. military.[39] Singlaub's time in the OSS established the central prism through which he came to view combat and politics. Effective opposition to totalitarian forces could only be achieved by arming the people themselves. This kind of warfare was heroic, individualistic, and efficient, accomplishing major goals without expending large amounts of American lives or resources.[40] Over the next few years, Singlaub had many chances to put those ideas into action. In August of 1944, as the U.S. Army began to break out of Normandy, he parachuted into the mountainous region of Massif Central, where he worked alongside the leaders of the rural French guerrillas known as the Maquis for two months.[41] In early 1945, he shipped out to Kūnmíng, situated in a hilly region in southwest China, where he and his men equipped and trained a small band of Vietnamese guerrillas from Ho Chi

Minh's forces with the help of the French Foreign Legion.[42] When the OSS disbanded after the war, Singlaub joined the newly formed Central Intelligence Agency. For the next two years, he fought alongside guerrillas allied with Jiang Jieshi's Guomindang in a failed quest to prevent the communists from taking power.[43] Like other OSS veterans who joined the CIA, Singlaub helped expand the CIA's mission from gathering intelligence to waging secret wars.[44]

His greatest undertaking came during the Vietnam War. In 1966, the U.S. Army commissioned him as commander for the Studies and Observation Group, or SOG, an ultra-secret multi-service unit charged with interdicting the flow of men and materiel along the Ho Chi Minh Trail and creating armed insurgencies inside North Vietnam.[45] Singlaub now commanded Army Green Berets, Navy SEALs, and Air Force Air Commandos, and answered directly to the Joint Chiefs of Staff in Washington, D.C.[46] He also partnered with the CIA, which was running its own paramilitary operations in the border areas of Laos and Cambodia.[47] The "essence" of his assignment, in his words, was to take "the war directly to the enemy's home and into his sanctuaries," a mission that flew in the face of the United States' official position that forbade U.S. forces from fighting inside North Vietnam, Laos, and Cambodia.[48] And so he worked in tandem with the intelligence services of Taiwan and South Korea to sponsor several bands of anticommunist guerrillas in Laos and Cambodia.[49]

Singlaub's Vietnam operation drew upon the skills he honed with the OSS in France and China, but on a dramatically larger scale.[50] In addition to U.S. soldiers, his unit comprised more than 8,000 Vietnamese commandos and collaborators.[51] It also had its own private air force of Taiwanese pilots who flew aircraft stripped of any insignia that linked them to the United States. The unit airdropped thousands of radios into North Vietnam that tuned only to their propaganda broadcasts and created phony documents that North Vietnamese soldiers picked up and treated as legitimate intelligence.[52] The SOG's most ambitious scheme was to create a fake guerrilla army known as the Sacred Sword of the Patriot League.[53] Singlaub sent teams of operatives up the coast to kidnap fishermen and peasants and bring them to a base on an island near Danang, where South Vietnamese soldiers posed as anticommunist guerrillas. Feeding and clothing his prisoners, he gave them "gift kits" that included soap, pencils, writing pads and other items that were hard to find in the North. After a while, Singlaub's soldiers would release their captives so they could spread word of the growing resistance movement that did not exist. He counted his fake army as one his major triumphs during the war.[54]

Even though Singlaub had wide latitude to wage covert warfare in Vietnam, he still clashed with U.S. diplomats. He believed that these men, ensconced in their air-conditioned rooms in the U.S. Embassy, the Pentagon, and the White House, had hampered his efforts. While SOG units of only a few dozen men had tied up thousands of North Vietnamese soldiers on the Ho Chi Minh Trail, they could not stop the flow of weapons and soldiers into the South.[55] Singlaub would blame that failure on the U.S. Ambassador to Laos, who prevented Singlaub from expanding the war into Laos, where most of the Ho Chi Minh trail ran. In his eyes, U.S. policymakers failed to understand the superiority of covert action to conventional warfare. Special operations soldiers and their indigenous allies were the only forces that could have destroyed the North Vietnamese "sanctuaries."[56]

For Singlaub, this failure to wage an effective covert war in Vietnam had undercut the United States' credibility as world leader. The mobilization of hundreds of thousands of American men in conventional units caused too many people in the United States to oppose the draft, the war, and its casualties. Their protests killed the war effort. In contrast, a covert, unconventional war would have obviated the need for American draftees and would have placed the burden on the South Vietnamese and their allies. It would also have kept the war out of the public eye, thereby ensuring that ordinary people, particularly those who opposed the war, would have had no role in determining its outcome. For many years after he left Southeast Asia, this failure would stick with Singlaub, because it indicated that the state—especially effete bureaucrats who knew nothing of combat—could not be counted upon to pursue best interests of the American people or their most devoted allies.[57]

At the same time, Singlaub's many years of clandestine service inducted him into a fraternity that praised, above all, a willingness to get the job done no matter the costs. This was a world of hard men doing hard things and making hard choices. They were good at their work and they enjoyed it. Few outsiders ever knew of their activities. For that reason, the United States' covert warriors felt that they, better than anyone, understood what the Cold War was really about. They had seen what the communists did to their enemies. And they had worked alongside those who hoped to fight back. They also believed that they best knew the costs that service to one's nation required because they had carried the heaviest burdens. That weight was most acutely felt in one's personal life. Fighting secret wars in faraway places kept men like Singlaub from their families for long periods of time. Being away from home and in possession of secrets they could not share with others, covert warriors formed particularly close bonds with one another. These friendships persisted long after they finished their service.

Singlaub's belief that diplomats and politicians could not be trusted only grew as he rose through the ranks of the U.S. Army establishment. By 1977, he had ascended to the rank of Major General, commanding all U.N. and U.S. military forces in South Korea.[58] However, shortly after Jimmy Carter took office, the president began to press for the removal of U.S. forces from South Korea over a five-year timetable, thereby fulfilling a major campaign pledge to reduce U.S. military commitments and defense spending in a time of fiscal crisis. When Singlaub heard this news, he vented his frustrations to a *Washington Post* reporter who then published them in a front-page article. Under the impression that he was speaking off the record, Singlaub chastised Carter's policy, claiming a troop withdrawal would inevitably "lead to war."[59] Carter responded to Singlaub's apparent insubordination by recalling him to Washington and revoking his commission.[60]

The following morning, headlines informed readers that Carter had "fired" Singlaub. Reporters likened the situation to President Harry Truman's removal of General Douglas MacArthur at the height of the Korean War.[61] Since Singlaub had spent thirty years in active duty around the world, his reassignment provoked a flurry of attacks from the Right.[62] In a typical tirade, conservative commentator Patrick Buchanan invoked old tropes about martial masculinity in the Cold War, calling Carter "spineless" and celebrating Singlaub's "moral courage" and "physical bravery" over his long military career.[63] Carter, hoping to quell such criticism, quickly shuffled Singlaub into a new commission, appointing him chief of staff for the U.S. Army Forces Command, which oversaw more than 300,000 active soldiers.[64]

In this role, however, Singlaub grew even more frustrated with civilian control over the defense establishment. When Carter recalled him to Washington again in 1978 to explain another public challenge, Singlaub decided to retire.[65] The circumstances surrounding Singlaub's exit from the Army—particularly the notion that a headstrong liberal president was removing any critic of his policies—made the general into a conservative hero.[66] The editors of the *Chicago Tribune* celebrated Singlaub for "deliberately and publicly" putting "his career on the line" to reveal the "incredible mistakes by an inexperienced president who fancies himself as a military master and, alas, is not."[67] In Congress, Senator Barry Goldwater said Singlaub deserved the "thanks of all Americans who are seriously concerned about the weaknesses in the policies of the Carter administration."[68] The American Conservative Union presented Singlaub with an award for Conservative of the Year. Happy to play to part, Singlaub told reporters that he had quit the Army rather than be part of a "cover-up of truth."[69]

Once retired, Singlaub parlayed his outstanding service record into the lucrative world of conservative political activism. While he had received many job offers in "business and industry," he later recalled, he wasn't "ready to trade" his "uniform for a pair of plaid golf pants." He still considered himself "bound by my officer's oath to 'support and defend the Constitution of the United States against all enemies, foreign and domestic.'"[70] Joining conservative think tanks and advocacy groups was, in his mind, the best way to continue his service. The first group to come calling was the American Security Council (ASC), the consortium of defense-industry lobbyists and military hardliners that had been working on U.S. foreign policy since the 1950s.[71] His contact was retired U.S. Army Lt. General Daniel O. Graham, a specialist in advanced weapons systems, whom Singlaub had known for more than a decade.[72] Like Singlaub, Graham had resigned at the peak of his career rather than support détente.[73] After leaving the Army, he used his experience to lobby for defense firms while serving as an expert on military affairs for conservative groups such as the ASC's Coalition for Peace through Strength.[74] Making friends in conservative circles, Graham formed a tight bond with Ronald Reagan, who tapped him to serve as his foreign policy adviser on his failed bid for the presidency in 1976.[75]

At Graham's urging, the ASC found room in its substantial $4 million budget to hire Singlaub as its Education Field Director in the spring of 1979.[76] By then, Singlaub was already a frequent visitor to the ASC's Freedom School, founded in the mid-1960s to train legions of anticommunist activists.[77] Singlaub toured the country speaking to civic organizations, veterans groups, and university audiences. He also began lecturing on behalf of the American Conservative Union, appearing as a talking head in documentaries such as "Soviet Might/American Myth: U.S. in Retreat."[78] Singlaub explained to a friend that he targeted "conservatives and veterans' organizations" because they were "independent people. They tend to want to do their thing by themselves." Only they could stand up to the "strong coalition of the Left"—mostly "peaceniks" and "antiwar activists" who were "very active in an anti-defense lobby."[79]

The primary thesis of Singlaub's talks echoed what many of Carter's critics were saying in the late 1970s. The United States needed to "reestablish its national defenses and strategic position as the leader of the free world, following the military debacle in Indochina and the political disaster of Watergate."[80] Moving beyond that script, Singlaub stressed how the United States' clandestine services had suffered in the wake of the Church Committee investigations. He lamented Stansfield Turner's "dismantling of the Human Intelligence and Covert Operations facilities of the CIA," and attacked Carter for relying too much on "reconnaissance satellites and electronic surveillance." Instead of high-tech gadgetry, the United States needed to use "military and non-military" to roll back communism, first in the "captive nations of the Soviet Empire" and then elsewhere. In other words, the United States needed to aid homegrown forces that could launch wars of national liberation in communist countries, whether in Eastern Europe, Asia, Latin America, or Africa. Although this argument mostly stemmed from Singlaub's combat experience behind enemy lines, it echoed what many others had been saying since the 1950s—that ordinary people with guns were the key to winning the Cold War. Thus, militant anti-communists from Asia and Eastern Europe found much to like in Singlaub. As he toured the United States, U.S.-based chapters of the Anti-Bolshevik Bloc of Nations, among other groups, began to see him as a potential ally.[81]

At the same time, Singlaub sought new ways to fight perceived enemies at home. In 1979 he joined the board of Western Goals, a private intelligence network run by Congressman Larry McDonald, the ultraconservative Republican from Georgia. Headquartered in Alexandria, Virginia, Western Goals maintained computer files on thousands of U.S. citizens that the group saw as potential subversives. Most were members of labor unions and the civil rights and the nuclear-freeze movements. A few were just liberal-leaning celebrities.[82]

Western Goals arose from McDonald's longstanding opposition to the civil rights and student movements, especially their radical strains.[83] A former president of the John Birch Society, McDonald had come to Washington in 1975 hoping to join the House Internal Security Committee, formerly known as the House Un-American Activities Committee. But that body disbanded just as he arrived, another casualty of the mid-decade intelligence scandals. For McDonald, the United States' failure to combat "communist terrorism"—his preferred phrasing—was all the more obvious when compared to Latin America's right-wing military regimes, which dealt with their enemies ruthlessly. Inspired by the Southern Cone dictatorships, McDonald thought the United States government should take similar actions against leftist militants such as the George Jackson Brigade, the Black Panthers, the Weather Underground, and the Symbionese Liberation Army, a small community of homegrown revolutionaries who served as the last great gasp of Sixties radicalism.[84]

Few of McDonald's congressional colleagues wanted to follow the path of the Southern Cone dictatorships since Operation Condor was a gruesome affair, killing scores of civilians.[85] And so, embittered by what he saw as weakness and complacency, McDonald founded Western Goals to take over where the state had apparently failed—a domestic dragnet free from congressional oversight or budgetary constraints. He hailed it as the "first and only public foundation" to "fill the critical gap caused by the crippling of the FBI, the disabling of the House Committee on Un-American Activities and the destruction of crucial government files."[86] After securing tax-exempt status, McDonald built an operating budget of approximately $90,000, accrued mostly through private donations ranging from $25 to $1000.[87] Because of the tax break, McDonald had to insist that Western Goals operated within the bounds of the law. Its intelligence, he claimed to the press, largely came from public records and the files of retired government employees "who choose to make their information available to us."[88] However, as subsequent investigations revealed, Western Goals acquired much of its data illegally, often by having U.S. police departments copy their files and transfer them to McDonald's outfit.[89]

Western Goals directed profits from its intelligence operations to sponsor seminars and publish newsletters about leftist subversion and terrorism in the Caribbean, Central America, and Africa.[90] Meanwhile, McDonald and Singlaub assembled a group of retired military brass to serve as fundraisers and board members, including the retired Joint Chiefs of Staff Chairman Thomas Moorer and Generals George S. Patton III and Lewis Walt.[91] Other members included Roger Milliken, a North Carolina textile magnate who had donated millions of dollars to conservative causes over the years, and Edward Teller, the physicist who helped create the hydrogen bomb.[92] With an illustrious board and generous donors, Western Goals joined the ASC and other conservative groups in challenging the human rights initiatives of the Carter administration and pressing for greater alliances with hardline anticommunist forces in Latin America and southern Africa. Within a few years, Western Goals had taken a more active role on Central America, passing information to the FBI about peace activists who traveled to El Salvador and other countries.[93]

Earning more friends on the U.S. Right, Singlaub also turned his attention to kindred movements abroad. In December 1979, he led an ASC delegation on a fact-finding mission to Guatemala. Since the 1960s, a succession of military governments backed by the country's conservative oligarchy—which controlled nearly all of Guatemala's arable land—had waged a genocidal war against the largely Mayan peasantry. Although a small Marxist guerrilla movement operated in the northern part of the country, most of those killed were not fighters but laborers who organized collectively for land rights and an end to the political violence.[94]

Singlaub and Graham enlisted themselves firmly on the side of the military regime. They met President Lucas García and members of the nation's ultraconservative business organizations, such as Amigos del País (Friends of the Country) and the Guatemalan Freedom Foundation.[95] Funded by the same wealthy landowners who propped up the military regime and controlled the death squads, these groups had been trying to improve their government's image in the United States.[96] They did not dismiss the extreme levels of violence—more than 500 dead a month—but instead argued that the human rights abuses committed by the army and the death squads were an unfortunate but necessary part of the war against communism. That argument did not sway many in Congress or the Carter administration, and so the Guatemalans turned their hopes to presidential hopeful Ronald Reagan, believing he would resume the military aid program that Congress had suspended a few years prior.[97]

During his visit, Singlaub learned from the Guatemalan oligarchy that those peasants who opposed their rule were "controlled by Cuban advisers" including "guerrilla warfare specialists." Even if most Guatemalans had suffered centuries of oppression, they'd nevertheless sold out their cause to the communists, undercutting their claims to land and power.[98] When he returned to the United States, Singlaub expounded upon the views of his allies in Guatemala. He said that he was "terribly impressed" by the Lucas regime's handling of popular discontent and the communist insurgency even as the Carter administration undercut the Guatemalan military. Singlaub urged a sympathetic understanding of the death squads, arguing that the Carter administration's "unwillingness to back the Lucas regime" was "prompting those who are dedicated to retaining the free enterprise system and to continuing progress toward political and economic development to take matters into their own hands."[99]

By 1980, then, as Singlaub surveyed the rise of armed leftist movements in Latin America and elsewhere, he found himself drawn to those who could do what was needed outside of formal state action. Others reached similar conclusions.

---

Theodore "Ted" Shackley left the CIA in 1979. Popular with his colleagues, he was nicknamed the Blond Ghost, for his fair hair and his ability to keep out of photographs. He'd won the agency's highest honor three times in his thirty-year career. In the 1950s, he ran spy networks in East Germany and Poland. Then he oversaw the United States' covert war against Cuba in the early 1960s.[100] During the Vietnam War, he managed a paramilitary army of more than 20,000 Laotian tribesmen, mostly from the highland-dwelling Hmong people, who fought against the Pathet Lao, a communist force supported by North Vietnam.[101] By 1970, Shackley was in charge of the CIA's station in Saigon, where he ran the assassination program known as Operation Phoenix.[102] Returning to the United States in 1972 to head the Latin American division, he oversaw a number of major operations, including the U.S.-backed coup that forced Chile's Salvador Allende from power. The following year, he received yet another promotion to head the East Asian division, just as the war in Vietnam was falling apart.[103] Many of Shackley's colleagues thought he was on the way to becoming director of the CIA. But the arrival of Stansfield Turner in early 1977 meant that his days in the agency were numbered. Shackley was precisely the kind of covert warrior that Turner hoped to purge from the Agency. In turn, Shackley viewed Turner as a bumbling amateur, hopelessly out of his depth.[104]

Disgruntled with the CIA's new boss, Shackley turned to former colleagues who had entered the private sector. He soon reached out to ex-CIA agent Edwin Wilson, who had built a new life as an arms dealer in the Islamic world.[105] For Wilson, "being in the CIA was like putting on a magic coat that forever made him invisible and invincible."[106] Retiring from government in 1976, Wilson monetized his knowledge of secretive shipping operations to sell weapons and explosives to Iran, Egypt, and Libya. He also set up private training missions for those nations' militaries. Amassing a personal fortune of millions of dollars, Wilson had a stable of exotic cars, apartments across Europe, and a sprawling 2,000-acre estate in northern Virginia.[107] His shady dealings would ultimately result in long prison sentences, but in the late 1970s many CIA officers looked favorably upon his activities, convinced that the private sector was better equipped to carry out secret operations in the era of Stansfield Turner.[108]

Shackley, for one, hoped to use Wilson's connections to bolster the agency's intelligence capabilities in the Middle East.[109] For a year, Wilson and his partner, another ex-CIA man, had been trying to sell the Iranians an expensive electronic surveillance system. Impressed, Shackley believed Wilson's contacts in Iran could make the CIA less reliant on intelligence reports from the Shah's notoriously corrupt secret police, known as SAVAK. But the whole plan collapsed when higher-ups in the CIA learned that Wilson was also selling weapons to Libya, in violation of U.S. law.[110] To Stansfield Turner, this proved Wilson was a renegade and a crook. It was inconceivable that an experienced and well-respected officer such as Ted Shackley could associate with someone like Wilson. When a bureaucratic job opened at the newly formed National Intelligence Tasking Center, Turner shuffled Shackley into the position, cutting him off from any role in planning clandestine operations.[111] Frustrated with more than three years of constant congressional and executive oversight of his activities, Shackley left the agency in early 1979, receiving his third Distinguished Intelligence Medal on the way out.[112]

Like John Singlaub, Shackley joined an informal network of ex–covert warriors who now plied their trade in the private sector. While former CIA men sometimes struggled to find employment, mostly because they could not tell potential employers about their work in the clandestine services, Shackley had a few colleagues whose businesses connections promised steady pay in retirement. Over the previous years, they had often discussed "getting out of the agency and making lots of money."[113] In the spring of 1979, Shackley teamed up with Tom Clines, one of his old friends from his days in Southeast Asia.[114] Clines had hatched a plan to sell weapons to the Egyptian government. Partnering with a former Egyptian official to create the Egyptian American Transportation and Services Company (EATSCO), Clines soon landed an exclusive contract to ship U.S. military hardware to Egypt.[115] He then brought in the recently retired Ted Shackley to manage the company, with an annual salary of about $50,000.[116]

In September 1980, Shackley struck out on his own. With the help of another colleague, a former CIA Soviet specialist, he founded Research Associates International, a "risk analysis company" that catered to the needs of oil companies operating in dangerous parts of the globe.[117] According to one colleague, Research Associates International was Shackley's revenge against Stansfield Turner, a competitive business that would siphon operations and agents from the CIA. Ever the spy, Shackley's firm cultivated an atmosphere of secrecy. His office, located on the top floor of a high-rise in the Washington, D.C., metropolitan area, could only be reached by taking a private elevator and then passing through heavy locked doors under camera surveillance.[118]

Laboring in the shadow of the state, Shackley became a popular commentator about the declining capabilities of the United States' clandestine services. In December 1980, he participated in a conference sponsored by a conservative think tank known as the National Strategy Information Center, joining a panel of congressional staffers, diplomats, and former spies who sought to shape the intelligence policies of the incoming Reagan administration. The big topic was covert action—the kinds of clandestine operations needed to counter what many perceived as Soviet ascendancy in the international arena.[119]

When Shackley rose to speak, he lectured about covert paramilitary actions in a changing world. "As the decade of the 1980s opens," he began, "Cuban mercenary armies sustain dictatorial governments in two large African nations, Angola and Ethiopia. In the Western Hemisphere, Cuban and Soviet-trained revolutionaries rule in Nicaragua. Their comrades threaten to seize neighboring El Salvador. Guatemala is in turmoil for it knows it is next in line to receive priority attention from Havana's and Moscow's guerrilla movements." He painted a picture of communist global expansion—the Soviet Army in Afghanistan, Vietnamese forces fighting in Cambodia and Thailand, Soviet-supported rebels in Honduras and Namibia. These mounting problems, Shackley opined, placed the United States in an increasingly untenable position. The stakes could not be higher. If the U.S. failed to counter Soviet military incursions and proxy insurgencies, then U.S. leaders might resort to nuclear warfare.[120]

But instead of retreating or launching an apocalyptic nuclear war, Shackley noted with hope, the United States had a "third option"—"the use of insurgency and counter insurgency techniques and covert action to achieve policy goals."[121] Simply put, the United States had to re-embrace paramilitary warfare. This required nothing less than an overhaul of the United States' clandestine services, which would reverse the recent changes made by Carter and Turner. In a book that expanded upon his conference lecture, Shackley argued that the "clandestine sponsorship of armed insurgencies" was the best means to roll back communist rule. Paradoxically, he was suggesting that the most effective means of counterinsurgency was in fact insurgency. By utilizing the same tactics and techniques that communist guerrillas had used, ordinary people could foment armed uprisings that would undermine communist rule from within. As the U.S. experience in Vietnam had indicated, a resilient guerrilla movement operating in remote areas and among a sympathetic population could topple a government, even one supported by an industrialized superpower with massive amounts of arms and hundreds of thousands of soldiers.[122]

Shackley's understanding of anticommunist guerrilla warfare harkened back to U.S. covert actions under the Truman, Eisenhower, and Kennedy administrations—some of which he had helped orchestrate. But he conceived of anticommunist guerrilla warfare on a far grander scale and with much loftier ambitions than most U.S. policymakers had, even in the heady days of the early Cold War. He did not want to contain communism to the Soviet Union and its satellites but instead eradicate it from the world. Yet that ambition hardly squared with the realities in most of the countries that Shackley examined. Armed actions against weak communist states could plausibly cause those regimes to collapse, especially in places where anticommunist guerrilla movements already existed, like Angola. But even if armed anticommunists did gain power, their war would have done little to transform the society they would now have to govern. More likely, it would have made governance more difficult, since war profoundly disrupts economic and political life, most obviously by killing people. In other words, guerrilla war could certainly oust a government, but it could not ensure that whatever regime took over would be able to improve the lives of its people.

Shackley's faith in anticommunist guerrilla warfare severed covert action from many of the policies and programs that it had accompanied in the early Cold War, especially the nexus of antipoverty schemes known as development. Since the late 1940s, American scientists and statesmen had allied themselves with nationalist elites and local leaders to reverse the spread of communism in the global South by moving poor, rural countries into a capitalist modernity modeled upon, and led by, the United States. That plan hinged on the presumption that widespread poverty and rurality in Asia, Africa, and Latin America was what made them "a breeding ground for violent revolution," as Harry Truman's foreign aid advisor once put it.[123] Often conceived as counterinsurgency—and at times implemented in conjunction with covert military actions—development programs, whether undertaken at the community level or through massive agricultural and architectural projects, promised to resolve the underlying conditions that caused poor people to embrace communism by reconstructing lives, livelihoods, and landscapes.[124]

Shackley sought nothing of the sort. Shorn of the impulse to modernize, the Third Option aimed not to ameliorate the conditions that generated violence but instead to exploit them. Development experts had it all wrong. The point was not to cure poverty but to transform popular frustrations into armed actions against Soviet-supported governments. This was a leaner and meaner approach to the problem of communism in the global South. Americans did not need to waste money setting up expensive modernization projects, let alone find ways to make them work. Instead, they just needed to give the right weapons to the right people and then get out of the way.

---

While Shackley and Singlaub joined think tanks and private firms, other ex–CIA officers also sought to revitalize the United States' covert war-making abilities by vigorously lobbying elected officials. The Association of Former Intelligence Officers (AFIO) led the way. Organized in 1975 at the height of the Church Committee hearings, the AFIO comprised retired members of the CIA, the FBI, the Defense Intelligence Agency, the National Security Agency, the State Department, the U.S. Treasury, and the WWII-era Office of Strategic Services.[125] Sharing a "deep concern over the gradual erosion of American Intelligence operations throughout the world," the AFIO petitioned members of Congress, wrote newspaper editorials, and engaged in grassroots politicking.[126] Many of the group's financial matters, especially its petitions for tax exemption, were handled by the ubiquitous conservative organizer Marvin Liebman—collaboration that highlights the overlap between the anticommunist activism of the 1950s and 1960s and that of ex–covert warriors who migrated into the private sector in the late 1970s.[127] Drawing from his decades of organizational experience, Liebman advised the AFIO leadership to form local "citizen's auxiliaries" through direct-mail techniques. Doing so would create a "broad-based public constituency which can provide funds—for the long run—and grassroots political action when it is required."[128] With Liebman's help, the AFIO managed a few major successes. Its greatest victory came in 1978, when it helped prevent the passage of the National Intelligence Reform and Organization Act, which would have further expanded congressional oversight of the United States' clandestine services.[129]

The work of the AFIO intersected with that of another organization known as the Citizens Legal Defense Fund for the FBI. Created in 1977 by former Senator James L. Buckley (brother of the *National Review*'s William F. Buckley), Claire Booth Luce, a former Congresswoman and widow of *Time/Life* magnate Henry Luce, and William E. Simon, a former Secretary of the Treasury, the group raised funds to "defend present and former FBI agents involved in civil and criminal litigation arising out of the performance of their duties."[130] Initially, the Citizens Legal Defense Fund rallied behind disgraced FBI agent James Kearney, indicted for illegal surveillance of leftist radicals.[131] Kearney had been a key part of the FBI's sprawling Counter Intelligence Program, known as COINTELPRO, which monitored and disrupted the activities of student groups, civil rights organizations, labor unions, and armed organizations like the Weather Underground, the Black Panther Party, and the Ku Klux Klan. COINTELPRO agents infiltrated groups, spread disinformation, and goaded their targets into committing acts of violence. They also resorted to unlawful methods of force, including break-ins, beatings, torture, and probably assassination, like that of Black Panther Party chairman Fred Hampton, shot dead by Chicago police as he lay in his bed.[132]

At the urging of organizer Marvin Liebman, the Citizens Legal Defense Fund initiated a direct-mail campaign that raised nearly $200,000 for Kearney's legal defense.[133] Its broadsides alleged his indictment was part of a "continuing effort afoot to weaken and neutralize the nation's law enforcement and intelligence gathering agencies through legal harassment." Some in the organization believed these attacks revealed the "efforts of the Soviet Union—unwittingly aided by all too many misinformed and misguided individuals in our own country—to wreck American intelligence and counter-intelligence activities." While members of the Citizen's Legal Defense Fund understood that Kearney and the FBI had skirted the law, they maintained that COINTELPRO had been necessary to combat the "notorious Havana-Hanoi backed terrorists of the Weatherman Underground organization" and other radical groups intent on subversion and violence.[134] Moreover, they argued, exposing agents like Kearney to indictment for their activities would have disastrous consequences. The "ultimate result" would "only be the weakening of law enforcement and intelligence gathering at a time when crime is rampant and the security of our nation is in jeopardy due to the growing restrictions on our intelligence agencies."[135]

Fearing that rising domestic crime was somehow linked to the declining abilities of U.S. intelligence agencies, the leaders of the Citizen's Legal Defense Fund expanded their aid to ex–CIA agents facing criminal charges. When the Justice Department announced that former CIA director Richard Helms would be indicted for perjury and obstruction of justice, stemming from his congressional testimony on the CIA's actions in Chile, the defense fund began raising money for Helms's legal fees.[136] As with Kearney, the fund's leaders argued that subversion, whether at home or abroad, demanded covert actions outside of the law. Revealing secrets and indicting those agents tasked with America's defense would only make life harder for the CIA and other clandestine agencies.[137]

Efforts to rehabilitate the CIA and resuscitate covert action crossed into the realm of fiction. In 1976, as his brother was assembling the Citizen's Legal Defense Fund, William F. Buckley launched a series of spy novels that reimagine the years of the high Cold War. His protagonist, Blackford Oakes, is a CIA officer in his mid-twenties who, over the course of nearly a dozen books, undertakes one perilous mission after another to save the world from communism. Having worked for the CIA in Mexico for "seven or eight months" in 1953, under the aegis of E. Howard Hunt, a key player in the Watergate bugging operation, Buckley poured much of himself into the character. Like Buckley, Oakes was also born to a rich family in 1925. Both went to an elite British school, served in World War II, and attended Yale where they were tapped by the CIA to serve as deep-cover agents.[138] "The training received by Blackford Oakes is, in exact detail, the training I received," Buckley once explained. The two dressed alike and shared the same basic worldview.[139] Indeed, Oakes "is often found reading Buckley's books" and articles from the *National Review*.[140]

As such, Oakes served as a vehicle for Buckley's personal fantasies about the CIA career he abandoned as a young man. The books are filled with henchmen and hijinks, damsels and double-crosses. Blond, blue-eyed, handsome, tanned, and powerfully built, Oakes romances a woman in every story, although Buckley, the prudent Catholic, offered only the barest glimpses of intimate relations, unlike many other authors in the spy genre. A prodigious traveler, Buckley drew upon his deep knowledge of foreign cities for his stories, places like London, Berlin, Budapest, Moscow, Havana, and Saigon. Thrust into the key flashpoints of the early Cold War, Oakes jockeys with fictionalized versions of Allen Dulles, John F. Kennedy, Che Guevara, Fidel Castro, and Nikita Khrushchev. He foils a plot to land Soviet missiles in Cuba, and is shot down while piloting a U-2 spy plane over Russia. He infiltrates communist circles in Moscow after Stalin's death, dodges Soviet troops during the Hungarian Uprising, and discovers the plans for the Sputnik satellite. He even beds the Queen of England, an affair that tips him off to a British agent that had been smuggling H-Bomb secrets to the communists.[141]

But Oakes was more than a projection of Buckley's adventurism and imagination. The character provided him with yet another outlet to outline the moral dimensions of the Cold War and explain why covert action was the key to winning it. Unlike John le Carré and Graham Greene, whose books condemn the entire world of Cold War espionage—American, British, and Soviet—as essentially amoral, Buckley offered precious few critiques of the CIA. He was adamantly opposed to what he called the "effete moral ambiguity of some of my contemporaries." As he put it in 1976, "There are good guys and there are bad guys," and the CIA were obviously the good guys.[142]

To a nation wracked by Watergate, the Church Committee, and other moments of humiliation and self-flagellation, Oakes offered a simple answer. As one reviewer explained, Oakes made it clear that "there are times when a nation needed to operate in secret and even times when those who carried out secret operations could legitimately refuse to answer questions about them before a Senate subcommittee hearing."[143] Rather than retreat from covert action, as the Church Committee recommended, the United States should engage in more of it. In places like Southeast Asia and southern Africa, Buckley said, Americans should "make it more a pain than a pleasure for the Russians to intervene."[144]

---

The idea that the United States could no longer wage covert war, and that private initiatives could take up the slack, radiated into other areas of American life in the late 1970s. In April of 1975, ex-Marine Bart Bonner founded Veterans and Volunteers for Vietnam to help South Vietnam fend off the invading armies of the communist North. Having served in Vietnam in 1965 and 1966, Bonner was disgusted by the United States' slow withdrawal from the war. As South Vietnam tottered on its last legs, Bonner sent letters to fellow servicemen asking them to join a paramilitary mission to return to Vietnam and continue the fight. He then reached out to the South Vietnamese military command about his plans. They sent back a muddled response, telling him that foreigners were not welcome in the South Vietnamese armed forces. They did not, however, reject his proposal outright. That was just fine, Bonner said, for his men "didn't intend to join their army." This was to be a private mission run by concerned

Americans, not a campaign to recruit U.S. nationals for a foreign armed service, which would violate U.S. law.[145] As he told one reporter, "We are going to make every effort to fight under the American flag." But if that couldn't be arranged, Bonner's troops would carry the Confederate banner—a "beautiful flag," in his words—into combat.[146] He told his men that they "must be willing to sacrifice everything, even their citizenship, if need be."[147]

Bonner boasted that his scheme attracted some two thousand Americans, including elite soldiers from the Green Berets, the Navy SEALs, and Air Force Commandos, along with a few hundred Canadians.[148] But he was better at selling his mission to the media than he was at planning it. He had no money to buy weapons, supplies, and transport. Still, he hoped that if his volunteers got themselves to "staging areas on the east and west coasts, funds could be obtained from private sources to charter a plane to fly to Saigon." And if Bonner managed to bring his men to Vietnam, perhaps they would be "issued weapons from the ARVN or use captured weapons." He summed up his impromptu approach nicely: "As far as logistics go, we'll make do with what is available."[149] Nothing ever became available. Bonner received no support from private sources let alone from the South Vietnamese government, which collapsed before he could muster his men. After the fall of South Vietnam, Bonner reworked his group as a "clearinghouse providing information on opportunities to fight communism," in Africa and Asia, though little seems to have come from that as well.[150]

When Bonner's Vietnam campaign fizzled, Americans sought armed action elsewhere. For most, Africa was the place to be. Indeed, much of the region was a battlefield in the late 1970s. By 1975, the white-supremacist government of Rhodesia faced a massive popular insurgency. In the early 1960s, Africans had formed two nationalist political movements—the Zimbabwe African People's Union (ZAPU) and the Zimbabwe African National Union (ZANU)—to advocate for independence along the lines of other African states. Clashes over ideology and strategy produced bitter conflict between ZANU and ZAPU, but white Rhodesians saw little difference between the two groups since they both mobilized large swaths of the black population against white rule and were backed by communist states.[151]

The fall of Portuguese Angola was equally troublesome. When a military coup and a popular uprising unseated the authoritarian Estado Novo regime in Portugal in April of 1974, the new socialist government began to dismantle its colonial state in favor of Angolan independence. Shortly thereafter, the country fell into civil war as three vaguely Marxist guerrilla groups, each controlled by a domineering leader, filled the void left by the retreating colonial regime.

In 1976, the most powerful group, the Movimento Popular de Libertação de Angola, or MPLA, established a government, forcing its rivals to retreat to the hinterlands, where they staged hit-and-run attacks against the new regime.[152]

Angola's simmering civil war, coupled with the nationalist movements fighting in Rhodesia, convinced leaders in the Ford Administration that the region was facing an all-out communist assault. The growing presence of Cuban soldiers in Angola prompted the administration, led by Henry Kissinger and CIA director William Colby, to send more than $50 million in covert aid to the FNLA (Frente Nacional Libertação de Angola) and UNITA (União Nacional para a Independência Total de Angola) starting in July 1975, using third-party states such as South Africa and Zaire as cover.[153] But many in Congress, still in the throes of the Church Committee hearings, were skeptical about initiating yet another covert operation to aid questionable forces abroad. And so, in early 1976, Congress passed the Clark Amendment, banning any U.S. military aid to the Angolan rebels.[154]

Glimpsing yet another dimension of U.S. weakness on the world stage, some American men sought to take matters into their own hands. A growing paramilitary subculture in the United States guided them to southern Africa, where they worked as mercenaries of sorts.[155] At the heart of that subculture was the magazine *Soldier of Fortune*, created by U.S. Army Reserve Lt. Col. Robert K. Brown in 1975. A former Special Operations soldier and mercenary freelancer, Brown had been involved in a succession of outlandish exploits, including plans to smuggle guns to Cuba and an abortive mission to overthrow the government of Haiti. Volunteering for Vietnam, Brown believed firmly in the United States' anticommunist crusade in Southeast Asia and elsewhere. He served in a few different special operations units, including John Singlaub's Studies and Observation Group, but grew bored with the life of a stateside reserve officer when the war ended.[156]

In 1975, while visiting an American friend who had joined the Rhodesian police, Brown had a life-changing revelation. Rhodesia, like many other countries, needed American volunteers to fight, yet few in the United States knew this. Realizing the potential of an untapped market, he created *Soldier of Fortune*—a "journal for professional adventurers" that sold the mercenary life through in-depth, first-person reporting about a host of armed conflicts spanning the globe. It was written by and for "those who have gone and done for those who go and do."[157] Indeed, many of its correspondents were veterans. But it also appealed to those armchair warriors who wished only to read about exciting wars in exotic places—in Brown's words, the "Walter Mitty market."[158] A hit at newsstands, Brown was selling more than 125,000 copies per issue by 1976.[159]

Under Brown's guidance, *Soldier of Fortune* became an ad-hoc labor market for aspiring soldiers-for-hire. The magazine's back pages were filled with job-seeking ads from anonymous men hoping to find adventure and fortune in Africa.[160] Beyond classified ads, *Soldier of Fortune* offered practical advice for veterans and thrill-seekers. Rhodesia was the main attraction. A passionate supporter of Ian Smith's regime, Brown hoped his magazine could take up the slack for the U.S. government while liberals equivocated in Congress. To that end, he interviewed the recruiting officer for the Rhodesian Army, Major Nick Lamprecht, who advised *Soldier of Fortune*'s American readers on how they could join his forces. It was not an easy job, Lamprecht explained, nor a particularly well-paying one. But it did offer disillusioned young men the chance to remake their life in a new land. "Rhodesia has many things to offer," Lamprecht noted. "Good Rhodesian beer, a friendly populace, and what I would describe as a free and easy, unhurried way of life, lots of wide open spaces."[161]

Rhodesia was, simply, a place where one could "Be a Man among Men," as the official recruitment poster urged Americans.[162] It also held out the possibility for romance—not just with war but with women as well. Since "wives have difficulty adjusting," Lamprecht explained, the single men preferred by recruiters could very well find a mate while serving abroad.[163] Indeed, according to one former Rhodesian soldier, foreign mercenaries were not motivated by money so much as they were the promise of adventure and freedom. "I think basically the conditions of life appealed to them," he said. "They wanted a few kicks out of life and they thought that was the way to get them."[164] Of course, the notion that American men had any right to fight in Rhodesia had obvious racist and paternalist underpinnings, and white mercenaries from the United States did not shy from saying so. "What we have here is an ideal core of white people who are able to raise the standard of living among the Africans," another American mercenary noted. "Without us, conditions will decline rapidly."[165]

The belief that Rhodesia represented a superior, even ideal, society often overlapped with Americans' concerns about life at home, especially the fate of Vietnam veterans in post-Vietnam America. The economic troubles of the late 1970s had created a large pool of skilled combat veterans with few prospects for stable and rewarding employment. As Brown opined in *Soldier of Fortune*'s first issue, "The Vietnam War has left the U.S. with the largest number of unemployed combat-trained soldiers in the world . . . I foresee most of the new mercenaries coming from here in the next few years."[166] Oil embargoes, energy crises, inflation, stagnation, and deindustrialization not only threatened ex-soldiers with joblessness but also a loss of masculinity as their breadwinner status diminished.[167] Disillusioned by the legacies of the civil rights, feminist, and student movements on mainstream American life, veterans also fretted about the decline of the one institution in which they still believed: the military. One American who fought in Rhodesia later said that he "became really disenchanted with what the Army became after the Vietnam era . . . I said to myself this wasn't the Army I joined and I'm getting the hell out."[168]

Fighting as mercenaries would allow these men to continue their wartime crusade against communism abroad while reclaiming the economic and social power they believed they had lost at home.[169] That point registered in numerous stories that *Soldier of Fortune* and other magazines published about Africa's most notorious mercenaries, "Mad" Mike Hoare and Bob Denard, both of whom had been fighting in one conflict after another since the early 1960s.[170] Promising a life of independence, adventure, and fortune with a bit of hard-drinking and womanizing on the side, those stories overlapped with a number of films about mercenaries that *Soldier of Fortune* eagerly promoted. The most successful was 1978's *The Wild Geese*, a fictionalized account of Mike Hoare's time in the Congo fighting for Moïse Tshombe, the secessionist anticommunist leader who so charmed U.S. conservatives in the 1960s. Starring Richard Burton and Roger Moore, the film tells the story of "50 steelhard mercs who undertake a terrifying mission" in "dangerous, sweltering Central Africa—very much like the Old Congo—to rescue and bring out a deposed and imprisoned black president." The film blurred the line between fiction and reality, not only in its plot but also its production. Mike Hoare, who was then planning an ill-fated coup in the Seychelles, somehow found time to serve as a "military and technical advisor" on set. Reflecting on the film, he explained that it offered a true depiction of what mercenaries were all about: "In a good mercenary outfit, they're all there because they want to be. All right, the motive is probably the high money they'll earn, but they all want to do it. They're all volunteers."[171]

Hoare talked of independence, adventure, and fortune, but the reality was far messier. Americans had to write to the Rhodesian Army, which would carefully vet their applications, weed out the "phonies," and send recruiting packets to those deemed fit for service. The Rhodesian government would then pay for their airfare and other travel expenses. Once the recruits completed basic training, they would join the army as conscripts. Those who failed would promptly receive plane tickets back to the United States. As a matter of routine, Lamprecht and other recruiters stressed that this was not mercenary work but instead formal enlistment. "Everyone joins our army under the same conditions and for three years. All are regular soldiers. All receive the same pay, the same type of equipment. There is no difference between an American joining the Rhodesian Army than there would be if a Rhodesian joined the

U.S. Army," he claimed.[172] That meant enlisting in Rhodesia did not make much financial sense for Americans. It was less lucrative than joining the U.S. military.[173] But there were other benefits beyond pay. Claiming a new homestead on the African savanna was one of them. The Rhodesian government expected those foreigners who joined its army to settle there as citizens, part of its attempt to rebuild its dwindling European-descended population after years of "white flight."[174]

Promises of land and power, coupled with the imagined bonds of whiteness, made Rhodesia a haven for mercenaries from Great Britain, New Zealand, Australia, and France who fought alongside their American counterparts in the Rhodesian military.[175] Some were veterans of paramilitary campaigns in the Congo in the early 1960s. Others were recent recruits, lured, like the Americans, to southern Africa by the possibility of adventure and fortune. A few had family connections in the country. No matter how they got there, white foreigners became significant parts of Rhodesia's fighting forces as well as the South African military and police.[176]

The experiences and assumptions that brought white American men to Rhodesia were most acutely shared by Britons. Like their American counterparts, white mercenaries from the United Kingdom faced dwindling jobs prospects in a changing industrial economy marked by inflation and stagnation. As in the United States, British industries such as manufacturing and mining declined significantly in the late 1970s just as the welfare state contracted. Stable, well-paying work started to disappear as firms embraced new technologies and searched for cheaper labor abroad.[177] The sight of long lines of British unemployed men, waiting to collect the dole, became commonplace.[178] For some of these men, left without work and a viable stake in society, fighting in Rhodesia or Angola offered a way to regain their economic power and their manhood.[179]

Rhodesian authorities were keen to play upon the sense of disillusionment and dissatisfaction that ran throughout white working-class communities on both sides of the Atlantic. As in the United States, the Rhodesian Information Office sent recruitment literature to sympathizers in the United Kingdom, who disseminated it amongst their friends.[180] It also mailed recruitment packets to active-duty soldiers at British military bases, particularly in West Germany, and to private British defense companies in Iran and elsewhere.[181]

As British men traveled to Rhodesia, the British government, which had never recognized Rhodesia's independence, struggled to stamp the flow of its citizens to the country. That was because the situation presented British leaders with a legal paradox. Did British citizens who traveled to Rhodesia with the intent of joining its military violate laws that forbade them from fighting in foreign armed services? If the government prosecuted them for doing so, it would mean that it recognized Rhodesia's sovereignty, insofar as any successful prosecution would hinge on the notion that Rhodesia was a foreign state rather than a member of the British Commonwealth engaged in an illegal yet temporary rebellion.[182] But if Rhodesia was indeed a member of the Commonwealth, and not a foreign state, then British citizens from the United Kingdom and elsewhere could legally enlist in its forces. After wrestling with the issue for months, government leaders decided to prohibit British citizens from fighting in Rhodesia under the 1968 embargo, which curtailed migration and commerce between the Commonwealth and Rhodesia. This choice gave the British legal maneuverability in case they wished to recruit their own mercenaries for future conflicts.[183] Still, the British government's threats of jail time and fines did not stop its citizens from fighting and dying in Rhodesia.[184]

In both the United States and Britain, then, the Rhodesian government's attempts to lure mercenaries to its country unfolded in an extralegal gray area, as it helped subsidize ostensibly private recruitment efforts organized by U.S. or British nationals. Meanwhile, a number of grassroots enterprises started their own recruitment schemes.[185] In 1976, a new group called American Aid for Rhodesia announced that it was searching for one thousand volunteers to fight ZAPU and ZANU.[186] Its founder, a former U.S. Army infantryman from El Paso, Texas, named Mike Gonzalez, hoped that his group could gather enough men to aid Ian Smith's regime in a time of crisis. He claimed he was not in it for the money but rather to stem the growing tide of communism in southern Africa while the U.S. government sat on its hands. "It's a paramilitary organization, but it's not composed of mercenaries," he noted to a reporter. "It will be set up as a non-profit. We would only fight as a last resort."[187] Other Americans went to Rhodesia as private security guards for large landowners, jobs that promised higher pay and less danger but still the chance to fight communists, terrorists, and bandits. Although pay on these ranches was often less than American men were making in the United States, they found them to be "challenging and personally rewarding" in ways that their previous jobs had not been.[188]

Those American men who took up arms in southern Africa shared a few common experiences. Most were familiar with weapons, often gained through service in the military or, less often, the police, but few were hardened combat veterans. Many were single or divorced. The majority were underemployed or unemployed.[189] Beyond that, many believed that they were carrying out the same anticommunist mission that the United States had undertaken in Vietnam—a mission that weak politicians had forsaken. Thus, in their self-understandings, American mercenaries were real men who could take over where effete policymakers had failed. As one American mercenary put it, "The West isn't doing its job. The U.S. especially isn't doing its duty. If they're too scared to fight the Communists, then people like me have to act independently. I consider it my duty to fight in Rhodesia. After Vietnam and Angola, we can't afford to lose any other countries."[190]

Their martial abilities, however, varied widely. Some, such as L. H. "Mike" Williams and Michael Pierce, two U.S. Army veterans who had joined Rhodesia's army in 1975 and 1978, respectively, were skilled soldiers who rose quickly through the ranks, earning praise for their leadership and combat acumen.[191] Others were not so successful. The realities of guerrilla warfare quickly disabused all but the most dedicated of their mercenary fantasies. As one *Soldier of Fortune* reporter noted in 1979, "The majority found the routine too rough to last more than a few months. The desertion rate among American citizens who have joined the Rhodesian army over the past two years is estimated to run about 80 percent."[192]

Deserters were the lucky ones. The unfortunate and foolhardy died. One was John Alan Coey, a medic from the outskirts of Cleveland, Ohio, who served with the Rhodesian Light Infantry. When he was killed by guerrillas in July 1975, *Soldier of Fortune* published a posthumous essay celebrating his courage and sacrifice. It quoted Coey on his time in combat: "Since coming to Rhodesia, I have often heard people remark that it's 'inevitable' for this country and all of southern Africa to follow the 'winds of change' and go the same way as other former colonies to the north. This is rubbish and only indicates a lack of fighting spirit, guts, and the will to rule a civilization built by better men."[193] After he died, and questions emerged about the legality of his time in Rhodesia, John Coey's mother maintained that her son was a hero and that the "ones who committed treason were the U.S. government officials" who involved "America in a no-win, undeclared war" in Vietnam.[194] Coey's parents soon received sympathy notes from the right-wing Liberty Lobby and Lester Maddox, the former governor of Georgia and a staunch civil rights opponent.[195]

Americans fared even worse in Angola, where the racial politics were not as clear as they were in Rhodesia. Unlike the Rhodesian Army, which was fighting for a white-supremacist state, both the UNITA and the FNLA guerrilla movements were almost entirely composed of black Africans seeking nationhood, and that cause did not inspire many white Americans. Practical difficulties also played a part. There were no official offices for either the FNLA or UNITA, and since both had been relegated to remote parts of the country, finding the guerrillas took considerable effort and luck. Hopefuls had to deal with con artists and swindlers who boasted lucrative opportunities and then failed to deliver. In Miami, a group of Cuban exiles had announced that they were recruiting a few hundred mercenaries for Angola. But when reporters picked up the story, they found that the Cubans were all talk.[196]

Other schemes bore out the same pattern. David Bufkin, a crop duster from California who transformed himself into a self-styled mercenary in the mid-1970s, claimed that he had contracts with several governments and paramilitary groups. Officials in the Ford administration described him as an "ex-soldier who has gone AWOL several times, been tried for rape and been in and out of jail."[197] Shortly after the start of Angola's civil war, Bufkin started taking out ads in local newspapers and *Soldier of Fortune* seeking between sixty and one hundred soldiers-for-hire. Bufkin said he had a contract worth $80,000, some of which, he hinted, was supplied by the CIA.[198] A few dozen Americans contacted him, willing to offer their services. But Bufkin's operation was mostly a ploy. His supposed CIA contract did not exist. As one disgruntled mercenary later recalled, "Bufkin obviously had no funds available. He operated out of motels. He had no office. Potential recruits had to pay their own travel expenses. It was definitely a shoestring operation."[199]

Nevertheless, Bufkin managed to get a few American mercenaries to Angola. Those who made it to the guerrilla's camps joined a withering effort to repel the powerful offensives of the MPLA government, now backed by nearly thirty thousand Cuban soldiers. They were unable to change the war in any meaningful way.[200] A few were quickly killed in combat. One of Bufkin's recruits, George Bacon, an ex-CIA officer and former member of John Singlaub's clandestine Studies and Observation Group, died in an assault in February 1976. Before coming to Angola, Bacon had tried to join Bart Bonner's Veterans and Volunteers for Vietnam.[201] When that group failed, Bacon turned to Angola, the "only area where American volunteers could be employed to fight communism." But Angola was hardly the place to win glory. As one of his friends lamented after his death, Bacon "went over there and found a half-a-dozen men trying to stop a Cuban armada. It was stupid and he should have just got out."[202]

Daniel Gearhart met the same fate. A Vietnam veteran from Maryland, besieged with financial debts, he had responded to one of Bufkin's ads in *Soldier of Fortune* against his wife's wishes. Angola was a bust for Gearhart too. Promised more than $1000 a week, he made less than $1700 in his entire time there.[203] His comrades-in-arms were poorly trained and equipped, and tired of years of fighting, which frustrated Gearhart to no end. In April 1976, MPLA forces captured him along with six other American and British mercenaries. A military tribunal sentenced him to death. His wife and family begged the Ford administration to intervene.[204] But the MPLA government could not be swayed. Gearhart was a "highly dangerous character," officials said. On July 10, 1976, government soldiers executed Gearhart and four of his British comrades.[205] The two Americans captured with Gearhart, Gary Acker and Gustavo Grillo, who had also been recruited by Bufkin, managed to escape the firing squads and spent the next six years in an Angolan prison.[206] In the months after the execution, *Soldier of Fortune* published a series of articles praising Gearhart's commitment to fighting communism and organized a relief fund for his widow and three children.[207]

Gearhart's highly publicized death fed mounting allegations that the U.S. government and the CIA were recruiting American mercenaries for Africa.[208] Congress decided to investigate. In August 1976, members of the House Committee on International Relations interviewed the Deputy Assistant Attorney General and the Assistant Secretary of State for Africa to find out just how many Americans were fighting in Rhodesia and Angola, and who exactly was paying them. The officials waffled under the limelight. They could not pin down the exact number of mercenaries fighting in Africa—there could be as few as ten in Angola and as many as four hundred in Rhodesia. But the officials did make it clear that the United States government was not recruiting or paying these men. It was largely unfolding through private channels, about which American policymakers knew precious little.[209] Subsequent investigations over the following years did not make matters any clearer.[210]

The thorniest issue was figuring out whether any of these individuals or groups broke the law. Publishing information about potential mercenary jobs, like *Soldier of Fortune* did, was not illegal. Actively recruiting them without registering as a foreign agent, however, was. Moreover, those Americans who became mercenaries, whether with the Rhodesian Army or Angolan guerrillas, were violating neutrality laws that forbade U.S. citizens from joining foreign armed forces.[211] The congressional inquiry generated some sensationalist press and was part of a larger international conversation about mercenaries, which culminated in a United Nations resolution calling on all countries to ban them from combat.[212] In terms of prosecutions and jail time, however, little came from the U.S. congressional investigations. And since the U.N. had few means to enforce its ban, it was mostly symbolic.

Meanwhile, U.S. mercenaries tried to soften their image. Robert Brown and human rights lawyer Luis Kutner talked of forming an international collective called World Veterans for Human Rights, which would "take the sting out of the connotation of 'mercenaries.'"[213] This failed bid at public relations masked the fact that many private mercenary recruiting networks remained in place, even as the conflicts in Africa died down. The Rhodesian government, after nearly fifteen years of constant fighting, began negotiating with the ZANU and ZAPU rebels in 1978, paving the way for a transition of power to Robert Mugabe and the new nation of Zimbabwe, which he soon turned into a dictatorship. In Angola, the MPLA government, aided by Soviet arms and a battalion of Cuban soldiers, crushed the FNLA and nearly destroyed UNITA, which retreated further into the hinterlands, barely surviving to fight another day. The mercenaries had failed.

---

Although U.S. mercenaries had at best marginal impacts on the wars in Rhodesia and Angola, their stories helped radicalize a small but growing pool of right-wing American men who saw in armed action a path to power. To those who had fought in southern Africa—or, more often, fantasized about it—the dissolution of Rhodesia's white supremacist government after 1978 foretold a frightening future that might befall the United States. Some right-wingers in the United States started to think that African Americans, liberals, communists, Jews, and foreigners were trying to establish a totalitarian state at home. Soon guns would be illegal, religion outlawed, and racial mixing compulsory.

White supremacist leader William Pierce drew those fears together in his 1978 novel, *The Turner Diaries*. Told from the perspective of a white government looking back on its triumph in the "Great Revolution," the book documents the life of Earl Turner, a hero from the war to save the white race. Recruited into a guerrilla movement known as the Organization, Turner battles the U.S. government—referred to as "the System"—which had confiscated Americans' weapons, done away with rape laws, and allowed African Americans and Jews to take over the country. For several years, Turner stages hit-and-run attacks against the System, blowing up the FBI's headquarters in Washington, D.C., and lobbing mortars at Congress. Those efforts induct Turner into the group's secret leadership, called the Order. After the "Day of the Rope," in which the Order lynches thousands of white media figures, academics, and women for betraying their race, it launches missiles at the Soviet Union, which sparks a nuclear war that cripples the System. Turner delivers the death blow when he flies a plane loaded with a nuclear warhead into the Pentagon. Advertised in *Soldier of Fortune* and other paramilitary periodicals, *The Turner Diaries* became a kind of bible for white supremacists in the United States, spurring the growth of numerous armed groups across the country that saw themselves as guerrillas arrayed against an increasingly totalitarian state.[214]

To other Americans, the apparent gutting of the United States' clandestine services in these same years suggested that paramilitary campaigns abroad would save the United States from a future of totalitarianism. And so, as the fighting in Africa waned, some U.S. mercenaries turned their gaze toward Central America, especially El Salvador and Nicaragua, where two leftist insurgencies threatened anticommunist regimes. They were appalled by the spread of communism to countries so close to the United States, as it indicated the United States would be the next to capitulate.

That was roughly the same picture retired covert warriors such as John Singlaub saw. Communist guerrillas in Central America signaled yet another failure of Carter and of détente, more proof of how far the United States had fallen. On the campaign trail, Ronald Reagan harnessed those sentiments. He promised to reverse this arc of national decline by restoring the United States' military capabilities, reclaiming its leading position in world affairs, and rolling back communism by any means necessary.[215]

For that last bit to happen, many on the right believed, the United States had to regain its ability to mount clandestine operations that could undermine communist states from within. But if the U.S. government was not up to the task, then the private sector should take over. In the Reagan era, John Singlaub and other retired covert warriors would turn to the anticommunist international to realize that conviction. First in Central America, and then elsewhere, they fashioned covert actions that united wealthy donors and aspiring mercenaries with a legion of foreign activists and paramilitaries.

## 5 | Private Wars in Central America

In May 1985, John Singlaub placed a call to his old friend Robert K. Brown, the brash editor of *Soldier of Fortune* magazine. He needed someone to assemble a team of veterans to train the beleaguered Contra guerrillas in Nicaragua. Their backs were against the wall, Singlaub told Brown. "Congress has cut off aid to them. They need you to take over where the CIA left off." Brown set about recruiting a unit of unconventional warfare specialists. He'd known most of them for years. Some were veterans of Rhodesia's bush war. Others had been working in Central America as private consultants for state security forces in El Salvador and Guatemala. A few days later, Brown flew his team to Boulder, Colorado. They assembled at a downtown hotel where Brown told his men to lay low, an admittedly difficult task. As he later recalled, "The daunting group of tall, muscular, mean-looking, scruffy-bearded men didn't have much chance of blending in with the dull, fatcat, suited-types booked into the prestigious hotel."[1] Singlaub requested to interview each man personally. Brown agreed and arranged transport to Singlaub's mountain home in nearby Fraser, Colorado, though he had little reason to think that Singlaub would second-guess his selections. This was all "just to humor" the aging general. He was sure that Singlaub "would accept my private little army at no cost to him."[2]

Once he was satisfied with the team, Singlaub laid out the plan. They were to travel to Tegucigalpa, Honduras, where they would reconvene with members of the Fuerza Democrática Nicaragüense (FDN), the largest and most powerful Contra army. Then they would make the difficult journey through remote jungles and rugged mountain passes to Camp Las Vegas, the FDN headquarters on the Nicaraguan-Honduran border. Once there, Brown's team was supposed to "train their elite commando unit for deep penetration operations into Nicaragua." The mission was to last ninety days. Singlaub offered a parting note: "Each one of you is an expert in your field, so you need not to be told what to do. Thank you, and good luck."[3]

Singlaub's plan was one of many private military ventures that conservative Americans launched in Central America in the 1980s. Convinced that the U.S. government, especially liberals in Congress, had forsaken the anticommunist struggle, they concluded foreign paramilitaries were the ideal proxy warriors who could conquer the Marxist threat once and for all. That conviction had its roots in the early Cold War, but Singlaub and those around him sharpened it into policy. Working behind the scenes in an array of think-tanks and organizations, they helped shape the impulses that guided the Reagan administration's low-intensity wars in Central America and, in subsequent years, Africa and Central Asia.

But lobbying efforts, largely visible to the public, were only part of their strategy. As the Reagan administration faced stiff resistance to its wars in Central America from Congress and the American public, not to mention the constraints of international diplomacy, many right-leaning Americans concluded that the private sector was best suited to channel money, weapons, supplies, and advisors to embattled paramilitary groups. Singlaub and other retired covert warriors organized rallies, sponsored television and radio programs, and published books, pamphlets, and articles to raise millions of dollars in private donations from wealthy individuals and businesses, international groups, and grassroots organizations. They used these funds to establish private military aid programs that they hoped would not only fill in for the United States military and intelligence services but do a better job for less money.

These efforts promised new power and profits by shifting war-making from the state to private actors. Secretive weapons sales, in particular, offered fresh revenue streams for arms manufacturers and all sorts of gunrunners, from sophisticated international operations to ill-conceived plots hatched by American white supremacist groups. At the same time, in attempting to privatize war, retired covert warriors and their allies sought to avoid congressional scrutiny and circumvent popular debate about U.S. foreign policy. By working along the margins of the state, they hoped to use extralegal channels to revitalize a form of combat to which they had dedicated their lives. Yet their endeavors revealed significant cleavages between the Reagan administration and its supporters about the role of government and the direction of U.S. foreign policy. While many shared Reagan's vision of a world free from communism, they often chastised his administration for not doing enough. Thus, the intervention of private groups was an attempt to manage and make sense of competing impulses about the state.

John Singlaub's forays into international activism dovetailed with his successes in the domestic arena. Having made a name in conservative circles in the months leading up to the 1980 election, some commentators predicted he would run for the nation's highest office.[4] Instead, he emerged as a prominent advocate for Ronald Reagan's presidential campaign.[5] In Reagan, Singlaub saw a true leader who would do whatever was needed to prevent the spread of communism in the Third World. He admired Reagan for his patriotism and single-mindedness, the fact that, "unlike Jimmy Carter, Reagan was not beset by doubts about a fundamental 'malaise' in American Society."[6] Reagan's celebrations of militarism, his strident anticommunism, and his denunciations of détente all indicated to Singlaub that he was the ideal candidate for president, tough enough to stand up to the communists.[7] This was not particularly surprising, given that Reagan cribbed many of his foreign policy talking points from hardliners such as Singlaub and his colleagues in the American Security Council and other hawkish groups. When they met for the first time on the 1980 campaign trail, Reagan told Singlaub, "General, you give me more material for my speeches than anybody else." In turn, Singlaub confessed that Reagan was "the only national politician who really understands what I am talking about."[8] Over the summer of 1980, Republican leaders tapped Singlaub as a key foreign policy adviser for Reagan's campaign, helping propel the actor-turned-governor to victory in November.[9]

Soon after Reagan took office, Singlaub received an invitation from the Asian Peoples' Anti-Communist League (APACL) to address their regional conference in Perth, Australia.[10] Speaking to hundreds of anticommunists from across Asia, including many of the APACL's old guard from the early 1960s, Singlaub reworked his domestic script. Titled a "Message of Hope and Optimism," Singlaub stressed that the Reagan administration "intended to strengthen the armed forces of the United States so that America would no longer be dominated by the Soviet Union." He also pointed out that Reagan had pledged his "support to our traditional allies in the region, South Korea and the Republic of China on Taiwan." Singlaub's hosts, especially members of the Taiwan chapter, received his message warmly, since the U.S. government had recently chosen to recognize the People's Republic of China over Jiang Jieshi's government. Before leaving Perth, Taiwan's Ku Chen Kang, the long-serving honorary chairman of the APACL and the World Anti-Communist League, invited Singlaub to attend the groups' fourteenth annual conference in Taipei in August 1981. There, Singlaub met activists and paramilitary leaders from across the globe—the Anti-Bolshevik Bloc of Nations, the Cuban militants of

Alpha 66, several bands of Afghan mujahedin, a group of Angolan guerrillas, and members of Guatemala's paramilitary Movimiento Liberación Nacional.[11]

Back in the United States, Singlaub hosted a meeting in Phoenix, Arizona, to establish a new U.S.-based WACL chapter. The previous one had shuttered in 1978 after a series of public exposés revealed that its leader, Roger Pearson, was an avowed anti-Semite and white supremacist.[12] Singlaub lamented that Pearson had tarnished the image of an otherwise respectable group. Ku told Singlaub his new chapter should avoid the extremist label that damned Pearson's outfit by recruiting retired "former military officers with distinguished records." Singlaub agreed, saying that his group would "avoid any half-baked theories of racial superiority." After all, he had "fought fascism in two theaters in World War II," and had no sympathy for "strutting Nazis."[13]

Receiving contributions from wealthy conservatives, Singlaub christened his group the United States Council for World Freedom (USCWF), recruiting a dozen retired members of the American defense-intelligence community. General Daniel Graham, former director of the Defense Intelligence Agency and the most ardent proponent of the Reagan administration's high-tech Strategic Defense Initiative, became the organization's vice-chairman. Retired Air Force colonel Albert Koen served as treasurer. General Lewis Walt, former commander of the Marine Corps in Vietnam, joined the advisory board. As Singlaub stocked the council with ex-military men, he also reached out to some of the most well-known and influential conservative organizers in the United States. Howard Philips, leader of the Conservative Caucus, a policy group that solicited millions in donations through direct-mail lists, joined in late 1981. So did Andy Messing, an ex–Green Beret and Vietnam veteran who now chaired the American Conservative Union, the largest conservative advocacy group in the United States. Messing, who also ran the National Defense Council, a policy group that studied guerrilla wars in Central America and southern Africa, had a penchant for militant rhetoric, boasting that "going to war was his favorite pastime."[14]

With the USCWF leadership in place, Singlaub began crisscrossing the globe, giving lectures to civic groups, universities, and grassroots activists. He often used these opportunities to hammer home the importance of "unconventional warfare" in fighting popular insurgency. In 1982, at a WACL meeting in Tokyo, he chaired panels about "Military Strategies to Counter Soviet Expansionism" and "Political, Economic, and Media Strategies to Counter Communist Expansionism" the latter of which featured Nguyen Cao Ky, the former prime minister of South Vietnam.[15] Later that year, he traveled to London to address the annual meeting of the ABN, the group of Eastern European exiles who had been working to foment "national liberation movements" in their home countries since the end of World War II. Taking the stage after Yaroslav Stetsko, the aging Ukrainian nationalist, Singlaub spoke of the challenges faced by insurgent forces battling Soviet and Cuban incursions into Latin America, Africa, and Asia, as well as the old battlegrounds of Eastern Europe. To truly counter communist expansion, he argued, Americans had to utilize the very same tactics the communists used. This was a dirty war, waged not by large-scale military forces but rather small paramilitary units engaged in an array of unconventional tactics including "terrorism, subversion, and guerrilla warfare," as well as "such covert and non-military activities as sabotage, economic warfare, support to resistance groups, black and gray psychological operations, disinformation activities, and political warfare."[16]

Blending his own experiences fighting secret wars behind enemy lines with the kinds of guerrilla warfare advocated by Che Guevara and Mao Zedong, Singlaub wanted to turn the doctrine of "people's war" against the Soviets and their allies.[17] The goal was not just to liberate subjugated nations from communist rule or to prevent leftist insurgencies from gaining power. Instead, Singlaub's strategy was an endgame for the Cold War itself. Just as Che Guevara had envisioned waging "two, three, many Vietnams" to defeat the United States in the 1960s, so Singlaub believed that resilient guerrilla movements would put increasing pressure on the Soviet Union and its allies until they finally collapsed, unable to bear the burden of fighting small wars around the world.

Others shared this view. Since the 1950s, members of the ABN—mostly old fighters from the partisan wars against Soviet rule in Eastern Europe—had worked year in and year out to launch guerrilla offensives in their homelands, often with few tangible results. In public gatherings in the United States, Western Europe, Asia, and Australia, and in the pages of its official publication which exiles smuggled behind the Iron Curtain, ABN leaders harkened back to their experiences fighting as insurgents during and after World War II.[18] Yaroslav Stetsko, for one, perennially celebrated the long-defunct Ukrainian Insurgent Army as the ideal model for "national liberation," a force of ordinary men who transformed into paramilitary warriors. Their willingness to fight and die made them into the true leaders of their nation.[19] Stetsko and other ABN leaders believed these guerrilla campaigns, which mobilized and armed thousands of civilians, should be replicated wherever communist forces impinged on free societies—places such as Nicaragua, Angola, and Afghanistan.[20] These were not distinct struggles, Stetsko opined, but rather a global plan to combat communism. Fighting only one war at a time would not do. Rather, as Stetsko often put it, anticommunists had to foment "synchronized national liberation revolutions."[21]

Many others saw in paramilitary warfare the path to power. At meetings of the WACL and other international gatherings, militant anticommunists talked of a shared "struggle for freedom waged by the peoples of Afghanistan, Africa, the Caribbean, El Salvador, the Chinese mainland, North Korea, Indochina, Poland, Ukraine, Lithuania and other nations under communist rule."[22] As activists and intellectuals preached about the growing armed resistance to communism, leaders of anticommunist guerrilla forces toured the international circuit of conferences, where they promoted their own forces and made pointed calls for private and state aid. Members of Cuban exile groups like Alpha 66, many of whom had been waging an extralegal war against Castro's regime since the 1960s, defended their clandestine acts and solicited private funds to continue their campaigns of sabotage and assassination.[23] Afghan guerrillas made their rounds too, condemning the recent Soviet invasion of their country and begging for military aid—arms, radios, and medical supplies.[24] Likewise, members of a group of guerrillas known as the Karen National Liberation Army, which had been fighting for nationhood for the Karen people in Burma, celebrated their "armed revolution" against the "totalitarian and communistic Rangoon government."[25] Exiled leaders from Angola's Frente Nacional de Libertação de Angola, which had been decimated in the late 1970s, expressed its "solidarity with the people of Afghanistan, Cambodia and Eritrea in their fight against Soviet expansionism" while insisting that it could still mount an offensive against the Marxist MPLA government.[26]

This was not simply a call to arms. It was also a reaction to widespread fears about American martial and masculine decline that had been a persistent feature of rightist discourse, both in the U.S. and abroad, since the late 1970s—what many commentators labeled the "Vietnam syndrome."[27] The United States' failure in Southeast Asia, whatever its causes, had made Americans weak and apathetic, unwilling to take up arms and maintain the fight against communism. Moreover, as John Singlaub put it, few Americans even understood the "West actually was at war—albeit a low-intensity conflict." Without American soldiers, the burden of fighting fell to armed anticommunist movements that possessed the will, if not yet the means, to roll back communist gains. But, even here, as Singlaub pointed out, the "Vietnam syndrome still crippled our efforts and dominated congressional oversight of our unconventional warfare operations."[28] By passing laws such as the Clark Amendment and reorganizing the U.S. intelligence community, the Carter administration and its allies in Congress had constrained the ability of the United States to provide covert aid to anticommunist guerrillas. To change that, Singlaub and other Americans started to work in the shadow of the state, laboring toward a more active engagement with guerrillas overseas.

---

While Singlaub built relationships with anticommunists abroad, his contacts in the Reagan administration offered him opportunities to shape U.S. foreign policy in a more direct fashion. National Security Advisor Richard V. Allen had heard his speeches about anticommunist guerrilla movements, and invited Singlaub to give his talk to leaders from the Pentagon, the Department of Defense, and the Joint Chiefs of Staff.[29] Again, Singlaub explained that the United States had to integrate its "economic, political, and military efforts in combined unconventional warfare just as effectively as the Soviets" did. Soon he was working as a kind of private adviser to the White House and the Pentagon, helping to convince policymakers to create the new Special Operations Division (SOD), which financed and coordinated most of the military's counterterrorist and covert-action units.[30] He later petitioned, unsuccessfully, to resume active duty so that he could lead this new command.[31]

During Singlaub's frequent visits to Washington, he often chatted with the new CIA director, William J. Casey, whom he'd known since their time together in World War II.[32] Like Singlaub, Casey was an aging covert warrior who had served in the OSS, the forerunner to the CIA. He had commanded a spy base in London that parachuted agents behind enemy lines to organize resistance groups in France, an experience that made him a passionate advocate for unconventional warfare. After retiring from the Army, Casey spent the following decades as a corporate attorney and financier. He taught wealthy Americans how to create tax shelters and made a fortune of millions.[33] During the Nixon and Ford administrations, Casey served in a few different executive posts but decided to retire from government in 1975.[34] But Reagan pulled him back to Washington to serve as his campaign adviser for the 1980 election, promising Casey a major position in government. His reward was the directorship of the CIA.[35]

Reagan brought Casey into the fold to reverse the changes Stansfield Turner had made to the CIA. Like many hardliners in Reagan's inner circle, Casey was convinced the Soviet Union had taken advantage of the United States' declining intelligence apparatus to press its interests and agents across the Third World.[36] Beyond funding leftist insurgencies and supporting proxy states, he said, the Soviets were also responsible for the wave of terrorist bombings, hijackings, kidnappings, and assassinations washing over Western Europe and the Americas. Casey's thoughts on this matter stemmed less from rigorous intelligence gathering and analysis and more from popular media. In 1981, journalist Claire Sterling published *The Terror Network*, which outlined a vast underworld of terrorists funded and controlled by the Soviets and their client states. Sterling asserted that nearly every major terrorist organization from Europe to the Middle East—the Irish Republican Army, the Italian Red Brigades, the German Red Army Faction, the Palestine Liberation Organization, Hezbollah, and the cells controlled by the infamous Abu Nidal and Carlos the Jackal—were all members of a "family" whose patriarch was none other than the KGB.[37] Although the CIA's intelligence indicated that nearly everything that Sterling wrote was at best hyperbolic and at worst outright fabrication, Casey and others insisted her book offered definitive proof of the Soviets' intentions to destroy the West through terrorism.[38] As Casey surveyed the shifting geopolitical terrain of the early 1980s, he concluded that the United States needed to counter the Soviets' moves with its own covert actions.

In their meetings in 1981 and 1982, Singlaub and Casey discussed these links between Soviet expansionism, leftist insurgencies, communist proxy states, and terrorist groups. Singlaub made a point of keeping Casey "informed on my speaking campaign" about unconventional warfare. In turn, Casey told Singlaub that his lectures had "partially inspired" the "emerging policy known as the Reagan Doctrine." Formulated by conservative defense intellectuals in the run-up to the 1980 election, the doctrine asserted that the United States had to roll back communism by supporting anticommunist rebels in the Third World while simultaneously revamping the United States' own clandestine forces. In its global reach, the Reagan Doctrine aimed to match the ambitions of the Soviets.[39] If the communists had assembled an international network of rebels and terrorists, then anticommunists must do the same.

When Reagan entered office, his leading advisers set about making the doctrine that bore his name a reality. In a March 1981 meeting of Reagan's National Security Planning Group, Casey proposed a CIA-directed program to provide covert aid to resistance movements in Afghanistan, Angola, Cambodia, Cuba, Grenada, Iran, Laos, Libya, and Nicaragua.[40] At the meeting, Casey remarked, "we need to be backing these movements with money and political muscle. If we can get the Soviets to expend enough resources, it will create fissures in the system. We need half a dozen Afghanistans."[41]

In calling for the United States to aid to anticommunist national liberation movements, Casey and other administration officials were giving form and substance to the imaginings of American paramilitary enthusiasts and retired covert warriors. One CIA officer who worked under Casey later recalled that the Reagan administration attracted "an awful lot of *Soldier of Fortune* readers."[42] Therefore, even though the Reagan Doctrine was ostensibly a covert action, it also served as a kind of public theater, a way for Reagan and his advisers to show the world just how committed they were to fighting communism. As Reagan's secretary of state George Schultz put it years later, "There was nothing covert about the Reagan doctrine. It was an articulated view that we were in favor of freedom . . . To the extent that there were people willing to stand up and fight, we were ready to help them."[43]

As the Reagan Doctrine took shape, Singlaub was pleased to hear that his efforts promoting paramilitary warfare were making waves in the administration. One night, while gazing out at Pennsylvania Avenue from Casey's office, he had a profound revelation. He realized that he "probably had more influence as a private citizen than I would have had as mid-level defense official struggling in the bureaucratic trenches."[44] Freed from the burdensome oversight and partisan infighting of government, he began to see himself as more than just an advocate for a cause. He started to imagine that he could make the Reagan Doctrine a reality by using the anticommunist international to arm, supply, and train the world's "freedom fighters."

---

Singlaub first turned his attention to Central America. He saw a region teetering on the edge of total communist control. Since the late 1970s, Central America had been wracked by popular convulsions and civil war. In Nicaragua, the half-century reign of the Somoza dynasty finally collapsed. Taking power after his brother Luis was assassinated in 1967, Anastasio Somoza Debayle maintained the patterns of corruption and dictatorial rule that had sustained his family's domination of Nicaragua since the early twentieth century. When a huge earthquake destroyed Managua in 1972, Somoza diverted the flood of international relief funds into his own coffers. In response, large sections of the Nicaraguan population threw their support behind the once-moribund guerrilla movement known as the Sandinistas. Despite a splintering leadership, the Sandinistas waged an effective hit-and-run campaign, slowly destabilizing Somoza's regime over the next six years.[45] In a last-ditch attempt to save his rule, Somoza unleashed the National Guard to level towns and massacre civilians. It failed. The widespread human rights abuses committed by his soldiers—rape, genital mutilation, torture, and mass murder—dissolved any international support that Somoza once had.[46]

The Sandinistas, now united under a moderate faction known as the *terceristas*, headed by the Ortega brothers Daniel and Humberto, formed a coalition government in late 1979. Blending Marxist doctrines, nationalism, and anti-American sentiments, the Sandinistas advocated a revolutionary program based primarily upon land reform and the nationalization of foreign-owned enterprises—ideas that enjoyed wide support amongst the workers and farmers but also alienated the Sandinistas' former allies in the bourgeoisie, who soon began to split from the coalition government.[47] While the Sandinistas struggled to implement their revolutionary vision, they entered into a year of fractious negotiations with the Carter administration. In mid-1980, talks broke down over the enormous debt accumulated by Somoza, and the Sandinistas started to look to the Soviet Union for much-needed humanitarian aid.[48] As Ronald Reagan castigated Nicaragua's revolution on the campaign trail, the Sandinistas sought weapons and heavy military equipment, both to protect their fledgling revolution from U.S. interference and, in time, allow them to export it to the rest of Central America.[49]

For the Sandinistas, the primary target was El Salvador, where the military government of José Napoleon Duarte struggled to maintain control after decades of mounting conflicts exploded into all-out civil war in the late 1970s. By 1980, five guerrilla factions had united to form an army of thousands of peasants, workers, students, and radicals called the Frente Farabundo Martí Liberación Nacional (FMLN). Inspired by the success of the Sandinistas, they aimed to overthrow the government, nationalize foreign-owned industries, distribute land, assert workers' rights, and stop political repression. To that end, they, too, sought help from Cuba and the Soviet Union, which offered substantial military and humanitarian aid. Meanwhile, members of El Salvador's unions, urban middle classes, and clergy grew more hostile to the military government—especially its collaboration with right-wing death squads that murdered thousands of civilians with impunity.[50]

The breaking point came in May 1980 when death-squad leader Roberto D'Aubuisson sent two hit men to assassinate Archbishop Oscar Romero as he led mass. For many, Romero, who had sided with peasants and workers, represented the best hope for a peaceful revolution.[51] His murder threw the country into chaos and generated broad support for the FMLN. Unsure of what to do, Duarte ordered the military to root out the insurgency by combing the countryside and razing villages. Meanwhile, large landowners hired the right-wing militias controlled by D'Aubuisson and others to eliminate any peasants who pressed for land reform.[52] By the summer of 1980, thousands were dying every month. El Salvador had become a killing field.[53]

John Singlaub, like most members of the Reagan administration, understood these developments in terms of Soviet and Cuban conquest. It was yet another example of the "communist strategy" to "exploit poverty and social upheaval." Although he recognized that the insurgencies in Central America had something to do with the inequalities created by centuries of oligarchic rule, he still saw the guerrillas as little more than proxy warriors for outside communist forces bent on establishing footholds close to the United States. These armies, which claimed to represent the people, were in fact "dominated by Cuban-trained communists" and funded with "hundreds of millions of dollars of military assistance" from the Soviet Union. Now in power, the Sandinistas were exporting their revolution, sending arms and advisers to El Salvador and Guatemala. Their goal was to create a "staging base for the 'liberation' of Central America and eventually Mexico."[54]

While Singlaub was appalled at the communist insurgency in Central America, he was equally troubled by the Reagan administration's response. Like many on the right, he had hoped that Reagan's election would pave the way for a swift American intervention.[55] Indeed, on the campaign trail and in his first year in office, Reagan and his advisors had said as much. The United States would finally "draw the line" in Central America to prevent the spread of international communism any further.[56] It would be a "test case" for Reagan's hardline foreign policy.[57] To promote intervention, the administration had published a widely circulated State Department White Paper, which laid out the links between the revolutions in Central America and the Soviet Union and Cuba.[58]

At first, the administration's tough talk pleased supporters in the United States as well as anticommunists in Central America. For the latter group, Reagan's election signaled that they would have the support needed to vanquish their enemies. In El Salvador, a week after the election, locals discovered the bullet-riddled bodies of two death-squad victims draped with signs that read "With Ronald Reagan the miscreants and guerrillas of Central America and El Salvador will be finished."[59] Likewise, a high-ranking member of Guatemala's military government told a reporter that "Mr. Reagan recognizes that a good deal of dirty work has to be done."[60]

Reagan's jeremiads about communist expansion in Central America, however, did not generate much support beyond the conservative faithful.[61] Many Americans had no desire to drag the United States into another unwinnable war like Vietnam. Others pointed out that U.S. support for dictatorships produced massive human rights violations. As a transnational movement coalesced to oppose U.S. intervention, congressional liberals voted to limit the scope of U.S. military missions in Central America, especially El Salvador.[62] They capped U.S. funding to the Salvadoran security forces and imposed strict regulations on the numbers and activities of U.S. military advisers. To Singlaub, this was the Vietnam Syndrome at work. Congressional liberals, "terrified of any U.S. military entanglement," put "an arbitrary limit of fifty-five U.S. trainers on our military assistance mission and severely restricted their freedom of movement in the small country."[63]

Believing this situation demanded action from conservative groups in the United States, Singlaub began making trips to the frontlines in Central America. He and Daniel Graham had already visited Guatemala several times in 1979 and 1980, talking politics and war with members of the ruling elite.[64] Now his trips took on a distinct paramilitary character. In August 1982, he toured El Salvador with Andy Messing, the former Green Beret who ran the Conservative Caucus, to observe Salvadoran military units in action. Dressed in fatigues, flying around the country in military helicopters and roaming the countryside with Salvadoran units, one could have easily mistaken them for U.S. soldiers.

They found a "very disturbing situation." The restrictions on U.S. military advisers had hampered the official mission. Meanwhile, the Salvadoran army was still organized "along conventional lines with clumsy battalion size units armed with heavy-caliber weapons." Recalling the failure of conventional American forces during the Vietnam War, Singlaub noted that the Salvadoran army was no match for the "hit-and-run tactics of the lightly armed guerrillas." He also discovered that the military lacked basic medical training and supplies. When guerrillas attacked the unit that Singlaub was touring with, he and Messing had to administer emergency aid to save the life of a young soldier because no one else knew what to do.[65]

All this was deeply troubling. The inability of the Salvadorans—and by extension the U.S. military—to mount an effective counterinsurgency campaign indicated that America was "making the same kinds of mistakes we had made in Vietnam." What the Salvadorans needed, he thought, were highly trained covert and paramilitary outfits capable of sabotaging the guerrillas from the inside out.[66] They also needed an "effective paramilitary rural constabulary," an "organization made up of local residents familiar with the geography and people of each village."[67] As he had done in Vietnam, Laos, Manchuria, and France, Singlaub hoped to turn ordinary people into a fighting force with the knowledge and training to fill in for the beleaguered state security forces, especially the national police.

Convinced the U.S. government was failing in its obligations to fight communism in Central America, Singlaub felt he was duty-bound to do something about it. When he returned home to Washington, he set up a meeting with a colleague, Nestor Sanchez, a former chief of the CIA's Latin American Directorate who was now working for the Department of Defense.[68] Singlaub informed Sanchez that he wanted to establish a "private support effort for the hard-pressed Salvadoran Army." Sanchez said it was a promising idea but stipulated it could only be humanitarian aid. Otherwise, Singlaub ran the risk of violating U.S. neutrality laws and could quickly wind up in jail, especially with all of the liberals on Capitol Hill searching for ways to hurt the administration.[69]

Encouraged, Singlaub spent the next few weeks soliciting donations from a few dozen "concerned conservative groups" to fund what he called a "private military assistance effort" in El Salvador. Foremost among these were Robert K. Brown and several staffers at *Soldier of Fortune* magazine. Singlaub knew Brown from their time together in Vietnam, serving together the Studies and Observation Group, and the pair remained close in retirement.[70] Together the two war buddies planned a multifaceted campaign that would offer both medical and military assistance. They soon began recruiting veteran doctors and trainers and shipping them down to El Salvador. They even found a "retired American parachute rigger to train dozens of counterparts in the Salvadoran airborne battalion." Singlaub was moved by Brown's "vigorous activities and funding." His magazine's financial networks and sponsored advertisements ensured that "dozens of private American non-combat trainers went to El Salvador to assist their military." Singlaub and Brown painted their endeavors as volunteer work, a charity that raised contributions for a worthy cause from private donors, rather than a moneymaking enterprise. As Singlaub later put it, Brown's men "demonstrated true patriotism and dedication to the principles of democracy and morality which refute the image of a crass mercenary so prevalent in media reports on his activities."[71] These men were not in it for the money, or at least not directly.

Humanitarian aid was just the beginning. As the war in El Salvador reached new peaks in 1983 and 1984, Brown and his team of veterans led a series of military training missions in the tiny country, a new endeavor for the magazine. While Brown had publicized mercenary jobs for the wars in Angola and Rhodesia in the 1970s, he had kept away from the actual fighting. When pressed by journalists or investigators, he could plausibly claim that his magazine had no real role in shaping combat operations, even though he and his staff frequently visited Rhodesian and South African units in the field. However, by 1982, Brown and his staffers had started to see themselves as a private military assistance outfit, capable of filling in the gaps in the United States' official military program. Because Congress refused to "provide the necessary funds and advisers," Brown hoped that private funds from individuals, businesses, church groups, and veterans' clubs could mitigate the Salvadoran army's many shortages.[72] Moreover, while Congress had forbade the fifty-five American military advisers from traveling in combat areas, let alone participating in battles, no such restrictions applied to the magazine's staff. They were largely free to do what they wanted so long as they did not kill anyone. As Brown later summed it up, "The bottom line was that with the 55 advisor limit that the U.S. had imposed, boots-on-the-ground training and maintenance were sadly neglected, and that's where the private sector (us) provided back-up."[73]

From late 1982 onward, Brown had teams of retired military officers in El Salvador "nearly year round."[74] They toured the countryside with the Salvadoran military's elite counterinsurgency units, offering training sessions on military tactics, medical aid, and civic action programs, many of which harkened back to their experiences in the Vietnam War. Retired Army Special Forces colonel Alex McColl, who had also served in Vietnam with Singlaub's clandestine Studies and Observation Group, instructed Salvadorans in combat and survival skills ranging from "machine gun marksmanship to water purification," and distributed supplies, uniforms, and handbooks.[75] Demolitions expert John Donovan taught the Salvadorans how to blow up all sorts of things.[76] Peter Kokalis, one of the world's leading small-arms experts, overhauled the weapons inventory of the Salvadoran army's elite counterinsurgency unit.[77] With John Early, another Special Forces Vietnam veteran, Kokalis also conducted three-day-long ambush and counter-ambush training programs.[78] Another American, former Marine Harry Caflin, trained the Salvadoran paratroopers, reworking courses from his Missouri-based Starlight Training Center, which taught U.S. civilians outdoor survival and parachute operations.[79]

Although these efforts straddled the line between legal and extralegal activities, many U.S. officials in Washington and El Salvador gave their tacit approval.[80] Before launching the first expedition in 1982, Brown met with Nestor Sanchez and members of the Pentagon who "condoned our Central America operation but could not offer any official sanction or assistance." But when problems arose, Sanchez pressured the U.S. Army's advisers to help the magazine's training program. Brown's men received Salvadoran IDs, "Get out of jail free cards," and press credentials that allowed them to "carry personal weapons on and off military bases and even arrest civilians on the street." At Ilopango airbase, near the capital San Salvador, they had their "own arms room, supply room, and ate at the officer's mess."[81] When they returned from the front lines, they often briefed the U.S. military group on how well the Salvadorans fought in the field. For American officials whose knowledge of the counterinsurgency campaign was blinkered by the congressional limits, these civilian warriors were providing a vital service. As one embassy spokesman told journalists,

"We want to encourage private, voluntary efforts to help the Salvadorans." Still, U.S. officials made it clear that the government was not hiring private contractors. Instead, as one pointed out, "Any contacts between this embassy and the *Soldier of Fortune* people have been informal, unofficial, and at their request."[82] In placing the burden at the feet of private citizens, the administration hoped to deflect any potential criticism that it was violating congressional limits.

Members of the Salvadoran state security forces were happy with the private assistance as well. Death-squad commander Roberto D'Aubuisson admitted that he would "prefer retired U.S. military personnel as trainers rather than additional official U.S. advisers." As he told an Associated Press reporter, "We have enough advisers, especially considering the conditions attached to their presence."[83] Another Salvadoran commander, Colonel Sigfredo Ochoa, contacted Brown in 1984 to "organize and train a small, elite special operations unit."[84] For their part, Brown's team maintained that their efforts were akin to that of volunteers working for a charity. "Don't call us mercenaries," said *Soldier of Fortune* adviser Alex McColl. They were simply "private citizens who wanted to fight communism."[85]

While in El Salvador, Brown and his comrades-in-arms spent much time with the Atlacatl Battalion, an elite rapid-response counterinsurgency unit.[86] Created by graduates of the U.S. military training center known as the School of the Americas in 1980, the battalion was the first of its kind in El Salvador's history.[87] It soon earned a reputation as the most fearsome of all the Salvadoran security forces. On December 11, 1981, Atlacatl marched into the tiny village of El Mozote to round up and execute guerrillas. Although the hamlet had remained neutral in the civil war, the battalion gathered eight hundred people in the central square and imposed a military curfew. The following day, they began pulling men from the houses to interrogate, torture, and murder them, often by cutting off their heads. In the afternoon, the soldiers turned on the women, raping them before filling them with bullets. Then they killed the children by slitting their throats and hanging their corpses from trees. With nearly eight hundred dead, the soldiers burnt the village to the ground. In August of 1982, the battalion massacred more than two hundred displaced peasants, shooting many, throwing some into rivers, and smashing babies on rocks. Although news of the massacres quickly reached American audiences, the Reagan administration and the Salvadoran government dismissed the claims of survivors, witnesses, and reporters as communist propaganda.[88]

*Soldier of Fortune* showed no awareness of these crimes when its staffers trained members of Atlacatl and other military units over the following years. Instead, the magazine's writers praised the battalion as a group of "battle hardened volunteers," commanded by a "charismatic leader."[89] Radiating martial power, the Salvadorans conferred it on their American allies. When weapons expert Peter Kokalis appeared on stage at the annual *Soldier of Fortune* convention in 1985, he shouted "I am from Atlacatl Battalion!" to thunderous applause.[90] A best-selling *Soldier of Fortune* poster featured the Atlacatl battalion commander standing shoulder-to-shoulder with Robert Brown against the backdrop of the Salvadoran jungle. The banner read, "Communism Stops Here."[91] While in El Salvador, Brown distributed to Atlacatl soldiers copies of the magazine and patches bearing the *Soldier of Fortune* logo, a skull wearing a beret and clenching a knife between its teeth.[92] Back in the United States, the magazine urged readers with an extra $79.99 to purchase their limited-issue "El Salvadoran Jump Wings," silver-colored replicas of the Salvadoran Airborne Squadron's insignia.[93]

In print, the magazine offered harrowing stories about guerrilla warfare in which the Salvadoran military were clearly the good guys. Most riffed on the central theme that the Salvadorans made up for their lack of expertise and weapons with supreme dedication to the cause, a willingness to fight to the last to save their country. They were hard men doing a hard job—especially the Atlacatl battalion. As one U.S. official intimated to a *Soldier of Fortune* reporter, Atlacatl soldiers were "Bad asses, the toughest unit in El Salvador . . . When they move in the Gees (guerrillas) move out or die."[94]

As Brown's teams worked with elite forces such as the Atlacatl, the bravery and toughness of the Salvadorans transferred to the *Soldier of Fortune* staff. Their articles, replete with dozens of glossy images showing Americans and Salvadorans marching through jungles, flying in helicopters, firing their weapons, and interacting with local people, demonstrated to readers just how committed *Soldier of Fortune* was to fighting communism.[95] While other journalists stayed in their hotels, drinking and writing poolside, the magazine's correspondents were willing to risk their lives in combat zones. As one *Soldier of Fortune* writer put it, "American journalists, while writing their stories in the El Camino Real Hotel, are quite fond of tacking the 9-to-5 label on the Salvadoran officer corps. Their numbers are correct but, in their drunken haze, they have transposed them."[96] In contrast, *Soldier of Fortune* practiced what Brown called "'participatory' journalism." "We would create the story, gin up a lot of action and then write about it for the glistening pages of our bad boy magazine," he later said.[97] This startling admission reveals how the magazine's missions in El Salvador operated on a different plane than reporting or charity work. In addition to monetizing the image of El Salvador's counterinsurgency forces by selling posters and paraphernalia, Brown saw the war itself as a way to make money for the magazine by providing more material for more sensational stories. Victory was perhaps less important than keeping the war going. As long there were "guerrillas" to kill, Brown could count on a steady stream of profits.

In this way, the *Soldier of Fortune* team crossed the line from observers to combatants. Their stories read like official after-action reports, filled with assessments about the strengths and operations of the Salvadoran army and the communists, as well as myriad technical observations about weapons. As sociologist James Gibson has noted, these reports allowed readers to imagine themselves as part of the struggle since the stories resembled secret intelligence dispatches from the front lines. Nearly every article "was written as *if* the reader was a soldier or mercenary going off to war tomorrow." The long descriptions of weapons and enemy troop movements gave the impression that "all these details were vitally important," and that one's life depended on knowing them.[98] While the majority of *Soldier of Fortune* readers would never travel to Central America to actually become mercenaries, their subscription enlisted them in the paramilitary campaign to defeat communism. They were privy to the real information and so they knew, better than most Americans, what the war was all about. By purchasing the magazine and its paraphernalia, and by donating money, they could imagine themselves as much-needed financiers backing the anticommunist forces while the U.S. government vacillated.

Despite its success in supplying and training El Salvador's security forces, *Soldier of Fortune*'s campaign paled in comparison to the network of wealthy Salvadoran exiles that channeled millions of dollars to right-wing vigilantes and death squads in the early 1980s.[99] Now based in Miami, these expatriates had grown up as members of the ruling oligarchy before abandoning the country for the safety of the United States. Dubbed the "Miami Six" by U.S. Ambassador Robert White, they helped "organize, fund, and direct the death squads" controlled by Roberto D'Aubuisson. In so doing, they became a major embarrassment for the Reagan administration and members of the State Department who had been working to marginalize the Salvadoran extreme Right.[100] In December 1983, National Security Advisor Robert "Bud" McFarlane urged the Department of Justice and the FBI to investigate and prosecute any Salvadoran exiles who were funding the death squads.[101] Their investigation revealed that D'Aubuisson and his ultra-right political party, the Alianza Republicana Nacionalista (ARENA), used funds raised in the United States to murder and intimidate their opponents, recruiting agents from an international network of foreign mercenaries. By 1985, several Cuban exiles and at least one former intelligence officer from Rhodesia were serving as hit men for the Salvadoran Right.[102] These links indicated that while Americans like Brown and Singlaub saw themselves as a crucial support network for El Salvador's anticommunist forces, a larger web of paramilitaries and mercenaries existed over which Americans had no control.[103]

There were other problems. The violence of El Salvador's right-wing paramilitaries—tens of thousands of dead civilians and many more tortured and intimidated—and their willingness to talk about even greater purges of Salvadoran society presented a problem for those in the United States who shared the Salvadoran Right's commitment to anticommunism and free enterprise but could not condone such bloodshed.[104] Singlaub, for one, had mixed feelings about the rightist paramilitaries commanded by D'Aubuisson and others. When pressed, he and his associates condemned the actions of the death squads and their covert support network.[105] Still, like members of the Reagan administration, he insisted that the leftist guerrillas were largely responsible for the extreme levels of violence, asserting that the FMLN posed as right-wing death squads to tarnish their opponent's image.[106] Subsequent investigations, however, showed that 85 percent of the nearly 75,000 people killed during the war died at the hands of government forces or those acting on behalf of state agents.[107]

In official circles, Singlaub blamed the death squads on liberals in Congress. In May 1984, at the behest of Undersecretary of Defense for Policy Fred Ikle, Singlaub assembled a lineup of "recognized experts in unconventional warfare," including Edward Lansdale and Heine Aderholt, to assess the situation in El Salvador. The so-called Singlaub Panel found that congressional restrictions on the CIA and the Pentagon had helped create the death squads. As Singlaub later wrote, "Over the previous decade liberals in Congress had prohibited American foreign aid from being used for police training... But without adequate training in counterinsurgency, police often fought assassination and kidnapping through illegal means. El Salvador's death squads were typical of this reaction."[108]

By this logic, the massive human rights violations committed by Salvadoran death squads were actually the fault of those American politicians who *opposed* military aid. They had prevented the government from creating "professional" security forces that could defeat the rebels and thereby make the death squads obsolete. But in drawing a clear distinction between "professional" police and military units and the death squads, Singlaub obscured the fact that many Salvadoran officers condoned, financed, armed, and often commanded rightist vigilante groups.[109] As one colonel in the Salvadoran Army explained in 1983, "Most laws are designed to deal with common crimes, but you can't fight subversion with the same methods. Subversion is a cancer which attacks slowly, and our judicial system isn't set up to deal with it."[110] The death squads, in other words, were useful precisely because they could do what the state could not. Moreover, as many observers pointed out at the time, El Salvador's death squads and rightist vigilantes dated back to the 1960s, long before Congress had imposed limits on U.S. military and police aid.[111] Their enduring presence in El Salvador underscored the death squads' ability to wage war outside the frame of formal state action.

Although his portrayal of the death squads was way off the mark, many in the defense establishment agreed with Singlaub's policy recommendations, especially his insistence that non-state organizations were in a better position to train and support the Salvadoran security forces.[112] By the summer of 1984, Singlaub was convinced that private military programs were helping the United States reverse "the stagnant drift of the post-Vietnam years" and set a course "to defend freedom and support democracy in our own hemisphere and throughout the world."[113]

---

As the race for the presidency heated up in 1984, Singlaub and other activists turned their attention to the civil war in Nicaragua. In the years since Somoza's fall, members of the deposed National Guard had joined with other opponents of the Sandinistas to form a few guerrilla armies that became known collectively as the Contras, short for *la contrarrevolución*, or the counterrevolution.[114] For a time, their primary foreign sponsor was not the United States but Argentina, which offered arms, advisers, and supplies, as well as military instruction in Buenos Aires.[115] The Argentine aid was part of the military junta's attempts to export its doctrine of the "national security state" and the expertise honed by its security forces during the Dirty War.[116]

As Somoza's regime collapsed and the ousted dictator fled to Paraguay, his lieutenants, mostly former National Guardsmen, turned to the Argentine military regime for help. Sometime in late 1979 and early 1980, Argentine military and intelligence officers agreed to train and finance the emerging Contra army. They did so not only to aid a kindred movement but also to assert greater control over the hemispheric anticommunist struggle in the apparent absence of firm U.S. leadership. Indeed, for many members of the Argentine junta, the inability of the CIA to mount effective covert operations in the wake of the Church Committee hearings proved that the United States had abandoned its anticommunist mission.[117] They concluded they would have to lead the charge. In Nicaragua, Honduras, and Costa Rica, the same officers who oversaw the Dirty War trained the nascent Contra army in guerrilla warfare, assassination, and demolition. Some of the advisers were members of special military units such as the Batallón de Inteligencia 601.[118] Others came from right-wing vigilante death squads such as the Alianza Anticomunista Argentina.[119]

As such, the Argentine advisers in Nicaragua represented a geographic expansion of Operation Condor, the transnational program of terror and assassination in South America. They shifted the ideas and techniques that had underpinned their purge of suspected subversives at home into a more ambitious program to wage covert war on multiple fronts. To make that happen, the Argentine military regime established an international network of gunrunners and front companies to move weapons throughout the Americas. The center of that network was in Miami, where Argentine military and intelligence officers trained many of the soldiers from the early Contra group known as the September 15th Legion.[120]

As they did so, the Argentines joined Miami's anticommunist underworld, working with exiles from Cuba, El Salvador, and other countries to plot paramilitary operations.[121] Those connections, particularly with Cuban paramilitary groups, also helped the Argentines manage clandestine financial transactions and purchase weapons and equipment that "could not be obtained through normal channels." They bought most of their guns from anticommunist stalwarts such as Taiwan, Thailand, and South Korea, but some also came from the United Kingdom and even East Germany, part of the Soviet Bloc.[122] Meanwhile, as the Argentine military regime lent its support to the Nicaraguan counterrevolution, other anticommunist states and groups followed suit.[123] In neighboring Honduras, where many of the Contras' camps were located, a former member of Somoza's National Guard who had also trained in an Argentine military school worked with the Honduran military to smuggle U.S.-made weapons and military equipment into Nicaragua.[124]

This hemispheric collaboration between Latin America's anticommunists was soon overshadowed by resurgent CIA operations under the Reagan administration. When Argentina became embroiled in the Falklands/Malvinas War and withdrew its advisers in 1982, CIA director William Casey seized the opportunity. Reagan had already authorized the CIA to create a 500-strong paramilitary force to interdict the flow of arms between Nicaragua and the Salvadoran guerrillas.[125] Now the CIA could expand the secret war. By the end of 1982, the Contras were receiving nearly $20 million worth of weapons and supplies annually from the CIA to destabilize the Sandinista government and provoke it into taking harsher measures against the Nicaraguan people.[126] The Contra army soon swelled to almost ten thousand, led by ex–National Guard officers and prominent Nicaraguans.[127] The rank-and-file pulled widely from peasant and Indian communities, some of whom were dissatisfied with the Sandinistas' land reforms and others who feared what would happen if they didn't join.[128] Based along the Honduran and Costa Rican borders, the Contras waged a low-intensity war of sabotage, assassination, and hit-and-run raids.

The Contras were never a unified force but rather a series of armed bands competing with one another over weapons, funds, and the right to say what their war truly meant. The closest thing to a common mission statement came from the largest and most powerful group, the Fuerza Democrática Nicaragüense. In a semi-secret document known as the "Blue and White Book," FDN leaders advocated an eclectic mixture of anticommunism, nationalism, free-market ideology, and religious zeal. They were fighting for "God, Motherland, (and) Democracy." Attempting to distance themselves from the legacy of the Somoza dictatorship, FDN leaders portrayed their movement as a "popular insurgency of the Nicaraguan people" fighting for an inclusive and pluralistic democracy. Although FDN leaders called for free elections and limited agrarian and labor reforms, their vision fell far short of an economic revolution. Instead, they insisted that "free enterprise and private property will be the basic foundations of the national economic system."[129]

Such rhetoric solidified the Contras' support amongst U.S. conservatives, who talked of the Nicaraguan "freedom fighters" in glowing terms. Singlaub referred to them as a "band of brave warriors" who "were often undertrained, always underarmed" and yet who managed to "attack and regularly defeat the largest army ever amassed on Central American soil."[130] In a famous remark, Reagan went so far as to deem the Contras the "moral equivalent of our Founding Fathers and the brave men and women of the French resistance."[131] Indeed, for many conservative Americans, the Contras stirred their historical imaginings of the American Revolution in which plucky bands of insurgents cast off the chains of imperialism and established a flourishing democracy. As such, Americans tended see much of themselves in the Contras. As Reagan said in his 1985 inaugural address, he and his supporters were leading a "second American Revolution" that would carry "beyond our shores the golden promise of human freedom."[132] Yet the metaphor of the American Revolution was poorly suited to Nicaragua's civil war. It also cut both ways. Critics of the Contras likened them not to the Founding Fathers but to the Hessians, a mercenary force hired by an imperial power to suppress a democratic revolution.[133]

Despite conservatives' affinity for the Contras, broad popular and congressional opposition created major obstacles for the administration's covert program. Many Americans were skeptical about helping deposed members of a totalitarian regime wage war against the Sandinistas, no matter how objectionable they found the new government. In 1982, Reagan's opponents in Congress, mostly Democrats led by House Speaker Tip O'Neill, passed the first Boland Amendment, stipulating that U.S. aid to the Contras could not be used to overthrow the Sandinista government. Two years later, Congress passed a stronger version of the amendment which cut off all U.S. funding to the anticommunist guerrillas. For Singlaub and others invested in the war in Nicaragua, this was a clear indication of how liberals subordinated important military issues to their own political ambitions. Echoing his time in Vietnam, Singlaub feared that the "entire CIA covert operation funding the Contras was threatened with defeat, not in the jungle mountains of Central America, but in the back rooms of Capitol Hill."[134]

When funding for the CIA's covert war in Nicaragua dried up, Singlaub and others decided that their private networks could fill the void. But they were not the first American civilians to enlist in the anticommunist struggle there. In the late 1970s, as dictator Anastasio Somoza's regime tottered on its last legs, dozens of Americans, mostly Vietnam veterans, worked as mercenaries for his security forces, fighting alongside a few militant Cubans who had been part of the Bay of Pigs invasion. Some had tenuous connections to the CIA but most were just freelancers migrating through an informal network of right-wing groups.[135] The most well-known was Mike Echanis, a Vietnam vet, expert knife-thrower, martial arts master, and survivalist guru who appeared frequently in the pages of *Soldier of Fortune*.[136] In the summer of 1977, Echanis arrived in Managua hoping to join Somoza's last-ditch assault against the Sandinista insurgency. He soon accepted an official contract to serve as Somoza's chief military adviser with a reported budget of $5 million.[137] But his tenure was short-lived. In September 1978, a plane carrying Echanis, another American consultant, a Nicaraguan general, and a mysterious Vietnamese mercenary crashed in the jungle. All died.[138] Echanis's death became a minor scandal for the Carter administration and the U.S. embassy but did not result in any significant investigations of or prohibitions against American mercenary activity in Central America.[139] For paramilitary enthusiasts in the United States, Echanis epitomized martial values and masculinity. One said that he was "a fine example of the men who make the word freedom meaningful." Another argued he "was down there to do something useful in the cause of freedom," explaining that if the Contras were successful, Nicaragua would have more "freedom ... than would be found in some Peoples' Peaceful Progressive Proletariat Paradise."[140]

The military program envisioned by Singlaub far exceeded the ambitions of Echanis and other American freelancers in Nicaragua. It more closely resembled the time in the 1850s when American citizens under the command of William Walker invaded the country, although it stemmed from very different impulses. While Walker had tried to set up his own slave-holding fiefdom, Singlaub only wished to help the Contras overthrow the Sandinista government and reestablish a non-Marxist government. Those differences notwithstanding, both men mobilized a pool of armed American men who believed they had the right and the duty to intervene in Nicaragua's affairs. And both campaigns had ambiguous relationships to the state.[141] For Singlaub, the big problem was whether the Reagan administration and the CIA, fearing backlash from Congress and the American public, would stand in his way. Again, he turned to CIA Director Bill Casey for advice and, he hoped, an official blessing. At a May 1984 reunion of Jedburgh soldiers, the clandestine units that trained paramilitary forces behind Nazi lines in World War II, Singlaub talked with Casey about how he could help fill the $20 million shortfall that the Contras were now facing. According to Singlaub, Casey shared his frustrations about the restrictions but, again, indicated that the White House could not publicly sanction any private fundraising and weapons-buying programs. Still, Casey did not say he would stop Singlaub. He just preferred not to know the details. Over the following years, Casey would threaten to throw Singlaub out of his office if he ever brought up his work with the Contras.[142]

Still, this was encouraging. Singlaub made several trips to Nicaragua, Honduras, and Costa Rica in the summer of 1984, meeting all of the major Contra leaders including Enrique Bermudez and Eden Pastora as well as Steadman Fagoth, commander of an army of Miskito Indians who opposed the Sandinistas on Nicaragua's Atlantic Coast. He formed a particularly close relationship with Adolfo Calero, a Nicaraguan businessman and lawyer who had run a Coca-Cola plant under the Somoza regime.[143] Educated at Notre Dame, Calero had a "special rapport with Americans," as one U.S. official put it.[144] By 1982, he had emerged as one of the leaders of the Fuerza Democrática Nicaragüense.[145] Aware of Singlaub's training and supply operations in El Salvador, Calero hoped he could provide similar aid to the FDN.[146] At first, he only asked for medical supplies, boots, and uniforms but soon made pleas for ammunition and rifles.[147] However, as Calero explained, the problem was larger than weapons and supplies. His forces could not repair their broken trucks and artillery let alone maintain long air-supply routes. All of this suggested that the CIA had not been very effective in turning the rag-tag guerrillas into an effective fighting force. The CIA had been crucial in getting the war started, but its "actual management of Contra operations and training of their troops had often been clumsy and inadequate."[148]

To fill that gap, Singlaub embarked upon a multifaceted program to solicit money from donors in the United States and abroad, purchase supplies and weapons from third-party states and secretive arms dealers, and then get them into the Contras' hands.[149] Railing about the congressional liberals who "ripped the ground from under the Nicaraguan freedom fighters," Singlaub said that the "American people" would "have to dig into their own pockets and contribute to the Freedom Fighters" no matter if it was "$10,000 or $10."[150] Yet when the news program *Frontline* showed up to one of his events in Phoenix, Singlaub dissembled about his activities. He was not "soliciting funds," he told the reporter. Instead, he was just serving as a liaison between concerned Americans with deep pockets and those folks overseas who could buy weapons and supplies. He told the audience, "If someone wanted to give money for bullets and bandages, they could see him after his speech and he would tell them what to do."[151]

Many took him up on his offer. One of Singlaub's wealthiest and most visible donors was Texas oil heiress Ellen Garwood. A socialite with extensive political and personal connections, Garwood saw Singlaub in religious terms, a patriot who "was undoubtedly sent by the Lord Almighty to help save freedom and the United States from the onrush of totalitarianism." She admired how he managed to avoid all of the complicated bureaucratic wrangling and legal red tape that the CIA had to deal with. "General Singlaub not only gets help for the Nicaraguan freedom fighters, he also takes it to them . . . no overhead, no middle man," she opined. "He collects no salary. His only salary is God's blessing."[152] When pressed by reporters, Garwood conceded that the U.S. government should supply the Contras. But she also explained that "when you have a Congress that doesn't do its duty, it's like when your house is burning down and the fire department doesn't come. The private citizen has to act." Garwood eventually gave $2.5 million to the Contras, including $65,000 to purchase an old Huey helicopter which the Contras soon christened Lady Ellen. She also petitioned her wealthy friends to give large sums of money.[153] While Garwood's donations made national news, other major backers, such as oil millionaire Nelson Bunker Hunt and beer brewing magnate Joseph Coors, preferred to stay out of the limelight, quietly channeling hundreds of thousands of dollars to private groups invested in the Nicaraguan war.[154]

Much of this money came from individuals and businesses that had lost assets in Nicaragua when the Sandinistas took power. For instance, when talking to a reporter about his European donors, Singlaub explained how "corporations that had their properties expropriated or nationalized" were eager to give to the Contras.[155] He also noted that funds came from shrewd businessmen who "wanted an 'in' with the new government" that the Contras hoped to install.[156] On another occasion, one of Singlaub's subordinates explained, "Our fundraising efforts have paid off best with people who used to work in the government who are now in corporations with defense contracts."[157] Aiding the Contras, in that sense, was a financial investment from which businessmen, former government officials, and arms manufacturers all hoped to reap major profits. That was certainly how the Contras' opponents in the American Left saw things. A journalist from the *Worker's World* newspaper wondered, "Is it any great surprise that it is the large U.S. corporations which are putting up the cash for the Contras, since these very same profiteering corporations are the ones on whose behalf the Reagan administration is waging the war against Nicaragua in the first place?"[158]

With a stream of donations flowing into his hands—more than $250,000 a year in 1984 and 1985—Singlaub began buying large quantities of military supplies for the Contras.[159] He also shepherded deals between the Contras, arms dealers, and foreign governments, including one in the spring of 1985 that totaled $5.3 million.[160] Through Singlaub, the Contras procured an arsenal of AK-47 and HK21 machine guns, 9mm pistols, rocket-propelled grenade launchers, claymore mines, antitank mines, and C-4 explosives.[161] Most of these weapons came through Singlaub's old contacts in South Korea and Taiwan, but sympathetic parties elsewhere in the world also contributed.[162] Since U.S. law forbade American citizens from raising money inside the United States for weapons to be sent abroad, Singlaub conducted these transactions through an array of overseas bank accounts.[163]

Around this time, Singlaub joined a private firm called GeoMiltech Consultants as "an unpaid advisor." The company had been started a few years prior by Barbara Studley, a right-wing radio-show host in Miami whose ardent support for the Nicaraguan "freedom fighters" made Singlaub a devoted fan.[164] Studley incorporated the company in Delaware, most likely to take advantage of the state's generous corporate tax code.[165] In official documents, Singlaub and Studley described GeoMiltech as an "international marketing consulting firm." Its purpose was to "advise on, and facilitate, the locating and supply of military, industrial, and agricultural products worldwide." Its greatest strength was its versatility. The company was able to work as a conduit "from government to government" but also between "government and foreign private enterprises and, when appropriate, between private companies." To bolster its relationships with foreign governments and businesses, the company kept offices in Washington, D.C., Seoul, Brussels, and Tel Aviv.[166] It also worked with a bank in Miami to hide money for arms purchases overseas.[167]

By 1985, GeoMiltech was serving as a front for several secretive deals between Singlaub, Studley, and a fascist-leaning German arms merchant named Ernest Glatt, who had made a career buying and selling weapons for the CIA. Glatt sold Singlaub a few hundred Polish-made AK-47s, along with the forged end-user certificates, and arranged for the weapons' transport on a Greek freighter. Singlaub didn't share Glatt's affinity for the Nazis, but he did like his low prices. While the going rate for a brand-new Polish-made AK-47 was between $200 and $300 in 1985, Glatt managed to procure them for only $135, which helped Singlaub stretch his limited funds.[168] This meant Singlaub was unable to turn a profit—unlike others who supplied the Contras with weapons. But that was not a problem since Singlaub said he was only "trying to advance the cause of freedom," not make money.[169]

Weapons-buying was only one part of the campaign. Since the Contras had become "orphans" when the CIA left in 1984, Singlaub thought he might serve as their foster father—a private military adviser.[170] He traveled to Nicaragua, Honduras, and Costa Rica several times a year to monitor the Contras' performance. Whenever he arrived, Contra leaders treated him as a guest of honor. In small patches of open land, they arranged their soldiers in ceremonial formations. At one gathering in 1986, Singlaub told the assembled fighters that he represented "hundreds of thousands of Americans who are sympathetic to your cause and want to help." Touring the front lines in a mud-splattered jeep, he spoke with ordinary soldiers and observed combat operations. Although he did not join in the fighting, his presence in an active war zone blurred the line between observer, contributor, and combatant. He could have been shot or blown up at any time.[171]

The Contras started to become an effective fighting force despite, or perhaps because of, the CIA's absence.[172] In a memo to the National Security Council, Singlaub opined that the "period of austerity was very useful in increasing their efficiency and effectiveness."[173] "In a way," he thought, "the funding hiatus of the Boland Amendment might prove to be a godsend for the Contras, weaning them from too strict American control." From what he had gathered, the "CIA advisers had been inflexible, often doctrinaire, and above all patronizing. They had not encouraged much initiative among the Contras."[174] This brought back bad memories of Vietnam. The CIA had been "treating these Central Americans much as they had treated Montagnard mercenaries in Indochina." But now that they were free from the CIA's domineering control, they could finally defeat the Sandinistas. To that end, Singlaub suggested that the Contras use pack mules to haul supplies and weapons over long distances, just as the North Vietnamese Army had done on the Ho Chi Minh Trail.[175]

Spending weeks in Central America, Singlaub began drafting war plans for various Contra units. His most ambitious scheme was the "Rainbow Plan," an invasion of Nicaragua by thousands of Miskito Indian guerrillas based in Honduras. The goal was to cut off the Atlantic Coast of Nicaragua from Sandinista control. The guerrillas would blow up a network of bridges and loading docks, mine several arterial roads, destroy Soviet aircraft, and attack forty different Sandinista camps. Advising the White House of his plan, Singlaub made it clear that he would provide "all of the necessary TOYS to implement (the) mission"—an arsenal that included five hundred pounds of C-4 explosives, as well as mortars, antitank land mines, claymore mines, grenades, and tens of thousands of rounds of AK-47 and M16 ammunition. In total, the supplies weighed more than 6,000 pounds. He also emphasized that he was in control. "Anything and everything will be at my disposal," he wrote.[176]

By May 1985, Singlaub had set his sights on forming private military training units.[177] Again he turned to Robert K. Brown, who grasped the gravity of the operation. Singlaub was asking him "to circumvent the U.S. Congress" in "defiance of left-wingers who had cut off aid to the Contras." He was asking them to "fill in for their CIA predecessors."[178] If they were successful, more operations would follow. This could mean a steady stream of stories for the magazine, as well as the chance to turn back the communist tide in the hemisphere. As Brown put it in a *Soldier of Fortune* editorial, "Qualified private sector aid is vital. Not to fight but to teach, to preserve hard won wisdom and put it to good use."[179] Brown contacted the most capable unconventional warriors that he knew. Most had been with him in El Salvador in 1982 and 1983. Others, such as Lieutenant Colonel John Boykin, were recently retired veterans who had worked in an official capacity for the United States MilGroup in El Salvador. The new recruits were well familiar with the world of private military training. Jack Thompson, the Vietnam vet who fought with the elite Selous Scouts in Rhodesia, was working as a private "security consultant" in Guatemala before Brown picked him for his team. John Harper, a retired CIA demolitions expert, had spent the late 1970s working with rogue ex-CIA agent Ed Wilson on a series of moneymaking schemes in Libya.[180]

The mission did not go as planned. When Brown and his men arrived in Tegucigalpa, Honduras, nobody was there to meet them. For several hours they sat on the airport tarmac with more than two tons of "illegal military supplies and bomb-making material" while incredulous customs officials glared at them. Finally, after Brown's men made some hasty phone calls, a Contra leader arrived and they loaded their guns, ammo, and supplies into a Toyota pick-up and set off for the border. The ride lasted fourteen hours, as they bumped along a hundred miles of backwoods roads, often in sight of the Sandinista's hillside bunkers. When they arrived in Camp Las Vegas, Contra commander Enrique Bermudez greeted them. As they got to know each other, Brown was astonished by what he saw as Bermudez's complete lack of preparation. When he asked about the unit's plans, Bermudez reportedly replied "PLON, PLON? We don't have no PLON?"

Over the next month, Brown's team—the "Wild Bunch," as he liked to call them—instructed the Contras in espionage, life-saving techniques, "weapons maintenance, marksmanship, and basic small unit tactics." But simple weapons training took up most of their time. They needed it badly, Brown thought. "These people had no military training at all," he later recalled. "Who knows what the CIA had been doing before we got there." The program went well enough for about four weeks until a Sandinista rocket attack destroyed the Las Vegas camp. Brown and his men packed their things and headed back to the United States shortly thereafter. Looking back on the mission, Brown noted that it "could hardly be called a resounding success." The would-be Contra spies whom they trained in espionage tried and failed to infiltrate the Sandinistas' regime in Managua. All were executed. Even still, Brown believed that the "four weeks of training we provided was better than the CIA bozos had given them, and we got a hell of a lot of the Contras' small arms up and running."[181]

Back in the United States, *Soldier of Fortune* ran a series of stories describing the Contra war from the frontlines.[182] They read much like the magazine's pieces about El Salvador—official after-action reports that described combat operations in vivid detail. However, unlike the El Salvador articles, Brown did not fully divulge his involvement in the Contra training missions at the time. To do so would have been too dangerous and given more ammunition to those who opposed private interventions in Nicaragua's war.[183]

A growing number of journalists picked up these stories. That put Singlaub in the awkward position of having to defend activities that skirted the law while at the same time soliciting more private aid.[184] He mostly did that by claiming an affinity with the Reagan administration's anticommunist foreign policy, while maintaining that he worked independently of the White House.[185] For instance, in a 1985 letter to the *New York Times*, he celebrated his organization's support for Nicaragua's embattled "liberators," a feat that was even more impressive because "U.S. public opinion and the opinion in Congress has not yet caught up with President Reagan's policy regarding the seriousness of the threat to continental security and the need to promote democracy on our continent."[186] Still, when pressed on the issue, he often struggled to explain the legality of his actions. In a television interview, Singlaub conceded that private support for foreign paramilitaries was a "fine point," a gray area between legal and illegal activity.[187]

Ambiguity thus characterized the relationship between Singlaub's private paramilitary campaigns and the Reagan administration. Officials often denied that the administration had any connection to, let alone control over, private groups aiding in the Contra cause.[188] And White House staffers and members of the State Department advised Reagan to avoid sending messages to Singlaub's USCWF and WACL meetings, as they could be easily misconstrued as open support for potentially illegal and certainly embarrassing activities.[189] Reagan, however, ignored these warnings and regularly sent Singlaub messages of support.[190] As he did in other forums, Reagan took the chance to explain the Cold War in religious terms. In one letter to Singlaub, penned in 1984, he explained, "The struggle between freedom and communism is, in its essence, not an economic conflict but a spiritual one. It is a struggle in which those who love God, country, family and freedom are pitted against those possessed by ideological zeal who seek absolute power."[191]

Reagan's letters served another purpose since Singlaub often brandished them at public meetings—evidence that the state looked favorably upon his activities as well as those donors who sent him money. In a message that Singlaub read aloud at a 1986 WACL meeting, Reagan wrote, "I call for you to do your part in this noble cause. Our combined efforts are moving the tide of history towards world freedom. We must persevere and never falter. I send you and all who help in your crusade for liberty my best wishes. God bless you."[192] In other communiqués, Reagan likened Americans' private military campaigns in Nicaragua to the actions of the Abraham Lincoln Brigade—the group of volunteers who fought Francisco Franco's forces in the Spanish Civil War of the late 1930s.[193] Yet Reagan never acknowledged that many veterans of the Abraham Lincoln Brigade faced stiff penalties, including jail time and loss of citizenship, for joining another country's war.

Other private conservative organizations in the United States supplemented the flow of arms and advisers into the region with a variety of non-lethal cargo, often administered as part of private humanitarian refugee resettlement programs.[194] The Connecticut-based Americares Foundation raised more than $14 million in medical supplies for the Contras.[195] The Texas-based group known as Freedom's Friends sent medicine and jeeps to members of the Nicaraguan insurgency. Composed primarily of wealthy oil families in Dallas and Houston, this group held semiannual fundraising seminars, which featured the leaders of anticommunist forces in Nicaragua and El Salvador as well as Afghanistan and Angola.[196] Protestant television evangelist Pat Robertson used his Christian Broadcasting Network to host Contra leaders and solicit small donations from millions of viewers.[197]

Through these spectacles, Freedom's Friends, the Christian Broadcasting Network, and other religiously oriented groups helped unite and mobilize evangelical Protestants and conservative Catholics by presenting the ongoing wars in the region as a spiritual struggle between Marxist atheism and Christianity.[198] By 1985, they had managed to raise more than $25 million for the Nicaraguan Contras as well as substantial funds for other right-wing regimes in Central America.[199] Even though much of this money paid for non-lethal cargo, those who donated had military goals in mind. Private relief funds and supplies would relieve the United States' burden of humanitarian aid, thereby freeing up more state money for weapons and advisers.[200]

The Reagan administration helped mobilize and unify these campaigns through a propaganda initiative known as the White House Outreach Working Group on Central America. Run by White House staffer Faith Whittlesey, it provided Americans with "extensive information and even lists of speakers to better proselytize and to affect public opinion" about the war in Nicaragua.[201] Enlisting private groups such as the American Security Council, the program disseminated publications and sponsored lectures across the United States. Audiences listened to businessmen, policy experts, and a few Contra commanders, like Eden Pastora, denounce the Sandinistas and explain why Americans could and should help the Contras.[202] Within a few years, the working group was also drumming up support for other anticommunist guerrilla movements in Asia and Africa.[203]

As the administration took a larger role in shaping private anticommunist initiatives, Singlaub's work collided with shady dealings going on in the White House. Since 1984, Lt. Colonel Oliver North, a staffer on the National Security Council, had organized a series of illicit arms deals to resupply the Contras, in violation of the Boland Act. Using secret bank accounts, North purchased weapons abroad and shipped them through a covert airline service run by retired intelligence officers Richard Secord and Ted Shackley. Reminiscent of the CIA's secret Air America program during the Vietnam War, their company, Southern Air Transport, used funds laundered through banks in Switzerland, South Africa, and Australia to fly military supply missions to the Contra camps in El Salvador, Honduras, and Costa Rica.[204] Violating numerous international laws, the operation "was for all purposes the clandestine air force of the Reagan White House," as one journalist later wrote. Beyond Central America, it flew covert shipments of weapons from the United States to Tel Aviv, after which other aircrafts carried the arms to Tehran—part of a broader scheme to finance the Contras with off-the-books arms sales to the Islamic Republic of Iran, an avowed enemy of the Reagan administration.[205]

While Secord and Shackley bought weapons and arranged transport, two Cuban exiles directed operations in Central America, landing flights at El Salvador's Ilopango airport and Costa Rica's Aguacate airfield.[206] One, Felix Rodriguez, had fought at the Bay of Pigs before joining the CIA. He led the operation that captured Che Guevara in Bolivia and then shipped off to Vietnam, where he worked as a helicopter pilot in Ted Shackley's ultra-secret Phoenix Program.[207] In Central America, Rodriquez worked with Luis Posada Carriles, a veteran of the Cuban paramilitary underground who had organized, among other violent acts, the bombing of a Cubana Airlines plane in 1976 that killed 73 civilians.[208] In addition to these Cuban exiles, Oliver North also turned to the right-wing mercenary underground, seeking out men who had fought under "Mad" Mike Hoare in Africa, and who had recently attempted a coup in the Seychelles, an archipelago country in the Indian Ocean.[209]

By March 1985, Singlaub was corresponding with North to discuss his own private ventures and coordinate their efforts.[210] Yet they started to clash. No doubt Shackley and Secord were capable covert operators, Singlaub thought. But they were driven by the wrong motives, especially Secord. Singlaub recalled how Secord had finished his career in intelligence in disgrace because of his contact with the rogue CIA-agent-turned-arms-dealer Ed Wilson, who had been convicted of illegally selling weapons to Libya in 1983.[211] He "hated to see the Contras involved with someone like Secord," who seemed to care more about profits than he did about the anticommunist cause.[212] Secord had convinced Oliver North to buy weapons from his Iranian-American partner, Albert Hakim, for prices that were dramatically higher than those offered by Singlaub's gunrunner, Ernest Glatt. To him, this meant that the Contras' thin weapons budget was being wasted on overpriced items to enrich the middlemen.[213]

Already worried that North's inconsistent support of the Contras indicated he was "not a real conservative," Singlaub also had growing concerns about other Americans bound up in North's networks.[214] He had heard "disturbing reports" that Carl "Spitz" Channell, a conservative fundraiser who ran a group called the National Endowment for the Preservation of Liberty, was purporting to raise millions of dollars for the Contras while actually lining his pockets.[215] Indeed, Channell was working in tandem with Oliver North, hosting fundraising meetings that homed in on "extremely wealthy donors," including many of the same men and women who had given to Singlaub, such as Ellen Garwood and Nelson Bunker Hunt. Through these meetings, Channell raised nearly $10 million for the Contras, yet less than $4 million ever reached their hands. The rest went into bank accounts controlled by Channell and Richard Secord, the latter of whom used the money to purchase missiles, illegally, for the Iranian government.[216] These conflicts over profits and motivation started to drive a wedge between Singlaub and the men leading the Reagan administration's secret Contra war. While they shared the same basic goal—to covertly aid the Contras during the funding hiatus—the unscrupulous actions of Oliver North's men threatened to bring everything crashing down.

---

Fashioning an international network of financiers and arms dealers propelled John Singlaub into domestic paramilitary culture. Since retiring from the army in 1978, Singlaub had rekindled his friendship with Mitchell WerBell IV, a former OSS operative with whom Singlaub had fought behind Japanese lines in Manchuria in the mid-1940s.[217] WerBell left the army after World War II but later worked for the CIA in Laos during the Vietnam War—or so he claimed. After his time in Vietnam, he fashioned himself into an international gunrunner and paramilitary adviser. His activities produced a series of scandals and indictments.[218] In 1970, federal authorities seized his shipment of communist weapons from Vietnam bound for Eglin Air Force Base in Florida.[219] Some speculated that WerBell meant to distribute the weapons to right-wing extremists in the United States. WerBell said they were just souvenirs.[220] A few years later, federal authorities charged him with smuggling thousands of pounds of marijuana from Colombia to Florida. But the case fell apart when the prosecutor revealed that DEA agents had enticed WerBell and his co-defendants to move the drugs.[221]

These brushes with the law did little to deter WerBell's money-making schemes. He started a few arms-manufacturing companies that, as one journalist noted, peddled "a range of firearms from machine guns to desk-sized cannons."[222] He also founded a paramilitary training school on a sixty-acre compound just outside of Atlanta, Georgia.[223] There, in the foothills of the Appalachians, WerBell taught, in Robert Brown's words, "outrageously expensive" personal security and counterterrorism courses to "an eclectic group of ever-changing arms dealers, rogues, veterans of various wars, law enforcement personnel," and other combat enthusiasts.[224] Singlaub visited these camps in the late 1970s, but he eventually soured on WerBell and his growing connections with the idiosyncratic extremist Lyndon LaRouche.[225]

By the mid-1980s, Singlaub was a regular feature at *Soldier of Fortune* conventions, urging attendees to support armed anticommunist guerrillas from Nicaragua to Angola to Afghanistan—groups that generally managed to send a few leaders to make personal pleas at the summits.[226] Singlaub also promoted himself as one of the United States' most experienced covert warriors at *Soldier of Fortune*'s conventions and camps, which attracted armchair warriors and glory-seekers who paid hefty sums to live out their combat fantasies. For instance, in October 1982, *Soldier of Fortune* sponsored a three-day meeting where more than 1,200 men fought mock battles. After the day's activities ceased, participants got to dine alongside Singlaub, as well as General William Westmoreland, the retired commander of all U.S. military operations in Vietnam, and Watergate burglar G. Gordon Liddy.[227] At the same time, Robert Brown's Paladin Press ran a clearinghouse of how-to books on guerrilla warfare, sniping, explosives, intelligence-gathering, and other clandestine arts, including Carlos Marighella's *Mini-manual of the Urban Guerrilla*, the bible for armed left-wing groups from the Weather Underground to Uruguay's Tupamaros. Generally promoted as key texts for understanding political violence in the late Cold War, these books could easily be read as guides for those wishing to take up arms overseas or at home.[228]

Similar for-profit enterprises appeared across the United States. As one *Soldier of Fortune* writer said, more and more people wanted combat experience "without having to enlist for six weeks of real boot camp and a four-year hitch. They opt instead for short, private training programs."[229] Some camps resembled condensed versions of military basic training while others stressed survival techniques in the wilderness, security measures, or counterterror tactics. Whatever their specialty, paramilitary enthusiasts and entrepreneurs claimed that these camps fulfilled two objectives that the U.S. government had failed to meet—to prepare Americans in the event of a Soviet invasion and to provide the truly daring with the skills necessary to become a mercenary. As one supposed ex-mercenary put it, "I've fought in Africa and Lebanon, but learned better assassination techniques at Merc School. If the government refuses to teach anti-communist freedom fighters how to defend in case of war, then by all means, let's have merc schools."[230]

But only a select few professed to train mercenaries for overseas action. Hardened combat veterans balked at the idea that civilians could learn all the skills they had acquired over decades after spending a few weeks playing war in the woods. Even *Soldier of Fortune*'s Robert Brown, the self-proclaimed "senior statesman of the popular paramilitary business in the United States," dismissed mercenary schools as little more than fantasy—albeit a lucrative one that his magazine encouraged. "The only thing you can learn to be in a 10-day mercenary school is a corpse," he wrote in 1985.[231] Still, mercenary schools posed a serious problem for federal authorities who worried they violated U.S. neutrality laws. In Vietnam veteran Frank Camper's ten-day course, situated on a rural compound in central Alabama, students paid $250 to run across rivers under live machine gun fire, fight each other with heavy sticks, and engage in what one journalist called "sadistic tactics of interrogation" against their fellow classmates.[232] Camper made a substantial profit from his camp for a few years until federal investigators shut it down when two graduates, Sikh militants from India, attempted to kill Indian prime minister Rajiv Gandhi. Two years later, Camper received convictions on charges of racketeering, criminal conspiracy, and the possession of illegal weapons after he conspired with two California women to blow up the cars of their disgruntled employees.[233]

On a broader ideological level, celebrations of covert warfare at these camps and conventions helped legitimize a growing movement of right-wing paramilitaries in the United States. These groups, too, imagined themselves as freedom fighters and their vigilante campaigns intersected with fears of national decline that permeated post-Vietnam America. For many disaffected white men, "lacking confidence in the government and the economy," and troubled by the changing racial and sexual order, paramilitary warfare offered a kind of redemption. As sociologist James Gibson put it, paramilitarism provided these men with a way to "reverse the previous twenty years of American history and take back all the symbolic territory that had been lost." Such endeavors, whether in the United States or abroad, offered them "the fantastic possibility of escaping their present lives, being reborn as warriors, and then remaking the world."[234]

For those who saw war against domestic enemies as the ultimate objective, they could turn to an overlapping network of armed groups spread across the United States. A patchwork of former and current Klansmen, neo-Nazis, so-called Christian patriots, paramilitary survivalists, and others, this network centered on an affinity for violence, though the specifics varied from group to group. For some, such as Louis Beam, a Vietnam veteran and Klansman from Texas, the key was a guerrilla-war strategy that he called "leaderless resistance." "There should be no doubt that all means short of armed revolution have been exhausted," he wrote in the early 1980s. Sensing that the armed Right in the United States had been fractured by years of infighting and infiltrators, Beam saw an opportunity. Rather than unite disparate bands under a single leader, he urged them to form an underground of independent cells, capable of working toward a common cause—the overthrow of the federal government—but self-reliant enough to withstand the collapse of other cells. Modeled on how Beam understood communist undergrounds, as well as a similar organization that featured in William Pierce's right-wing fantasy novel, *The Turner Diaries*, "leaderless resistance" signaled a shift unfolding within the armed Right.[235]

Just as Americans like John Singlaub saw guerrilla war as the best means to defeat enemies abroad, Beam and those around him sought a similar path at home. Much like the Contras, they hoped armed men would lead the struggle against totalitarianism.

The growth of the domestic paramilitary movement in the early 1980s provided a fertile breeding ground for U.S. mercenaries.[236] In 1981, several Klan members and neo-Nazis in Louisiana hatched a plot to invade of the tiny Caribbean nation of Dominica and overthrow its new, democratically elected government. Dubbed the "Bayou of Pigs" by the press, this ill-conceived coup attempt was mostly organized through classified advertisements in *Soldier of Fortune* that attracted disgruntled Vietnam veterans, Klansmen, and a drug-dealing neo-Nazi from Canada. Foiled at the last minute by an FBI infiltrator, "Operation Red Dog," as its participants called it, sought to reinstate the deposed black ruler Patrick John and use the island nation as a base for a hemispheric offensive against leftist governments in the Caribbean and Latin America. Although exceptional in many ways, the plot exposed some of the links between a rapidly militarizing right-wing movement at home and the glorification of mercenary adventures abroad. But it also revealed how ideological motives could be suborned to the hope for easy money. For many of the men, the most attractive thing about Operation Red Dog was how it was supposed to make them the rich barons of a tiny island nation. They expected to receive large parcels of land upon which they could build casinos and hotels. And so it didn't really matter to them, despite their affinity for white supremacy, that they were trying to put a black man in power, nor were they troubled by the fact that their operation's success hinged on their cooperation with the island's radical Rastafarian movement known as the Dreads.[237]

By mid-decade, a few hundred American mercenaries were working in Central America. Some of these men served only in support capacities, running weapons and supplies along Nicaragua's borders, while others joined combat units.[238] In either case, private mercenaries became important parts of the Reagan administration's covert wars in Central America. In one notable instance, the CIA used American mercenaries from Alabama, operating under the name of Civilian Military Assistance (CMA), to smuggle arms, train Contras, and participate in operations in Honduras and Nicaragua. Led by a white supremacist named Tom Posey, the group comprised Vietnam veterans and National Guardsmen from the U.S. South, some of whom were tied to the Klan. Many had also trained at Frank Camper's paramilitary school in Alabama. In 1984, the CMA secured several CIA contracts through its liaison with the U.S. Ambassador in Honduras, John Negroponte.[239] But the operation collapsed later that year when the Sandinistas shot down a CMA supply flight, killing two Americans and causing a brief scandal for the Reagan administration.[240]

Although the full extent of administration officials' involvement was not known at the time, the Sandinistas and their supporters in the United States generally regarded Posey's band of mercenaries as official contractors working for the White House. Senator Barry Goldwater saw things differently. "A private citizen of this country has the right to volunteer in any cause or country any place in this world to help them, and there's nothing we can do to stop them," he said. "It's been going on forever and ever," likening Posey's band to other Americans who fought as volunteers in Spain, China, and Israel.[241] Following that line of thought, Posey stressed that his men were volunteers who received next to nothing for risking their lives. "Those people do not fight for money or train for money," he said. "99 percent of what we do is out of our own pockets.... The only thing they got out of it was some beans and rice."[242]

Paramilitary enthusiasts in the U.S. were thrilled by these exploits. After the crash, *Soldier of Fortune* magazine honored the dead CMA members with posthumous "heroism awards" at its 1984 national convention.[243] A few found the CMA mission to be so inspiring that they joined Posey's outfit. Sam Hall was one. A former Olympic diver who could not fight in Vietnam due to an injured leg, Hall had spent the war in the United States drinking, taking drugs, chasing women, and contemplating suicide.[244] The terrorist attacks at the 1972 Olympics changed all of that. He decided to become a counterterrorist and a mercenary. According to his boastful and unreliable memoir, Hall trained with Israeli commandos, and attended mercenary schools in England, West Germany, and Holland. Then he went to South Africa to recruit mercenaries to rescue American POWs in Vietnam.[245] When that failed, he decided to test his fate as a spy in El Salvador and Nicaragua. He dreamed up an elaborate scheme to create a private unit of counterterrorists that could serve government contracts. His contact in the Joint Chiefs of Staff told him there was no money in that and instead advised him to join Posey's band. He linked up with the CMA and also made contact with John Singlaub and Oliver North. But he could not get any of them to support his plan to blow up bridges in Nicaragua.[246] On his final reconnaissance mission, Hall was captured by the Sandinistas and imprisoned for months. They let him go when they found out he was little more than a mercenary imposter.[247] Recalling the incident a couple of years later, Singlaub pitied Sam Hall and his ilk—"I think he suffered from a Walter Mitty type complex, and I felt sorry for him, really."[248]

By 1985, as Singlaub and those around him looked toward Central America, they could be pleased with their efforts. Their work on behalf of the Salvadoran security forces had resulted in major defeats for the leftist guerrillas. FMLN leaders had started to talk about laying their arms down. Meanwhile, the private Contra campaign was a major success. Singlaub and others had helped assemble an international network of foreign leaders, wealthy Americans, grassroots groups, and arms dealers which could not be easily identified let alone stopped by policing agencies. In the process, the Contras had become a better fighting force, creating major problems for the Sandinistas.[249] Meanwhile, hundreds of American men had joined the wars in Central America as mercenaries of sorts, running guns, training troops, and even fighting in combat. Soon, they hoped, the leftists would be out of power.

As Singlaub ran these private paramilitary operations, he maneuvered behind the scenes in the World Anti-Communist League. He wanted to become chairman of the entire group and make it into something more than a bunch of ideologues and intellectuals who wrung their hands about communism and did little else.[250] He hoped he could turn it into an action-oriented group that could conduct covert operations on a truly global scale.[251] After all, anticommunist insurgents in Africa, Asia, and Eastern Europe needed help too and the U.S. government couldn't be counted upon to get the job done. Perhaps the private sector could.

## 6 | Rebels for the Cause

In June 1985, the leaders of armed anticommunist movements from Nicaragua, Afghanistan, and Laos gathered at the remote stronghold of the paramilitary group known as UNITA (União Nacional para a Independência Total de Angola) in Jamba, Angola. Organized by a group of American activists, the meeting was, in a certain sense, a right-wing version of the Tri-Continental Conference of 1966, at which leftist revolutionaries from a dozen countries had gathered in Havana to proclaim their solidarity with one another.[1] In Jamba, anticommunist guerrilla leaders discussed how they could join forces to reverse the spread of communism in Asia, Africa, and Latin America. Proclaiming themselves the Democratic International, they promised to "cooperate to liberate our nations from the Soviet imperialists."[2] Jonas Savimbi, the leader of the Angolan rebels, predicted that "our guns, our faith and our determination" would spark a global revolution that would save the world.[3]

Two months later in Dallas, Texas, John Singlaub took the stage at an upscale hotel for the eighteenth annual conference of the World Anti-Communist League. Like the meeting in Angola, Singlaub's featured guests were the leaders of a half-dozen armed anticommunist movements from around the world—places such as Nicaragua, Afghanistan, Angola, Mozambique, Laos, Cambodia, and Vietnam.[4] He had invited them to Dallas where they could make their case directly to wealthy Americans hoping to make a difference in the world. They were seated amongst representatives from more than one hundred anticommunist groups from Asia, Latin America, Europe, and Africa—and a handful of aspiring mercenaries.[5] Many had already given to Singlaub's aid program in Nicaragua. One had sent $25,000 for weapons. Another had donated $65,000 to buy the Nicaraguan Contras a helicopter.[6] Now Singlaub wished to channel these funds to the world's anticommunist rebels—without the involvement of the U.S. government or any other state body.[7] Guerrilla leaders showed up with shopping lists for AK-47s, bazookas, and surface-to-air missiles.[8] All of this signified, in Singlaub's words, the beginnings of a "counter-offensive for world freedom."[9]

Although separated by thousands of miles, these two events marked the highpoint of the anticommunist international. For decades, Americans had tried to use private funds to fight communism abroad, channeling resources to kindred movements spread across the global south. They often dreamed of launching guerrilla wars but generally settled for lecture tours, conferences, training academies, and publications. While those efforts did fashion an imagined community of anticommunist activists, they fell short of creating the global revolution U.S. conservatives so desired.

Things changed in the 1980s. Anticommunist guerrillas were now chic. The Nicaraguan Contras had become darlings of the American Right, alongside other rebel groups like the Afghans, the Angolans, the Cambodians, and so on. This enthusiasm had a strong strategic component, as the rebels were viable partners in the struggle against the Soviet Union, capable of combatting its troops or those of its allies. More than that, these armed movements served as reflections of Americans' self-understandings. At rallies and fundraisers, they wore buttons that proclaimed "I'm a Contra too."[10] Activist and direct-mail pioneer Richard Viguerie put it in starker terms in 1986. "We used to be just a rag-tag band of guerrillas ourselves," he said. "Now we have the President and the White House."[11] Those ideas redounded in popular culture, most clearly in the *Rambo* and *Missing in Action* blockbuster film franchises, which further blurred the line between Americans and anticommunist guerrillas. In these imaginings of an international anticommunist crusade, armed Americans and their allies abroad were brothers-in-arms, rebels for the cause, each doing their part in the global revolution.

During the first years of the Reagan administration, faith in the power of armed men guided the ideas and impulses that comprised the Reagan Doctrine.[12] It called for the arming of rebel groups who could defeat communists' proxy states and, ultimately, bring about the collapse of the Soviet Union by dragging it into a series of unwinnable wars. As Reagan entered his second term, conservative activists strove to make that plan into a reality. They traveled to Afghanistan, Angola, and Southeast Asia to meet anticommunist guerrillas in the field. They solicited donations from individuals, businesses, churches, and international groups to lobby Congress. And they tried to give rebel groups whatever material support they could. Combined, all of this activity constituted a "relatively unpublicized, private, and multinational military operation," as one journalist later put it.[13]

Meanwhile, rebel leaders made their rounds on the circuit of international anticommunist conferences. They shrewdly used the rhetoric of Soviet imperialism that resonated with audiences in the United States and Europe to promote their own interests. They also sought legitimacy by claiming affinity with other armed groups in other parts of the world. Afghan rebels made common cause with Angola's UNITA paramilitaries who in turn celebrated the struggles of Nicaragua's Contras and Cambodia's Khmer People's National Liberation Force. This vision of a globe-spanning network of guerrillas in opposition to the Soviet Union enthralled a generation of U.S. conservatives. Their dream of a global anticommunist revolution, built from the ground up by ordinary people, finally seemed to be coming true.

It was not to be. Yet their work was gesturing toward something new—a form of military intervention that relied less upon the state than it did upon the private sector. While the dream of a global anticommunist revolution would soon come to an abrupt end, that conviction, only partially realized in the Reagan era, persisted for years to come.

---

In 1984, John Singlaub secured election as chairman of the World Anti-Communist League. Winning over and then managing so many people and organizations took considerable effort and patience. With more than 100 chapters spread across five continents, the group's members held a variety of conflicting opinions about strategy. But Singlaub hoped that his U.S. chapter, composed of retired military officers and prominent conservative activists, would provide new direction to the group, moving it from "passive anticommunism to active support of the pro-democratic resistance movements fighting Communist totalitarianism" in Africa, Asia, and Latin America.[14]

First, he would have to improve the WACL's image. Since the late 1970s, investigative reporters had been monitoring the activities of its members, especially those in Latin America. Mexican journalist Manuel Buendía spent more than a decade researching and writing about the WACL and its links to armed right-wing groups in Latin America—until he was murdered by Mexican intelligence officers in 1984 for exposing corruption in the Mexican government.[15] When he died, the *Washington Post*'s Jack Anderson picked up on his work, tracing the connections between death squad leaders in Guatemala, El Salvador, Argentina, and the Confederación Anticomunista Latinoamericana, the regional affiliate of the World Anti-Communist League.[16] He was on the right track. The CAL was filled with members of paramilitary groups and state security officials from Central and Southern America, heirs to the Operation Condor network.[17]

While members of the CAL often denied their relationship to death squads to the press, they celebrated them in private. For instance, when leftist guerrillas in El Salvador assassinated CAL member Adolfo Cuellar in 1980, his colleagues mourned the passing of a true member of the "active resistance," who had fought "with weapons, with the pen," and "with the spoken word."[18] Cuellar had been a leader in the Salvadoran paramilitary group commanded by ultra-rightist Roberto D'Aubuisson, which helped murder thousands of Salvadorans.[19] He was just the latest CAL leader with links to the Central American death squads to be killed by leftist guerrillas.[20]

Journalists in the United States also scrutinized the Anti-Bolshevik Bloc of Nations, the group of ex-partisans from Eastern Europe.[21] Since the mid-1960s, Croatian exiles from the ABN had carried out a string of high-profile bombings and murders in Western Europe and Latin America.[22] Others had become thorns in the side of Soviet intelligence authorities. ABN leaders claimed that they were under constant surveillance from the KGB and that its members had been targeted for assassination. That brought back memories of the murder of Stepan Bandera, the Ukrainian partisan who had helped found the organization in the 1950s before Soviet agents gunned him down in Munich in 1959.[23]

All of this generated much unwanted attention as Singlaub attempted to take charge of the WACL and its affiliates. It may also have threatened his life. According to a CBS news report, a group of "Palestinian guerrillas" associated with terrorist Abu Nidal had drawn up a "hit list" with Singlaub on it, as well as Oliver North and members of right-wing think tanks such as the Heritage Foundation.[24] Whether that was true was less important than the credibility it lent Singlaub and other anticommunist activists. If Palestinian terrorists were plotting to kill John Singlaub, his supporters concluded he was probably doing something right.

In confronting all this violence and radicalism, Singlaub was struggling with the same dilemma that perplexed a previous generation of Americans—how to aid the forces of anticommunist revolution while excluding extremist elements from the Far Right. For years, Americans had tried and failed to walk the fine line separating those whom they deemed respectable anticommunists and the radicals and fanatics who moved in the same circles. John Singlaub wanted to break that pattern. As he eyed the chairmanship of the WACL in early 1983, he realized he had to deal with its awful reputation.[25] He aimed to do so by purging its most unsavory characters, those "neo-Nazis, racists, and other non-democratic elements" who had proven themselves to be a liability in previous years.[26]

To gain a greater understanding of the group's members and activities, Singlaub reached out to the head of the Belgian WACL chapter, retired General Robert Close, a senator in the Belgian parliament and a representative to the European parliament.[27] Like Singlaub, Robert Close had fought an unconventional war against the Nazis during World War II. He had served as a member of the Belgian resistance and was captured and imprisoned in a Nazi concentration camp.[28] That was why Singlaub sought him out—"No one could accuse him of being a fascist," he later wrote. After chairing a panel at a WACL conference in Tokyo, Singlaub invited Close to his mountain home in Colorado, where they pored over files, researching the "backgrounds of hundreds of League members and dozens of organizations which had applied for membership." He soon realized the CAL "would have to go"—not so much for its links to death squads in Central and South America but rather for the strident anti-Semitism that underpinned its crusade against communism.[29] The same went for "several British and European groups who had infiltrated League chapters" with their "half-baked theories of racial supremacy."[30]

In May 1983, Singlaub and Close released what they called the Tabernash Report, demanding that the WACL expel any "extremist, neo-Nazi, neo-Fascist, racist, or similar organizations."[31] To make the group more transparent, Singlaub started inviting members of the Anti-Defamation League of B'nai B'rith to observe its conferences. At the same time, he wrote letters to the editors of major newspapers protesting any negative publicity that the group received.[32] As a public relations maneuver, it worked. A correspondent for the *New Republic* noted that Singlaub's efforts had won the WACL and its affiliates "newfound respectability"—even though many of the group's extremist elements continued to show up at its meetings.[33]

Singlaub's efforts secured his bid to chair the entire WACL. He promised to bring the group's 1984 conference to San Diego, where its members could meet face-to-face with leaders from armed anticommunist movements from four continents and create a global strategy for private aid.[34] That meeting set the stage for the larger summit that Singlaub convened in Dallas the following year, at which guerrilla leaders, hopeful mercenaries, and conservative activists talked of their joint struggle against communism and made plans to help one another overthrow communist regimes, to lead a global revolution for the Right.[35]

Drumming up support for these gatherings, Singlaub crisscrossed the globe on a marathon tour of speaking engagements and meetings. He spoke to members of Anti-Bolshevik Bloc of Nations in London and Toronto, with chapters of the Asian Peoples' Anti-Communist League in Tokyo and Taiwan, and other groups in Brazil, Paraguay, Luxembourg, Australia, and elsewhere.[36] All of this came on top of the work Singlaub was doing in Central America—soliciting donations from individuals, businesses, activist groups, and third-party states to buy weapons and supplies, meeting with guerrilla leaders in the field, and overseeing private military advising teams in Nicaragua and El Salvador.[37] Emboldened by his success in Central America, Singlaub sought to use those same methods to help anticommunist paramilitaries in other parts of the globe. As he told one reporter, "I can go into any country in the world and know that I have a friend there who can help me get in touch with the people I need."[38]

As he traveled, Singlaub made closer connections with guerrilla commanders from Afghanistan, Angola, Laos, and Cambodia.[39] To be sure, these groups had already been sending delegates to meetings of the WACL for years, and so Singlaub was mostly capitalizing on the work of other activists, particularly Mexico's Rafael Rodriguez, who had brought many of them into the fold.[40] Starting in the late 1970s, leaders from Angola's UNITA movement, several Afghani guerrilla factions, the Khmer People's National Liberation Force, and the Ethnic Liberation Organization of Laos began touring the United States for speaking engagements and other events, including the annual Conservative Political Action Conference, the premier fundraiser for the right wing of the Republican Party.[41] They also traveled to WACL-sponsored conferences in Taiwan, the Philippines, Britain, and West Germany.[42]

Despite differences in the scale and nature of their conflicts, guerrilla leaders from Asia, Africa, and Latin America routinely expressed solidarity with one another.[43] So did those Americans invested in their success. Each armed anticommunist movement was a crucial part of a larger global struggle. John Singlaub summed it up when speaking to a group of Cuban exiles in Miami. While the world's armed anticommunist movements "may seem widely separated geographically and culturally, they all have three very significant similarities. First, they are all fighting the same enemy, International Communism. Second, all are engaged in a citizens' rebellion against the Communist tyranny which has been imposed on them by force of arms and against their will. And third, all are receiving inadequate support from the governments of the Free World because of the obstructionist tactics of a few left-wing legislators."[44]

For Singlaub, the rise of these anticommunist insurgencies was the "most significant international political development of the last 40 years."[45] Their existence indicated the start of a tectonic shift in geopolitics—"the rollback of communism throughout the world." Americans did not have to fight this war. Rather they needed to "exploit the successes represented by these active resistance movements" to defeat the Soviet Union and its allies by dragging them into a series of unwinnable and unconventional wars.[46] That entailed several things. "To be effective, each resistance movement must know that they are receiving support and encouragement from all parts of the Free World," he told the audience at the 1984 annual *Soldier of Fortune* conference. "This not only enhances the morale of the freedom fighters but it [also] greatly complicates the Communist problem of stopping the support." It was thus "equally important" to "provide *coordinated*, relevant support to all of the resistance movements at the same time. We must not allow Moscow, Peking, and Havana the opportunity to deal with these resistance movements one at a time."[47]

This was an ambitious scheme to synchronize several guerrilla wars separated by thousands of miles and distinct historical trajectories. For those reasons, it only seemed achievable by working through the U.S. government, with its vast resources and virtual monopoly on the sale of weapons abroad. Yet Singlaub insisted that the state could not be counted upon. In his view, the "fuzzy-minded liberals in the House of Representatives" had "almost immobilized the decision making processes of the Executive Branch."[48] It was, therefore, up to citizens to "carry forward the aims of the administration," to "roll back communism" through the "private sector."[49] Instead of using "funds from the taxpayer," Singlaub aimed to replace the state with an international network of private donors and arms merchants.[50] In so doing, he hoped to skirt popular debate and congressional authority, while moving beyond the covert war-making powers of the executive branch, particularly the CIA.

To that end, Singlaub announced he had established committees to determine the needs of anticommunist resistance movements in seven countries: Afghanistan, Angola, Mozambique, Ethiopia, Laos, Cambodia, and Vietnam.[51] After conferring with rebel leaders, Singlaub's committees would form a "series of regional action programs" that would provide material support to "freedom fighters" in communist-controlled countries.[52] He also proposed a global "information service" that would "provide up-to-the-minute reports from the worldwide freedom fighters fronts," thereby "circumventing the liberal media establishment."[53] When pressed by reporters on the details of his action programs, the old general remained tight-lipped.[54] But those who knew of Singlaub's operations in Nicaragua and El Salvador could be confident that they would encompass a variety of covert war strategies, including weapons smuggling, propaganda, and the training of paramilitary warriors.

Ordinary Americans had an important role in all of this. By contributing money, time, and energy to private paramilitary endeavors, Singlaub liked to say, a concerned individual would "become more than a spectator." He or she would now be a "participant in the new counteroffensive" spreading across battlefields in Latin America, Asia, and Africa.[55] They would demonstrate that Americans could and would help their brothers-in-arms abroad, even if the U.S. government was not quite up to the task. Singlaub found many who agreed with him—concerned citizens with some extra cash or weapons, the armchair warriors who showed up at *Soldier of Fortune* conventions, and the hopeful mercenaries and military advisers already at work in Central America. He had "people calling everyday" offering "guns, ammunition, everything."[56]

Around Washington, D.C., Singlaub found kindred spirits amongst the suit-wearing policy wonks working in conservative think tanks. The most influential was the Heritage Foundation, founded in 1973 by the wealthy beer magnate Joseph Coors and his political partner Paul Weyrich, with an annual operating budget of more than $10 million.[57] Like Singlaub, the Heritage Foundation believed foreign guerrillas should lead the way in the unfolding global struggle. In a widely circulated policy proposal, the group urged the Reagan administration to "employ paramilitary assets to weaken those communist and non-communist regimes that may already be facing the early stages of insurgency in their borders and which threaten U.S. interests."[58] These ideas echoed in proposals offered by other think tanks. For instance, the Georgetown University's Center for Strategic and International Studies—a haven for retired intelligence officers that was chaired by Ray Cline, former Deputy Director of Operations for the CIA—published studies and held conferences that called for the arming of anticommunist guerrilla forces in key conflicts in Asia, Africa, and Latin America.[59]

Of those wars, one was starting to assume ever greater importance as *the* place where the tide would turn against the Soviets. In Afghanistan, the religious warriors of the mujahedin were not just fighting communism. They were killing Soviet soldiers.

---

As Reagan entered his second term, the war in Afghanistan had been raging for years. It began in 1978, after the Marxist People's Democratic Party of Afghanistan overthrew the short-lived government of modernizer Mohammed Daoud Khan. After the coup, the Afghan communists set about transforming their country along Soviet lines, a difficult task in one of the world's poorest countries, where years of U.S.-led agricultural and hydrological projects had borne little fruit.[60] Establishing closer relations with Moscow, they used Soviet aid to build agricultural programs, communications networks, and a centralized state.[61] Championing their regime as an ideological and territorial extension of the Soviets' October 1917 revolution, Afghanistan's Marxists soon replaced religious laws with secular ones and initiated land reforms and literacy campaigns designed to win the loyalty of the poor and landless.[62] Solidifying their grasp on power—at least in Kabul and a few other major cities—they utilized a growing number of Soviet military and intelligence advisors to crack down on their enemies.[63]

By early 1979, the communists' program of modernization, secularization, and repression had brought the state into the lives of ordinary Afghanis in an unprecedented fashion, generating strident opposition from many quarters. At the vanguard were Islamist radicals who had been gaining ground in many parts of the country, drawing adherents from a patchwork of literate young people and traditional tribal leaders.[64] The Islamists' challenge was underwritten by the Pakistani military, which expanded its funding for religious schools and training camps along the Afghan frontier in hopes of using the Islamist rebels to promote its own interests. With this support, the Islamists initiated a guerrilla war.[65] The first salvos, such as the abortive rebellion in the western city of Herat that left thousands dead, should have made it clear to the Afghan communists that armed Islamist groups were now a serious threat to their regime.[66] Yet the communists failed to deal with this new enemy. Instead, they competed with one another for power. All the while, their Soviet allies grew ever more frustrated.[67]

Soon the country was in the throes of an all-out civil war.[68] The Soviet politburo chose to intervene.[69] By January 1980, tens of thousands of Soviet soldiers, tanks, and helicopters had crossed the border.[70] But the introduction of Soviet troops only galvanized the guerrillas, who solidified their alliances with local military commanders. Even though many tribal leaders were skeptical about the idea of an Islamic state, they seized the opportunity to wage war against an invasive secular government supported by foreigners.[71]

The Soviet invasion caught most U.S. leaders off guard. However, President Jimmy Carter's national security advisor, Zbigniew Brzezinski, thought the moment opportune, a "major watershed" in the conflict between the United States and the Soviet Union.[72] He convinced Carter that the Afghan Islamist resistance could be turned into a weapon against the Soviet Union, a way to punish the USSR by tying Soviet troops down in a prolonged guerrilla war, much like the United States had experienced in Vietnam.[73] In late 1979, Carter authorized the CIA to aid the Afghan rebels.[74]

In the aftermath of the Church Committee hearings and the debacle of the hostage rescue mission in Iran, Carter sought a limited program that was inexpensive and would not generate much popular or congressional scrutiny.[75] CIA leaders assured him that could be done by channeling military aid though the Pakistani government, thereby providing plausible deniability that the United States was involved in Afghanistan's affairs. Over the next year—Carter's last in office—CIA agents built a delicate alliance with the Pakistani intelligence service known as ISI (Inter-Services Intelligence). By early 1981, their shipments had expanded to include hundreds of thousands of British bolt-action rifles, Chinese-made AK-47s, mortars, and rocket-propelled grenade launchers.[76]

From these modest beginnings, the CIA's covert program to aid the mujahedin would become its most expensive and, arguably, most successful. By the end of the year, the guerrillas had gained control over much of the countryside and many towns, killing thousands of Soviet soldiers in the process. Still, in the first few years of the Reagan presidency, until 1983, the CIA's aid to Afghanistan's rebels remained within the framework established by the Carter administration—channeling modest amounts of weapons through Pakistan, which controlled their distribution in Afghanistan.[77] U.S. aid during this time was dwarfed by that of Saudi Arabia and a few other Arab countries. Soon, however, congressional hardliners from both sides of the aisle began calling for greater investment in the covert program. The most influential was Charlie Wilson, a conservative Texas Democrat with a reputation for hard drinking and womanizing. Working with both parties, Wilson made the Afghan covert-aid program his pet project. He traveled to Afghanistan, met tribal leaders and CIA officers, and discussed strategy with high-ranking members of the Pakistani military.[78]

Back in Washington, Bill Casey, Reagan's CIA director and a lover of clandestine and paramilitary operations, also started to see Afghanistan as the place where the tide of communism could be turned back. While the CIA's covert war in Nicaragua encountered ever more opposition on Capitol Hill, the situation in Afghanistan looked better with every death of a Soviet soldier. "Usually it looks like the big bad Americans are beating up on the natives," he once explained. "Afghanistan is just the reverse. The Russians are beating up on the little guys. We don't make it our war. The Mujahedin have all the motivation they need. All we have to do is give them help only more of it."[79] Starting in January 1984, the CIA's Afghan task force expanded its aid to encompass hundreds of millions of dollars' worth of arms, supplies, vehicles, and training camps.[80]

As the war in Afghanistan intensified, the mujahedin beguiled many Americans.[81] In John Singlaub's words, the mujahedin were precisely the kind of force needed to defeat the Soviet Union and its proxies—"anti-Communist forces already engaged in conflict."[82] But getting them the right aid was a difficult task,

Singlaub argued, because "our capability in this UW (unconventional warfare) area" had been "so enfeebled" by liberal American lawmakers in the late 1970s. To get around that problem, Singlaub believed that "our efforts to support the Afghans must be handled through third parties" even if this meant sacrificing "adequate supervision or direction." Fighting the Soviets in Afghanistan, as elsewhere, demanded ugly alliances and off-the-books operations.[83]

Beyond these strategic impulses, Americans were mesmerized by the Afghans' supreme dedication and sacrifice.[84] In the newsletter of Singlaub's United States Council for World Freedom, one author described how "the Afghan's will and courage is unbroken. Nurtured and supported by people who forage for food and till the fields under cover of darkness, the mujahedin fight on. Armed with obsolete weapons and short of basic supplies, they still control more than 80% of the territory. Even in the cities, the Soviets dare not venture out except in large, well-armed groups."[85] In light of the guerrillas' courage, as well as the widespread suffering and famine that caused ordinary Afghans to flee their homes, Americans had a "moral obligation to help a people who are fighting for their freedom."[86]

Many U.S. conservatives saw in the mujahedin reflections of themselves—deeply religious, truly masculine, and highly motivated champions of the anticommunist cause. They were, as one *Soldier of Fortune* writer declared, "brave holy warriors . . . who set the example for future generations of freedom fighters, those who will shun the easy road for a more difficult and noble task. To live like a man. And to die like one."[87] Another writer explained, "History teaches that freedom goes hand-in-hand with bravery. The people of Afghanistan are, above all things, brave . . . the fight for freedom is the fiercest of passions, an ideal so consuming it rides rough-shod over doubt. It is a faith."[88]

Such narratives, in which Americans and Afghans shared the cause of fighting communism, radiated throughout American popular culture. They found clearest expression in John Milius's 1984 film *Red Dawn*. Set in the dusty mountains surrounding a small Colorado town, the film tells the story of a Soviet and Cuban invasion of the United States and the willingness of ordinary Americans to pick up arms after the U.S. government failed its people. When communists overrun the town, a band of high school students retreat to the mountains where they, like the mujahedin, wage a guerrilla war against the invaders. Calling themselves the Wolverines, after the high school mascot, the youngsters pick off Russian soldiers, capture their weapons, destroy tanks and heavy artillery, and battle fearsome Soviet helicopters. They even start to look like the mujahedin, dressed in a mixture of flowing robes, scarves that resemble keffiyehs, and Soviet uniforms pulled from dead soldiers. And like most popular representations of the mujahedin, the Wolverines are motivated by simple concerns—love of family, home, and country—rather than abstract political or religious ideas. While most of the Wolverines perish, their sacrifice, as the film's closing narration explains, helped spur others to action and ultimately defeat the communist invaders.[89]

Imagining that the Afghans were only doing what patriotic Americans would do in the same situation—picking up arms and becoming guerrillas—Americans embarked upon a series of private aid missions to the mujahedin. They had four related goals. First, they worked to lionize the Afghan "freedom fighters" in U.S. political culture, thereby legitimizing their war against the Soviet invaders. Next, they sought to prod Congress into spending more money on weapons and supplies for the mujahedin, especially the shipment of high-tech weaponry that could destroy Soviet tanks and helicopters. Third, they devised humanitarian programs to ease the suffering of Afghanistan's war refugees, which numbered in the hundreds of thousands.[90] Finally, they attempted to fund and supply the Afghan rebels with donations from conservative groups in the United States and elsewhere. Those programs led a few adventure-seeking Americans to Afghanistan to join the mujahedin's fight.

The first goal—to create an "atmosphere of support"—was the easiest.[91] Of course, Reagan was a frequent cheerleader for the mujahedin. In a typical pronouncement, he told of how "the courageous Afghan freedom fighters battle modern arsenals with simple hand-held weapons," thereby serving as an "inspiration to those who love freedom. Their courage teaches us a great lesson—that there are things in this world worth defending."[92] Yet fondness for Afghanistan's guerrillas extended far beyond the executive office. Of all of the covert actions undertaken by the United States in the 1980s, the war in Afghanistan was far and away the most popular among U.S. policymakers from both major parties, mostly because they liked the idea of killing Soviet soldiers without sacrificing American lives.[93] Hence the Reagan administration's covert war in Afghanistan never provoked much opposition in Congress or in the public sphere—certainly not on par with the hostility leveled at the administration's activities in Nicaragua. As former CIA director Stansfield Turner summed it up in 1984, "This nation, today, is not agreed on what we should do about Nicaragua. It is agreed . . . in what we should do about Afghanistan and therein lies the difference."[94]

Such widespread affinity for the mujahedin amongst American leaders derived from more than Reagan's rhetoric or idealized visions of what the war was accomplishing. It was, in many ways, the result of sustained lobbying efforts from conservative activists and their deep-pocketed backers. Utilizing many of the same connections that had funded their other international projects in the early 1980s, they worked to persuade policymakers of the war's merits and maintain that support as the conflict in Afghanistan evolved.

The premier avenue for that activism was the Committee for a Free Afghanistan (CFA), founded in 1981 by Reed Irvine, director of the conservative watchdog group Accuracy in Media, and Charles Moser, an activist and intellectual who had outlined a general theory of anticommunist revolution.[95] Irvine and Moser selected retired U.S. Army General Theodore Mataxis, a counterinsurgency expert who had led the United States' paramilitary operations in Cambodia during the Vietnam War, to head the organization.[96] Like John Singlaub, Mataxis thought he still had something to accomplish in retirement. He later recalled, "I felt very sorry for the Afghans . . . I thought rather than sitting around and grousing at the club, watching the pine cones fall, I would try to do something to help."[97]

But Mataxis was more of a figurehead than a dedicated activist. The real work of the CFA was done by Karen McKay, a lieutenant colonel in the U.S. Army Special Forces Reserve who had been interning for Reed Irvine's Accuracy in Media.[98] One of the few women involved in the male-dominated world of anticommunist internationalism, McKay had a tough time convincing some of her male peers that she was up to the task.[99] But she was an accomplished soldier, having completed the U.S. Army's grueling Airborne School. Often dressed in battle fatigues and a green beret, McKay exuded martial power.[100]

McKay reached out to wealthy donors, including many of the same patrons who were then financing conservatives' undertakings in Central America.[101] With a growing network of contacts in the world of New Right think tanks and advocacy groups, she published articles and editorials and embarked on a litany of speaking engagements to hammer home the importance of the war.[102] In her words, Afghanistan was the "Soviet Union's soft underbelly. That's where they are vulnerable. . . . Afghanistan is the case of naked imperialistic aggression and if we're going to fight the Soviets anywhere, that is the place to do it."[103]

Pro-mujahedin activism quickly registered in the White House. Responding to pressure from the CFA and similar groups, the Reagan administration declared March 21 as Afghan National Day. As Reagan announced, it would "commemorate the valor of the Afghan people" and "condemn the continuing Soviet invasion of their country." Beyond that, the day was to remind Americans of the principles that had guided their own revolution two centuries before—the struggle of a people "for the freedom to determine its own future, the right to be free of foreign interference and the right to practice religion according to the dictates of conscience."[104] In 1982, activists observed the occasion by gathering in front of the Soviet embassy in Washington, D.C., where they carried placards, made speeches, flew Afghan kites, and listened to traditional music including songs from a man known as "Afghanistan's Frank Sinatra."[105]

The CFA also sought to bring the Afghan war into the minds of U.S. policymakers in a more direct fashion. From 1983 through 1987, McKay and Mataxis traveled regularly to Peshawar and the Afghan-Pakistan border to make contact with mujahedin leaders from nearly every major faction, often by visiting refugee camps.[106] Although Americans were forbidden from crossing the border, McKay did so many times because no one really knew where the border was. But it was more than the region's imprecise geography that enabled McKay to travel inside Afghanistan. As she later recalled, her missions to meet the mujahedin had the full blessings of CIA Director Bill Casey, Secretary of Defense Caspar Weinberger, and President Reagan.[107] Even with official support, this was dangerous work. As McKay well knew, foreign reporters often died in Afghanistan.[108]

After making connections with rebel commanders in Pakistan, McKay arranged for them to visit the United States. Meeting members of Congress, officials from the State Department and the Pentagon, and private groups such as the American Legion and the Reserve Officers Association, the mujahedin described their struggle and made pointed pleas for more U.S. aid.[109] Other activists helped engineer a series of sit-downs between President Reagan and leaders of the mujahedin factions, which made for awkward photo opportunities of a smiling Reagan addressing stoic guerrilla leaders garbed in traditional Afghan dress.[110] As the members of the CFA shuffled their Afghan clients around Washington, they were careful to point out that their work was intended to supplement—not supplant—the programs of the U.S. government. As McKay put it, "We stand ready to cooperate with our administration in any way we can to increase popular support for the more positive U.S. policies suggested by . . . President Reagan."[111]

Americans were not the only ones invested in the war in Afghanistan. The Soviet invasion and the mujahedin's armed response served as a rallying cry across world. At meetings in the United States, France, Germany, Canada, Taiwan, and South Korea, paramilitary groups from Cuba, Burma, and Angola made solemn pledges to support their Afghan brothers-in-arms, to champion their cause in the West, and to pressure states into more active programs of assistance. They talked of the Afghan struggle as part of their own—"an example of a heroic and unrelenting fight in facing the huge USSR war apparatus," which was simultaneously being carried out by other "rebel forces" around the world.[112]

The Afghans held special significance for the exiled partisans in the Anti-Bolshevik Bloc of Nations. Unlike other anticommunist rebels elsewhere, the Afghans were actually fighting the Soviets, an experience that guerrilla warriors from Eastern Europe felt only they had fully understood. For them, the Red Army in Afghanistan represented both Soviet tyranny *and* the long history of Russian conquest over non-Russian peoples along its periphery. In their minds, the Afghans were experiencing the same history of Russian colonization and domination that Ukrainians, Poles, Belarusians, and Lithuanians shared.[113] Thus, in the Afghans, exiles from Eastern Europe tended to see themselves. Like them, the Afghans were part of the anticommunist revolutionary vanguard, the "true representatives of the subjugated nations," "the real spokesmen of the disenfranchised nations behind all Curtains." That kinship led ABN leaders to invite Karen McKay and several Afghan guerrilla leaders to their meetings in the West.[114]

The ABN also sent emissaries into Afghanistan, where they reported on the war.[115] Their dispatches focused on the limited supplies and weapons used by the Afghans, and urged the U.S. government and other states to provide more "military aid in guerrilla warfare" especially "arms, mine detectors, and radio broadcasting equipment." But they also noted that this aid "must be offered without any preconditions which may fluctuate by changes in policy of the Western countries."[116] The Afghans needed weapons and supplies, not high-minded talk about human rights or restraints on their tactics.

Mujahedin leaders capitalized on this international fascination with their war. Starting shortly after the Soviet invasion, bands of Afghan rebels began sending delegates to anticommunist conferences abroad.[117] They spoke in an array of languages, Pashtu and Urdu but also English and French. Often dressed in traditional garments—baggy trousers, flowing robes, and wrapped head coverings—they appeared as the authentic voice of the guerrilla war. Speaking before audiences in Switzerland, Belgium, Korea, Japan, Canada, and the United States, they generally began their talks by describing the suffering of their people and the brutalities of the Soviet army.[118] Then they would make their pitch for more and better weapons. Lest their audiences forget, Afghan rebel leaders made it clear that they were fighting for more than themselves. As one French-speaking representative put it to a crowd in Switzerland, "If the Afghan resistance emerges victorious, the myth of Soviet invincibility will be destroyed. The balance of power is going to change. So if you're interested in your freedom, your civilization, I beg you to . . . help the Afghan resistance because, by helping the Afghan resistance, we will help you."[119]

This image of a united Afghan resistance fighting to save civilization, carefully constructed by those guerrilla leaders who appeared in the United States and Western Europe, belied the persistent conflict that divided rebel groups in Afghanistan. From the start of the insurgency, Afghan Islamist leaders clashed with one another over the meaning of the war and for access to the weapons flowing through Pakistan—enmity best evidenced in the rivalry that developed between the two most powerful mujahedin factions. The first was the Pakistani's preferred client, Gulbuddin Hekmatyar, a university student who abandoned his studies to join the resistance, having been radicalized by the militant Islamic doctrines that filtered across college campuses in the 1970s. Hekmatyar led a fierce band of rebels in the mountains north of Kabul. In his eyes, the Afghan war was only the beginning of a global jihad that would create a new Islamic caliphate. His main rival was Ahmed Shah Massoud, who had also left university to join the guerrillas. By the age of thirty, he had repelled "six direct assaults by the world's largest army" in the strategically important Panjshir Valley north of Kabul. The CIA regarded him as a military genius and the Afghans called him the "Lion of Panjshir." Massoud was by no means a secular leader, but he did not advocate the rigid Islamist doctrines that Hekmatyar did. Massoud and Hekmatyar occasionally collaborated but more often clashed, sometimes attacking each other's forces with the same ferocity they unleashed on the Soviets.[120] Other, smaller bands did much of the same. Rather than a united resistance, the Afghan rebels were a shifting community of allies and adversaries who rarely agreed on tactics, let alone the overarching goals of the war.[121]

For those Americans who hoped to aid the Afghan resistance, conflicts between mujahedin factions threatened to derail the war against the Soviets.[122] As one contributor to *Soldier of Fortune* magazine lamented, "a single, unified Afghan resistance front might drive the Russians from Afghanistan" but "that potential is a virtual impossibility given the inevitable division of the Freedom Fighter factions along familial, tribal, ethnic, linguistic, religious and political lines." They needed a "strong, charismatic leader" to "form one organization" that could "find new sources of funding and resources for their struggle."[123]

Some hoped that would be Pir Sayyid Ahmed Gailani, a Pashtu businessman from the east of the country. After the Soviet invasion, Gailani had fled to Peshawar, Pakistan, where he founded the National Islamic Front of Afghanistan, which ran guerrilla operations in southern and eastern Afghanistan.[124] His group was largely secular in its political program, causing his American supporters to think he was the ideal candidate to lead a coalition of guerrillas that absorbed the radical Islamist groups into a more unified and more moderate fighting force.[125] American and Pakistani intelligence officers thought otherwise. Gailani's group always received far fewer weapons and supplies from the ISI/CIA program than did the Islamist radicals.[126] This infuriated Gailani, who decried how his troops carried weapons captured from dead Soviet soldiers rather than those supplied by foreign benefactors.[127] To make that point resonate with Americans, Gailani frequently traveled to the United States, where he complained to members of the Reagan administration and Congress about this relative lack of support and insisted that he alone could unite the competing rebel factions.[128]

While he worked the formal channels of the state, Gailani developed a close relationship with McKay. Starting in 1984, he and members of his command, including his son Hasan, regularly appeared alongside her at meetings of the CFA. They also traveled to John Singlaub's WACL conferences in San Diego and Dallas, as well as *Soldier of Fortune* magazine's annual convention in Las Vegas.[129] At these gatherings, Gailani made the same complaints—the CIA/ISI supply operation was insufficient and ineffective.[130] His fighters did not have enough automatic rifles, medical sundries, ammunition, or camping supplies. For McKay and Singlaub, this was yet another failure of the American intelligence community, on par with its poor training of the Nicaraguan Contras.[131]

To those on the inside of the CIA's operation, Gailani's charges rang hollow. The CIA's operation was not only the most expensive in agency history; it had also expanded into training programs in urban terror methods such as car bombings and assassinations. Moreover, many in the intelligence community regarded Ahmed Gailani as something of a fraud. Based in Peshawar for years, he dressed in "silk-and-cashmere suits," rarely strayed into Afghanistan, and had only the most tenuous connections to his guerrilla commanders in the field.[132] CIA officers felt that Gailani's American supporters didn't understand who they were dealing with and what was really going on with the Afghan insurgency.

This disconnect between Americans enamored with Afghan guerrillas and the CIA officers tasked with their support stemmed from the very nature of covert actions. Although the dollar amount of the United States' covert aid was widely known, the breadth of CIA's program remained a high-level secret—nobody in the agency or the White House wanted the Soviets to know just how deeply the U.S. was involved in supplying and training the Afghan rebels, or just what its agents were doing in Afghanistan and Pakistan. Pro-mujahedin activists in the United States were out of the loop. Closed off from the clandestine activities of the CIA—at least in part—they became the agency's harshest critics. Ironically, as journalist George Crile writes, while the "CIA threw itself into arming, training, and funding the largest Muslim jihad in modern history, the only ones to register their outrage" were those "who seemed to believe that the CIA's support was so meaningless as to constitute a betrayal of the Afghans."[133]

To overcome the perceived failures of the CIA, conservative activists from the United States embarked upon a series of private schemes to help the mujahedin. By 1983, McKay had established a medical-aid program whereby wounded mujahedin fighters could receive treatment in the United States and American military bases in Western Europe before returning to the war. She also helped refugees resettle outside of Afghanistan, but only women, children, the elderly, and the disabled. In her view, it was the duty of all able-bodied Afghan men to remain in their country and fight.[134]

Other activists labored to supply to the mujahedin with war materiel, in an operation that closely mirrored Americans' work in Nicaragua. John Singlaub was a key player, soliciting donations through international anticommunist groups, conservative think tanks, and paramilitary enthusiasts. Here, too, Singlaub likened his activities to that of a humanitarian charity rather than a military aid mission, one that aimed to alleviate the suffering of the Afghan people. At speaking engagements and in conservative periodicals, Singlaub described how the Afghan guerrillas marched across mountains in bare feet, clothed themselves in rags, and slept on the ground. To remedy that, he asked the AFL-CIO to organize a program wherein construction workers could donate their old work boots to the mujahedin.[135]

Singlaub also made direct pleas to concerned citizens, imploring them to send their used footwear, blankets, clothes, and other sundries.[136] If they didn't have those items, then money would suffice. Singlaub set up a hotline from his office in Phoenix and urged concerned Americans to phone in their donations or mail him checks.[137] He also told his supporters they could help fight Afghanistan's atheist invaders by purchasing Korans which his agents would then smuggle into the country—much like "anticommunist Christians" had done behind the Iron Curtain.[138] While making these pleas, Singlaub assured contributors that their money would only be used for "non-military" items such as medicines, gasoline, clothing, bedding, and uniforms—which would then be "personally distributed" and to "the people who need it."[139] Still, as in Nicaragua, non-lethal aid served lethal purposes. It would make the Afghans into a more efficient fighting force.

The editors of *Soldier of Fortune* magazine were more ambitious. They urged readers to become members of their Freedom Fighters Fund by mailing cash to the magazine's offices in Colorado—hard currency, they said, was easier to get in the Afghans' hands "due to customs and distance restrictions."[140] In full-page advertisements celebrating the Fund as "the charity of the decade," the magazine pledged this money would be "used for arms, ammunition, and supplies," an endeavor that threatened to violate U.S. laws forbidding Americans from purchasing weapons for foreign military and paramilitary forces.[141]

Beyond soliciting supplies, the magazine also encouraged its subscribers to write their congressmen and urge them to provide more money to the CIA's program.[142] The campaign inspired many readers. One laid it out in simple terms—"All our allies ask is some U.S. greenbacks that won't be worth anything in a few years anyway. They ask no sacrifice, no life on the line, only a few hours' pay." This was money well-spent because "every Ivan a freedom fighter zaps is one less you have to face in the years to come," an argument which linked the actual war in Afghanistan to an imagined invasion of the United States by communist troops.[143]

Beyond raising money, the *Soldier of Fortune* staff traveled to Afghanistan to observe the mujahedin in battle. As with the magazine's private aid missions in El Salvador and Nicaragua, publisher Robert K. Brown and others saw the war as a chance for good adventure and good stories, a way to drum up publicity while helping out some anticommunist allies.[144] The magazine's reports often read like official intelligence dispatches, replete with detailed passages on weapons and troop movements, thick descriptions that allowed readers to imagine that they understood the conflict far better than those who got their information from liberal-biased media outlets such as the *New York Times* and the *Washington Post*.[145] Meanwhile, at *Soldier of Fortune*'s annual conventions, staff writers chaired educational panels about the war in Afghanistan, sometimes featuring commanders from Ahmed Gailani's forces or other rebel outfits. All of this was, as one writer put it, "the best (information) that can be obtained without a Top Secret security clearance."[146]

Believing *Soldier of Fortune* was disseminating the real facts about the war, Brown led a series of intelligence-gathering missions in Pakistan and Afghanistan. He desperately wanted to get his hands on a new version of the Soviet Automat Kalashnikov assault rifle, the AK-74, and its ammunition.[147] So far, no Americans, CIA or otherwise, had procured one. If Brown could do it, he would beat the leading American intelligence service to the punch. Before departing for South Asia, he met with an arms dealer who agreed to smuggle the weapon and its bullets into the United States. He then cut a deal with the U.S. Army's Foreign Science and Technologies Center, an intelligence unit that specialized in enemy weapons, to buy them, asking for payment in cash or gold so that he could use it to finance new missions to Afghanistan.[148] With this plan set, he assembled a team of retired specialists in unconventional warfare to accompany him on a trip to Pakistan.[149]

Brown's first trip to the Afghanistan-Pakistan border in December 1980 served as an introduction to the complex and delicate relationship between the mujahedin, Pakistani intelligence, the CIA, and the U.S. State Department. The *Soldier of Fortune* team flew into Karachi and then made their way to the U.S. embassy in Islamabad to meet a young lieutenant colonel who promised Brown some additional pay if his team was successful. They hired a taxi, bumped across the road from Islamabad to Peshawar, and began scouring the arms markets of nearby towns in the tribal areas of Pakistan. After days of futile searches, they chanced upon 5,000 rounds of AK-74 ammo in the town of Barra. Brown's men purchased the bullets for about $3500, but they never found the gun they were looking for.[150]

Now they faced the task of getting the ammunition into the right hands without being arrested and thrown into a Pakistani prison for smuggling. The U.S. Consulate in Peshawar, the closest government office, wasn't interested. Brown later wrote, "I was sorely tempted to tell the gutless State Department puke to take the 5,000 rounds of ammo and insert them into the body orifice of his choosing."[151] Brown hired a taxi to take himself, his men, and the bullets back to Islamabad, hoping someone from the U.S. embassy would buy his contraband. The journey, he later recalled, was nearly a disaster. He suspected his driver was a police informant. When they encountered a military roadblock, Brown planned to rat him out, hoping he'd be "sent to jail with us" so Brown "could pound his scrawny ass twice a day." Fortunately for the driver, they made it past the checkpoint and arrived in Islamabad hours later. The next morning a U.S. military attaché bought the bullets from Brown, netting him the paltry sum of $1,500, not even enough to cover the cost of the mission.[152]

Still, Brown was pleased. For him, it wasn't about money but rather getting the intelligence that the government had failed to acquire, showing that his private warriors were more effective than the CIA. At a press conference on Capitol Hill weeks later, Brown announced his "intelligence coup" to a group of reporters. "Score: Soldier of Fortune, one—CIA, zero," he proclaimed.[153] Back in the United States, Brown disseminated his reports to officials in the Defense Intelligence Agency and sold videos of his men testing the new Soviet weapons to his subscribers for $39.95—a small price for those who wanted the inside scoop on the latest enemy weaponry.[154]

Over the next few years, Brown made several more trips to Afghanistan with his "A-Team" of retired unconventional warfare specialists.[155] In 1982, they once again slipped into the country from Pakistan after making contact with members of Sibghatullah Mojaddedi's Afghan National Liberation Front, one of the main CIA- and Pakistani-supplied guerrilla outfits. Brown's men had the same goal as in 1980—to procure hard-to-find Soviet weapons and sell them to the U.S. government.[156] Unlike their previous mission, where they mostly just rumbled around the tribal areas visiting bazaars, this time they followed the mujahedin into combat, risking their lives and livelihoods. If they didn't get shot, they could wind up in prison for violating U.S. neutrality laws. They attempted to conceal themselves by donning traditional Afghan dress, growing their beards, and dyeing their hair.[157] On the road from Peshawar to Afghanistan, they passed through five Pakistani military checkpoints where they feigned sleep in the back of a jeep to avoid detection. Next to them lay a small arsenal from the CIA and ISI—British rifles, antitank mines, mortar rounds, and ammunition for a captured Russian heavy machine gun. Although this was proof that the CIA's covert program had generated a steady stream of weapons for the Afghans, Brown was not impressed. The mortar rounds didn't fire and the rifles appeared to be ancient.[158]

Having slipped across the border, Brown and his men joined the rebels as they attacked a Soviet army outpost. On the first day, the *Soldier of Fortune* team just watched the Afghans pump machine gun rounds and mortars into the base with no real effect. But over the following week, Brown and his men slowly became part of the fighting, joining the guerrillas' raids on Soviet positions and advising them on their tactics. They shot heavy artillery and small arms. They dodged bullets and hid from Soviet patrols. They slept and ate with the mujahedin. In so many ways, they became guerrillas too.[159]

Brown counted his team's adventures as successes, even though they didn't generate any profits or have a decisive impact on the war. His team had crossed into Afghanistan, fought alongside the mujahedin, showed them some new techniques, and through it all managed to stay alive. It "wasn't bad for a week's work," he later wrote. "We had whetted our appetites for adventure and expressed our support for the Freedom Fighter's cause."[160] From 1982 through 1988, Brown's men returned nearly a dozen times to Afghanistan, where they did much of the same—searched for Soviet weapons, offered the guerrillas advice, and joined their operations.[161] Every time, the *Soldier of Fortune* team found the same opportunities and obstacles—dedicated guerrillas and exciting action but also stubborn commanders, poorly trained fighters, and complex rivalries. The greatest challenge, however, was the condition of the Afghans' weaponry. In article after article, *Soldier of Fortune* denounced the CIA's program as ineffective, offering only outdated or broken weapons that prevented the guerrillas from launching offensives and blowing Soviet choppers out of the sky.[162] Although accurate, those stories tended to gloss over the scope of the CIA/ISI operation, which supplied a variety of small arms and ammunition through an increasingly complex network of third-party states and private arms dealers.

Nevertheless, the notion that the CIA's covert supply operation was failing led other Americans into Afghanistan. One was a former Green Beret, Andrew Eiva, who founded the American Afghan Education Fund to gather information about the guerrillas' fighting capabilities and pressure Congress to expand the CIA's program. A descendant of Lithuanian immigrants who had fled Soviet repression in the 1940s, Eiva felt a personal bond with the Afghans. Some of his parents' friends had died fighting the Soviets.[163] Believing it his duty to follow a similar path, he quit his commission in the U.S. Army for a hardscrabble existence as a lobbyist for the mujahedin. His budget was miniscule, the product of small donations from Paul Weyrich of the Heritage Foundation and a militant Mormon group called Free the Eagle, the latter of which gave him a few thousand dollars to rent an office and produce mimeographed newsletters.[164] To make ends meet Eiva worked as a taxi driver. He somehow rustled enough money to finance several trips to Pakistan and Afghanistan, where he met guerrilla leaders, observed them in action, and offered tactical advice. When he returned to the United States, he roamed the halls of Congress, denouncing the CIA's program to anyone who would listen. After months of that, he managed to persuade Senators Paul Tsongas and Gordon Humphrey to present resolutions calling for more and better aid to the Afghans, especially Stinger missiles that could shoot down Soviet HIND helicopters.[165] Yet Eiva frequently clashed with other activists invested in the Afghan war, especially Karen McKay, who began to think that Eiva was spying for the Soviets or perhaps the Islamist faction run by Gulbuddin Hekmatyar.[166]

Members of the CIA's Afghan program, as well as their closest allies in Congress like Charlie Wilson, also grew frustrated with Eiva. His operation was a joke, they thought, run by an outsider with little knowledge of the struggle in Afghanistan or the CIA's program. But Eiva threatened to derail Wilson's efforts in Congress. When Eiva went on *Nightline* with Senator Gordon Humphrey to accuse the CIA of "selling out the freedom fighters," the agency's Afghan task force decided to act. In the spring of 1985, CIA officer Gust Avrakatos invited Humphrey to "a dog and pony show" at the CIA's base at Camp Peary, Virginia, where the senator got a first-hand look at the vast arsenal assembled by the CIA and heard tales from paramilitary specialists who had trained guerrillas in Pakistan and Afghanistan.[167] By co-opting the senator, the CIA undercut the charges made by outsiders like Eiva that the agency was failing in Afghanistan.

And so, even though activists such as Singlaub, Brown, McKay, and Eiva helped spur congressional support for the CIA's supply program, they remained bit players in the actual war in Afghanistan. Their efforts paled in comparison to those of the CIA, the Pakistani ISI, and sympathetic donors from Saudi Arabia and other countries in the Middle East. In part, this was because Afghanistan was so remote that it was nearly impossible for most ordinary Americans to get there. In contrast, getting to Nicaragua and linking up with the Contras was not especially difficult for the determined. The United States had friendly relations with all of its neighbors and, as Reagan liked to say, the country was "just as close to Miami, San Antonio, San Diego, and Tucson as those cities are to Washington."[168] A short plane ride and the right connections were often all that was needed to join the Contras.

Joining the Afghan mujahedin, however, required traveling to Pakistan, avoiding local authorities and Soviet spies, finding a secretive guerrilla organization in a frontier town such as Peshawar, persuading its leaders to hire a mercenary, and then sneaking across the border. And then, of course, one had to avoid getting killed or captured—not only by the Soviets but by rival bands of mujahedin, particularly the Islamist factions.[169] Afghanistan was not for the faint of heart. Moreover, the CIA had a close—if frequently strained—relationship with the Contras, even during the years when Congress suspended official American aid. The CIA's links to the Afghan guerrillas, on the other hand, were much more tenuous and generally dependent upon the Pakistani intelligence service, ISI. Beyond that, CIA officers had little desire to help Americans join the fighting as volunteers. To so do would generate more scrutiny of the agency's actions from its harshest critics. Even worse, if the CIA was caught sending mercenaries into Afghanistan, such actions might prompt a Soviet reprisal elsewhere.

Without the quasi-official channels that guided Americans to Central America, aspiring Americans had few resources to get them into Afghanistan. Still, many dreamed of making the trip and joining the insurgents in battle. In the pages of *Soldier of Fortune* magazine and at its conventions, American men talked of going to Afghanistan to show the communists a thing or two.[170] Some managed to make it to Peshawar hoping to link up with the guerrillas. According to Ted Mataxis, head of the Committee for a Free Afghanistan, the town was filled with "plenty of Walter Mitty types . . . young men who drift in here and want to grab the elephant by the tail. They are on their way to Afghanistan to test themselves. They want to see how they will react under fire."[171] There is little evidence, however, that American civilians ever made it into the ranks of the mujahedin in significant numbers. A few Afghans who had been raised in the United States did, but the flow of Afghans out of the country was always much greater than the trickle of Afghan exiles returning home to take up arms.[172] Robert Brown, John Singlaub, and others who knew the difficulties of guerrilla war treated Americans' paramilitary dreams with skepticism. The war in Afghanistan was best left to the Afghans. They should be the ones to fight and die.

As it turned out, the real foreign volunteers for the war in Afghanistan came not from the United States—or for that matter anywhere in the West—but from madrassas across Saudi Arabia and other Arab countries, which produced a steady stream of young, radical men who saw the conflict as the start of a global jihad.[173] Fearing upheaval from Islamists in their own countries, the oil-rich and conservative monarchies of Saudi Arabia and the Gulf States hoped that Afghanistan would serve as a Sunni alternative to the Iranian Revolution.[174] The Saudis, especially, harnessed those sentiments, and mobilized them through financial largesse and formidable recruitment networks to stir popular enthusiasm for the Afghan cause. Roughly 30,000 Arab men—many of whom were well-educated, multi-lingual, and tech-savvy—joined the war in Afghanistan, first as members of humanitarian aid programs, but increasingly as combatants. Their impact on the struggle against the Red Army was not great, but their experience of war inducted them into international Islamist networks and sharpened their convictions about jihad.[175]

One was Osama Bin Laden. The scion of an ultrawealthy Saudi family, he devoted himself to mujahedin. In 1982, he established a base of operations in Peshawar, where he shepherded Arab volunteers from Saudi Arabia, Egypt, and Algeria through boarding houses, training camps, and ultimately, into Islamist rebel units. By 1989, as the Soviet Army withdrew from Afghanistan, Bin Laden had built a computer database of all the militants who had passed through his network. Its Arabic title, Al Qaeda, formed the core of a new movement that sought jihad on a grander, global scale.[176]

That was not something that mujahedin's American supporters had ever really considered, let alone something they had wished for. But it was not entirely unpredictable either.

---

While Afghanistan and Nicaragua dominated news headlines in the 1980s, U.S. conservatives and their allies abroad also focused on southern Africa. Since the late 1970s, they had witnessed a series of setbacks in the region. The harshest was the fall of Rhodesia's white-dominated government in 1978, giving way to the authoritarian regime of Robert Mugabe, a black Marxist revolutionary. The situation in Angola was not much better. There the fall of the Portuguese empire led to the rise of a communist state under the Movimento Popular de

Libertação de Angola (MPLA). Supported by a majority of the population, and backed by more than 30,000 Cuban soldiers, the MPLA soon began aiding a growing insurgency in Angola's southern neighbor, Namibia, a vast and sparsely populated desert that South Africa had ruled as a colony for nearly thirty years.[177]

As Ronald Reagan entered office, some Americans started to pin their hopes to Jonas Savimbi, who led the Angolan paramilitary group known as the UNITA (União Nacional para a Independência Total de Angola), the only guerrilla force with any chance of unseating the Marxist government. A charismatic commander who was fluent in English and who often appeared for interviews in a leather jacket and battle fatigues, Savimbi quickly developed into a darling of the New Right. Yet he was an unlikely candidate to become a conservative icon. He began his military career in the late 1960s as an opponent of capitalism and Euro-American colonialism, looking to black revolutionaries such as Frantz Fanon and the Black Panthers for ideological inspiration.[178] But as Portuguese rule collapsed in the mid-1970s, Savimbi stopped talking about revolution and began collaborating with the retreating colonial regime. Portuguese leaders came to see him as their most valuable weapon in the fight against the Marxist MPLA movement, which was then emerging as the most powerful military force in Angola.[179]

By 1981, Savimbi had transformed into an ardent anticommunist. This was not the result of any meaningful change in his convictions but instead part of his strategy to woo the incoming Reagan administration and its supporters to his cause. When Reagan took office, Savimbi told a team of reporters who were visiting his base in Angola that this "was the best news we had heard since we launched our struggle against Soviet-Cuban imperialism five years ago."[180] Savimbi began celebrating his soldiers as anticolonial freedom fighters on par with the Afghan mujahedin. At the same time, he spoke of reopening Angola to foreign capital, though he still maintained the state should play a role in shaping investment and wealth distribution.[181] He was never as much of a free marketer as his American supporters wished him to be. Nor was he the preferred client of all ex-CIA officers, especially those who had grown critical of feckless covert actions in Africa in the late 1970s. For instance, John Stockwell, who had run CIA operations in the Congo and Angola, said that "Savimbi has no ideology. He believes in nothing beyond his own selfish ambitions, and fighting has become a way of life."[182]

Nevertheless, Savimbi's newfound worldview swayed influential conservatives in the United States.[183] They believed he could overthrow the communists and build a new Angola, based upon privatization and Western finance.

More than that, Savimbi's guerrillas might give hope to other anticommunist warriors. As a pair of commentators noted, "a Savimbi victory in Angola—evidently within the realm of possibility—obviously would be a great boost to morale, and might serve notice to other countries that the wind may be beginning to flow from the West at long last."[184]

But Savimbi and the UNITA were hardly in a position to claim power. The 1976 Clark Amendment still prohibited the CIA from aiding Savimbi's forces, leaving him with few resources to mount major offensives. Moreover, the UNITA garnered far less support from ordinary Angolans than the Marxist MPLA government did. Its primary base of power was amongst the Ovimbundu ethnic group in a little-populated stretch of land in the southeastern part of the country. There, Savimbi established a working government and staged hit-and-run battles against the MPLA and the Cubans. Without the intervention of South Africa in the late 1970s, the UNITA probably would have fallen apart. Indeed, by 1980, the majority of Savimibi's military equipment came from the apartheid state, which offered him weapons, advisors, and mercenaries to continue his guerrilla war against the Angolan government.[185] While this alliance undercut Savimbi's image as a true anticolonialist amongst many observers in the West, Savimbi argued that his relationship to South Africa was not borne out of any affinity for white supremacy but simply out of necessity. In his telling, his soldiers only "accepted South African assistance because of the geopolitical realities of southern Africa in which South Africa is the dominant military and economic power."[186]

South Africa's aid was not enough. Savimbi always saw it as a stop-gap measure—sufficient to launch raids and defend the UNITA's strongholds, to stave off defeat and prolong the war. What he really desired was the recognition of the U.S. government and the resumption of official, if covert, American military aid. So Savimbi began sending his lieutenants to conservative gatherings in the United States and other countries.[187] At meetings of the WACL, conventions put on by *Soldier of Fortune* magazine, and banquet dinners sponsored by conservative think tanks, UNITA officials described how their war fit into the larger struggle against communism and chastised American leaders for not doing enough to help them.[188] At a 1979 meeting of the American Enterprise Institute, UNITA political officer Ernesto Mulato spelled out the central arguments.[189] Taking the stage after Jeane Kirkpatrick, a neoconservative hawk whom Reagan would later appoint as ambassador to the United Nations, Mulato lamented how the political scandals of the mid-1970s had crippled the U.S. government's ability to wage covert warfare in Africa. "At one time we were allies against the biggest war machine Africa has ever seen," he said. But "the

US government was paralyzed by Watergate and the investigations of the CIA when it cut off support to us." As these scandals chipped away at Americans' will to fight communism, Savimbi and the UNITA had no choice but to go "our own way."[190]

Savimbi made the same points when he visited the United States in 1981 for a series of meetings with conservative organizations and congressional leaders.[191] After making his rounds at the Heritage Foundation in Washington, D.C., Savimbi headed out to Palm Springs, California, where he rubbed elbows with golf-playing Republican supporters who had given at least $10,000 to the GOP.[192] In these appearances, and in lengthy columns in major American newspapers, Savimbi pleaded his case. The UNITA was just like the Nicaraguan Contras and the Afghan mujahedin, he explained. They, too, were trying to "raise the costs of foreign occupation" until "the Cubans and the Soviets can no longer bear the burden." But Savimbi had an additional advantage—his past life as a Marxist. He knew their strengths and weaknesses. "From Mao and the Communists I learned how to fight and win a guerrilla war. I also learned how not to run an economy or a nation," he later wrote in the conservative daily newspaper the *Washington Times*. In other words, he was equipped to use the "tactics of guerrilla warfare developed by the communists" in order to "defeat the Soviets and their political ideology."[193]

This translated into a series of sustained lobbying campaigns for the UNITA during Reagan's first term. By 1985, the Heritage Foundation, the American Security Council, the American Enterprise Institute, the Conservative Caucus, and the United States Council for World Freedom were all working on behalf of Savimbi's guerrillas.[194] Their passion, as journalist Thomas Frank has noted, operated much like the student Left's celebration of Ho Chi Minh and Che Guevara in the 1960s, but in reverse. Conservatives saw Savimbi as a towering muscular figure with a beard and bandolier, ready to forge a new path in the global South. He was "one of the few authentic heroes of our time," said Jeane Kirkpatrick at a Heritage Foundation fundraiser.[195] John Fisher, the long-serving head of the American Security Council, dubbed him the "foremost freedom-fighter against Soviet expansion."[196] Howard Phillips, the chairman of the Conservative Caucus, went so far as to speculate that "if Jonas Savimbi were an American citizen, he would be the Presidential candidate of the conservative movement in 1988."[197] He was a guerrilla that conservatives could love, an armed anticommunist with all the right talking points who could offset conservatives' support for apartheid.

For all of the ways in which Savimbi helped U.S. conservatives appear less racist, his struggle was always bound up with apartheid South Africa's anticommunist mission. And Americans understood that. As Howard Phillips argued, "The real issue ... is whether we will permit the Soviet Union to replace South Africa as the dominant power in the region."[198] Moreover, Americans' love for Savimbi elided the messier details of his past—his life as a Marxist, his continued faith in state economic planning, his collaboration with the Portuguese, and his frightful record of human rights abuses, including the recruitment of soldiers by force, the destruction of public marketplaces and private farms, and the kidnapping and assassination of civilians, foreign aid workers, and rivals.[199]

Americans managed Savimbi's questionable history by celebrating his physicality. Of all of the anticommunist guerrillas they championed in the 1980s, none received so much attention to his body as Savimbi did. A writer from *Soldier of Fortune* offered a typical description. After meeting Savimbi for the first time, he wrote "Physically, Savimbi is an impressive specimen: barrel-chested and narrow-hipped, clear-eyed with teeth that are large, white and very even; he has a broad nose, skin the color of well rubbed ebony and a curly black beard. Tieless and wearing a black leather jacket Savimbi strode into Washington's posh International Club on the balls of his feet, like a panther stalking its prey: Wary, alert and prepared for any challenge."[200] Such descriptions were commonplace, as Americans imagined Savimbi as a kind of superman whose very body indicated his martial prowess and, by extension, that of his troops. At the same time, if Savimbi's muscles and weapons showed his power, his blackness underscored his authenticity, for it made him a more credible and less racist voice of anticommunism in southern Africa, so often associated with white supremacy.

Beguiled by Savimbi, a handful of American activists and paramilitary enthusiasts flocked to his base in Angola. They toured the bush and watched Savimbi's troops in action, bringing back stories of courage and desperation. Predictably, *Soldier of Fortune* led the way. Robert Brown's correspondents had made their first contacts with Jonas Savimbi and his men in the late 1970s and they returned to Angola many times to give readers updates on his war against communism. They were among a very small number of foreign journalists to cover the war from inside the country.[201] *Soldier of Fortune*'s reporters would travel to South Africa, rendezvous with Savimbi's lieutenants, and then fly to Angola in small planes owned by sympathetic South Africans. When they arrived in Savimbi's camps, they were generally appalled by the poor quality of the UNITA's weapons. But they remained confident that, despite a serious lack of arms and supplies, the guerrillas were a feisty bunch on the verge of victory—if only the Reagan administration would give the right kind of covert aid and let them get on with their war.[202]

Travelogues about Savimbi's war in Angola might have gratified his diehard supporters, but they did little to change official U.S. policy during Reagan's first term. Without the legal basis to aid UNITA, Reagan administration officials, particularly CIA director Bill Casey, urged American citizens to work with third-party states and channel money through private networks and front companies. The Saudi royal family was initially the most forthcoming, offering on several occasions to "set up a company [and] channel funds through it, and buy equipment and supplies for anti-communist movements" in Angola and elsewhere—although those plans were never completed. Instead, the Saudis paid for UNITA soldiers to receive training in Morocco, whose monarchy was a close ally of the Saudi royal family.[203]

Despite attempts to circumvent it, the Clark Amendment prevented U.S. aid to the UNITA well into 1985. To change that, Savimbi decided to do what so many American businesses did when they wanted new legislation—he hired an expensive Beltway lobbyist. That was the law firm run by Paul Manafort, known as Black, Manafort, and Stone, which specialized in lobbying on behalf of authoritarian rulers.[204] To serve as Savimbi's voice in Washington, D.C., it requested $600,000 a year, which Savimbi met with profits from UNITA-controlled diamond mines where poor laborers—essentially slaves—pulled minerals from the earth under threat of violence.[205]

Savimbi made a wise choice in selecting Manafort's firm. His handler, lawyer Christopher Lehman, had just finished a stint in the White House helping Reagan line up support for arms sales to the Nicaraguan Contras. His campaign to sell Savimbi to Congress would be a kind of second act. After visiting Savimbi near his bush headquarters in Angola—which was then under siege by MPLA troops—Lehman created a multifaceted public-relations strategy. He shuffled Savimbi and his lieutenants around Washington to meet policymakers and private citizens. He sent monthly updates to Savimbi's headquarters in the remote southeastern corner of Angola. He gave the guerrilla leader pointers on his public image, on how to "answer his critics and compliment his patrons." He even helped Savimbi avoid quarrels with the Congressional Black Caucus, which regularly protested the UNITA's links to the apartheid state of South Africa.[206] Soon Savimbi started making regular appearances at meetings of the American Conservative Union and the annual Conservative Political Action Conference.[207]

While Savimbi's lieutenants toured Washington, his American sympathizers planned an international summit of freedom fighters deep inside UNITA-held territory. There they hoped guerrilla leaders from Asia, Africa, and Latin America would unite for the final push against global communism. Although touted as an authentic expression of international anticommunist solidarity, the meeting was actually the brainchild of two American activists. The first was Lewis Lehrman, a millionaire economist and businessman who ran a group called Citizens for America, which lobbied for conservative congressional candidates.[208] The other was Jack Wheeler, a self-styled professional adventurer who had spent the early 1980s on a tour of guerrilla wars in Nicaragua, Afghanistan, Mozambique, Cambodia, and elsewhere.[209] He spent so much time in rebel camps that his admirers christened him the "Indiana Jones of the right."[210]

If the world's anticommunist guerrillas were to make common cause, they would first have to meet face-to-face. Wheeler decided that the UNITA's headquarters in Jamba would be an ideal location for such a summit. It was not. Jamba was far away from international airports and there were few paved roads to get there—the "end of the world," as one reporter put it.[211] And, obviously, the Angolan government had no reason to grant visas to a bunch of guerrilla leaders who wished to make an alliance with their main enemy. So Lehrman and Wheeler turned to South Africa's National Student Federation—a front organization run by the South African military intelligence branch—which helped them fly their clients from airports in Cape Town and Johannesburg to Savimbi's remote fiefdom.[212]

The leaders of four major guerrilla movements gathered in Jamba—the Fuerza Democrática Nicaragüense, a faction of Afghan mujahedin, the Ethnic Liberation Organization of Laos, and of course Angola's UNITA.[213] A group of Cambodian guerrillas also sent a delegation, but they were unable reach Jamba due to problems with their visas. Rebels from Mozambique hoped to attend, but they got bogged down fighting.[214] Those who did make it to Jamba spent three days talking of the need to consolidate their forces. While their "liberation movements began as national struggles," Jonas Savimbi explained in his keynote speech, the rebels now recognized the "international solidarity" of all their causes. They all faced "the same enemy, the only empire that exists at the moment: the Soviet empire."[215]

Savimbi heralded the assembled delegates as the founding members of a Democratic International, each pursuing the "common goals of liberty and constitutional democracy" against the imperialist designs of the Soviet Union.[216] When Lewis Lehrman took the stage, he read a letter from President Reagan, conferring the official blessing of the White House. "Around the world," Reagan wrote, "we see people joining together to . . . free their countries from outside domination and alien ideology. It is a global trend and it is one of the most hopeful of our times."[217] News of the conference spread back to the United States, where paramilitary outfits such as Alabama's Civilian Military Assistance—then engaged in sending weapons and mercenaries to the Nicaraguan Contras—republished the rebels' declaration of solidarity in a monthly newsletter.[218]

The journalists who covered the Jamba conference treated it as a strange curiosity, a collection of guerrillas and activists sleeping in thatched huts, eating bush meat, and watching a Jimi Hendrix impersonator belt out tunes.[219] The Soviets dismissed it as a "meeting of counter-revolutionary scum and professional killers."[220] Yet many on the American Right imagined it as a major turning point in the Cold War, indeed in modern history. It was, in Jack Wheeler's estimation, an "historic meeting," proof that "these freedom fighters represent the most significant geopolitical development of our times."[221] Soon it would reach a critical mass, and the Soviets would be unable to respond. "By the time the Kremlin tries to stop it, the snowball will be too big," Wheeler predicted.[222]

The Jamba summit, in the words of journalist Thomas Frank, cemented U.S. conservatives' "identification with revolution" because it allowed them to imagine themselves as part of the guerrilla wars in Angola, Afghanistan, Nicaragua, and elsewhere—if not as soldiers, then as sympathizers and benefactors.[223] Beyond that ideational bond, the meeting legitimized new Washington-based think tanks devoted entirely to the world's freedom fighters. One was the Freedom Research Council, which Jack Wheeler founded to study to the problems of anticommunist guerrillas in Africa, Asia, and Latin America. Its monthly newsletter, the *Freedom Fighter*, published monthly reports of the Democratic International's wars in a half-dozen countries.[224] Sponsored by the Heritage Foundation's Paul Weyrich, the group also published a book-length study of the world's anticommunist insurgencies. Titled *Combat on Communist Territory*, it attempted to outline a "theory of anti-communist insurgency" that drew upon communist doctrines, particularly those of Mao Zedong, but also explained how armed anticommunists faced unique historical circumstances.[225]

After the Jamba conference, the Freedom Research Foundation started to work with another new group, the International Freedom Foundation, founded by conservative activist Jack Abramoff in 1986 to lobby on behalf of the South African apartheid government.[226] Although Abramoff told reporters that his group was a privately funded think tank, it was financed almost entirely by South Africa's military intelligence branch to the tune of $1.5 million a year. With those funds, it disseminated propaganda that portrayed all opponents to apartheid as Soviet puppets and celebrated the military operations of the

UNITA and the South African Defense Force in Angola. It also served as a dragnet for South African intelligence, gathering information about supporters of the African National Congress in Britain and the United States.[227]

The International Freedom Foundation gave Jack Abramoff the capital to write and produce the action movie *Red Scorpion*, in which the hulking actor Dolph Lundgren plays an elite Soviet soldier ordered to kill a rebel leader clearly based upon Jonas Savimbi. When he fails his mission, the Soviets imprison and torture Lundgren. But the blonde giant escapes to the African bush. He meets up with the guerrillas, learns of their struggle, turns anticommunist, and helps them win the day. Although the film's plot was an unoriginal mixture of several movies about guerrilla warfare in Africa, it was more than just another fantasy. Shot in the active warzone of Namibia with South African soldiers as extras, *Red Scorpion* fittingly illustrated the overlap between "private" anticommunist groups and secretive state agencies invested in the region's armed struggles.[228]

Despite all that, the Jamba conference did not result in any lasting alliance between rebel leaders in Asia, Latin America, and Africa. The Democratic International was mostly for show. Its members did not commit themselves to exchanging funds or weapons, or collaborating on military operations. They simply showed up in the bush, made some speeches, and went back to their own wars. Meanwhile their American supporters talked them up as part of a global revolution without offering much tangible aid—money, weapons, supplies, and the like—to make it happen.

However, the Jamba summit did enhance Savimbi's image in the United States.[229] Along with the speaking engagements and expensive banquet dinners sponsored by conservative groups, the conference helped more congressional leaders learn of his struggle. They started to put pressure on the president and officials from the Department of Defense and the CIA, calling for a resumption of U.S. military aid. If the Afghan mujahedin and the Nicaraguan Contras were worthy of American weapons, they asked, why not the Angolan guerrillas too?[230] They pointed out the gap between the rhetoric of the Reagan Doctrine, which proclaimed an offensive of anticommunist paramilitaries around the world, and the reality on the ground in Angola, where U.S. aid was sorely lacking.[231] Reading the Reagan Doctrine against the administration, they said it would only work if each rebel force could actually take on the communists and, if not defeat them outright, at least drag the Soviets into further conflict. After a sustained push from conservative legislators and their supporters in private groups, Congress voted to repeal the Clark Amendment in July 1985.[232]

The amendment's repeal paved the way for a resumption of American military aid. In early 1986, as Savimbi visited Washington on a trip sponsored by the American Security Council, he and Reagan met for the first time. The minutes of their White House talk remain classified. But a couple of weeks later, the administration announced that it would soon provide "covert aid" to Savimbi's rebel forces.[233] This was an awkward statement, an overt announcement of covert aid which, as some in the Reagan administration pointed out, undercut the whole purpose of clandestine operations. Covert action, they said, was supposed to remain a secret, not told to the entire world.[234] But Savimbi didn't mind. Back in Jamba, he erected a thirty-foot-tall banner depicting his meeting with Reagan in the Oval Office.[235]

The new U.S. aid program for Savimbi's guerrillas, like the one in place in Afghanistan, unfolded as an open secret. Americans, Soviets, Cubans, and Angolans—and everybody else for that matter—knew the administration was supporting Savimbi's forces even if they were not aware of the specifics, which involved smuggling weapons through the military of the Congo's dictator, Joseph Mobutu, a longtime friend of the United States. The notion of an overt covert assistance program thus operated not on a plane of strategy but of symbolism. It signified the Reagan administration's willingness to match the tough talk of the Reagan Doctrine with tangible aid for Angola's anticommunists. Aiming to please Savimbi's inflexible American allies, it obscured the aid's actual management from their gaze.

Despite Reagan's professed affinity for Savimbi and his announcement of the covert aid program, his administration moved cautiously after 1986. Many in the State Department, especially Assistant Secretary of State Chester Crocker, remained skeptical about Savimbi's potential to overthrow the MPLA. They were even less sanguine about his ability as a national leader.[236] Covert military aid to the UNITA was, therefore, not meant for waging an all-out war. Rather, it was to give the rebels just enough weapons to force the MPLA to a diplomatic settlement in which all parties would share power.[237] Predictably, these limits provoked the ire of Savimbi's faithful in the United States. They began calling for an open military program in the tens of millions of dollars. Some even advised Savimbi to refuse any covert military aid from the Reagan administration, though Savimbi was wise enough to accept whatever help he could get.[238]

In calling for an open aid program, Savimbi's supporters reversed the logic that had undergirded their efforts in Angola so far—as well as similar campaigns to aid guerrillas in Nicaragua and Afghanistan. Whereas many had argued for covert aid to the Contras and the mujahedin, especially programs run exclusively through the executive branch or through private organizations, an open aid program would be subject to debate on the floor of Congress, where it could be killed by liberal opponents. Ironically, as the Reagan administration and its allies in Congress overturned a decade-long ban and began sending millions of dollars' worth of weapons and supplies to the UNITA rebels, Jonas Savimbi's supporters insisted that the administration had abandoned him.

The divisions that emerged between Savimbi's hardline supporters and the Reagan administration over military aid radiated into concerns about U.S. businesses in Angola, and revealed similar contradictions. The Angolan economy depended heavily on the export of petroleum. During the era of Portugal's rule, the U.S.-based Gulf Oil Company, a subsidiary of Chevron, had operated major oil fields off the coast of the Cabinda province. When the MPLA took power, the company negotiated a new contract with the new regime.[239] This deal generated significant revenue for the Angolan state, helping the MPLA strengthen its grasp on power. Of course, Savimbi was aghast that an American company would operate in a communist country. It reminded him of Vladimir Lenin's dictum that capitalists "will sell the rope by which they hang themselves."[240] The deal also dismayed those Americans who had thrown their weight behind Savimbi and the UNITA. They questioned why the U.S. government prevented American firms from doing business in South Africa, a stout anticommunist ally, but allowed them to work with a Marxist regime in Angola.[241]

The uproar over the Gulf Oil contract reversed the logic of the free market for which U.S. conservatives claimed to be fighting. After all, Chevron/Gulf was only doing what any good capitalist enterprise should do—exploiting an opportunity for financial gain. Yet here was a scenario in which the omniscient hand of the market had failed to distribute wealth in the right way. John Singlaub and others called for a boycott of Chevron/Gulf, hoping to pressure the corporation into renouncing its contract with the MPLA regime.[242] Jack Wheeler went so far as to urge Savimbi to attack Gulf Oil's property. It was an absurd scenario—an American activist asking an Angolan guerrilla to attack the property of an American company in the name of democracy and the free market.[243] Although some members of the Reagan administration tried to dissuade U.S. corporations from doing business with the MPLA government, their efforts had no meaningful effect on business in Angola.[244] The oil kept flowing.

The Chevron/Gulf controversy was soon overshadowed by the UNITA's meager results on the battlefield. While the $20 million in U.S. military aid had helped Savimbi's men mount some large offensives against the MPLA, they never seriously challenged the regime's power. The war remained stalemated for the next few years, even as the Reagan administration expanded the sum of covert aid to $40 million. During this time, Savimbi's diehard supporters in the United States maintained their calls for an open aid program, but they found few in the White House or Congress willing to listen. Nevertheless, their lobbying on behalf of Savimbi had helped put his struggle in the minds of American lawmakers and that had translated into a significant covert aid program, reversing a decade-long ban on sending arms to Angola.

Their work, however, was far less ambitious than their efforts in Nicaragua, where private groups had managed to raise serious money for weapons, supplies, training programs, and where Americans had served as private military advisers or mercenaries. The remoteness of the conflict in Angola and the complexity of the region's politics prompted Americans to direct their efforts primarily through domestic channels—particularly lobbying groups that raised awareness and pressured the U.S. government to act. Their campaign to help Jonas Savimbi's freedom fighters made them feel a part of his war. But it also showed the limits of what privately funded anticommunist activism could do, even in the Reagan era.

---

The notion that the U.S. government was failing to support anticommunist rebels—and that private groups could fill in for the state—emerged in other conflicts, with ever diminishing results. In Southeast Asia, Americans turned their efforts to several armed groups engaged in a string of conflicts known as the Third Indochina War.[245] In 1978, the Vietnamese army invaded neighboring Cambodia to force the Khmer Rouge, a brutal Marxist regime that murdered more than a million of its own citizens, from power. After a year of fighting, the triumphant Vietnamese had relegated the Khmer Rouge to the countryside, from which it launched periodic guerrilla attacks against the new Vietnamese-supported state, the People's Republic of Kampuchea. Just as the ousted communists began their counterattacks, remnants of Cambodia's former monarchy started their own guerrilla campaigns. So did antiroyalist and anticommunist rebel groups, such as the Khmer People's National Liberation Front. By 1980, a half dozen rebel factions were fighting in Cambodia, against the new government and with each other.[246] In Laos, the communist Pathet Lao took power in 1975 after decades of fighting with anticommunist guerrillas, particularly among the highland-dwelling Hmong people, who had been armed and trained by the CIA.[247] As the Pathet Lao consolidated power and collectivized land holdings, many began to resist. In turn, the Laotian communists turned to Vietnam for support. The Vietnamese leadership sent a few battalions of soldiers to help their neighbor combat the growing popular resistance, especially the resilient bands of anticommunist guerrillas operating in the mountains.[248]

Although these wars were complex and shifting affairs, the Reagan administration and its supporters saw a clear pattern of Soviet expansionism. In their eyes, Vietnam was not helping kindred nationalist movements but rather serving as a proxy for Soviet efforts to gain a greater foothold in Southeast Asia. As such, the United States needed to find a way to counter their moves without making the same mistakes of the Vietnam War, particularly the escalating use of U.S. soldiers. Shortly after Reagan took office, Bill Casey and the CIA began flirting with the idea of sending aid to anticommunist guerrillas in Laos and Cambodia. But it was not until 1982 that the agency received the green light to send non-lethal covert aid to the three main resistance groups in Cambodia, which had recently formed a quarrelsome coalition.[249] The amount of U.S. aid, however—roughly $5 million a year—was almost meaningless, only able to purchase a small number of vehicles, food, uniforms, medicine, and other supplies.[250] It mostly served as a symbol of the administration's willingness to fight communism through covert warfare, to carry out the pledges of the Reagan Doctrine. Many in the administration were far more concerned with other conflicts, especially Nicaragua and Afghanistan, and did not want to upset the delicate balance of support they had built in Congress for those covert actions. Cambodia, then, was a sideshow to more important struggles elsewhere. Laos hardly mattered, as U.S. policymakers rarely considered sending covert aid to the Laotian resistance. For the most part, the Reagan administration followed the lead of the Association of Southeast Asian Nations (ASEAN), which sought a diplomatic rather than military solution to the armed conflicts in Southeast Asia.[251]

Outgunned and outmanned, rebel groups in Laos and Cambodia turned to the anticommunist international to press their cause. In the early 1980s, the Khmer People's National Liberation Front (KPNLF) began sending delegates to meetings of the WACL and other events, where they constructed themselves in the same terms as guerrillas in Nicaragua, Afghanistan, Angola, and elsewhere. Laotian rebels made their rounds too, traveling to conferences in San Diego, Dallas, Luxembourg, and Taiwan, and exchanging letters with John Singlaub and other conservative leaders in the United States.[252] At the same time, rebel commanders from Southeast Asia sought to pressure the Reagan administration by writing to the president and high-ranking officials. For instance, Son Sann, a politician who had returned to Cambodia after a lengthy exile to start the KPNLF, maintained an impassioned if sporadic correspondence with Reagan. In his letters, he portrayed his people's fight as a "sacred struggle for national liberation, for the restoration of peace, justice, freedom, independence, neutrality, and non-alignment in Cambodia, and for the re-establishment of peace stability, and security in the Southeast Asian region."[253] He, like other rebel leaders in Southeast Asia and their supporters in the United States, wanted to know whether Reagan would "consider taking such powerful measures like those [he had] taken in Latin America" in their own countries.[254]

At the same time, rebel groups rallied their exiled countrymen in the United States and elsewhere. They played to exiles' memories of home, participating in the construction of what historian Her Vang has termed "refugee nationalism."[255] Laotian rebel leader Pa Kao Her, of the Ethnic Liberation Organization of Laos, canvassed Hmong communities in California and Minnesota, presenting his "liberation strategies to Hmong leaders" and outlining a "plan to run Laos once the country was independent."[256] The royalist and anticommunist factions of the Cambodian resistance did the same, meeting with their kinfolk in California and elsewhere.[257] As rebel leaders reached out to exile communities, they attempted to build grassroots fundraising programs in which ordinary people could donate small sums from their paychecks to purchase much-needed weapons and supplies—paramilitary remittances, in a certain sense. One such campaign, run from a KPNLF office in Thailand, asked for donations of $40 to purchase "basic personal equipment" and other sundries.[258] Similar pleas for donations appeared in *Soldier of Fortune* magazine.[259] As one writer put it, "Any private citizen who wants to give more than just moral support to help the KPNLF rebels can send money. Forty dollars will buy two uniforms, one pair of shoes, two pairs of socks, knapsack, plastic sheet and a scarf for one soldier. That's not a bad deal."[260]

By funneling resources through these paramilitary networks, Americans and their allies in Southeast Asian exile communities believed they could sidestep the cumbersome apparatus of government, not unlike donating to a private charity. As one writer put it, "Contributions will not be channeled through any bureaucratic organization. Your money will reach the destination where it will do the most good."[261] Yet the editors at *Soldier of Fortune* were also aware that numerous hurdles stood in their way. When one reader questioned, "How come you bleeding hearts don't smuggle guns to the people so they can protect themselves?," a staffer—possibly Robert Brown—responded that is was "easier said than done. Look at a map of SE Asia. Obtaining weapons is only half of the problem. Assuming one could obtain a large quantity of weapons ... the cost of inserting them into a denied area would be tremendous."[262]

As Laotian and Cambodian guerrillas raised money for war, they also sought common cause with armed rebels in Vietnam. They wrote letters to one another and made furtive plans for joint operations, most of which never got off the ground.[263] Instead, the Vietnamese guerrillas received most of their funds, limited as they were, from exile communities in Los Angeles, San Diego, San Francisco, and other West Coast cities.[264] In these enclaves, a stream of wild-eyed dreamers and ex-military men—most notably Nguyen Cao Ky, former prime minister of South Vietnam—talked about returning home, organizing the scattered pockets of resistance that remained, and then taking on the communist government.[265] In their imaginings, a small band of exiled guerrillas could incite tens or perhaps hundreds of thousands in Vietnam to join their war.[266] As a matter of routine, exiled Vietnamese leaders, like other hopeful guerrillas, stressed their plans would not require the sacrifice of American lives.[267] "Give me the guns, and we'll kick them out," Ky liked to say.[268]

That militancy was matched by a penchant for action at home. In the 1980s, Vietnamese exiles in Los Angeles, San Francisco, and other cities often clashed with one another, sometimes resorting to murder to silence a critic or squelch a rival. Such was the fate of Nguyen Van Luy, a left-wing editor who had opposed U.S. intervention in Vietnam. In 1984, a right-wing Vietnamese paper in Orange County accused him of being a communist. A few days later someone shot him and his wife. He survived but she died. A group calling itself the Vietnamese Organization to Exterminate Communists and Restore the Nation claimed responsibility. "The war is still going on here," explained one San Jose police officer tasked with investigating political violence within Vietnamese exile communities.[269]

The violence in California was real enough, but most privately organized plots in Vietnam, Laos, and Cambodia never went anywhere. The few that did were utter failures—as when, in 1987, 200 fighters, mostly "American citizens of Vietnamese origin and Australian-Vietnamese," attempted an incursion into Vietnam's Quang Tri province only to be routed by Vietnamese regulars. According to intelligence reports, more than three-quarters died. The operation prompted American officials to ask, "Who's behind this extremely ill-planned venture?"[270] That same year, the leader of the largest group of exiled Vietnamese paramilitaries, the National Liberation Front of Hoang Co Minh, was killed by communist soldiers while leading his men though the jungles of Laos. The reality in Vietnam was that it was "nearly impossible to foment a mass uprising against the Hanoi regime."[271]

Guerrillas in Laos and Cambodia fared better than their counterparts in Vietnam, mostly because the new communist regimes in those countries were never able to gain full military control of their hinterlands, where the guerrillas operated. Still, their overseas organizations struggled to have any meaningful impact on the wars in Laos and Cambodia. Campaigns that targeted exile communities generated little in the way of private donations. To be sure, the persistent lobbying efforts by Cambodia's royalist and anticommunist factions did procure more official aid from the U.S. government, which helped the guerrillas press for a power-sharing agreement in the late 1980s.[272] But they had failed in their primary objective—forcing the communists from power.

American interest in the wars in Cambodia, Laos, and Vietnam often had less to do with the aspirations of anticommunist rebels than it did with concerns about the fate of the United States' missing servicemen from the Vietnam War. After the war, many Americans—Vietnam veterans, the families of missing servicemen, and others—came to believe that the United States government had abandoned several thousand U.S. soldiers and pilots in Vietnam. That idea was voiced most persistently by the families of missing soldiers who organized the National League of Families, demanding that American officials locate and rescue their loved ones. Activists assembled a mosaic of evidence—the recollections of former POWs and dubious reports from sources claiming to have seen Americans in prison camps long after the war's end—to prove that American officials were lying about the United States' POWs and MIAs to protect the peace with communist Vietnam.[273]

A few retired covert warriors and Vietnam veterans decided that if the government was not going to rescue the abandoned soldiers, they would—a conviction that led them into the messy wars in Cambodia and Laos. One of these paramilitary patriots was Lt. Colonel James "Bo" Gritz, an ex-Green Beret and Vietnam veteran who organized a series of private missions to save Americans POWs trapped in Vietnam. In 1981, with the backing of the Reagan administration and funds from the National League of Families, Gritz and a few other Vietnam veterans traveled to Laos to photograph the prison camps and collect intelligence.[274] Although that expedition brought back scant evidence, Gritz persisted.[275] The following year he led a team of four Americans and fifteen Laotian rebels in a mission to rescue American POWs who were supposedly interned along the border between Laos and Vietnam. They failed again. Ambushed by a local militia and then run out of the country by the Pathet Lao, Gritz lost two Laotian rebels and left an American behind.[276] He and other Americans mounted several more private rescue missions over the next few years with the same disappointing results.[277]

The only winners in these schemes were rebel groups in Laos who managed to secure large sums of cash from concerned Americans by promising to find missing servicemen and then never doing anything.[278] Still, Gritz's popularity within POW/MIA circles boosted his political appeal at home. In 1987, Willis Carto, the white supremacist who ran the Liberty Lobby, tapped Gritz to join the presidential ticket of Klansman David Duke. Although, the campaign "more often resembled a circus act on a circuit for paramilitary advocates" than a genuine bid for the nation's highest office, Gritz used his celebrity to sell the rights to his life story, which actors Clint Eastwood and William Shatner bought for $40,000.[279]

The tale of Bo Gritz never made it to the silver screen, but other films offered similar stories. Actor Chuck Norris made the POW/MIA issue into a cottage industry, starring in a trio of films, the *Missing in Action* franchise, in which he uses stealth tactics and superior firepower to rescue U.S. soldiers from Vietnam.[280] Better known—and better scripted, shot, acted, and directed—was *Rambo: First Blood Part II*. In it, Sylvester Stallone reprises his role as John Rambo, a Vietnam veteran tortured by the experience of war without victory, who embarks on a mission to save U.S. soldiers in Southeast Asia. Throughout the film, Rambo lays waste to the predictable enemies, Vietnamese soldiers and their Soviet commanders. But his main foe is an American named Murdock, an archetypically effete bureaucrat who intends to betray Rambo and close the POW/MIA issue forever. Operating against orders, Rambo fights to save his comrades before the government can pull the plug.[281] Wildly popular with audiences, *Rambo: First Blood Part II* harnessed the antigovernment sentiment that propelled Bo Gritz's real-life campaigns, while offering an unmistakably macho vision of how Americans should deal with their enemies. Reagan loved the film for precisely that reason. Screening it in the White House, he remarked, "Boy, after seeing 'Rambo' last night, I know what to do the next time this happens," jokingly referring to the ongoing hostage crisis in Lebanon, where militants held dozens of Americans for ransom for months on end.[282]

*Rambo: First Blood Part II* and its lesser counterparts also bore out the same assumptions that motivated Americans' real-life paramilitary campaigns to rescue abandoned soldiers. In both realms, Asians served as little more than props in a story of American suffering and salvation, revenge and redemption. Seizing upon popular fascination with POW/MIAs, Gritz made himself into the poster boy for the cause, but his faulty reports and foolish actions generated opprobrium from others concerned about America's missing servicemen. John Singlaub was one. Having spent three years in Vietnam, he was heavily invested in the POW/MIA issue and devoted significant effort raising awareness and soliciting funds for other private intelligence-gathering and rescue missions. Singlaub always doubted Gritz's sincerity and the accuracy of his intelligence, and despised Gritz's connections with Willis Carto.[283]

So did the staff at *Soldier of Fortune* magazine. For much of the 1980s, Robert Brown and his colleagues ridiculed Gritz, not so much for his intentions—after all, *Soldier of Fortune* was a primary outlet for information and rumors about POWs and MIAs—but for taking money from the families of missing servicemen and then failing to deliver.[284] With funds from the National League of Families, *Soldier of Fortune* launched its own missions to unearth proof of living American soldiers, as well as the remains of the deceased, taking over where the "prissy lethargic bureaucrats" and the "bungling private operatives had failed."[285] Like Gritz's abortive incursions, the magazine's missions never brought back definitive proof that American soldiers had been left behind, let alone rescue any of them.[286] They did, however, generate stimulating stories about the smoldering guerrilla war in Laos. Bob Brown and his team of Americans fought with the faction known as the Lao United Liberation Front, efforts that earned Brown an honorary commission as major general in the guerrilla outfit.[287]

The Reagan administration alternately offered support and disdain for these private paramilitary endeavors. Behind closed doors, high-ranking officials encouraged such missions and sometimes gave state resources to make them happen—support that probably led Gritz to construct himself as an agent of the U.S. government in his dealings with Laotian rebels.[288] But when Gritz's schemes failed, the administration quickly distanced itself from his ill-planned adventures. As one official told Gritz's supporters, "private cross border forays such as this are a major obstacle to progress," both in the search for American POWs and MIAs and the United States' larger foreign-policy goals in Southeast Asia.[289]

The administration's two-track policy served mainly as public theater, as did its support for private paramilitary missions in Nicaragua, Afghanistan, Angola, and other parts of the world. By lending rhetorical and material support to these missions, the administration demonstrated to its supporters just how far it was willing to go to fulfill their hopes and dreams. At the same, by outsourcing the functions of the state to private groups, the administration sought to avoid any potential punishment or embarrassment that may have come from the missions. Since the executive branch did not run these programs, or at least not entirely, administration officials believed they could avoid responsibility for their misdeeds. They were wrong about that.

---

The private paramilitary campaigns launched by Americans in the 1980s represented the most concerted effort to make the anticommunist international a true force in geopolitics. Since the 1950s, Americans and their overseas allies had talked of fomenting wars of national liberation to defeat communism once and for all. In the 1980s, a globe-spanning network of activists, retired soldiers, mercenaries, and guerrillas others harnessed those discourses, moving the anticommunist international from propaganda to paramilitary action. By linking wealthy American donors to the world's anticommunist rebels, they sought to circumvent those parts of the state they believed to be ineffective, obstructionist, or hostile—Congress, the State Department, the Justice Department, and so on. And they hoped that by doing so, they could wield some of the power and influence that governments and militaries possessed, but without any real accountability.

That was what made anticommunist guerrillas so attractive to conservative activists in the Reagan era, and why they spent so much time, effort, and money working on their behalf. In the rebels of Nicaragua, Afghanistan, Angola, Cambodia, Vietnam, and Laos, Americans saw an idealized vision of combat in which ordinary people took up arms to defend their homes and nations from the totalitarian forces that threatened them. This was a world in which civilians could do something to defeat communism, to become independent agents of historical change on the global stage. Meanwhile, as conservative activists, wealthy donors, retired covert warriors, and others worked to aid anticommunist guerrillas around the world, they were simultaneously attempting to manage and make sense of their own place within the United States, their own roles as revolutionaries at home. So they drew upon and contributed to a vein of paramilitary culture in the United States.

Yet their hope for an international anticommunist revolution was never fully realized. In part, that was because Americans never really understood just what their allies abroad wanted out of their relationships. Confronted with disparate rebel groups, American conservatives saw a global struggle in the offing. But it was more than an inability to grasp complex geopolitics that doomed their paramilitary endeavors. Many of their campaigns broke the law. That was, ultimately, what did them in. The revelations of the Iran-Contra scandal put an end to the Right's armed anticommunist revolution before it ever really got going. If indeed if it ever could have.

# Conclusion

## The Twilight of the Anticommunist International

On the morning of October 6, 1986, a C-123 aircraft departed from a secret CIA base in El Salvador loaded with ten tons of ammunition and gear. Behind the controls were two CIA men and a seventeen-year-old Nicaraguan radio operator. In the back of the plane, Eugene Hasenfus, an ex-Marine from Wisconsin who had served in Vietnam, prepared to kick the supplies out of the cargo bay.[1] Hasenfus had traveled down to Nicaragua after being laid off from his job as a steelworker, hoping to find some of the adventure he had missed since returning from Vietnam.[2] He was the only one wearing a parachute, which he had borrowed from his brother.[3]

Shortly after the plane entered Nicaraguan airspace, Sandinista troops shot it out of the sky with a surface-to-air missile. As the plane careened out of control, Hasenfus leapt out and pulled the cord on his chute. The others had mocked him for his caution, but it saved his life. He tried to flee the crash site, but Sandinista soldiers found him the next day.[4] They handcuffed Hasenfus, marched him back to their base, and began showing him off to the media.[5] Within a few hours, Hasenfus's capture made international news. In captivity, he revealed everything he knew about the secret supply operations. His testimony, combined with revelations coming out of Lebanon, Iran, and Washington, confirmed what so many had alleged over the previous two years—that the Reagan administration was still supporting the Contras, in defiance of Congress.[6]

At the time, John Singlaub was on the other side of the world in the Philippines, supposedly working out a murky deal as a private security consultant for a group of ex-military men seeking sunken Japanese treasure. Others said he was there trying to persuade the Philippine Army to hire U.S. "advisers and trainers" in its fight against a band of resilient leftist guerrillas.[7] Whatever his true purpose, the news of the ill-fated CIA flight and the capture of Hasenfus proved a major distraction. The CIA and Oliver North had failed yet again, he thought. In his eyes, the flight was plagued by poor planning from the start. It should have been done at night. They should have used a smaller plane. They should have left their wallets and identity cards at home, along with the log book of other clandestine supply flights. Singlaub was sure that these mistakes never would have happened on one of his shipments.[8]

And so he was shocked a few days later when major news outlets began to report that the plane was a part of his Contra operation. Some unnamed Reagan administration officials had told the *New York Times* and other papers that Singlaub owned the plane and was running the whole show.[9] The White House, they claimed, had nothing to do with it.[10] By pinning the downed plane on Singlaub, the administration was trying to pull media attention away from the illegal operation run by Oliver North and other administration officials while they destroyed as much incriminating evidence as possible.[11] Singlaub's notoriety within the anticommunist international made him an easy scapegoat. After all, he had spent the last few years touring the world as a private citizen, raising money to buy weapons and supplies for the Contras and other anticommunist guerrillas. His efforts did more than just help anticommunists abroad. It also took "the heat off of those who were trying to be more covert in their actions"—men such as Oliver North and CIA Director Bill Casey. But now, as the scandal that would become Iran-Contra erupted, Singlaub spurned the role of fall guy.[12]

The administration's ruse did not stop the deluge of inquiries. Within a few weeks, investigators revealed a conspiracy of startling proportions. Starting in 1984, when the congressional ban on U.S. aid to the Contras went into effect, administration officials had sold arms to Iran to free American hostages in Lebanon and then used the proceeds to fund the Contras. Known by its participants as the Enterprise, the scheme utilized an "elaborate private network" to circumvent congressional authority and, in so doing, violated many U.S. laws—not to mention Reagan's avowed policy of not dealing with terrorists or their supporters.[13]

As congressional leaders began a year-long investigation into the Iran-Contra operation, they first focused on how far up the executive command chain it went. Their most burning questions centered upon President Reagan: How much did he know and when did he know it? Did he give the orders? If not, what was his actual role? However, after a presidentially appointed body tasked with the initial inquiries into Iran-Contra released a report spotlighting Reagan's "lax management style" and "diminished mental acuity," congressional investigators shifted their attention to lower-ranking members of the administration who ran the day-to-day operations—Oliver North; his deputy in the field, Robert Owen; Elliot Abrams, Assistant Secretary of State for Inter-American affairs; and Lewis Tambs, U.S. Ambassador to Costa Rica. These men were the primary architects of Iran-Contra operation. How, investigators wondered, did they concoct an intricate funding scheme, run an international arms pipeline, and manage a parallel foreign policy without any official mandate from Congress?

These were important questions that targeted some of the most troubling aspects of Reagan's presidency—the eagerness of administration officials to circumvent the system of checks-and-balances and their reliance upon paramilitary enterprises to do so.[14] In the end, however, almost all of the guilty parties avoided jail time, whether through stymied prosecutions, plea bargains, weak sentences, successful appeals, or presidential pardons. And Reagan survived the most serious challenge to his presidency even though investigators placed the "ultimate responsibility for the events" at his feet.[15]

Thus, the Iran-Contra investigations and prosecutions failed to punish, or even hold accountable, many of the operation's key players. But they also failed another way. For their overwhelming focus on the Reagan administration's role in the Iran-Contra operation obscured the world of anticommunist internationalism that surrounded it. In so doing, Congress missed many opportunities to examine how American citizens—conservative activists, mercenaries, retired military officers like John Singlaub, and others—had worked with an array of people outside of the United States to support anticommunist guerrillas abroad, not only in Nicaragua but also Angola, Afghanistan, Laos, Cambodia, and elsewhere. Moreover, congressional leaders were unable to see that activism as part of a movement dating back to the 1950s. Without that context, they tended to attribute conservatives' private anticommunist initiatives to the malfeasance of the Reagan administration, an error that exaggerated the power of White House officials and diminished that of folks who labored in the shadow of the state.

But the paramilitary endeavors undertaken by U.S. conservatives and their overseas allies in the 1980s were not simply an outgrowth of the Reagan administration's extralegal operations. Instead, they culminated decades of international collaboration between anticommunist Americans and kindred forces abroad. Since the late 1950s, when Marvin Liebman organized a congress of anticommunist groups from four continents, U.S. conservatives had dreamt of using private money to build a global movement which they would then lead to victory. The paramilitary activities of the Reagan era did not break with that history. Rather, activists like John Singlaub took those impulses and ideas—particularly the notion that private groups could succeed where state institutions failed—and extended them further into the realms of covert warfare.

Iran-Contra halted these campaigns. For the scandal required their ringleaders, John Singlaub among them, to spend long periods of time testifying in Congress and preparing legal defenses rather than working overseas. Within a few years, the collapse of the Soviet Union made the anticommunist international all but obsolete, a relic of a struggle that no longer existed. Although guerrilla wars still raged in many parts of the world, leftists in Asia, Africa, and Latin America could no longer count on the Soviet Union for aid. As Soviet weapons, supplies, and advisors vanished from the world stage, so did the anticommunist international.

---

Even though the Iran-Contra hearings did not spur a serious reckoning with what had gone wrong at the highest levels of U.S. foreign policymaking, they made for remarkable spectacle. For months on end, witnesses appeared before Congress describing secret arms deals, shadowy go-betweens, misfit mercenaries, executive cover-ups, and a general contempt for U.S. and international law. Televised nationally, the hearings offered two competing narratives about the role of the state under the Reagan administration. Depending on one's politics, Iran-Contra signified either systemic disregard for the law amongst the highest ranks of the administration or the lengths to which true American patriots would to go to defend the United States and its allies. One of the Senate's lead counsels summed up the latter view—the Iran-Contra affair stemmed from a "mentality" that "made it patriotic to lie to Congress, to circumvent checks and balances through covert actions, and to create the Enterprise to do what the CIA was not permitted to do."[16]

The hearings held more particular meanings for those called as witnesses. To them, the congressional spotlight was an occasion to defend their actions and condemn those of others. Their disagreements centered on three things—strategies, motives, and profits. John Singlaub expressed his views over several days in May 1987. He appeared before Congress unrepentant, mostly because Special Prosecutor Lawrence Walsh had already told Singlaub he would not face criminal charges. His time before the committee was also made easier by the nearly universal respect that its members gave him. They knew of his storied career as a special-operations soldier in France, Manchuria, and Vietnam, and seemed reticent to challenge such a dedicated serviceman.[17]

Confident with that appreciation, Singlaub began by explaining his actions as those of a private citizen, albeit one with "combat experience in four wars."[18] He was not working as an adjunct of the Reagan administration, nor had he been hired by Oliver North. His attempts to aid the Contras—and the rest of the world's anticommunist guerrillas, for that matter—stemmed from his convictions about freedom, democracy, and the like.[19] But his activities were never as private as he claimed. His work was often more like that of a contractor hired to do a job than a volunteer working for a charity—even though he did manage to secure large amounts of private donations for the Contras.[20]

To defend himself from such charges, Singlaub went on the offensive. He spent much of his time before Congress offering withering critiques of the administration and of Oliver North's operation. In his eyes, retired Air Force general Richard Secord, who had managed the Enterprise's supply flights, like the one carrying Eugene Hasenfus, was a profiteer, gouging millions from the arms deals to line his own pockets.[21] The same went for cronies like Carl "Spitz" Channell, who siphoned millions of dollars from the Enterprise into a maze of personal bank accounts. As for the rogues' gallery of Iranian, Israeli, and Lebanese arms merchants and middlemen that made the secret transactions of the Enterprise possible, Singlaub testified that covert operations required dealing with shady characters. But he still believed that Oliver North had chosen his collaborators unwisely.

Singlaub reserved his harshest words for North, who emerged as a conservative icon during the hearings. For many right-leaning Americans, North was a hero. Good-looking, knowledgeable, and articulate, he was a devoted Catholic, family man, and career soldier who exuded a beguiling air of masculinity and faith, confidence and belligerence.[22] But Singlaub knew a man who was willing to lie and impugn others to advance his own aspirations. Moreover, North seemed incapable of running a successful covert operation. He had failed by the most important measure—getting caught. Beyond that, North's scheme to channel weapons to the Iranian government and Lebanese terrorists imperiled the security of the United States.[23] Singlaub later wrote that he "had learned too much" about North's "moral courage to ever respect him again."[24]

Even though North's operation had revealed many of the problems that emerged when one tried to privatize covert operations, Singlaub still insisted that such schemes were the way forward. When Congress brought up his plan to "create a conduit for maintaining a continuous flow of Soviet weapons and technology to be utilized by the United States in support of Freedom Fighters in Nicaragua, Afghanistan, Angola, Cambodia, Ethiopia, et cetera," Singlaub defended it in no uncertain terms. By using private money to wage secret wars, Singlaub said, his scheme did not require "funds from the taxpayer in order to carry out the national policy of this country." Thus, it enabled the administration and concerned civilians to undertake operations "which are generally covert" to support the "democratic Resistance forces around the world."[25] This meant removing Congress, and all of its bureaucratic infighting, from the equation. As one senator summed it up, Singlaub's plan, if "fully developed," would produce a "flow of weapons ... all over the world without the knowledge of Congress or the State Department ... and without accountability."[26]

---

Yet John Singlaub's plan was never fully developed. In the final months of 1985, nearly a year before the Iran-Contra scandal erupted, the Internal Revenue Service had already begun investigating the tax-exempt status of Singlaub's United States Council for World Freedom on the basis that the group was clearly not a charity and was possibly engaged in illegal or extralegal activities.[27] As the IRS targeted his group, Singlaub also found himself in the crosshairs of a pair of investigative journalists. In early 1986, Scott Anderson and Jon Lee Anderson (no relation) published a book-length exposé that delved into the history of the World Anti-Communist League and Singlaub's relationship to it. The frontispiece, excerpted from a letter the authors received from a former League member, said it all: "In considering the World Anti-Communist League you have entered a world of ideological fanaticism, radicalism, ignorance, and fear which is almost beyond comprehension of the average American ... your subject matter is a collection of oriental fascists, militarists, right-wing terrorists who put bombs in civilian airliners, death squads, assassins, criminals and many people who are as much opposed to democracy as they are to communism. You are in some danger yourself."[28]

The book, however, was better at documenting connections between right-wing groups from different parts of the world than explaining them. It gave little attention to the historical processes that enabled those connections, let alone the larger world of the international Right in which they evolved. Much of it simply catalogued the most distasteful people who had shown up at WACL meetings over the years. It also tended to hyperbolize some of the League's activities while glossing over the many conflicts that erupted between its members. At times, the WACL appeared as a vast right-wing conspiracy. Its more quotidian and symbolic features—the planning of international conferences and speaking tours, for instance—rarely appeared in the book's analysis of what the WACL was all about.

Still, the authors' vignettes about the Nazi collaborators in the Anti-Bolshevik Bloc of Nations and the death squad-leaders in the Confederación

Anticomunista Latinoamericana evoked the violence and extremism that had become hallmarks of the anticommunist international. For that reason, the book caused a stir among the American Left, triggering yet more hostile articles about Singlaub's activities in major newspapers and publications such as the *Covert Action Information Bulletin*.[29] Predictably, the book had far less influence within conservative circles in the United States. Most commentators on the right simply dismissed its claims, easy enough since its authors provided scant evidence.[30] As Singlaub explained to a reporter, "these charges have surfaced before from people who spend all their waking hours trying to spike the work of the WACL. Each time, these charges have been successfully proven to be false."[31]

Popular scrutiny fed conspiracy theories. In early 1986, just as *Inside the League* hit bookshelves, a newly formed legal group called the Christic Institute filed a civil lawsuit in a Florida court alleging that John Singlaub, Richard Secord, Ted Shackley, and other ex–covert warriors had been operating as a "secret team," controlling the clandestine branches of American foreign policy. They were, as one reporter put it, a "shadow government, arming international vigilantes and carrying on an outlaw foreign policy, secure in the belief that the White House will shield them."[32] Going back to the Vietnam War, the Christics said, these men had been running all sorts of illegal covert operations. When they left the armed services and the CIA, they had started smuggling weapons into Central America and drugs into the United States on the return flights.[33] There was some truth to these assertions, yet the Christics wrongly fingered Singlaub and those around him as cocaine traffickers.[34] But for the Christics, drug smuggling was just the tip of the iceberg. They alleged that Singlaub and others had even conspired to murder those who got too close to their operation. For proof of that, they pointed to a 1984 bombing at a Contra outpost in Nicaragua that claimed the lives of three journalists and injured several more. The Christics placed the blame for the bombing at the feet of the "secret team" and asked for $24 million in damages.[35] Pressed forward by left-leaning activists and lawyers, the Christics' suit ironically received warm support from Bo Gritz, the right-wing paramilitary patriot, who somehow slotted Singlaub and his fellow defendants into a global plot to establish a "one-world government."[36]

Over the next two years, the Christic lawsuit made major headlines in the press and major headaches for its targets. Singlaub and the other defendants struggled to raise hundreds of thousands of dollars for their legal defenses, often by soliciting donations from concerned citizens and conservative groups.[37] Many of those who gave money did so not only to defend the accused but also to protect the very idea of "private anti-communist initiatives," as one donor confessed.[38] With that money, along with personal funds from John Singlaub and Ted Shackley, the defendants hired a few high-profile lawyers. They mounted an effective if expensive defense, pointing out major gaps in the plaintiff's evidence and conclusions.[39] In 1988, the judge threw out the suit for lack of proof and ordered the Christics to pay $1 million in damages.[40] But the idea of a vast conspiracy continued to echo. The persistence of such thinking stemmed from the inability of many contemporaries to see Singlaub and his allies in the anticommunist international in their appropriate historical context.

Simply put, they mistook a movement for a conspiracy. While Singlaub and others had indeed managed clandestine operations in Vietnam and elsewhere, they were not part of a "secret team" that pulled the strings of U.S. foreign policy from the shadows. Rather, they were part of a political mobilization, one that stretched back to the earliest years of the Cold War. Like previous generations of anticommunist activists from the United States and abroad, they, too, shared the conviction that the U.S. government was failing in its mission to fight communism, and that the private sector could take up the slack. They trafficked in similar ideas and worked to similar ends.

What differentiated the private anticommunist campaigns of the 1980s from earlier ones was the shift from propaganda to paramilitary warfare. In so doing, Singlaub and those around him had tried to harness the weapons and technologies that states used without the public accountability that came with formal state action. And yet, despite those affinities, the private-sector players in the Iran-Contra operation were never working entirely in concert with one another—let alone running a shadow government as a cabal of seemingly omnipotent policymakers. As the hearings revealed, they often clashed with one another about prices, motives, allies, goals, and a host of other concerns. And while some of their activities unfolded in secret—particularly arms deals— many were quite public, like Singlaub's globetrotting tours to raise funds for the world's anticommunist rebels or his efforts to lobby Congress on their behalf.

More importantly, Singlaub and other ex–covert warriors did not create or command the global network of private anticommunist groups that operated at the base of the Iran-Contra scandal. For that network extended far beyond Americans' attempts to free hostages and arm guerrillas. Because of its breadth, it was diffuse and contentious, always more contingent on the aims and actions of people outside the United States than most Americans ever acknowledged.

That dynamic was still at play in the 1980s, even as men like John Singlaub imagined themselves at the forefront of a global anticommunist crusade. Therefore, despite the time, money, and effort that Singlaub and others invested in their attempts to aid the world's anticommunist guerrillas, they never were able to control them or their allies. Armed groups, whether in Nicaragua, Angola, Afghanistan, or Cambodia, had their own plans. Their talk of an international crusade against communism was rarely heartfelt. More often, it was designed to win the hearts and minds of Americans, particularly wealthy conservatives who could donate to their cause or influence U.S. policymakers. In that sense, John Singlaub and other ex–covert warriors struggled to confront the same problem that had doomed previous attempts to foment a global anticommunist revolution—the international Right was much older, larger, and more complex than they had assumed. That was what made John Singlaub's dream of an anticommunist international fighting wars of national liberation on three continents so difficult to realize.

The dream died when the Cold War ended. Within a few years, many of the groups that had formed the core of the anticommunist international disappeared. Others tried to adjust to new geopolitical realities. Leaders from the World Anti-Communist League, for instance, sought to keep up with the times by rechristening their organization the World League for Freedom and Democracy.[41] Without a clear enemy, however, the group lost its purpose. By the mid-1990s, shorn of its overarching mission and international elements, it had been reduced to little more than a lobbying group for Taiwan's government and business leaders. Likewise, leaders of the Anti-Bolshevik Bloc of Nations rejoiced at the fall of communism in Eastern Europe. But since they had aged considerably or died by the 1990s, they played little part rebuilding post-Soviet governments in their homelands, although some became national heroes.[42]

In the United States a similar process unfolded. Almost overnight, the network of private anticommunist groups, which had been growing in fits and starts since Marvin Liebman and others laid its foundations in the 1950s, closed up shop. While many conservative activists remained passionate about a particular struggle in one part of the world or another, especially Nicaragua and Afghanistan, they felt less of a need to build an international movement. As Americans withdrew from the overseas circles in which they had been working for decades, the anticommunist international unraveled from within. If the most important thread that tied that movement together was the shared conviction that communism had to be defeated, then the collapse of the Soviet Union made such a mission all but obsolete.

To put it simply, the anticommunist international could not survive the end of the Cold War because it was based upon a mutual sense of what its members were against, not what they were for. Other concerns were always present—most obviously Christian salvation and free-market triumphalism—

but they never served as paramount goals and, for that reason, were more fully realized when loosed from the overarching framework of anticommunist internationalism. Indeed, neoliberal acolytes and evangelical missionaries were better suited to shaping what came after communism than they were at working toward its defeat. They found leaders in formerly communist countries to be far more receptive to their ideas—particularly neoliberal "shock therapy"—than they ever imagined during the Cold War.[43]

The deeply rooted conviction that international communism was a one-size-fits-all explanation for the world's conflicts never encompassed, or even acknowledged, the complexity of different struggles in different parts of the world. Instead, it sought to draw them into a grand historical narrative of freedom versus tyranny. Enduring armed conflict after the Cold War, however, revealed that narrative as wishful thinking. As U.S. aid for the world's scattered anticommunist guerrillas evaporated after 1991, many of those groups continued to fight on, finding new allies and new enemies. But few in the United States seemed to care now that the Soviets were gone. So the anticommunist international vanished from our historical memory just as the Cold War ended.

---

Although the anticommunist international died, the impulses that animated its paramilitary campaigns in the Cold War persisted. Nowhere was that more clear than in the rise of private military firms (PMFs), colloquially known as military contractors. For some Americans, the connections between Cold War anticommunist activism and these new for-profit ventures were self-evident. Looking back on his time in Central America, Robert Brown of *Soldier of Fortune* magazine believed his training units "were the first modern 'contractors,' as we provided combat experienced military personnel—former Marine Recon, SEALs, Special Forces, Rangers, etc.—to assist the U.S. in both El Salvador and against the Sandinistas."[44] Over the following decade, the magazine continued to send teams of retired special operations soldiers to teach others how to fight, most notably in crumbling Yugoslavia, where the *Soldier of Fortune* staff trained Croatian military and paramilitary units.[45]

Yet the magazine's haphazard missions, funded by donations and undertaken without a clear profit incentive, were hardly the wave of the future. They were quickly overshadowed by large-scale market-driven approaches to war. Rather than a dozen ex-soldiers working informally with whichever armed group they could find, as was generally the case with the *Soldier of Fortune* missions, these new enterprises operated as sizable corporations with thousands of employees serving lucrative contracts for governments, often in several different countries at the same time. In the 1990s and early 2000s, an array of PMFs appeared on the international stage, mostly from the United States, Britain, France, Germany, and South Africa. These enterprises derived primarily from the attempts of retired military and intelligence officers to manage and monetize the armed conflicts that emerged as the Cold War ended. Believing the private sector could wage better—and cheaper—wars than states could, those who started PMFs promised two major advantages over traditional militaries. First, they enhanced the abilities of governments, including the United States, to pursue geopolitical interests without deploying their own armies, thereby removing war-making from the realm of popular debate and citizen sacrifice. Second, by shielding their operations from public scrutiny, PMFs offered new ways for states to clandestinely support unpopular or undemocratic regimes with horrendous human rights records.[46]

American PMFs evolved in dialogue with similar enterprises in other parts of the world. The most influential early private military firm appeared in South Africa in the late 1980s. Known as Executive Outcomes, its origins and development mirrored the migration of American covert warriors into private enterprises in the 1970s and 1980s, but with much greater success. Founded in 1989, Executive Outcomes was almost entirely composed of retired soldiers from the elite units of the South African Defense Force (SADF). Its director, Eeben Barlow, had spent his career fighting guerrilla wars in Angola, Namibia, Rhodesia, and South Africa. As the apartheid state collapsed and the SADF faced large personnel cuts, Barlow started Executive Outcomes and set about recruiting soldiers who were now out of work. More than a thousand signed on.[47]

The firm soon found its first payday in Angola. Although the company was run by soldiers who had spent most of their careers fighting African nationalists and defending apartheid, their new work in the private sector had no consistent ideology beyond making money. In Angola, Executive Outcomes took a contract with the vaguely Marxist MPLA government to launch an assault against Jonas Savimbi's UNITA strongholds. A few years before, when the Cold War paradigm held sway for South Africa's military leadership, Savimbi had been a firm ally. Now, in 1992, with the Cold War over and serious profits up for grabs, the Executive Outcomes leadership had no qualms about switching sides. By 1994, Barlow had taken another lucrative contract in Sierra Leone to fight the rebels of the Revolutionary United Front, who had taken control over many of the country's diamond mines. In both places, Executive Outcomes managed every aspect of war-making. By most accounts the firm was far superior to the troops of the Angolan and Sierra Leonean governments.[48] Yet international observers were troubled by the creation of a powerful private army in Africa, and pressured Angola and Sierra Leone to end their contracts. Executive Outcomes shut up shop in 1998, though Barlow and other commanders quickly started new enterprises.[49]

In the United States, right-leaning ex-military men found inspiration in the Executive Outcomes model. Here was a solution to the problems that had doomed paramilitary endeavors in the 1980s. By forming contracts with the state, for-profit private military ventures moved from an extralegal realm to a legal one. In the mid-1990s, a series of PMFs appeared in the United States. Some such as DynCorp, headquartered just outside of Washington, D.C., had been working for decades as contractors for the U.S. military and simply expanded their operations into new terrains such as logistical support for American soldiers, security services for VIPs, and the training of military and police forces in Iraq and Afghanistan.[50] Others, such as Military Professional Resources Incorporated, were new companies that built their businesses by advising military operations in the Balkans—efforts that often overlapped with those of private arms dealers who maintained the flow of weapons into these conflicts despite United Nations' restrictions.[51] In both cases, American PMFs derived from the idea that the private sector could take over the state's war-making capabilities, and that retired Special Forces soldiers, in particular, should lead such endeavors.

Erik Prince, founder and owner of Blackwater and its latter-day successors, showed that. Prince was the son of a wealthy businessman from western Michigan, a man who spent much of his fortune funding conservative causes—work that his children continue to this day.[52] He grew up in the lap of luxury, but in his own telling, always chose the hard and righteous path.[53] So he joined the Navy, serving first as a junior officer, and then as a member of the Navy's elite special-operations force, the SEALs. Yet his time in the service convinced him that governmental bureaucracies and complex interagency rivalries caused "shocking dysfunction," impeding effective military operations. The only solution, in his eyes, was to "return to what made America great in the first place: individual initiative and competition."[54]

Prince's convictions about the beneficence of markets and their fundamental role in shaping U.S. history echoed a previous generation of Americans who had sought to use private means in pursuit of foreign-policy goals. So did his belief that the United States' ability to wage covert warfare had declined precipitously since the 1970s—the same argument that John Singlaub and others made decades before. But whereas Singlaub's efforts to privatize covert operations had at best a mixed record of success, Blackwater was by any measure a major triumph. In the early 2000s, Prince transformed his company from a small outfit offering training to cops and soldiers at a rural North Carolina facility into one of the world's largest private military firms serving contracts in more than a dozen nations in Asia, Africa, and the Middle East. Initially, Blackwater troops supplemented U.S. military operations but soon they took on their own missions.[55]

Most of Blackwater's men had served in combat with the U.S. military and had signed on with the firm in the hopes of securing better pay than they had received in the service of the U.S. government.[56] But for Prince and his allies in the CIA and Defense Department, Blackwater was not simply offering combat veterans better pay and better lives. More importantly, the firm promised a new and more efficient way to make war. "Where the Pentagon needs a hundred men to get a job done, a private company can do it with ten," he wrote in 2013. Blackwater "saved the taxpayers money" since market mechanisms kept the firm "focused on delivering a great product at a competitive price."[57] Beyond cost efficiency, Prince liked to think of his outfit as part of the United States' long history of "outsourcing" military professionals dating back to the Revolutionary War and continuing thereafter—although Prince conveniently elided the messy details of the Iran-Contra operation and the Reagan Doctrine.[58]

For all of Prince's certainty that private firms were more efficient than state-run military and intelligence forces, he rarely acknowledged that his company could not have come into existence, let alone thrived, without state resources—and not just lucrative government contracts. After all, his troops had received the bulk of their training and combat experience as part of the United States military. That was what made them effective soldiers in the first place. Moreover, the firm, like many other defense contractors and private military companies, benefitted from direct and indirect links with state officials—relationships best exemplified in Prince's decision to hire former CIA Director Cofer Black to run a new intelligence wing of Blackwater.

Blackwater was, of course, only one of many private military firms founded by Americans as the Cold War ended. While it endured years of national and international scrutiny over the actions of its employees in Iraq, most other companies worked under the radar, serving contracts with little fanfare or oversight. Sometimes, the links between these new endeavors and the paramilitary undertakings of the Iran-Contra operation were obvious.

Such was the case of Duane "Dewey" Clarridge, a CIA officer who had been a central part of the Enterprise, having mined Nicaragua's harbors in 1984. In the aftermath of the Iran-Contra hearings, Clarridge was indicted on seven counts of perjury and making false statements, though President George H. W. Bush granted him a pardon in 1992 before his trial finished. In the years afterwards, Clarridge kept a low profile, writing a memoir about his exploits as a spy. In 1998, while working as a private consultant for the Department of Defense, he authored a plan to insert thousands of Iraqi exiles and American commandos into Iraq to bring down Saddam Hussein's regime—a throwback to the Nicaraguan Contras that never went anywhere. Growing dissatisfied with the CIA and its human intelligence capabilities, he dreamt of starting his own intelligence firm, which would be leaner and meaner than the CIA since it would be free from government oversight and bureaucratic wrangling. As journalist Mark Mazzetti writes, "It would be like the Office of Strategic Services but updated for the world of the twenty-first century—a world dominated by corporations, loose multinational criminal and terror networks, and multinational institutions."[59]

Most of the CIA's leadership had turned its back on Clarridge, but he maintained a few relationships with retired special-operations veterans. Teaming up in 2009, they created the American International Security Corporation and assembled a network of Americans, Britons, Pakistanis, and Afghanis whom Clarridge hoped would serve as spies, moving undetected in the underworlds of Kabul, Peshawar, and elsewhere. Clarridge worked out a multimillion-dollar contract with an official in the Defense Department to set up an "off the books spy operation" that sent intelligence back into official channels. But the CIA grew worried that Clarridge's network was providing faulty intelligence. His information had prompted an errant drone strike that killed several Arab men who were serving as double-agents for Pakistani intelligence. In 2010, the CIA and the U.S. military broke ties with Clarridge and revoked the company's contract.[60] When all of this became public, an unnamed American official explained that "it's generally a bad idea to have freelancers running around a war zone pretending to be James Bond."[61]

Growing public outcry about the use of PMFs in Iraq, Afghanistan, and elsewhere has unfolded in conversation with academics, mostly political scientists and international relations experts, who seek to explain how and why such enterprises became a regular feature of combat in the post–Cold War era. Most scholars tend to view the rise of private military firms such as Blackwater as simply the latest incarnation of mercenaries, part of a long history that stretches back thousands of years. They emphasize that the modern age in which states supposedly gained monopoly over war-making, the last two hundred years or so, now appears to have been both short-lived and incomplete. The end of the Cold War, in this narrative, brought about a reversion to an earlier model of war-making, in which states hire mercenaries to do their bidding. The downsizing of militaries around the world after the Cold War, and the subsequent flow of their weapons onto a global black market, hastened that shift.

Such a perspective has many merits. But it is insufficient to fully explain the rise of PMFs. Viewing them as both a post–Cold War phenomenon and a return to pre-modern past obscures how they are actually a product of the Cold War itself, of the ways in which civilians and retired soldiers sought to change the world.[62] As this story has shown, the major historical forces that triggered the rise of PMFs—the migration of soldiers into private firms and the growing conviction that such enterprises were better suited than states to wage war—had deep roots in the Cold War, particularly its later stages.

Those forces did not cease after 1991. Rather, the end of the Cold War accelerated and redirected them into new arenas. During the Cold War, the anticommunist international was a main outlet for a number of private military endeavors. When it ended, the ideological and institutional successors of those endeavors—corporatized private military firms—turned to new conflicts. But they did so without the overriding political mission that had unified previous attempts. In other words, the end of the Cold War shifted the impulse to privatize war onto a more diverse ideological terrain populated with competing concerns about politics and profits.

The rise of private military firms has, ironically, done little to quell Americans' fantasies of getting foreigners to fight their wars—the core of the Reagan Doctrine. In 2014, as the Islamic State gained control over large swaths of territory in Iraq and Syria, U.S. leaders struggled for a response.[63] After more than a decade of war in Iraq and Afghanistan, few thought that U.S. soldiers could or should be called upon to fight the Islamic State. That caused Fox News anchor Bill O'Reilly to present a plan for a "volunteer mercenary army" of tens of thousands of fighters drawn from all over the world. "We would select them, special forces would train them," he explained. It would be a "25,000-man force to be deployed to fight on the ground against worldwide terrorism. Not just ISIS."[64] O'Reilly's plan was immediately ridiculed by many commentators, including his guest on that particular program, Tom Nichols, a professor of military strategy and a former Army officer, who told O'Reilly this was a "terrible idea not just as a practical matter but a moral matter. It's a morally corrosive idea to try to outsource our national security."[65]

Yet when viewed through the lens of the anticommunist international, it is easy to spot in O'Reilly's plan the same kind of thinking that undergirded conservatives' paramilitary campaigns in the Cold War, especially its later years. The United States was not up to the task of fighting this new global threat, and so Americans needed someone else to do it. "We need ground forces," O'Reilly explained. "However, the American people, perhaps rightly so, don't want to send any more of our troops into these chaotic countries. What about a mercenary army, elite fighters well paid, well trained to defeat terrorists all over the world?"[66]

What indeed. Shorn of the overarching project of anticommunist internationalism, the impulse to pay foreigners to do the United States' dirty work took on a more defensive and more nationalistic posture in the Global War on Terror. Bill O'Reilly and John Singlaub might have agreed on means, but their ends were starkly different. Singlaub conceived of a global revolution, and talked in the idioms of national liberation. His was a lofty project, something that would propel a fundamental shift in the course of human history. O'Reilly, on the other hand, spoke only of American problems and American goals. Foreign fighters may share some convictions about the need to fight "worldwide terrorism" with their American paymasters, but what really mattered was securing U.S. geopolitical interests. His was an international project solely for American aims.

---

The ideas and impulses that sustained the paramilitary campaigns of the 1980s also redounded in unpredictable ways in the United States. The notion that ordinary men and women could become independent agents of historical change by picking up arms—another key element of the Reagan Doctrine—inspired a series of right-wing radical groups whose violent campaigns escalated in the late 1980s and early 1990s. And like earlier efforts, these groups also drew upon the experience and skills of disgruntled Americans soldiers. More than that, they trafficked in similar tropes about the U.S. government, particularly its inability to protect its citizens and pursue their best interests.[67] Some guarded the U.S.-Mexico border, hoping to capture migrants entering the country illegally—private volunteer border patrols that straddled the line between overnight camps for wannabe soldiers and deadly interdiction forces.[68]

Other right-wing groups took the notion that the U.S. government could not be trusted a few giant leaps further. In their visions, the state was not just incapable. It was irreparably malevolent. In the mid-1980s, as American men cycled back from Nicaragua and other overseas battlegrounds, several right-wing paramilitary groups in the United States were preparing for an apocalyptic showdown with the federal government. They believed the state had been taken over by Jews, communists, African Americans, foreigners—or some combination of those groups—and was now bent on crushing individual freedom by levying unjust taxes, passing gun-control laws, allowing interracial marriage, preaching multiculturalism, and a host of other concerns. For years, those ideas had circulated throughout an underground press and right-wing novels—above all, *The Turner Diaries*, William Pierce's fantasy tale about a guerrilla war against the totalitarian incarnation of the U.S. state known as the System.[69]

In Michigan, Montana, Missouri, and elsewhere, right-wing groups drilled their members, shot their weapons, and talked of the war to come. While most just practiced combat, a few enacted their guerrilla fantasies, mostly with dismal results. Members of a group called The Covenant, the Sword, and the Arm of the Lord, based in rural Missouri, stockpiled a vast arsenal to fight what they called the Zionist Occupation Government, but the group's leaders were soon rounded up by the FBI, charged with weapons violations, and issued lengthy prison sentences.[70] The same went for the white-separatist group known as The Order. Named after the guerrilla organization in the *Turner Diaries*, its members robbed banks and armored cars, murdered Jewish talk-radio host Alan Berg, and tried to establish a "White Sovereign National State" in the Pacific Northwest. The group fell apart after a violent clash with federal authorities on an Idaho compound that killed The Order's leader, a neo-Nazi named Bob Matthews. But others carried on, hoarding weapons and preparing for war.[71]

As the Cold War ended, these armed Americans grew convinced that the forces of totalitarianism were gaining ground in the United States. For proof of that, they pointed to two events which rippled like shockwaves through the Far Right. In 1992, on a remote mountaintop in Ruby Ridge, Idaho, federal agents had tried to serve white separatist Randy Weaver a warrant for weapons violations. A standoff ensued, marked by occasional shots from both sides. When the smoke cleared, Weaver's son and wife and a federal agent lay dead.[72] The following year, in Waco, Texas, federal authorities engaged in a standoff with the Branch Davidians, a millenarian Christian sect with a cache of illegal weapons on a fortified compound. After fifty-one days, the Bureau of Alcohol, Tobacco, and Firearms (ATF) launched a military-style raid, sparking a fire that gutted the compound, killing at least seventy-six people, including twenty-one children.[73] To the armed Right—the survivalists, the militias, the Christian Identity groups, and so on—these events signaled the start of a war.[74]

That was how Timothy McVeigh, a Gulf War veteran, Army Ranger washout, and militia sympathizer, saw things. Having witnessed the siege at Waco from the hood of his car, he wanted to strike back. On April 19, 1995, McVeigh used a fertilizer bomb to blow up the federal building in Oklahoma City. A state trooper arrested him a few hours later, discovering photocopies of the

*Turner Diaries* in his car.[75] McVeigh's act of terror, which tore the side off the building, killing 169 people, caused Americans of all stripes to search for its meaning. Commentators on the right condemned him for killing innocents but nevertheless contended that the real cause for his anger and violence was the federal government itself, which had ridden roughshod over Americans' constitutional liberties, religious freedoms, and their right to arms. To be sure, that worldview had been coalescing in right-wing publications for decades. But the events at Waco and Ruby Ridge made it real and brought it into the minds of millions. As historian Garry Wills wrote in 1995, Waco and Ruby Ridge took all of the Right's fears and rolled them into one: "People protecting their own families on their own property were killed by governmental agencies, including the hated anti-gun agency, for trying to defend their religious beliefs with constitutionally protected firearms." At Waco and Ruby Ridge, "Freedom lovers confronted the jackbooted thugs," and paid the ultimate price for it.[76]

In many ways, the resilient belief that armed civilians could vanquish the federal government was firmly rooted in what many right-leaning Americans understood about the guerrilla wars of the Cold War. In the wake of Ruby Ridge and Waco, Wayne LaPierre, the long-serving head of the National Rifle Association, analogized American gun ownership to an array of overseas conflicts going back to the 1950s. "The claim that an armed populace cannot successfully resist assault stems from an unproven theory," he wrote in 1994. "The twentieth century provides *no example* of a determined populace with access to small arms having been defeated by a modern army. The Russians lost in Afghanistan, the United States lost in Vietnam, and the French lost in Indo-China. In each case, it was the poorly armed populace that beat the 'modern' army. In China, Cuba, and Nicaragua, the established leaders Chiang Kai-Shek, Batista, and Somoza lost. Modern nations like Algeria, Angola, Ireland, Israel, Mozambique, and Zimbabwe only existed because guerrilla warfare can triumph over modern armies."[77] LaPierre's reading of history was specious since most of the guerrillas he referred to "had tanks, missiles, the organization of 'modern armies,' and the help of outside governments," as Garry Wills pointed out.[78] Nevertheless, by omitting those details, LaPierre offered a simplified, generalized, and idealized vision of guerrilla combat, one that was inspired as much by communist guerrillas as their anticommunist counterparts. Resuscitating an old idea on the right, LaPierre insisted that ordinary men with guns were the only real guarantors of freedom.

The Oklahoma City bombing was exceptional, but only in its scale and toll, not its ideological thrust. In recent years, other Americans have embraced the same basic assumptions that McVeigh clung to while also linking them to new fears. Some think the United States government is really a front for a tyrannical conspiracy called the New World Order, or NWO, which wants to strip U.S. citizens of their rights—starting with their right to keep and bear arms. Once Americans are rendered defenseless, the theory holds, they, too, will be enslaved by the NWO.[79] Today, the Oath Keepers, a heavily armed militia comprised of former and active soldiers and police officers, arrays itself against the power of the federal government, while many of its members subscribe to the New World Order theory. Oath Keepers have been present at a number of recent flashpoints—Ferguson, Missouri, the Bundy Ranch in Nevada, and the 2015 seizure of a Bureau of Land Management wildlife refuge in Oregon—preaching that armed insurrection is the only option left for true American "patriots."[80]

For all of their novelty, right-wing militias have continued the paramilitarism that had emerged in many different arenas of American life throughout the Cold War. Like private military firms, they form another point along the historical trajectory by which war-making shifted from states to non-state actors in the closing decades of the Cold War. More than that, they illuminate, alongside SWAT teams and other forms of paramilitary policing, the increasingly inward turn of the militarization that undergirded the United States' quest for global leadership since 1945.[81]

Despite their intense inward focus and fierce racial nationalism, the militias and their acolytes are also a part of global history. For when the Cold War ended, they drew closer to similar groups in Europe. But they did so without the glue of anticommunism. Instead, they reinvigorated older discourses and assumptions of a shared racial identity. Making the case that white people in the United States and Europe inherited a common ethnic, cultural, and religious past—and therefore faced similar challenges in the post–Cold War era—they utilized the internet to network across borders and attract new adherents. They circulated texts, populated chat rooms and message boards, and planned gatherings. They denounced immigrants and nonwhites as inferior and unassimilable, and ranted about Jewish conspiracies for world domination. Neo-Nazi bands sold each other's records and played shows together. Holocaust deniers hosted joint conferences. Klan leaders visited Britain and Germany, and German and British neo-fascists toured the United States. William Pierce published *The Turner Diaries* in French and German.[82]

In their world, rights and nationhood stemmed from blood and soil and violence. Therefore, white nationalists in the United States and Europe had to work together to achieve the same goals in separate nations. As one British fascist put it, "It is not an American fight, or a British fight, or a German fight. It is a white fight, and we've got to win it."[83] That worldview reinforced an affinity for ethnic cleansing of the kind that wracked Yugoslavia and other post-communist states in Europe. Indeed, some 200 American neo-Nazis had traveled to Croatia in 1992, where they fought with the paramilitaries of the Croatian Defense Forces, joining right-wingers from France, Germany, Austria, and elsewhere who had also volunteered.[84] More often, far-right groups targeted enemies at home. Americans were better armed, and thus amassed a greater body count, since stronger gun laws in most European countries prevented their citizens from acquiring large amounts of weapons. Europeans generally preferred beatings, stabbings, and arson over large-scale paramilitary action. But that was not always the case. In 2011, Norway's Anders Breivik set off a car bomb in downtown Oslo before massacring dozens of teenagers at an island retreat, actions that left 79 people dead and more than 300 wounded.[85] At his trial, Breivik explained that he had been inspired by Timothy McVeigh.[86] His rambling 1,500-page manifesto, plagiarized in large part from other sources, often quoted American Richard Spencer, a history PhD dropout and leading light in the unfolding "alt-right" movement.[87]

The Right's revolution persists in other ways. Ideological and material collaboration between individuals and groups in the United States and Europe has helped propel the recent rise of what many commentators on both sides of the Atlantic call "right-wing populism." Although most of these movements seek change through the ballot rather than the bullet, they nevertheless call for a "revolution" against a world system supposedly dominated by multiculturalists and economic elites who champion globalization, migration, and interconnectedness over race and nation. France's National Front leader Marine Le Pen promises a "revolution" against the "globalists" based on "patriotism, proximity, liberty."[88] Dutch far-right politician Geert Wilders claims he's leading a "patriotic revolution" so his followers can "fight for the preservation of their own people."[89]

In the United States, President Donald J. Trump and his supporters used the same words. Guided to office—at least in part—by lawyer and lobbyist Paul Manafort, who had spent the 1980s working on behalf of the late Angolan guerrilla leader Jonas Savimbi, Trump pledged to lay siege to the U.S. political establishment.[90] "This is a revolution," one supporter gushed in the heady moments after Trump's surprise Electoral College victory. The conservative daily *Washington Times* went further, editorializing that this was a "new American Revolution," and that Trump was ready to lead the country in a "war for the nation's future," a war in which the main enemies were at home—"Mrs. Clinton, Mr. Obama and the Democrats"—not overseas.[91] Another talked of a "Trump revolution" against "leftist cockroaches" that would "save the world from the path of self-destruction by the vices of our own virtues"—whatever that meant.[92] Meanwhile, Trump elevated to his inner circle "alt-right" ideologue Steve Bannon—a man who fancies himself a Leninist revolutionary and who is obsessed with the thought of a "cleansing war."[93]

Such claims speak to the power of revolution as a metaphor, as well as its implicit violence. But they also reveal how much it has changed over the last few decades. If we are to make sense of what the Right's revolution means today, then we must reckon with its past. It is not a pleasant history, but it is a necessary one.

# Acknowledgments

A vibrant and supportive community of scholars, colleagues, friends, and family helped me bring this story to the page. My deepest gratitude goes to Michael Sherry of Northwestern University, who shepherded this book from its earliest stages. His patience, generosity, and ceaseless support guided me at every turn. And his confidence that this story was important and that it needed telling always kept my spirits high during the tough moments of academic life. Beyond that, he is a peerless scholar. His work continues to illuminate and inspire.

Others at Northwestern provided invaluable advice and apt critiques. Daniel Immerwahr read several drafts and helped me see the broader implications of my work, especially how it connects to other histories of internationalism. His wise council also helped me navigate the publishing world. Michael Allen sharpened my thinking on paramilitary violence and conservativism, and the relationship between the two. Kathleen Belew, whose research dovetails with my own, sent me down many useful paths of inquiry. Other members of the Department of History made me a better historian. Alex Owen transformed my understanding of history. Tim Breen made me a stronger writer. Susan Pearson and Deborah Cohen guided my study of imperialism. Gerry Cadava supported my interests in U.S.–Latin American relations and transnational history. Scott Sowerby, Lane Fenrich, Caitlin Fitz, and Kevin Boyle all helped me become a better teacher. I am also deeply grateful that Sarah Maza and the Chabraja Center for Historical Studies pulled me back to Northwestern for the 2017–2018 academic year.

I had the good fortune to spend a semester as the Agnese N. Haury Postdoctoral Scholar at New York University's Tamiment Library and the Center for the United States and the Cold War. A hub of intellectual and political activity, the Center provided crucial support as I revised the manuscript. I am especially grateful to Tim Naftali, who brought me to NYU and who provided invaluable feedback on several portions of the manuscript. While at NYU, I got to know the late Marilyn Young. She was a true force of nature in the field, and was kind enough to review the manuscript for UNC Press. Her praise and suggestions meant the world to me. She is missed. I am also grateful for the camaraderie and insights of the other fellows at the Center—Sean Fear and Andrea Chiampan—as well as Michael Koncewicz, who made my time in New York easy and productive. Participants and presenters at the Center's seminars provided a stimulating environment to test new ideas, receive feedback, and immerse myself in the work of others. It's hard to imagine a more exciting place to write Cold War history.

While completing this project, I've been honored to teach and write as a member of Temple University's Center for the Study Force and Diplomacy. I am deeply indebted to Richard Immerman for his thoughts, critiques, and mentorship. Petra Goedde, Bryant Simon, Greg Urwin, and Peter Gran guided and encouraged my work, while Jay Lockenour provided me with every resource needed. While at Temple, I also enjoyed getting to know several outstanding scholars through CENFAD's colloquia, including Aaron O'Connell, Kate Epstein, and Joseph Fronczak, whose work I very much admire and who offered sound and timely advice.

A number of other scholars have shared their thoughts and time over the last few years. Gerald Horne reviewed the book for UNC, offering a raft of useful critiques and suggestions. Theresa Keeley, Jeff Perry, and Jeremy Kuzmarov also read the manuscript in whole, and their suggestions strengthened my arguments and tightened my prose. Ángel Alcalde, Dirk Bonker, Tim Borstelmann, Jonathyne Briggs, Olivier Burtin, Nick Cullather, Brian DeLay, David Fitzgerald, Paul Gillingham, Tanya Harmer, David Hollinger, Kim Philips-Fein, Marc Selverstone, Stuart Schrader, and Aileen Teague offered prudent suggestions and kindly encouragement. Audiences in Berkeley, Chicago, Jacksonville, London, New York, Philadelphia, San Diego, and elsewhere provided excellent sounding boards as I wrote and revised chapters. Other scholars guided my work through their incisive and inspiring scholarship, especially Greg Grandin, Ariel Armony, Patrice McSherry, Piero Gleijeses, Odd Arne Westad, and Naomi Klein.

I would not have become a historian without the advice and faith of my undergraduate mentors at the University of South Florida—especially David K. Johnson, Fraser Ottanelli, and Scott Ickes. Moreover, it was David Johnson who first encouraged me, nearly a decade ago, to explore the relationship between American conservativism and paramilitary violence.

I could not have tracked down all of the materials needed to tell this story without the help of many archivists. I owe the greatest debt to Rosa Palau, who runs the Archive of Terror, as it is colloquially known, in Asunción, Paraguay. Rosa helped me navigate a vast amount of material and provided digital copies for every document I wished to have—a first in my many years of research. Moreover, she made my partner and me feel welcome as we made our way in a new country. Carol Leadenham at the Hoover Institution for War, Revolution, and Peace guided me through a staggering amount of documents and collections. Other archivists at the Reagan, Carter, and Ford Presidential Libraries, the National Security Archive at George Washington University, the Bancroft Library at the University of California, the Chicago Historical Society, the University of Kansas's Spencer Research Library, NYU's Tamiment Library, Columbia University's Rare Book and Manuscript Library, and the British National Archives helped me access materials I never would have found on my own and, in many cases, propelled me down new avenues of research. The staff at Northwestern University's library helped me find rare books and forgave about a thousand dollars' worth of late fines.

Karen McKay shared her memories and documents with me, and prevented me from making some serious errors. She might not agree with my arguments, but I am nonetheless grateful that she spent so many hours talking with me—all the more so since most of my historical subjects refused my requests for interviews or documents.

I received crucial financial support from several institutions. Northwestern University's Buffet Institute for International Studies, Latin American and Caribbean Studies Center, Chabraja Center for Historical Studies, and Graduate School all contributed thousands of dollars to finance my research in the United States, Latin America, and Britain. The Society for Historians of American Foreign Relations provided a yearlong fellowship to complete the first draft of the manuscript. New York University's Center for the United States and the Cold War and Temple University's Center for the Study of Force and Diplomacy provided ample time and resources for me to finish the book.

At UNC Press, I am deeply grateful to have worked with my editor, Brandon Proia. His unflagging enthusiasm has encouraged me at every step, and his sharp suggestions made this a much stronger—and shorter—book. Jay Mazzocchi, Matthew Somoroff, and others at UNC Press have made the publishing process a breeze, and I thank them for all their hard work on the manuscript.

Along the way, I've been surrounded by wonderful friends and colleagues. Andy Baer and Matt June listened to me talk about this project for more hours than they probably would have liked. They also read early versions of the book and offered many valuable suggestions. Wen-Qing Ngoei read large portions of the manuscript and gave key advice. Alvita Akiboh, Kevin Baker, Ryan Burns, Andrea Christmas, Brian Druchniak, Mariah Hepworth, Alex Hobson, Zachary Jacobson, Ashley Johnson, Don Johnson, Matt Kahn, Amanda Kleintop, Sam Kling, Alex Lindgren-Gibson, Keith Rathbone, Aram Sarkisian, Ian Saxine, and Leigh Soares all enriched my time at Northwestern through working groups, seminars, conversations, and, most importantly, karaoke nights. Beyond making this a better story, they helped make Chicago home. The same goes for Brian O'Camb, Erica Krutsch, Marcus Parker, Ashley Telman, Jonah Radding, Gaia Radding, and Sasha and Madeline June. A special round of thanks must go to the Tuesday-night trivia stalwarts who helped me unwind nearly every week for longer than I care to say. Thanks as well to Jeremy, Andrea, and Michelle at the bygone Pumping Company, who always offered friendly faces and stiff drinks. Leaving Chicago wasn't easy, and so I am all the more grateful for the community of promising scholars at Temple University—Minju Bae, Mathias Fueling, Brian McNamara, Ariel Natalo Lifton, Eric Perinovic, Gary Scales, and Silke Zoller—who made me feel welcome in Philadelphia.

My last words must go to my family and friends, for without them none of this would have been possible. My mother and father, Bill and Collette Burke, have always inspired me through their hard work, love, and sacrifice. They are the most resilient people I know. They have labored all of their lives so I could pursue my ambitions. I can never repay them for that, but I offer this book as a small token of my endless gratitude. My brother Tim has been my best friend since I was born and he remains so to this day. My godparents, Larry and Kathy Moore, have been a constant source of support, and their devotion to public education has inspired me to follow a similar path. My grandmothers, Ida Burke and Rita Marsland, beyond supporting my academic ambitions, have always sustained my interest in history through stories about our family. I also gained a new family while writing this book. Jerry, Audrey, and Cary Tignanelli—and the rest of the clan—have offered love and encouragement over the last few years as they opened their homes and their lives to me. And Brian Richter, Greg Saldana, Vinnie Tricarico, Josh Jamieson, Keenan Sanz, and Eric Blattler provided much-needed respite from research and writing on my visits back home. To all of my family and friends—thanks for everything.

Most importantly, my wife, Nina, has sustained and nurtured me with her unwavering support, kindness, and love. Her passion for teaching inspires me every day. What is more, she's never flinched at the many hardships my career has imposed on our lives—not just my long absences and late hours but also our moves from Tampa to Chicago, Chicago to Philly, Philly to Chicago, and wherever else the future may deliver us. Our beautiful and bright daughter,

Norah, arrived as I was completing the first draft of the manuscript. That was more than two years ago. The book has been part of her life since she was born, and she, like her mother, has already had to sacrifice too much for its realization, especially trips to the park. But I could not have done it without either of them. For they have enriched my world in more ways than I could have imagined and in far more ways than I could ever count here.

# Note on Sources

This story delves into a shadowy world of people who tried to shield their activities from outside view. Unsurprisingly, they left behind a partial, scattered, and sometimes deceptive paper trail which presents a serious challenge for researchers. To navigate that obstacle, I have pulled widely from U.S. and international sources, including governmental records and documents, private correspondence, congressional hearings and reports, direct-mail broadsides, newsletters, magazines, newspapers, radio and television programs, films, and reports from international human-rights organizations.

Insofar as this story has an archival spine, it comes from the Hoover Institution for War, Revolution, and Peace, housed at Stanford University. This archive offered thousands of pages of documents about the people who made up the international anticommunist movement and their role in shaping the guerrilla wars of the global South. Especially helpful were the many files of correspondence between Americans and their allies in Asia, Africa, Europe, and Latin America, and the internal reports of private anticommunist groups. Other U.S. archives, such as the National Security Archive at George Washington University, the Bancroft Library at the University of California, the Chicago Historical Society, the University of Kansas's Spencer Research Library, Columbia University's Rare Book and Manuscript Library, and New York University's Tamiment Library and Robert F. Wagner Archives, offered further insight into how and why American conservatives sought common cause with anticommunists abroad, and what those connections amounted to. I have tried to gain a better sense of what U.S. policymakers thought and did about these groups by visiting the Reagan, Carter, and Ford Presidential Libraries, and by mining declassified reports from the Department of State, the Department of Defense, and the CIA. While many files remain closed to researchers, these archives offer a fuller understanding of just how much—or more often how little—the U.S. government was involved with private anticommunist initiatives.

Overseas archives also proved crucial to this study. The most important was Paraguay's Centro de Documentación y Archivo para la Defensa de los Derechos Humanos, colloquially known as the Archive of Terror. Discovered in an abandoned house in suburban Asunción in 1992, three years after the fall of Paraguay's right-wing dictator Alfredo Stroessner, the archive remains the most complete documentary record of the anticommunist crusade of Latin America's southern cone military regimes, especially their transnational program of kidnapping, torture, and murder called Operation Condor. Beyond documenting collaboration between the secret intelligence branches of Paraguay, Chile, Argentina, Uruguay, Brazil, and several other countries, the Archive of Terror also holds thousands of documents about the activities of private anticommunist groups in Latin America, Asia, and Europe. These files offered new vistas into what non-Americans thought about their allies in the United States, as well as insights into organizations in which Americans played no significant part.

Other overseas archives helped fill in this story. The National Archives of the United Kingdom offered many declassified reports from British intelligence services about guerrilla groups in Eastern Europe in the 1950s and mercenaries in Rhodesia and Angola in the 1970s. South Korea's Syngman Rhee Institute, in partnership with the Woodrow Wilson Center for International Studies, has built an online archive with hundreds of documents from anticommunist groups in South Korea, Taiwan, South Vietnam, and other states. I have used these files to better explain how private groups and state officials from across Asia interacted with one another, as well as how they collaborated with people from Europe, Latin America, and Africa.

I have also made extensive use of the Central Intelligence Agency's online archive of declassified documents, in addition to CIA documents that I received through Freedom of Information Act requests. While the agency's staff redacted many of these reports for "reasons of national security," the documents nonetheless shed much light onto many of the actors and organizations that moved through the global anticommunist underworld. The Digital National Security Archive, through the peerless declassification efforts of its archivists, offered a more complete view of CIA operations in the global South and their links to private anticommunist groups.

The online archives of the Foreign Broadcast Information Service, a federal body that monitored and disseminated the reports of hundreds of foreign news outlets during the Cold War, helped me gain a better understanding of what people in Asia, Africa, Europe, and Latin America said about the anticommunist international and its dreams of global revolution. This archive also sheds some light onto what Soviet officials thought about my subjects, as it holds translated dispatches from the USSR's official propaganda agencies.

I have supplemented this material with many articles from the official publications of anticommunist groups in Taiwan, West Germany, Mexico, and elsewhere, as well as newspaper articles and other published materials from a dozen countries in Latin America, Asia, Africa, and Europe. I owe a special debt to the many journalists from the *New York Times, Washington Post, Los Angeles Times*, and other publications whose tireless investigative reporting made clear so many aspects of this story.

Combined, these documents have allowed me tell a story about a world of people who hoped to hide their actions from the scrutiny of outsiders and the judgement of history. Many of its protagonists died thinking they had done exactly that. Many of those still alive endeavored to do so by denying my requests for interviews and documents. And so, by reconstructing their actions, I have sought not only to cast light onto darkness, to reveal what they wish to keep hidden. Much more than that, I have tried to explain what it all means.

# Notes

**Abbreviations**

| | |
|---|---|
| *AO* | *Asian Outlook* (Taipei, Taiwan) |
| APACL | Asian Peoples' Anti-Communist League Collection |
| *BG* | *Boston Globe* |
| BL | Bancroft Library, University of California Berkeley |
| CDADDH | Centro de Documentación y Archivo para la Defensa de los Derechos Humanos |
| CHC-UM | Cuban Heritage Collection, University of Miami Library Digital Collections |
| CHM | Chicago History Museum |
| CIA-FOIA | Central Intelligence Agency Freedom of Information Act Reading Room |
| CMP | Clarence Manion Papers |
| *CT* | *Chicago Tribune* |
| CWIHP | Cold War International History Project |
| DNSA | Digital National Security Archive |
| DOD-FOIA | United States Department of Defense Freedom of Information Act Reading Room |
| FBI-FOIA | Federal Bureau of Investigation Freedom of Information Act Reading Room |
| FBIS | Foreign Broadcast Information Service |
| *FCA* | *Free China and Asia* (Taipei, Taiwan) |
| FCO | Foreign and Commonwealth Office (United Kingdom) |
| *FRUS* | Foreign Relations of the United States |
| GFPL | Gerald Ford Presidential Library |
| GRR | Group Research Inc. Records |

| | |
|---|---|
| HIWRP | Hoover Institution for War, Revolution, and Peace |
| HPP | Herbert Philbrick Papers |
| KDP | Kyrill Drenikoff Papers |
| LAT | *Los Angeles Times* |
| LOC | Library of Congress |
| MLP | Marvin Liebman Papers |
| NR | *National Review* |
| NYT | *New York Times* |
| RBML | Rare Books and Manuscript Library, Columbia University |
| RRPL | Ronald Reagan Presidential Library |
| SOF | *Soldier of Fortune* |
| TLRWLA | Tamiment Library and Robert F. Wagner Labor Archives |
| UKNA | United Kingdom National Archives |
| USCWF | United States Council for World Freedom |
| USD-FOIA | United States Department of State Freedom of Information Act Reading Room |
| WCCPM | Wilcox Center for Contemporary Political Movements, University of Kansas |
| WHORM | White House Office of Records Management |
| WP | *Washington Post* |
| WRP | William Rusher Papers |
| WT | *Washington Times* |

## Introduction

1. Doyle McManus, "Rightist Crusade Finds Its Way into the Spotlight," *LAT*, September 16, 1985.

2. For a partial list of the conference's speakers and attendees, see Panel List, September 5, 1985 folder World Anti-Communist League, box 339, GRR, RBML.

3. Anthony Bouscaren, "WACL Conference Great Success," and Dr. Ku Chen Kang, "... A Future Bright with Freedom," *World Freedom Report: The USCWF Newsletter* 3, no. 5 (October 15, 1985), WCCPM. See Anderson and Anderson, *Inside the League*, 207–10.

4. PBS *Frontline*, "Who's Running This War?," March 18, 1986.

5. Doyle McManus, "Rightist Crusade Finds Its Way into the Spotlight," *LAT*, September 16, 1985.

6. Shirley Christian, "Rich Texans Rub Elbows with Rebels," *NYT*, September 15, 1985.

7. Doyle McManus, "Rightist Crusade Finds Its Way into the Spotlight," *LAT*, September 16, 1985.

8. Liebman, *Coming Out Conservative*, 119.

9. The scholarship on grassroots conservatism has become a sophisticated subfield. The best work includes Perlstein, *Before the Storm*; McGirr, *Suburban Warriors*; Frank, *What's the Matter with Kansas?*; Kruse, *White Flight*; Martin, *With God on Our Side*; Lassiter, *The*

*Silent Majority*; Critchlow, *Phyllis Schlafly and Grassroots Conservatism*; Crespino, *In Search of Another Country*; Perlstein, *Nixonland*; Lichtman, *White Protestant Nation*; Frank, *The Wrecking Crew*; Dochuk, *From Bible Belt to Sunbelt*; Kabaservice, *Rule and Ruin*; and Nickerson, *Mothers of Conservatism*.

10. For businessmen's support for free enterprise, and their opposition to the civil rights, labor, and feminist movements, see MacLean, *Freedom Is Not Enough*; Phillips-Fein, *Invisible Hands*; Shermer, *Sunbelt Capitalism*; and Fones-Wolf, *Selling Free Enterprise*. See also Nash, *Conservative Intellectual Movement in America*.

11. See Cowie, *Stayin' Alive*; McCartin, *Collision Course*; and Edsall and Edsall, *Chain Reactions*.

12. On the importance of crime and other social panics in the rise of conservatism, see Jenkins, *Decade of Nightmares*; Flamm, *Law and Order*; and Lancaster, *Sex Panic and the Punitive State*. On the broader punitive turn in American life since the late 1960s see Sherry, "Dead or Alive"; and Thompson, "Why Mass Incarceration Matters."

13. On Latin America, see Grandin, *Empire's Workshop*; Moreton, *To Serve God and Wal-Mart*; and Turek, "To Support a "Brother in Christ." On China, see Mao, *Asia First*. On southern Africa, see Horne, *From the Barrel of a Gun*. On Vietnam, see Allen, *Until the Last Man Comes Home*; and Scanlon, *The Pro-War Movement*.

14. For an international history of conservative evangelicals, see Preston, "Evangelical Internationalism." On transatlantic relationships between free-market economists, see Burgin, *The Great Persuasion*. For broader collections of scholarship on the transnational right, see Durham and Power, eds., *New Perspectives on the Transnational Right*; and van Dongen, Roulin, and Scott-Smith, eds., *Transnational Anti-Communism and the Cold War*.

15. European fascists came close to building an international movement, but their collaboration always hinged on the direct support of Adolf Hitler's regime, especially in countries the Nazis conquered. Therefore, it had marginal influence outside continental Europe. See Hobsbawm, *Age of Extremes*, 109–41; Rustsila, "International Anticommunism before the Cold War"; and Bauerkämper, "Interwar Fascism in Europe and Beyond." On American sympathizers and collaborators with Nazi Germany in the 1930s, see Ribuffo, *Old Christian Right*; and Bernstein, *Swastika Nation*. On Nazi exiles in the Cold War, see Lee, *The Beast Reawakens*. The rise of a transatlantic right in the 1930s mirrored and responded to Popular Front activists who formed a global left in these same years. See Fronczak, "Popular Front Movements"; and Fronczak, "Local People's Global Politics."

16. Robin, "You Say You Want a Counterrevolution," 372.

17. For overviews of U.S. imperialism, see Kramer, "Power and Connection"; and McMahon, "The Republic as Empire."

18. For an overview of the global cold war, Westad, *The Global Cold War*. On Africa, see Gleijeses, *Conflicting Missions*; and Gleijeses, *Visions of Freedom*. On Latin America, see Harmer, *Allende's Chile and the Inter-American Cold War*; and McSherry, *Predatory States*. On China, see Chen Jian, *Mao's China and the Cold War*.

19. For an overview of how transnational actors shaped geopolitics in the late twentieth century, see Sargent, *A Superpower Transformed*. On human rights activism, see Snyder, *Human Rights Activism and the End of the Cold War*; Iriye, Goedde, and Hitchcock, eds. *The Human Rights Revolution*; and Moyn, *The Last Utopia*. On transnational peace and solidarity movements, see Peace, *A Call to Conscience*; Smith, *Resisting Reagan*; and Gosse, "El Salvador Is Spanish for Vietnam." This work on non-governmental organizations built upon that of historians who studied the anticolonial efforts of African Americans, though those scholars generally did not conceive of their work as dealing with NGOs. See, for example, Von Eschen, *Race against Empire*.

20. Summing up that view, one of the leading theoreticians of conservatism, Corey Robin, sees it as a "mode of counterrevolutionary practice," or a "reaction" against modern revolutionary and emancipatory movements, especially those of the Left. Still, Robin does acknowledge that the Right, "in the course of conducting its reaction," has also "consistently borrowed from the left." Robin, *The Reactionary Mind*, 1–60, quotes from 17 and 35. Yet some historians of the extreme Right, such as Robert Paxton, have argued that fascism, particularly its German version, can be considered "revolutionary," but only in a "special sense, far removed from the word's meaning as usually understood from 1789 through 1917." Fascism carried out "some changes profound enough to be called 'revolutionary,'" including the expansion of state power, changing practices of citizenship through "mass ceremonies of public affirmation," collapsing the boundaries between private and public life, and the release of "aggressive emotions hitherto only known in Europe during war or social revolution." See Paxton, *Anatomy of Fascism*, 11.

21. John Singlaub, Speech to the Anti-Bolshevik Bloc of Nations/European Freedom Council Conference, London, Great Britain, September 24–26, 1982, folder 5, box 54, KDP, HIWRP.

22. The key texts about U.S. race relations on the global stage of the Cold War include Borstelmann, *The Cold War and the Color Line*; Borstelmann, *Apartheid's Reluctant Uncle*; Dudziak, *Cold War Civil Rights*; von Eschen, *Race against Empire*; and Noer, *Cold War and Black Liberation*.

23. Indeed, the vast majority of those who comprised the international anticommunist movement were men, and they understood war and politics, even the kinds undertaken by citizens, to be inherently masculine enterprises. Thus, very few women joined the movement, and most of those who did were married to male activists. The clearest example is Slava Stetsko, wife of Yaroslav Stetsko, head of the Anti-Bolshevik Bloc of Nations. Slava served as her husband's secretary and the editor of the ABN's publications for four decades. She frequently attended conferences with her husband and in later years, as his health failed, spoke in his stead.

24. In this sense, the international anticommunist movement drew upon and contributed to a rich vein of discourse through which many people constructed the Cold War in terms of masculinity and sexuality. On the centrality of gender in Cold War political culture and policymaking, see May, *Homeward Bound*; Rotter, "Gender Relations, Foreign Relations"; Gibson, *Warrior Dreams*; Sherry, *In the Shadow of War*; Costigliola, "'Unceasing Pressure for Penetration'"; Dean, *Imperial Brotherhood*; McAlister, *Epic Encounters*; Johnson, *The Lavender Scare*; Cuordileone, *Manhood and American Political Culture in the Cold War*; Jacobs, *America's Miracle Man in Vietnam*; and Canaday, *The Straight State*.

25. See Gibson, *Warrior Dreams*; and Belew, *Bring the War Home*.

26. The United States Neutrality Act, first passed in 1794 and revised several times thereafter, forbids American citizens from waging war against any nations with which the United States is at peace. Since 1939, the act has been enforced under the U.S. Code 22 § 441–57. The United States Foreign Agents Registration Act, passed in 1938, "requires persons acting as agents of foreign principals in a political or quasi-political capacity to make periodic public disclosure of their relationship with the foreign principal, as well as activities, receipts and disbursements in support of those activities." See Foreign Agents Registration Act, U.S. Code 22 §611 et seq.

## Chapter 1

1. Liebman recalled that he made his trip in August, but official APACL documents indicate that the conference met from March 27 through April 1, 1957. Liebman, *Coming Out Conservative*, 119.
2. Ibid., 119–20.
3. See list of representatives in "Asian Peoples' Anti-Communist League Third Annual Conference: Speeches and Reports," March 27, 1957, B-393–002, APACL, CWIHP.
4. Address by the President of the Republic of South Vietnam in "Asian Peoples' Anti-Communist League Third Annual Conference: Speeches and Reports," March 27, 1957, B-393–002, APACL, CWIHP.
5. Liebman, *Coming Out Conservative*, 119.
6. See Address by General Ferenc Farkas de Kisbarnaki, delegate of the Hungarian Liberation Movement, and Address by Yaroslav Stetsko, delegate of the Anti-Bolshevik Bloc of Nations, in "Asian Peoples' Anti-Communist League Third Annual Conference: Speeches and Reports," March 27, 1957, B-393–002, APACL, CWIHP.
7. Address by Ku Chen Kang, Chief Chinese Delegate, in "Asian Peoples' Anti-Communist League Third Annual Conference: Speeches and Reports," March 27, 1957, B-393–002, APACL, CWIHP.
8. Address by Dr. Chin Hang Kong, Chief Delegate of the Republic of Korea, in "Asian Peoples' Anti-Communist League Third Annual Conference: Speeches and Reports," March 27, 1957, B-393–002, APACL, CWIHP.
9. See Roy, *Taiwan*, 38–40, 78–80.
10. See Kerr, *Formosa Betrayed*, chaps. 5–14. U.S. press coverage of incident was rather limited. See, for example, Christopher Rand, "Formosa Riots Are Reported to Have Spread," *New York Herald Tribune*, March 4, 1947; and "Formosa Is Reported in Grip of Rebellion," *NYT*, March 2, 1947.
11. Tucker, *Strait Talk*, 67–75.
12. See Logevall and Campbell, *America's Cold War*, 103–4.
13. On China's role as a market for U.S. goods and a source of cheap labor, see Jacobsen, *Barbarian Virtues*, 26–38, 75–85.
14. For an overview of Americans' fascination with China, starting in the late eighteenth century, see Chang, *Fateful Ties*. For missionaries and religious orientalism, see Yoshihara, *Embracing the East*; Klein, *Cold War Orientalism*; and Miller-Davenport, "'Their Blood Shall Not be Shed in Vain.'"
15. Some officials in the Pentagon had the same hopes, transforming Jiang's grandiose hopes for reconquering the mainland into a set of detailed but never enacted military plans. See Lin, *Accidental State*.
16. See Mao, *Asia First*, 5–7.
17. Lichtman, *White Protestant Nation*, 154. Kohlberg also used his wealth to fight communism at home. The same year that he founded the American China Policy Association, Kohlberg began funding a private company run by three former FBI agents called American Business Consultants that exposed potential subversives by investigating leftist publications, membership lists, and petitions. See Everitt, *A Shadow of Red*, 37–46.
18. On the success of Kohlberg, see Bachrcak, *The Committee of One Million*; and Keely, *China Lobby Man*. Many reporters in the United States alleged that the GMD was funding the China Lobby, causing the Truman administration to carry out its own probe through a joint effort of several executive departments. However, the investigation could not unearth legal proof that this money had actually been exchanged between Chinese Nationalist sympathizers

and American political personalities. See Charles Wertenbacker, "The China Lobby," *The Reporter*, April 15, 1952, 2–24; and Philip Horton, "The China Lobby: Part II," *The Reporter*, April 29, 1952, 5–24. See also William S. White, "Acheson Proffers Data for Inquiries into 'China Lobby,'" *NYT*, June 9, 1951; "Truman Orders Investigation of China Lobby," *Daily Boston Globe*, June 10, 1951; Koen, *The China Lobby in American Politics*, 27; and Accinelli, *Crisis and Commitment*, 77, 284, n.33.

19. Liebman, *Coming Out Conservative*, 19–32.

20. See Bérubé, *Coming Out under Fire*.

21. Liebman, *Coming Out Conservative*, 33–47.

22. Ibid., 80–85.

23. Lipper's book was published by conservative media magnate Henry Regnery. See Lipper, *Eleven Years in Soviet Prison Camps*.

24. Liebman, *Coming Out Conservative*, 84–87, quote from 87.

25. "Chinese in New York Rallying to Aid of Intellectuals," *NYT*, July 5, 1952; "Resettlement Hope Dim for Chinese Intellectuals," *NYT*, August 16, 1952.

26. Liebman, *Coming Out Conservative*, 89–90.

27. On Judd's missionary work and advocacy for Jiang and the GMD, see Edwards, *Missionary for Freedom*.

28. Harold L. Oram, "Report on Mission to Hong Kong and Taiwan, 1952," folder 10, box 1, Aid Refugee Chinese Intellectuals Records, HIWRP.

29. "U.S. Group Expands its Aid to Asians," *NYT*, July 30, 1952. On CIA funding for the Committee for A Free Asia, see Warren Unna, "State Dept. to Ask Congress for Asia Foundation Funds," *WP*, February 26, 1968. APACL leaders praised the work of the Committee for a Free Asia. See Speech by Jose M. Hernandez, "We Have Communism on the Run in the Philippines," June 16, 1954, B-387–023, APACL, CWIHP.

30. Liebman, *Coming Out Conservative*, 100–101.

31. See Committee of One Million, "Shall the Chinese Communists Shoot their Way into the UN?," *NYT*, April 12, 1955. See also Bachrcak, *Committee of One Million*, 110–12. On Americans' hopes that Jiang Jieshi could retake the mainland, see Mao, *Asia First*, 31.

32. Bachrcak, *Committee of One Million*, 3.

33. The APACL grew out of discussions between state leaders and anticommunist activists from Taiwan, South Korea, and South Vietnam in the spring and summer of 1954. See "Proposals for the Establishment of an Anti-Communist Union of the Peoples of Asia," June 1954, B-389–060, APACL, CWIHP; and "Resolutions Adopted by the Chinhae Conference, June 17, 1954: Principles of the Asian Peoples' Anti-Communist League," *Free China Review* (Taipei), July 1954, 60–63; "Rhee Offers ROK Troops for Indochina," *WP*, June 16, 1954. For a brief overview of the APACL's founding and early years see, "From APACL to WACL," *AO*, April 1974.

34. Anderson and Anderson, *Inside the League*, 54–55. The CIA denied the author's FOIA request for mandatory declassification review of all CIA documents relating to the APACL in March 2013. It also denied his appeal in May 2013.

35. "Anti-Communist Congress Aims Doomed," *Voice of Vietnam* (Hanoi), September 1, 1956 in *FBIS*, Foreign Radio Broadcasts, Communist Indochina, FBIS-FRB-56–181.

36. See speech of Ku Chen Kang in "Asian Peoples' Anti-Communist Conference, Minutes of the Opening Session," June 15, 1954, B-387–039, APACL, CWIHP.

37. See "General Report of APACL/ROC Activities," *FCA*, August 1958, 14. APACL leaders reported that they had "been constantly exchanging material with the US Psychological Warfare Office and the psychological warfare organizations in the Philippines and other countries. Particularly intensive is its exchange of anti-communist materials with the NTS

and the ABN. The exchanged materials, besides being used for broadcasting purposes, are also for reprinting either in part or in condensed form in each other's own publications."

38. See "Reports of the Committees, Asian Youth & Students Anti-Communist Conference," October 16, 1956, B-392–020, APACL, CWIHP.

39. See Speech by Chief Delegate of Macau in "Asian Peoples' Anti-Communist League Third Annual Conference: Speeches and Reports," March 27, 1957, B-393–002, APACL, CWIHP.

40. Rhee speech quoted in "Asian Peoples' Anti-Communist Conference, Provisional Summary Record of the Fourth Session," June 16, 1954, B-387–027, APACL, CWIHP.

41. See list of representatives in "Asian Peoples' Anti-Communist League Third Annual Conference: Speeches and Reports," March 27, 1957, B-393–002, APACL, CWIHP.

42. Ku Chen Kang was third in command of the GMD's Central Standing Committee. He was also the head of the Free China Relief Association, a program sponsored by the Taiwanese government to send food and medical supplies to the mainland. See Wu, "The Kuomintang and Political Development in Taiwan since 1968," 138; and "Vice President and Premier Chen Cheng's Statement on Flight of Refugees into Hong Kong," *FCA*, May 1962.

43. See I-Cheng Loh, "Asian Peoples Unite for Freedom," *FCA*, July 1960. From 1971 to 1986, Bagatsing served as the mayor of Manila—the longest serving mayor in the city's history.

44. Anderson and Anderson, *Inside the League*, 56–58.

45. APACL leaders routinely urged Asian states to "strengthen their respective counterespionage activities and the mutual exchange of information, experiences, measures, and techniques relative thereto." See "Minutes of Workshop a on Subject of Communism in Govt. Agencies," March 12, 1956 in "Materials from the Asian Peoples' Anti-Communist League Conference, Manila," March 9–12, 1955, B-392–001, APACL.

46. "On a Global Anti-Communist Strategy," *FCA*, August 1962.

47. Much of this clandestine activity depended upon material and financial support from the Central Intelligence Agency and the U.S. State Department's police training programs. See Kuzamarov, *Modernizing Repression*, esp. 79–120.

48. See Taylor, *Generalissimo's Son*, 206. In 1951, Jiǎng Jīngguó also established a new Political Staff College to train GMD officers in clandestine propaganda work. See the largely celebratory account in Marks, *Counterrevolution in China*, 136–81.

49. See McCoy, *Policing America's Empire*, 374–79.

50. See, for instance, the speech by Jose M. Hernandez, "We Have Communism on the Run in the Philippines," June 16, 1954, B-387–023, APACL, CWIHP.

51. While U.S. trainers claimed they were professionalizing and modernizing South Korea's security forces, their efforts resulted in widespread suffering, terror, and political murder. Police and military units colluded with right-wing political groups to spy on Korean citizens, smash leftist organizations, and suppress working-class activism. See Kuzamarov, *Modernizing Repression*, 91–98.

52. As this campaign of collaboration and covert war expanded into other parts of Asia in the late 1950s, the Asian Peoples' Anti-Communist League followed. Within a few years, it had incorporated chapters from Australia, Burma, Iraq, Iran, Malaya, New Zealand, Pakistan, Singapore, and Turkey. Letter from Tran Tam to Senator Thomas Dodd, February 16, 1962, folder APACL, box 8, MLP, HIWRP.

53. See for instance "The Consequences of the So-called Asian-African Peoples' Solidarity Conference," *FCA*, December 1958; and "Formation of SEATO," in "A Brief History of the Asian Peoples' Anti-Communist League," March 5, 1956, B-392–008, APACL, CWIHP.

54. See for instance, Ku Chen Kang, "Asian Peoples' Anti-Communist Conference, Annex to the Summary Record (APACC/SR.2)," June 17, 1954, B-387–044, APACL, CWIHP.

55. See Dorril, *MI6*, 226–28.

56. Bandera's faction became known as the OUN/B and adopted a paramilitary structure. Flush with funding and weaponry from the German military intelligence, the OUN/B carried out a campaign of assassinations, culminating in the murder of Polish Interior Minister Bronislaw Pieracki in 1934, which caused Polish authorities to imprison Stetsko and several other OUN leaders in Warsaw. Yet Stetsko managed to escape from prison in the mayhem that followed the Nazi invasion of Poland in September 1939. He soon traveled to western Ukraine and then to Berlin to organize tens of thousands of partisan forces to combat the Red Army and the NKVD, the Soviet intelligence apparatus. On Stetsko's early life see, Berkhoff and Carynnyk, "Organization of Ukrainian Nationalists."

57. Like the Nazis, the OUN linked anti-Semitism and anticommunism. "Although I consider Moscow to be the main and decisive enemy," Stetsko wrote in 1941, "I nonetheless fully appreciate the undeniably harmful and hostile role of the Jews, who are helping Moscow to enslave Ukraine. I therefore support the destruction of the Jews and the expedience of bringing German methods of exterminating Jewry to Ukraine, barring their assimilation and the like." Stetsko quoted in Berkhoff and Carynnyk, "Organization of Ukrainian Nationalists," 153.

58. See Snyder, *Bloodlands*, 161.

59. Memo from Deputy Director, CIA to U.S. Dept. of State, "Yaroslav Stetsko," July 1 1957, CIA-FOIA, at https://www.cia.gov/library/readingroom/docs/STETSKO,%20YAROSLAV_0092.pdf; and Memo from Deputy Director, CIA to United States Secretary of State John Foster Dulles, July 1957, CIA-FOIA, http://www.foia.cia.gov/sites/default/files/document_conversions/1705143/STETSKO%2C%20YAROSLAV_0093.pdf.

60. See Brietman and Goda, *In Hitler's Shadow*, 73–97.

61. See Snyder, *Bloodlands*, 160–61, 187–223.

62. See British Foreign Office report, "Request for an interview to discuss results achieved and aims of the Anti-Bolshevik Bloc of Nations," July 12, 1950, FO 371/86154, UKNA. On postwar Munich and exiled partisans, see Weiner, *Legacy of Ashes*, 74–76, 129–30.

63. As late as 1949, American and British intelligence officers believed that exile groups such as the ABN could be used in covert actions—"propaganda, economic warfare . . . subversion against hostile states, including assistance to underground movements, guerrillas, and refugee liberation groups." See National Security Council Directive 10/2, June 18, 1948, in Etzold and Gaddis, eds., *Containment*, 127. For British intelligence and the ABN, see Dorril, *MI6*, 234–40. For the CIA and the ABN, see Brietman and Goda, *In Hitler's Shadow*, 73–97. For a useful overview of the CIA's failures in fomenting guerrilla war in the Eastern bloc, see Weiner, *Legacy of Ashes*, 44–54.

64. As a British Foreign Office report noted in 1950, the ABN's links with guerrillas in Ukraine and elsewhere were "increasingly hard to maintain." See "Report of Interview with M. Stetsko, President of the "Anti-Bolshevik Bloc of Nations," London, March 10, 1950, and March 22, 1950, FO 371/86154, UKNA. British intelligence made a few attempts to arm Ukrainian insurgents but, by 1951, most of these operations failed due to double agents who disclosed classified information to Soviet authorities. See Dorril, *MI6*, 243–47. For its part, the CIA surmised that the ABN "might have been penetrated by Soviet[s] through certain Ukrainian personalities." See the CIA memo regarding the ABN, July 27, 1951, CIA-FOIA, http://www.foia.cia.gov/sites/default/files/document_conversions/1705143/STETSKO%2C%20YAROSLAV_0034.pdf, accessed October 21, 2013.

65. Yaroslav Stetsko, "The Perspective of Our Campaign," *ABN Correspondence* (Munich), March/April 1953.

66. As Stetsko wrote in 1964, the "armed fight which was put up twenty years ago may

serve as a two-fold guide for freedom-loving mankind—that is to say, as both a political and military strategic guide." Yaroslav Stetsko, "The Light of Freedom from the Forests of Ukraine," *The Ukrainian Review*, no. 1, 1964, 53–59.

67. See Yaroslav Stetsko, "Possibility of National Revolution Behind the Iron Curtain," *ABN Correspondence*, May-June 1959, 7–8.

68. Holian, *Between National Socialism and Soviet Communism*, 129–30.

69. See Memo from J. H. Peck, February 12, 1951, FO 371/94964, UKNA.

70. Holian, *Between National Socialism and Soviet Communism*, 129–30.

71. A rival Ukrainian group argued that the ABN continued the "tradition of Hitler and Goebbels" by fostering "chauvinism and blind hatred towards the Russian peoples." Ukrainian Liberation Movement, "What Is ABN," no date, folder 10, box 45, HPP, LOC.

72. Levy, "Madison, Wilson, and Eastern European Federalism," 315–16. For a list of ABN leaders, see U.S. State Department Memo from John A. Russell, "STETSKO, Yaroslav and the Anti-Bolshevik Bloc of Nations," March 1, 1971 in U.S. Department of State Electronic Reading Room, http://foia.state.gov/Search/results.aspx?searchText=%22stetsko%22&beginDate=&endDate=&publishedBeginDate=&publishedEndDate=&caseNumber, accessed September 30, 2014.

73. On the early collaboration between the ABN and the APACL, see "American, National Chinese, and Korean Politicians Support the Ideology of the ABN," *ABN Correspondence*, May/September 1954; Stephen C. Y. Pan, "National China and the ABN," *ABN Correspondence*, May/September 1954; "Free China and Vanguard in the Anti-Communist Struggle," *ABN Correspondence*, January/March 1956; "The Union of the Anti-Communist Front in the East and the West," *ABN Correspondence*, January/March 1956; and "An Anti-Communist World League," *ABN Correspondence*, August/September 1956.

74. For Stetsko's meeting with Franco, see "President of the Central Committee of the ABN Visits Spain," *ABN Correspondence*, March/April 1955. For Jiang, see "The Democracies Must Strengthen their Mutual Defense in Asia," *ABN Correspondence*, January–March 1956. For Walter Judd, see "Americans for ABN: Freedom and Peace through Liberation Congress in Washington," *ABN Correspondence*, October–December 1956.

75. See British Foreign Office report, "Convention of Delegates of the ABN held in Edinburgh," FO 371/86154, UKNA. For an overview of Stetsko's collaboration with Stewart see "Obituary: John F. Stewart, Champion of the Enslaved Nations," *ABN Correspondence*, September/October 1958; "Coexistence or a Policy of Liberation," *ABN Correspondence*, October/November 1955. See also Dorril, *MI6*, 441–42.

76. See John F. Stewart, "Economic and Military Strength and Weakness of Red Russia and the Independence Movements in the USSR," (Scottish League for European Freedom), FO 371/94964, UKNA.

77. See, for example, Fuller, *Russia Is Not Invincible*; and Fuller, *How to Defeat Russia*. See also Searle, "Was There a 'Boney' Fuller after the Second World War?"

78. For instance, when Stetsko applied for a U.S. visa in 1956, internal CIA memorandums noted that the ABN "although strongly anticommunist has engaged in methods considered objectionable by this agency and has furthered objectives detrimental to this interests of this agency." CIA Memorandum, Subject Stetzko, June 13, 1956, CIA-FOIA, http://www.foia.cia.gov/sites/default/files/document_conversions/1705143/STETSKO%2C%20YAROSLAV_0081.pdf, accessed November 19, 2013.

79. R. S. Faber, Report on Meeting of Scottish League for European Freedom in June 1950, June 12, 1950, FO 371/94964, UKNA.

80. Memo from J. H. Peck, February 12, 1951, FO 371/94964, UKNA.

81. Memo from Deputy Director, CIA to U.S. Dept. of State, "Yaroslav Stetsko," July 1

1957, CIA-FOIA, https://www.cia.gov/library/readingroom/docs/STETSKO,%20YAROSLAV_0092.pdf, accessed June 6, 2017.

82. Memorandum of Discussion at the 132d Meeting of the National Security Council, Washington, February 18, 1953, document 71, *FRUS, 1952–1954*, vol. VIII, Eastern Europe, Soviet Union, Mediterranean; Record of Meeting of the Ad Hoc Committee on NSC 143, Monday, March 23, 1953, document 75, *FRUS, 1952–1954*, vol. VIII, Eastern Europe, Soviet Union, Mediterranean; and CIA Report, "Communist Reactions to US Establishment of a 'Volunteer Freedom Corps,'" April 13, 1953, CIA-FOIA, at https://www.cia.gov/library/readingroom/document/0000269304, accessed December 14, 2016.

83. Carafano, "Mobilizing Europe's Stateless," quotes from 77.

84. Dulles quoted in Herring, *From Colony to Superpower*, 667. On the United States and the Hungarian Uprising, see Békés, Rainer, and Byrne, eds., *The 1956 Hungarian Revolution*; and Granville, "'Caught with Jam on Our Fingers.'" On the ABN and Hungary, see "The Activity of the ABN in Connection with the Revolution in Hungary," *ABN Correspondence*, January/February 1957, 6.

85. This network centered on a "nuclei of exiled leaders from various countries who were, at times, able to coordinate their activities and mobilize 'foot soldiers'—exiles living throughout the region." See Gleijeses, "Juan Jose Arevalo and the Caribbean Legion," 134–35; and Moulton, "Building Their Own Cold War in Their Own Backyard."

86. "Report from the Preparatory Conference for the World Anti-Communist Congress for Freedom and Liberation," *FCA*, April 1958, 6–11; "Groundwork for World Anti-communist Congress for Freedom and Liberation Laid by [Preparatory] Conference in Mexico City," *Ukrainian Quarterly* 14 (March 1958): 63–76. During the 1950s and early 1960s, Jorge Prieto Laurens was financing several anticommunist student groups in Monterrey and Guadalajara. See Pensado, "Political Violence and Student Culture in Mexico," 172, 309–10. On Prieto Laurens's beliefs, see Prieto Laurens, *El Complot Comunista*; and Prieto Laurens, *El Comunismo en México*.

87. See CIA Report, "Preside El Sr. Jorge Prieto Laurens," May 30, 1954, CIA-FOIA, http://www.foia.cia.gov/sites/default/files/document_conversions/89801/DOC_0000922999.pdf, accessed September 30, 2014; "Salazar Foresees Guatemalan Revolt," *The Palm Beach Post*, May 29, 1954; and "Las Armas Guatemala Punto Principal del Primer Congreso Anti-Comunista," *La Nación* (Mexico City), May 26, 1954.

88. See CIA Memo from Jerome C. Dunbar to Chief of Hemisphere, "KUGORN Operation: Congreso Panamericano Anticomunista," April 14, 1954, CIA-FOIA, at http://www.foia.cia.gov/sites/default/files/document_conversions/89801/DOC_0000916380.pdf, accessed October 2, 2014.

89. See CIA Dispatch HUL-W-370 from Chief, WH to Chief of Station, LINCOLN, "Anti-Communism in Mexico: Frente Popular Anti-Comunista de Mexico," May 21, 1954, CIA-FOIA, at http://www.foia.cia.gov/sites/default/files/document_conversions/89801/DOC_0000923420.pdf, accessed September 28, 2014.

90. The CIA also offered funds to Guatemalan exiles to help finance the conference. See Aaron Colton McCoy, "Los Hijos de Ubico: Dissident Guatemalan Exiles and the Transnational Counter-Revolution against the Guatemalan Revolution, 1944–1954," paper delivered at the Latin American Studies Association Conference, San Juan, Puerto Rico, May 27–30, 2015, in author's possession.

91. CIA Dispatch HUL-A-76 from LINCOLN to Chief, Western Hemisphere, "KUGORN-PBSUCCESS: Hemisphere Conference in Mexico City, April 1954," February 22, 1954, CIA-FOIA, http://www.foia.cia.gov/sites/default/files/document_conversions/89801/DOC_0000928364.pdf, accessed October 2, 2014. CIA Dispatch HUL-A-822 from Lincoln to

[redacted], "KUGORN Summit: Guatemalan Delegation, May 19, 1954, CIA-FOIA, http://www.foia.cia.gov/sites/default/files/document_conversions/89801/DOC_0000923527.pdf, accessed October 3, 2014. See also "Meeting Urges Action against Guatemala," *Ciudad Trujillo* in Spanish to the Dominican Republic, May 31, 1954, in *FBIS*, Foreign Radio Broadcasts FBIS-FRB-54-105 on 1954-06-01.

92. See Botto, *O Que é o comunismo?*; and *Como se desenvolve a Ofensiva Comunista*.

93. On the links between IACDC leaders and the APACL, see Jorge Prieto Laurens, "Incredible Blindness in the Case of Russianized Cuba," *Free China & Asia* (Taipei), August 1961. On their visits to ABN conferences in Munich and other cities see, Adm. Carlos Penna Botto, "Sheer Force Is the Only Argument," *ABN Correspondence*, September/October 1957; "A Further Stage in the World Crusade Against Bolshevism," *ABN Correspondence*, September/October 1957; and Jorge Prieto Laurens, "World Tragedy of Our Day," *ABN Correspondence*, September/October 1957, folder 6, American Friends of the Anti-Bolshevik Bloc of Nations, Box 34, HPP LOC.

94. See Letter from Marvin Liebman to Francis J. McNamara, October 16, 1958, folder Special Folder: World Anti-Communist Congress, Box 106, MLP, HIWRP. He did not want it to "be seen as an American operation," believing it "would be best if it seemed to come from Latin America." To create that illusion, he convinced Jorge Prieto Laurens to send invitations and handle the logistics from his offices in Mexico City, sending him a few thousand dollars from the Committee of One Million's coffers. Liebman, *Coming Out Conservative*, 134–35.

95. See "Report from the Prepatory Conference for the World Anti-Communist Congress for Freedom and Liberation," *FCA*, April 1958, 6–11.

96. "Principles Governing the Organization of the World Anti-Communist Congress for Freedom and Liberation," *FCA*, April 1958, 13; "Political statement: Adopted at the Preparatory Conference for the World Anti-Communist Congress for Freedom and Liberation, held in Mexico City, March 20–25, 1958," *Ukrainian Bulletin*, April 15, 1958, 4–6. U.S. press coverage for the conference was limited to a few short articles in major publications. See, for example, "World Anti-Red Conference Set," *NYT*, March 23, 1958.

97. "Principles Governing the Organization of the World Anti-Communist Congress for Freedom and Liberation," *FCA*, April 1958, 13.

98. Marvin Liebman, "Comments on the Mexico City Preparatory Conference for the World Anti-Communist Congress for Freedom and Liberation," *FCA*, April 1958, 17.

99. Memo from Marvin Liebman to Steering Committee, Secretariat, and Participants in Mexico City Conference of the World Anti-Communist Congress for Freedom and Liberation, July 14, 1958, folder World Anti-Communist Congress, box 106, MLP, HIWRP.

100. Liebman, *Coming Out Conservative*, 135. At the time, he confessed to his American friends that the conference "was a good try, but I'm glad we're out of it." Letter from Marvin Liebman to Francis J. McNamara, October 16, 1958, folder World Anti-Communist Congress, box 106, MLP, HIWRP.

101. Letter from Lev Dobriansky to Marvin Liebman, August 14, 1958, folder World Anti-Communist Congress, box 106, MLP, HIWRP.

102. Liebman, *Coming Out Conservative*, 136.

103. Memo from Marvin Liebman to Steering Committee, Secretariat, and Participants in Mexico City Conference of the World Anti-Communist Congress for Freedom and Liberation, July 14, 1958; and J. Howard Pew, Financial Report, World Anti-Communist Congress for Freedom and Liberation, no date, folder World Anti-Communist Congress, box 106, MLP, HIWRP.

104. Members from the APACL wanted Ku Chen Kang to chair the group while those from IACDC called for Admiral Botto and the ABN pressed Yaroslav Stetsko forward. See

the responses to Marvin Liebman's July 14, 1958 letter, folder World Anti-Communist Congress, box 106, MLP, HIWRP.

105. For instance, Marvin Liebman participated in the 5th APACL conference in Seoul in 1959. See Letter from Marvin Liebman to Ku Chen Kang, May 21, 1959; Travel Information for Marvin Liebman, May 28, 1959; and Program for the 5th Conference of the APACL, June 1–10, 1959, Seoul, Republic of Korea in folder Asian People's Anti-Communist League, box 11, MLP, HIWRP.

## Chapter 2

1. Clarence Manion on "We Are at War: Will We Fight or Will We Surrender?," *Manion Forum*, January 15, 1961, folder 1, box 83, CMP-CHM.
2. See McGirr, *Suburban Warriors*; Perlstein, *Before the Storm*; Kruse, *White Flight*; Lassiter, *Silent Majority*; Crespino, *In Search of Another Country*; Perlstein, *Nixonland*; and Nickerson, *Mothers of Conservatism*. The two most important contemporary explanations of the Goldwater campaign and its historical trajectory were Richard Hofstadter, "The Paranoid Style in American Politics," *Harper's*, November 1964; and Bell, ed. *The Radical Right*.
3. On the role of wealthy individuals, corporations, and think tanks in propelling the rise of the Right, see Fones-Wolf, *Selling Free Enterprise*; MacLean, *Freedom Is Not Enough*, esp. chapter 7; and Phillips-Fein, *Invisible Hands*.
4. Liebman later recalled, "Only three times in my life has anyone had such an immediate impact on me." See Liebman, *Coming Out Conservative*, 86.
5. See Phillips-Fein, *Invisible Hands*, 78.
6. Hunt had Buckley translate the work of a former Chilean Marxist, Eudocio Ravines, into English. See Hunt, *American Spy*, 48, 53, 59.
7. See Buckley, *God and Man at Yale*; and Buckley, *McCarthy and His Enemies*.
8. On the fusion of conservative philosophies see, Nash, *Conservative Intellectual Movement in America*.
9. Burnham made similar calls in his books. See Burnham, *Struggle for the World*; Burnham, *Coming Defeat of Communism*; and Burnham, *Operation Rollback*.
10. In 1926, for instance, Manion authored a textbook, titled *American History* and organized around the premise that an overly powerful central government quashes individual freedom. On his biography, see Carolyn Manion, "A Life worth Living," unpublished paper, Georgetown Visitation Junior College, 1957, folder 11, box 74, CMP-CHM. See also Hoplin and Robinson, *Funding Fathers*, 88–90.
11. See Hemmer, "Messengers of the Right," 33–43. On the America First Committee's support for the fascist powers, see Horne, *Color of Fascism*.
12. See Hemmer, "Messengers of the Right," 48–51; Perlstein, *Before the Storm*, 8–11.
13. See "Manion Ousted by White House as Head of Governmental Survey," *NYT*, February 18, 1954; "Dr. Manion Departs," *Chicago Daily Tribune*, February 19, 1954; Phillip Dodd, "Manion Tells Story of Ouster," *Chicago Daily Tribune*, February 22, 1954.
14. Manion's start-up funds came from thousands of business owners, large and small, who responded to his pleas for donations. See Form Solicitation Letters, folder 1, box 98, CMP-CHM. For the creation of the *Manion Forum* see Perlstein, *Before the Storm*, 8–11; and Phillips-Fein, *Invisible Hands*, 83–84.
15. For *Manion Forum* funding and listenership figures, see Group Research Inc., "Report on the Manion Forum," 1966, folder 8, box 88, CMP-CHM.
16. Perlstein, *Before the Storm*, 61–62.
17. He and his guests railed about government intrusion into the labor market, the ty-

rannical power of unions, the oppression of the federal income tax, and wasteful federal expenditures on interstates, housing projects, and agricultural subsidies. They pled for local control of schools, states' rights, and right-to-work laws. Manion's advocacy for right-to-work laws reached a peak in 1957 when he enlisted his show in the cause of Wisconsin industrialist Herbert Kohler, who was facing a massive a United Auto Workers strike. The *Manion Forum* broadcasted Kohler's anti-union diatribe which, in turn, caused several local stations affiliated with the Mutual Broadcasting System to drop his show. See "Network Bars Kohler's Talk on UAW Strike," *CT*, October 1, 1957. See also Phillips-Fein, *Invisible Hands*, 120–26.

18. See "Foreign Aid to the Communist Conquest," *Manion Forum*, March 18, 1956, folder 14, box 81; "Foreign Aid Program Full of Danger," *Manion Forum*, September 16, 1956, folder 2, box 82; "Foreign Aid Design for National Suicide," *Manion Forum*, January 27, 1957, folder 3, box 82; Will Hungary Rouse Us to Real Anger," *Manion Forum*, December 2, 1956, folder 2, box 82; "Peace Impossible While Captive Nations Remain in Bondage," *Manion Forum*, March 2, 1958, folder 6, box 82; "We Must Declare for Independence of Captive Nations," *Manion Forum*, July 3, 1960, folder 12, box 82, CMP-CHM.

19. On Kennedy, Castro, and the Bay of Pigs invasion, see Fursenko and Naftali, *"One Hell of a Gamble,"* 77–100.

20. "Who Is Betraying the Efforts to Free Cuba from Communism?," *Manion Forum*, January 20, 1963, folder 5, box 83, CMP-CHM.

21. Luis V. Manrara, "The Truth about Cuba Committee: Its Motives, Organization, and Goals," September 22, 1988, folder 2, box 118, Truth about Cuba Committee Records, CHC-UM.

22. On Cuban exiles and the U.S. government's reception, see Garcia, *Havana, USA*, 24–45.

23. For Manrara's biography, see Truth about Cuba Committee brochure, "Brief Biographical Data of Mr. Luis V. Manrara," November 1967, folder 7, box 123, Truth about Cuba Committee Records, CHC-UM. On his view of Castro's turn towards communism, see Typescript of "Castro Admits Cuba Is Communist," 1961, folder 8, box 119, Truth about Cuba Committee Records, CHC-UM. See also "Castro's Cuba—A Dagger Aimed at the Heart of the United States," *Manion Forum*, August 12, 1962, folder 4, box 83, CMP-CHM.

24. "Cuban Exile Group Works to Help Refugees," *St. Petersburg Times*, April 11, 1980. By mid-decade Manion was providing free legal services to the Truth about Cuba Committee. See letter from Luis V. Manrara to Clarence Manion, March 27, 1964, folder 10, box 74, Truth about Cuba Committee Records, CMP-CHM.

25. Jorge Bosch, the long-serving president of the Bacardi Corporation also served as the group's vice president. See the biographical data in Truth about Cuba Committee brochure, "Objectives, Plans," November 1961; and Truth about Cuba Committee brochure, "Background on The Truth about Cuba Committee, Inc.," 1961, folder 4, box 119, Truth about Cuba Committee Records, CHC-UM.

26. "Castro's Cuba—A Dagger Aimed at the Heart of the United States," *Manion Forum*, August 12, 1962, folder 8, box 83, CMP-CHM.

27. Luis Manrara, "The Tri-Continental Conference: A Declaration of War," pamphlet of speech given before various civic clubs in Puerto Rico, 1966, quotes from 12–13, folder 43, box 123, Truth about Cuba Committee Records, CHC-UM.

28. For a list of the many exile groups operating in the 1960s, see Cuban Freedom Committee report, "Groups, Collaborators, and Individuals in the United States," 1967, folder Groups—United States, box 33, Cuban Freedom Committee Papers, HIWRP. On the Cuban Freedom Committee as a CIA front see Schoultz, *That Infernal Little Cuban Republic*, 440.

29. Mario Lazo, "Decision for Disaster," September 1964, published by Truth about Cuba Committee, folder 7, box 84, HPP, LOC.

30. See "Ex-Castro Officers Build Force in U.S.," *NYT*, April 19, 1962.

31. For an internal history of Alpha 66, see "Los Principios Ideologicos de Alpha 66," July 21, 1972, folder 2, box 57, KDP, HIWRP. See also Garcia, *Havana, USA*, 93, 128–29.

32. See "U.S. Jury Acquits 4 Foes of Castro," *NYT*, June 5, 1966; "Cuban-Exile Terrorist Ring Smashed as FBI Arrests 9," *WP*, October 12, 1968; "Cuban Exiles Guilty in Ship Conspiracy," *NYT*, November 16, 1968; and "Cuban Terrorist Gets Ten Years for Firing on Vessel in Miami," *NYT*, December 14, 1968.

33. Released from prison in 1972, Bosch quickly resumed his paramilitary activities. See William Turner, "A Sordid Tale of the Most Unforgiving Cuban of Them All," *The Sun* (Baltimore), October 31, 1976.

34. As a member of the Council of Foreign Relations, Braden made several highly publicized speeches calling for Eisenhower to oust Arbenz. He also helped facilitate connections between United Fruit and the U.S. government to members of the Guatemalan and Nicaraguan armies. See Immerman, *The CIA in Guatemala*, 127–28; and Streeter, *Managing the Counterrevolution*, 17. See also Murray Illison, "Spruille Braden, Former Official of State Department, Is Dead at 83," *NYT*, January 11, 1978.

35. See, for example, "We Must Fight to Oust Communism from Cuba," *Manion Forum* 327, January 1, 1960, folder 10, box 82, CMP-CHM.

36. "Nicaraguan President Urges Blockade of Cuba," *Manion Forum*, April 30, 1961, folder 1, box 83, CMP-CHM.

37. See Grandin, *Last Colonial Massacre*, 51–52, 67, 76–77.

38. See Schlesinger and Kinzer, *Bitter Fruit*; and Streeter, *Managing the Counterrevolution*, 72–77, 81–91.

39. See Pastor, *Condemned to Repetition*, 35–37; and Gambone, *Eisenhower, Somoza, and the Cold War in Nicaragua*.

40. See Grandin, *Last Colonial Massacre*, 73–80.

41. See Weiner, *Legacy of Ashes*, 186.

42. "The Menace of Communism in Cuba," *Manion Forum*, February 26, 1961 and "Will Communism Take over the United States via South America?," *Manion Forum*, January 31, 1960, folder 1, box 83, CMP-CHM.

43. The Menace of Communism in Cuba," *Manion Forum*, February 26, 1961, folder 1, box 83, CMP-CHM.

44. For instance, in 1962, Ydígoras asked U.S. business-owners and bankers to aid his government by making available private long-term loans that would "encourage the development of agriculture, light industry, transportation, and culture." "The Menace of Communism in Cuba," *Manion Forum*, February 26, 1961, folder 1, box 83; "How the Communists Plan to Take Over this Hemisphere," *Manion Forum*, December 16, 1962, folder 4, box 83, CMP-CHM.

45. See "Are We Pledged to Protect Communism in Cuba? Ask Congress to Find Out," *Manion Forum*, folder 4, box 83, CMP-CHM. See also Lichtman, *White Protestant Nation*, 235.

46. Founded in 1947 by a Catholic priest, Jose Joaquin Salcedo Guarin, Acción Cultural Popular aimed to counter the propaganda of communist agents who had supposedly infiltrated the countryside. See the English- and Spanish-language promotional literature for the Acción Cultural Popular, distributed by the Inter-American Literacy Foundation, folder 1, box 6, CMP-CHM.

47. "The Menace of Communism to Central America," *Manion Forum*, December 9, 1962, folder 4, box 83, CMP-CHM.

48. "How the Communists Plan to Take Over this Hemisphere," *Manion Forum*, December 16, 1962, folder 4, box 83, CMP-CHM.

49. "The Menace of Communism to Central America," *Manion Forum*, December 9, 1962, folder 4, box 83, CMP-CHM.

50. "A New Sanctuary for Subversion," *Manion Forum*, May 23, 1965, folder 7, box 83, CMP-CHM.

51. "Exhibitionism on the Campus: Headlines Hide Widespread Student Commitment to Conservatism," *Manion Forum*, May 9, 1965, folder 7, box 83, CMP-CHM.

52. On the success of Jiang's government, see Jean Baylot, "Formosa and the Defense of Free Asia," *NR*, March 11, 1961. Baylot praised Taiwan for having the fastest growing economy and the "best land laws of any nation in the Far East." For Taiwan's importance in the global anticommunist struggle, see James Burnham, "Fulcrum for a Lever," *NR*, June 3, 1961.

53. Marvin Liebman, "An Interview with Jiang Jieshi," *NR*, June 17, 1961.

54. See Kwan Soo Park, "Look Straight on the Situation in Southeast Asia: Let Us Rise Up for the Defense of Freedom," *FCA*, March 1962, 5–8.

55. Letter from Ku Chen Kang to Marvin Liebman, January 31, 1961, folder Asian Peoples' Anti-Communist League, Box 11, MLP, HIWRP.

56. "Volunteers for Vietnam," *FCA*, November 1961, 7–11.

57. See Memorandum of Conversation, "KMT Troops in Burma," July 31, 1951, CI00787, U.S. Intelligence and China: Collection, Analysis, and Covert Action collection, DNSA.

58. See Weiner, *Legacy of Ashes*, 66–70.

59. Senator Thomas J. Dodd, a conservative Democrat from Connecticut, declared his enthusiasm for the Free Asian Brigade in a speech before the seventh annual APACL conference in Manila in June 1961. Dodd later wrote to CIA director Allen Dulles about the plan, but nothing came from that. See Letter from Allen Dulles to Sen. Thomas J. Dodd, October 10, 1961, CIA-FOIA, http://www.foia.cia.gov/sites/default/files/document_conversions/5829/CIA-RDP80B01676R000700190034-0.pdf, accessed October 17, 2013.

60. On conservatives' interests in Vietnam before 1963, see Scanlon, *Pro-War Movement*, 18–42.

61. The best overview of the Vietnamese independence movement and the First Indochina War is Logevall, *Embers of War*. On U.S. support for Ngo Dinh Diem, and his appeal as a Catholic anticommunist, see Jacobs, *America's Miracle Man in Vietnam*. On the origins of the NLF as a popular insurgency in South, and its relationship to North Vietnam, China, and the Soviet Union, see Brigham, *Guerrilla Diplomacy*. For an overview of the war's escalation and the introduction of U.S. combat troops see, among other works, Young, *The Vietnam Wars*, 60–172; and Herring, *America's Longest War*, 89–170.

62. See "Address by Former U.S. President Richard M. Nixon," *Proceedings of the 10th APACL Conference* (Saigon: Secretariat of the APACL, 1964), 22–24.

63. On de Jaegher's life, see "Raymond de Jaegher, A Catholic Missionary in China and Vietnam," *NYT*, February 8, 1980. De Jaegher first became involved with the APACL in 1959 when he visited Taiwan to speak with several local anticommunist groups. By 1964, he was a regular feature at its conferences as well as a frequent correspondent with Jiang Jieshi. See "Activities of the APACL," *FCA*, March 1959; and "10th APACL Conference a Success," *FCA*, December 1964.

64. See "2+2 Doesn't Equal 4 Any More," *Manion Forum*, June 5, 1966, folder 8, box 83, CMP-CHM.

65. "World Freedom Depends upon a Free China," *Manion Forum*, February 19, 1967, folder 9, box 83, CMP-CHM.

66. "The Short, Straight Line—Quick Military Victory the Only Way out of Vietnam," *Manion Forum*, March 13, 1966, folder 8, box 83, CMP-CHM.

67. See "Issues for '64—Foreign Aid and Southeast Asia," *Manion Forum*, June 28, 1964, folder 6, box 83, CMP.

68. See Lyons's report, "World Freedom Depends upon a Free China," *Manion Forum*, February 19, 1967, folder 9, box 83, CMP-CHM.

69. The lecture circuit also featured Walter Judd and few other holdovers from the China Lobby. See letter from Raymond de Jaegher to Clarence Manion, December 21, 1966, folder 11, box 58, CMP-CHM.

70. Appy, *American Reckoning*, 185.

71. Varon, *Bringing the War Home*, 123.

72. For YAF membership information, see Lichtman, *White Protestant Nation*, 241–42. For broader histories of the YAF, see Andrew, *Other Side of the Sixties*; and Schneider, *Cadres for Conservatism*.

73. See "First Things First—Young Americans Plan Worldwide Effort Aimed at the Feet of Communism," *Manion Forum*, March 6, 1966, folder 8, box 83, CMP-CHM; and "Newsletter, Republic of China Chapter, APACL," *AO*, September 1965.

74. See Letter from Tom Huston to Members of the Senior Advisory Council, WYFC, April 29, 1966, folder WYC 4/29/1966 (551), box 108, MLP, HIWRP. See also Schneider, *Cadres for Conservatism*, 98.

75. Letter from David Keene to Senior American Advisory Council, Contributors, and Associates, no date, folder World Youth Crusade for Freedom, Inc., box 107, MLP, HIWRP.

76. Gerald S. Berger, International Youth Crusade for Freedom in Vietnam: Report on Examination from the Period November 29, 1965 to June 16, 1966, folder Financial Matters, box 107, MLP, HIWRP; World Youth Crusade for Freedom, Inc., "A Report and Prospectus," World Youth Crusade for Freedom—A Report and Prospectus, box 107, MLP, HIWRP.

77. Letter from Marvin Liebman to Council for International Youth Crusade for Freedom, March 18, 1966, folder Financial Matters, box 107, MLP, HIWRP.

78. Gerald S. Berger, International Youth Crusade for Freedom in Vietnam: Report on Examination from the Period November 29, 1965 to June 16, 1966, folder Financial Matters, box 107, MLP, HIWRP.

79. "S. Vietnam Youth Applaud YAF Stand on War," *CT*, Jan 8, 1966.

80. "First Things First—Young Americans Plan Worldwide Effort Aimed at the Feet of Communism," *Manion Forum*, March 6, 1966, folder 8, box 83, CMP-CHM.

81. Liebman, *Coming Out Conservative*, 185. Emphasis in original.

82. Once selected by Huston and Rusher, these students underwent a rigorous one-week training seminar at Yale University, run by Professor David Nelson Rowe, an expert on China and frequent participant in APACL activities in Taiwan and South Korea. "First Things First—Young Americans Plan Worldwide Effort Aimed at the Feet of Communism," *Manion Forum*, March 6, 1966, folder 8, box 83, CMP-CHM.

83. Tom Charles Huston, "The Third Dimension of International Conflict," *WYFC Report*, vol. 1, no.2, November 1966, folder World Youth Crusade for Freedom, box 107, MLP, HIWRP. Chapter leaders included Rama Swarup (India), Jose Hernandez (Philippines), and Ku Chen Kang (Taiwan). Letter from Tom Huston to All Freedom Corps Fellows, June 20, 1966, folder WYCF 6/20/66 (583), box 108, MLP, HIWRP.

84. Schneider, *Cadres for Conservatism*, 99.

85. "Campus Conservatives on the Move," *Manion Forum*, May 28, 1967, folder 9, box 83, CMP-CHM.

86. Liebman, *Coming Out Conservative*, 186.

87. Institution for American Strategy pamphlet, "Freedom Studies Center: The Private

Freedom Academy," no date, folder Friends of Rhodesian Independence, box 29, MLP, HIWRP.

88. Fisher had made a career in the FBI's so-called Red Squads, where he spent decades investigating suspected communists. See Juan de Onis, "Lobbying Body to Push Congress for a Nuclear Edge over Soviet," *NYT*, January 6, 1981.

89. Brian Kelly, "Virginia Manor House Is 'West Point' of the Cold War," *Washington Star*, November 25, 1969.

90. See Memo from Edward Lansdale to John M. Fisher, July 14, 1965, folder Freedom Studies Center, Boston Virginia, box 11, Edward Lansdale Papers, HIWRP. Lansdale had been kicking the idea around since 1963. See Memo from Edward Lansdale, November 29, 1963, folder Freedom Studies Center, Boston Virginia, box 11, Edward Lansdale Papers, HIWRP.

91. See Pamphlet for the Freedom Studies Center, 1975, folder Freedom Studies Center of the Institution for American Strategy, box 111, MLP, HIWRP. The school's "overseas affiliates" included the Asian Peoples' Anti-Communist League, the Inter-American Committee for the Defense of the Continent, the Brazilian Anti-Communist Crusade, the Alianza Revolucionaria Democrática Cubana, and several Anti-Bolshevik Bloc of Nations offshoots. See the pamphlet for the Freedom Studies Center of the Institution for American Strategy, 1966, folder Freedom Studies Center, box 11, Edward Lansdale Papers, HIWRP.

92. Edward Lansdale, "Freedom Academy: Preliminary Working Study," 1965, folder "Freedom Academy," June 1965 typescript, box 74, Edward Lansdale Papers, HIWRP.

93. See Pamphlet for the Freedom Studies Center, 1975, folder Freedom Studies Center of the Institution for American Strategy, box 111, MLP, HIWRP; and J. Reagan Kerney, "The Cold War Campus: Boston, Va. Estate Is Home of American Security Council," *WP*, January 8, 1979.

94. See Immerman, *The Hidden Hand*, 93–94.

95. Brian Kelly, "Virginia Manor House Is 'West Point' of the Cold War," *Washington Star*, November 25, 1969.

96. On Katanga's mineral riches and the Belgian company Union Minière, see de Witte, *Assassination of Lumumba*, 31–32.

97. As Irish diplomat Conor Cruise O'Brien once noted, Katanga was where the "Winds of Change" encountered the "escarpment of a relatively solid area of European settlement and rule. The 30,000 or so Europeans of Katanga felt themselves to be backed by the 300,000 or so Rhodesians and by more than 3,000,000 in South Africa." O'Brien quoted in Hughes, "Fighting for White Rule in Africa," 596.

98. According to a 1961 CIA report, Katanga "presently receives about $44 million annually in tax revenues and dividends from the Union Minière and related companies. These contributions are paid to Katanga, via Brussels, and are used for Tshombe's military and other expenditures. Tshombe also receives considerable advice and guidance from the Union Minière managers in Katanga; they, in turn, are to some extent dependent upon him for protection and for the right to continue to operate." See Special National Intelligence Estimate, "Possible Developments in Katanga," December 7, 1961 document 152, *FRUS*, vol. XX, Congo Crisis.

99. Schmidt, *Foreign Intervention in Africa*, 61.

100. On the United States' growing opposition to Lumumba, see Westad, *Global Cold War*, 137–41; and Gleijeses, *Conflicting Missions*, 60–64. For witnesses' reactions to the public beating of Lumumba, see "Lumumba Beaten in Shift to New Prison in Katanga," *NYT*, January 19, 1961.

101. Conor Cruise O'Brien quoted in Gibbs, "Dag Hammarskjold, the United Nations, and the Congo Crisis of 1960–1961," 166.

102. Gleijeses, *Conflicting Missions*, 60–64.

103. These included William F. Buckley, L. Brent Bozell (Buckley's brother-in-law), Eugene Lyons, Alfred Kohlberg, Herbert Kohler, Russell Kirk, Victor Lasky, William Loeb, Clarence Manion, and Ralph de Toledano. See "Organize U.S. Committee to Back Katanga," *NYT*, December 14, 1961; and "New U.S. Group Backs Katanga against U.N.," *LAT*, December 14, 1961.

104. In the words of Penny Von Eschen, Yergan's shift to the right was "perhaps the most pronounced political about-face among African American activists and intellectuals of the Cold War era." See Von Eschen, *Race against Empire*, 115. See also Anthony, *Max Yergan*, 231–70.

105. Yergan also drew other prominent black conservatives, such as George Schuyler, editor of the *Pittsburgh Courier* and member of the CIA-front known as the Congress for Cultural Freedom, into his international work. See Campbell, *Middle Passages*, 265–66; and Anthony, *Max Yergan*, 261.

106. Telegram from Marvin Liebman to Moïse Tshombe, December 8, 1961, folder Katanga and Miscellaneous, box 56, MLP; Telegram from Moïse Tshombe to the ACAKFF, December 11, 1961, folder Katanga and Miscellaneous, box 56, MLP; Statement submitted by President Moïse Tshombe to the ACAKFF, no date, folder Katanga and Miscellaneous, box 56, MLP; and Press release from the ACAKFF, December 14, 1961, folder Katanga and Miscellaneous, box 56, MLP, HIWRP. See also American Committee for Aid to Katangan Freedom Fighters ad, *NYT*, December 14, 1961.

107. Press release from the ACAKFF, December 14, 1961, folder Katanga and Miscellaneous, box 56, MLP, HIWRP.

108. Activists in Europe made similar arguments. A fascist-leaning paramilitary group composed of former Belgian colonists and paratroopers who fled in 1961—known as Mouvement d'Action Civique—used funds from Union Minière to attack the United Nations and press Tshombe's cause in the Belgian Parliament. See Bale, "'Black' Terrorist International," 108–9.

109. Ibid. See also Memorandum from Max Yergan to Friends of the Katanga Freedom Fighters, March 26, 1962, folder American Committee for Aid to Katanga Freedom Fighters, box 6, GRR, RBML.

110. Max Yergan, "A Petition to the United States Congress," no date, folder Washington Post Ad, box 56, MLP, HIWRP.

111. On the mercenaries' motivation, see Special Correspondent, "Why Mercenaries Fight for Tshombe," *The Observer* (London), April 29, 1962; and Mockler, *New Mercenaries*, 35–55.

112. Hoare quoted in John Latz, "White Mercenaries Calm African Terror," *CT*, October 4, 1966. See also Hoare, *Congo Warriors*.

113. In a series of letters, Liebman explicitly advised van den Haag that his research was to "indicate (the) committee's estimate of (the) situation correct." See memo from Marvin Liebman to Ernest van den Haag, December 28, 1961, folder Katanga and Miscellaneous, box 56, MLP, HIWRP.

114. Van den Haag, *War in Katanga*, 12. Describing the refugee camp on the outskirts of Elizabethville, van den Haag offered the following: "Conditions in the camp are miserable to western eyes. But many primitive Congo tribes still prefer leisure to the comforts that can be achieved by giving it up. Hence, the camp may be more attractive to them than it would appear to people conditioned by an industrial civilization," 26.

115. Van den Haag, *War in Katanga*, 12.

116. See Memo from Max Yergan to Friends of the ACAKFF, October 12, 1962, folder Katanga: UN Secret Memorandum, box 56, MLP, HIWRP.

117. Van den Haag, *War in Katanga*, 22.

118. Schraeder, *United States Foreign Policy toward Africa*, 69–70.

119. See Telegram from the Department of State to the Embassy in the Congo, August 10, 1964, document 207; and Memorandum from the Chief of the Africa Division, Directorate of Plans, Central Intelligence Agency (Fields) to the Deputy Director for Plans (Fitzgerald), document 427, *FRUS*, vol. XXIII, Congo, 1960–1968.

120. See Memorandum for the Record, February 18, 1965, document 399, *FRUS*, vol. XXIII, Congo, 1960–1968; Central Intelligence Agency, "Short Term Prospects for Tshombe in the Congo," Special National Intelligence Estimate, August 5, 1964, CIA-FOIA, http://www.foia.cia.gov/sites/default/files/document_conversions/89801/DOC_0000011837.pdf, accessed November 7, 2013. See also Gleijeses, *Conflicting Missions*, 70–75. Tshombe's use of mercenaries was well known in the American press. See for example, J. Anthony Lukass, "Tshombe's Mercenaries: Congo Leader Uses Them for Immediate Action," *NYT*, August 30, 1964. Western writers responded to these claims by painting Tshombe as an ally of the "free world" trying to build a "modern, orderly country in accordance with Western standards." For a summary of both perspectives, see Max Clos, "Why Africans Hate Tshombe," *NYT*, January 10, 1965.

121. See "Tshombe Is Ousted as Premier," *CT*, October 14, 1965; "Moïse Tshombe Ousted in Congo," *Chicago Daily Defender*, October 14, 1965; and "Tshombe Fired by Kasavubu in Congo Row," *LAT*, October 14, 1965.

122. Tshombe's plots to take back the Congo, and his relationships with financiers and mercenaries was best outlined in Sandro Viola, "Double Crisscross: The Case of Moïse Tshombe," *atlas*, October 1967, folder Moïse Tshombe Articles, box 104, MLP, HIWRP.

123. See Tad Szulc, "Tshombe Confident He Will Displace Mobutu Soon," *NYT*, September 11, 1965; and Thomas F. Fenton, "Return Home Is to Congo Is Tshombe Aim," *Baltimore Sun*, August 1966.

124. As a U.S. official in the Congo wrote, "Right now Belgian, French, Spanish and English mercenaries, backed by Belgian financial interests, are engaged in all-out effort to overthrow Mobutu govt. These groups will spare no efforts to overthrow DGRC." Telegram from the Embassy in the Congo to the Department of State, July 6, 1967, document 505, *FRUS*, vol. 23, Congo, 1960–1968. See also Gibbs, *Political Economy of Third World Interventions*, 167–68; and "Tshombe Rebels Crushed in Congo," *Chicago Daily Defender*, September 27, 1966.

125. As historian David N. Gibbs has pointed out, "No satisfactory account has been written on the hijacking affair, and it is still not clear who arranged it. Various reports have attributed the kidnapping to French intelligence, the KGB, and or the CIA." See Gibbs, *Political Economy of Third World Interventions*, 168. U.S. conservatives generally asserted that a French intelligence agent with a murky past, François Bodenan, hijacked the plane. See Memo from Marvin Liebman to All Concerned, August 4, 1967, folder 15, box 80, CMP-CHM.

126. These events made for a stream of sensationalist headlines in the U.S. See for example "Tshombe Reported Kidnapped in Air, Flown to Algeria," *NYT*, July 2, 1967; and "Algiers Holds Tshombe after Kidnap in the Air," *BG*, July 2, 1967.

127. Memo from Marvin Liebman to John Ashbrook, Spurille Braden, William F. Buckley, John Chamberlain, John Dos Passos, Charles Edison, Eugene Lyons, Clarence Manion, William Rusher, George Schuyler, Ralph de Toledano and Max Yeargan, July 7, 1967, folder Report of Activities sent to Members of Tshombe Emergency Committee, box 105, MLP, HIWRP. Telegram from William F. Buckley et al. to Marvin Liebman, no date, Report of Activities sent to Members of Tshombe Emergency Committee, box 105, Marvin Liebman Papers, HIWRP. Liebman, for his part, was not sure about how "such funds would be effectively utilized" but nonetheless believed it was urgent to get some money together "for use if and when they might be needed." See Memo from Marvin Liebman to John Ashbrook et al, July 7, 1967, folder 15, box 80, CMP-CHM. Contributions ranged from $10 to $1,000 and

came from donors in New York, Virginia, Texas, Pennsylvania, South Carolina, Missouri, California, Michigan, and elsewhere. See the donation letters in folder Tshombe Emergency Fund (SP VIP), box 105, MLP, HIWRP.

128. See William F. Buckley, "Will Anyone Stand Up for Tshombe?," *BG*, July 8, 1967; William F. Buckley, "Who Speaks for Tshombe?," *BG*, July 26, 1967; William F. Buckley, "The End of Moïse Tshombe," *Washington Star*, July 27, 1967; Editorial, "Tshombe Needs Saving," *Chicago Daily News*, August 9, 1967; and Anthony T. Bouscaren, "Tshombe and the Congo Story," *American Security Council Washington Report*, July 31, 1967, folder Moïse Tshombe Articles, box 104, MLP, HIWRP.

129. See Excerpts from Petition of Madame Ruth Tshombe For and On Behalf of Moïse Tshombe for a United Nations Writ of Habeas Corpus, to the Members of the General Assembly, Economic and Social Council, and Human Rights Commission, July 27, 1967, folder 15, box 80, CMP-CHM.

130. Confidential Memo from Harry H. Lipsig and Panfil A. Riposanu to Marvin Liebman, no date, folder 15, box 80, CMP-CHM.

131. Remarks of Strom Thurmond, "The Kidnapping of Tshombe and the Untold Story of the Congo Crisis," by Senator Thomas Dodd, *Congressional Record*, July 21, 1967, folder Moïse Tshombe Articles, box 104, MLP, HIWRP. Dodd's participation, however, was probably more harmful than helpful. Over the summer of 1967, the Senate's Ethics Committee had opened censure proceedings against Dodd. They found evidence that he had spent more than $100,000 of campaign contributions for personal purposes. On Dodd's censure hearings, see Andrew Glass, "'I'm Telling the Truth,' Sen. Dodd Swears," *WP*, June 15, 1967. On Dodd's harm to the Tshombe campaign, see Willard Edwards, "Capital Views," *CT*, July 8, 1976. I am indebted to Matthew June, who provided the following documents: Letter from Thomas J. Dodd to Lyndon Johnson, April 25, 1964; and Letter from Thomas J. Dodd to Lyndon Johnson, July 7, 1964 in folder CO 52: Congo, Republic of (1964), box 8, White House Central Files—Confidential Files, CO-52, Lyndon Baines Johnson Presidential Library, Austin, TX.

132. The source—who signed the letters as a "Loyal Friend"—demanded that Liebman and Kutner deliver £10,000 and $5,000 in hard currency to their "emissary in New York City" as "evidence of good faith." The source demanded that an additional £20,000 be transferred into an anonymous account at the Bank of Switzerland. And finally, Liebman and Kutner were to bring another £20,000 to the international airport in Zurich on August 15. See Letter from "A Loyal Friend" to Luis Kutner, July 28, 1967, folder 15, box 80, CMP-CHM.

133. Memo from Marvin Liebman to Organizers and Friends, October 31, 1967, folder 15, box 80, CMP-CHM.

134. "Moïse Tshombe—RIP," *Washington Intelligence Report* 2, no. 7 (July 1969), folder 10, box 191, HPP, LOC. In a syndicated editorial column, William F. Buckley lamented that this was yet another reminder of how "conservatives do not retrieve their wounded." See William F. Buckley, "Tshombe's Lonely Death in Exile," *BG*, July 5, 1969.

135. Holmes Alexander, "A Needed Evaluation of the Congo," *Human Events*, August 4, 1962.

136. John Boland, "Sorenson—From White House to White Mercenary," *Human Events*, March 4, 1967.

137. Brownell, *Collapse of Rhodesia*, 15.

138. This summary of Rhodesian history and politics draws from White, *Unpopular Sovereignty*, 5–10; Horne, *From the Barrel of a Gun*, 34–39; and Darwin, *Empire Project*, 616–32, 645–47.

139. Brownell, *Collapse of Rhodesia*, 3.

140. Ian Smith quoted in Borstelmann, *The Cold War and the Color Line*, 196; and "1964: Not in my Lifetime; 1976: Within Two Years," *WP*, September 25, 1976.

141. On economic sanctions against Rhodesia see Horne, *From the Barrel of a Gun*, 169–79.

142. For British colonization in Africa see Thompson, *History of South Africa*, 110–53; Pakenham, *Scramble for Africa*; Meredith, *Diamonds, Gold, and War*.

143. See Irwin, "Wind of Change? White Redoubt and the Postcolonial Moment."

144. Gleijeses, *Conflicting Missions*, 274.

145. Their efforts expanded upon the previous work of Marvin Liebman, who had been working as a paid lobbyist for the colonial government of Southern Rhodesia since 1962. But since Liebman was so focused on other endeavors at the time, his work for Southern Rhodesia was limited to a handful of advertisements and editorials in major American newspapers. However, after Smith declared independence in 1965, Liebman and others threw themselves into activism on behalf of the white regime. See Letter from Marvin Liebman to Max Yergan, January 26, 1962, folder Southern Rhodesia, box 56, MLP, HIWRP.

146. Form letter from Robert R. Richardson, January 7, 1966, folder Friends of Rhodesian Independence, box 29, MLP, HIWRP; and FORI Flyer, "Come to Rhodesia—August 30-Septmeber 20, 1966," folder 8, box 169, HPP, LOC.

147. Anthony, *Max Yergan*, 266–67.

148. See Memo from William A. Rusher and Max Yergan to Directors and Members, June 21, 1967, folder 2, box 129; and Dr. Warnell Jacobs, James J. Kirkpatrick, and Rene Wormser, "Report on Rhodesia: April 1967," American-African Affairs Association, folder 5, box 131, WRP, LOC. A condensed version of the report appeared as Warnell Jacobs, James J. Kirkpatrick, and Rene Wormser, "Rhodesia: A Case History," *NR*, May 16, 1967.

149. See Report, "South Africa Trip, 1968," folder 6, box 80; and Letter from Daniel Lyons to Clarence Manion, February 22, 1967, folder 11, box 58, CMP-CHM.

150. Luis V. Manrara, Truth about Cuba Committee pamphlet, "Report on South Africa," 1966, folder 68, box 123, Truth about Cuba Committee Records, CHC-UM.

151. Rhodesian Department of Information Services pamphlet, "Rhodesia: Progress in African Education," no date, folder 13, box 135, Donald Dozer Papers, HIWRP.

152. "Rhodesia: A Profile in Courage," *Manion Forum*, March 5, 1967, folder 9, box 83, CMP-CHM.

153. Ibid.

154. "Rhodesia," *Dan Smoot Report*, February 27, 1967, vol. 13, no. 9, folder Rhodesia, box 286, GRR, RBML.

155. "Communist Objectives in Rhodesia, *Manion Forum*, March 12, 1967, folder 9, box 83, CMP-CHM.

156. "Apartheid or Annihilation," *Manion Forum*, January 5, 1969, folder 1, box 84, CMP-CHM.

157. "Rhodesia: A Profile in Courage," *Manion Forum*, March 5, 1967, folder 9, box 83, CMP-CHM.

158. Letter from Clyde M. Wood to President Richard Nixon, May 18, 1967, folder Rhodesia, box 286, GRR, RBML.

159. Ralph de Toledano, "Is Race the Issue in Rhodesia?," *Human Events*, February 26, 1966.

160. Dr. Warnell Jacobs, James J. Kirkpatrick, and Rene Wormser, "Report on Rhodesia: April 1967," American-African Affairs Association, folder 5, box 131, WRP, LOC.

161. One author argued that the Black Panthers looked to Red China and Cuba for their models of national liberation and were receiving weapons and training from communist nations. See for example, Robert Bailey, "Who Are the Black Panthers?," *Human Events*,

September 7, 1968. For the shift from non-violent protest to armed defense in the civil rights movement, see Tyson, *Radio Free Dixie*; Hill, *Deacons for Defense*; Jeffries, *Bloody Lowndes*; and Murch, *Living for the City*.

162. "Racial Riots: One Front in a Worldwide War," *Manion Forum*, August 13, 1967, folder 9, box 83, CMP-CHM.

163. See "Method in their Madness," *Christian Anti-Communist Crusade Newsletter*, September 4, 1967, folder 4, box 66; and "The Philosopher of Racial Violence," *Christian Anti-Communist Crusade Newsletter*, January 29, 1968, folder 5, box 66, HPP, LOC.

164. The idea that black America represented an internal colony dated back to at least the 1920s. By the 1960s, many African-Americans, including Malcolm X, Stokely Carmichael, Angela Davis, and Martin Luther King Jr., had offered "updated variations on the internal colony thesis." See Malloy, "Uptight in Babylon: Eldridge Cleaver's Cold War," quote from 541. See also Singh, *Black Is a Country*.

165. "Communism and Race Riots," *Christian Anti-Communist Crusade Newsletter*, August 14, 1967, folder 4, box 66, HPP, LOC.

166. On the Klan in the 1960s, see Wade, *Fiery Cross*, 307–67; Drabble, "FBI, COINTELPRO-WHITE HATE and the Decline of Ku Klux Klan Organizations in Mississippi"; Drabble, "'To Ensure Domestic Tranquility'"; and Cunningham, *Klansville, USA*.

167. See Geary and Sutton, "Resisting the Wind of Change: The Citizens' Councils and European Decolonization." For a comparative history of white racial violence in the United States and South Africa at the turn of the twentieth century, see Strobel, "'We Are All Aimed and Ready.'"

168. "Klan Feared Operating in South Africa," *WP*, April 26, 1959; "S. Africa's Got a Ku Klux Klan Too, Reports Say," *Atlanta Daily World*, February 20, 1959.

169. "Ku Klux Klan Seeking Branch in South Africa," *WP*, May 5, 1967.

170. Westad, *Global Cold War*, 207–14.

171. "Rhodesia: A Profile in Courage," *Manion Forum*, March 5, 1967, folder 9, box 83, CMP-CHM.

172. See Connelly, "Taking off the Cold War Lens."

173. On détente as a conservative attempt to quell global protest and undercut leftist national liberation movements in the late 1960s and early 1970s, see Suri, *Power and Protest*, 1–5, 213–59.

## Chapter 3

1. The "ad hoc" national delegation for the United States consisted of Marvin Liebman, David N. Rowe, Walter Judd, Lev Dobriansky, Kim Combs, and six others. Reverends Daniel Lyons, Raymond de Jaegher, and David Head attended as members of the Free Pacific Foundation. Reverends James Colbert and David C. Colbert came as delegates for the Christian Anti-Communist Crusade. See "Partial List of Participaters [sic] of the First WACL Conference," *AO*, September 1967, 21–27.

2. See ibid.; "ABN Joins World Anti-Red League," *ABN Correspondence* (Munich), November 1967; and World Anti-Communist League, Republic of China chapter, *Proceedings of the First Conference of the World Anti-Communist League*, September 26–29, 1967. To manage the linguistic challenges of an international gathering, each delegate received an earphone in which translators broadcast speeches from a dozen languages into English, French, and Spanish. See "The First World Anti-Communist League Conference: A Great Splendid Success," *AO*, October 1967, 29–33.

3. See Editorial, "Freedom Will Win Definitely, Communism Perish Absolutely," *AO*,

October 1967, 3–4; "Declaration of the First World Anti-Communist League," *AO*, October 1967, 13–16.

4. Other messages came from Ferdinand Marcos of the Philippines, Konstantin Kollias of Greece, and Joaquin Balaguer of the Dominican Republic. See "Special Documents," *AO*, November 1967, 6–11.

5. "A New Development of the World-wide Anti-Communist Struggle," *AO*, May 1967, 1–3. The WACL's mission drew heavily upon that of its predecessor, the Asian Peoples Anti-Communist League (APACL). For its founding mission, see APACL, "Documents on Asian Peoples' Anti-Communist Conference," June 15, 1954, B-390–001, APACL, CWIHP.

6. Liebman, *Coming Out Conservative*, 119.

7. On the growing transnational connections between leftist radicals and revolutionaries in the 1960s and 1970s, see Chamberlain, *Global Offensive*; Varon, *Bringing the War Home*; Byrne, *Mecca of Revolution*; and Malloy, *Out of Oakland*.

8. For brief overviews of the WACL's founding and activities, see "From APACL to WACL," *AO*, April 1974; and "The Development of APACL and WACL," 1982, WHORM: Subject File ME 002, casefile 112422, RRPL.

9. Most of this work was the product of collaboration between the Free Pacific Association, run by Lyons and de Jaegher, and the WACL's Freedom Center, an anticommunist cadre school in South Korea. See, for example, Hsu Fu-teh, "My Report from the Freedom Center," *AO*, December 1968, 34–35.

10. For instance, at a meeting in November 1969, American Stefan Possony of Stanford's Hoover Institution explained that the Guomindang's leftover armies in Burma and Thailand were in the best position to end the war in Vietnam. This was roughly the same argument that the GMD leadership had been making since the early 1950s. See George Chen, "One of the Significant Activities of WACL: Report on Participation in the Second WACL Seminar on People's War," *AO*, February 1970, 49–51. This conference formed the basis for Stefan Thomas Possony, "Peoples' War: The Art of Combining Partisan-Military, Psycho-Social, and Political Conquest Techniques," (Taipei: WACL Republic of China Chapter, 1970), Deering Library Special Collections, Northwestern University, Evanston, Ill.

11. Memo from David N. Rowe et al., February 13, 1970, folder 4, box 33, HPP, LOC.

12. Others who were involved in international work included John Fisher, head of the American Security Council, and David Keene, a former president of the Young Americans for Freedom and the World Youth Crusade for Freedom. See Memo from Herbert A. Philbrick to S.A. Edward C. Rudiger, March 17, 1970, folder 4, box 33, HPP, LOC.

13. See "Anti-Red Meeting Draws Big Crowds," *LAT*, March 9, 1961; Louis Fleming, "Probe Into 'Muzzling' of Military Asked: 15,700 at Anti-Red School Rally," *LAT*, August 31, 1961; and Charles Grutzner, "Reports of Dr. Schwarz' Anti-Communist Crusade Show $1,273, 492 Collected," *NYT*, June 24, 1962.

14. On the CACC's work in India and Taiwan, see Fundraising letter from Fred Schwarz, July 15, 1959; Fred C. Schwarz, "Distribution of *You Can Trust the Communists to Be Communists* to India"; and Letter from Rev. Ch. Devananda Rao to Fred Schwarz, in *Christian Anti-Communist Crusade News Letter*, October 1, 1967, folder 9, box 65, HPP, LOC. On Latin America, see Fundraising letter from Fred Schwarz, August 5, 1964, folder 1, box 66, HPP, LOC. Schwarz also reached out the exiled Cubans by holding a series of schools in Miami to address Fidel Castro's regime and its potential threat to other Latin American countries. See "Schwarz to Talk at Cuba Rally," *LAT*, December 11, 1962. For a summary of all the CACC's international projects, including its work in South Africa, see Christian Anti-Communist Crusade Solicitation Flyer, no date, folder 9, box 65, HPP, LOC; and Hubert Villeneuve, "Teaching Anti-Communism," 497–517.

15. See Rabe, *U.S. Intervention in British Guiana*, 155; and Villeneuve, "Teaching Anti-Communism," 518–27.

16. For debates about the founding of the ACWF, see Memo from Herbert A. Philbrick to S.A. Edward C. Rudiger, March 17, 1970, folder 4, box 33, HPP, LOC.

17. Walter Judd, Stefan Possony, Daniel Lyons, and Lee Edwards rounded out the executive committee. These debates are recounted in the meeting minutes enclosed in a letter from John Fisher to Herbert Philbrick, March 11, 1970, folder 4, box 33, HPP, LOC.

18. Tan Tien, "Establishment of the American Council for World Freedom," *AO*, April 1970, 34–35.

19. See Turse, *Kill Everything That Moves*; Sherry, *In the Shadow of War*, 267–68; and Adas, *Dominance by Design*, 310–13, 319–20.

20. On the goals and failures of Nixon's Vietnamization program, see Herring, *America's Longest War*, 281–88.

21. The connections between these issues were outlined at an ACWF meeting in June 1971. See Minutes for American Council for World Freedom Board Meeting, June 12, 1971, folder 4, box 33, HPP, LOC.

22. Fundraising letter from Ku Chen Kang, April 21, 1966, folder Asian People's Anti-Communist League, box 33, GRR, RBML.

23. Tan Tien, "Establishment of the American Council for World Freedom," *AO*, April 1970, 34–35.

24. Stefan Possony, "ACWF-WACL Relationship," no date, folder 8, box 212, HPP, LOC.

25. In press releases, John Fisher, the first ACWF chairman, hailed it as a "new national organization to promote communication and cooperation among organizations active in the field of international affairs," comprised of "distinguished scholars, journalists, and foreign affairs experts," but said little more. Press Release, "New 'Council' Will Promote Communication and Cooperation in International Affairs," March 1 1970, folder 4, box 33, HPP, LOC.

26. See American Council for World Freedom, "Red China and Its American Friends: A Report on the Red China Lobby," 1971, folder American Council for World Freedom, box 9, GRR, RBML. For an earlier iteration of this idea, which many conservatives had repeated since the early 1960s, see William D. Pawley, "A Way Out of Vietnam," American Security Council Washington Report, December 1, 1969, folder 4, box 33, HPP, LOC.

27. See Frank Ching, "Chinese Groups in Confrontation Here," *NYT*, September 22, 1971; and "Dr. McIntire and 2,500 protest in D.C.; Denver Arrests Anti-War Veteran at Parade," *Baltimore Sun*, October 24, 1971. By 1971, Asian members of the WACL had grown concerned about Nixon's relations with communist China and they expressed their dissatisfaction in writing. For an encapsulation of their views, see "WACL's Letter to Nixon," *AO*, December 1971.

28. Minutes for American Council for World Freedom Board Meeting, March 2, 1971, folder 4, box 33, HPP, LOC.

29. Some Americans still had reservations about joining the WACL. One argued that the group's conferences had become a "routine operation, repetitive and unproductive of anything substantive." See Memorandum from David Rowe to WACL Executive Committee, no date, folder 4, box 33, HPP, LOC.

30. Letter from Walter Judd to David N. Rowe, January 17, 1972, folder 6, box 226, Walter Judd Papers, HIWRP.

31. Letter from Fred Schlafly to Clarence Manion, September 13, 1973, folder 6, box 79, CMP-CHM.

32. Letter from Clarence Manion to Fred Schlafly, April 25, 1974, folder 7, box 79, CMP-CHM. Dorothy Collin, "Phyllis Schlafly's Husband Is More Than That," *CT*, September 24,

1976. See also American Council for World Freedom brochure, circa 1973, folder 7, box 79, CMP-CHM.

33. The most prominent was the Cardinal Mindszenty Foundation. Named after a Hungarian Catholic leader who had been imprisoned by communists for nearly a decade, the group sponsored working groups across the country to draw U.S. Catholics into the struggle against communism in Eastern Europe and elsewhere—efforts inducted the Schlaflys into the world of anticommunist internationalism. See Critchlow, *Phyllis Schlafly and Grassroots Conservatism*, 31–35, 81–83.

34. Memorandum from Lee Edwards to Board of Directors, February 6, 1974, folder 5, box 33, HPP, LOC.

35. Minutes of ACWF Executive Committee Meeting, March 9, 1973, folder 5, box 33, HPP, LOC. On Viguerie's pioneering use of computerized direct-mailing lists, see Philips-Fein, *Invisible Hands*, 213–21.

36. For an overview of the WACL's activities and the addition of new member groups, see American Council for World Freedom Pamphlet, "Peace Is Freedom and Justice for All," 7th WACL Conference, April 8–11, 1974, folder 7, box 57, KDP, HIWRP.

37. Shokyo Rengo was founded by Ryoichi Sasakawa and Yoshio Kodoma, who were cellmates in Sugamo Prison during the U.S. occupation of Japan. Both were major figures in postwar Japan's ultra-rightist circles and organized crime syndicates. On the creation of Shokyo Rengo, see Kaplan and Dubro, *Yakuza*, 64–65. On their prosecution as war criminals and time in Sugamo prison, see Dower, *Embracing Defeat*, 454, 511. For American views of the Japanese WACL chapter, see Stefan Possony, "WACL and APACL Meeting at Kyoto and Tokyo, Japan," September 1970, folder 8, box 212, HPP, LOC.

38. Stefan Possony, Confidential American Council for World Freedom report, "The 1972/73 Leadership of WACL," enclosed in a letter from Geoffrey Stewart-Smith to Thomas Lane, January 9, 1974, folder 6, box 226, Judd Papers, HIWRP.

39. See Letter from Geoffrey Stewart-House to Gen. Thomas A. Lane, January 9, 1974, folder 6, box 226, Walter Judd Papers, HIWRP; and Minutes of Annual Meeting of American Council of World Freedom, April 7, 1973, folder 5, box 33, HPP, LOC.

40. Their dissatisfaction with Vietnam overlapped with domestic concerns. As Nixon aide Bob Haldeman pointed out, "right-wing Republican unhappiness" was "because we're not adequately cutting spending, welfare, etc. and they feel we're softening on Vietnam." See Scanlon, *The Pro-War Movement*, 110.

41. Ibid., 169–83.

42. See "Groups Rap Nixon's Trip," WP, August 23, 1971, folder World Anti-Communist League, box 339, GRR, RBML.

43. Richard Nixon quoted in Sargent, *Superpower Transformed*, 66. For the original quote, see "Memorandum for the President's Files," May 8, 1972, in *Foreign Relations of the United States, 1969–1976*, Vol. 8, Vietnam, January–October 1972, no. 131.

44. See ACWF Pamphlet, "For a Free World in Peace . . . The World Anti-Communist League," marked as February 2, 1974, folder American Council for World Freedom, box 9, GRR, RBML.

45. The estimated cost was $193,000, of which $70,000 went to food and hotel rooms. See Estimated budget for the 7th World Anti-Communist League Conference, April 8–11, 1974, folder 4, box 227, Judd Papers, HIWRP. The ACWF presented "Freedom Fighter of the Year" awards to Soviet dissidents Alexander Solzhenitsyn and Valentyn Moroz as well as Cardinal Mindszenty, the Hungarian cleric who had come to international fame in 1956 for his opposition to the Soviet invasion of Hungary. See Program of the 7th World Anti-Communist League Conference, Washington, D.C., April 8–11, 1974, R108F 1423, CDADDH.

46. Memorandum from Lee Edwards to Board of Directors, February 6, 1974, folder 5, American Council for World Freedom 1972–1975, box 33, HPP, LOC.

47. American Council for World Freedom Pamphlet, "Peace Is Freedom and Justice for All," from the 7th WACL Conference, April 8–11, 1974, folder 7, box 57, KDP, HIWRP.

48. Ibid.

49. On Nixon's attempt to secure "peace with honor," see Herring, *America's Longest War*, 271–76.

50. Remarks of Yaroslav Stetsko to the 7th WACL conference, April 9, 1974, R108F 1468–R108F1509, CDADDH.

51. See Letter from Geoffrey Stewart-Smith to Gen. Thomas A. Lane, January 9, 1974; Letter from Thomas A. Lane to Geoffrey Stewart-Smith, January 14, 1974; and Letter from Geoffrey Stewart-Smith to Thomas Lane, January 28, 1974, folder 6, box 226, Walter Judd Papers, HIWRP. See also, Peter Deeley, "Anti-'Red' Crusaders Fall Out," *The Observer*, January 13, 1974.

52. See Stefan Possony, Confidential American Council for World Freedom report, "The 1972/73 Leadership of WACL," enclosed in a letter from Geoffrey Stewart-Smith to Thomas Lane, January 9, 1974, folder 6, box 226, Walter Judd Papers, HIWRP.

53. Letter from David Martin to Thomas Lane, March 22, 1974, folder 3, box 58, KDP, HIWRP.

54. Some members of the ACWF had invited the Brazilian Catholic organization known as Tradition, Family, and Property (TFP), a group with a deeply conservative and anticommunist bent, to join the WACL. CAL leaders Rafael Rodriguez and Raimundo Guerrero vehemently opposed this, less for ideological reasons than for personal disputes with the TFP's leadership.

55. See FEMACO, "Gravismos Inconvenientes que se Derivarian para la WACL si se apreuda la admison de la socided brasilena de defense de la tradicion, la familia, la propiedad," document no. 2, no date, folder 4, box 58, KDP; and Carlos Filho Barbieri, circular letter 007/75, "Conferencia Interamericana pro Libertad y Seguridad," September 1975, R0198F 2610, CDADDH.

56. Jorge Prieto Laurens, "Look out, Peoples and Governments of the American Continent," flyer published by the Conferderacion Interamericana de Defense del Continente, no date, folder 4, box 58, KDP, HIWRP.

57. See World Youth Anti-Communist League Executive Committee resolutions, February 22–23, 1975, R198F 2574, CDADDH.

58. See Letter from Fred Schlafly to Clarence Manion, August 1, 1975, folder 7, box 79, CMP-CHM.

59. For an overview of these guerrilla wars, see Wright, *Latin America in the Age of the Cuban Revolution*, chapters 5 and 6.

60. These included the Feminine Anticommunist Alliance, the Popular Anticommunist Alliance, the Mexican Student Force, the Association for Intellectual Freedom, the League for the Defense of Free Enterprise Against Communism, and the Independent Association of Industrial Businessmen. See FEMACO pamphlet, "Foundation of the Mexican Anticommunist Federation," circa 1972, folder 1, box 52, KDP, HIWRP.

61. On the Cristeros, see Meyer, *Cristero Rebellion*. On the links between the Cristeros and the Tecos, see Stefan Possony, Confidential American Council for World Freedom report, "The 1972/73 Leadership of WACL," enclosed in a letter from Geoffrey Stewart-Smith to Thomas Lane, January 9, 1974, folder 6, box 226, Walter Judd Papers, HIWRP.

62. López Macedonio, "Historia de una colaboración transnacional anticomunista," 136–38.

63. Ibid., 136.

64. Buendía, "Lo que pasa en la UAG," *El Día* (México City), May 31, 1976, reprinted in Buendía, *La Ultraderecha en México*, 61–62.

65. He added that "on this continent, it's probable that only in Argentina, Brazil, Uruguay, Paraguay, Chile exist more centers and major organizations." See Manuel Buendía, "Lo que significa UAG," *El Sol de México*, August 11, 1977, reprinted in Buendía, *La Ultraderecha en México*, 74–76.

66. See Ávila, "Las guerrillas blancas."

67. These included the Frente Universitario Anticomunista at the Universidad de Puebla, the Movimiento Universitario de Renovadora Orientación at the Universidad Nacional Autónoma de México, and the Organización Nacional del Yunque. See Ávila, "Las guerrillas blancas," 5–26.

68. See Romero, "El movimiento fascista en Guadalajara," 51.

69. Buendía, "Advertencia a los Tecos," *El Sol de México*, August 9, 1977, reprinted in Buendía, *La Ultraderecha en México*, 71–72. Likewise, American journalists concluded that the Tecos were responsible for "innumerable acts of violence, including dozens of political assassinations." See Anderson and Anderson, *Inside the League*, 71.

70. See López Macedonio, "Historia de una colaboración transnacional anticomunista," 143.

71. FEMACO, "Resolución Presentada al Sexto Conferencia de la Liga Mundial Anticomunista por la Federación Mexicana Anticomunista sobre la creación de la Confederación Anticomunista Latinoamericana, organismo regional del WACL," México City, August 25–28, 1972, folder 1, box 57, KDP, HIWRP.

72. Despite its ambitions, the Organization of Solidarity with the People of Asia, Africa and Latin America was "largely ineffective as a functioning collective organization," though it carried major symbolic importance. See Harmer, *Allende's Chile and the Inter-American Cold War*, 36.

73. While the early 1970s did indeed represent a time of triumph for communists, these successes were due in large part to particular local and national circumstances rather than a truly international assault led by the Soviet Union, communist China, or Cuba. Moreover, while the Cuban and Vietnamese struggles inspired leftist movements in Asia, Africa, and the Americas, this inspiration was "more indirect than direct, and at times based on a very superficial knowledge of the Cuban and Vietnamese revolutions." See Westad, *Global Cold War*, 158.

74. FEMACO, "Resolución Presentada al Sexto Conferencia de la Liga Mundial Anticomunista por la Federación Mexicana Anticomunista sobre la creación de la Confederación Anticomunista Latinoamericana, organismo regional del WACL," Mexico City, August 25–28, 1972, folder 1, box 57, KDP, HIWRP. See also, "Communique of the Sixth Conference of the World Anti-Communist League," *AO*, 8–9.

75. Members of the Inter-American Confederation for the Defense of the Continent also called for a "regional command and a management team all within the structure of the WACL." See Proposcion del Comite Internacional Pro-Defense de La Democracia at the 6th WACL Conference, Mexico City, August 25–28, 1972, folder 1, box 57, KDP, HIWRP.

76. Guerrero had met most of these men during the First Secret Congress of the Confederación Anticomunista Latinoamericana in Mexico City on August 28, 1972. Delegations came from Argentina, Bolivia, Brazil, Chile, Colombia, Costa Rica, the Dominican Republic, Guatemala, Mexico, Panama, Peru, Nicaragua, Paraguay, El Salvador, Uruguay, and Venezuela. For the full list of these delegates, see List of Delegates and Observers at the VI Conference of the World Anti-Communist League, folder 2, box 56, KDP, HIWRP.

77. Rafael Rodriguez was also the second-in-command of FEMACO. See Stefan Possony, Confidential American Council for World Freedom report, "The 1972/73 Leadership of

WACL," enclosed in a letter from Geoffrey Stewart-Smith to Thomas Lane, January 9, 1974, folder 6, box 226, Walter Judd Papers, HIWRP.

78. CAL leaders were solidifying the structure that they had planned at the August 1972 meeting in Mexico City. For that structure, see Confederación Anticomunista Latinoamericana, "Leyes Fundamentales de la Confederación Anticomunista Latinoamericana," August 29, 1972, R108F 1543–1565, CDADDH.

79. See Memorandum, "Segundo Conferencia Secreto de la Confederación Anticomunista Latinoamericana," May 28 to June 1, 1973, R108F 2069, CDADDH.

80. See Marvin Howe, "Latin Anti-Communists Plan Tactics," *NYT*, January 26, 1974.

81. On U.S. military and police training programs in Latin America, see Gill, *School of the Americas*; Huggins, *Political Policing*; and Kuzamarov, *Modernizing Repression*, 208–31.

82. La Técnica was short for the benign-sounding La Dirección Nacional de Asuntos Técnicos or the National Directorate of Technical Matters.

83. Campos Alum worked with U.S. Army Lieutenant Colonel Robert K. Thierry. See "Falleció Antonio Campos Alum, director de centro detención clandestina stronista," *ABC Color* (Asunción), February 14, 2012; and Calloni, *Los años del lobo: Operación Cóndor*, 169–71.

84. McSherry, *Predatory States*, 80.

85. "La Fiscalía promoverá jucio a Campos Alum y Saldivar," *Ultima Hora* (Asunción), December 28, 1992, R0246F0003, CDADDH. La Técnica cast its net widely. Few of those who suffered in its prisons were hardcore revolutionaries. Most were teachers, students, and labor leaders. The author has reviewed hundreds of arrest orders signed by Campos Alum over the course of three decades. See files R238F0001 through R238F0515, CDADDH.

86. See Nickson, *La Guerra Fría y El Paraguay*, 57–58.

87. For example, the head of the Brazilian chapter, Carlos Barbieri Filho, was a medical doctor who ran a private intelligence service in Sao Paulo known as SEPES, short for Sociedade de Estudos Políticos, Econômicos e Sociais. See "Instalado o Congresso da Confederação Anticomunista," *O Dia* (Rio de Janerio), January 25, 1974, folder 1, box 56, KDP, HIWRP.

88. Dinges, *Condor Years*, 41.

89. The literature on Latin America's leftist guerrillas is vast. For useful overview of Argentina's guerrilla movements, particularly the Ejército Revolucionario del Pueblo and the Montoneros, see Lewis, *Gods and Generals*, esp. 33–70. On Chile's guerrilla group, the Movimiento Izquierda Revolucionario, which supported the government of Salvador Allende in the early 1970s, see Constable and Valenzuela, *Nation of Enemies*, 15–39.

90. As historian Piero Gleijeses has ably documented, Cuba feared the consequences of armed intervention in Latin America, especially after Che Guevara's disastrous guerrilla war in Bolivia, which led to his death in 1967. Instead, Cuba focused its revolutionary struggle on sub-Saharan Africa. See Gleijeses, *Conflicting Missions*, 377.

91. On Allende's political beliefs, see Harmer, *Allende's Chile and the Inter-American Cold War*, 30–39.

92. See "Instalado o Congreso de Confederação Anticomunista," *O Dia* (Rio de Janiero), January 23, 1974, folder 1, box 56, KDP, HIWRP.

93. These included General Silvio Frota and Colonel Pedro Braga from the army and Admiral Joaquim Américo dos Santos and Captain Jose Augusto Machedo from the navy. See "Instalado na Guanbara o II Congreso Anticomunista," *A Noticíca* (Porto Alegre), January 25, 1974, folder 1, box 56, KDP, HIWRP.

94. See Marvin Howe, "Latin Anti-Communists Plan Tactics," *NYT*, January 26, 1974. Others, including a Soviet correspondent, noted that the "public was not admitted and journalists were carefully checked." See "Article Ridicules Latin American Anticommu-

nist Meeting," *Isvestiya* (Moscow), January 29, 1974, in *FBIS*, Daily Report, Soviet Union, FBIS-SOV-74–025.

95. See "Planes contra subversión roja tratará el II Congreso del CAL," *Prensa Gráfica* (Costa Rica); and "CAL reúne lideres anticomunistas para II Congreso no Rio," *O Globo* (Rio de Janeiro), January 23, 1974, folder 1, box 56, KDP. The Archbishop of a rural Brazilian diocese went so far as to call the spread of Marxism into the Church the most pressing problem in Latin America. See Dom Geraldo de Provença Siguad, Archbishop of Diamantina, Minas Gerais, "Discurso de abertura do II Congresso da Confederação Anticomunista Latino-americana-CAL," *Arena do povo* (Brazil), 2nd quinzena de Janeiro de 1974, folder 1, box 56, KDP, HIWRP.

96. "Segundo Congreso de la Confederación Anticomunista Latinoamericana," *brújula* (official paper of the Alianza Popular Anticomunista), February 1974, folder 1, box 56, KDP, HIWRP. Pinochet's delegation to the CAL conference included key members of the military *junta*, including Ambassador Sergio Onofre Jarpa and Air Force General Gustavo Leigh Guzmán. See "Buzaid abre reunião Anticomunista no Rio," *Folha de S. Paulo*, January 24, 1974; and "Se Prepara Activamente del Congreso Anticomunista de Brasil," *¡Alerta!* (Guatemala), January 20, 1974, in folder 1, box 56, KDP, HIWRP.

97. Konstantin Karenin, "Commentary on Anticommunist Forces in Latin America," January 26, 1974, in *FBIS*, Daily Report, Soviet Union, FBIS-SOV-74–108.

98. The widely accepted number of deaths and disappearances is 3,197. See Kornbluh, *Pinochet File*, 162. The Chilean National Commission for Truth and Reconciliation cited 2,279 deaths and disappearances by state security forces while noting the actual number was higher. See Comisión Nacional de Verdad y Reconciliación, *Report of the Chilean National Commission for Truth and Reconciliation*, vol. 1, 1122. For the number of exiles in the Pinochet years, see Zúñiga, "Chilean Political Exile," 31.

99. On the arrest, disappearance, torture and murder of political prisoners, see Constable and Valenzuela, *Nation of Enemies*, 31–37. On the Caravan of Death, see Verdugo, *Chile, Pinochet, and the Caravan of Death*.

100. As one U.S. embassy official noted, the Chilean security forces operated with a "determination to cleanse and rejuvenate Chile." See Davila, *Dictatorship in South America*, 93.

101. These numbers come from Klein, *Shock Doctrine*, 93–94.

102. "Se Recomienda la Creación de Grupos Paramilitares," *El Día* (Mexico City), January 28, 1974, folder 1, box 56, KDP, HIWRP.

103. "Rio de Janeiro: Sede del Segundo Congreso de la Confederación Anticomunista Latinoamericana," *¡Alerta!* (Guatemala), January 20, 1974, folder 1, box 56, KDP, HIWRP.

104. "Se Recomienda la Creación de Grupos Paramilitares," *El Día* (Mexico City), January 28, 1974, folder 1, box 56, KDP, HIWRP.

105. After the WACL meeting in Washington, the heads of the CAL met in Guadalajara, Mexico to lay out their plans for collaboration. See Memorandum from la Policía Federal de Argentina, "Informé la reunion Consejo Coordinador de la Confederación Anticomunista Latinoamericana," October 14, 1974, R0013F 0298, CDADDH. The first major Condor meeting was held the following October in Santiago Chile. See "Primera Reunión de Trabajo de Inteligencia Nacional," October 28, 1975, R022F 155—R022F 165, CDADDH. The "parallel state" of Operation Condor was the result of clandestine activities and conspiratorial thinking amongst Latin Americans that stretched back to the late 1960s, if not earlier. These networks were distinct from, but shared links with, the European "stay-behind armies" that political scientist Patrice McSherry has traced. McSherry argues the logic of Operation Condor stretched back to the end of the Second World War, when the CIA set up several

covert forces to prevent leftists from gaining power in the postwar order. These secret armies were comprised of former military officers, including former Nazis and Nazi collaborators, as well as right-wing civilians and paramilitary groups in Italy, Greece, and elsewhere. See McSherry, *Predatory States*, 38–46.

106. For a useful overview of the Southern Cone dictatorships, see Dávila, *Dictatorship in South America*.

107. See McSherry, *Predatory States*, 41, 43, 197–98; and Lee, *Beast Reawakens*, 184.

108. An extensive secret intelligence report from 1975 detailed the formation and operations of the JCR. Amongst other things, it revealed how the JCR linked leftist guerrillas from Argentina, Chile, Uruguay, Paraguay, and Bolivia with exiles living in Paris and other major European cities. Military leaders concluded that the JCR's goal was the "communization of all of Latin America." See Secret Report, "Conferencia Bilateral de Inteligencia Paraguay—Argentina," 1975, R046F 1344—R046F 1377; and Benito Guanes Serrano, "Acción Subversiva Combinada," secret memorandum, October 20 1975, R021F 1578–R021F 1584, CDADDH. See also Dinges, *Condor Years*, 50–54.

109. Dávila, *Dictatorship in Latin America*, 116.

110. As Tanya Harmer has documented in Chile, members of the junta were deeply disillusioned by the fall of South Vietnam, which they perceived as an ally, as well as Kissinger's lukewarm support for political repression. The election of Jimmy Carter only exacerbated their fears that the United States had abandoned anticommunism. See Harmer, "Fractious Allies," 136–43.

111. This statement was made by General Guillermo Carlos Suarez Mason, commander of the Argentine intelligence service known as Batallón de Inteligencia 601, at a CAL conference in Buenos Aires in 1980. See "Suarez Mason Insisto a la Unión ante el Comunista," *La Nación* (Buenos Aires), September 4, 1980.

112. For an overview of Operation Condor, see McSherry, *Predatory States*, 1–33.

113. See Dinges, *Condor Years*, 73–78. Townley admitted his guilt in the assassination years later while on trial for killing Chilean diplomat Orlando Letelier. See Federal Bureau of Investigation, "Directorate of National Intelligence (DINA)," January 21, 1982, in National Security Electronic Briefing Book no. 8, DNSA, http://www2.gwu.edu/~nsarchiv/NSAEBB/NSAEBB8/nsaebb8.htm, accessed October 16, 2014.

114. McSherry, *Predatory States*, 97.

115. U.S. Embassy, Argentina, Office of the Federal Bureau of Investigation Attaché, Secret, Cable, September 28, 1976, TE00555, Terrorism and U.S. policy, 1968–2002, DNSA.

116. McSherry, *Predatory States*, 9–10, 71–72, 95–96.

117. U.S. Department of State, SECRET, "Conversation with Argentine Intelligence Source," April 7, 1980, in National Security Archive Electronic Briefing Book No. 416, DNSA. Numerous reports from Paraguay's Archive of Terror document these kinds of transnational disappearances. See, for example, Servicio Inteligencia de Naval de Argentina, "Ingreso de Terroristas argentinos a su país a través del nuestro," July 10, 1980, R0019F 0876, CDADDH.

118. For instance, at the 1975 CAL conference in Brazil, the head of the Brazilian chapter, Carlos Filho Barbieri, met with General Gustavo Leigh, General Sergio Arellano Stark, and other high-ranking officials from Chile's military and intelligence services. See Circular Letter no. 9 from Carlos Filho Barbieri to All Members of the WACL, September 1975, folder 4, box 58, KDP, HIWRP. See also Zoglin, "Paraguay's Archive of Terror," 64–67.

119. For an example of these meetings, see Memorandum from la Policía Federal de Argentina, "Informé la reunion Consejo Coordinador de la Confederación Anticomunista Latinoamericana," October 14, 1974, R0013F 0298, CDADDH, Palacio de Justicia, Asunción, Paraguay. Beyond semi-annual conferences, CAL leaders often met with military dictators

and heads of state security agencies for private meetings. For instance, in 1976, Brazil's Carlos Filho Barbieri held summits with Paraguay's Alfredo Stroessner and members of Uruguayan military. He also gave a lecture to six hundred members of Stroessner's Colorado Party, which was broadcast on national television. See Circular Letter no. 4 from Carlos Filho Barbieri to All WACL Members, March 1976, folder 2, box 59, KDP, HIWRP.

120. For instance, a 1976 CIA memo about Operation Condor planning noted that the intelligence services of Argentina and Paraguay had been "deeply involved security arrangements for the third congress of the Latin American Anti-Communist Confederation." See CIA Memorandum, Comments by Paraguayan Security Official on Operation Condor," no date, c. 1976, CIA-FOIA, http://www.foia.cia.gov/sites/default/files/document_conversions/89801/DOC_0000887275.pdf, accessed February 13, 2014. For messages of support from Stroessner and Videla see, for instance, "Congreso Anticomunista," *La Nación* (Buenos Aries), September 2, 1980.

121. These included Argentina's Rafael Videla and Paraguay's Alfredo Stroessner. See "Habló el Presidente de la Liga Anticomunista Mundial," *ABC Color* (Asunción), February 25, 1976, R234F 054; "Anticomunistas del Mundo al Paraguay," *Patria* (Asunción), February 12, 1979, R142F 1059; and "Delegados Paraguayos Asistieron al Primer Encuentro Anticomunista en la Argentina," *Patria* (Asunción), December 15, 1979, R229F 0184, in CDADDH. See also "Suarez Mason insitió a la unión ante el comunismo," *La Nación* (Buenos Aires) September 2, 1979; and List of Latin American Anti-Communist Politicians, folder 24, box 9, Philip Agee Papers, TLRWLA.

122. Rafael Rodriguez, "Regional Report of Latin America," 9th WACL Conference, Seoul, South Korea, April 29 to May 4, 1976, folder 3, box 59, KDP, HIWRP.

123. Ibid. Some of the CAL's members had even been murdered by the Sandinista guerrillas in Nicaragua. See Confederación Anticomunista Latinoamericana Flyer for Chester Escobar Martinez and Dr. Francisco Buitrago Martinez, no date, folder 5, box 61, KDP, HIWRP.

124. The MLN joined the CAL in same year as Paraguay's Colorado Party, the party of dictator Alfredo Stroessner, and the Cuban exile paramilitary group Alpha 66. See Report of the Secretary General of the World Anti-Communist League, Presented at the 7th WACL Conference, Washington, D.C., R108F1348, CDADDH.

125. See Villagrán Kramer, *Biografía política de Guatemala*, 144.

126. See Central Intelligence Agency report, "Guatemala: Political Violence Up," in National Security Archive Electronic Briefing Book No. 363, ed. Kate Doyle, http://www2.gwu.edu/~nsarchiv/NSAEBB/NSAEBB363/, accessed October 20, 2014.

127. On this shift, see Grandin, *Last Colonial Massacre*, 86–89.

128. Grandin, *Empire's Workshop*, 154–55.

129. As historian Greg Grandin writes, by the "mid-1960s the MLN had shed its progressive posture and turned into a vengeful protector of planters, its earlier language of justice and modernization degenerating into the virulent idiom of 'armed struggle without quarter, a true national crusade.'" See Grandin, *Last Colonial Massacre*, 89.

130. On the relationship between the MLN and the La Mano Blanco death squad, see Rothenberg, ed., *Memory of Silence: The Guatemalan Truth Commission Report*, 112–13.

131. See Norman Gall, "Guatemala: Death in the Hills," *The Economist*, June 10, 1967; Gall, "Slaughter in Guatemala," *New York Review of Books*, May 20, 1971; "Guatemala Guerrillas Slaughtered: Church Objects to Bloodbath," *National Catholic Reporter*, June 7, 1967.

132. Grandin, *Last Colonial Massacre*, 88.

133. See Victor Perera, "Guatemala: Always La Violencia," *NYT*, June 13, 1971.

134. Anderson and Anderson, *Inside the League*, 173.

135. U.S. officials were aware of this at the time. In one declassified cable, the U.S. Em-

bassy in Guatemala noted that Sandoval "frequently sends representatives to international anti-communist congresses." See Cable from U.S. Embassy-Guatemala to Secretary of State, September 17, 1976, USD-FOIA, http://foia.state.gov/searchapp/DOCUMENTS/FOIADocs/00004F47.pdf, accessed May 9, 2017.

136. See Text of speech given by Mario Sandoval Alarcón to the 11th WACL Conference, Washington, D.C., April 27, 1978, folder 2, box 60, KDP; and Text of speech given by Mario Sandoval Alarcón at 12th WACL Conference, Asunción, Paraguay, April 27, 1979, folder 2, box 60, KDP, HIWRP.

137. In May 1977, the government of Guatemala joined El Salvador and Nicaragua in refusing U.S. military aid "so long as Washington tries to pass judgments on its human rights policies." See "Guatemala, El Salvador, Join 3 Rejecting U.S. Aid," *The Sun* (Baltimore), March 18, 1977. This stance was more of a symbolic protest as these regimes continued to receive arms-buying credits and other covert military aid from the United States. See Grandin, *Last Colonial Massacre*, 188.

138. See "Congreso anticomunista," *La Nación* (Buenos Aires), September 1, 1979; "Suarez Mason insitió a la unión ante el comunismo," *La Nación* (Buenos Aires) September 2, 1979; and Armony, *Argentina, the U.S., and the Anti-Communist Crusade*, 87, 92–93. See also, Stella Calloni, "Muere Guillermo Suárez Mason, feroz represor de la dictadura argentina," *La Jornada* (Mexico City), June 22, 2005; and "Pulling Out of Central America: Alfonsin Puts an End to Anti-Communist Crusade," *Latin America Weekly Report*, February 3, 1984, folder 26, box 9, Philip Agee Papers, TLRWLA.

139. According to a Guatemalan journalist, "In the late [19]70s, Sandoval sought help from abroad. He got it, too, principally from Taiwan. The MLN's leaders go there with frequency where they get advice in psychological warfare and money." See Anderson and Anderson, *Inside the League*, 173. See also James Baron, "Taipei's Central American Skeletons," *Taipei Times*, June 2, 2014.

140. See LeoGrande, *Our Own Backyard*, 159.

141. D'Aubuisson was part of the intelligence branch Agencia Nacional de Servicios Especiales (known by its acronym ANSESAL), which worked with ORDEN and other groups to maintain a network 80,000 informants, or one out of every sixty Salvadorans. See Laurie Becklund, "Salvador Death Squads: Deadly Other War," *LAT*, December 18, 1983.

142. See Central Intelligence Agency, Directorate of Intelligence, "El Salvador: Controlling Right-wing Terrorism," February 1985, file El Salvador Death Squads, box 132, Oliver North Files, RRPL; and LeoGrande, *Our Own Backyard*, 159;

143. See Armony, *Argentina, the U.S., and the Anti-Communist Crusade*, 87.

144. These included ORDEN (Organización Democrática Nacionalista) and La Mano Blanca, the name of which was inspired by Guatemala's most notorious vigilante outfit. See LeoGrande, *Our Own Backyard*, 48–50; and Allan Nairn, "Behind El Salvador's Death Squads," *The Progressive*, May 1984, folder 11, box 9, Philip Agee Papers, TLRWLA.

145. For the activities of right-wing death squads in El Salvador, see Central Intelligence Agency, Directorate of Intelligence, "El Salvador: Controlling Right-wing Terrorism," February 1985, file El Salvador Death Squads, box 132, Oliver North Files, RRPL. On the broader history of El Salvador's death squads in the 1980s see Danner, *Massacre at El Mozote*; and Bonner, *Weakness and Deceit*. See also Anne-Marie O'Connor, "Participant in 1980 Assassination of Romero in El Salvador Provides New Details," *WP*, April 6, 2010.

146. According to retired American soldier Stan Fulcher, who worked in El Salvador from 1974 through 1977, Salvadoran officers took instruction in a variety of tactics, including "population control through psychological warfare, the development and control of agents provocateurs, the development of political cadres within the officer corps, and the placement

of military officers in the civilian security forces." See Valentine, *Phoenix Program*, 422. For instance, Lt. Colonel Domingo Monterrosa, commander of the elite rapid-response unit known as the Atlacatl Battalion trained at the Political Warfare Cadres Academy in Peitou, Taiwan, in 1978. See Danner, *Massacre at El Mozote*, 143.

147. See McSherry, *Predatory States*, 212.

148. These groups included Brigade 2506, the Cuban National Liberation Front, and the Cuban Nationalist Movement. Exiles publicized their clandestine acts, celebrating their successes and lamenting setbacks to journalists from major newspapers. See, for instance, the list of raids and acts of sabotages in the Alpha 66 Pamphlet, "Los Principios Ideologicos de Alpha 66," July 21, 1972, folder 2, box 57, KDP, HIWRP. See also "Exiles Say Guerrillas Open 2 'Fronts' in Cuba," *WP*, April 21, 1970; and "Exiles Claim Cuba Fighting," *WP*, July 17, 1970.

149. This figure comes from an FBI report cited in Burrough, *Days of Rage*, 5. For analyses of Cuban exile groups within the context of other domestic terrorist movements, see Jenkins, *Decade of Nightmares*, 56–58; and Perlstein, *Nixonland*, 339–40.

150. Isaac M. Flores, "Cuban Liberation Movement Talks about Hard Times," *LAT*, December 15, 1971.

151. See "FBI Raids Miami Office of Group Opposing Castro," *NYT*, May 27, 1970; and Kenneth Reich, "Exiles Bitter at U.S. Attitudes on Cuba Raids," *LAT*, July 15, 1970; and "Six Seized of Florida on Boat Carrying Load of Ammunition," *NYT*, September 7, 1971.

152. Pinochet also promised aid from Paraguay and Uruguay. See McSherry, *Predatory States*, 159.

153. CORU was led by a fanatical anticommunist named Orlando Bosch who channeled funds from state and private sources to his forces. For instance, in 1976, Bosch organized a $1000-a-plate fundraiser in Caracas to finance CORU activities. See CIA, Secret Intelligence Cable, "Activities of Cuban Exile Leader Orlando Bosch During his Stay in Venezuela," October 14, 1976, in the National Security Electronic Briefing Book no. 157, DNSA, http://www2.gwu.edu/~nsarchiv/NSAEBB/NSAEBB157/19761014.pdf, accessed February 18, 2014.

154. The most notable assassination in which Cuban exiles played a part was that of exiled Chilean diplomat Orlando Letelier, discussed later in this chapter. See also McSherry, *Predatory States*, 158.

155. Report of the Secretary General of the World Anti-Communist League, presented at the 7th WACL Conference, Washington, D.C., April 8–11, 1974, folder 1, box 58, KDP, HIWRP.

156. Rafael Rodriguez, "Regional Report of Latin America," 9th WACL Conference, Seoul, South Korea, April 29 to May 4, 1976, folder 3, box 59, KDP, HIWRP.

157. Felipe Sin Garciga, "United Cubans in the Anti-Communist Struggle," address at the 11th WACL Conference, Taipei, Taiwan, April 18–22, 1977, folder 7, box 59, KDP, HIWRP.

158. On the Red Army Faction and its links to the PLO, see Varon, *Bringing the War Home*, 69–70; and Aust, *Baader-Meinhof*, 65–79, 72–74, 239, 268.

159. Dinges, *Condor Years*, 129.

160. On the origins of the HOP, its clashes with rival émigré groups, and its influence in exile communities, see CIA National Foreign Assessment Center, memorandum, "Yugoslav Émigré Extremists," May 29, 1980 CIA-FOIA, https://www.cia.gov/library/readingroom/docs/CIA-RDP85T00287R000101220002-6.pdf, accessed June 6, 2017. See also Tanner, *Croatia*, 141–67; McCormick, *Croatia under Pavelić*, 176–77; Clarkson, *Fragmented Fatherland*, 60; and Tokić, "The End of 'Historical-Ideological Bedazzlement.'"

161. CIA National Foreign Assessment Center, memorandum, "Yugoslav Émigré Extremists," May 29, 1980 CIA-FOIA, https://www.cia.gov/library/readingroom/docs/CIA-RDP85T00287R000101220002-6.pdf, accessed June 6, 2017. For press coverage of these acts and the response of Western policing agencies, see Malcolm Browne, "Yugoslavs Press

for Curb on Foes," *NYT*, June 12, 1976; Malcolm Browne, "Croatian Exiles and Tito's Police Fight Clandestine War Worldwide," *NYT*, September 12, 1976; Associated Press, "Croatian Nationalists Have Waged a Long Fight for Autonomy," *BG*, September 12, 1976; Stewart Harris, "Concern in Canberra over Terrorist Bombings," *The Times* (London), September 2, 1972.

162. See Resolution passed by the Commission of Anticommunist Civic Bodies at the 3rd CAL Conference, Asunción Paraguay, March 28–30, 1977, R0145F 0996, CDADDH.

163. See, for example, Croatian Liberation Movement, "The Croatian Christian Martyrs," announcement at the 9th WACL Conference, Seoul, South Korea, April 29 to May 4, 1976; and Croatian Liberation Movement, "Croatia Demands Freedom," announcement at the 9th WACL Conference, Seoul, South Korea, April 29 to May 4, 1976, folder 2, box 59, KDP, HIWRP.

164. The link between the HOP and the Paraguayan and Argentine state security forces was Miro Baresic. See Memorandum to Pastor Coronel, Chief of Investigations, Judicial Department, Asunción, Paraguay, July 18, 1979, R0046F 2029, CDADDH. See also Luis Veron, "Terrorista y héroe," *ABC Revista* (Asunción), July 24, 2011; "Terrorista e instructor militar," *ABC Revista* (Asunción), March 22, 2009; and Alan Riding, "Paraguay Accepts Terrorist and Stir Is Minor," *New York Times*, December 27, 1987.

165. While journalist John Dinges has argued that the heads of Operation Condor, particularly Chile's Manuel Contreras, "created a network of civilians recruited from right-wing terrorist groups in Europe and the United States," the reality was messier than that. Operation Condor leaders did not create this so much as they sought to enlist it for their own purposes. See Dinges, *Condor Years*, 127.

166. Damjanovic's involvement in prior terrorist acts formed a central part of subsequent legal proceedings against him. See Letter from the Vice President of the FRG Bundeskriminalamt to Pastor Coronel, Chief of Investigations, Judicial Department, Asunción, Paraguay, June 24, 1976, R0046F 0163, CDADDH.

167. In the deportation hearings that followed Damjanovic's murder, Croatian exiles admitted to sending between $30,000 to $50,000 from exile communities in Canada, Germany, and Australia. See Unaddressed Letter from Dinko Sakic, July 27, 1977, R0028F 0556-R0028F 0561, CDADDH. Some claimed that Sakic was the "moral father" of the assassination. See Confidential Cable from U.S. Embassy, Paraguay to U.S. Secretary of State, April 4, 1977, in Wikileaks Public Library of U.S. Diplomacy, at https://wikileaks.org/plusd/cables/1977ASUNCI01335_c.html, accessed October 23, 2014.

168. See Memorandum from Daniel Coronel, Inspector General, Policía del Capital, June 7, 1976, R0022F 0077, CDADDH.

169. Associated Press, "Croat Who Killed Uruguayan Ambassador by Mistake 16 Years Ago, Freed," Associated Press, December 2, 1992, at http://www.apnewsarchive.com/1992/Croat-Who-Killed-Uruguayan-Ambassador-by-Mistake-16-Years-Age-Freed/id-fd8d888b4677ca5d9ffea0ebfea2bbf9, accessed October 23, 2014.

170. In the late 1950s, he founded the Northern League, a neo-Nazi group with chapters in Britain and West Germany, which hoped to save the Nordic race from "annihilation" and "mongrelization." See Northern League, "Aims and Principles of the Northern League for Pan-Nordic Friendship," no date, folder 58, box 44, Church League of America Collection of the Research Files of *Counterattack*, the Wackenhut Corporation, and Karl Baarslag, Tamiment Library and Robert F. Wagner Archives, New York University, New York City, NY. See Roger Pearson, "Immigration to Britain," *The Northlander* 1, no. 1, April 1958; and "League Policy Outlined—Ethnic Heritage Must Be Preserved!," *The Northlander* 1, no. 2, June 1958, in the Institute for the Study of Academic Racism, http://www.ferris.edu/isar/pictures/northlan/, accessed February 10, 2014.

171. The Liberty Lobby financed Pearson's first visit to the United States in 1958. See "Roger Pearson to Tour United States," *Right*, June 1959, 1; and "Northern League Concludes Successful U.S. Tour," *The Northlander* 2, no. 3, June–July 1959, in the Institute for the Study of Academic Racism, http://www.ferris.edu/isar/pictures/northlan/, accessed February 10, 2014. On the merging of the Liberty Lobby and the Northern League, see Bellant, *Old Nazis, the New Right, and the Republican Party*, 60.

172. See Pearson, *Race and Civilization*; and *Eugenics and Race*. Pearson taught at the University of Southern Mississippi and the Montana College of Mineral Science and Technology. See Southern Poverty Law Center profile, "Roger Pearson," https://www.splcenter.org/fighting-hate/extremist-files/individual/roger-pearson, accessed June 6, 2017.

173. Pearson formed a particularly close bond with Edwin Fuelner, president of the Heritage Foundation think tank, with whom Pearson coauthored several articles and a book about communist China. See Fuelner, *China: The Turning Point*.

174. In 1975, Pearson and McDonald traveled to Asunción, Paraguay, to discuss Marxist insurgencies with dictator Alfredo Stroessner, military leaders, and prominent civilians. "Congressman Investigates Possibility of Guerrilla Warfare in Chile," *Council on American Affairs Newsletter*, July 1975, folder Council on American Affairs, box 104, KDP, HIWRP.

175. See Text of speech given by Jesse Helms at the 8th WACL Conference, Rio de Janeiro, April 25, 1975, folder 5, box 227, Walter Judd Papers, HIWRP. Helms also met with CAL leaders, such as Brazil's Carlos Filho Barbieri, when they traveled to the United States. See Circular Letter no. 11 from Carlos Filho Barbieri to All Members of the WACL, September 1975, folder 4, box 58, KDP, HIWRP.

176. See Woo Jae-Sung, Office of Secretary General, World Anti-Communist League, Korean Chapter, Circular Letter No. 4, May 25, 1978, folder 2, box 60, KDP, HIWRP. The conference featured speeches by two U.S. Senators—Jake Garn and James A. McClure. See World Anti-Communist League, Korean Chapter, Office of Secretary General, Woo Jae-Sung, Circular Letter No. 4, May 25, 1978, folder 2, box 60, KDP, HIWRP; and Text of speech delivered by U.S. Senator James McClure at 11th WACL Conference, Washington, D.C., April 28, 1978, folder 3, box 60, KDP, HIWRP.

177. See Paul Valentine, "The Fascist Specter behind the World Anti-Red League," *WP*, May 28, 1978. The CAL leaders met with members of the Italian Social Movement- National Right and the masonic lodge Propaganda Due (P-2), an "anticommunist organization with close links to military and intelligence organizations." On the links between Italian neo-fascist paramilitary groups and Latin American dictatorships, see McSherry, *Predatory States*, 42–44.

178. Paul Valentine, "The Fascist Specter behind the World Anti-Red League," *WP*, May 28, 1978.

179. See U.S. government cable from Executive Secretary to Department of State, "Reported Anti-Communist Meetings in Washington DC," April 4, 1974, in Henry Kissinger Cables, WikiLeaks' Public Library of US Diplomacy, https://wikileaks.org/plusd/cables/1974STATE068009_b.html, accessed October 2, 2014.

180. Valentine, "The Fascist Specter," *WP*, May 28, 1978.

181. In the weeks after the conference, Pearson castigated journalists for their biased coverage. See Letter from Roger Pearson to All WACL chapters, July 8, 1978, folder 2, box 60, KDP, HIWRP.

182. The most well-known murder of an American citizen by the Chilean junta is that of Charles Horman, who was disappeared shortly after the coup and then executed in the Estadio Nacional. See Hauser, *Execution of Charles Horman*.

183. See Harmer, "Fractious Allies," 136.

184. Liebman, *Coming Out Conservative*, 212–13.

185. Ibid., 213.

186. See for instance, Nena Ossa, "Chile's Che Guevara," *NR*, March 23, 1971; Nena Ossa, "Chilean Notes," *NR*, November 5, 1971; Nena Ossa, "The End of the Line," *NR*, March 16, 1973; Nena Ossa, "What Now?," *NR*, April 13, 1973; and "Never a Dull Moment," *NR*, August 3, 1973.

187. These included Raymond de Jaegher, Ralph de Toledano, Walter Judd, David Keene, and David Rowe. For the position of chairman, Liebman reached out to retired American ambassador Spruille Braden, who had helped orchestrate the 1954 Guatemalan coup. See the list of members in the ACC advertisement, "Why Chile?," *Washington Weekly*, February 12, 1980, box 123, MLP, HIWRP.

188. Liebman, *Coming Out Conservative*, 213.

189. Letter from Nena Ossa to Marvin Liebman, January 2, 1975, folder Ossa to Liebman, October 14, 1974–December 21, 1976, box 121, MLP, HIWRP.

190. Letter from Marvin Liebman to William F. Buckley, October 30, 1974, folder Justice Department exhibit originals, box 123, MLP, HIWRP. To get the money from into the United States without provoking inquiry from the U.S. government, Ossa suggested a scheme whereby attendants on Braniff Airways smuggled cash in their luggage on flights between Santiago and New York City. Letter from Nena Ossa to Marvin Liebman, January 2, 1975, folder Ossa to Liebman, October 14, 1974-December 21, 1976, box 121, MLP, HIWRP.

191. See Newsletter (labeled "Confidential Memorandum") from ACC by Marvin Liebman, December 8, 1976, folder Consejo Chileno Norteamericano, box 111, MLP, HIWRP.

192. Ossa, aware of the sensitive nature of these visits, advised Liebman in one letter that "it is better not to ever name a particular type of friends who may visit you, such as my friend who is supposed to call you and visit you around April 1. Somebody may start wondering if they see his name written down." Liebman later insisted that he knew nothing of the Chilean government's involvement with the CCNA and the ACC, but this correspondence reveals that as a lie. Letter from Nena Ossa to Marvin Liebman, April 1, 1975, folder Ossa to Liebman, October 14, 1974-December 21, 1976, box 121, MLP, HIWRP.

193. See Letter from Marvin Liebman to Michael Milwee, May 3, 1977, folder Nicaragua, box 141, MLP, HIWRP.

194. For example, one pamphlet recounted a series of elaborate plans laid by Allende to subvert the democratic process, round up political opponents and business-owners, and import revolutionaries from other socialist states. See Victor Lavsky, "The Soviet Offensive against Chile," CAA pamphlet, September 2, 1975, folder Lavsky Pamphlet, box 121, MLP, HIWRP.

195. See fundraising letter from Congressman Robert Bauman, January 1, 1976, folder Justice Department exhibit originals, box 123, MLP, HIWRP. This letter was almost certainly penned by an ACC staffer such as Liebman or Lynn Bouche and not Congressman Bauman.

196. See the draft of the fundraising letter from U.S. Senator James McClure, March 26, 1976, folder Justice Department exhibit originals, box 123, MLP, HIWRP. On Kissinger and Operation Condor, see Grandin, *Kissinger's Shadow*, 147–54.

197. See Valdes, *Pinochet's Economists*.

198. See Klein, *Shock Doctrine*, 100–104.

199. Jeffrey Hart, "Chilean Spring?," *NR*, March 3, 1978, folder Jeffrey Hart, box 112, MLP, HIWRP.

200. Ibid.

201. Letter from William Rusher to U.S. Ambassador John Davis Lodge, March 15, 1978, folder 7, box 131, WRP, LOC.

202. Larry P. McDonald, "Let's Help Our Friends- Not Our Enemies," *Conservative Digest*,

February 1976, folder Larry P. McDonald reprint, box 121, MLP, HIWRP. Under decree no. 521, DINA had the right to detain any individual so long as there was a declared state of emergency. See McSherry, *Predatory States*, 71.

203. This was known as the "martyr theory," and it gained wide circulation in the U.S. press. DINA alleged that left-wing terrorists had killed Letelier to discredit the Pinochet regime. See Dinges, *Condor Years*, 193.

204. Liebman, *Coming out Conservative*, 214.

205. See "Trial by Speculation, Leaks, and Plants," American Chilean Council Report, July 1978, folder ACC Report July, box 118, MLP, HIWRP.

206. The influence of these thinkers should not be overstated. Proponents of unrestrained capitalism often mined the works of Hayek, von Mises, and Friedman for ideas they liked and discarded those they did not. That forms a central theme of Burgin, *Great Persuasion*.

207. See for instance, Kenneth Freed, "Chile's Strongman Sets Out to Reshape His Nation," *LAT*, September 28, 1980.

208. Letter from Marvin Liebman to William Rusher, May 17, 1978, folder 7, box 131, WRP, LOC.

209. Liebman, *Coming Out Conservative*, 119.

210. Kenneth Bredemeier, "Justice Dept. Says Group Illegally Lobbies for Chile," *WP*, December 19, 1978.

211. Liebman, *Coming Out Conservative*, 215. The Justice Department ordered the ACC to close shop in early 1979, forcing Liebman to publish an advertisement in major American newspapers in which he revealed the ACC's links to the Chilean government. See "American Chilean Council Held Illegal Agent of Chile Dictator," *WP*, June 1, 1979.

212. See United States District Court for the District of Columbia, Final Judgment of Permanent Injunction and other Ancillary Relief Fund as the American-Chilean Council, November 8, 1979, folder 7, box 131, WRP, LOC.

## Chapter 4

1. From 1944 through 1978, Singlaub saw action in four campaigns—France and Manchuria during World War II, the Korean War, and the Vietnam War—and received a litany of awards including the Distinguished Service Medal with Oak Leaf Cluster, the Silver Star, the Legion of Merit with two Oak Leaf clusters, the Bronze Star with Oak Leaf cluster, the Air Medal with Oak Leaf cluster, the Army Commendation Medal, and the Purple Heart. His foreign decorations include the French Croix de Guerre, as well as medals from the Republic of China, the Netherlands, and South Vietnam.

2. See American Security Council Education Foundation, "Newly Retired Singlaub, Sumner Speak Out," *Washington Report*, July 1978; and Singlaub and McConnell, *Hazardous Duty*, 428–35.

3. Americans also learned that the CIA ran a "massive illegal domestic intelligence operation" that targeted antiwar protestors and other critics of the Nixon administration. The agency tapped Americans' phones, opened their mail, and broke into their houses, businesses, and meeting places to steal records and maintained files on more than 10,000 U.S. citizens. These actions clearly violated the agency's charter, which forbade spying in the United States. See Seymour Hersh, "Huge CIA Operation Reported in U.S. against Anti-War Forces, Other Dissidents," *NYT*, December 22, 1974. See Olmsted, *Challenging the Secret Government*; de Vries, "1967 Central Intelligence Agency Scandal"; and Saunders, *Cultural Cold War*.

4. Colby and Forbath, *Honorable Men*, 391.

5. After Nixon left office in 1974, President Gerald Ford sought to distance himself from

the CIA. He also attempted to stave off a congressional investigation by appointing his own body to review Hersh's allegations. But since no congressional leaders wanted to participate, Ford settled for a commission chaired by Vice President Nelson Rockefeller. Yet, in the wake of the Watergate scandal, few trusted executive inquiry. "Like the media," historian Laura Kalman writes, "Congress treated the president's blue-ribbon commission, which included Ronald Reagan and various individuals linked to the national security establishment, as a joke." See Kalman, *Right Star Rising*, 79.

6. Most notably, Church sponsored the Cooper-Church Amendment which sought to end funding to U.S. ground troops and military advisors in Cambodia and Laos, bar air operations in Cambodian airspace in direct support of Cambodian forces without congressional approval, and end U.S. support for Republic of Vietnam forces outside territorial South Vietnam. See Schmitz, *United States and Right-wing Dictatorships*, 121.

7. Ibid., 128.

8. See U.S. Congress, *Covert Action in Chile: 1963–1973*; U.S. Congress, *Final Report*; U.S. Congress, *Hearings on Covert Action*; and U.S. Congress, *Alleged Assassination Plots Involving Foreign Leaders*.

9. On the Church Committee and conspiracy theories about the CIA, see Olmsted, *Real Enemies*, 160–66.

10. See "Assassination and Foreign Policy," *LAT*, November 23, 1975.

11. See Memorandum of conversation between Gerald Ford, Brent Scowcroft, and Henry Kissinger, June 26, 1975, KT01684, The Kissinger Transcripts, 1969–1977, DNSA.

12. Transcript of *Face the Nation*, November 9, 1975, box 64, Ron Nessen Files, GFPL.

13. U.S. Congress, *Covert Action in Chile: 1963–1973*, 54–56.

14. See "Divided Intelligence Panel Issues Final Report," *Congressional Quarterly Almanac* 32 (1976), 304–7.

15. Agee, *Inside the Company*.

16. Colby quoted in "The Spooks Who Rush to Print," *Newsweek*, January 27, 1975.

17. The most important ex-CIA agents' memoirs published in the mid-1970s include Marchetti, *CIA*; Ayers, *War That Never Was*; and Hunt, *Give Us This Day*.

18. See Jenkins, *Decade of Nightmares*, 53.

19. Schmitz, *United States and Right-Wing Dictatorships*, 7.

20. On Carter's foreign policy and human rights, see Schmitz and Walker, "Jimmy Carter and the Foreign Policy of Human Rights"; and Schmidli, "Institutionalizing Human Rights."

21. See "President Names Adm. Turner as Director of CIA," *WP*, February 8, 1977.

22. See David Binder, "Personnel Cuts Are Begun in CIA's Clandestine Units," *NYT*, November 13, 1977. Quote from David Binder, "Cutbacks by CIA's New Director Creating Turmoil within the Agency," *NYT*, December 10, 1977.

23. Richard Harwood, "CIA's Spy Section Facing Big Cutback," *LAT*, November 13, 1977.

24. Henry S. Bradsher, "CIA Morale Sags; Director Turner's 'Bureaucracy' Is Hit," *CT*, December 25, 1977.

25. Richard Harwood, "CIA Begins a Purge of Spy Division," *WP*, November 12, 1977.

26. David Binder, "Personnel Cuts Are Begun in CIA's Clandestine Units," *NYT*, November 13, 1977.

27. As one journalist summed it up, "To hear Turner and other intelligence authorities, the agency will be smaller, with more sharply focused analysis, and with covert operations scaled down and sparingly used." See "Shaping the CIA," *Time*, February 6, 1978.

28. See David Binder, "Cutbacks by CIA's New Director Creating Turmoil within the Agency," *NYT*, December 10, 1977.

29. Henry S. Bradsher, "CIA Morale Sags; Director Turner's 'Bureaucracy' Is Hit," *CT*, December 25, 1977.

30. Patrick Buchanan, "CIA Firings to Leave 800 Out in the Cold," *CT*, November 17, 1977.

31. "Has Church Panel Jeopardized U.S. Agents," *Human Events*, May 29, 1976.

32. Francis J. McNamara, "How Congress and the Media Are Destroying the CIA," *Human Events*, February 28, 1976. McNamara served as an intelligence officer in China during World War II. When he returned to the United States in 1948, he went to work for American Business Consultants, a private security firm that monitored suspected subversives in the United States. He later edited *Counterattack*, a leading anticommunist newsletter, before serving as the head of the Veterans of Foreign Wars' National Security Program. That experience led him into HUAC, where he first worked as a research director and later as a staff director.

33. Speech given by Bill James Hargis to the 9th World Anti-Communist League Conference, Seoul, South Korea, December 12, 1975, folder 6, box 62, KDP, HIWRP.

34. See Harmer, "Fractious Allies."

35. American Enterprise Institute, "A Conversation with Ernest Mulato: The Political and Military Struggle in Angola," March 2, 1979, folder Revolutionary Movements UNITA Reports, box 4, Angola Subject Collection, HIWRP.

36. As Philip Agee wrote in 1979, "Only two months ago, an unusually high number of CIA employees chose to accept early retirement rather than to serve the embattled agency to the end of normal careers." Philip Agee, "The U.S. Intelligence System," March 31, 1979, folder 71, box 17, Philip Agee Papers, TLRWLA.

37. As historian Robert Dean argues, many of the United States' covert warriors, as well as policymakers such as John F. Kennedy, viewed "American diplomats and foreign aid bureaucrats as soft, lazy men, ignorant of the local languages, huddling in their enclaves enjoying a comfortable lifestyle of colonial privilege." In contrast, "salvation lay in the few hard, bright, committed American men willing to sacrifice ease and complacency by beating the Communists at their own game"—men such as John Singlaub. See Dean, "Masculinity as Ideology," 39.

38. The caption under his yearbook photo read "Military man with learned technique . . . Jack is never feminine . . . the Colonel just wants to kill Japs." From John Singlaub's UCLA *Southern Campus* yearbook, 1943, on Ancestry.com, accessed January 24, 2014.

39. See Singlaub and McConnell, *Hazardous Duty*, 28–40.

40. See Woods, *Shadow Warrior*, 243.

41. Singlaub was part of Operation Jedburgh. For their operations and their work the British Special Operations Executive in France, see Irwin, *Jedburghs*, 37–38, 60–69. For a summary of the Jedburgh activities in France, see Memo from William Donovan to Franklin Roosevelt, October 31, 1944, 72–194, microfilm, Selected OSS Documents, 1941–1945, Director's Office Files, Records of the Office of Strategic Services 1940–1946, Record Group 226, National Archives, Washington, D.C. See also Singlaub and McConnell, *Hazardous Duty*, 45–69.

42. Singlaub and McConnell, *Hazardous Duty*, 72. Emphasis in original.

43. Ibid., 151–85.

44. The CIA shared much of the same mission as the OSS—to collect intelligence and conduct espionage though its mandate to wage covert warfare was unclear from the start. It also shared most of the same personnel as OSS veterans comprised the first generation of CIA agents and station chiefs. On the creation of the CIA, see Weiner, *Legacy of Ashes*, 26–29.

45. Although it had already been in existence for two years, leaders in the Pentagon and the White House hoped to dramatically expand the unit's operations as the conventional war reached new heights. Formerly known as the Special Operations Group, the SOG was

formed in 1964 to "execute an intensified program of harassment, diversion, political pressure, capture of prisoners, physical destruction, acquisition of intelligence, generation of propaganda, and diversion of resources, against the Democratic Republic of Vietnam." See Department of Defense, "Military Assistance Command Vietnam Special Operations Group (MACVSOG) Command History 1971 to 1972," A-1, in DOD-FOIA, http://www.dod.mil/pubs/foi/International_security_affairs/vietnam_and_southeast_asiaDocuments/396.pdf, accessed September 9, 2014.

46. See Kelley, "Misuse of the Studies and Observation Group as a National Asset in Vietnam," 5; and Singlaub and McConnell, *Hazardous Duty*, 92.

47. On Singlaub's work with the CIA, see Secord and Wurts, *Honored and Betrayed*, 65.

48. Singlaub and McConnell, *Hazardous Duty*, 295.

49. Years later, Singlaub would turn to these connections as a private citizen to help arm and supply anticommunist guerrillas in a half dozen nations. See Testimony of John Singlaub, in *Joint Hearings before the Senate Subcommittee on Secret Military Assistance to Iran and the Nicaraguan Opposition*.

50. Department of Defense, Military Assistance Command Studies and Observation Group Documentation Study: Appendix C, A-14.

51. This figure comes from Woods, *Shadow Warrior*, 242.

52. See United States, Department of Defense, "Report on Selected Air and Ground Operations in Cambodia and Laos," September 10, 1973, U.S. Policy in the Vietnam War, 1969–1975, DNSA.

53. John Singlaub oral history interview in Appy, *Patriots*, 92. SOG officers created an elaborate backstory for the Sacred Sword of the Patriot League that stretched back to the 1930s. See Department of Defense, Military Assistance Command Studies and Observation Group Documentation Study: Appendix C, A-14.

54. See Singlaub and McConnell, *Hazardous Duty*, 296–97; and Kelley, "Misuse of the Studies and Observation Group," 60. Internal MACV documents revealed that some North Vietnamese officials believed that not only was the SSPL real but that it was controlled by two former South Vietnamese Army colonels who had defected to the Soviet Union. See Gillespie, *Black Ops, Vietnam*, 29.

55. Former SOG soldier John Plaster counted this as the SOG's greatest accomplishment. In his view, SOG's "investment of less than a company-sized U.S. force tied down the equivalent of four-plus divisions in Laos and Cambodia, an economy of force unparalleled in U.S. history, perhaps without precedent in world military history." See Plaster, *SOG*, 466.

56. Singlaub was most frustrated by the American ambassador to Laos, William Sullivan, who insisted that he authorize every covert action attempted by Singlaub's unit. See Singlaub and McConnell, *Hazardous Duty*, 284–319.

57. Ibid., 319.

58. Ibid., 358.

59. John Saar, "U.S. General: Korea Pullout Risks War," *WP*, May 19, 1977.

60. Singlaub and McConnell, *Hazardous Duty*, 397–98.

61. Austin Scott, "President Fires Gen. Singlaub as Korea Staff Chief," *WP*, May 22, 1977, 1; Jack Nelson, "Carter Removes General Who Opposed Korea Policy: President Takes Swift Action Against Singlaub," *LAT*, May 22, 1977.

62. George C. Wilson, "Administration Used Singlaub Firing as Signal to S. Korea," *WP*, May 24, 1977; Editorial, "Beyond General Singlaub," *Wall Street Journal*, May 24, 1977.

63. Patrick J. Buchanan, "The General Deserves Respect," *CT*, May 26, 1977.

64. Times Wire Services, "Singlaub Gets Plum Post in Army's Biggest Command," *LAT*, May 27, 1977. Carter was also worried about his defense credentials as a round of Strategic

Arms Limitation Treaty talks approached. See memo from Hamilton Jordan to Jimmy Carter, folder John Singlaub, box 37, Office of the Chief of Staff Files, Hamilton Jordan's Confidential Files, JCPL.

65. Singlaub and McConnell, *Hazardous Duty*, 400–414. In April 1978, Singlaub again vented his grievances the media, this time about Carter's negotiations with Panama over control of the canal. See "Singlaub in Jam for New Remark," *WP*, April 28, 1978. His subsequent rebuke in Washington was the final straw. Singlaub retired a few days later. On Singlaub's retirement announcement see, "General Who Blasted Carter Agrees to Retire," *LAT*, April 28, 1978.

66. "Gen. Singlaub becomes Newest Right-wing Hero," *Group Research Report*, June 27, 1978, folder Singlaub, box 298, GRR, RBML.

67. "General Singlaub Speaks Again," *CT*, May 6, 1978.

68. Barry Goldwater in *Congressional Record*, 95th Cong., 2nd Sess., 1978, vol. 124, pt. 13: 16819.

69. "Carter's Foreign Policy Naïve, Singlaub Says," *BG*, June 2, 1978.

70. Singlaub and McConnell, *Hazardous Duty*, 423.

71. John K. Singlaub, "I Intend to Continue to Speak Out," *Human Events*, July 8, 1978.

72. Graham had been an intelligence officer on General William Westmoreland's staff in Saigon during the Vietnam War, and later headed the Defense Intelligence Agency, where he honed his knowledge on strategic issues and advanced weapons systems. Graham became the key proponent behind the Reagan administration's Strategic Defense Initiative. See Daniel O. Graham, "The High Frontier," no date, folder American Security Council Speakers and Coalition for Peace through Strength, box 1, Morton Blackwell files, Series I, RRPL.

73. See Weiner, *Legacy of Ashes*, 407–8.

74. See Sandra G. Boodman, "Retired Generals Enlist in Solid Brass Network for Reagan," *WP*, October 23, 1980.

75. See Leslie H. Gelb, "Top Experts Helping Guide Candidates Views," *NYT*, March 27, 1976.

76. Thomas Oliphant, "Singlaub's 'All on the Record' Now," *BG*, June 11, 1978. On the ASC's budget see Juan de Onis, "Lobbying Body to Push Congress for Nuclear Edge over Soviet," *NYT*, January 6, 1981.

77. On the school's campus in the bucolic rural town of Boston, Virginia, Singlaub joined a "parade of hundreds of congressional aides, retired military officers, and corporate executives who arrived" to talk about "the Pentagon, the Soviet Union, and ultimately, World War III." J. Reagan Kerney, "The Cold War Campus: Boston, Va. Estate Is Home of American Security Council," *WP*, January 8, 1979.

78. On Singlaub's film appearances, see Senator Philip M. Crane, "Soviet Might/American Myth: U.S. in Retreat," *Atlanta Daily World*, April 26, 1979. The documentary, which also featured Alexander Solzhenitsyn and Senator Barry Goldwater, generated more than $100,000 in donations after its screenings in major U.S. cities. See "Conservatives' Film," *WP*, September 17, 1978.

79. "SOF Interviews General John K. Singlaub," *SOF*, January 1979.

80. Singlaub and McConnell, *Hazardous Duty*, 425. See also, "Capitol Briefs," *Human Events*, May 13, 1978; George C. Wilson, "Singlaub in Retirement Continues Assault on Carter Military Policies," *WP*, June 3, 1978; and M. Stanton Evans, "Gen. Singlaub Blasts Carter on Muzzling," *Human Events*, June 24, 1978.

81. By the early 1980s, Singlaub was a regular feature at meetings of the ABN as well as the APACL. See text of speech given by John Singlaub to the Anti-Bolshevik Bloc of Nations/European Freedom Council Conference, London, Great Britain, September 24–26, 1982, folder 5, box 54, KDP, HIWRP.

82. See "Vigilantism by Computer," *LAT*, May 26, 1983. For information about the LAPD investigation, see Joel Sappel, "Grand Jury Gets Files in LAPD Spy Case," *LAT*, September 30, 1983.

83. See Larry P. McDonald, "Communists Organize Support for Criminals," *Congressional Record*, Extension of Remarks, August 5, 1976, E 4378–4379.

84. See Larry P. McDonald, "George Jackson Brigade Continues Terrorism in Pacific Northwest," *Congressional Record*, Extension of Remarks, June 30, 1977; "Terrorism and Subversion in Latin America," *Congressional Record*, Wednesday July 13, 1977, 22869–22880; "Congressman Investigates Possibility of Guerrilla Warfare in Chile," *Council on American Affairs Newsletter*, July 1975, folder Council on American Affairs, box 104, Drenikoff Papers, HIWRP; Larry P. McDonald, "Let's Help Our Friends—Not Our Enemies," *Conservative Digest*, February 1976, folder Larry P. McDonald reprint, box 121, MLP, HIWRP; and Circular Letter no. 11 from Carlos Filho Barbieri to All Members of the WACL, September 1975, folder 4, box 58, KDP, HIWRP.

85. Some Operation Condor agents had even conspired to murder U.S. Congressman Ed Koch. See Letter from Ed Koch to U.S. Attorney General Edward Levi, October 19, 1976 in National Security Electronic Briefing Book no. 112, DNSA, http://nsarchive.gwu.edu/NSAEBB/NSAEBB112/, accessed May 24, 2017; and Dinges, *Condor Years*, 214–18.

86. Mary Battista, "Congressman's Foundation Targets Communist 'Threat,'" *WP*, August 22, 1981.

87. For Western Goals budget figures, see the "Deposition of Barbara Newington," in Senate Select Committee on Secret Military Assistance to Iran and the Nicaraguan Opposition, *Report of the Congressional Committees Investigating the Iran-Contra Affair with Supplemental, Minority, and Additional Views*, 367.

88. Mary Battista, "Congressman's Foundation Targets Communist 'Threat,'" *WP*, August 22, 1981.

89. In Los Angeles, for example, a detective from the LAPD's Public Disorder Intelligence Division sent Western Goals discs with secret files on hundreds of suspected subversives. See "L.A. Detective Is Linked to Private Subversives Study," *LAT*, August 12, 1983; and Joel Sappell, "LAPD Role in Study of Subversive: Detective Got Okay to Work for Right-wing Group, Officer Says," *LAT*, August 12, 1983. The discs included files on celebrities such as Joan Baez, Jackson Browne, Bonnie Raitt, Richard Dreyfuss, Susan Sarandon, and other well-known actors, directors, and musicians. See "Western Goals Enjoined from Using LAPD Spy Files," *WP*, April 19, 1984. LAPD detective Jay Paul's wife reportedly received $30,000 a year from Western Goals. See Joel Sappell, "Grand Jury Gets Files in LAPD Spy Case," *LAT*, September 30, 1983.

90. For a partial list of titles, see Western Goals Endowment Fund and Western Goals, "Annual Report 1982/83," folder 1, Western Goals Issuances, HIWRP.

91. Mary Battista, "Congressman's Foundation Targets Communist 'Threat,'" *WP*, August 22, 1981.

92. See "Roy Cohn Joins Board of Anti-Communist Group," *NYT*, May 15, 1982. Since the 1950s, Milliken had been a key financial backer of William F. Buckley's *National Review* and Clarence Manion's *Manion Forum of Opinion*, as well as many other conservative media outlets and activist organizations. See Philips-Fein, *Invisible Hands*, 78–80, 127–28.

93. After 1981, Western Goals became part of the Reagan administration's campaign against the Committee in Solidarity with the People of El Salvador, which opposed U.S. military aid to the Salvadoran government, which used it to kill thousands of civilians every year. See Grandin, *Empire's Workshop*, 138; and Mary Battista, "Congressman's Foundation Targets Communist 'Threat,'" *WP*, August 22, 1981.

94. On Guatemala's civil war and the genocidal policies of its military government, see Grandin, *Last Colonial Massacre*; and Garrard-Burnett, *Terror in the Land of the Holy Spirit*.

95. As one commentator put it in 1980, "The Amigos del País is equivalent to the John Birch Society and the Guatemalan Freedom Foundation is even more to the right." See "Reagan Aides Guatemalan Connections Investigated," *Pittsburgh Press*, September 8, 1980.

96. See Martin and Sikkink, "U.S. Policy and Human Rights," 346–47; and Raymond Bonner, "'Why Guatemala?' Some Answers to the Question," *NYT*, January 3, 1982.

97. To that end, they hired the public relations firm of Michael Deaver—a future Reagan administration staffer—to serve as their registered agent in the United States. See Stephen Kinzer, "Guatemala Pushes for a New Image," *BG*, May 3, 1981; Stephen Kinzer, "Latin Rightists Hope for Reagan Win," *BG*, October 7, 1980; and Stephen Kinzer, "Guatemala Pushes for a New Image," *BG*, May 3, 1981. Deaver resigned from his position in the firm, Deaver and Hannaford, to become Reagan's Deputy Chief of Staff in 1981.

98. Singlaub and McConnell, *Hazardous Duty*, 441.

99. Singlaub relayed these comments to journalist Allan Nairn in a telephone conversation. See Allan Nairn, "Controversial Reagan Campaign Links with Guatemalan and Private Sector Leaders," Council on Hemispheric Affairs Research Memorandum, October 30, 1980, online at Princeton University's Digital Library, http://pudl.princeton.edu/objects/rv042v23j, accessed June 26, 2017.

100. See Corn, *Blond Ghost*, 67–151.

101. Commanded by General Vang Pao, the secret army stretched back to at least 1960, when CIA agent Edgar "Pop" Buell met Vang Pao, who told him that he could assemble an army of guerrillas that would be more effective than the Royal Lao Army. See Jacobs, *Universe Unraveling*, 198–200. As Shackley ran the paramilitary war in Laos, he coordinated his station's operations with John Singlaub's Studies and Observations Group. See Corn, *Blond Ghost*, 141; and Singlaub and McConnell, *Hazardous Duty*, 284–319.

102. Over time, Shackley transferred the management of the Phoenix Program to the intelligence branch of the Military Assistance Command Vietnam (MACV). See Valentine, *Phoenix Program*, 277.

103. Corn, *Blond Ghost*, 240–67. On the role of the CIA and ITT in the Chilean coup, see U.S. Congress, *Covert Action in Chile: 1963–1973*.

104. See Corn, *Blond Ghost*, 300–322.

105. Hired by the agency in 1955, Wilson had formed a series of front companies to spy on labor unions and monitor the movement of goods around the world, always making sure that his fake companies generated not only intelligence but also personal profit. After leaving the agency in 1971, Wilson went to work for the Naval Intelligence Center, where he opened yet more companies. On his work with the CIA and NIC, see Maas, *Manhunt*.

106. Douglas Martin, "Edwin P. Wilson, the Spy Who Lived It Up, Dies at 84," *NYT*, September 22, 2012.

107. See also Goulden, *Death Merchant*; and Trento, *Prelude to Terror*. See also *United States of America vs. Edwin Paul Wilson*, United States District Court, Southern District of Texas, Criminal Case H-82–139, Opinion on Conviction in Ancillary Civil Action H-97–831.

108. See Douglas Martin, "Edwin P. Wilson, the Spy Who Lived It Up Dies at 84," *NYT*, September 22, 2012. Wilson's arrest and trial made major headlines in the early 1980s, and offered a brief glimpse into the world of ex-spies and -soldiers who now plied their trade in the private sector. See for instance Joanna Omang, "Ex-CIA Agent Lured from Libya, Arrested," *WP*, June 16, 1982; Phillip Smith, "Wilson Convicted of Smuggling Guns to Libya," *WP*, November 18, 1982; and Philip Taubman, "Ex-Agent Given Fifteen Years in Prison," *NYT*, December 21, 1982.

109. The pair had known each other for years and had rekindled their friendship in 1972, as Shackley was intrigued by Wilson's knowledge of international arms market and his relationships with foreign intelligence services. See Maas, *Manhunt*, 52–53.

110. See Corn, *Blond Ghost*, 318–26.

111. Shackley's removal from ADDO generated little press reaction. See "Top Operations Official to Be Replaced," *WP*, December 29, 1977; and Corn, *Blond Ghost*, 346–48.

112. See Trento, *Prelude to Terror*, 132–33.

113. See Corn, *Blond Ghost*, 396.

114. These companies included Systems Services International, which traded weapons, and API Distributors, an oil-equipment dealer. See Patrick E. Tyler and Al Kamen, "Relationship with CIA Aide Gave Credibility to Arms Seller," *WP*, September 10, 1981.

115. See Philip Taubman, "Ex-CIA Agent's Associates Run Arms Export Concerns," *NYT*, September 6, 1981.

116. See "Deposition of Theodore Shackley," in Senate Select Committee on Secret Military Assistance to Iran and the Nicaraguan Opposition, *Report of the Congressional Committees Investigating the Iran-Contra Affair With Supplemental, Minority, and Additional Views*, 13. For Shackley's salary, see Corn, *Blonde Ghost*, 354–56.

117. Most of RAI's money came from a contract with Trans-World Oil, an oil trading company based in New York and the Bahamas. See "Deposition of Theodore Shackley," in Senate Select Committee on Secret Military Assistance to Iran and the Nicaraguan Opposition, *Report of the Congressional Committees Investigating the Iran-Contra Affair With Supplemental, Minority, and Additional Views*, 17–21. See also Philip Taubman, "Ex-CIA Agent's Associates Run Arms Export Concerns," *NYT*, September 6, 1981.

118. See Corn, *Blond Ghost*, 348.

119. The papers presented at the symposia appeared in Godson, ed., *Intelligence Requirements for the 1980s*.

120. Shackley quoted in Corn, *Blond Ghost*, 360–61.

121. Ibid.

122. Shackley, *Third Option*, 16.

123. Isador Lubin, foreign aid advisor to President Harry S. Truman, quoted in Cullather, *Hungry World*, 79.

124. On development and modernization schemes, see Cullather, *Hungry World*; Immerwahr, *Small World*; Ekbladh, *The Great American Mission*; Latham, *The Right Kind of Revolution*; and Gilman, *Mandarins of the Future*.

125. See Association of Former Intelligence Officers, "Statement of Purposes of the Citizen's Auxiliary of the AFIO," no date, folder AFIO, box 135, MLP. See also "ARIO Convention," *SOF*, Winter 1977.

126. Association of Former Intelligence Officers press statement, no date, folder AFIO, box 135, MLP, HIWRP.

127. Letter from Marvin Liebman to Jack Coakley, March 2, 1978, folder AFIO, box 135, MLP, HIWRP.

128. Letter from Marvin Liebman to Jack Coakley, April 26, 1978, folder AFIO, box 135, MLP, HIWRP.

129. See, for example, Statement of Gen. Richard Giles Stilwell, president, Association of Former Intelligence Officers, Senate Select Committee on Intelligence, *National Intelligence Reform and Organization Act: Hearings on S. 2525*, 308–445. On the bill's failure, see George Lardner Jr., "As Congress' Resolve Faded, So Did Proposed CIA Charter," *WP*, May 5, 1980; and Alfred B. Prados, "Intelligence Reform Issues," Congressional Research Services Issue

Brief, February 6, 1989, EP01148, U.S. Espionage and Intelligence, 1947–1996 collection, DNSA.

130. "Citizens Fund Established to Aid FBI Agents Indicted by U.S.," *NYT*, May 17, 1977.

131. "Defense Fund formed by GOP Conservatives," *WP*, May 18, 1977.

132. The links between Fred Hampton's death and the FBI's COINTELPRO were exposed in a suit filed by the Peoples' Law Office in 1976 and 1977, which revealed the FBI had cased Hampton's apartment before the Chicago Police raid. See G. Flint Taylor, "'Nothing but a Lynching': The Assassination of Fred Hampton," *Huffington Post*, December 5, 2012, at http://www.huffingtonpost.com/g-flint-taylor/fred-hamptom-death_b_2234651.html, accessed May 19, 2017; and Enclosure to Bureau, Instructions furnished to Bureau Lab Personnel at CG," December 22, 1969, 35–40, FBI-FOIA, at https://vault.fbi.gov/Fred%20Hampton/Fred%20Hampton%20Part%201%20of%202/view, accessed May 19, 2017.

133. Memorandum from Marvin Liebman to Sponsors and Friends of the Citizen's Legal Defense Fund for the FBI, June 3, 1977, folder Release to Sponsors, box 124, MLP. For fundraising figures, see Mary McGrory, "FBI, Helms Cases Presenting a Legal and Political Dilemma," *BG*, August 24, 1977.

134. Citizen's Legal Defense Fund for the FBI press release, September 20, 1977, folder FBI publicity photos, box 124, MLP, HIWRP.

135. Citizen's Legal Defense Fund for the FBI advertisement, no date, folder FBI publicity photos, box 124, MLP, HIWRP.

136. See "Defense Fund Drive for Ex-FBI Agent Would Aid Helms, Simon Says," *NYT*, September 20, 1977.

137. Memorandum from Marvin Liebman to Sponsors and Friends of the Citizen's Legal Defense Fund for the FBI, October 21, 1977, folder Release to Sponsors, box 124, MLP, HIWRP.

138. Their military service was, however, markedly different. Buckley served stateside in the U.S. Army while Oakes was a decorated fighter pilot who flew missions across Europe.

139. Carey Winfrey, "Buckley at Home," *NYT*, May 14, 1978. Winfrey also noted that Buckley appeared for his interview "dressed like Blackford Oakes . . . in a blue blazer over charcoal slacks."

140. Michael Malone, "Send in the Tanks: *The Story of Henri Tod* by William F. Buckley," *NYT*, February 5, 1984.

141. These plots come from the first six books of the Blackford Oakes series: *Saving the Queen; Stained Glass; Who's on First; Marco Polo, if You Can; The Story of Henri Tod;* and *See You Later, Alligator*.

142. Hugh Hebert, "Mr. Buckley Plays for a Royal Flush," *Guardian*, March 9, 1976.

143. Carey Winfrey, "Buckley at Home," *NYT*, May 14, 1978.

144. Hugh Hebert, "Mr. Buckley Plays for a Royal Flush," *Guardian*, March 9, 1976.

145. See "Ex-Marine Plans for Viet Combat," *LAT*, April 24, 1975.

146. "100 Ready to Fight for Viet: ex-Marine," *CT*, April 23, 1975.

147. "Ex-Marine Plans for Viet Combat," *LAT*, April 24, 1975.

148. "100 Ready to Fight for Viet: ex-Marine," *CT*, April 23, 1975.

149. Bonner also reported that the governments of Thailand and South Korea also expressed interest in the VVV coming to train their elite units but nothing ever happened. See "Soldier of Fortune Interviews VVV: Veterans and Volunteers for Viet Nam," *SOF*, Summer 1975, 9–11, 75.

150. See Robert K. Brown and Robert Himber, "The Story of George Bacon: A Twentieth Century Crusader," *SOF*, Fall 1976, 13–18, 76–77.

151. From the late 1960s onward, ZAPU relied mostly upon material and military support from the Soviet Union and the Eastern Bloc, particularly the German Democratic Republic, while ZANU received its weapons and supplies from communist China. See Horne, *From the Barrel of a Gun*.

152. See Gleijeses, *Conflicting Missions*, 236; Miller, "Yes, Minister."

153. Since the United States did "enjoy the same freedom to raise levels of support as do the Soviets," any "assistance would have to be covert, and military assistance would have to be channeled through third parties." See National Security Council Meeting, June 27, 1975, box 2, folder: NSC Meeting, 6/27/1975, National Security Adviser's NSC Meeting File, GFPL.

154. See Schmitz, *United States and Right-wing Dictatorships*, 134. Without U.S. support, the rebels looked increasingly towards South Africa to continue their fight against the MPLA government. See Miller, "Yes, Minister." Meanwhile, leading conservative figures renewed their propaganda campaigns for Rhodesia. In 1976, Marvin Liebman and William Rusher partnered with former CIA officer David Atlee Philips, founder of the Association of Former Intelligence Officers, to form a new pro-Rhodesian lobbying group called the American-Rhodesian Association. Like the Friends of Rhodesian Independence and its kindred groups had done in the 1960s, the American-Rhodesian Association disseminated materials from the Rhodesian government's Information Office and raised money through grassroots channels to send Americans to southern Africa. See Letter from Marvin Liebman to William Rusher, April 5, 1978; and Letter from David Atlee Philips to Marvin Liebman, April 12, 1978, folder Africa, box 135, MLP, HIWRP. Others included Clarence Manion and William F. Buckley. For Manion's work, see "The Real Rhodesia: Part I," September 18, 1977 and "The Real Rhodesia: Part II," September 25, 1977, folder 9, box 84; "South Africa in Perspective: American Legion Fact-Finding Mission Results in Comprehensive Report," *Manion Forum*, August 6, 1978, folder 10, box 84, CMP-CHM. On Buckley's activism, see William F. Buckley and Ian Smith, "The Question of Rhodesia," *Firing Line*, March 15, 1974; and Judis, *William F. Buckley*, 357.

155. As James William Gibson and Kathleen Belew have documented, this subculture—composed of films, novels, magazines, training camps and gun shows—helped many American men envision themselves as warriors fighting the United States' enemies at home and abroad. See Belew, *Bring the War Home*; and Gibson, *Warrior Dreams*.

156. See Brown and Spencer, *I Am Soldier of Fortune*, 44–104.

157. Brown quoted in Michael Marchino and Robert K. Musil, "The American Mercenaries," *The Nation*, April 10, 1976.

158. Dorothy Conlin, "Publisher Shoots for Blood, Guts Set: Magazine for Mercenaries," *CT*, September 7, 1975.

159. Michael Marchino and Robert K. Musil, "The American Mercenaries," *The Nation*, April 10, 1976.

160. Often, those who placed the ads constructed themselves as accomplished soldiers with experience in one or several of the U.S. military's elite branches. One ad from a man in Pittsburgh read "former Airborne, Ranger, Special Forces, RA officer seeks military employment anywhere; all offers considered." Another, from Brownsville, Texas: "Former Green Beret offers extensive military experiences to interested parties." Michael Marchino and Robert K. Musil, "The American Mercenaries," *The Nation*, April 10, 1976.

161. "SOF Interview: Major Nick Lamprecht, Rhodesian Recruiting Officer," *SOF*, Summer 1977.

162. See the Rhodesian army advertisement on the back cover of the fall 1976 issue of *Solider of Fortune*; and "SOF Interviews Rhodesian Recruiting Officer," *SOF*, spring 1977.

163. Major Robert K. Brown, "American Mercenaries in Africa," *SOF*, Summer 1975.

164. Ex-Rhodesian Army member interviewed in Cohen, "The War in Rhodesia," 493.

165. Ibid.

166. Robert K. Brown, "Requiem for Three Nations," *SOF*, Summer 1975.

167. On the links between the economic crises of the 1970s, breadwinner status, and notions of white masculinity see Self, *All in the Family*, 17–19, 41–45. Those links also form a central theme of Cowie, *Stayin' Alive*.

168. This comes from John Coleman, an American who fought in Rhodesia for four years. See T. W. McGarry, "Parallels, Differences in Vietnam, Rhodesia Wars Noted by Veteran of Both," *LAT*, August 18, 1983.

169. Gibson, *Warrior Dreams*, 11.

170. See "Mad Mike Hoare Attempts to Retake Angola," *SOF*, Summer 1975; "War in Angola: Mercs in Action," *SOF*, Spring 1976; and "War in Rhodesia," *SOF*, Fall 1976.

171. *Soldier of Fortune* hailed the film as the "first motion picture to present an authentic, explosive, no-punches pulled portrayal of modern merc soldiers; their recruitment, training, comradeship, and way of life. It includes glimpses of their terrors and triumphs, their sweat and sorrows, their living and their dying, as well as the kind of camaraderie that goes with the personality of these dogs of war." Al J. Venter, "The Wild Geese Fly Again," *SOF*, January 1979. On Hoare's plotting of the Seychelles coup, which earned him a lengthy prison sentence, see "Crooked Goose: Mad Mike Gets Ten Years," *Time*, August 1982; and Hoare, *Seychelles Affair*. For the film, see *Wild Geese*, dir. Andrew V. McLaglen.172. "SOF Interview: Major Nick Lamprecht, Rhodesian Recruiting Officer," *SOF*, Summer 1977.

173. For pay figures, see James McManus, "Mercenary Trial Raises Rhodesia Connection," *The Guardian*, June 9, 1976; Robin Wright, "Speaking Out: Americans in Rhodesia," *WP*, September 12, 1976; and "US Vets Fight for Rhodesia," *BG*, December 10, 1976.

174. See Major Robert K. Brown, "American Mercenaries in Africa," *SOF*, Summer 1975. On "white flight" in Rhodesia, see Horne, *From the Barrel of a Gun*, 87.

175. See James McManus, "Mercenary Trial Raises Rhodesian Connection," *The Guardian*, June 9, 1976.

176. See Mockler, *New Mercenaries*, 149–70. Contemporary sources claimed that 800 foreigners fought as mercenaries in Rhodesia. See Memo "Recruitment of Mercenaries for Rhodesia and the Diplock Report," November 24, 1976, CP 050/1 Part E 243, FCO 36/1876, Mercenaries and Recruitment for Rhodesia, UKNA.

177. In 1975, Britain experienced what contemporaries dubbed the "Great Inflation." The following year, the value of British sterling collapsed. See Sandbrook, *Seasons in the Sun*, 206–7, 344–59, 421–22, and 691–92.

178. Margaret Thatcher and the Tories famously used that image, under the headline "Labour Isn't Working," to promote her 1979 campaign. See Ibid., 663–66.

179. For British soldiers, fighting with the Rhodesian armed forces was actually more lucrative than serving with their nation's forces. See David Pallister, "Mercenaries Get Rhodesia Offer," *The Guardian*, March 16, 1976.

180. Most of this recruiting came through Lamprecht's Rhodesian Information Office, an arm of the Rhodesian government that published propaganda and made contacts with sympathetic groups in the United States and, to a lesser extent, the United Kingdom. See Rhodesian Army recruiting packet from Nick Lamprecht, "Recruiting: Rhodesian Army (Regular Force)," CP 050/1 Part A 28, FCO 36/1872, Mercenaries and Recruitment for Rhodesia, National Archives, London, UK; and Letter from P. J. Barlow to Green, March 18, 1976, CP 050/1 Part A 22, FCO 36/1872, Mercenaries and Recruitment for Rhodesia, UKNA.

181. One of these firms was defense contractor Millbank Technical Services, a group of ex-British servicemen who trained the Shah of Iran's security forces. Several Millbank employees later served as mercenaries in Rhodesia. See Letter from G. B. Chalmers to I. T. M.

Lucas, June 30, 1976, CP 050/1 Part C 151, FCO 36/1874, Mercenaries and Recruitment for Rhodesia, UKNA.

182. Many British officials already viewed the Foreign Enlistment Act as problematic and outdated—for instance, it had not been enforced in the 1930s when British citizens fought in the Spanish Civil War. See Letter from P. J. Barlow to Porter, March 11, 1976, CP 050/1 11, FCO 36/1872, Mercenaries and Recruitment for Rhodesia, UKNA.

183. See Letter from M.E. Heath to A. Duff, December 17, 1976, CP 050/1 Part E 257, FCO 36/1876, Mercenaries and Recruitment for Rhodesia, UKNA.

184. British government sources placed the total number of foreign mercenaries in Rhodesia at around 800. See Memo "Recruitment of Mercenaries for Rhodesia and the Diplock Report," November 24, 1976, CP 050/1 Part E 243, FCO 36/1876, Mercenaries and Recruitment for Rhodesia, UKNA.

185. Nick Lamprecht once told Bob Brown that of the 450 Americans who served with the Rhodesian armed forces, seventy-five percent had joined because of articles published in his magazine. See Brown and Spencer, *I Am Soldier of Fortune*, 115.

186. "More Rhodesian Recruiting," *SOF*, Fall 1976.

187. "Texas Group Seeks Troops for Rhodesia," *CT*, May 23, 1976.

188. Rhodesian ranches offered contracts to American "bounty hunters" for $450 a month plus room and board. See Wyatt Earp Jr., "Pros at Work: Bounty Hunting in Africa," *SOF*, March 1978, 36–40.

189. See James Howe, "Soldier of Fortune," *Illustrated Life of Rhodesia* 11, no. 6, (October 26, 1976), 14–15; "US Vets Fight for Rhodesia," *WP*, December 10, 1976; and "Mercenaries in South Africa: Interview with Professor Lars Rudebeck, Member of the International Commission of Enquiry on Mercenaries," *Review of African Political Economy*, no. 6, May-August 1976. See also Horne, *From the Barrel of a Gun*, 29.

190. Robin Wright, 'Speaking Out: Americans in Rhodesia," *WP*, September 12, 1976.

191. See, for instance, "American Mercs in Rhodesia," *SOF*, Summer 1975; "American with Rhodesian Gray Force," *SOF*, November 1978. Mike Williams later recounted his Rhodesian exploits in a book written by *Soldier of Fortune* report Robin Moore. See Moore, *Major Mike*.

192. A. J. Venter, "Rhodesia Tragic Terrorist War: The End Is Near," *SOF*, June 1979.

193. "Killed in Action," *SOF*, Spring 1976.

194. David Anable, "The Return of the Mercenaries," *Africa Report*, December 1975, CP 050/1 Part A W32, FCO 36/1872, Mercenaries and Recruitment for Rhodesia, UKNA.

195. See Horne, *From the Barrel of a Gun*, 226. The right's affinity for Coey resulted in the posthumous publication of his Rhodesian journals. See Coey, *A Martyr Speaks: Journal of the Late John Coey*.

196. See Laurence Stern, "The Angola Mercenary Caper: Instead of Fortune, Soldiers of Fortune Meet the Press," *WP*, January 10, 1976.

197. See Memorandum for the Record, February 3, 1976, document 173, *FRUS, 1969–1976*, vol. 28, Southern Africa.

198. See Tendayi Kumbula, "'Bad Boy' Mercenary Tells of His Adventures," *LAT*, May 25, 1977; and "Green Berets for Sale," *Mother Jones*, July 1977.

199. Robert K. Brown and Robert Himber, "The Story of George Bacon: A Twentieth Century Crusader," *SOF*, Fall 1976.

200. Gleijeses, *Conflicting Missions*, 342–43.

201. "Soldier of Fortune Interviews VVV: Veterans and Volunteers for Viet Nam," *SOF*, Summer 1975.

202. Robert K. Brown and Robert Himber, "The Story of George Bacon: A Twentieth Century Crusader," *SOF*, Fall 1976.

203. Pay figures from Eileen Brennan, "Epitaph for a Dead Mercenary," *People*, August 23, 1976.

204. Press Briefing Paper, "American Mercenaries in Angola," June 29, 1976, folder Angola, box 121, Ron Nessen Papers, GFPL; and Memorandum from Roger Harrison to Brent Scowcroft, June 29, 1976, folder Daniel Gearhart, box 1, National Security Advisor, Presidential Name File, 1974–77, GFPL. Robert Brown also put pressure on the administration to no avail. See also World Human Rights Committee, Press Release, May 19, 1976, folder Col. Robert Brown, Luis Kutner Papers, HIWRP.

205. See "Mercenaries are Executed by Angolans," *WP*, July 11, 1976.

206. See Wilfred Burchett, "Angola Mercenary Trial Begins," *Guardian*, June 23, 1976; and Jay Ross, "Angolans Free 3 Americans in Prisoner Swap," *WP*, November 17, 1982, folder Revolutionary Movements: UNITA News Clippings and Articles, Angola Subject Collection, HIWRP.

207. See John J. Tooney, letter to the editor, *SOF*, September 1977. Sheila Gearhart's attorney informed readers that *Soldier of Fortune*'s story generated approximately $1000 for the widow and her four children.

208. See for example the pamphlet, published by the ZANU lobby group, the Zimbabwe Support Committee, *Guns for Hire: How the CIA and the U.S. Army Recruit Mercenaries for White Rhodesia* (no publication information, circa 1977) in the Melville J. Herskovits Africana Library, Northwestern University, Evanston, Ill. See also Ramesh Jaura, "Mercenaries for Rhodesia," *Economic and Political Weekly*, May 22, 1976.

209. See U.S. Congress, *Mercenaries in Africa*, 15–18.

210. See House Subcommittee on Africa, Committee on Foreign Affairs, *Economic Sanctions against Rhodesia*; and House Subcommittee on Africa, Committee on International Relations, *U.S. Policy toward Rhodesia*.

211. See U.S. Congress, *Mercenaries in Africa*, 4–5, 9–11.

212. See "U.N. Seeks Mercenary Ban," *The Sun* (Baltimore), July 11, 1976; and Tom Lambert, "Ban on the Enlisting of Mercenaries in Britain Urged," *LAT*, August 4, 1976. For a broader discussion of the legal issues regarding mercenaries in Rhodesia and Angola, see Burmester, "Recruitment and Use of Mercenaries in Armed Conflicts."

213. See Letter from Luis Kutner to Robert K. Brown, February 14, 1977; Letter from Luis Kutner to Robert K. Brown, July 12, 1976; and Letter from Luis Kutner to Robert K. Brown, September 7, 1976, folder Mercenary Law, box 39, Luis Kutner Papers, HIWRP.

214. Pierce published the book under the pen name Andrew MacDonald. See Pierce, *Turner Diaries*; and Gibson, *Warrior Dreams*, 220–27.

215. Speaking before the Veterans of Foreign Wars in Chicago, Reagan talked of how "Cuban and Soviet-trained terrorists are bringing civil war to Central American countries" and how "in the face of declining American power, the Soviets and their friends are advancing." See Ronald Reagan, "Address to the Veterans of Foreign Wars Convention in Chicago," August 18, 1980. Online by Gerhard Peters and John T. Woolley, *The American Presidency Project*, http://www.presidency.ucsb.edu/ws/?pid=85202, accessed September 5, 2015.

## Chapter 5

1. Brown with Spencer, *I Am Soldier of Fortune*, 282–83. See also See Harry Caflin, "SOF Trains Contras," and Robert K. Brown, "Questions for the CIA," *SOF*, October 1990.

2. Brown with Spencer, *I Am Soldier of Fortune*, 282–83.

3. Ibid.

4. On speculation about Singlaub's presidential campaign, see "Politics '80: Singlaub," *Human Events*, August 11, 1979.

5. "SOF Interviews General John K. Singlaub," *SOF*, January 1979. His talks hit familiar notes for many audiences. In the wake of the Iranian Revolution, when the helicopters carrying U.S. soldiers to rescue American hostages in Tehran crashed in the desert, Singlaub, like many other conservative critics, blamed Carter for this debacle, since the president had cut the Pentagon's budgets for Army and Navy unconventional warfare units. To prevent such catastrophes in the future, Singlaub called for the creation of a "permanent, well-funded, independent Special Operations Command that would combine the assets of all four services, as well as civilian covert action personnel." See Singlaub and McConnell, *Hazardous Duty*, 435.

6. Singlaub and McConnell, *Hazardous Duty*, 436.

7. On Reagan's celebrations of militarism, see Sherry, *In the Shadow of War*, 392–98.

8. Singlaub and McConnell, *Hazardous Duty*, 435.

9. At the National Republican Convention in Detroit in the summer of 1980, four months before the election, Singlaub teamed up with Generals Alexander Haig and Daniel Graham to insert what they called the "peace-through-strength policy" into the Republican Party's national platform. The plank echoed what Singlaub and others on the Right had been saying throughout the dark days of détente. The only way to reverse the arc of American national decline and defeat communism once and for all was to initiate an all-out war against the Soviet Union and its allies. To that end, Singlaub and other members of the American Security Council organized the Coalition for Peace through Strength, bringing together former military officers and ambassadors, college presidents, and intellectuals to lobby members of Congress to tear down nuclear arms limitation treaties, expand defense expenditures, and overturn congressional limits to U.S. military aid to anticommunist guerrillas. See "SOF Interviews General John K. Singlaub," *SOF*, January 1979; American Security Council, "Coalition for Peace Through Strength," *Washington Report*, October 1978; American Security Council, "The Anti-Defense Lobby," *Washington Report*, December 1978; American Security Council, "An Analysis of SALT II," *Washington Report*, May 1979; and American Security Council, "The Marxist Threat to Central America," *Washington Report*, August 1979. Singlaub also served as a foreign policy adviser to Newt Gingrich and Paul Gann. See "Singlaub Speak for Gingrich," *Atlanta Daily World*, September 18, 1980; and "3 Ex Generals Aid Gann on Foreign Policy," *LAT*, September 22, 1980; Ernest B. Ferguson, "Ultra Hard Liners Surface at Republican Gathering," *The Sun* (Baltimore), July 15, 1980.

10. Testimony of John K. Singlaub to U.S. Select Committee on Secret Military Assistance to Iran and the Nicaraguan Opposition, *Report of the Iran Contra Affair*, 911.

11. For Singlaub's invitation, see Singlaub and McConnell, *Hazardous Duty*, 436–37. For the conference's attendees, see Report of the WACL Secretary-General to the 14th WACL General Conference, August 1, 1981; Report by Prof. Rafael Rodriguez, CAL Secretary-General, given to 14th WACL Conference, August 1, 1981; and Report of the Anti-Bolshevik Bloc of Nations given at the 14th WACL General Conference in Taipei, Taiwan, August 3–7, 1981 in folder 4, box 61, KDP, HIWRP. See also "President Chiang's Message to Anti-Red Leagues," *China Post*, August 4, 1981; and "Carter's Mistakes Have Created Great Danger," *China Post*, August 4, 1981, folder WACL Clippings, box 55, KDP, HIWRP.

12. Paul W. Valentine, "The Fascist Specter behind the World Anti-Red League," *WP*, May 28, 1978.

13. Singlaub and McConnell, *Hazardous Duty*, 439.

14. Ibid., 436–40. Other members of the advisory board included longtime WACL associates, many of whom had been in the first U.S. chapter in the early 1970s, including Walter Chopiwskj, Anthony Bouscaren, Ann Chennault, Lev Dobriansky, Anthony Kubek, Stefan

Possony, and Fred Schlafly. The full list of USCWF personnel can be found on the group's official letterhead. See, for example, Letter from John Singlaub to Ronald Reagan, May 18, 1984, White House Office and Records Management (WHORM): Subject File ME 002, case file 345378, RRPL. See also Letter from Marx Lewis to John Singlaub, October 30, 1985, folder 31, box 2, Marx Lewis Papers, HIWRP. Andy Messing quoted in John Dillon and Jon Lee Anderson, "Who's Behind the Aid to the Contras," *The Nation*, October 6, 1984, folder 29, box 9, Philip Agee Papers, TLRWLA.

15. On Singlaub's appearances at the Tokyo conference, see Woo Jae Sung, Korean WACL Chapter, Circular Letter no. 12, December 30, 1982, folder 5, box 61, KDP, HIWRP.

16. See Text of speech given by John Singlaub to the Anti-Bolshevik Bloc of Nations/European Freedom Council Conference, London, Great Britain, September 24–26, 1982, folder 5, box 54, KDP, HIWRP. Propaganda is usually classified into three categories. Black propaganda claims to be one from one source but is in fact from another (e.g. a leaflet created by the U.S. military that resembles an official communication from the North Vietnamese government to its citizens). Gray propaganda has no identifiable source or author (an erroneous piece of information given to a reporter that accuses a political leader of malfeasance). White propaganda openly discloses its source and generally uses methods of persuasion (brochures distributed by U.S. soldiers that explain to Iraqi civilians that the United States will help them).

17. See Singlaub and McConnell, *Hazardous Duty*, 445–46.

18. In 1973, Stetsko noted that the ABN had helped start underground publications in Ukraine and elsewhere in Eastern Europe. See Opening address by Yaroslav Stetsko to the Conferences of the Anti-Bolshevik Bloc of Nations and the European Freedom Council, August 24–27, 1973, London, folder 14, box 53, KDP, HIWRP.

19. See, for example, the four-part series on the Ukrainian Insurgent Army published by Stetsko in 1982–1983: "The Ukrainian Insurgent Army: Part I," *Ukrainian Review* 29, no. 2 (1982): 3–26; "The Ukrainian Insurgent Army: Part II," *Ukrainian Review* 29, no. 3 (1982): 3–28; "The Ukrainian Insurgent Army: Part III," *Ukrainian Review* 29, no. 5 (1982): 54–72; and "The Ukrainian Insurgent Army: Part IV," *Ukrainian Review* 30, no. 1 (1983): 68–84.

20. See Report of the Anti-Bolshevik Bloc of Nations given at the 14th WACL General Conference in Taipei, Taiwan, August 3–7, 1981, folder 4, box 61, KDP, HIWRP.

21. Quote from Maria Riccardi, "Yaroslav Stetsko: The Lonely Patriot," *WP*, July 21, 1981.

22. Joint Communiqué of the WACL Executive Board and the APACL Executive Committee, Taipei, Republic of China, April 18, 1982, folder 2, box 62, KDP, HIWRP.

23. Report by Prof. Rafael Rodriguez, CAL Secretary-General, given to 14th WACL Conference, August 1, 1981, folder 4, box 61, KDP, HIWRP.

24. Speech given by Dr. Houmayoun Shah Assefy, Afghan Resistance, at 13th WACL Conference, Geneva, Switzerland, no date, folder 1, box 61, KDP, HIWRP.

25. Statement of the Karen National Union at the 15th WACL Conference, December 6–9, 1982, folder 5, box 61, KDP, HIWRP.

26. Speech given by FNLA representative at 13th WACL Conference, Geneva, Switzerland, no date, folder 1, box 61, KDP, HIWRP.

27. On the origins and effects of the "Vietnam syndrome" on U.S. foreign policy in the 1980s, see Young, *Vietnam Wars*, 314–15; and Herring, *America's Longest War*, 250–53.

28. Singlaub and McConnell, *Hazardous Duty*, 445.

29. Jay Perkins, "Reagan Security Aid Holds Secret Parley with Singlaub," *Toledo Blade*, June 3, 1981.

30. Formally created in February 1981, the Special Operations Division was the predecessor of the Special Operations Command, which currently oversees nearly all special operations

components of the United States Army, Navy, Marines, and Air Force. See McClintock, *Instruments of Statecraft*, 340–42.

31. This strategy would encompass all of the "assets of our covert intelligence activities, black and gray psychological operations, information campaigns, and economic warfare." To do so, Singlaub said, the U.S. "would have to revitalize" the capabilities of the CIA and other clandestine units that had been "stripped away by Carter's CIA Director, Stansfield Turner." Singlaub and McConnell, *Hazardous Duty*, 446. See also Memo from Oliver North to William P. Clark, November 4, 1982, WHORM Subject File ND 017, casefile 1126073, RRPL.

32. Singlaub and McConnell, *Hazardous Duty*, 446.

33. On Casey's time with the OSS during World War II, see Woodward, *Veil: The Secret Wars of the CIA*, 51–53.

34. Casey was chairman of the Securities and Exchange Commission, then Under Secretary for of State for Economic Affairs, and then head of the Export-Import bank. He was subject to a perjury investigation in 1973 for possibly shielding wealthy backers of Nixon's 1972 campaign from investigation. See David E. Rosenbaum, "Casey's Nomination Held Up in Senate over Role on ITT," *NYT*, December 13, 1973.

35. Woodward, *Veil: The Secret Wars of the CIA*, 33–34, 69–70.

36. Casey referred to them as a "noose tightening, a rope woven of communist victories around the globe." See Persico, *Casey: From the OSS to the CIA*, 217.

37. Sterling, *Terror Network*, 15.

38. When Casey's subordinates confronted him with the CIA's intelligence reports, he reportedly told them to "read Claire Sterling's book, and forget this mush. I paid $13.95 for this and it told me more than you bastards whom I pay $50,000 a year." See Woodward, *Veil: The Secret Wars of the CIA*, 126; and Gibson, *Warrior Dreams*, 270–71.

39. For an overview of the formulation of the Reagan Doctrine, see Scott, *Deciding to Intervene*, 14–39.

40. Ibid., 19.

41. Casey quoted in Schweizer, *Victory*, 23.

42. Former CIA officer Frank Anderson quoted in Coll, *Ghost Wars*, 125.

43. Miller Center, "Interview with George P. Shultz," University of Virginia, December 18, 2002, millercenter.org/oralhistory/interview/george-shultz, accessed March 1, 2016.

44. Singlaub and McConnell, *Hazardous Duty*, 447.

45. On the Sandinista's war, see Kinzer, *Blood of Brothers*.

46. LeoGrande, *Our Own Backyard*, 14–15.

47. See Westad, *Global Cold War*, 341.

48. LaFeber, *Inevitable Revolutions*, 225–42.

49. See Westad, *Global Cold War*, 342.

50. The best overview of the relationship between the death squads, the Salvadoran state, and wealthy civilians is Stanley, *Protection Racket State*.

51. D'Aubuisson's role in the murder, widely rumored at the time, was confirmed by postwar investigations. See United Nations, *From Madness to Hope: The 12-Year War in El Salvador*, 127–31. See also Anne-Marie O'Connor, "Participant in 1980 Assassination of Romero in El Salvador Provides New Details," *WP*, April 6, 2010.

52. As a CIA top-secret report noted in 1985, D'Aubuisson and ARENA's "internal terrorist network" was "one component of a much broader phenomenon of rightist violence in El Salvador, the party's attitudes and goals probably influence extremist perspectives in general and, by extension, help determine the prospects for resurgent violence by less organized and ad hoc groupings of both civilian and military." See Central Intelligence Agency, Directorate of Intelligence, "El Salvador: Controlling Right-wing Terrorism," February 1985,

file El Salvador Death Squads, box 132, Oliver North Files, RRPL. See also Stanley, *Protection Racket State*, 110–11.

53. See Bonner, *Weakness and Deceit*.

54. Singlaub and McConnell, *Hazardous Duty*, 441.

55. Singlaub was one of many conservative hardliners who wanted to revitalize American military power at home and abroad, along with figures such as Jeanne Kirkpatrick, Alexander Haig, and Jesse Helms. See Grandin, *Empire's Workshop*, 71–78; and Wilentz, *The Age of Reagan*, 156.

56. The notion of "drawing the line" was repeated by many members of the administration and its supporters in Congress. See Don Oberdorfer, "El Salvador Is 'The Place to Draw the Line' on Communism, Percy Says," *WP*, February 20, 1981; Abraham F. Lowenthal, "Drawing the Line in El Salvador," *LAT*, February 25, 1981; John M. Goshko, "Drawing a Hard Line against Communism," *WP*, February 22, 1981; and Karen de Young, "El Salvador: Where Reagan Draws the Line," *WP*, March 9, 1981. See also LeoGrande, *Our Own Backyard*, 80.

57. See Joshua M. Goshko, "U.S. Prepares to Aid El Salvador in First Test Issue of Reagan Policy," *WP*, February 14, 1981; and Bernard Gwertzman, "El Salvador: A Test Issue," *NYT*, February 14, 1981.

58. The paper was largely based upon rhetorical links rather than hard evidence, as subsequent analyses showed. See U.S. Department of State, *Communist Interference in El Salvador*, Special Report No. 80, February 23, 1981. On its factual errors, see Jon Dinges, "White Paper of Blank Paper?," *LAT*, March 17, 1981; and Robert G. Kaiser, "White Paper on El Salvador Is Faulty," *WP*, June 9, 1981.

59. See Alan Riding, "Reagan Impact Felt in Central America," *NYT*, November 16, 1980.

60. Unnamed Guatemalan official quoted in Sklar, *Washington's War on Nicaragua*, 83.

61. See Sherry, *In the Shadow of War*, 410.

62. On the transnational opposition to U.S. intervention in Central America, see Peace, *Call to Conscience*; Smith, *Resisting Reagan*; Gosse, "El Salvador Is Spanish for Vietnam"; and Martin, *Other Eighties*, 25–44.

63. Singlaub and McConnell, *Hazardous Duty*, 442.

64. These trips were financed by the Friends of Guatemala, a collection of wealthy landowners and industrialists who hoped to improve their nations' human rights image and garner the support of the Reagan administration before the election. See "Guatemalan 'State Terrorism,' Reaganites Linked," *Barricada* (Nicaragua), July 21, 1981, in *FBIS, Latin America*, FBIS-LAM-81-139. According to journalist Stephen Kinzer, future administration members such as National Security Advisor Richard Allen and Deputy Secretary of State William Clark also met with the Friends of Guatemala to ensure them of Reagan's support. See Stephen Kinzer, "Guatemala Pushes for New Image," *BG*, May 3, 1981.

65. Singlaub and McConnell, *Hazardous Duty*, 442–43.

66. Ibid., 442. That the United States lost the war in Vietnam because "we failed to understand the nature and totality of unconventional warfare" was a touchstone of Singlaub's public speeches. See for instance, John Singlaub, "How and Where World War III Will Be Fought," text of speech given at the "Racing to the Year 2000" conference, September 26, 1985, republished in *World Freedom Report: The USCWF Newsletter* 3, No. 6 (November 15, 1985), WCCPM.

67. Singlaub and McConnell, *Hazardous Duty*, 450.

68. On Sanchez's career with the CIA, see T. Rees Shapiro, "Nestor D. Sanchez, 83: CIA Official Led Latin American Division," *WP*, January 26, 2011.

69. Singlaub and McConnell, *Hazardous Duty*, 443.

70. Singlaub appeared periodically in the magazine's page for interviews about American

military and foreign policy matters. See "SOF Interviews General John K. Singlaub," *SOF*, January 1979. By the early 1980s, Singlaub was also a regular feature at the annual *Soldier of Fortune* convention in Las Vegas, Nevada. See Gibson, *Warrior Dreams*, 167.

71. Singlaub and McConnell, *Hazardous Duty*, 443.

72. Robert K. Brown, "Embattled El Salvador—Has the U.S. Forgotten to Win a War?," *SOF*, September 1983.

73. Brown with Spencer, *I Am Soldier of Fortune*, 274.

74. Ibid., 273.

75. Robert J. McCartney, "Soldiers of Fortune Lend a Hand in El Salvador," *WP*, August 29, 1983.

76. Brown, "Embattled El Salvador," *SOF*, September 1983.

77. Peter G. Kokalis, "Arming El Salvador: U.S. Gives Brave Warriors Worn-out Weapons," *SOF*, September 1983. See also, Peter G. Kokalis, "Appendix A: My War in El Salvador," in Brown with Spencer, *I Am Soldier of Fortune*, 389–92.

78. John E. Padgett, "Morazan Sitrep: SOF A-Team Reports Gains in El Salvador," *SOF*, June 1984.

79. On the Starlight Training Center see, James L. Pate, "Starlight Training Center: Civvies Get a Quick Taste of Boot Camp," *SOF*, February 1986.

80. As *Soldier of Fortune* adviser Alex McColl said in 1984, "What we are doing here has been briefed to senior political officials in Washington. They are aware of what we are doing and they approve. They have not told us to stop. In fact they seem grateful for the private initiatives." See John Dillon and Jon Lee Anderson, "Who's Behind the Aid to the Contras," *The Nation*, October 6, 1984, folder 29, box 9, Philip Agee Papers, TLRWLA.

81. Brown with Spencer, *I Am Soldier of Fortune*, 270–71.

82. Robert J. McCartney, "Soldiers of Fortune Lend a Hand in El Salvador," *WP*, August 29, 1983.

83. Ibid.

84. This operation, known as Grupos Operaciones Especiales (GOE), eventually became a regular part of the Salvadoran military and, as such, received substantial support from the CIA and U.S. military advisory group. See Brown with Spencer, *I Am Soldier of Fortune*, 275.

85. Robert J. McCartney, "Soldiers of Fortune Lend a Hand in El Salvador," *WP*, August 29, 1983.

86. See "Blood Brothers," *Mother Jones*, November 1983, 10.

87. See Gill, *School of the Americas*, 6, 137.

88. On El Mozote, see Danner, *Massacre at El Mozote*. Danner's reporting and collected testimonies were crucial parts of the investigation conducted by the Salvadoran government in 1992. See United Nations, *From Madness to Hope*, 114–21. For the El Calabozo massacre, see *From Madness to Hope*, 125.

89. Peter G. Kokalis, "Arms and the Atlacatl: SOF Trains Salvadoran Immediate Reaction Battalion," *SOF*, January 1984, 55.

90. Kokalis quoted in Gibson, *Warrior Dreams*, 151.

91. Brown with Spencer, *I Am Soldier of Fortune*, 271.

92. See the photograph on the contents page of the January 1984 issue of *Soldier of Fortune*.

93. See the ad for "El Salvadoran Jump Wings," *SOF*, January 1984, 87.

94. Peter G. Kokalis, "Arming El Salvador: U.S. Gives Brave Warriors Worn-out Weapons," *SOF*, September 1983.

95. *Soldier of Fortune*'s work with the Atlacatl formed the core of several stories from 1984. See Peter Kokalis, "Arms and the Atlacatl: SOF Trains Salvadoran Immediate Reaction Battalion," *SOF*, January 1984; Jim Graves, "Medical Mission in Morazán: Treating the

Symptoms, Battling the Disease," *SOF*, January 1984; and John E. Padgett, "Morazan Sitrep: SOF A-Team Reports Gains in El Salvador," *SOF*, June 1984.

96. See Peter Kokalis, "Arms and the Atlacatl: SOF Trains Salvadoran Immediate Reaction Battalion," *SOF*, January 1984, 55.

97. Brown with Spencer, *I Am Soldier of Fortune*, 269.

98. See Gibson, *Warrior Dreams*, 147–48.

99. See Memo from Robert McFarlane to William French Smith and William H. Webster, December 1, 1983, folder El Salvador Death Squads (3), box 132, Oliver North Files; Memo from Jeffery H. Smith to James H. Michael, December 8, 1983, folder El Salvador Death Squads (3), box 132, Oliver North Files; Memo from William French Smith with Robert C. McFarlane, December 9, 1983, folder El Salvador Death Squads (3), box 132, Oliver North Files, RRPL; and Telegram from U.S. Embassy El Salvador to Secretary of State, subject "Millionaires Murder Inc.?," January 6, 1981, El Salvador: 1980–1984, DNSA.

100. U.S. Ambassador Robert White quoted in LeoGrande, *Our Own Backyard*, 50. See also, Joel Brinkley, "Ex-Envoy Accuses 6 Salvador Exiles," *NYT*, February 3, 1984.

101. On the beginnings of Department of Justice's investigation, see Memo from Robert McFarlane to William French Smith and William H. Webster, December 1, 1983, folder El Salvador Death Squads (3), box 132, Oliver North Files; Memo from Jeffery H. Smith to James H. Michael, December 8, 1983, folder El Salvador Death Squads (3), box 132, Oliver North Files, RRPL; and Memo from William French Smith with Robert C. McFarlane, December 9, 1983, folder El Salvador Death Squads (3), box 132, Oliver North Files, RRPL.

102. Central Intelligence Agency, Directorate of Intelligence, "El Salvador: Controlling Right-wing Terrorism," February 1985, file El Salvador Death Squads, box 132, Oliver North Files, RRPL.

103. That network was older and larger than Brown and Singlaub knew. It dated back to at least the mid-1970s, when the Confederación Anticomunista Latinoamericana had established a hemispheric program of collaboration between right-wing groups in Central and South America. Those connections allowed the Salvadoran death squads to receive weapons and training from the Argentine military junta. See chapter 2.

104. On the murders committed by right-wing death squads, see Central Intelligence Agency, Directorate of Intelligence, "El Salvador: Controlling Right-wing Terrorism," February 1985, file El Salvador Death Squads, box 132, Oliver North Files, RRPL.

105. As members of the Salvadoran American Association, Singlaub and others "vigorously denounce[ed] violence and those who financially or in any other way make violence possible." See Letter from Fernando Quinoez-Meza to Andy Messing, December 7, 1983, folder El Salvador- Violent Right (2), box Cable 2, Latin American Affairs Directorate, NSC Records, RRPL.

106. Juan Williams, "Salvadoran Rebels Imitate Rightists, President Suggests," *WP*, December 3, 1983, folder El Salvador-Violent Right, box Cable 2, Latin American Affairs Directorate, National Security Council Records, RRPL.

107. See Wood, *Insurgent Collective Action*, 8.

108. Singlaub and McConnell, *Hazardous Duty*, 449–50.

109. Of these, D'Aubuisson, a major in the Salvadoran Army and leader of the ultra-right Alianza Republicana Nacionalista (ARENA) party, was the most notorious. See Stanley, *Protection Racket State*, 164, 192, 228–29.

110. Rep. James Oberstar et al, "El Salvador, 1983: Report of a fact-finding mission sponsored by the Unitarian Universalist Service Committee," April 1983, folder 11, box 9, Philip Agee Papers, TLRWLA.

111. See CIA, National Foreign Assessment Center, "El Salvador: The Right Wing,"

March 18, 1981, in El Salvador, 1980–1984, Digital National Security Archive (hereafter DNSA); and CIA, Directorate of Intelligence, "El Salvador: Controlling Right-wing Terrorism," February 1985, 2, file El Salvador Death Squads, box 132, Oliver North Files, RRPL; and Allan Nairn, "Behind El Salvador's Death Squads," *The Progressive*, May 1984.

112. Singlaub asserted that "Non U.S. personnel and retired or reserve U.S. personnel should be considered for specialized military functions in order to reduce the profile of U.S. military presence and offset the current shortage of active-duty U.S. personnel." See Memorandum for the Secretary of Defense, "El Salvador Security Assistance, Expert Review—Information Memorandum," May 1984, item no. EL00401 in El Salvador, 1980–1984, DNSA.

113. Singlaub and McConnell, *Hazardous Duty*, 450.

114. See Westad, *Global Cold War*, 339–44.

115. Argentine leaders were already deeply invested in shaping Nicaraguan society. Before the Sandinistas took power, the military junta had been training and supplying Somoza's National Guard.

116. See McSherry, *Predatory States*, 211. As discussed earlier in chapter three, Argentine advisors had trained paramilitary groups in El Salvador and Guatemala in the late 1970s, often relying upon international organizations like the Confederación Anticomunista Latinoamericana to forge relationships across the hemisphere.

117. As historian Jerry Dávila writes, Argentine military regime saw itself as a "crucial defender of freedom against a global communist menace." See Dávila, *Dictatorship in South America*, 116–17, quote from 130.

118. As discussed in chapter 3, Batallón de Inteligencia 601 was commanded by Guillermo Suarez Mason, who was also a leading figure in the Confederación Anticomunista Latinoamericana.

119. Indeed, many of the Argentines who arrived in the border areas of Nicaragua, where the Contras operated, were veterans of the secret intelligence units that had been fighting against insurgent groups in Argentina. See Armony, *Argentina, the United States, and the Anti-Communist Crusade*; and Juan José Salinas, "Los mercenarios argentinos," *El Porteño* (Buenos Aires), August 1988, 35–36.

120. See Armony, *Argentina, the United States, and the Anti-Communist*, 148–50. Much of Armony's information about the Florida operation comes from the testimony of an Argentine civilian who set up the Florida base and helped smuggle weapons, launder money, and work with exiled paramilitary groups. See U.S. Congress, Testimony of Leandro Sánchez before the Subcommittee on Terrorism, Narcotics, and International Operations of the Senate Committee on Foreign Relations, July 23, 1987, II; and Guy Gugliotta, "Anti-Sandinistas claim Argentine Aid," *Miami Herald*, March 25, 1982, folder Contra Aid Non-U.S., container 12, Nicaraguan Information Center Records, BL.

121. See Jo Thomas, "Latin Exiles Focus on Nicaragua as They Train Urgently in Florida," *NYT*, December 23, 1981.

122. See Armony, *Argentina, the United States, and the Anti-Communist Crusade*, 150–51.

123. For instance, the Confederación Anticomunista Latinoamericana began working with "Nicaraguan organizations to bring together the forces in exile and those within the country, knowing that their time is limited for recuperating their country before the Soviet Union openly takes it over." See Report by Rafael Rodriguez, CAL Secretary-General, given to 14th WACL Conference, August 1, 1981, folder 4, box 61, KDP, HIWRP.

124. LeoGrande, *Our Own Backyard*, 116.

125. See National Security Decision Directive 17, "Cuba and Central America," January 4, 1982 in Ronald Reagan Presidential Library National Security Decision Directives, 1981–1989, http://www.reagan.utexas.edu/archives/reference/Scanned%20NSDDS/NSDD17.pdf accessed May 12, 2014.

126. See Kornbluh, "Nicaragua," 138–39.

127. See LeoGrande, *Our Own Backyard*, 308.

128. See U.S. Department of State resource paper, "Groups of the Nicaraguan Democratic Resistance: Who Are They?," April 1985, Iran-Contra Affair, DNSA. The best on-the-ground account of the Contras' early years is Dickey, *With the Contras*.

129. Fuerza Democrática Nicaragüense, "Blue and White Book," folder Manual Nicaraguan Resistance, box 4, Oliver North Files, RRPL.

130. Testimony John K. Singlaub, in *Joint Hearings before the Senate Subcommittee on Secret Military Assistance to Iran and the Nicaraguan Opposition*, 72.

131. Ronald Reagan, "Remarks at the Annual Dinner of the Conservative Political Action Conference," March 1, 1985, online by Gerhard Peters and John T. Woolley, *The American Presidency Project*, http://www.presidency.ucsb.edu/ws/?pid=38274. See also Gerald M. Boyd, "Reagan Terms Nicaraguan Rebels 'Moral Equivalent of Founding Fathers,'" *NYT*, March 2, 1985.

132. See George Skelton, "Reagan Appeals to Public in Battle to Help Contras," *LAT*, February 17, 1985; Raymond Coffey and Storer Rowley, "A 2nd American Revolution," *CT*, February 7, 1985; and Ronald Reagan, "Address Before a Joint Session of the Congress on the State of the Union," February 6, 1985, online by Gerhard Peters and John T. Woolley, *The American Presidency Project*, http://www.presidency.ucsb.edu/ws/?pid=38069, accessed June 6, 2017.

133. See, for instance, Colman McCarthy, "They Are Less than Freedom Fighters," *WP*, March 2, 1985.

134. Singlaub and McConnell, *Hazardous Duty*, 453.

135. See Sklar, *Washington's War in Nicaragua*, 22.

136. See "Mike Echanis—Personal Bodyguard to Somoza," *SOF*, September 1977; and Robert K. Brown, "SOF Interview Mike Echanis: One of the New Breed of American Warriors," *SOF*, November 1977.

137. N.E. MacDougal, "A Tribute to a Professional Warrior: Michael Echanis, 16 Nov 1950—8 Sept 1978," *SOF*, February 1979.

138. "Somoza's Army Chief Killed in Plane Crash," *CT*, September 9, 1979.

139. See United States Embassy, Nicaragua, "Alleged American Mercenaries," secret cable, April 12, 1978, Nicaragua Collection, DNSA.

140. See "Flak: Echanis Tributes," *SOF*, February 1979.

141. On William Walker's filibusters, see May, *Manifest Destiny's Underworld*, 40–49; and Greenberg, *Manifest Manhood and Antebellum American Empire*, 135–69.

142. Singlaub and McConnell, *Hazardous Duty*, 454. On Casey's threats to throw Singlaub out of his office, see Testimony of John Singlaub, *Joint Hearings before the Senate Subcommittee on Secret Military Assistance to Iran and the Nicaraguan Opposition*, 88. Still, Singlaub noted that he told Casey about his work with Contras at a "social activity," and also that he felt free to discuss his "activity in other parts of the world" while in Casey's office.

143. Calero testified that he preferred working with Singlaub over other Americans who were aiding the Contras, and that the "friendship and affection he had for General Singlaub is difficult to have with other people." Testimony of Adolfo Calero, *Joint Hearings before the Senate Subcommittee on Secret Military Assistance to Iran and the Nicaraguan Opposition*, 35.

144. North, *Under Fire*, 243–44.

145. Singlaub quickly relayed this information to Oliver North, Robert McFarlane, and other members of the National Security Council. See Top Secret Memorandum from Oliver North to Robert C. McFarlane, December 4, 1984, Iran-Contra Affair, DNSA.

146. See Testimony of John K. Singlaub, in *Joint Hearings before the Senate Subcommittee on Secret Military Assistance to Iran and the Nicaraguan Opposition*, 71, 78.

147. Singlaub and McConnell, *Hazardous Duty*, 456.
148. Ibid., 463.
149. PBS *Frontline*, "Who's Running this War?," March 18, 1986, produced by Martin Smith.
150. Many of these pleas appeared in the pages of the USCWF's official newsletter. See for example "Freedom Fighters Betrayed," *World Freedom Report*, May 15, 1985, 5–6, WCCPM. See also "How You Can Help the Freedom Fighters," *Human Events*, May 4, 1985.
151. PBS *Frontline*, "Who's Running This War?," March 18, 1986.
152. Ibid.
153. See "'Lady Ellen' Reaches Freedom Fighters," *World Freedom Report: The Official USCWF Newsletter* 3, no. 12 (May 15, 1986), WCCPM; Bernard Gwertzman, "U.S. Approves of Contra Copter," *NYT*, April 30, 1986; and "A Copter Called Lady Ellen," *NYT*, August 13, 1985. On her total contributions to the Contras, see "Obituary: Ellen Garwood, A Prominent Donor to the Contras," *NYT*, March 23, 1993. For her work with other Dallas conservatives, see Robert Tomsho, "Part-time Revolutionaries," *Dallas Life Magazine*, February 9, 1986, folder 26, box 106, Communist Party of the United States of America Files, TLRWLA.
154. Alfonso Chardy, "Wealthy Donors Aiding Rebels in Nicaragua," *Miami Herald*, January 21, 1985.
155. Shirley Christian, "Ex-General Tells of Nicaragua Role," *NYT*, August 10, 1985.
156. Peter Stone, "'Contras of the World Unite': World Anti-Communist League Launches 'Counter-Offensive for World Freedom,'" *Sunday Times* (London), September 15, 1985.
157. John Lee Anderson and Lucia Annunziata, "A Fragile Unity Is Born," *The Nation*, March 9, 1985, folder 29, box 9, Phillip Agee Papers, TLRWLA.
158. Sharon Shelton, "CIA hand seen in 'private' war on Nicaragua," *Workers World*, September 20, 1984, folder 27, box 9, Phillip Agee Papers, TLRWLA.
159. Testimony of John K. Singlaub, in *Joint Hearings before the Senate Subcommittee on Secret Military Assistance to Iran and the Nicaraguan Opposition*, 179. Some journalists put the figure as high as $500,000 a month, but the actual amount was lower. See Fred Hiatt, "Private Groups Press 'Contra' Aid," *WP*, December 10, 1984.
160. Testimony of John K. Singlaub, in *Joint Hearings before the Senate Subcommittee on Secret Military Assistance to Iran and the Nicaraguan Opposition*, 85, 181.
161. For a copy of this list, see "Initial Military Supplies Shipped by John Singlaub to Adolfo Calero," May 1985, item no. IC01091, Iran-Contra Affair, DNSA. See also Testimony of Adolfo P. Calero, in *Joint Hearings before the Senate Subcommittee on Secret Military Assistance to Iran and the Nicaraguan Opposition*, 444–49.
162. During the hearings, investigators and witnesses generally referred to Taiwan and South Korea as Country Three and Country Five, respectively. On Singlaub's fundraising efforts among his old military contacts in Taiwan and South Korea, see ibid., 90, 169, 171–73, 178, 180, 186.
163. Singlaub and McConnell, *Hazardous Duty*, 464–66.
164. Testimony of John K. Singlaub, in *Joint Hearings before the Senate Subcommittee on Secret Military Assistance to Iran and the Nicaraguan Opposition*, 171–72. GeoMiltech was incorporated in Delaware in 1983. See "GeoMiltech Certificate of Incorporation," August 13, 1983, item no. IC00170, Iran-Contra Affair, DNSA.
165. See "GeoMiltech Certificate of Incorporation," August 13, 1983, item no. IC00170, Iran-Contra Affair, DNSA.
166. See "GeoMiltech Corporation Precis," January 1985, item no. IC00678, Iran-Contra Affair, DNSA.
167. See "Suit Filed against Barbara Studley and John Singlaub Claiming Bank Fraud," October 26, 1988, IC04304, Iran-Contra Affair, DNSA.

168. On Singlaub and Glatt's relationship, see Silverstein, *Private Warriors*, 88–93. These prices were confirmed in official GeoMiltech documents made public during the Iran-Contra hearings. See "List of Soviet Bloc Weapons Made Available by GeoMiltech, Handwritten Note Attached," July 28, 1986, item no. IC03207, Iran-Contra Affair, DNSA.

169. As he testified before Congress in 1987, he "did not make any money" from his deals. Instead, he was only interested in "trying to advance the cause of freedom." Testimony of John K. Singlaub in *Joint Hearings before the Senate Subcommittee on Secret Military Assistance to Iran and the Nicaraguan Opposition*, 175.

170. Singlaub and McConnell, *Hazardous Duty*, 469.

171. For images of Singlaub with Contra forces in Honduras and Costa Rica, see PBS Frontline, "Who's Running this War?," March 18, 1986.

172. Singlaub was "impressed by the courage and morale of individual guerrillas, the leadership qualities of the commanders, and the relatively high professionalism of the FDN general staff." Memo from John Singlaub to Oliver North, March 14, 1985, item no. IC00943, Iran-Contra Affair, DNSA.

173. Ibid.

174. Singlaub and McConnell, *Hazardous Duty*, 469.

175. Ibid., 469–70. Singlaub commented on the effectiveness of mule transportation, which obviated the need for air resupply operation, in his communications with Oliver North. See Memo from John Singlaub to Oliver North, titled "John Singlaub Trip Report on Visit to Contra Camps in Honduras," March 14, 1985, item no. IC00943, Iran-Contra Affair, DNSA.

176. Strategy Paper, "Mission to Cut Off Atlantic Coast from Sandinista Control," May 1, 1985, item no. IC01093, Iran-Contra Affair, DNSA. Emphasis in original.

177. Brown with Spencer, *I Am Soldier of Fortune*, 283.

178. Ibid., 285.

179. Robert K. Brown, "Command Guidance," *SOF*, October 1986.

180. Brown with Spencer, *I Am Soldier of Fortune*, 282–83.

181. Ibid., 290.

182. See Steve Salisbury, "Contra Communist Cow Roundup: SOF has Beef with ARDE," *SOF*, February 1984; Dale A. Dye, "ARDE Aims for Action South of the Lake," *SOF*, June 1985; "Assignment ARCE: Yanks Volunteer for Down-South Duty," *SOF*, July 1986; and John Prester, "Gringo Merc: Contras, Cammies, and Pinstripes in Central America," *SOF*, February 1990.

183. Brown finally revealed to readers the extent of their training mission in 1990. See Harry Caflin, "SOF Trains Contras," and Robert K. Brown, "Questions for the CIA," *SOF*, October 1990.

184. For an example of this public pressure, see Alfred P. Rubin, letter to the editor, "Contra's Helpers on the Wrong Side U.S. and World Law," *NYT*, September 25, 1985.

185. See "Singlaub Denies Reagan Aided Contra Fund," *WP*, October 10, 1985.

186. See, for example, John Singlaub's letter to the *New York Times*, "One Group's Role in the Struggle for Central American Democracy," *NYT*, September 19, 1985.

187. PBS Frontline, "Who's Running this War?," March 18, 1986.

188. For instance, Reagan staffer Harold Heilsnis informed a constituent inquiring about Singlaub and the USCWF that the "United States Government does not interfere in the legal activities of private citizens nor does it monitor them." See letter from Harold Heilsnis to Le Van, August 31, 1988, WHORM Subject Files ND 007, Casefile 608990, RRPL.

189. See Memo from Paul Bremer to William P. Clark, November 11, 1982, WHORM: Subject File ME 002, casefile 112422; and Memo from Bud McFarlane/DEX to Admiral Poindexter, December 3, 1982, WHORM: Subject File ME 002, casefile 112422, RRPL.

190. Reagan, acting on the advice of his staff, never accepted Singlaub's invitations to appear at USCWF or WACL gatherings. See Letter from John Singlaub to Ronald Reagan, May 18, 1984; and Memo from Claudia Korte to Debbie Hutton, 8/28/1984, WHORM: Subject File ME 002, casefile 345378, RRPL.

191. Letter from Ronald Reagan to John Singlaub, August 31 1984, WHORM: Subject File ME 002, casefile 345378, RRPL.

192. *PBS Frontline*, "Who's Running this War?," March 18, 1986. See also Letter from Ronald Reagan to John Singlaub, June 2, 1986, WHORM Alphabetical File John Singlaub, RRPL.

193. See "Private Pipeline to the Contras; A Vast Network," *NYT*, October 22, 1986.

194. For instance, Singlaub sent Texas evangelist Bill Murray to Nicaragua to deliver a shipment of "supplies for the Freedom Fighters" in 1985. See Robert Ward, "Nicaragua, Part I," *World Freedom Report* 3, no. 3 (August 15, 1985), WCCPM. The Nicaraguan Refugee Fund used donations to deliver "goods and services" to Nicaraguans displaced by the war. See "How You Can Help the Nicaraguan Refugees," *Human Events*, May 4, 1985.

195. Peter H. Stone, "Private Group Steps Up Aid to Contras," *WP*, May 3, 1985.

196. Dave Denison, "Freedom's Friend's," *The Sun* (Baltimore), April 24, 1986.

197. George D. Moffitt, "Private Groups Channel Aid to the Contras," *Christian Science Monitor*, June 5, 1986.

198. On the broader relationship between Catholics and U.S. policies in Central America, see Keeley, "Reagan's Gun-Toting Nuns." For U.S. evangelicals and Guatemala, see Garrard-Burnett, *Terror in the Land of the Holy Spirit*.

199. Shirley Christian, "Nicaraguan Rebels Reported to Raise Up to $25 Million," *NYT*, August 13, 1985. See also Diamond, *Spiritual Warfare*, 169–76.

200. See Fred Hiatt, "Private Groups Press 'Contra' Aid," *WP*, December 10, 1984.

201. Francis X. Clines, "The White House: Propaganda, Propagation, or Just Prop," *NYT*, June 15, 1984. For an overview of the White House Outreach Working Group, see Grandin, *Empire's Workshop*, 150.

202. Letter from Faith Ryan Whittlesey to John Fischer, November 11, 1983; and Letter from Faith Whittlesey to Eden Pastora, November 21, 1983, folder White House Outreach Working Group on Central America (1), Blackwell Morton Files, RRPL.

203. See Meeting Agenda: White House Outreach Working Group on Central America, March 20, 1985, folder Outreach Working Group on Central America 3/20/1985, box OA13157, Robert Reilly Files, RRPL.

204. Richard Halloran, "CIA Denies Role—Points to Private Rightist Organization," *NYT*, October 8, 1986.

205. David Truong D.H., "The Reagan White House's Private Air Force," *Covert Action Information Bulletin* 27 (Spring 1987), quote from 64. Truong's reporting drew upon congressional testimonies about the Iran-Contra scandal. See Testimony of Adolfo P. Calero, in *Joint Hearings before the Senate Subcommittee on Secret Military Assistance to Iran and the Nicaraguan Opposition*, 407, 543. See also "Southern Air Transport Recap of [Excised] and Tel Aviv Activity," January 22, 1987 item no. IC04133, Iran-Contra Affair, DNSA.

206. See Memo from John Singlaub to Oliver North, March 14, 1985, IC00943; and Memorandum for the Record, "Meeting with Oliver North," August 6, 1986, IC03427, Iran-Contra Affair, DNSA. See also North, *Under Fire*, 255.

207. See Rodriguez and Weisman, *Shadow Warrior*. For a hagiographic account, see Jay Nordlinger, "The Anti-Che," *NR*, August 5, 2013.

208. See "Luis Posada Carriles: The Declassified Record," National Security Archive Electronic Briefing Book no. 153, May 10, 2005; and Bardach, *Cuba Confidential*, 171–223.

209. See Oliver North Notebook Entries for August 30, 1984, IC00553, Iran-Contra Affair, DNSA.

210. Singlaub and McConnell, *Hazardous Duty*, 473.

211. See Joanna Omang, "Ex-CIA Agent Lured from Libya, Arrested," *WP*, June 16, 1982; Phillip Smith, "Wilson Convicted of Smuggling Guns to Libya," *WP*, November 18, 1982; and Philip Taubman, "Ex-Agent Given Fifteen Years in Prison," *NYT*, December 21, 1982.

212. Singlaub and McConnell, *Hazardous Duty*, 474. Beyond that, Secord's work with the Iranian government—an avowed enemy of the United States—showed he exercised poor judgement in recruiting overseas allies. Singlaub had been in touch with an anticommunist movement known as the Iranian National Army, who "were absolutely opposed" to the Iranian government and business figures that Secord and North were dealing with. See Testimony of John K. Singlaub in *Joint Hearings before the Senate Subcommittee on Secret Military Assistance to Iran and the Nicaraguan Opposition*, 179.

213. Testimony of John K. Singlaub in *Joint Hearings before the Senate Subcommittee on Secret Military Assistance to Iran and the Nicaraguan Opposition*, 81.

214. See "Report Critical of Oliver North's Conservative Credentials, Two Pages Withheld—Found in Barbara Studley's Safe," c. 1986, IC02051, Iran-Contra Affair, DNSA.

215. Singlaub and McConnell, *Hazardous Duty*, 478.

216. See Byrne, *Iran-Contra*, 139–41.

217. See "Soldier of Fortune Mitchell WerBell Dies," *LAT*, December 18, 1983.

218. In 1965 he was in the Dominican Republic, helping dictator Rafael Trujillo battle a popular revolution. In 1966 he was scheming to overthrow the government of Haiti and use the island as a base to attack Cuba. The following year he was indicted for plotting with Cuban exiles to oust Fidel Castro. The scheme became known as the "CBS Invasion" after a local news crew filmed WerBell's men training in Florida. See Jack Nelson, "Figure in Gun Inquiry Is Soldier of Fortune," *LAT*, December 3, 1969.

219. See "'Death Wizard' WerBell Now in Semi-retirement," *LAT*, June 17, 1981.

220. Roger Williams, "Mitch WerBell: Gun Smith to the 'Right,'" *WP*, December 27, 1970.

221. See Tom Duncan, "The Great Pot Plot," *SOF*, Winter 1977; and "5 Cleared of Plotting to Import Marijuana," *WP*, September 5, 1976.

222. Roger Williams, "Mitch WerBell: Gun Smith to the 'Right,'" *WP*, December 27, 1970.

223. Richard Beene, "Arms Expert, Ex-CIA Aid Runs Anti-terrorism School," *LAT*, April 22, 1970. According to one reporter, the school offered classes in the "use of .45- and .38-caliber pistols, countersniper techniques . . . unconventional weapons (bow and arrow, crossbow, and throwing knives and axes), medical emergencies, martial arts (hand-to-hand combat), cardiopulmonary resuscitation, a shotgun 'stress' course, counterterrorist procedures, bomb search techniques, building search, security analysis, convoy techniques, electronic countermeasures, risk analysis, 'survival in the cultural environment,' escapes and evasive driving maneuvers." See Beau Cutts, "The Lesson at Cobray Is: 'You Kill or Be Killed,'" *BG*, October 12, 1981.

224. Brown with Spencer, *I Am Soldier of Fortune*, 100.

225. For instance, Singlaub was staying with WerBell when *Soldier of Fortune* interviewed him in 1979. See "SOF Interviews General John K. Singlaub," *SOF*, January 1979. On the rift between Singlaub and WerBell, see Singlaub and McConnell, *Hazardous Duty*, 439.

226. Gibson, *Warrior Dreams*, 167.

227. "Paramilitary Group Holds Big Maneuver," *Group Research Report* 21, no. 9, October 1982, 35.

228. See, for instance, the Paladin Press Catalog in *SOF*, March 1979.

229. James L. Pate, "Starlight Training Center: Civvies Get a Quick Taste of Boot Camp," *SOF*, February 1986.

230. Letter to Editor, S. Zeitchyk, "Merc School . . . ," *SOF*, February 1986.

231. Brown regularly dismissed mercenary schools but nonetheless let them advertise in his pages. He also lent his support to the Starlight Training Center, run by his friend Jeff Cooper, who had served on several of the magazines training endeavors in El Salvador and Nicaragua. For Brown's comments, see Robert K. Brown, "Command Guidance," *SOF*, October 2, 1985; and Gibson, *Warrior Dreams*, 204.

232. Larry Martz and Vincent Coppola, "The Shadowy World of America's Mercenaries," *Newsweek*, November 3, 1986. See also Timothy K. Smith, "In Alabama Woods, Frank Camper Trains Men to Repel Invaders," *Wall Street Journal*, August 19, 1985.

233. See U.S. Senate Subcommittee on Security and Terrorism, Committee on the Judiciary, *Mercenary Training Camps*, 99–591. On the convictions, see Jane Applegate, "Jury Convicts Camp Owner of Two Firebombings," *LAT*, April 14, 1987. Camper's involvement with the Sikhs became a major news item in India. See "Camper School May Close Down Soon," *Times of India*, September 15, 1985; J. N. Parimoo, "Camper to Testify: Plot to Kill Rajiv," *Times of India*, February 27, 1986; and "Frank Camper Arrested," *Times of India*, May 22, 1986.

234. Gibson, *Warrior Dreams*, 11, 14, 196.

235. On Louis Beam and "leaderless resistance," see Belew, *Bring the War Home*; and Zeskind, *Blood and Politics*, 88–93

236. On the resurgence of right-wing extremists in the 1980s, see Gibson, *Warrior Dreams*; Stern, *Force Upon the Plain*; Levitas, *The Terrorist Next Door*; D. J. Mulloy, *American Extremism*; and Wright, *Patriots, Politics, and the Oklahoma City Bombing*.

237. See Ken Lawrence, "Behind the Klan's Karibbean Koup Attempt," *Covert Action Information Bulletin*, no. 13, July–August 1981; Ken Lawrence, "Klan's Karibbean Koup Part II," *Covert Action Information Bulletin*, no. 16, March 1982; and Bell, *Bayou of Pigs*.

238. Ken Lawrence, "From the Hessians to the Contras: Mercenaries in the Service of Imperialism," *Covert Action Information Bulletin*, no. 22, Fall 1984.

239. CMA contacts with Negroponte and the CIA are documented in a series of cables from U.S. Embassy in Honduras. See cable from U.S. Embassy Honduras to U.S. Secretary of State, January 11, 1984, folder DRF/Contra-Military Activities 7, box 4, Oliver North Files; Cable from U.S. Embassy El Salvador to U.S. Secretary of State, January 26, 1984, folder DRF/Contra-Military Activities 7, box 4, Oliver North Files; Cable from U.S. Embassy Honduras to U.S. Secretary of State, September 3, 1984, folder DRF/Contra-Military Activities 7, box 4, Oliver North Files; Memo from CIA/DDO 7 to Robert McFarlane, September 11, 1984, folder DRF/Contra-Military Activities 6, box 4, Oliver North Files, RRPL.

240. On the CMA crash and the public outcry that followed, see Michael Hirsley, "Paramilitary Freelancers under Fire in Nicaragua," *CT*, September 23, 1984.

241. "Senators Hear Official Story of Fatal Nicaraguan Adventure," *San Francisco Chronicle*, September 11, 1984, folder Contra Aid Private Groups, Container 12, Nicaraguan Information Center Records, BL.

242. Don Oberdorfer, "Two Americans Called Volunteers," *WP*, September 5, 1985.

243. See Iver Peterson, "Mercenaries in Fatigues Meet in Nevada Glitter," *NYT*, September 26, 1984; and James L. Pate, "CMA in Central America: The Private Sector Suffers Two KIA," *SOF*, January 1985.

244. He later wrote, "After the discharge, I felt empty with an ache that stayed with me long after the grief of a death or a divorce or a lover's loss. It was impossible to shake the sadness and it tinged very joy that came after." See Hall et al., *Counter-Terrorist*, 35.

245. See John Singlaub, United States Council for World Freedom, "Press Statement on Sam Hall Accusations to CBS 60 Minutes," December 21, 1986, IC04069, Iran-Contra Affair, DNSA.

246. See Testimony of John K. Singlaub, in *Joint Hearings before the Senate Subcommittee on Secret Military Assistance to Iran and the Nicaraguan Opposition*, 188–89. See also John Singlaub, United States Council for World Freedom, "Press Statement on Sam Hall Accusations to CBS 60 Minutes," December 21, 1986, IC04069, Iran-Contra Affair, DNSA.

247. See Gibson, *Warrior Dreams*, 205–6, 209–11.

248. See Testimony of John K. Singlaub, in *Joint Hearings before the Senate Subcommittee on Secret Military Assistance to Iran and the Nicaraguan Opposition*, 188–89.

249. Westad, *Global Cold War*, 346.

250. He once referred to it as a group that would "meet, eat, and retreat." See Anderson and Anderson, *Inside the League*, 155.

251. Testimony of John K. Singlaub, in *Joint Hearings before the Senate Subcommittee on Secret Military Assistance to Iran and the Nicaraguan Opposition*, 70.

## Chapter 6

1. See Paul Dean, "Adventurer Helps Rebel Groups Fight Communist Forces," *LAT*, August 1, 1985; and Sidney Blumenthal, "Jack Wheeler's Adventures with the Freedom Fighters," *WP*, April 16, 1986.

2. See Alan Cowell, "Four Rebel Units Sign Anti-Soviet Pact," *NYT*, June 6, 1985; and Alfonso Chardy, "Rebels of Four Nations form Anti-Leftist Front," *WP*, June 6, 1985.

3. Jonas Savimbi, "Alocução Aquando do Encerramento da Conferencia da International Democratica," June 2, 1985, in Savimbi, *Por Um Futuro Melhor*, 169–82, quote from 173.

4. See Anthony Bouscaren, "WACL Conference Great Success," and Dr. Ku Chen Kang, "... A Future Bright with Freedom," *World Freedom Report: The USCWF Newsletter* 3, no. 5 (October 15, 1985), WCCPM. See also Anderson and Anderson, *Inside the League*, 207–10. PBS *Frontline*, "Who's Running this War?," March 18, 1986, produced by Martin Smith.

5. See Shirley Christian, "Rich Texans Rub Elbows with Rebels," *NYT*, September 15, 1985; Peter Stone, "'Contras of the World Unite': World Anti-Communist League Launches 'Counter-Offensive for World Freedom,'" *Sunday Times* (London), September 15, 1985; and Doyle McManus, "Rightist Crusade Finds Its Way into the Spotlight," *LAT*, September 16, 1985.

6. Charles R. Babcock, "Dallas Hosts Anti-Communist League: Diverse Group Hears Insurgents Plead for 'No-Strings' Funding," *WP*, September 17, 1985.

7. Shirley Christian, "Rich Texans Rub Elbows with Rebels," *NYT*, September 15, 1985.

8. Jerry Sanders, "The Terminators," *Mother Jones*, August/September 1985.

9. Peter Stone, "'Contras of the World Unite': World Anti-Communist League Launches 'Counter-Offensive for World Freedom,'" *Sunday Times* (London), September 15, 1985.

10. Sidney Blumenthal, "The Contra Conclave: 'Freedom Fighters' Gather in Washington," *WP*, July 17, 1986.

11. "Guerrilla Chic," *Newsweek*, March 17, 1986, folder World Anti-Communist League, box 339, GRR, RBML.

12. As columnist Sidney Blumenthal wrote in 1986, "Like supply-side economics, the Reagan Doctrine of never-ending warfare against pro-Soviet regimes in the Third World is the product of a small coterie of conservative thinkers and activists." See Sidney Blumenthal, "The Reagan Doctrine's Strange History," *WP*, June 29, 1986.

13. Ross Gelbspan, "Worldwide Rightist Unit Spotlighted," *BG*, May 31, 1987, folder John Singlaub, box 2, Douglas Valentine Vietnam Collection, National Security Archive, George Washington University, Washington, D.C.

14. Testimony of John K. Singlaub, in *Joint Hearings before the Senate Subcommittee on Secret Military Assistance to Iran and the Nicaraguan Opposition*, 70. See also Singlaub and McConnell, *Hazardous Duty*, 440. See also Anderson and Anderson, *Inside the League*, 155.

15. See Raymundo Riva Palacio, "Crimen de Estado," *El Universal* (México City), May 30, 2007; and "27 Years after the Murder of Journalist Manuel Buendía, Dossiers on the Case are Finally Made Public," Inter-American Press Association, http://en.sipiapa.org/notas/1146326-27-years-after-the-murder-of-journalist-manuel-buendia-dossiers-on-the-case-are-finally-made-public, accessed May 11, 2017.

16. See Jack Anderson, "Death Squads Continue Despite U.S. Pressures," *WP*, January 26, 1984; Jack Anderson, "Nazi Concepts Survive Among Latin Rightists," *WP*, February 9, 1984; and Jack Anderson, "Mexican Group said to Promote Neo-Nazi Cause," *WP*, September 11, 1984.

17. A partial list of these groups and individuals can be found in List of Latin American Anti-Communist Politicians, folder 24, box 9, Phillip Agee Papers, TLRWLA.

18. Report by Prof. Rafael Rodriguez, CAL Secretary-General, given to 14th WACL Conference, August 1, 1981, folder 4, box 61, KDP, HIWRP.

19. This group was known as known as ORDEN (Organización Democrática Nacionalista) and included 100,000 paramilitaries and informants at its peak. See LeoGrande, *Our Own Backyard*, 48–49.

20. Others included Chester Escobar Martinez and Dr. Francisco Buitrago Martinez, members of Nicaraguan dictator Anastasio Somoza's inner-circle. See CAL Flyer for Chester Escobar Martinez and Dr. Francisco Buitrago Martinez, no date, folder 5, box 61, Drenikoff Papers, HIWRP; and Resolution 13 in "Joint Communique of 13th General Conference of the World Anti-Communist League, Geneva, July 27, 1980," *ABN Correspondence* (Munich), September/October 1980, 45. Cuellar's death prompted one CAL leader to lament how the "forces of Communism" used "assassins to impose their bloody rule over our peoples," around the world—"Soviet soldiers in Afghanistan, Cuban soldiers in Angola, or Latin American terrorists in El Salvador." Letter from Rafael Rodriguez to All World Anti-Communist League Officers and Members, January 17, 1980, folder Confederación Anticomunista Latinoamericana, box 104, KDP, HIWRP.

21. See "Neo-Fascism Seen in Take-Over of WACL," *Group Research Report* 17, no. 5 (May 30, 1978), folder World Anti-Communist League 1987, box 339, GRR, RBML; Paul Valentine, "The Fascist Specter behind the World Anti-Red League," *WP*, May 28, 1978; and Charles Krause, "Even U.S. Suspect at Anti-Red Gathering," *WP*, May 5, 1979; and Ukrainian Liberation Movement pamphlet, "What Is ABN," no date, folder 10, box 45, HPP, LOC.

22. As described in chapter 3, American conservatives were well aware of these activities. That was one of the main reasons why they decided to cut ties with the World Anti-Communist League in the mid-1970s. See Letter from David Martin to Thomas Lane, March 22, 1974, folder 3, box 58, KDP, HIWRP; and Stefan Possony, Confidential American Council for World Freedom report, "The 1972/73 Leadership of WACL," enclosed in a letter from Geoffrey Stewart-Smith to Thomas Lane, January 9, 1974, folder 6, box 226, Walter Judd Papers, HIWRP.

23. The head of the ABN, Yaroslav Stetsko, often claimed that his life was in danger due to his anticommunist activities. See Maria Riccardi, "The Lonely Patriot," *WP*, July 21, 1981, folder 3, box 61, KDP, HIWRP. On the ABN's views of Bandera's murder, see "Why Did They Kill Stepan Bandera," *ABN Correspondence*, September/October 1984, 8.

24. See "Terrorist Group Hit List," *World Freedom Report: The USCWF Newsletter* 3, no. 12 (May 15, 1986), WCCPM.

25. Singlaub had met many of the WACL's most distasteful figures at the organizations' conferences in the early 1980s. For instance, in 1982, Singlaub chaired panels with Rafael Rodriguez, head of the Confederación Anti-Communist Latinoamericana, and Yaroslav Stetsko, leader of the Anti-Bolshevik Bloc of Nations. See Woo Jae Sung, Korean WACL Chapter, Circular Letter no. 12, December 30, 1982, folder 5, box 61, KDP, HIWRP. He also made regular appearances at ABN meetings from 1981 onwards. See text of speech given by John Singlaub to the Anti-Bolshevik Bloc of Nations/European Freedom Council Conference, London, Great Britain, September 24–26, 1982, folder 5, box 54, KDP, HIWRP; and John K. Singlaub, "You Can Trust the Communists (to Behave as Barbarians)," *ABN Correspondence*, March/April 1984, 10–16.

26. Singlaub and McConnell, *Hazardous Duty*, 447.

27. Close's background is described in a declassified CIA report, "IR 2 237 0117 85 Bio Info, BE Liberal Party," August 21, 1985, Freedom of Information Act (FOIA) request, released February 18, 2014, in author's possession.

28. "Robert Close: Un Anticomuniste Militant," *Pour* (Paris), folder 16, box 9, Phillip Agee Papers, TLRWLA. Close was best known for his books and lectures that claimed the Soviet Union was poised to take over Europe.

29. The Tokyo panel was entitled "Military Strategies to Counter Soviet Expansionism." See Woo Jae Sung, Korean WACL Chapter, Circular Letter no. 12, December 30, 1982, folder 5, box 61, KDP, HIWRP; and Singlaub and McConnell, *Hazardous Duty*, 447. See also "WACL Finally Expels One Pro-Fascist Organization," *Public Eye*, June 1984, folder World Anti-Communist League, box 339, GRR, RBML; and Jack Anderson, "Anti-Red Group Ousts Infamous Latin Affiliate," *WP*, February 18, 1984.

30. Singlaub and McConnell, *Hazardous Duty*, 439, 447.

31. Ibid., 447.

32. See, for example, John Singlaub's letter to the *New York Times*, "One Group's Role in the Struggle for Central American Democracy," *NYT*, Sep. 19, 1985. On Singlaub invited members of B'nai B'rith, see Singlaub and McConnell, *Hazardous Duty*, 447; and Robert Reinhold, "General Aiding Contras Hints at Broader Role," *NYT*, October 14, 1986.

33. See Craig Pyes, "Private General, Mystery Man of the Reagan Administration," *New Republic*, September 30, 1985; and "WACL Finally Expels One Pro-Fascist Organization," *Public Eye*, June 1984, folder World Anti-Communist League, box 339, GRR, RBML.

34. On the planning of the conference, see Singlaub and McConnell, *Hazardous Duty*, 447. For Singlaub's solicitation of private, tax-deductible donations for freedom fighters at the 1984 conference, see "Funds for Freedom," *World Freedom Report: The USCWF Newsletter* 2, no. 4 (September 15, 1984), WCCPM. The 1984 conference was an expanded version of summits that Singlaub had held around the United States since 1982. He had already made connections with several armed anticommunist groups from Vietnam, Angola, and Afghanistan. See Letter from Basil Mailat to Kyrill Drenikoff, June 14, 1982, folder 6, box 54, KDP, HIWRP; and "160 Attend League Conference," *ABN Correspondence* (Munich), July–October 1982, 88–90.

35. For a description of the conference's attendees and program, see Antony T. Bouscaren, "Resistance Leaders Meet at 17th WACL Conference," *World Freedom Report: The USCWF Newsletter* 2, no. 5 (October 15, 1984), WCCPM.

36. On Singlaub's travel to meetings of the ABN, APACL, and other affiliated groups, see Woo Jae Sung, Korean WACL Chapter, Circular Letter no. 12, December 30, 1982, folder 5, box 61, KDP, HIWRP; Press release, "International Freedom Group Ends Meeting," April 24, 1982, folder 2, box 62, KDP, HIWRP; Text of speech given by John Singlaub to the Anti-

Bolshevik Bloc of Nations/European Freedom Council Conference, London, Great Britain, September 24–26, 1982, folder 5, box 54, KDP, HIWRP; Joint Communiqué of the United States Council for World Freedom, Scottsdale, Arizona, April 24, 1982, folder 2, box 62, KDP, HIWRP; and Report of the National Captive Nations Committee, July 1983, folder 5, box 62, KDP, HIWRP. On Singlaub's travels to Paraguay and Brazil, see Letter from Gen. Alberto Cantero to Pastor Coronel, November 23, 1985, R095F1288; and Letter from Ofic. Inspector Oscar Luis Ojeda to Amado Said Luque, November 23, 1985, R163F1086, CDADDH.

37. See Julia Preston, "Rebels Press their Effort without aid from U.S.," *BG*, March 18, 1985; and James LeMoyne, "War Is Never Far Away for Nicaraguan Rebels," *NYT*, March 24, 1985.

38. Doyle McManus, "Rightist Crusade Finds its Way into the Spotlight," *LAT*, September 16, 1985; and "Dallas on Path of Most Resistance," *CT*, August 11, 1985.

39. See Conference Program, "A Global Strategy to Safeguard Human Freedom," December 6–9, 1982, folder 5, box 61, KDP, HIWRP.

40. Letter from Rafael Rodriguez to All WACL and WYACL Members, October 5, 1978, folder Confederación Anticomunista Latinoamericana, box 104, KDP, HIWRP; Resolution by the Cuban Chapter to 14th WACL Conference, Taipei Taiwan, August 3–7, 1981, folder 4, box 61, KDP, HIWRP; Resolution presented by Nicaraguan Chapter to 14th World Anti-Communist League Conference, Taipei Taiwan, August 3–7, 1981, folder 4, box 61, KDP; Resolution presented by the Confederación Anticomunista Latinoamericana to the 14th WACL Conference, Taipei Taiwan, August 3–7, 1981, folder 4, box 61, KDP, HIWRP; and Joint Communiqué of the WACL Executive Board and the APACL Executive Committee, Taipei, Republic of China, April 18, 1982, folder 2, box 62, KDP, HIWRP.

41. Sydney Blumenthal, "The Contra Conclave: 'Freedom Fighters' Gather in Washington," *WP*, July 17, 1986.

42. Letter from John Singlaub to Ronald Reagan, May 18, 1984, WHORM: Subject File ME 002, Case file 345378, RRPL. See also "League Backs Freedom Fighters," *LAT*, September 8, 1984; Peter H. Stone, "Private Groups Step up Aid to Contras," *WP*, May 3, 1985.

43. These expressions of solidarity became regular features of WACL meetings and other international gatherings from the late 1970s onwards. For Angolan views, see Speech given by Frente Nacional de Libertação de Angola representative at 13th WACL Conference, Geneva, Switzerland, no date, folder 1, box 61, KDP. For those of Afghan guerrillas, see Speech given by Dr. Houmayoun Shah Assefy, Afghan Resistance, at 13th WACL Conference, Geneva, Switzerland, no date, folder 1, box 61, KDP, HIWRP. For those of Central and South American anticommunists, see Resolution presented by CAL to 14th WACL Conference, Taipei Taiwan, August 3–7, 1981, folder 4, box 61, KDP, HIWRP; and for those of the Karen guerrillas in Burma, see Statement of the Karen National Union at the 15th WACL Conference, December 6–9, 1982, folder 5, box 61, KDP, HIWRP.

44. Major General John K. Singlaub, "The Counteroffensive for Freedom," text of speech given to the Central American and Caribbean Freedom Forum, Miami FL, February 3, 1985, republished in *World Freedom Report: The USCWF Newsletter* 2, no. 10 (March 15, 1985), WCCPM.

45. Shirley Christian, "Rich Texans Rub Elbows with Rebels," *NYT*, September 15, 1985.

46. Letter from John K. Singlaub to President Ronald Reagan, May 18, 1984, WHORM: Subject File ME 002, Case file 345378, RRPL.

47. Major General John K. Singlaub, "A Plan for Victory," text of speech delivered to the 1984 *Soldier of Fortune* convention is Las Vegas Nevada on September 22, 1984, republished in *World Freedom Report: The USCWF Newsletter* 2, no. 5 (October 15, 1984), WCCPM. Emphasis in original.

48. Ibid.

49. "Let's Go to Work," *World Freedom Report: The USCWF Newsletter* 2, no. 6 (November 15, 1984), WCCPM.

50. Testimony of John K. Singlaub, in *Joint Hearings before the Senate Subcommittee on Secret Military Assistance to Iran and the Nicaraguan Opposition*, 193–94.

51. See Doyle McManus, "Rightist Crusade Finds its Way into the Spotlight," *LAT*, September 16, 1985 and "Dallas on Path of Most Resistance," *CT*, August 11, 1985.

52. Letter from John K. Singlaub to President Ronald Reagan, May 18, 1984, WHORM: Subject File ME 002, Case file 345378, RRPL.

53. Dubbed the International Information Service, Singlaub proposed that it would reach 400 major radio markets and another 600 to 800 markets through audio cassettes. See "Executive Director's Report," *World Freedom Report: The USCWF Newsletter* 3, no. 9 (February 15, 1986), WCCPM.

54. See Doyle McManus, "Rightist Crusade Finds Its Way into the Spotlight," *LAT*, September 16, 1985.

55. Major General John K. Singlaub, "A Plan for Victory," text of speech delivered to the 1984 *Soldier of Fortune* convention is Las Vegas Nevada on September 22, 1984, republished in *World Freedom Report: The USCWF Newsletter* 2, no. 5 (October 15, 1984), WCCPM.

56. Larry H. Tifverberg quoted in Robert Reinhold, "General Aiding Contras Hints at Broader Role," *NYT*, October 14, 1986.

57. See Kim Philips-Fein, *Invisible Hands*, 169–73.

58. Richard Schultz, "Low Intensity Conflict."

59. On the activities of the Center for Strategic and International Studies, see Jerry Sanders, "The Terminators," *Mother Jones*, August/September 1985. For Ray Cline's work with the APACL and WACL, see "Expanding International Anti-Communist Battlefield," *Asian Outlook* 15, no. 8 (August 1980); and WACL Panel List, September 5, 1985, folder World Anti-Communist League, box 339, GRR, RBML.

60. See Cullather, *Hungry World*, 108–33.

61. See Westad, *Global Cold War*, 299–305.

62. See U.S. Embassy Afghanistan, confidential cable, "Khalqi Regime Identifies Afghan Revolution as an Extension of the USSR's October Revolution," November 15, 1978, cable no. 09145, AF00304, Afghanistan Collection, DNSA.

63. See Ewans, *Afghanistan*, 142; and Goodson, *Afghanistan's Endless War*, 51.

64. On the growth of Afghanistan's Islamist movement, or more precisely movements, see Coll, *Ghost Wars*, 39–40, 110–13.

65. Pakistani support for the Afghan Islamist rebels dated back to the early 1970s. See U.S. Department of State, Bureau of Intelligence and Research confidential report, "The Afghan Resistance Movement," March 16, 1982, AF01328, Afghanistan Collection, DNSA. See also Coll, *Ghost Wars*, 61–62.

66. See Cable from US Embassy Kabul to US Secretary of State, "Situation in Herat," March 17, 1979, cable no. 02043, AF00516, Afghanistan Collection, DNSA.

67. The mounting Soviet frustrations with the Afghan communists are documented in Westad, *Global Cold War*, 316–26.

68. See U.S. Embassy Afghanistan, confidential cable, "Current Status of the Insurgency in Afghanistan," October 6, 1979, cable no. 07350, AF00688, Afghanistan Collection, DNSA.

69. See Personal memorandum from Yuri Andropov to Leonid Brezhnev, December 1, 1979, Soviet Invasion of Afghanistan collection, CWIHP; and Dmitri F. Ustinov and Nikolai Ogarkov, "Directive 312/12/00," December 24, 1979, Soviet Invasion of Afghanistan collection, CWIHP. Initially, Soviet leaders wished only to send an elite force to root out militants and discipline the Afghan communist regime. By the end of December 1979, they had shifted

towards large-scale military intervention. These debates within the Soviet Politburo are documented in a series of declassified reports. See "Extract from CPSU CC Politburo Decision," December 6, 1979, Soviet Invasion of Afghanistan collection, CWIHP.

70. See telegram from the U.S. Embassy in Afghanistan to the U.S. Department of State, "Massive Soviet Air Operations into Kabul Continue," December 26, 1979, document 244; and "Summary of Conclusions of a Special Coordination Committee Meeting," January 2, 1980, document 251, *FRUS, 1977–1980: Vol. 6, Soviet Union*.

71. Westad, *Global Cold War*, 326.

72. Brzezinski, *Power and Principle*, 429.

73. See Confidential Memo from Zbigniew Brzezinski to Jimmy Carter, "Reflections on Soviet Intervention in Afghanistan," December 26, 1979, National Security Archive Electronic Briefing Book No. 39, October 13, 2012, National Security Archive, Washington, D.C. Quote from Immerman, *Hidden Hand*, 118.

74. Coll, *Ghost Wars*, 58.

75. On January 10, 1980—the day the first shipment of U.S. arms arrived in Afghanistan—the Afghanistan Task Force released a brief in which researchers asserted that Carter's ability to intervene was limited by the Vietnam Syndrome—a "national mood of withdrawal from globalism, and the military implications of such a role." See Afghanistan Task Force brief, "Afghanistan: Soviet Invasion and US Response," January 10, 1980, AF00789, Afghanistan Collection, DNSA.

76. See Coll, *Ghost Wars*, 53–70.

77. Westad, *Global Cold War*, 352.

78. On Wilson's fascination with, and involvement in, the Afghan war, see Crile, *Charlie Wilson's War*.

79. Casey quoted in Persico, *Casey: From the OSS to the CIA*, 26.

80. Reagan authorized this expansion of the CIA's covert aid program in National Security Decision Directive (NSDD) 166, "US Policy, Programs, and Strategy on Afghanistan," March 27, 1985, National Security Decision Directives archive, RRPL.

81. Memo from Morgan Norval to Congressman John Le Boutillier, April 27, 1981, folder Afghanistan, box 1, Morton Blackwell files, Series I, RRPL. Norval ran the Selous Foundation, which borrowed its name from the Rhodesian military's elite Selous Scouts unit, and which studied anticommunist insurgencies.

82. Singlaub and McConnell, *Hazardous Duty*, 445.

83. Major General John K. Singlaub, "A New Strategy for the 1980s: Address at the United States Council for World Freedom and North American Region of the World Anti-Communist League in Phoenix, Arizona, April 23, 1982," *ABN Correspondence* (Munich), July–October 1982, 24–29.

84. That was the key theme of the glossy pamphlet published by the United States Information Service, *Afghanistan: The Struggle Continues*, 1983, folder 150000–199999, WHORM Subject File CO 002, RRPL.

85. John Barron, "Soviets Maim Afghan Children," United States Council for World Freedom, *World Freedom Report: The USCWF Newsletter* 3, no. 7 (December 15, 1985), WCCPM. See also Leon Poullada, "Special Feature: Afghans Buy Time for America," *Free Afghanistan Report*, no. 2, April 1982 (reprinted from *Soldier of Fortune*), folder Afghanistan, box 1, Morton Blackwell files, Series I, RRPL.

86. Memo from Morgan Norval to Congressman John Le Boutillier, April 27, 1981, folder Afghanistan, box 1, Morton Blackwell files, Series I, RRPL.

87. David C. Isby, "Old Foes, New Tactics: Rebels Rout Kremlin's Afghan Army," *SOF*, September 1986.

88. Jim Coyne, "SOF Staffer Inside Afghanistan," *SOF*, May 1981.

89. See *Red Dawn*, directed John Milius, MGM/UA Entertainment Co., 1984. A few film critics made the association between this imagined guerrilla war against communist invaders and the real one taking place in Afghanistan but they did so only in passing. See Larry Kart, "Apocalypse Tomorrow? Milius Claims 'Red Dawn' Is Actually Anti-War," *CT*, August 12, 1984; and Kevin Thomas, "John Milius' Vision of an Invasion," *LAT*, August 10, 1984.

90. Humanitarian programs included health programs in Pakistan, shipments of food and medical sundries, and funds to help Afghans migrate to the West. See Memo from William Clark to William K. Sadleir, February 1, 1983, folder 046000–069999, WHORM Subject File CO 002, RRPL.

91. David B. Ottaway, "Groups Fostered Atmosphere Conducive to Giving Rebels Modern Weapons," *WP*, February 12, 1989.

92. Ronald Reagan, "Message on the Observance of Afghanistan Day," March 21, 1983, online by Gerhard Peters and John T. Woolley, *American Presidency Project*, http://www.presidency.ucsb.edu/ws/?pid=41078, accessed January 23, 2015.

93. Scott, *Deciding to Intervene*, 77.

94. Transcript of *This Week with David Brinkley*, ABC News, October 28, 1984, folder 27, box 9, Phillip Agee Papers, TLRWLA.

95. Author interview with Karen McKay, former director of the Committee for a Free Afghanistan, July 20, 2015.

96. See Loyn, *In Afghanistan*, 230.

97. Rone Tempest, "Peshawar: Many Lured by Intrigue," *LAT*, May 12, 1986.

98. Author interview with Karen McKay, former director of the Committee for a Free Afghanistan, July 20, 2015.

99. Ibid. McKay recalled that Paul Weyrich, the director of the Heritage Foundation, which housed McKay's office, felt she wouldn't be able to do the job. McKay was a skilled soldier, but Weyrich believed that women should not serve in the army. Moreover, in Weyrich's view, a woman—even one with an accomplished military record such as McKay—would not be able to work within the religiously conservative and masculine world of the mujahedin.

100. Journalist George Crile wrote that McKay had undergone "limited jump-school training and would sometimes appear at conservative gatherings in uniform, wearing a green beret." See Crile, *Charlie Wilson's War*, 329.

101. See Committee for a Free Afghanistan Fundraising Letter from Karen McKay, February 9, 1985, folder 2, box 29, HPP, LOC. The group also part of the White House Outreach Working Group on Central America. See Speakers for White House Outreach Working Group on Central America, circa 1983, CIA-FOIA, https://www.cia.gov/library/readingroom/docs/CIA-RDP85M00364R001803590011-7.pdf, accessed May 22, 2017.

102. Author interview with Karen McKay, former director of the Committee for a Free Afghanistan, July 20, 2015. See also "Q&A: Afghan Freedom Fighters Mature as Support Holds," *WT*, March 21,1984; Karen McKay, "What Afghan Freedom Forces Seek," *WT*, September 12, 1985; Caryle Murphy, "U.S. Doctor Aids Afghan Guerrillas," *WP*, July 25, 1984; "CFA Brings Wounded Afghans to U.S. for Treatment," and "Working for Freedom," *Free Afghanistan Report*, published by the Committee for a Free Afghanistan, no. 8, September 1985; Letter from Karen McKay to Rep. Don Ritter, in *Congressional Record*, May 9, 1984, 11644–11645.

103. Karen McKay quoted in Eric Brodin, "Afghanistan: The Forgotten War," *ABN Correspondence* (Munich), May–August 1984, 52–53.

104. Ronald Reagan, "Proclamation 4908 - Afghanistan Day," March 10, 1982, online by Gerhard Peters and John T. Woolley, *American Presidency Project*, http://www.presidency.ucsb.edu/ws/?pid=42249, accessed January 22, 2015. Other U.S.-based groups such as Af-

ghan Action helped pressure the administration as well. See Letters from William Clark to Don Ritter et al, January 7, 1982, folder 046000–069999, WHORM Subject File CO 002, RRPL.

105. See Letter from Charles Moser to William Clark, February 27, 1982, folder Afghanistan, box 1, Morton Blackwell files, Series I, RRPL. See also Joseph McLellan, "A Day for Afghans," *WP*, March 19, 1982; and Jean M. White, "Rallying for Afghanistan," *WP*, March 22, 1982.

106. Raymond Coffey, "Afghanistan: No End in Sight," *CT*, May 18, 1986.

107. McKay later recalled that she maintained friendly relations all of the major mujahedin factions except for that of Islamist leader Gulbuddin Hekmatyar. Author interview with Karen McKay, former director of the Committee for a Free Afghanistan, July 20, 2015. Declassified CIA documents confirm Casey's knowledge of her actions. See Memo from Debbie to William Casey, "Committee for a Free Afghanistan," March 16, 1984, CIA-FOIA, https://www.cia.gov/library/readingroom/docs/CIA-RDP88B00443R001500030117-3.pdf, accessed May 22, 2017.

108. McKay's office often reported on the fate of other Americans who ventured into Afghanistan and were injured or killed. See "3 From U.S. Reported Alive in Afghanistan," *NYT*, October 4, 1985.

109. See Letter from Karen McKay to Elizabeth Dole, March 24, 1983, folder Afghanistan, box 1, Morton Blackwell files, Series I, RRPL.

110. See "Reagan Meets with Freedom Fighters," *Free Afghanistan Report*, published by the Committee for a Free Afghanistan, no. 5, May 1983; and "Reagan Meets with Afghan Unity," *Free Afghanistan Report*, published by the Committee for a Free Afghanistan, no. 10, September 1986.

111. See Letter from Karen McKay to Elizabeth Dole, March 24, 1983, folder Afghanistan, box 1, Morton Blackwell files, Series I, RRPL.

112. Quote from Resolution presented by Confederación Anticomunista Latinoamericana to 14th WACL Conference, Taipei Taiwan, August 3–7, 1981, folder 4, box 61, KDP, HIWRP. See also Speech given by Angola's Frente Nacional de Libertação de Angola (FNLA) representative at 13th WACL Conference, Geneva, Switzerland, no date, folder 1, box 61, KDP, HIWRP; and Letter from Lt. Gen. Bo Mya, Karen National Union, December 2, 1981, folder 5, box 61, Drenikoff Papers, KDP, HIWRP.

113. As one writer put it, "Afghanistan has always been in the historical plan of Russian imperialism, regardless of whether this plan was formulated by the Russian tsarists or Bolshevik regimes." See E. Orlowskyj, "The 'Afghan, Crisis,' or the Global Crisis of the West?," *ABN Correspondence* (Munich), May–June 1980, 1–8.

114. See, for instance, Alexandra Radkewycz, "Anti-Soviet Nationalists Laud Afghan Resistance," *The Globe and Mail* (Toronto), November 24, 1986. McKay recalled her appearance as the keynote speakers at an ABN conference circa 1985. Author interview with Karen McKay, former director of the Committee for a Free Afghanistan, July 20, 2015.

115. See Askold Krushelnytsky, "Night Attack with Engineer Mahmoud," *ABN Correspondence* (Munich), September/October 1980, 26–29. It's possible that "Engineer Mahmoud" was in fact Ahmed Shah Massoud, a mujahedin leader who had studied engineering at the Polytechnical University of Kabul. See also and Jeremy Gaylard, "United Front Urged to Topple Soviet Imperialism," *New York City Tribune*, May 24, 1985, folder American Friends of the Anti-Bolshevik Bloc of Nations, OA 8631, Linas Kojelis Files, RRPL.

116. See Report of the Anti-Bolshevik Bloc of Nations given at the 14th WACL General Conference in Taipei, Taiwan, August 3–7, 1981, folder 4, box 61, KDP, HIWRP.

117. They also wrote in international publications, such as the Anti-Bolshevik Bloc of

Nations' *ABN Correspondence*. See Afghan Association of Freedom Fighters, "In God We Trust," *ABN Correspondence* (Munich) March/April 1980, 7.

118. See for instance the republished speech of Bashir Zikria, an Afghan rebel leader who appeared at a USCWF conference in Toronto in 1981, "The Guerrilla Movement Covering the Country," *ABN Correspondence*, July–October 1982, 63–64; text of speech delivered by M.A. Naim at an Anti-Bolshevik Bloc of Nations conference in London, September 24–26, 1982, entitled "Movement for Solidarity, Reconciliation and Resistance of Afghanistan," *ABN Correspondence*, November/December 1982, 11–12.

119. Speech given by Dr. Houmayoun Shah Assefy, Afghan Resistance, at 13th WACL Conference, Geneva, Switzerland, no date, folder 1, box 61, KDP, HIWRP.

120. Coll, *Ghost Wars*, 107–24.

121. As one Afghan guerrilla leader put it, "Afghan individualism makes every Afghan a party." Ahmed Gailani quoted in "Disunity Hampers Anti-Soviet Afghans in the U.S.," *NYT*, June 8, 1980.

122. See, for instance, Stuart Ayerbach, "Afghan Rebels Bottle Up Army Troops, Battle Each Other," *WP*, November 2, 1979; Tyler Marshall, "Afghan Rebels Remain Divided," *LAT*, September 1, 1980; and Tyler Marshall, "Afghan Rebels Divided but Confident They Won't Fall," *LAT*, August 31, 1981.

123. Jim Graves, "The Afghan Freedom Fighters' Organization," *SOF*, January 1985, 88–89.

124. The title "Pir" is conferred on masters in the Sufi tradition. The title "Sayyid" denoted Ahmed Gailani's ancestral lineage going back to the prophet Mohammed. Ahmed Gailani was also a descendant of Abdul-Qadir Gilani, the founder of the Qadiriyyah, a sect of the Sufi religion. See Goodson, *Afghanistan's Endless War*, 62; and M. Afzal Khan, "With the Afghan Rebels," *NYT*, January 13, 1980.

125. Some said that Gailani was "an avid reader of *Soldier of Fortune* magazine." See David Isby, "Soviet BG-15: Kunar Carry-out Bags a Blooper," *SOF*, July 1985, 26–31.

126. Coll, *Ghost Wars*, 175.

127. Kay Withers, "Leader of Afghan Resistance Group Says West Falls Short on Aid," *The Sun* (Baltimore), June 10, 1983.

128. See "Afghan Freedom Fighters' Plea," *World Freedom Report: The USCWF Newsletter* 2, no. 12 (May 15, 1985), WCCPM. See also "Afghan Rebel Has Aid Talks in US," *The Guardian*, February 25, 1981; and Cable from United States Embassy. Belgium to US Secretary of State, "Representatives of Afghan Resistance Movements Appear at European Parliament," July 14, 1980, cable no. 11609, AF00996, Afghanistan Collection, DNSA.

129. Letter from George Burn to Richard Allen, August 24, 1981, folder Begin-045999, WHORM Subject File CO 002, RRPL.

130. See September 5, 1985 Panel List, folder World Anti-Communist League, box 339, GRR, RBML; "Afghanistan Update," *SOF*, July 1981; and Bill Guthrie, "SOF Convention: Laying Siege in Las Vegas," *SOF*, January 1985, 26–31.

131. For Singlaub's views on the failures of the CIA's training of the Nicaraguan Contras, see Memo from John Singlaub to Oliver North, titled "John Singlaub Trip Report on Visit to Contra Camps in Honduras," March 14, 1985, item no. IC00943, Iran-Contra Affair, DNSA; and Singlaub and McConnell, *Hazardous Duty*, 469.

132. This comes from Milt Bearden, a former CIA officer who worked on the Afghan program. See Bearden and Risen, *Main Enemy*, 235, 238. See also Coll, *Ghost Wars*, 175.

133. Crile, *Charlie Wilson's War*, 338.

134. Author interview with Karen McKay, former director of the Committee for a Free Afghanistan, July 20, 2015.

135. The AFL/CIO program is described in Ted Abbott, "Project Boots," *World Freedom Report* 3, no. 2 (July 15, 1985), WCCPM, UKS.

136. See the "Staff Opinion" that follows John Barron, "Soviets Maim Afghan Children," *World Freedom Report* 3, no. 7 (December 15, 1985), WCCPM, UKS.

137. See "The Old Still Fight," *World Freedom Report: The USCWF Newsletter* 3, no. 2, (August 15, 1985), WCCPM, UKS.

138. This call appeared in Maj. Gen. John Singlaub, "Freedom and Nuclear War," *World Freedom Report: The USCWF Newsletter* 2, no. 1 (June 15, 1985), WCCPM, UKS.

139. See "You Can Help" *World Freedom Report: The USCWF Newsletter* 3, no. 2 (August 15, 1985), WCCPM, UKS.

140. See the advertisement "Freedom Fighters Fund," *SOF*, January 1984, 16. Those who contributed money or supplies often received mention in the magazine. See, for instance, "Afghan Collection," *SOF*, January 1985, 10; "Freedom Fighters," *SOF*, February 1985, 8.

141. See the advertisement "Afghan Freedom Fighters," *SOF*, December 1981, back cover.

142. See Bob Poos, "Support Afghanistan, Write Washington," *SOF*, May 1981, 76.

143. The notion that killing Soviets in Afghanistan would prevent an eventual communist invasion in the United States was a ubiquitous feature of the Afghan Freedom Fighter Fund campaign. As this particular writer lamented "only being able to send $20 from this paycheck," he also noted how was preparing to "stave off the Red Menace when they try to invade our homeland." See letter-to-the-editor from N.W., "Freedom Fund Praised," *SOF*, February 1981, 8.

144. Brown had been concerned with the Afghan war since at least 1980, when his magazine began publishing articles about the brutality of the Soviet invasion and the courage of the Afghan guerrillas. See Galen Geer, "More than the Bear Bargained For," *SOF*, October 1980.

145. *Soldier of Fortune* was one of a select few publications to send reporters into Afghanistan. As one commentator noted, "No major American newspaper saw fit to station a reporter in Peshawar, Pakistan, the base of rebel political and military operations, and American television crews rarely ventured up to the Khyber Pass for a glimpse of the war." Steve Galster, "The Making of U.S. Foreign Policy, 1973–1990," folder 1, box 10, Phillip Agee Papers, TLRWLA. See also Gibson, *Warrior Dreams*, 147–48. Starting in 1984, the magazine had reporters in country nearly year round, mostly with Ahmed Shah Massoud's forces in the Panjsher Valley. See, for example, David C. Isby, "Panjsher VII: Soviets Smash Afghan Resistance in Vital Valley," *SOF*, February 1985; Mike Winchester, "Irritating Ivan: Massoud's Men Keep the Pressure on the Panjsher," *SOF*, June 1985; Mike Winchester, "Afghan Jihad: Hard Pressed Massoud Holds Panjsher," *SOF*, August 1985. For other reports, see Philip Edwards, "Daylight raid: Freedom Fighters Batter Kabul Fort," *SOF*, October 1985, 38–43.

146. Bill Guthrie, "SOF Convention: Laying Siege in Las Vegas," *SOF*, January 1985, 26–31.

147. Soviet weapons designers hoped that the Automat-Kalashnikov, Model 74 (AK-74) would replace its predecessor, the better known AK-47, arguably the most popular assault rifle in the world.

148. According to Brown's memoir, the agent at the Army's Foreign Science and Technology Center promised to pay $1.00 per pound of AK-74 ammunition. Other items for which the FSTC was willing the pay included a grenade launcher ($65,000) and a container of nerve gas ($250,000). See Brown with Spencer, *I Am Soldier of Fortune*, 205, 211.

149. They included John Donovan, a master in explosives and demolitions, and Peter Kokalis, one of the world's small arms experts, both of whom Brown would partner on subsequent missions to El Salvador and Nicaragua. See Robert K. Brown, "Embattled El Salvador—Has the U.S. Forgotten to Win a War?," *SOF*, September 1983; Peter G. Kokalis,

"Arming El Salvador: U.S. Gives Brave Warriors Worn-out Weapons," *SOF*, September 1983; John E. Padgett, "Morazan Sitrep: SOF A-Team Reports Gains in El Salvador," *SOF*, June 1984; Peter G. Kokalis, "Arms and the Atlacatl: SOF Trains Salvadoran Immediate Reaction Battalion," *SOF*, January 1984, 55; and Robert J. McCartney, "Soldiers of Fortune Lend a Hand in El Salvador," *WP*, August 29, 1983; Galen Geer, "More than the Bear Bargained For," *SOF*, October 1980; and Brown with Spencer, *I Am Soldier of Fortune*, 198.

150. "Robert K. Brown, "AK-74: SOF's publisher fires Russia's new rifle," *SOF*, February 1981, 33–34.

151. Brown with Spencer, *I Am Soldier of Fortune*, 217.

152. Ibid., 218–19.

153. Henry Allen, "All's Fair in Soldier Of Fortune: Writing a Good Fight," *WP*, June 12, 1980.

154. Brown with Spencer, *I Am Soldier of Fortune*, 221.

155. Brown also paid for American activists to visit the mujahedin in the field. Sometimes he pulled on connections with the Committee for a Free Afghanistan to facilitate these trips, as when the magazine sent two Yale journalism students, one of whom was the son of U.S. circuit judge Robert Bork, to the country in 1984. See Charles Bork and Gregory D'Elia, "Afghan 101: Yale Journalist Tours Jihad Battlegrounds," *SOF*, January 1984, 46–49.

156. Robert K. Brown, "SOF inside Afghanistan," *SOF*, November 1982, 46–55.

157. For instance, Brown appeared on the cover of the November 1982 issue of *Soldier Fortune*, sitting astride a camel, wearing a turban, his moustache died black, and brandishing an AK-47, surrounded by smiling Afghan guerrillas.

158. Brown, "SOF inside Afghanistan," *SOF*, November 1982, 46–55.

159. Brown with Spencer, *I Am Soldier of Fortune*, 226.

160. Ibid., 229.

161. See Mark Warman, "Afghan Elite Forces: Mujahedin Unite to Train Crack Troops," *SOF*, December 1983, 62–71; Mark Warman, "Combat in Kunar," *SOF*, January 1985, 83–113; Gene Scroft, "Holy War Combat Tour: American Merc Join the Mujahedeen," *SOF*, December 1986, 74–79, 109; Harry Bateson, "Assignment Afghanistan," *SOF*, April 1988, 20–29; David C. Isby, "Four Battles in Afghanistan," *SOF*, April 1988, 30–37; and Louis Dupree and David C. Isby, "Endgame in Afghanistan," *SOF*, April 1988, 38–43.

162. For instance, in 1981, Hasan Gailani, Ahmad Gailani's brother and a commander of the National Islamic Front of Afghanistan, told readers that his forces had "no anti-tank rockets, no anti-aircraft weapons," and this prevented them from launching assaults on Kabul on other Soviet strongholds. See "Afghanistan Update," *SOF*, July 1981, 2.

163. Years later, in 1990, Eiva would return to Lithuania to train dissidents in guerrilla warfare as the Soviet Union collapsed. See Vincent J. Schodolski, "American Helps Lithuanians Prepare for Guerrilla Warfare," *CT* Jan 18, 1991.

164. See Leslie H. Gelb, "From One Kind of Army to Another," *NYT*, January 18, 1983.

165. See Mathiak, "American Jihad," 51–56; Mark Tran, "Reagan Meets Afghan Rebels," *Guardian* (London), June 17, 1986; and Jack Anderson and Dale Van Atta, "CIA Mismanages Afghan Aid," *WP*, April 29, 1987.

166. Author interview with Karen McKay, former director of the Committee for a Free Afghanistan, July 20, 2015

167. Crile, *Charlie Wilson's War*, 330–31.

168. Ronald Reagan, "Address Before a Joint Session of the Congress on Central America," April 27, 1983, online by Gerhard Peters and John T. Woolley, *American Presidency Project*, http://www.presidency.ucsb.edu/ws/?pid=41245, accessed February 3, 2015.

169. For instance, Karen McKay recalled that Islamist leader Gulbuddin Hekmatyar had

tried to kidnap and kill her on at least one occasion. Author interview with Karen McKay, former director of the Committee for a Free Afghanistan, July 20, 2015.

170. See Fred Reed, "'Kill Them All and Let God Sort Them Out': At the Soldier of Fortune Convention, the Talk Was Cheap and the Bellies were Big," *Washington Post Magazine*, December 7, 1986.

171. Rone Tempest, "Peshawar: Many Lured by Intrigue," *LAT*, May 12, 1986.

172. Author interview with Karen McKay, former director of the Committee for a Free Afghanistan, July 20, 2015.

173. See Coll, *Ghost Wars*, 144–64, 200–203, 227, 230.

174. See Kepel, *Jihad*, 137.

175. See Roy, *Globalized Islam*, 291–95.

176. See Kepel, *Jihad*, 315–16.

177. Cuba's military intervention in Angola was remarkable because, as historian Piero Gleijeses writes, "no other Third World country had projected its military power beyond its immediate neighborhood." Gleijeses, *Visions of Freedom*, 9. As one CIA officer who served in Angola noted, the MPLA's success can be attributed to the fact that it was "the least tribal" of all of the guerrilla groups, and its members were "more effective, better educated, better trained and better motivated. The rank and file also were better motivated (particularly the armed combatants, who fought harder and with more determination)." See "Interview with Robert W. Hultslander, Last CIA Station Chief in Luanda, Angola," 1998, CWIHP, http://digitalarchive.wilsoncenter.org/document/118163, accessed May 11, 2017.

178. At the 1968 UNITA central committee meeting, Savimbi stated, "Our struggle against colonialists in Africa is at one with that of black people in America who are containing America's imperialists which are Portugal's suppliers of money and military equipment to destroy the black people of Angola. We re-affirm that we are conscious of the profound value and scope of the struggle of all black brothers in the Americas. We must combine our struggle." See UNITA pamphlet, "The Armed Struggle in Angola," no date, folder Revolutionary Movements UNITA Reports, box 4, Angola Subject Collection, HIWRP.

179. See Gleijeses, *Visions of Freedom*, 68–69.

180. Arnaud de Borchgrave and Michael Ledeen, "Reagan's African Army: Jonas Savimbi Awaits Help from Washington," *The Sun* (Baltimore), January 13 1981.

181. See Jack Wheeler's interview with Jonas Savimbi, "Angola Is the Key to Africa," *Human Events*, July 7, 1984.

182. "Stockwell Scores Savimbi," *Covert Action Information Bulletin*, no. 7, December 1979–January 1980, folder 3, box 10, Phillip Agee Papers, TLRWLA.

183. On Savimbi's transformation into a free market warrior, see John A. Markum, "The Politics of Survival: UNITA in Angola," *Africa Notes*, no. 8, February 18, 1983.

184. Arnaud de Borchgrave and Michael Ledeen, "Reagan's African Army: Jonas Savimbi Awaits Help from Washington," *The Sun* (Baltimore), January 13, 1981.

185. See Gleijeses, *Conflicting Missions*, 275–76; and Gleijeses, *Visions of Freedom*, 66. In 1978, Savimbi had also established an alliance with the king of Morocco, who, after prodding from a French intelligence officer, created an international fund with $15 million from donors in France, Iran, Saudi Arabia, and Morocco. See Minter, *Apartheid's Contras*, 151–52.

186. UNITA news release, Remarks of Jonas Savimbi before luncheon with black journalists, May Flower Hotel, Washington, D.C., February 2, 1986, folder Speeches and Writing by Jonas Savimbi, box 4, Angola Subject Collection, HIWRP.

187. Savimbi's visits to the United States were also encouraged by South Africa officials such as Foreign Minister Pik Botha who thought these trips were an "excellent idea" because would

"Savimbi would come across excellent on television." See cable from American Consulate, Cape Town to Assistant Secretary of State Chester Crocker, "SAG Proposal for Meeting with Savimbi," October 15, 1981, CO01076, CIA Covert Operations 1977–2010 collection, DNSA.

188. See Bernard Gwertzman, "Angolan Rebel Chief Sees Schultz and Weinberger," *NYT*, January 30, 1986, folder Revolutionary Movements: UNITA News Clippings and Articles, Angola Subject Collection, HIWRP; Memo, Schedule of Jonas Savimibi's visit to the United states, no date, folder American Security Council Speakers and Coalition for Peace through Strength, box 1, Morton Blackwell files, Series I, RRPL; and Charles R. Babcock, "Dallas Host Anti-Communist League," *WP*, September 17, 1985.

189. The American Enterprise Institute, originally called the American Enterprise Association, was founded in 1943 to challenge the New Deal and other forms of Keynesian thought in American life. By the late 1970s, it was one of the premier business organizations using private funds to create a world of free markets and unfettered capitalism. On its origins and activities, see Phillips-Fein, *Invisible Hands*, 60–67, 166–69, 171–75.

190. American Enterprise Institute, "A Conversation with Ernest Mulato: The Political and Military Struggle in Angola," March 2, 1979, folder Revolutionary Movements UNITA Reports, box 4, Angola Subject Collection, HIWRP.

191. The trip almost didn't happen due to persistent attempts by the State Department to deny Savimbi a visa, which only relented after sustained pressure from members of the American Security Council. See Letter from Senator Roger Jepsen to President Ronald Reagan, November 17, 1981, CO01090, CIA Covert Operations 1977–2010, DNSA; Letter from John Fischer to Ronald Reagan, December 9, 1981, folder American Security Council Speakers and Coalition for Peace through Strength, box 1, Morton Blackwell files, Series I, RRPL; and Memo, Schedule of Jonas Savimibi's visit to the United states, no date, folder American Security Council Speakers and Coalition for Peace through Strength, box 1, Morton Blackwell files, Series I, RRPL; Letter from Morton Blackwell to John Fischer, December 10, 1981, folder American Security Council Speakers and Coalition for Peace through Strength, box 1, Morton Blackwell files, Series I, RRPL.

192. See Steve Muffon, "Angolan Leader Courts U.S. Aid," *Wall Street Journal*, December 17, 1981.

193. Jonas Savimbi, "Angola: The Munich of Africa?," *WT*, December 30, 1985, folder Speeches and Writing by Jonas Savimbi, box 4, Angola Subject Collection, HIWRP.

194. Bernard Gwertzman, "Angolan Rebel Chief Sees Schultz and Weinberger," *NYT*, January 30, 1986, folder Revolutionary Movements: UNITA News Clippings and Articles, Angola Subject Collection, HIWRP. See also Scott, *Deciding to Intervene*, 126–30.

195. Kirkpatrick quoted in Frank, *Wrecking Crew*, 65.

196. Letter from John Fischer to Ronald Reagan, December 9, 1981, folder American Security Council Speakers and Coalition for Peace through Strength, box 1, Morton Blackwell files, Series I, RRPL.

197. R.W. Apple Jr. "Conservatives Push for U.S. Aid to Angola," *NYT*, December 16, 1985.

198. Ibid.

199. On the human rights abuses committed by Savimbi and UNITA, see Minter, *Account from Angola*, 7–8; and Gleijeses, *Visions of Freedom*, 300–302.

200. Smith Hepstone, "The War the World Forgot: SOFer in Angola, Part I," *SOF*, July 1981.

201. As Piero Gleijeses writes, Angola was "far away, hard to get to, and the Angolan government rarely granted visas to Americans." See Gleijeses, *Visions of Freedom*, 297.

202. See Smith Hempstone, "The War the World Forgot," *SOF*, August 1981.

203. See Testimony of Sam Joseph Bamieh, in *Possible Violation or Circumvention of the*

*Clark Amendment*, Hearing before the House Subcommittee on Africa, 100th Cong., 1st Sess., July 1, 1987, 1–2, 94–96; Neil A. Lewis, "Saudis Linked to Donations to Angola Rebels," *NYT*, July 2, 1987; and Ed Magnunson, "Yet Another Saudi Connection," *Time*, June 29, 1987.

204. See Franklin Foer, "The Quiet American," *Slate*, April 28, 2016.

205. Edward Nielan and George Archibald, "Angola's Struggle like DC Home Rule Fight," *WT*, February 3, 1986, folder Revolutionary Movements: UNITA News Clippings and Articles, Angola Subject Collection, HIWRP.

206. Patrick E. Tyler and David Ottaway, "The Selling of Jonas Savimbi: Success and a $600,000 Tab," *WP*, February 9, 1986.

207. See David B. Ottaway and Patrick E. Tyler, "Angolan Rebel Chief to Receive U.S. Praise, and Possibly Aid," *WP*, January 26, 1986. On the Black Caucus's opposition to Savimbi, see Simon Anekwe, "Caucus Warns Reagan over Angolan Relations," *New Amsterdam News*, December 19, 1981.

208. At its peak in 1986, Citizens for America had lobbyists in every congressional district. On Lehrman's past and the founding of Citizens for America, see Don Irwin, "Reagan Gives Backing to Conservative Group," *LAT*, August 4, 1983; and Suzanne Garment, "Conservatives Slowly Begin to Grow Up," *Wall Street Journal*, January 27, 1984.

209. As a young man, Wheeler had climbed the Matterhorn, hunted tigers in Vietnamese jungles, and founded a safari adventure company—experiences that made him see himself as something of a global citizen. See "Biographical Summary: Dr. Jack Wheeler," folder Outreach Working Group on Central America 3/20/1985, box OA13157, Robert Reilly Files, RRPL; Paul Dean, "Adventurer Helps Rebel Groups Fight Communist Forces," *LAT*, August 1, 1985. Wheeler was perhaps best known for his time Mozambique with the RENAMO guerrillas. See Jack Wheeler, "RENAMO: Winning One in Africa," *SOF*, February 1986; and Jack Wheeler, "RENAMO: Winning One in Africa Part II," *SOF*, March 1986.

210. Wheeler's travels led him to conclude that these were not isolated phenomena. He "was witnessing a spontaneous worldwide rejection of Soviet imperialism." Sidney Blumenthal, "Jack Wheeler's Adventures with the Freedom Fighters," *WP*, April 16, 1986.

211. Savimbi was, as one U.S. reporter put it, a "Rambo at the end of the world." Patrick E. Tyler, "'Rambo' at the End of the World," *WP*, July 30, 1986. Another reporter noted that "Jamba has no telecommunications or official air links with the outside world." Journalists who attended were stranded there for thirty hours, waiting for a charter plane. See "Foreign Resistance Group Forms New Organization,'" June 6, 1985, in *Foreign Broadcast Information Service Daily Report*, Middle East & Africa, FBIS-MEA-85–109. See also Walter Shapiro and Peter Younghusband, "Lehrman's Contra Conclave," *Newsweek*, June 17, 1986.

212. On Citizens for America's collaboration with the National Student Federation, see "The World This Week," *Mail and Guardian* (Johannesburg), June 14, 1984.

213. The mujahedin faction was controlled by Ghulam Wardak, whom Karen McKay had invited and shepherded to the conference. Author interview with Karen McKay, former director of the Committee for a Free Afghanistan, July 20, 2015.

214. These movements were represented by Nicaragua's Adolfo Calero, a major leader of the FDN Contras; Ghulam Wardak, a commander of the Afghan rebel group run by Gulbuddin Hekmatyar, known as Hezb-e-Islami; and Pa Kao Her, leader of the Ethnic Liberation Organization of Laos.

215. Jonas Savimbi, "Alocução Aquando do Encerramento da Conferencia da International Democratica," June 2, 1985, in Savimbi, *Por Um Futuro Melho*, 169–82, quotes from 171.

216. Ibid.

217. Alan Cowell, "Four Rebel Units Sign Anti-Soviet Pact," *NYT*, June 6, 1985. White

House staffer Patrick Buchanan convinced Reagan to send the letter, noting the president "is the single world figure to whom all of these movements (Nicaraguan Resistance, Afghans, etc.) look to for inspiration." See Memo from Patrick Buchanan to Robert C. McFarlane, "Freedom Fighters International," May 12, 1985, document no. IC01124; and Memo from Dana Rohrabacher to Patrick Buchanan, "Freedom Fighters," May 3, 1985, document no. IC01106, Iran-Contra Affair, DNSA.

218. See "Jamba Declaration of June 1985," *Civilian Military Assistance Newsletter* 1, no. 1, June 1985, document no. IC01094, Iran-Contra Affair, DNSA.

219. Author interview with Karen McKay, former director of the Committee for a Free Afghanistan, July 20, 2015.

220. Telegraph Agency of the Soviet Union in Russian for abroad (TASS), "'Anti-Communist Alliance' Formed by CIA 'Mercenaries,'" June 7, 1985, in *British Broadcasting Company Summary of Foreign Broadcasts*, USSR, International Affairs, General and Western Affairs, SU/7971/A1/1.

221. Jack Wheeler, letter to the editor, "Too Many Contras," *LAT*, July 26, 1985.

222. Jack Wheeler quoted in Paul Dean, "Adventurer Helps Rebel Groups Fight Communist Forces," *LAT*, August 1, 1985.

223. Frank, *Wrecking Crew*, 65.

224. The full run of the *Freedom Fighter* can be found at the Hesburgh Library at the University of Notre Dame, South Bend, Ind. For its donation campaign, see Fundraising Letter from Charles A. Moser to *Freedom Fighter* readership, November 1987, folder World Anti-Communist League 1987, box 339, GRR, RBML.

225. See Moser, ed., *Combat on Communist Territory*, 190–211.

226. For an overview of the IFF's founding and activities, see Frank, *Wrecking Crew*, 111–24. Frank also documents how the IFF emerged as leading voice of neoliberal economic policies in the developing world after the Cold War ended.

227. The International Freedom Foundation was part of the South African Military Intelligence (MI) branch's Operation Babushka. Established "to combat sanctions and undermine the African National Congress," it also "supported Jonas Savimbi and his rebel Angolan movement, UNITA." It was the brainchild of South African military intelligence officer Craig Williamson and South African politician Russell Crystal. See "A Blast from the Past," *Mail and Guardian* (Johannesburg), January 24, 2006; and Truth and Reconciliation Commission of South Africa, *Truth and Reconciliation Commission*, vol. 2, 526.

228. Abramoff received credits both as producer and writer. See *Red Scorpion*, dir. Joseph Zito, Abramoff Production/Scorpion Film Production, 1988. Abramoff insisted that the film was financed by private investors. But Craig Williamson told reporters that the South African military assisted in the movie's production in neighboring Namibia, "providing tanks and logistical support." See Phillip Van Niekerk, "How Apartheid Conned the West," *The Observer* (London), July 16, 1995.

229. As William Minter writes, "the UNITA lobby largely had its way with Congress" in late 1985 and early 1986, as their efforts to repeal the Clark Amendment led to their press for the resumption of U.S. military aid. See Minter, *Apartheid's Contras*, 154.

230. Jonas Savimbi, "Angola: The Munich of Africa?," *WT*, December 30, 1985, folder Speeches and Writing by Jonas Savimbi, box 4, Angola Subject Collection, HIWRP.

231. See Heritage Foundation, "Angola and the US: The Shape of a Prudent Compromise," *Heritage Foundation Backgrounder*, May 2, 1984, folder Revolutionary Movements UNITA Reports, box 4, Angola Subject Collection, HIWRP.

232. David B. Ottaway, "President Pledges to Help Savimbi," *WP*, January 31, 1986, and

Jeremiah O'Leary and Thomas D. Brandt, "Savimbi Gets Help but No Specifics," *WT*, January 31, 1986, in folder Revolutionary Movements: UNITA News Clippings and Articles, Angola Subject Collection, HIWRP.

233. Savimbi also met with Secretary of State George Shultz and Secretary of Defense Caspar Weinberger. See Bernard Gwertzman, "Angolan Rebel Chief Sees Schultz and Weinberger," *NYT*, January 30, 1986; and David B. Ottaway, "President Pledges to Help Savimbi," *WP*, January 31, 1986.

234. Gleijeses, *Visions of Freedom*, 307.

235. Patrick E. Tyler, "Rebel Success Turns on South African Aid," *WP*, July 30, 1986.

236. See Crocker, *High Noon in Southern Africa*. See also David B. Ottaway and Patrick Tyler, "DIA Alone in Optimism for Savimbi, CIA and DOD Fear UNITA Failure," *WP*, February 7, 1986.

237. See Scott, *Deciding to Intervene*, 149–51.

238. James Morrison, "Don't Make a Deal for Covert Aid, Conservatives Tell UNITA Leader," *WT*, January 30, 1986, folder Revolutionary Movements: UNITA News Clippings and Articles, Angola Subject Collection, HIWRP.

239. See Gleijeses, *Visions of Freedom*, 159–60.

240. Jonas Savimbi, "Angola: The Munich of Africa?," *WT*, December 30, 1985, folder Speeches and Writing by Jonas Savimbi, box 4, Angola Subject Collection, HIWRP.

241. See Robert S. Greenberg, "Right-Wing Groups Join in Capitol Hill Crusade to Help Savimbi's Anti-Communists in Angola," *Wall Street Journal*, November 25, 1985; and David B. Ottaway, "Savimbi Warns Oil Firms in Angola: Rebel Would Cancel Attack if They Stop 'Lobbying' Against Him," *WP*, February 4, 1986.

242. For instance the USCWF called for a national boycott of all Gulf/Chevron products to "counter oil company support of a communist government." See Maj. Gen. Henry Mohr, "Gulf Oil and Angola," *World Freedom Report: The USCWF Newsletter* 3, no. 3 (August 15, 1985); and Ted Abbott, "Angola, the Critical Domino," *World Freedom Report: The USCWF Newsletter* 3, no. 8 (February 15, 1986), WCCPM, UKS. See also John Hutchinson, "Angola Recommendations," 17th WACL Conference, San Diego, CA, September 3–7, 1984, folder World Anti-Communist League, box 339, GRR, RBML.

243. Jack Wheeler, "How UNITA Can Win," *Human Events*, February 8, 1986.

244. See Gleijeses, *Visions of Freedom*, 311.

245. See Westad and Quinn-Judge, eds., *Third Indochina War*.

246. National Security Intelligence memorandum, "Perspectives on Laos and Kampuchea," June 29, 1979, HN01958, National Security Agency: Organization and Operations, 1945–2009 collection, DNSA.

247. The origins of the secret army stretched back to at least 1960, when CIA agent Edgar "Pop" Buell met Vang Pao who told him that he could assemble an army of guerrillas that would be more effective than the Royal Lao Army. See Jacobs, *Universe Unraveling*, 198–200. The best overviews of the secret war are Warner, *Back Fire*; and Ahern, *Undercover Armies*, 1961–1973.

248. See National Security Intelligence memorandum, "Perspectives on Laos and Kampuchea," June 29, 1979, HN01958, National Security Agency: Organization and Operations, 1945–2009 collection, DNSA.

249. Scott, *Deciding to Intervene*, 87–89.

250. As one writer pointed out, the $5 million in U.S. aid paled in comparison with the $4 billion that Vietnam received from the Soviet Union. See Parris Chang, "America's Cambodian Dilemma," *Newsweek*, September 16, 1985.

251. The administration outlined this policy in National Security Decision Directive

158, "United States Policy in Southeast Asia (The Kampuchea Problem)," January 9, 1985, CH00688, China and the United States collection, DNSA. See also, Barbara Crossette, "U.S. Official Rules Out Arms for Cambodia Rebels," *NYT*, January 19, 1985.

252. See Vang, "Dreaming of Home, Dreaming of Land," 239.

253. Letter from Son Sann to Ronald Reagan, December 16, 1983, file 190000–359999, CO 081, WHORM Subject File, RRPL.

254. Letter from Mech Sary to Ronald Reagan, July 2, 1983, file Begin-189999, CO 081, WHORM Subject File, RRPL.

255. See Nguyen, "The People of the Fall."

256. Vang, "Dreaming of Home, Dreaming of Land," 238.

257. Son Sann of the KPNLF also lobbied members of the Heritage Foundation, which supported some of his travels. See Letter from Edwin J. Fuelner to William P. Clark, August 12, 1983, file Begin-189999, CO 081, WHORM Subject File, RRPL.

258. This campaign is described in "Kampuchea Chronology," *Voice of Indochina*, January 1986, folder Vietnam Resistance (1), RAC box 13, Richard T. Childress Files, RRPL.

259. The magazine had been raising money for anticommunist rebel groups since as early as 1979. As one 1979 ad claimed, *Soldier of Fortune* is "joining individuals concerned with Cambodia's fate and is organizing a fundraising campaign to assist Cambodian resistance forces operating inside that Southeast Asian nation. Readers are invited to contribute financial donations to this most worthy cause." See "Holocaust Again," *SOF*, January 1979.

260. David Mills and Dale Andrade, "Hanoi Hits Hard and Holds: A New Wrinkle along the Thai-Cambodian Border," *SOF*, July 1985, 51. See also Mike Winchester, "Vietnam's Vietnam: Players Change, The Game's the Same," *SOF*, February 1985, 41–47, 87; and Calhoun, "On the Side of Pol Pot," 37–40.

261. "Holocaust Again," *SOF*, January 1979.

262. See "Bleeding Hearts," *SOF*, April 1979.

263. See Patrice de Beer, "Hanoi Defectors Unite," *Far Eastern Economic Review*, March 13, 1981; Jacques Bekaert, "Key VN Exiles to form Anti-Hanoi Movement," *The Nation*, December 23, 1980; and Jacques Bekaert, "Sihanouk Meets VN Dissident," *The Nation*, January 11, 1981.

264. See Richard Sandza, "Refighting the Vietnam War," *Newsweek*, November 26, 1984, folder 42, box 10, Phillip Agee Papers, TLRWLA.

265. These schemes began almost immediately after the fall of South Vietnam. See George McArthur, "S. Viet Resistance Forces Estimated in Thousands," *LAT*, December 8, 1975. By 1985, a number of groups were claiming they were ready "to open up a home font inside Vietnam to carry out both psywar and armed operations." See Vietnam National Salvation Committee, "War or Peace in Indochina," no date, folder 023545 (2), CO 172, WHORM Subject File, RRPL

266. See Gary Jarlson, "Viet Struggle Gaining, Says Rebel Leader," *LAT*, January 27, 1985; and Guy Wright, "The Fall of Saigon," *San Francisco Examiner*, May 5, 1985.

267. As one Vietnamese activist was aware, "The people of the United States and Westerners in general are still reacting against the Vietnam War; they do not want to get involved in a similar conflict again." Letter from Doan Van Toai to Richard V. Allen, November 23, 1981, folder 023546–077999, CO 172, WHORM Subject File, RRPL.

268. Joanne Omang, "'Little Saigons' in U.S. Foster Hopes of Toppling Hanoi," *WP*, January 16, 1983

269. Richard Sandza, "Refighting the Vietnam War," *Newsweek*, November 26, 1984, folder 42, box 10, Phillip Agee Papers, TLRWLA.

270. Cable from National Security Council to Richard Childress, October 3, 1987, folder Vietnam resistance (1), RAC box 13, Richard T. Childress Files, RRPL.

271. Phuong Nguyen, "People of the Fall," 147.

272. See Scott, *Deciding to Intervene*, 109–11.

273. Allen, *Until the Last Man Comes Home*, 8–9.

274. The mission, ostensibly authorized by the Reagan administration, began after satellite imagery revealed shadows that "looked too long for Asians but just right for Caucasians." See Allen, *Until the Last Man Comes Home*, 222; and George C. Wilson and Art Harris, "Mercenaries Sent to Laos Seeking MIAs: U.S. Financed Team that Tried in Vain to Find Americans in Laos," *WP*, May 21, 1981.

275. See Art Harris and George C. Wilson, "MIA's Families Undeterred by Failure of Raid," *WP*, May 22, 1981.

276. A few weeks later, the Pathet Lao traded the American for a few thousand dollars and some forty boxes of medicine, "raising obvious questions as to why Laotian officials would not similarly ransom American POWs if they held them." See Allen, *Until the Last Man Comes Home*, 221. See also United Press International, "Private Raid on Laos Reported," *NYT*, February 1, 1983; and William Branigin, "Thai's Probe Adventurers Search for POWs in Laos," *WP*, February 22, 1983.

277. An outline of Gritz's activities from 1979–1978 can be found in Memo for Jack L. Courtemanche to Colin M. Powell, December 24, 1987, file Gritz (2), box 16, Richard T. Childress Files; and National Security Council, "Activities of James Gritz, U.S. Army Retired," no date, file Gritz (2), box 16, Richard T. Childress Files, RRPL.

278. Allen, *Until the Last Man Comes Home*, 225.

279. Zeskind, *Blood and Politics*, 297; Allen, *Until the Last Man Comes Home*, 222.

280. See *Missing in Action*, dir. Chuck Zito; *Missing in Action 2: The Beginning*, dir. Lance Hool; *Braddock: Missing in Action III*, dir. Aaron Norris.

281. See *Rambo: First Blood Part II*, dir. George P. Cosmatos. On *Rambo* and similar films as narratives of male violence in the post-Vietnam era, see Franklin, *MIA, Or Mythmaking in America*, esp. 150–55; and Gibson, *Warrior Dreams*.

282. See "Reagan Gets Idea from 'Rambo' for Next Time," *LAT*, July 1, 1985. In Reagan's mind, the need to save those hostages, more than any other concern, was what justified Oliver North's extralegal scheme to free them by secretly selling weapons to Iran. As historian Michael Allen writes, "Captivity served as the link between Vietnam and Iran-Contra for Reagan and those around him." Allen, *Until the Last Man Comes Home*, 227.

283. Singlaub was a major backer of Project Freedom, which published information about missing soldiers. For a summary of his views, which condemned how the Reagan administration had given "little visibility" to the issue since "he came to office," see "The POW/MIA Issue," *World Freedom Report: The USCWF Newsletter* 3, No. 9 (February 15, 1986). See also Col. Laird Gutterson, "POWs—The Forgotten Ones," *World Freedom Report: The USCWF Newsletter* 3, No. 4 (September 15, 1985), WCCPM, UKS.

284. See Jim Graves, "Hoaglund Hoax: Gritz Caught in War Lie," *SOF*, Spring 1983, 51–53.

285. Brown with Spencer, *I Am Soldier of Fortune*, 143.

286. See Testimony of James Patrick Coyne, in Senate Committee on Veterans' Affairs, *Live Sightings of Americans Listed Missing in Action in Southeast Asia*, 146–61.

287. Brown with Spencer, *I Am Soldier of Fortune*, 148–49, 178–89.

288. See Gritz's forged Letter of Promise and Authorization, October 23, 1985, file Gritz (1), box 16, Richard T. Childress Files, RRPL.

289. Letter from Richard T. Childress to Ms. Segault, November 25, 1983, file Gritz (1), box 16, Richard T. Childress Files, RRPL.

## Conclusion

1. U.S. Congress, *Report of the Congressional Committees Investigating the Iran-Contra Affair*, 144.

2. Hasenfus claimed to friends and family that he worked for the CIA's clandestine Air America service, which flew weapons into Laos and Vietnam, which allowed him to make "more money than the law allows." See Andrew H. Malcolm, "Captured American Recalled as Seeker of Adventure," *NYT*, October 9, 1986.

3. See Maura Dolan, "Survivor an Ex-Marine and Skydiver," *LAT*, October 8, 1986; and LeoGrande, *Our Own Backyard*, 478.

4. U.S. Congress, *Report of the Congressional Committees Investigating the Iran-Contra Affair*, 144.

5. In a photo circulated around the world, a Sandinista soldier marched Hasenfus through the jungle with his hands tied. The photo first appeared under the headline "Se atrevieron... y así quedaron," ("He dared... And there he is"), *Barricada* (Nicaragua), October 8, 1986.

6. Although Hasenfus insisted he did not know who ran the operation, his testimony provided many details about key players such as Richard Secord and locations like the secret airbase in Ilopango, El Salvador. See James LeMoyne, "Hasenfus Says He Does Not Know Who Ran Nicaragua Operations," *NYT*, October 20, 1986; and Marjorie Miller, "Caught in U.S.-Sandinista Struggle, Hasenfus Says," *LAT*, October 25, 1986.

7. For allegations that Singlaub was in the Philippines arming and training paramilitaries, see "Philippine Army Officer Reveal Singlaub Offer," *Christian Science Monitor*, November 23, 1987; C. S. Manegold, "Singlaub linked to Private Bid to Aid Manila in War on Rebels," *BG*, February 16, 1987; and Sheila Coronel, "Opposition, U.S. Rightists Reportedly Linked," *Manila Chronicle*, October 25, 1987, in *Foreign Broadcast Information Service*, Daily Report, East Asia, FBIS-EAS-87-207.

8. See Singlaub and McConnell, *Hazardous Duty*, 504.

9. See Doyle McManus, "Singlaub Played Double Role in Aid to Contras," *LAT*, October 13, 1986; and "Private Pipeline to the Contras: A Vast Network," *NYT*, October 22, 1986; Peter Dale Scott, "Nicaragua: A Dubious Innocence," *Baltimore Sun*, October 13, 1986; and Peter Dale Scott, "Tracing CIA Ties to Singlaub and Southern Air," *The Post* (no publication information), October 19, 1986 folder Singlaub, container 12, Nicaraguan Information Center Records, BL.

10. See "Schultz Denies Link to Downed Plane," *LAT*, October 7, 1986.

11. Oliver North later claimed that he engineered the deception to protect the lives of his American agents and their allies in Nicaragua, Honduras, El Salvador, and Costa Rica. See U.S. Congress, *Report of the Congressional Committees Investigating the Iran-Contra Affair*, 144–50.

12. Testimony of John K. Singlaub, in *Joint Hearings before the Senate Subcommittee on Secret Military Assistance to Iran and the Nicaraguan Opposition*, 196.

13. Byrne, *Iran-Contra*, 289.

14. Ibid., 286, 289–306.

15. U.S. Senate Select Committee on Secret Military Assistance to Iran and the Nicaraguan Opposition, and House Select Committee to Investigate Covert Arms Transactions with Iran, *Report of the Congressional Committees Investigating the Iran-Contra Affair*, 21.

16. Arthur R. Liman quoted in Byrne, *Iran-Contra*, 289.

17. Testimony of John K. Singlaub, in *Joint Hearings before the Senate Subcommittee on Secret Military Assistance to Iran and the Nicaraguan Opposition*, 72–73.

18. Ibid.

19. As Singlaub put it, his work arming the Contras was "in no way suggested or directed by anyone in the U.S. government." Ibid., 71.

20. According to Edgar Chamorro Coronel, who ran the Contras' media operations, "one of our most important operations . . . was to create the impression that our funding came from 'private' sources, rather than the CIA." Although he didn't name the specific private sources, there is reason to believe that he was referring to Singlaub, since Singlaub was one of the leading fundraisers for the Contras.

21. Testimony of John K. Singlaub, in *Joint Hearings before the Senate Subcommittee on Secret Military Assistance to Iran and the Nicaraguan Opposition*, 85, 181–82.

22. On conservatives' adulation of North, see Gibson, *Warrior Dreams*, 283–85; and Jeffords, *Hard Bodies*, 57.

23. Singlaub and McConnell, *Hazardous Duty*, 505.

24. Ibid., 517.

25. Testimony of John K. Singlaub, in *Joint Hearings before the Senate Subcommittee on Secret Military Assistance to Iran and the Nicaraguan Opposition*, 193–94.

26. Ibid., 193.

27. See U.S. Department of Justice National Office Technical Advice Memorandum, IRS Report on Withdrawing U.S. Council for World Freedoms Tax Exemption, Unclassified, Memorandum. November 25, 1987, IC 04294, Iran-Contra Affair, DNSA; "USCWF under Attack," *World Freedom Report: The USCWF Newsletter* 3, no. 5 (October 15, 1985); and "IRS Audit Costly," *World Freedom Report: The USCWF Newsletter* 3, no. 7 (December 15, 1985), WCCPM.

28. Anderson and Anderson, *Inside the League*.

29. See Jack Anderson and Joseph Spear, "Anti-Communist League Unleashed," *WP*, August 9, 1986; Fred Clarkson, "Behind the Supply Lines," *Covert Action Information Bulletin*, no. 25 (Winter 1986): 56, 50–53; Fred Clarkson, "God Is Phasing Out Democracy," *Covert Action Information Bulletin*, no. 27 (Spring 1987): 36–46; and Howard Goldenthal, "Moonies, WACL, and Vigilantes: The Religious Right in the Philippines," *Covert Action Information Bulletin*, no. 29 (Summer 1987): 21–24.

30. Contemporary commentators made this same point. See Larry Ceplair, "Review: *Inside the League*," *LAT*, September 28, 1986.

31. See "Warning on New Book," *World Freedom Report: The USCWF Newsletter* 3, no. 9 (February 15, 1986), WCCPM.

32. Beatrice Eastman "Singlaub's Plots in Southeast Asia," no publication info, folder Singlaub, container 12, Nicaraguan Information Center Records, BL.

33. In one pamphlet, the Christics described how, "for a quarter century, a Secret Team of U.S. military and CIA officials, acting both officially and on their own, have waged secret wars, toppled governments, trafficked in drugs, assassinated political enemies, stolen from the U.S. government, and subverted the will of the Constitution, Congress, and the American people." See Christic Institute pamphlet, "Behind the Iran/Contra Affair," no date, folder Christic Institute, container 12, Nicaragua Information Center Records, BL.

34. For instance, while Singlaub visited the Costa Rican ranch of American expatriate John Hull, where Contras shipped weapons and drugs, no evidence has ever emerged that Singlaub knew of, let alone directed, such activities. But the issue of Contra cocaine smuggling is a black hole of historical inquiry. In the late 1980s and early 1990s, many former Contras testified that they smuggled drugs into California and elsewhere, and that the CIA endorsed and enabled their activities. Their testimonies formed the most damning parts of a 1989 Senate report, chaired by John Kerry, which briefly made news headlines. In 1996, Gary Webb, a journalist at the *San Jose Mercury*, resuscitated these claims in a series of articles based

upon new evidence, mostly from the federal trial testimony and depositions of a convicted Nicaraguan smuggler-turned-informant named Danilo Blandón. Webb traced the smuggling operation from Colombia through Nicaragua and, finally, to the streets of Los Angeles and San Francisco where gangs sold it as crack. His reporting generated a widely held theory that the CIA itself smuggled cocaine into black communities, perhaps with the intent of destroying them from within. But Webb always maintained his story didn't prove that. And as historian Peter Kornbluh has documented, that narrative overstated the power of the CIA and its intentions. The cocaine ended up in California because the CIA looked the other way while Nicaraguans and Colombians smuggled it. It did not get there because CIA officers brought it in themselves. Moreover, there is no credible evidence to suggest the CIA had a nefarious plan to poison black America with crack cocaine. Rather, CIA leaders did not think about black communities at all. On the Contras, the CIA, and cocaine trafficking, see Senate Committee on Foreign Relations, *Drugs, Law Enforcement, and Foreign Policy*; Gary Webb, "America's 'Crack' Plague Has Roots in Nicaragua War," *San Jose Mercury*, August 18, 1996; "Shadowy Origins of Crack Epidemic," *San Jose Mercury*, August 19, 1996; "War on Drugs Has Unequal Impact on Black Americans," *San Jose Mercury*, August 20, 1996; and Webb, *Dark Alliance*; and Kornbluh, "Contras, Crack, and the CIA," 35–39.

35. See *Tony Avirgan and Martha Honey, Plaintiffs, v. John Hull, et al., Defendants*, Case No. 86–1146-CIV-KING, United States District Court for the Southern District of Florida, 705 F. Supp. 1544; 1989.

36. See James Ridgeway, "The Trial that Wasn't: Christics Struggle to Stay in Court," *Village Voice*, January 10, 1989; and Zeskind, *Blood and Politics*, 296.

37. See Fundraising Letter from Thomas R. Spencer for Singlaub's Legal Defense, February 29, 1989, folder Singlaub, box 298, GRR, RBML.

38. Letter to Linas Kojelis, no date, folder Jack Singlaub, OA 18286, Linas Kojelis Files, RRPL. For another defense of Singlaub and Shackley, as well as condemnation of the Christic suit, see Cliff Kincaid, "The Christic Institute's Legal Terrorism," *Human Events*, November 28, 1987, folder Singlaub, box 298, GRR, RBML. For conservatives' attempts to destroy the Christic Institute, see Cyrus Sanai, "Conservatives and a Contra Celebration," *WP*, August 3, 1988.

39. For a summary of their arguments, see "The Christic Mystics: Dealing in Fantasy, Not Fact," *WP*, October 8, 1988, folder Singlaub, box 298, GRR, RBML; see also Singlaub and McConnell, *Hazardous Duty*, 509.

40. See *Tony Avirgan and Martha Honey, Plaintiffs, v. John Hull, et al., Defendants*, Case No. 86–1146-CIV-KING, United States District Court for the Southern District of Florida, 705 F. Supp. 1544; 1989; and "Legal Fees Granted to Defendants in Contra Arms Case," *WP*, February 4, 1989.

41. On that shift, see Lee Edwards, "Remaining Vigilant," *BG*, August 13, 1990, folder World Anti-Communist League 1987, box 339, GRR, RBML.

42. Today, the ABN is a historical touchstone for nationalists in many Eastern European countries who draw links between the anti-Soviet fervor of the Cold War and contemporary ire over Russian intervention in and annexation of Ukrainian territory. For instance, in April 2015, Ukrainian politicians sought to memorialize the Anti-Bolshevik Bloc of Nations and the Ukrainian Insurgent Army. See Zenon Zawada, "Rada Approves Historic Bills to Part with Soviet Legacy," *Ukrainian Weekly*, April 17, 2015.

43. Insofar as a truly global conservative or right-wing movement exists today, it is composed of neoliberal economists and their acolytes. The most compelling analysis of their collaboration on the world stage is Klein, *Shock Doctrine*.

44. Alexander Provan, "Interview with Lt. Col. Robert K. Brown, founder, editor, and publisher of Soldier of Fortune," *Magazine Bazaar*, http://bidoun.org/articles/magazine-

bazaar-interview-with-lt-col-robert-k-brown-founder-editor-and-publisher-of-soldier-of-fortune, accessed May 11, 2017.

45. See Rob Krott, "Looking for War in All the Wrong Places," *SOF*, September 1992; Robert C. McKenzie, "Combat Zone: Croatia," *SOF*, February 1992; Robert K. Brown, "Soldier of Fortune Trains the King's Cadre," *SOF*, April 1993.

46. See Silverstein, *Private Warriors*, 145.

47. See Barlow, *Executive Outcomes*, 408. For an overview of Executive Outcome's war in post–Cold War Africa, see Cilliers and Mason, *Peace, Profit, or Plunder*.

48. See Al J. Venter, "Market Forces: How Hired Guns Succeeded where the United Nations Failed," *Jane's International Defense Review*, March 1998.

49. For the best overview of Executive Outcomes' organization and operations, see Singer *Corporate Warriors*, 101–18.

50. See Renae Merle, "Looking beyond the Warzones: DynCorp, Big in Iraq and Afghanistan, Seeks to Diversify," *WP*, November 6, 2000; and Marilyn Alva, "DynCorp International: Falls Church, Virginia Contractor Helps the Military in the World's Most Troubled Places," *Investor's Business Daily*, August 5, 2009.

51. For instance, in the former Yugoslavia, Military Professional Resources Incorporated trained the Croat military which was simultaneously receiving arms from a network of private weapons dealers. See Ken Silverstein, "Privatizing War," *The Nation*, July 7, 1998.

52. On the Prince family's history and relationship to the conservative movement, see Scahill, *Blackwater*, 1–24.

53. Prince with Coburn, *Civilian Warriors*, 14.

54. Ibid., x.

55. Blackwater launched raids and captured suspected insurgents. It protected important bases, factories, and power plants, as well as a slew of American leaders, including Paul Bremer, the head of the American occupation in Iraq, and then-Senator Barack Obama. On Blackwater's rise, see Scahill, *Blackwater*, 25–90; and Prince and Coburn, *Civilian Warriors*, chapter 4.

56. On the motivations of former U.S. soldiers who joined private military firms, see Pelton, *Licensed to Kill*.

57. Prince and Coburn, *Civilian Warriors*, 98.

58. Ibid., 62–63.

59. Mazzetti, *Way of the Knife*, 204.

60. Ibid., 207–11.

61. Unnamed U.S. official quoted in Dexter Filkins and Mark Mazzetti, "Contractors Tied to Efforts to Track and Kill Militants," *NYT*, March 14, 2010.

62. Indeed, most historical explanations that link PMFs to the older world of mercenaries skip over the Cold War altogether. For instance, in his otherwise excellent study of private military firms, P. W. Singer devotes only a few paragraph to the Cold War, in which discusses the work of "individual ex-soldiers" who became mercenaries, of which the white mercenaries hired by Belgian companies in the Congo in the early 1960s serve as the most useful illustration. See Singer, *Corporate Warriors*, 37–38. See also McFate, *Modern Mercenary*; and Schaub and Kelty, eds., *Private Military and Security Contractors*.

63. See Warrick, *Black Flags*; Cockburn, *The Rise of the Islamic State*; Unnamed author and Ben Hubbard, "Life in a Jihadist Capital: Order with a Darker Side," *NYT*, July 23, 2014; Katie Zavadski, "ISIS Now Has a Network of Military Affiliates in 11 Countries around the World," *New York Magazine*, November 23, 2014; Mary Anne Weaver, "Her Majesty's Jihadists," *NYT Magazine*, April 14, 2015; and Rukmini Callimachi, "ISIS and the Lonely Young American," *NYT*, June 27, 2015.

64. Jean Song, "Bill O'Reilly Proposes Mercenary Army to Fight Terror," *CBS News*, September 23, 2014, http://www.cbsnews.com/news/bill-oreilly-on-creating-mercenary-army-with-troops-from-across-world-to-fight-terror/, accessed August 7, 2015.

65. Quoted in Jose Coscareli, "President Bill O'Reilly Has His Own Insane Plan to Destroy ISIS: 25,000 Mercenaries," *New York Magazine*, September 24, 2014, http://nymag.com/daily/intelligencer/2014/09/president-bill-oreilly-has-a-plan-to-fight-isis.html, accessed August 7, 2015.

66. Bob Cesca, "Bill O'Reilly's Outlandish Proposal for an Army of 25,000 Mercenaries," *The Daily Banter*, September 24, 2014, http://thedailybanter.com/2014/09/bill-oreilly-proposes-a-mercenary-army-to-fight-isis/, accessed August 7, 2015.

67. See Belew, *Bring the War Home*; Gibson, *Warrior Dreams*; Stern, *Force Upon the Plain*; Levitas, *Terrorist Next Door*; Mulloy, *American Extremism*; and Wright, *Patriots, Politics, and the Oklahoma City Bombing*.

68. See Shapira, *Waiting for José*.

69. First published in 1978 by white supremacist William Pierce (pen name Andrew MacDonald), the book remains a key text for many racist, right-wing militia groups today. See Pierce, *The Turner Diaries*.

70. See the Federal Bureau of Investigation declassified file on the Covenant, the Sword and the Arm of the Lord, 100-HQ-487200, FBI-FOIA, https://vault.fbi.gov/The%20Covenant%20The%20Sword%20The%20Arm%20of%20the%20Lord%20, accessed February 11, 2016.

71. See Tom Stites and James Coates, "Siege Over, Neo-Nazis Surrender," *CT*, April 23, 1985; Wayne King, "23 in White Supremacist Group Are Indicted on Federal Charges," *NYT*, April 6, 1985; Wayne King, "Neo-Nazi Dream of a Racist Territory in Pacific Northwest Refuses to Die," *NYT*, July 1986; and Zeskind, *Blood and Politics*, 96–106.

72. See John E. Yang, "Idaho Siege Ends as Fugitive Gives Up in Killing of Marshall," *WP*, September 1, 1992; Ashley Dunn, "Surrender Ends Mountain Siege," *LAT*, September 1, 1992; Zeskind, *Blood and Politics*, 301–7; and Jess Walter, *Ruby Ridge*.

73. See Levitas, *Terrorist Next Door*, 301–4; Zeskind, *Blood and Politics*, 329–31.

74. See Wright, *Patriots, Politics, and the Oklahoma City Bombing*, 139–65.

75. On McVeigh's belief in the New World Order, see Jon Ronson, "Conspirators," *The Guardian*, May 5, 2001; and Berlet, *Right-wing Populism in America*, 301–3.

76. Garry Wills, "The New Revolutionaries," *New York Review of Books*, August 10, 1995.

77. LaPierre, *Guns, Crime, and Freedom*, 19–20. Emphasis in original.

78. Wills, "The New Revolutionaries."

79. That theory spread across right-wing militia literature, but its leading proponent was Pat Robertson, a popular conservative evangelical preacher and media figure, who published *The New World Order* in 1991.

80. Anti-Defamation League, "The Oath Keepers: Anti-Government Extremists Recruiting Police and Military," 2015, at http://www.adl.org/assets/pdf/combating-hate/The-Oath-Keepers-ADL-Report.pdf, accessed February 11, 2016. The last action resulted in a months-long standoff that only ended after a violent clash between self-proclaimed patriots and federal agents—though a jury soon acquitted the protestors. The acquittal of the self-proclaimed patriots who took over the Oregon compound suggests that many Americans supported their actions. See Courtney Sherwood and Kirk Johnson, "Bundy Brothers Acquitted in Takeover of Oregon Wildlife Refuge," *NYT*, October 27, 2016.

81. On the inward turn of militarization at the end of the Cold War, see Sherry, *In the Shadow of War*. On the rise of SWAT teams and paramilitary policing, see Balko, *Rise of the Warrior Cop*.

82. In the fall of 2001, the Southern Poverty Law Center devoted an entire issue of its *Intelligence Report* to documenting and explaining how the "radical right has become increasingly international in scope." See SPLC, *Intelligence Report*, no. 103 (Fall 2001). See also Zeskind, *Blood and Politics*, 205–57; and Lee, *Beast Reawakens*, 237–383. Some had connections to the anticommunist international. A white supremacist from Atlanta named Sam Dickson, who attended the 1979 World Anti-Communist League conference in Paraguay, traveled across Europe to network with Germany's neo-Nazi National Democratic Party, Italy's openly fascist Forza Nuova, the Russian Imperial Movement, and other members of Europe's white-nationalist extreme Right. See "American Racists Join European Counterparts at Russian Meeting," Southern Poverty Law Center, *Intelligence Report* (Summer 2015); and Alexander Zaitchik, "From Atlanta to Asunción," Southern Poverty Law Center, *Intelligence Report* at https://www.splcenter.org/fighting-hate/intelligence-report/2015/atlanta-asunci%C3%B3n, accessed June 6, 2017.

83. Mark Cotterill quoted in Mark Potok, "The New Internationalism," Southern Poverty Law Center, *Intelligence Report* (Fall 2001).

84. Lee, *Beast Reawakens*, 297–98.

85. The best account of Breivik's massacre is Seierstad, *One of Us*.

86. "Norway Mass Killer Anders Behring Breivik Studied al Qaeda, Oklahoma City Bombing before Rampage," *CBS News*, April 2, 2012, at http://www.cbsnews.com/news/norway-mass-killer-anders-behring-breivik-studied-al-qaeda-oklahoma-city-bombing-before-rampage, accessed May 15, 2017.

87. Scott Shane, "Killings in Norway Spotlight Anti-Muslim Thought in U.S.," *NYT*, July 24, 2011; Spencer likes to talk of "an ethno-state that would be a gathering point for all Europeans." C. J. Ciaramella, "Some Well-dressed White Nationalists Gathered in DC Last Weekend," *Vice News*, October 29, 2013, https://www.vice.com/en_us/article/some-well-dressed-white-nationalists-gathered-in-dc-last-weekend, accessed June 6, 2017.

88. Elaine Ganley, "'Revolution for France': Le Pen Promises the 'Wind of History' has turned with Trump and Brexit," *The Independent* (Dublin), May 15, 2007, at http://www.independent.ie/world-news/europe/revolution-for-france-le-pen-promises-the-wind-of-history-has-turned-with-brexit-and-trump-35425188.html, accessed May 15, 2017.

89. Dale Hurd, Interview with Geert Wilders, "Wilders Could Take Netherlands Out of EU," *CBS News*, February 2, 2017 at http://www1.cbn.com/cbnnews/world/2017/february/exclusive-interview-wilders-will-take-netherlands-out-of-eu, accessed May 15, 2017.

90. On Manafort's career since the 1980s, see Franklin Foer, "The Quiet American," *Slate*, April 28, 2016, at http://www.slate.com/articles/news_and_politics/politics/2016/04/paul_manafort_isn_t_a_gop_retread_he_s_made_a_career_of_reinventing_tyrants.html, accessed June 17, 2017. Manafort resigned his position as Trump's campaign chairman in August 2016, after allegations surfaced about his business dealings in Ukraine and his efforts on behalf of the Russian government. See Maggie Haberman and Johnathan C. Martin, "Paul Manafort Quits Donald Trump's Campaign after a Tumultuous Run," *NYT*, August 19, 2016. As of this writing, Manafort remains under investigation for his activities in Ukraine and a raft of other financial matters. See Associated Press, "Special Counsel's Investigation Includes Manafort Case," *LAT*, June 26, 2017.

91. Richard Fausset, "For Trump Voters, Uncertainty Mixes with Elation," *NYT*, November 9, 2016; Monica Crowley, "Donald Trump and the New American Revolution," *WT*, November 9, 2016. Even Trump's critics employed the same terms: "We may as well call this what it is: a revolution." See Richard Wolffe, "Donald Trump's Victory Is Nothing Short of a Revolution," *Guardian*, November 9, 2016.

92. Nick Adams, "Trump Revolution Could Be More Incredible than Reagan Revolution," Townhall.com, March 23, 2016, https://townhall.com/columnists/nickadams/2016/03/23/trump-revolution-could-be-more-incredible-than-reagan-revolution-n2138333, accessed May 15, 2017.

93. See Jeremey W. Peters, "Bannon's Worldview," *NYT*, April 8, 2017; and Tara Isabella Burton, "Steve Bannon Shares a Fascist's Obsession with Cleansing, Apocalyptic War," *The Telegraph* (London), February 7, 2017.

# Bibliography

## Archival Sources

Paraguay

Centro de Documentación y Archivo para la Defensa de los Derechos Humanos, Asunción, Paraguay

United Kingdom

United Kingdom National Archives, Kew Gardens, London, United Kingdom
- FCO 36/1872
- FCO 36/1873
- FCO 36/1874
- FCO 36/1875
- FCO 36/1876
- FO 371/86154
- FO 371/94964

United States

Bancroft Library, University of California, Berkeley, Calif.
- Nicaraguan Information Center Records

Chicago History Museum, Chicago, Ill.
- Clarence Manion Papers

Columbia University Rare Books and Manuscripts Library, New York, N.Y.
- Group Research Inc. Records

Gerald Ford Presidential Library, Ann Arbor, Mich.
- Leo Cherne Papers
- National Security Adviser, NSC Latin American Affairs Staff: Files, 1974–77
- National Security Adviser, Presidential Agency File, 1974–77
- National Security Adviser, Presidential Country Files for Africa, 1974–77
- National Security Adviser, Presidential Name File, 1974–77
- Ron Nessen Files
- White House Central Files Name Files
- White House Central Files Subject Files

Hoover Institution on War, Revolution, and Peace, Palo Alto, Calif.
- Afghanistan Subject Collection

    Angola Subject Collection
    Enrique Bermudez Papers
    William J. Casey Papers
    Cuban Freedom Committee Papers
    Donald Dozer Papers
    Kyrill Drenikoff Papers
    Walter Judd Papers
    Luis Kutner Papers
    Edward Lansdale Papers
    Marx Lewis Papers
    Marvin Liebman Papers
Jimmy Carter Presidential Library, Atlanta, Ga.
    Office of the Chief of Staff Files
        Hamilton Jordan's Confidential Files
Library of Congress, Washington, D.C.
    Herbert Philbrick Papers
    William A. Rusher Papers
National Security Archive, George Washington University, Washington, D.C.
    Center for National Security Studies Document Collection
    Douglas Valentine Vietnam Collection
Ronald Reagan Presidential Library, Simi Valley, Calif.
    David S. Addington Files
    Morton C. Blackwell Files
    Richard T. Childress Files
    Linas Kojelis Files
    Constantine Menges Files
    Oliver North Files
    Robert Reilly Files
    Faith Whittlesey Files
    National Security Council Records
        African Affairs Directorate
        Latin American Affairs Directorate
    NSC Country Files—Central America
    White House Legal Task Force Record
    White House Office of Records Management Subject Files
        Subject File C002
        Subject File C006
        Subject File C081
        Subject File C172
        Subject File ME 002
        Subject File ND 007
        Subject File ND 017
    White House Office of Records Managements Alphabetical Files
        John Singlaub
Tamiment Library and Robert F. Wagner Labor Archives, New York University, New York, N.Y.
    Philip Agee Papers
    Church League of America Collection

Communist Party of the United States of America Files
Wilcox Collection of Contemporary Political Movements, Spencer Research Library,
    University of Kansas, Lawrence, Kans.

## Digital Archives

Digital National Security Archive, George Washington University, Washington, D.C.
    Afghanistan Collection
    CIA Covert Operations, 1977–2010
    El Salvador, 1980–1984
    Iran-Contra Affair
    National Security Agency: Organization and Operations, 1945–2009
    Nicaragua Collection
Cold War International History Project, Wilson Center for International Studies and the
        Smithsonian Museum, Washington, D.C.
    Soviet Invasion of Afghanistan Collection
Cold War International History Project, Wilson Center for International Studies and
        Syngman Rhee University, Seoul, South Korea
    Asian Peoples Anti-Communist League documents
University of Miami Libraries Digital Collections, Miami, Fla.
    Cuban Heritage Collection
        Truth about Cuba Committee Records

## Government Documents

Department of Defense. *Military Assistance Command Studies and Observation Group Documentation Study.* Appendix C, A-14
U.S. Congress. House of Representatives. *Report of the Congressional Committees Investigating the Iran-Contra Affair.* H.R. Rept. 100-433, S. Rept. 100-216, 100th Congress, 1st Sess., November 17, 1987.
U.S. Congress. House Special Subcommittee on Investigations of the Committee on International Relations. *Mercenaries in Africa.* 94th Cong., 2nd Sess., August 9, 1976.
U.S. Congress. House Subcommittee on Africa, Committee on Foreign Affairs. *Economic Sanctions against Rhodesia.* 94th Cong., 2nd Sess., May 14, 16, 21, 1976.
U.S. Congress. House Subcommittee on Africa, Committee on International Relations. *U.S. Policy toward Rhodesia.* 95th Cong., 1st Sess., Jun. 8, 1977.
U.S. Congress. Senate Committee on Foreign Relations. *Drugs, Law Enforcement, and Foreign Policy.* Hearings. 100th Cong., 1st Sess., May 27, July 15, and October 30, 1987
U.S. Congress. Senate Committee on Veterans' Affairs. *Live Sightings of Americans Listed Missing in Action in Southeast Asia.* Hearings. 99th Cong., 2nd sess., 1986.
U.S. Congress. Senate Select Committee on Intelligence, National Intelligence Reform and Organization Act: Hearings on S. 2525, 95th Cong., 2nd Sess., 1978.
U.S. Congress. Senate Select Committee on Secret Military Assistance to Iran and the Nicaraguan Opposition. *Report of the Congressional Committees Investigating the Iran-Contra Affair with Supplemental, Minority, and Additional Views.* S. Rept. No. 100-216, 100th Cong., 1st Sess., 1987.
U.S. Congress. Senate Select Committee to Study Governmental Operations with Respect to Intelligence Activities. *Alleged Assassination Plots Involving Foreign Leaders.* Washington, D.C.: U.S. Government Printing Office, 1975.

———. *Covert Action in Chile: 1963–1973.* Washington, D.C.: U.S. Government Printing Office, 1976.

———. *Final Report.* Washington, D.C.: U.S. Government Printing Office, 1976.

———. *Hearings on Covert Action.* Washington, D.C.: U.S. Government Printing Office, 1975.

U.S. Congress. Senate Subcommittee on Secret Military Assistance to Iran and the Nicaraguan Opposition and House Select Committee to Investigate Covert Arms Transactions with Iran. *Joint Hearings before the Senate Subcommittee on Secret Military Assistance to Iran and the Nicaraguan Opposition and House Select Committee to Investigate Covert Arms Transactions with Iran.* 100th Cong., 1st sess. May, 20, 21, 27, and 28, 1987.

U.S. Congress. Senate Subcommittee on Security and Terrorism, Committee on the Judiciary, *Mercenary Training Camps,* S. Hrg. 99–591, 99th Cong., 1st Sess., 1985.

U.S. Department of State. *Foreign Relations of the United States.* Washington, D.C.: U.S. Government Printing Office, various volumes.

United Nations. *From Madness to Hope: The 12-Year War in El Salvador.* Report of the Commission on the Truth for El Salvador, United Nations Document S/25500. New York: Department of Public Information, 1993.

## U.S. Newspapers, Magazines, and Other Periodicals

Atlanta Daily World
Atlanta Journal Constitution
Boston Globe
Chicago Daily Defender
Chicago Tribune
Christian Science Monitor
Covert Action Information Bulletin
The Daily Banter
Group Research Report
Human Events
International Business Times
Investor's Business Daily
Los Angeles Times
Miami Herald
The Nation
The National Catholic Reporter
National Review
Newsweek
New York Herald Tribune
New York Magazine
New York Review of Books
New York Times
New York Times Magazine
Palm Beach Post
Ramparts
The Reporter
San Francisco Examiner
San Jose Mercury
Soldier of Fortune
St. Petersburg Times
The Sun (Baltimore)
Time
Toledo Blade
Ukrainian Bulletin (New York)
Ukrainian Quarterly (New York)
U.S. News and World Report
Village Voice (New York)
Wall Street Journal
Washington Post
Washington Report
Washington Star
Washington Times
Worker's World

## Foreign Newspapers, Magazines, and Other Periodicals

ABC Color (Asunción, Paraguay)
ABC Revista (Asunción, Paraguay)
ABN Correspondence (Munich, Germany)
Arena do Povo (Sao Paulo, Brazil)
Asian Outlook (Taipei, Taiwan)
Barricada (Nicaragua)

*El Día* (Mexico City, Mexico)
*El Sol* (Mexico City, Mexico)
*El Universal* (Mexico City, Mexico)
*Far Eastern Economic Review* (Hong Kong)
*Free China and Asia* (Taipei, Taiwan)
*Free China Review* (Taipei, Taiwan)
*The Globe and Mail* (Toronto, Canada)
*O Globo* (Rio de Janeiro, Brazil)
*The Guardian* (London, United Kingdom)
*The Independent* (Dublin, Ireland)
*Jane's International Defence Review* (London, United Kingdom)
*La Nación* (Buenos Aires, Argentina)
*La Nación* (Mexico City, Mexico)
*Mail and Guardian* (Johannesburg, South Africa)
*The Observer* (London, United Kingdom)
*Patria* (Asunción, Paraguay)
*Prensa Gráfica* (San José, Costa Rica)
*Sunday Times* (London, United Kingdom)
*Taipei Times*
*The Telegraph* (London, United Kingdom)
*Times of India* (Mumbai, India)
*Ukrainian Review* (London, United Kingdom)

## Films

Cosmatos, George P., dir. *Rambo: First Blood Part II*. TriStar Pictures, 1985.
Hool, Lance, dir. *Missing in Action 2: The Beginning*. Cannon Group, 1985.
McLaglen, Andrew V., dir. *The Wild Geese*. Richmond Film Productions (West) Ltd., Varius Entertainment Trading A.G., 1978.
Milius, John, dir. *Red Dawn*. MGM/UA Entertainment Co., 1984.
Norris, Aaron, dir. *Braddock: Missing in Action III*. Cannon Group, 1988.
Zito, Joseph, dir. *Missing in Action*. Warner Bros., 1984.
———, dir. *Red Scorpion*. Abramoff Production/Scorpion Film Production, 1988.

## Books, Book Chapters, and Articles

Accinelli, Robert. *Crisis and Commitment: United States Policy towards Taiwan, 1950–55*. Chapel Hill: University of North Carolina Press, 1996.
Adas, Michael. *Dominance by Design: The Technological Imperatives and America's Civilizing Mission*. Cambridge: Belknap Press of Harvard University, 2006.
Agee, Philip. *Inside the Company: A CIA Diary*. New York: Stonehill, 1975.
Ahern, Thomas. *Undercover Armies, 1961–1973: CIA and Surrogate Warfare in Laos*. Washington, D.C.: Center for the Study of Intelligence, 2006.
Allen, Michael. *Until the Last Man Comes Home: POWs, MIAs, and the Unending Vietnam War*. Chapel Hill: University of North Carolina Press, 2009.
Amsden, Alice C. "Taiwan's Economic History: A Case of Etatisme and a Challenge to Dependency Theory." *Modern China* 5, no. 3 (July 1979): 341–80.
Anderson, Scott, and Jon Lee Anderson. *Inside the League: The Shocking Exposé of How Terrorists, Nazis, and Latin American Death Squads Have Infiltrated the World Anti-Communist League*. New York: Dodd, Mead, and Company, 1986.
Andrew, John A. *The Other Side of the Sixties: The Young Americans for Freedom and the Rise of Conservative Politics*. New Brunswick: Rutgers University Press, 1997.
Anthony, David Henry, III. *Max Yergan: Race Man, Internationalist, Cold Warrior*. New York: New York University Press, 2006.
Appy, Christian. *American Reckoning: The Vietnam War and Our National Identity*. New York: Penguin, 2015.
———. *Patriots: The Vietnam War Remembered from All Sides*. New York: Penguin, 2004.

———. *Working-class War: American Combat Soldiers in Vietnam*. Amherst: University of Massachusetts Press, 1993.

Armony, Ariel. *Argentina, the U.S., and the Anti-Communist Crusade in Central America, 1977–1984*. Athens: Ohio University Center for International Studies, 1997.

Aust, Stephen. *Baader-Meinhof: The Inside Story of the R.A.F.* Translated by Anthea Bell. London: Bodley Head, 2008.

Ávila, Luis Alberto Hernán. "Las guerrillas blancas: anticomunismo transnacional e imaginarios de derechas en Argentina y México, 1954–1972." *Quinto Sol* 19, no. 1 (January–April 2015): 1–26.

Ayers, Bradley Earl. *The War That Never Was: An Insider's Account of CIA Operations against Cuba*. Indianapolis: Bobbs-Merrill, 1976.

Bachrcak, Stanley D. *The Committee of One Million: "China Lobby Politics," 1953–1971*. New York: Columbia University Press, 1976.

Balko, Radley. *The Rise of the Warrior Cop: The Militarization of America's Police Forces*. New York: Public Affairs, 2014.

Bardach, Ann Louise. *Cuba Confidential: Love and Vengeance in Miami and Havana*. New York: Vintage, 2002.

Barlow, Eeben. *Executive Outcomes: Against All Odds*. Alberton, South Africa: Galago Books, 2007.

Bauerkämper, Arnd. "Interwar Fascism in Europe and Beyond: Toward a Transnational Radical Right." In *New Perspectives on the Transnational Right*, edited by Martin Durham and Margaret Power, 39–68. New York: Palgrave Macmillan, 2010.

Bearden, Milt, and James Risen. *The Main Enemy: The Inside Story of the CIA's Final Showdown with the KGB*. New York: Random House, 2003.

Békés, Csaba, János Rainer, and Malcolm Byrne, eds. *The 1956 Hungarian Revolution: A History in Documents*. Budapest: Central European University Press, 2000.

Belew, Kathleen. *Bring the War Home: The White Power Movement and Paramilitary America*. Cambridge: Harvard University Press, forthcoming.

Bell, Daniel, ed. *The Radical Right*. Garden City, N.Y.: Doubleday, 1963.

Bell, Stewart. *Bayou of Pigs: The True Story of an Audacious Plot to Turn a Tropical Paradise into a Criminal Paradise*. Mississauga, Ontario: John Wiley & Sons Canada, 2008.

Bellant, Russ. *Old Nazis, the New Right, and the Republican Party*. Boston: South End Press, 1988.

Berkhoff, Karel C., and Marco Carynnyk. "The Organization of Ukrainian Nationalists and Its Attitude toward Germans and Jews: Iaroslav Stetsko's 1941 *Zhyttiepys*." *Harvard Ukrainian Studies* 23, no. 4 (December 1999): 149–84.

Berlet, Chip. *Right-wing Populism in America: Too Close for Comfort*. New York and London: Guilford Press, 2000.

Bernstein, Arnie. *Swastika Nation: Fritz Kuhn and the Rise and Fall of the German American Bund*. New York: St. Martin's Press, 2014.

Bérubé, Allan. *Coming Out under Fire: The History of Gay Men and Women in World War II*. New York: Free Press, 1990.

Black, George, Milton H. Jamail, and Norma Stoltz Chinchilla, eds. *Garrison Guatemala*. New York: Monthly Review Press, 1984.

Blaufarb, Douglas. *The Counterinsurgency Era: U.S. Doctrines and Performance*. New York: Free Press, 1977.

Blum, William. *Killing Hope: U.S. Military and CIA Interventions since World War II*. New York: Black Rose Books, 2000.

Bonner, Raymond. *Weakness and Deceit: U.S. Policy and El Salvador*. New York: Times Books, 1984.
Borstelmann, Thomas. *Apartheid's Reluctant Uncle: The United States and Southern Africa in the Early Cold War*. Oxford: Oxford University Press, 1993.
———. *The Cold War and the Color Line: American Race Relations in the Global Arena*. Cambridge: Harvard University Press, 2003.
Botto, Carlos Penna. *Como se desenvolve a Ofensiva Comunista*. Petropolis, Brazil: Editôra vozes limitada, 1961.
———. *O Que é o comunismo?* Petrópolis, Brazil: Editôra vozes limitada, 1961.
Brigham, Robert. *Guerrilla Diplomacy: The NLF's Foreign Relations and the Viet Nam War*. Ithaca: Cornell University Press, 1999.
Brietman, Richard, and Norman J. Goda. *In Hitler's Shadow: Nazi War Criminals, U.S. Intelligence and the Cold War*. College Park, Md.: National Archives and Records Administration, 2010.
Brown, Robert K., with Vann Spencer. *I Am Soldier of Fortune: Dancing with Devils*. Haverstown, Pa.: Casemate, 2013.
Brownell, Josiah. *The Collapse of Rhodesia: Population Demographics and the Politics of Race*. London: I.B. Tauris, 2011.
Brzezinski, Zbigniew. *Power and Principle: Memoirs of the National Security Adviser*. New York: Farrar, Straus, and Giroux, 1983.
Buckley, William F. *God and Man at Yale*. New York: Regnery, 1951.
———. *McCarthy and His Enemies*. New York: Regnery, 1954.
Buendía, Manuel. *La Ultraderecha en México*. Mexico City: Oceano, 1984.
Burgin, Angus. *The Great Persuasion: Reinventing Free Markets Since the Depression*. Cambridge: Harvard University Press, 2012.
Burmester, H. C. "The Recruitment and Use of Mercenaries in Armed Conflicts." *American Journal of International Law* 72, no. 1 (January 1978): 37–56.
Burnham, James. *The Coming Defeat of Communism*. New York: John Day, 1950.
———. *Operation Rollback: America's Secret War behind the Iron Curtain*. New York: John Day, 1952.
———. *The Struggle for the World*. New York: John Day, 1947.
Burns, Jennifer. *Goddess of the Market: Ayn Rand and the American Right*. Oxford: Oxford University Press, 2011.
Burrough, Bryan. *Days of Rage: America's Radical Underground, the FBI, and the Forgotten Age of Revolutionary Violence*. New York: Penguin, 2015.
Byrne, Jeffrey James. *Mecca of Revolution: Algeria, Decolonization, and the Third World Order*. Oxford: Oxford University Press, 2016.
Byrne, Malcolm. *Iran-Contra: Reagan's Scandal and the Unchecked Use of Presidential Power*. Lawrence: University of Kansas Press, 2014.
Calloni, Stella. *Los años del lobo: Operación Cóndor*. Buenos Aires: Ediciones Continente, 1999.
Campbell, James T. *Middle Passages: African American Journeys to Africa, 1787–2005*. New York: Penguin, 2006.
Canaday, Margot. *The Straight State: Sexuality and Citizenship in Twentieth-Century America*. Princeton: Princeton University Press, 2009.
Carafano, James Jay. "Mobilizing Europe's Stateless: America's Plan for a Cold War Army." *Journal of Cold War Studies* 1, no. 2 (Spring 1999): 61–85.
Chamberlain, Paul Thomas. *The Global Offensive: The United States, the Palestinian

Liberation Organization, and the Making of the Post-Cold War Order. Oxford: Oxford University Press, 2012.

Chamorro Coronel, Edgar. *Packaging the Contras: A Case of CIA Disinformation.* New York: Institute for Media Analysis, 1987.

Chang, Gordon H. *Fateful Ties: A History of America's Preoccupation with China.* Cambridge: Harvard University Press, 2015.

Chávez, Joaquín M. "How Did the Civil War in El Salvador End?" *American Historical Review* 120, no. 5 (December 2015): 1784–1979.

Chen, Jian. *Mao's China and the Cold War.* Chapel Hill: University of North Carolina Press, 2001.

Cilliers, Jakkie, and Peggy Mason. *Peace, Profit, or Plunder: The Privatisation of Security in War-torn African Societies.* Pretoria, South Africa: Institute for Security Studies, 1999.

Clarkson, Alexander. *Fragmented Fatherland: Immigration and Cold War Conflict in West Germany, 1946–1980.* New York: Berghahn Books, 2013.

Cockburn, Patrick. *The Rise of the Islamic State: ISIS and the Sunni Revolution.* London: Verso, 2015.

Coey, John. *A Martyr Speaks: Journal of the Late John Coey.* Fletcher, N.C.: New Puritan Library, 1988.

Cohen, Barry. "The War in Rhodesia: A Dissenter's View." *African Affairs* 76, no. 305 (October 1977): 483–94.

Colby, Jason M. *The Business of Empire: United Fruit, Race, and U.S. Expansion in Central America.* Cornell: Cornell University Press, 2013.

Colby, William, and Peter Forbath. *Honorable Men: My Life in the CIA.* New York: Simon and Schuster, 1978.

Coll, Steve. *Ghost Wars: The Secret History of the CIA, Afghanistan, and Bin Laden, from the Soviet Invasion to September 10, 2001.* New York: Penguin, 2005.

Comisión Nacional de Verdad y Reconciliación (Chile). *Report of the Chilean National Commission on Truth and Reconciliation.* Translated by Philip E. Berryman. South Bend: Notre Dame University Press, 1993.

Connelly, Matthew. "Taking off the Cold War Lens: Visions of North-South Conflict during the Algerian War for Independence." *American Historical Review* 105, no. 3 (June 2000): 739–69.

Constable, Pamela, and Arturo Valenzuela. *A Nation of Enemies: Chile under Pinochet.* New York: W. W. Norton, 1993.

Corn, David. *Blond Ghost: Ted Shackley and the CIA's Crusades.* New York: Simon and Schuster, 1994.

Costigliola, Frank. "'Unceasing Pressure for Penetration': Gender, Pathology, and Emotion in George Kennan's Formation of the Cold War." *Journal of American History* 83, no. 4 (March 1997): 1309–39.

Cowie, Jefferson. *Stayin' Alive: The Last Days of the American Working Class.* New York: New Press, 2012.

Crespino, Joseph. *In Search of Another Country: Mississippi and the Conservative Counterrevolution.* Princeton: Princeton University Press, 2007.

Crile, George. *Charlie Wilson's War: The Extraordinary Story of How the Wildest Man in Congress and a Rogue CIA Agent Changed the History of Our Times.* New York: Grove Press, 2003.

Critchlow, Donald. *Phyllis Schlafly and Grassroots Conservatism: A Woman's Crusade.* Princeton: Princeton University Press, 2005.

Crocker, Chester. *High Noon in Southern Africa: Making Peace in a Rough Neighborhood* New York: W. W. Norton, 1992.
Cullather, Nick. *Hungry World: America's Cold War Battle against Poverty in Asia.* Cambridge: Harvard University Press, 2010.
Cunningham, David. *Klansville, USA: The Rise and Fall of the Civil-Rights Era Ku Klux Klan.* Oxford: Oxford University Press, 2013.
———. *There's Something Happening Here: The New Left, the Klan, and FBI Counterintelligence.* Berkeley: University of California Press, 2005.
Cuordileone, K. A. *Manhood and American Political Culture in the Cold War.* New York: Taylor and Francis, 2005.
Danner, Mark. *Massacre at El Mozote: A Parable of the Cold War.* New York: Vintage Books, 1994.
Darwin, John. *The Empire Project: The Rise and Fall of the British World System, 1830–1970.* Cambridge: Cambridge University Press, 2009.
Davila, Jerry. *Dictatorship in South America.* Chichester, U.K.: Wiley-Blackwell, 2013.
Dean, Robert. *Imperial Brotherhood: Gender and the Making of Cold War Foreign Policy.* Amherst: University of Massachusetts Press, 2001.
———. "Masculinity as Ideology: John F. Kennedy and the Domestic Politics of Foreign Policy." *Diplomatic History* 22, no. 1 (Winter 1998): 29–62.
DeBenedetti, Charles. *An American Ordeal: The Antiwar Movement of the Vietnam Era.* Syracuse: Syracuse University Press, 1990.
Diamond, Sara. *Spiritual Warfare: The Politics of the Christian Right.* Boston: South End Press, 1988.
Dickey, Christopher. *With the Contras: A Reporter in the Wilds of Nicaragua.* New York: Touchstone, 1987.
Dinges, John. *The Condor Years: How Pinochet and His Allies Brought Terror to Three Continents.* New York: New Press, 2004.
Dochuk, Darren. *From Bible Belt to Sunbelt: Plain Folk Religion, Grassroots Politics, and the Rise of Evangelical Conservatism.* New York: W. W. Norton, 2012.
Donner, Frank. *Protectors of Privilege: Red Squads and Police Repression in Urban America.* Berkeley: University of California Press, 1990.
Dorril, Stephen J. *MI6: Inside the Covert World of Her Majesty's Secret Service.* New York: Free Press, 2000.
Dower, John. *Embracing Defeat: Japan in the Wake of World War II.* New York: W. W. Norton, 2000.
Drabble, John. "The FBI, COINTELPRO-WHITE HATE, and the Decline of Ku Klux Klan Organizations in Mississippi, 1964–1971." *Journal of Mississippi History* 66, no. 4 (Winter 2004): 353–401.
———. "'To Ensure Domestic Tranquility': The FBI, COINTELPRO-WHITE HATE, and Political Discourse, 1964–1971." *Journal of American Studies* 38, no. 2 (August 2004): 297–328.
Dudziak, Mary. *Cold War Civil Rights: Race and the Image of American Democracy.* Princeton: Princeton University Press, 2000.
Durham, Martin, and Margaret Power, eds. *New Perspectives on the Transnational Right.* New York: Palgrave Macmillan, 2010.
Edsall, Thomas Byrne, with Mary C. Edsall. *Chain Reactions: The Impact of Race, Rights, and Taxes on American Politics.* New York: W. W. Norton, 1982.
Edwards, Lee. *Missionary for Freedom: The Life and Times of Walter Judd.* Oakcrest, Minn.: Paragon House, 1990.

Ekbladh, David. *The Great American Mission: Modernization and the Construction of the American World Order*. Princeton: Princeton University Press, 2011.

Ellis, Stephen, and Tsepo Sechaba. *Comrades against Apartheid: The ANC and the South Africa Communist Party in Exile*. Bloomington: Indiana University Press, 1992.

Etzold, Thomas H., and John Lewis Gaddis, eds. *Containment: Documents on American Policy and Strategy, 1945–1950*. New York: Columbia University Press, 1978.

Evans, Grant, and Kelvin Rowley. *Red Brotherhood at War: Vietnam, Cambodia and Laos Since 1975*. London: Verso, 1984.

Everitt, David. *A Shadow of Red: Communism and the Blacklist in Radio and Television*. Chicago: Ivan R. Dee, 2007.

Ewans, Martin. *Afghanistan: A Short History of Its People and Politics*. New York: HarperCollins, 2002.

Flamm, Michael. *Law and Order: Street Crime, Civil Unrest, and the Crisis of Liberalism in the 1960s*. New York: Columbia University, 2007.

Fones-Wolf, Elizabeth. *Selling Free Enterprise: The Business Assault on Labor and Liberalism, 1945–1960*. Urbana: University of Illinois, 1994.

Frank, Thomas. *What's the Matter with Kansas? How Conservatives Won the Heart of America*. New York: Metropolitan Books, 2004.

———. *The Wrecking Crew: How Conservatives Rule*. New York: Metropolitan Books, 2008.

Franklin, H. Bruce. *MIA, Or Mythmaking in America*. New Brunswick: Rutgers University Press, 1993.

Fraser, Steve, and Gary Gerstle, eds. *The Rise and Fall of the New Deal Order, 1930–1980*. Princeton: Princeton University Press, 1989.

Fronczak, Joseph. "Local People's Global Politics: A Transnational History of the Hands-Off Ethiopia Movement of 1935." *Diplomatic History* 39, no. 2 (April 2015): 245–74.

Fuelner, Edwin J. *China: The Turning Point*. Washington, D.C.: Council on American Affairs, 1976.

Fuller, J. F. C. *How to Defeat Russia*. London: Eyre and Spottiswoode, 1951.

———. *Russia Is Not Invincible*. London: Eyre and Spottiswoode, 1951.

Fursenko, Alexsandr, and Timothy Naftali. *"One Hell of a Gamble": Khrushchev, Castro, and Kennedy, 1958–1964*. New York: Norton, 1997.

Gambone, Michael D. *Eisenhower, Somoza, and the Cold War in Nicaragua*. New York: Praeger, 1997.

Garcia, Maria Cristina. *Havana, USA: Cuban Exiles and Cuban Americans in Miami*. Berkeley: University of California Press, 1997.

Garrard-Burnett, Virginia. *Terror in the Land of the Holy Spirit: Guatemala under General Efraín Ríos Montt, 1982–1983*. Oxford: Oxford University Press, 2010.

Geary, Daniel, and Jennifer Sutton. "Resisting the Wind of Change: The Citizens' Councils and European Decolonization." In *The U.S. South and Europe*, edited by Cornelis A. van Minnen and Manfred Berg. Lexington: University of Kentucky Press, 2013.

Gibbs, David N. "Dag Hammarskjold, the United Nations, and the Congo Crisis of 1960–1961: A Reinterpretation." *Journal of Modern African Studies* 31, no. 1 (March 1993): 163–74.

———. *The Political Economy of Third World Interventions: Mines, Money, and U.S. Policy in the Congo Crisis*. Chicago: University of Chicago Press, 1991.

Gibson, James William. *Warrior Dreams: Violence and Manhood in Post-Vietnam America*. New York: Hill and Wang, 1994.

Gibson, Richard Michael, and Wen H. Chen. *The Secret Army: Chiang Kai-Shek and Drug Warlords of the Golden Triangle*. New York: Wiley and Sons, 2011.
Gifford, Laura Jane, and Daniel K. Williams, eds. *The Right Side of the Sixties: Reexamining Conservatism's Decade of Transformation*. New York: Palgrave MacMillan, 2012.
Gill, Lesley. *School of the Americas: Military Training and Political Violence in the Americas*. Durham, N.C.: Duke University Press, 2004.
Gillespie, Robert M. *Black Ops, Vietnam: The Operational History of MACVSOG*. Annapolis: Naval Institute Press, 2011.
Gilman, Nils. *Mandarins of the Future: Modernization Theory in Cold War America*. Baltimore: Johns Hopkins University Press, 2007.
Gilman, Nils, Jesse Goldhammer, and Steven Weber, eds. *Deviant Globalization: Black Market Economy in the 21st Century*. New York: Continuum, 2011.
Gleijeses, Piero. *Conflicting Missions: Havana, Washington, and Africa, 1957–1976*. Chapel Hill: University of North Carolina Press, 2002.
———. "Juan Jose Arevalo and the Caribbean Legion." *Journal of Latin American and Caribbean Studies* 21, no. 1 (February 1989): 133–45.
———. *Shattered Hope: The Guatemalan Revolution and the United States, 1944–1954*. Princeton: Princeton University Press, 1992.
———. *Visions of Freedom: The United States, Havana, Pretoria, and the Struggle for Southern Africa*. Chapel Hill: University of North Carolina Press, 2013.
Godson, Roy, ed. *Intelligence Requirements for the 1980s: Covert Action*. Washington, D.C.: National Strategy Information Center, 1981.
Goodson, Larry P. *Afghanistan's Endless War: State Failure, Regional Politics, and the Rise of the Taliban*. Seattle: University of Washington Press, 2001.
Gosse, Van. "El Salvador Is Spanish for Vietnam: A New Immigrant Left and the Politics of Solidarity." In *The Immigrant Left in the United States*, edited by Paul Buhle and Dan Georgakas, 302–31. Albany: State University of New York Press, 1996.
Goulden, Joseph C. *The Death Merchant: The Rise and Fall of Edwin P. Wilson*. New York: Simon and Schuster, 1984.
Grandin, Greg. *Empire's Workshop: Latin America, the United States, and the Rise of the New Imperialism*. New York: Holt Paperbacks, 2006.
———. *Kissinger's Shadow: The Long Reach of America's Most Controversial Statesman*. New York: Picador 2015.
———. *Last Colonial Massacre: Latin America in the Cold War*. Updated ed. Chicago: University of Chicago Press, 2011.
Grandin, Greg, and Gilbert Joseph, eds. *A Century of Revolution: Insurgent and Counterinsurgent Violence during Latin America's Long Cold War*. Durham, N.C.: Duke University Press, 2010.
Granville, Johanna. "'Caught with Jam on Our Fingers': Radio Free Europe and the Hungarian Uprising of 1956." *Diplomatic History* 29, no. 5 (November 2005): 811–39.
Greenberg, Amy S. *Manifest Manhood and Antebellum American Empire*. Cambridge: Cambridge University Press, 2005.
Hall, Sam, with Larry Hussman and Felicia Lewis. *Counter-Terrorist*. New York: Donald I. Fine, 1987.
Harmer, Tanya. *Allende's Chile and the Inter-American Cold War*. Chapel Hill: University of North Carolina Press, 2011.
———. "Fractious Allies: Chile, the United States, and the Cold War, 1973–1976." *Diplomatic History* 37, no. 1 (January 2013).

Hauser, Thomas. *The Execution of Charles Horman: An American Sacrifice*. New York: Harcourt Brace, 1978.

Herring, George. *America's Longest War: The United States and Vietnam, 1950–1975*. 4th ed. New York: McGraw Hill, 2002.

———. *From Colony to Superpower: U.S. Foreign Relations since 1776*. Oxford: Oxford University Press, 2008.

Hill, Lance. *Deacons for Defense: Armed Resistance and the Civil Rights Movement*. Chapel Hill: University of North Carolina Press, 2004.

Hoare, Mike. *Congo Warriors*. London: Hale, 1991.

———. *The Seychelles Affair*. Reprint ed. Boulder, Colo.: Paladin Press, 2008.

Hobsbawm, Eric. *The Age of Extremes: A History of the World, 1914–1991*. New York: Vintage Books, 1994.

Holian, Anna. *Between National Socialism and Soviet Communism: Displaced Persons in Postwar Germany*. Ann Arbor: University of Michigan Press, 2011.

Hoplin, Nicole, and Ron Robinson. *Funding Fathers: The Unsung Heroes of the Conservative Movement*. Washington, D.C.: Regnery Publishing, 2008.

Horne, Gerald. *From the Barrel of a Gun: The United States and the War against Zimbabwe, 1965–1980*. Chapel Hill: University of North Carolina Press, 2001.

———. *The Color of Fascism: Lawrence Dennis, Racial Passing, and the Rise of Right-wing Extremism in the United States*. New York: New York University Press, 2006.

Huggins, Martha. *Political Policing: The United States and Latin America*. Durham, N.C.: Duke University Press, 1998.

Hughes, Matthew. "Fighting for White Rule in Africa: The Central African Federation, Katanga, and the Congo Crisis, 1958–1965." *International History Review* 23, no. 5 (September 2003): 592–615.

Hunt, E. Howard. *American Spy: My Secret History in the CIA, Watergate, and Beyond*. New York: Wiley & Sons, 2007.

———. *Give Us This Day: The Inside Story of the CIA and the Bay of Pigs Invasion . . . by One of Its Key Organizers*. New Rochelle, N.Y.: Arlington House, 1973.

Ignatieff, Michael. *Blood and Belonging: Journeys into the New Nationalism*. New York: Farrar, Straus, and Giroux, 1993.

Immerman, Richard. *The CIA in Guatemala: The Foreign Policy of Intervention*. Austin: University of Texas Press, 1982.

———. *The Hidden Hand: A Brief History of the CIA*. Chichester, U.K.: Wiley-Blackwell, 2014.

Immerwahr, Daniel. *Small World: The United States and the Lure of Community Development*. Cambridge: Harvard University Press, 2015.

Iriye, Akira, Petra Goedde, and William Hitchcock, eds. *The Human Rights Revolution: An International History*. Oxford: Oxford University Press, 2012.

Irwin, Ryan. "Wind of Change? White Redoubt and the Postcolonial Moment, 1960–1963." *Diplomatic History* 33, no. 5 (November 2009): 897–925.

Irwin, Will. *Jedburghs: The Secret History of the Allied Special Forces, France 1944*. New York: PublicAffairs, 2005.

Jacobs, Seth. *America's Miracle Man in Vietnam: Ngo Dinh Diem, Religion, Race, and U.S. Intervention in Southeast Asia*. Durham, N.C.: Duke University Press, 2005.

———. *The Universe Unraveling: American Foreign Policy in Cold War Laos*. Ithaca: Cornell University Press, 2012.

Jacobsen, Matthew Frye. *Barbarian Virtues: The United States Encounters Foreign Peoples at Home and Abroad, 1876–1917*. New York: Hill and Wang, 2000.

Jeffords, Susan. *Hard Bodies: Hollywood Masculinity in the Reagan Era.* New Brunswick: Rutgers University Press, 1993.

Jeffries, Hasan. *Bloody Lowndes: Civil Rights and Black Power in Alabama's Black Belt.* New York: New York University Press, 2009.

Jenkins, Philip. *Decade of Nightmares: The End of the Sixties and the Making of Eighties America.* New York: Oxford University Press, 2006.

Johnson, David K. *The Lavender Scare: The Cold War Persecution of Gays and Lesbians in the Federal Government.* Chicago: University of Chicago Press, 2004.

Jones, Rhodri-Jeffrey. *The CIA and American Democracy.* 3rd ed. New Haven: Yale University Press, 2003.

Judis, John B. *William F. Buckley: Patron Saint of the Conservatives.* New York: Simon and Schuster, 1988.

Kabaservice, Geoffrey. *Rule and Ruin: The Downfall of Moderation and the Destruction of the Republican Party from Eisenhower to the Tea Party.* Oxford: Oxford University Press, 2012.

Kalman, Laura. *Right Star Rising: A New Politics, 1974–1980.* New York: W. W. Norton, 2010.

Kaplan, David E., and Alex Dubro. *Yakuza: Japan's Criminal Underworld.* Berkeley: University of California Press, 2003.

Keely, Joseph. *China Lobby Man: The Story of Alfred Kohlberg.* New Rochelle, N.Y.: Arlington House, 1969.

Kepel, Gilles. *Jihad: The Trail of Political Islam.* Cambridge: Harvard University Press, 2002.

Kerr, George H. *Formosa Betrayed.* Boston: Houghton Mifflin, 1965.

Kinzer, Stephen. *Blood of Brothers: Life and War in Nicaragua.* New York: Putnam, 1991.

———. *Overthrow: America's Century of Regime Change from Hawaii to Iraq.* New York: Times Books, 2006.

Klein, Christina. *Cold War Orientalism: Asia in the Middlebrow Imagination, 1945–1961.* Berkeley: University of California Press, 2003.

Klein, Naomi. *The Shock Doctrine: The Rise of Disaster Capitalism.* New York: Picador, 2007.

Koen, Russ. *The China Lobby in American Politics.* New York: Harper and Row, 1976.

Kornbluh, Peter. "The Contras, Crack, and the CIA: The Storm over 'Dark Alliance.'" *Columbia Journalism Review* 35 (January/February 1997): 35–39.

———. "Nicaragua: U.S. Pro-Insurgency Warfare against the Sandinistas." In *Low Intensity Warfare: How the USA Fights Wars without Declaring Them,* edited by Michael T. Klare and Peter Kornbluh, 136–85. New York: Pantheon, 1988.

———. *The Pinochet File: A Declassified Dossier on Atrocity and Accountability.* New York: New Press, 2003.

Kramer, Paul. "Power and Connection: Imperial Histories of the United States." *American Historical Review* 116, no. 5 (December 2011): 1348–91.

Kruse, Kevin. *White Flight: Atlanta and the Making of Modern Conservatism.* Princeton: Princeton University Press, 2005.

Kuzamarov, Jeremy. *Modernizing Repression: Police Training and Nation-Building in the American Century.* Amherst: University of Massachusetts Press, 2012.

LaFeber, Walter. *Inevitable Revolutions: The United States in Central America.* 2nd ed. New York: W. W. Norton, 1993.

LaPierre, Wayne. *Guns, Crime, and Freedom.* New York: HarperPerennial, 1995.

Lancaster, Roger. *Sex Panic and the Punitive State.* Berkeley: University of California Press, 2011.

Latham, Michael E. *The Right Kind of Revolution: Modernization, Development, and U.S. Foreign Policy from the Cold War to the Present*. Ithaca: Cornell University Press, 2010.
Lassiter, Matthew. *The Silent Majority: Suburban Politics in the Sunbelt South*. Princeton: Princeton University Press, 2006.
Lee, Martin A. *The Beast Reawakens*. Boston: Little, Brown, and Company, 1997.
LeoGrande, William. *Our Own Backyard: The United States in Central America, 1977–1992*. Chapel Hill: University of North Carolina Press, 1998.
Levitas, Daniel. *The Terrorist Next Door: The Militia Movement and the Radical Right*. New York: St. Martin's Press, 2002.
Lewis, Paul H. *Gods and Generals: The "Dirty War" in Argentina*. Westport, Conn.: Praeger, 2002.
Lichtman, Allan. *White Protestant Nation: The Rise of the American Conservative Movement*. New York: Grove Press, 2008.
Liebman, Marvin. *Coming Out Conservative: An Autobiography*. San Francisco: Chronicle Books, 1992.
Lin, Hsiao-ting. *Accidental State: Chiang Kai-Shek, the United States, and the Making of Taiwan*. Cambridge: Harvard University Press, 2016.
Lipper, Elinor. *Eleven Years in Soviet Prison Camps*. Chicago: Regnery, 1951.
Logevall, Fredrik. *The Embers of War: The Fall of an Empire and the Making of America's Vietnam*. New York: Random House, 2014.
Logevall, Fredrik, and Craig Campbell. *America's Cold War: The Politics of Insecurity*. Cambridge: Belknap Press of Harvard University Press, 2009.
López Macedonio, Mónica Naymich. "Historia de una colaboración transnacional anticomunista: Los Tecos de la Universidad Autónoma de Guadalajara y el gobierno de Chiang Kai-Shek de los principios de los años setentas." *Contemporánea: Historia y problemas del siglo XX* 1 (2010): 133–57.
Loyn, David. *In Afghanistan: Two Hundred Years of British, Russian, and American Occupation*. New York: Palgrave MacMillan, 2009.
Maas, Peter. *Manhunt: The Incredible Pursuit of a CIA Agent Turned Terrorist*. New York: Random House, 1986.
MacLean, Nancy. *Freedom Is Not Enough: The Opening of the American Workplace*. Cambridge: Harvard University Press, 2006.
Malloy, Sean. *Out of Oakland: Black Panther Party Internationalism during the Cold War*. Ithaca: Cornell University Press, 2017.
———. "Uptight in Babylon: Eldridge Cleaver's Cold War." *Diplomatic History* 37, no. 3 (June 2013): 538–71.
Mao, Joyce. *Asia First: China and the Making of Modern American Conservatism*. Chicago: University of Chicago Press, 2015.
Marchetti, Victor. *The CIA: The Cult of Intelligence*. New York: Knopf, 1974.
Marks, Thomas A. *Counterrevolution in China: Wang Sheng and the Kuomintang*. London: Frank Cass, 1998.
Martin, Bradford D. *The Other Eighties: A Secret History of America in the Age of Reagan*. New York: Hill and Wang, 2011.
Martin, Lisa L., and Kathryn Sikkink. "U.S. Policy and Human Rights in Argentina and Guatemala, 1973–1980." In *Double Edge Diplomacy: International Bargaining and Domestic Policy*, edited by Peter B. Evans, Harold K. Jackson, and Robert D. Putnam. Berkeley: University of California Press, 1993.
Martin, William. *With God on Our Side: The Rise of the Religious Right in America*. Rev. ed. New York: Broadway, 2005.

May, Elaine Tyler. *Homeward Bound: American Families in the Cold War Era*. New York: Basic Books, 1989.

May, Robert E. *Manifest Destiny's Underworld: Filibustering in Antebellum America*. Chapel Hill: University of North Carolina Press, 2002.

Mazzetti, Mark. *The Way of the Knife: The CIA, a Secret Army, and a War at the End of the Earth*. New York: Penguin, 2013.

McAlister, Melani. *Epic Encounters: Culture, Media, and U.S. Interests in the Middle East, 1945–2000*. Berkeley: University of California Press, 2001.

McCartin, Joseph A. *Collision Course: Ronald Reagan, the Air Traffic Controllers, and the Strike That Changed America*. Oxford: Oxford University Press, 2013.

McClintock, Michael. *Instruments of Statecraft: U.S. Guerrilla Warfare, Counter-Insurgency, and Counter-Terrorism, 1940–1990*. New York: Pantheon Books, 1992.

McCormick, Robert. *Croatia under Pavelić: America, the Ustashe, and the Croatian Genocide*. London: I. B. Tauris, 2014.

McCoy, Alfred. *Policing America's Empire: The United States, the Philippines, and the Rise of the Surveillance State*. Madison: University of Wisconsin Press, 2009.

———. *The Politics of Heroin: CIA Complicity in the Global Drug Trade*. New York: Lawrence Hill, 1991.

McFate, Sean. *The Modern Mercenary: Private Armies and What They Mean for World Order*. Oxford: Oxford University Press, 2016.

McGirr, Lisa. *Suburban Warriors: The Origins of the New American Right*. Princeton: Princeton University Press, 2002.

McMahon, Robert J. "The Republic as Empire: American Foreign Policy in the 'American Century.'" In *Perspectives on Modern America: Making Sense of the Twentieth Century*, edited by Harvard Sitkoff, 80–100. Oxford: Oxford University Press, 2001.

McSherry, Patrice. *Predatory States: Operation Condor and Covert War in Latin America*. Lanham, Md.: Rowman and Littlefield, 2005.

Meredith, Martin. *Diamonds, Gold, and War: The British, the Boers, and the Making of South Africa*. London: Simon and Schuster, 2007.

Meyer, Jean. *The Cristero Rebellion: The Mexican People between Church and State, 1926–1929*. Cambridge: Cambridge University Press, 1976.

Miller, Jamie. "Yes, Minister: Reassessing South Africa's Role in the Angolan Civil War." *Journal of Cold War Studies* 15, no. 3 (Summer 2013): 4–33.

Miller-Davenport, Sarah. "'Their Blood Shall Not be Shed in Vain': Evangelical Missionaries and the Search for God and Country in Post–World War II Asia." *Journal of American History* 99, no. 4 (March 2013): 1109–32.

Minchin, Timothy J. *After the Dream: Black and White Southerners since 1965*. Lexington: University of Kentucky, 2011.

Minter, William. *Account from Angola: UNITA as Described by Ex-Participants and Foreign Visitors*. Amsterdam: African European Institute, 1990.

———. *Apartheid's Contras: An Inquiry into the Roots of War in Angola and Mozambique*. London: Zed Books, 1994.

Mockler, Anthony. *The New Mercenaries*. London: Sidgwick and Jackson, 1985.

Moore, Robin. *Major Mike: Major Mike Williams as Told to Robin Moore*. New York: Charter, 1981.

Moreton, Bethany. *To Serve God and Wal-Mart: The Making of Christian Free Enterprise*. Cambridge: Harvard University Press, 2010.

Moser, Charles, ed. *Combat on Communist Territory*. Lake Bluff, Ill.: Regnery Gateway, 1985.

Moulton, Aaron Coy. "Building Their Own Cold War in Their Own Backyard: The Transnational, International Conflicts in the Greater Caribbean Basin, 1944–1954." *Cold War History* 15, no. 2 (2015): 135–54.

Moyn, Samuel. *The Last Utopia: Human Rights in History*. Cambridge: Belknap Press of Harvard University Press, 2010.

Mulloy, D. J. *American Extremism: History, Politics, and the Militia Movement*. New York: Routledge, 2004.

Murch, Donna. *Living for the City: Migration, Education, and the Rise of the Black Panther Party in Oakland California*. Chapel Hill: University of North Carolina Press, 2010.

Nash, George H. *The Conservative Intellectual Movement in America: Since 1945*. New York: Basic Books, 1976.

Nickerson, Michelle T. *Mothers of Conservatism: Women and the Postwar Right*. Princeton: Princeton University Press, 2012.

Nickson, Andrew. *La Guerra Fría y El Paraguay*. Asunción: El Lector, 2014.

Noer, Thomas J. *Cold War and Black Liberation: The United States and White Rule in Africa, 1948–1968*. Columbia: University of Missouri Press, 1985.

North, Oliver, with William Novak. *Under Fire: An American Story*. New York: HarperCollins, 1991.

Olmsted, Kathryn. *Challenging the Secret Government: The Post-Watergate Investigations of the CIA and the FBI*. Chapel Hill: University of North Carolina Press, 1996.

———. *Real Enemies: Conspiracy Theories and American Democracy, World War I to 9/11*. Oxford: Oxford University Press, 2009.

Pakenham, Thomas. *The Scramble for Africa: White Man's Conquest of the Dark Continent from 1876–1912*. New York: Random House, 1991.

Pastor, Robert. *Condemned to Repetition: The United States and Nicaragua*. Princeton: Princeton University Press, 1987.

Paxton, Robert. *The Anatomy of Fascism*. Reprint. New York: Vintage, 2005.

Peace, Roger. *A Call to Conscience: The Anti-Contra War Campaign*. Amherst: University of Massachusetts Press, 2012.

Pearson, Roger. *Eugenics and Race*. London: Clair Press, 1966.

———. *Race and Civilization*. London: Clair Press, 1966.

Pelton, Robert Young. *Licensed to Kill: Hired Guns in the War on Terror*. New York: Broadway Books, 2007.

Perlstein, Rick. *Before the Storm: Barry Goldwater and the Unmaking of the American Consensus*. New York: Nation Books, 2001.

———. *The Invisible Bridge: The Fall of Nixon and the Rise of Reagan*. New York: Simon and Shuster, 2014.

———. *Nixonland: The Rise of a President and the Fracturing of America*. New York: Scribner, 2008.

Persico, Joseph E. *Casey: From the OSS to the CIA*. New York: Viking, 1990.

Phillips-Fein, Kim. *Invisible Hands: The Making of the Conservative Movement from the New Deal to Reagan*. New York: W. W. Norton, 2009.

Pierce, William Luther [Andrew MacDonald, pseud.]. *The Turner Diaries*. Fort Lee, N.J.: Barricade Books, 1978.

Plaster, John. *SOG: A Photo History of the Secret Wars*. Boulder, Colo.: Paladin Press, 2000.

———. *SOG: The Secret Wars of America's Commandos in Vietnam*. New York: Simon and Schuster, 1997.

Preston, Andrew. "Evangelical Internationalism: A Conservative Worldview for the Age of Globalization," in *The Right Side of the Sixties: Reexamining Conservatism's Decade of Transformation*, edited by Laura Jane Gifford and Daniel K. Williams, 221–42. New York: Palgrave MacMillan, 2012.

Prieto Laurens, Jorge. *El Complot Comunista*. Mexico: n.p., 1951.

———. *El Comunismo en México*. Mexico City: Federación Mexicana Anticomunista, 1961.

Prince, Erik, with David Coburn. *Civilian Warriors: The Inside Story of Blackwater and the Unsung Heroes of the War on Terror*. New York: Portfolio/Penguin, 2013.

Rabe, Stephen. *U.S. Intervention in British Guiana: A Cold War Story*. Chapel Hill: University of North Carolina Press, 2005.

Ribuffo, Leo. *Old Christian Right: The Protestant Far Right from the Great Depression to the Cold War*. Philadelphia: Temple University Press, 1983.

Richards, Lawrence. *Union-Free America: Workers and Anti-Union Culture*. Urbana-Champaign: University of Illinois Press, 2010.

Robertson, Pat. *The New World Order*. Dallas: World Publishing, 1991.

Robin, Corey. *The Reactionary Mind: Conservatism from Edmund Burke to Sarah Palin*. Oxford: Oxford University Press, 2011.

———. "You Say You Want a Counterrevolution, Well, You Know, We All Want to Change the World." In *A Century of Revolution: Insurgent and Counterinsurgent Violence during Latin America's Long Cold War*, edited by Greg Grandin and Gilbert Joseph, 371–80. Durham, N.C.: Duke University Press, 2010.

Rodriguez, Felix I., and John Weisman. *Shadow Warrior: The CIA Hero of a Hundred Unknown Battles*. New York: Simon and Schuster, 1989.

Romero, Laura. "El movimiento fascista en Guadalajara." In *Perspectivas de los movimientos sociales en la región Centro-Occidente*, edited by Jaime Tamayo. Guadalajara: Instituto de Estudios Sociales de la Universidad de Guadalajara, 1986.

Rosenfeld, Seth. *Subversives: The FBI's War on Student Radicals and Reagan's Rise to Power*. New York: Picador, 2013.

Rothenberg, Daniel, ed. *Memory of Silence: The Guatemalan Truth Commission Report*. New York: Palgrave-MacMillan, 2012.

Rotter, Andrew J. "Gender Relations, Foreign Relations: The United States and South Asia, 1947–1964." *Journal of American History* 81 (September 1994): 518–42.

Roy, Denny. *Taiwan: A Political History*. Ithaca: Cornell University Press, 2002.

Roy, Olivier. *Globalized Islam: The Search for a New Ummah*. New York: Columbia University Press, 2006.

Rustsila, Markku. "International Anticommunism before the Cold War: Success and Failure in the Building of a Transnational Right." In *New Perspectives on the Transnational Right*, edited by Martin Durham and Margaret Power, 11–38. New York: Palgrave Macmillan, 2010.

Sandbrook, Dominic. *Seasons in the Sun: The Battle for Britain, 1974–1979*. London: Penguin, 2013.

Sargent, Daniel. *A Superpower Transformed: The Remaking of American Foreign Relations in the 1970s*. Oxford: Oxford University Press, 2015.

Saunders, Frances Stonor. *The Cultural Cold War: The CIA and the World of Arts and Letters*. 2nd ed. New York: The New Press, 2013.

Savimbi, Jonas. *Por Um Futuro Melhor*. Lisbon: Nova Nordica, 1986.

Scahill, Jeremy. *Blackwater: The Rise of the World's Most Powerful Mercenary Army*. New York: Nation Books, 2007.

Scanlon, Sandra. *The Pro-War Movement: Domestic Support for the Vietnam War and the Making of Modern American Conservatism*. Amherst: University of Massachusetts Press, 2013.

Schaub, Gary, and Ryan Kelty, eds. *Private Military and Security Contractors: Controlling the Corporate Warrior*. Lanham, Md.: Rowman and Littlefield, 2016.

Schlesinger, Stephen, and Stephen Kinzer. *Bitter Fruit: The Story of the American Coup in Guatemala*. Rev. ed. New York: Rockefeller Center for Latin American Studies, 2005.

Schmidli, William Michael. "Institutionalizing Human Rights in U.S. Foreign Policy: U.S.-Argentine Relations, 1976–1980." *Diplomatic History* 35, no. 2 (April 2011): 351–77.

Schmitz, David F. *Thank God They're on Our Side: The United States and Right-wing Dictatorships, 1921–1965*. Chapel Hill: University of North Carolina Press, 1999.

———. *The United States and Right-wing Dictatorships, 1965–1989*. Cambridge: Cambridge University Press, 2006.

Schmitz, David F., and Vanessa Walker. "Jimmy Carter and the Foreign Policy of Human Rights." *Diplomatic History* 28, no. 1 (January 2004): 113–43.

Schmidt, Elizabeth. *Foreign Intervention in Africa: From the Cold War to the War on Terror*. Cambridge: Cambridge University Press, 2013.

Schneider, Greg. *Cadres for Conservatism: The Young Americans for Freedom and the Rise of the Contemporary Right*. New York: New York University Press, 1999.

Schoultz, Lars. *That Infernal Little Cuban Republic: The United States and the Cuban Revolution*. Chapel Hill: University of North Carolina Press, 2009.

Schraeder, Peter J. *United States Foreign Policy toward Africa: Incrementalism, Crisis and Change*. Cambridge: Cambridge University Press, 1994.

Schultz, Richard. "Low Intensity Conflict." In *Mandate for Leadership II*, edited by Stuart Butler, Michael Sanera, and W. Bruce Weinrod. Washington, D.C.: Heritage Foundation, 1984.

Schweizer, Peter. *Victory: The Reagan Administration's Secret Strategy That Hastened the Collapse of the Soviet Union*. New York: Atlantic Monthly Press, 1994.

Scott, James M. *Deciding to Intervene: The Reagan Doctrine and American Foreign Policy*. Durham, N.C.: Duke University Press, 1996.

Searle, Alaric. "Was There a 'Boney' Fuller after the Second World War? Major-General J. F. C. Fuller as Military Theorist and Commentator, 1945–1966." *War in History* (July 2004): 327–57.

Secord, Richard, and Jay Wurts. *Honored and Betrayed: Irangate, Covert Affairs, and the Secret War in Laos*. New York: John Wiley and Sons, 1992.

Seierstad, Åsne. *One of Us: The Story of Anders Breivik and the Massacre in Norway*. Translated by Sarah Death. New York: Farrar, Straus, and Giroux, 2013.

Self, Robert O. *All in the Family: The Realignment of American Democracy since 1960*. New York: Hill and Wang, 2013.

Shackley, Theodore. *The Third Option: An American View of Counterinsurgency Operations*. New York: Reader's Digest Press, 1981.

Shapira, Harel. *Waiting for José: The Minutemen's Pursuit of America*. Princeton: Princeton University Press, 2013.

Shermer, Elizabeth Tandy. *Sunbelt Capitalism: Phoenix and the Transformation of American Politics*. Philadelphia: University of Pennsylvania Press, 2013.

Sherry, Michael S. "Dead or Alive: American Vengeance Goes Global." *Review of International Studies* 31 (December 2005): 245–63.

———. *In the Shadow of War: The United States since the 1930s*. New Haven: Yale University Press, 1995.

Silverstein, Ken. *Private Warriors*. London: Verso, 2000.

Simpson, Bradley R. *Economists with Guns: Authoritarian Development and U.S.-Indonesian Relations, 1960–1968*. Stanford: Stanford University Press, 2008.

Singer, P. W. *Corporate Warriors: The Rise of the Privatized Military Industry*. Ithaca: Cornell University Press, 2003.
Singh, Nikhil Pal. *Black Is a Country: Race and the Unfinished Struggle for Democracy*. Cambridge: Harvard University Press, 2004.
Singlaub, Major General John K., and Malcolm McConnell. *Hazardous Duty: An American Soldier in the Twentieth Century*. New York: Summit Books, 1991.
Sklar, Holly. *Washington's War on Nicaragua*. Boston: South End Press, 1988.
Small, Melvin. *Antiwarriors: The Vietnam War and the Battle for America's Hearts and Minds*. Lanham, Md.: Rowman and Littlefield, 2002.
Smith, Christian. *Resisting Reagan: The U.S. Central America Peace Movement*. Chicago: University of Chicago Press, 1996.
Snyder, Sarah B. *Human Rights Activism and the End of the Cold War: A Transnational History of the Helsinki Network*. Cambridge: Cambridge University Press, 2013.
Snyder, Timothy. *Bloodlands: Europe between Hitler and Stalin*. New York: Basic Books, 2010.
Stanley, William. *The Protection Racket State: Elite Politics, Military Extortion, and Civil War in El Salvador*. Philadelphia: Temple University Press, 1996.
Sterling, Claire. *The Terror Network*. New York: Holt/Readers' Digest, 1981.
Stern, Kenneth S. *Force upon the Plain: The American Militia Movement and the Politics of Hate*. New York: Simon and Schuster, 1996.
Streeter, Stephen M. *Managing the Counterrevolution: The United States and Guatemala, 1954–1961*. Athens: Ohio University Press, 2001.
Strobel, Christoph. "'We Are All Aimed and Ready': Reactionary Insurgency Movements and the Formation of Segregated States in the American South and in South Africa." *North Carolina Historical Review* 80, no. 4 (October 2003): 430–52.
Sugrue, Thomas J. *Sweet Land of Liberty: The Forgotten Struggle for Civil Rights in the North*. New York: Random House, 2008.
Suri, Jeremi. *Power and Protest: Global Revolution and the Rise of Détente*. Cambridge: Harvard University Press, 2003.
Tanner, Marcus. *Croatia: A Nation Forged in War*. New Haven: Yale University Press, 1997.
Taylor, Jay. *The Generalissimo's Son: Chiang Ching-kuo and the Revolution in China and Taiwan*. Cambridge: Harvard University Press, 2000.
Thompson, Heather Ann. "Why Mass Incarceration Matters: Rethinking Crisis, Decline, and Transformation in Postwar American History." *Journal of American History* 97 (December 2010): 703–58.
Thompson, Leonard. *A History of South Africa*. New Haven: Yale University, 2000.
Tokić, Mate Nikola. "The End of 'Historical-Ideological Bedazzlement': Cold War Politics and Émigré Croatian Separatist Violence, 1950–1980." *Social Science History* 36, no. 3 (Fall 2012): 421–45.
Trento, Joseph J. *Prelude to Terror: Edwin P. Wilson and the Legacy of America's Private Intelligence Network*. New York: Basic Books, 2006.
Tristán, Eduardo Rey. *A La Vuelta de La Esquina: La Izquierda Revolucionaria Uruguaya, 1955–1973*. Montevideo: Editorial Fin de Siglo, 2006.
Truth and Reconciliation Commission of South Africa. *Truth and Reconciliation Commission of South Africa Report*. 2 vols. London: MacMillan Reference, 1999.
Tucker, Nancy Bernkopf. *Strait Talk: United States-Taiwan Relations and the Crisis with China*. Cambridge: Harvard University Press, 2011.
Turek, Laura Frances. "'To Support a Brother in Christ': Evangelical Groups and U.S.-Guatemalan Relations during the Ríos Montt Regime." *Diplomatic History* 39, no. 4 (September 2015): 689–715.

Turner, Stansfield. *Burn before Reading: Presidents, CIA Directors, and Secret Intelligence.* New York: Hyperion, 2005.

Turse, Nick. *Kill Everything That Moves: The Real American War in Vietnam.* New York: Picador, 2013.

Tyson, Timothy B. *Radio Free Dixie: Robert F. Williams and the Roots of Black Power.* Chapel Hill: University of North Carolina Press, 1999.

Valdes, Juan Gabriel. *Pinochet's Economists: The Chicago School in Chile.* Cambridge: Cambridge University Press, 1995.

Valentine, Douglas. *The Phoenix Program.* New York: William Morrow and Company, 1990.

Van den Haag, Ernest. *The War in Katanga.* New York: American Committee to Aid Katangan Freedom Fighters, 1962.

Van Dongen, Luc, Stéphanie Roulin, and Giles Scott-Smith, eds. *Transnational Anti-Communism and the Cold War: Agents, Activities, and Networks.* New York: Palgrave MacMillan, 2014.

Varon, Jeremy. *Bringing the War Home: The Weather Underground, the Red Army Faction, and Revolutionary Violence in the Sixties and Seventies.* Berkeley: University of California Press, 2004.

Verdugo, Patricia. *Chile, Pinochet, and the Caravan of Death.* 1st English ed. Translated by Marcelo Montecino. Coral Gables, Fla.: North-South Center Press, 2001.

Villagrán Kramer, Francisco. *Biografía política de Guatemala: Los pactos políticos de 1944 a 1970.* Guatemala City: FLASCO, 1993.

Von Eschen, Penny. *Race against Empire: Black Americans and Anticolonialism, 1937–1957.* Ithaca: Cornell University Press, 1997.

Vries, Tity de. "The 1967 Central Intelligence Agency Scandal: Catalyst in a Transforming Relationship between State and People." *Journal of American History* 98, no. 4 (March 2012): 1075–92.

Wade, Wyn Craig. *The Fiery Cross: The Ku Klux Klan in America.* New York: Simon and Schuster, 1987.

Warner, Roger. *Back Fire: The CIA's Secret War in Laos and Its Link to the War in Vietnam.* New York: Simon and Schuster, 1995.

Warrick, Joby. *Black Flags: The Rise of ISIS.* New York: Anchor Books, 2016.

Webb, Gary. *Dark Alliance: The CIA, the Contras, and the Crack Cocaine Explosion.* Reprint. New York: Seven Stories Press, 2014.

Weigert, Stephen L. *Angola: A Modern Military History, 1964–2002.* New York: Palgrave Macmillan, 2011.

Weiner, Tim. *Legacy of Ashes: The History of the CIA.* New York: Anchor Books, 2008.

Westad, Odd Arne. *The Global Cold War: Third World Interventions and the Making of Our Times.* Cambridge: Cambridge University Press, 2007.

Westad, Odd Arne, and Sophie Quinn-Judge, eds. *The Third Indochina War: Conflict between China, Vietnam, and Cambodia, 1972–1979.* London: Routledge, 2006.

White, Louise. *Unpopular Sovereignty: Rhodesian Independence and African Decolonization.* Chicago: University of Chicago Press, 2015.

Wilentz, Sean. *The Age of Reagan: A History, 1974–2008.* New York: Harper, 2010.

Witte, Lude de. *The Assassination of Lumumba.* London: Verso, 2001.

Wood, Elisabeth Jean. *Insurgent Collective Action and Civil War in El Salvador.* Cambridge: Cambridge University Press, 2003.

Woods, Jeff. *Black Struggle, Red Scare: Segregation and Anti-Communism in the South, 1948–1968.* Baton Rouge: Louisiana State University Press, 2004.

Woods, Randall B. *Shadow Warrior: William Egan Colby and the CIA*. New York: Basic Books, 2013.
Woodward, Bob. *Veil: The Secret Wars of the CIA*. New York: Simon and Schuster, 1987.
Wright, Stuart A. *Patriots, Politics, and the Oklahoma City Bombing*. Cambridge: Cambridge University Press, 2007.
Wright, Thomas C. *Latin America in the Age of the Cuban Revolution*. Westport, Conn.: Praeger, 2001.
Wright, Thomas C., and Rody Oñate Zúñiga. "Chilean Political Exile." *Latin American Perspectives* 34, no. 4 (July 2007): 31–49.
Yoshihara, Mari. *Embracing the East: White Women and American Orientalism*. New York: Oxford University Press, 2003.
Young, Marilyn. *The Vietnam Wars: 1945–1990*. New York: Harper, 1991.
Zeskind, Leonard. *Blood and Politics: The History of the White Nationalist Movement from the Margins to the Mainstream*. New York: Farrar, Straus, Giroux, 2009.
Zoglin, Kate. "Paraguay's Archive of Terror: International Cooperation and Operation Condor." *Inter-American Law Review* 32, no. 1 (Winter–Spring 2001): 57–82.

## Dissertations and Theses

Bale, Jeffrey McKenzie. "The 'Black' Terrorist International: Neo-fascist Paramilitary Networks and the 'Strategy of Tension' in Italy, 1968–1974." Ph.D. diss., University of California, Berkeley, 1994.
Fronczak, Joseph. "Popular Front Movements: Antifascism and the Makings of a Global Left during the Depression." Ph.D. diss., Yale University, 2014.
Hemmer, Nicole. "Messengers of the Right: Media and the Modern Conservative Movement." Ph.D. diss., Columbia University, 2010.
Keeley, Theresa. "Reagan's Gun-Toting Nuns: Catholicism and U.S.–Central American Relations." Ph.D. diss., Northwestern University 2013.
Kelley, U.S. Army Major Danny M., II. "The Misuse of the Studies and Observation Group as a National Asset in Vietnam." Master's thesis, U.S. Army Command and General Staff College, 2005.
Levy, Johnathan. "Madison, Wilson, and Eastern European Federalism." Ph.D. diss., University of Cincinnati, 2006.
Mathiak, Lucy J. "American Jihad: The Reagan Doctrine as Policy and Practice." Ph.D. diss., University of Wisconsin, 2000.
Nguyen, Phuong. "The People of the Fall: Refugee Nationalism in Little Saigon." Ph.D. diss., University of Southern California, 2010.
Pensado, Jaime. "Political Violence and Student Culture in Mexico: The Consolidation of *Porrismo* during the 1950s and 1960s." Ph.D. diss., University of Chicago, 2008.
Vang, Her. "Dreaming of Home, Dreaming of Land: Displacements and Hmong Transnational Politics." Ph.D. diss., University of Minnesota, 2010.
Villeneuve, Hubert. "Teaching Anti-Communism: Fred C. Schwarz, the Christian Anti-Communism Crusade, and American Postwar Conservatism." Ph.D. diss., McGill University, 2011.
Wu, Wen-Cheng. "The Kuomintang and Political Development in Taiwan since 1968." Ph.D. diss., Columbia University, 1987.

# Index

Abraham Lincoln Brigade, 146
Abramoff, Jack, 185&86
Abrams, Elliot, 199
Afghanistan, 1, 4, 6, 9, 92, 122, 123, 125, 155, 160, 161, 178, 190, 196, 199, 205, 208, 210, 211, 214; Central Intelligence Agency and, 163&64, 171, 173, 174; Committee for a Free Afghanistan and, 167, 168, 171, 172; communists in, 162&63; mujahedin in, 121, 123, 157, 163&75; origins of war in, 162&63; as parable for Soviet invasion of the United States, 165, 173; Reagan administration and, 180, 181, 182, 183, 184, 187, 186; Reagan Doctrine and, 164; *Soldier of Fortune* in, 172&75; Soviet Union and, 110, 163
Afghan mujahedin, 92, 121, 123, 157, 171, 184; anticommunist international and, 1, 6, 9, 146, 149, 155, 156, 160, 161, 168–69; conflicts among, 169–70, 171; private support programs for, 167, 172–75; Saudi support for, 164, 177, 178; U.S. conservatives' fascination with, 164–66, 167, 170, 176. *See also* Afghanistan; Committee for a Free Afghanistan; McKay, Karen
Afghan National Day, 167–68
Afghan National Liberation Front, 174
African National Congress, 53, 186
Agee, Philip, 89
Aide Refugee Chinese Intellectuals (ARCI), 16–17

Alianza Republicana Nacionalista (ARENA), 73–74, 134
Allende, Salvador, 64, 66, 67, 70, 80, 81, 82, 88, 99
Alpha 66 (Cuban exile group), 34, 121, 123; Confederación Anticomunista Latinoamericana and, 74–75; Mexican Far Right and, 63. *See also* Bay of Pigs; Brigade 2506; Cuban exiles
Al Qaeda, 178
American Afghan Education Fund, 176
American Aid for Rhodesia, 112
American-Chilean Council, 79–84; finances of, 80; founding of, 79; Letelier assassination and, 82–83; views of Allende, 80–81; views of Pinochet, 81–82; violation of Foreign Agents Registration Act, 84
American China Policy Association, 15
American Committee to Aid Katangan Freedom Fighters (ACAKFF), 44–46. *See also* Tshombe, Moïse; Tshombe Emergency Committee
American Conservative Union, 95, 96, 121, 183
American Council for World Freedom (ACWF), 57–58; relationship with World Anti-Communist League, 59–62; struggles of, 58. *See also* Schlafly, Fred; World Anti-Communist League
American International Security Corporation, 210

American Security Council, 42, 43, 50, 57, 58, 77, 86, 96, 98, 120, 147, 181, 187. *See also* Fisher, John; Freedom Studies Center
Anderson, Jack, 157
Anderson, Scott and Jon Lee, 202–3
Angola, 1, 4, 9, 45, 46, 53, 101, 102, 122, 160, 123, 161, 196, 199; independence struggles of, 107–8; Movimento Popular de Libertação de Angola (MPLA in), 108, 114–15, 116, 123, 179, 180, 183, 187, 188, 207; Reagan administration and, 180, 181, 182, 183, 184, 187, 186, 188; South African Defense Force in, 185; União Nacional para a Independência Total de Angola (UNITA) in, 91, 108, 113, 116, 155, 157, 160, 179–84, 186, 187, 188, 207; U.S. mercenaries in, 111, 113–15. *See also* Savimbi, Jonas
Anti-Bolshevik Bloc of Nations (ABN), 20–24, 25–26, 27, 61–62, 76, 120, 158; Afghan mujahedin and, 169; British relationship to, 21, 23, 24; chapters of, 22; decline of, 205; ethnic policies, 22; guerilla warfare strategy, 21, 61, 122; links to Asian Peoples' Anti-Communist League, 22, 24; origins of, 20–22; publications of, 22; Singlaub and, 121, 159–60; U.S. relationship to, 23; views of Soviet Union, 22; World Anti-Communist League and, 61, 158. *See also* Stetsko, Yaroslav
Anticommunist internationalism, 2, 11, 13, 26, 27, 28, 29, 30, 43, 53, 54, 55, 56, 57, 58, 59, 61, 62, 77, 79, 83, 84, 85, 117, 126, 156, 167, 190, 195, 196, 198, 199, 200, 203, 204–5, 211; comparison to NGOs, 8; conflicts within, 7, 26–27, 54, 61–62, 158–59; conservatism and, 5–6; decline of, 205–6; guerilla warfare and, 7, 8–9; U.S. state power and, 6. *See also* Asian Peoples' Anti-Communist League; Liebman, Marvin; Singlaub, John; World Anti-Communist League; *specific guerilla movements*
Apartheid, 46, 49, 51, 78, 180, 181, 183, 185, 207. *See also* South Africa

Arbenz, Jacobo, 25, 35, 72
Argentina, 35, 56, 69, 70, 76; Confederación Anticomunista Latinoamericana and, 72, 157; guerrillas in, 66, 69, 71; military dictatorship in, 65, 66, 68; Operation Condor and, 70–72, 73, 74; training of Nicaraguan Contras by, 136–37
Armas, Castillo, 25,
Arms trafficking, 10, 119, 137, 142–43, 155–56, 160, 164, 175–76, 191, 201–2, 203, 204
Asian Peoples' Anti-Communist League (APACL), 12, 18–20, 22, 25, 27, 37–39, 41, 42; covert action and, 19; founding of, 18; guerrilla warfare in China and, 37–38; leadership of, 19; Singlaub and, 120–21; views on Vietnam War, 38–39. *See also* Ku Chen Kang
Asian Speakers Bureau, 40
Atlacatl Battalion, 132–33
Avrakatos, Gust, 176

Bacon, George, 114
Bagatsing, Ramón, 19, 37
Bandera, Stepan, 20–21, 158
Bannon, Steve, 217
Barlow, Eeben, 207–8
Bay of Pigs invasion, 32–33, 34, 35, 139, 148. *See also* Central Intelligence Agency: Cuban exiles and
"Bayou of Pigs" invasion, 152
Beam, Louis, 151–52
Bermudez, Enrique, 140, 145
Bin Laden, Osama, 178
Binstock, Susana, 71
Black, Cofer, 209
Black Power, 52
Blackwater, 208–9, 210
Boland Amendment, 139, 143, 147
Bolivia, 65, 66, 69, 148; Operation Condor and, 70
Bonner, Bart, 106–7, 114. *See also* Veterans and Volunteers for Vietnam
Bosch, Orlando, 34, 261n153. *See also* Cuban exiles; Insurrectional Movement for the Recovery of the Revolution

Braden, Spruille, 35
Branch Davidians, 213
Brazil, 25, 57, 65, 66, 160; military dictatorship in, 68; Operation Condor and, 70, 71, 72
Breivik, Anders, 216
Brigade 2506, 32. *See also* Alpha 66; Bay of Pigs invasion; Cuban exiles
British Guiana, 57
British Union of Fascists, 23. *See also* Mosley, Oswald
Brown, Robert K., 108; in Afghanistan, 172–75, 178; domestic paramilitary culture and, 150–51; in El Salvador, 130–34; founding of *Soldier of Fortune*, 108; in Laos, 195; in Nicaragua, 118, 144–45; private military training programs of, 118–19, 132–34, 144–45, 173–75; relationship to Singlaub, 118–19, 130, 144, 149–50; in Rhodesia, 108–9; Vietnam War experience, 108. *See also* Singlaub, John; *Soldier of Fortune*
Brzezinski, Zbigniew, 163
Buchanan, Patrick, 91, 95
Buckley, James L., 104
Buckley, William F., 2, 29, 30, 31, 32, 34–35, 36, 37, 40, 41, 47, 60; American-Chilean Council and, 79; Blackford Oakes novels of, 105–6; early life of, 30; and *National Review*, 30
Buendía, Manuel, 157
Bufkin, David, 114–15
Burnham, James, 30
Bush, George H. W., 209

Calero, Adolfo, 140
Cambodia, 4, 37, 125, 155, 160, 161, 196, 199; Khmer Peoples' National Liberation Front (KPNLF) in, 157, 189, 190, 191; origins of Third Indochina War and, 189; private military support for rebels in, 191; *Soldier of Fortune* and, 191
Camper, Frank, 151, 152
Campiglia, Horacio, 71
Campos Alum, Antonio, 65, 72

Carriles, Luis Posada, 148
Carter, Jimmy, 3, 62, 73, 79, 86, 89, 96, 102, 117, 120, 163; clashes with Singlaub, 95
Carter administration, 95, 98, 99, 123, 127, 139, 164; Central Intelligence Agency and, 90–92; foreign policy of, 62, 89; human rights and, 69
Carto, Willis, 77, 194
Casey, William J., 124, 183, 190, 197, 198; Afghan mujahedin and, 164, 168; Nicaraguan Contras and, 137; Reagan Doctrine and, 125; relationship with Singlaub, 124–25, 126, 140; views on guerrilla warfare, 124–25
Castro, Fidel, 2, 28, 29, 31–32, 33, 34, 35, 36, 74, 75, 88, 105, 123; support for Latin American revolutionaries, 66
Catholic Church: anticommunism and, 24, 30, 38, 39, 50, 55, 56, 63, 147, 201, Liberation Theology and, 67, 68
Center for Strategic and International Studies, 50, 162
Central Intelligence Agency, 3, 4, 7, 17, 20, 21, 24, 27, 32, 34; in Afghanistan, 163–64, 166, 170, 171, 172; in Angola, 108, 180, 183; Anti-Bolshevik Bloc of Nations and, 21, 24; Asian Peoples' Anticommunist League and, 18, 20; and Bay of Pigs invasion, 32; in Cambodia, 88; in China, 38; Church Committee and, 88–89; clashes with Carter administration and Stansfield Turner, 90–92; in the Congo, 44, 46; conspiracy theories about, 88; Cuban exiles and, 32–33, 34; in El Salvador, 129; in Guatemala, 72; in Laos, 88; mass firings of agents in, 90–92; in Nicaragua, 137, 140, 143; in Paraguay, 65; Operation Condor and, 70–71; Reagan Doctrine and, 125; in Vietnam War, 93
Channell, Carl "Spitz," 148, 201
Chile, 56, 65; assassination of Orlando Letelier, 82; free-market revolution of, 81; military dictatorship in, 66–67, 68, 79; U.S. conservatives' support for, 80–84. *See also* American-Chilean

Council; Confederación Anticomunista Latinoamericana; Operation Condor; Pinochet, Augusto

China (Peoples' Republic of China), 13, 15, 17, 18, 30, 37, 39, 59, 60, 61; American visions of, 14. *See also* Taiwan (Republic of China)

China Lobby, 15. *See also* American China Policy Association; Committee of One Million; Kohlberg, Alfred; Liebman, Marvin

Christian Anti-Communist Crusade, 57, 58. *See also* Schwarz, Fred

Christic Institute, 203–4

Church, Frank, 87–89

Church Committee, 87–89, 91–92, 96, 103, 106, 108, 136, 163. *See also* Church, Frank

Citizens' Legal Defense Fund for the FBI, 104–5

Civilian Military Assistance, 152–53, 185

Civil rights movement, 5, 6, 29, 36, 43, 51, 97, 104, 109

Clark Amendment, 108, 123, 180, 183, 186

Clarridge, Duane "Dewey," 209–10

Cline, Ray, 162

Clines, Tom, 101

Close, Robert, 159

Coey, John, 113

COINTELPRO (FBI Counter Intelligence Program), 104–5

Colby, William, 43, 87, 89, 108

Colombia, 36, 149

Committee for a Free Afghanistan, 167; Afghan mujahedin and, 167, 168, 171, 172, 177. *See also* Afghanistan; Afghan mujahedin; McKay, Karen

Committee for a Free Asia, 17

Committee for the Monroe Doctrine, 36

Committee of One Million, 17–18, 26, 58

Confederación Anticomunista Latinoamericana, 157–58, 159; Cuban exiles and, 74–75; in El Salvador, 73–74; founding of, 64–65; in Guatemala, 72–73; Operation Condor and, 68, 71–72; in Paraguay, 65; second conference of, 66–67; view of Pinochet's Chile, 68

Congo, the, 28, 29, 43–48

Consejo Chileno de Norte America (CCNA), 80, 84

Conservatism, 4–5; anticommunist revolution and, 8–9; international dimensions of, 5–6; in Latin America, 65–66; origins of U.S. movement, 28–29. *See also* Buckley, William F.; Goldwater, Barry; Liebman, Marvin; Manion, Clarence; Reagan, Ronald

Conservative Caucus, 121, 129, 181

Conservative Political Action Conference, 160, 183

Contreras, Manuel, 70, 82–83. *See also* Dirección Inteligencia Nacional

Coordination of United Revolutionary Organizations (CORU), 75

Coors, Joseph, 141, 162

Council on American Affairs, 77

Covenant, Sword, and the Arm of the Lord, The, 213

Crile, George, 171

Croatia, 216

Croatian Liberation Movement (*Hrvatski oslobodilački pokret*, HOP), 76–77

Cuba, 31–35, 53, 125, 137; support for kindred forces in Central America, 127; support for MPLA in Angola, 108, 114, 116, 179, 180

Cuban exiles, 31–34, 114, 123, 134, 137, 139, 148, 160; Confederación Anticomunista-Latinoamericana and, 74–75. *See also* Alpha 66; Bay of Pigs invasion; Brigade 2506

Cuban Revolution, 28, 31

Cuellar, Adolfo, 158

Damjanovic, Jozo, 77. *See also* Croatian Liberation Movement

D'Aubuisson, Roberto, 132, 158; founding of ARENA, 73; as death squad commander, 73–74, 127, 134, 135; work with Confederación Anticomunista Latinoamericana

and World Anti-Communist League, 74. *See also* Alianza Republicana Nacionalista
Dávila, Jerry, 69
Death squads, 35, 68, 69, 73, 74, 88, 98, 99, 127, 128, 132, 134, 135, 136, 137, 157, 158, 159, 202
De Jaegher, Raymond, 39–40, 56
Democratic International, 155, 184–86
Denard, Bob, 110
Détente, 54, 60–61, 62, 69, 73, 78, 81, 89, 96, 117, 120
Diem Ngo Dinh, 12, 38, 39, 88
Dirección Inteligencia Nacional (DINA), 70, 75, 76, 82–83
Dominica, 152
Domino Theory, 18
Donovan, John, 131
Drug smuggling, 203, 310n34
Duarte, José Napoleon, 127
Duke, David, 194
Dulles, Allen, 105
Dulles, John Foster, 24
DynCorp, 208

Eastwood, Clint, 194
Echanis, Mike, 139
Edwards, Lee, 56
Eiva, Andrew, 176. *See also* American Afghan Education Fund
Egypt, 100–101, 173
Egyptian-American Transportation and Services Company (EATSCO), 101
Eisenhower, Dwight D., 23, 24, 31
Eisenhower administration, 14, 15, 20, 23, 24, 31, 32, 44, 102
El Mozote massacre, 132. *See also* Atlacatl Battalion
El Salvador, 9, 25, 36, 65, 72, 98, 117, 118, 123, 157, 161, 173, 197; death squads in, 73–74, 127, 135; exiles from, 134; failure of state security services in, 129; human rights in, 128, 132; origins of civil war, 127–28; support for Reagan in, 128; U.S. paramilitary missions in, 130–34
Ethiopia, 1, 4, 101, 161, 201

Ethnic Liberation Organization of Laos, 160, 184, 191, 304n214. *See also* Laos
Executive Outcomes, 207–8

Fascism, 21, 23, 25, 31, 60, 62, 63, 67, 78, 121, 143, 159, 202, 215; in Latin America, 69. *See also* Nazi Germany; Neo-Nazis
Federación Mexicana Anticomunista, 62–63; World Anti-Communist League and, 64
Federal Bureau of Investigation (FBI), 43, 65, 71, 75, 91, 97, 98, 103, 104, 116, 134, 152, 213
Fellers, Bonner, 39–40
Fisher, John M., 43, 57, 181
Ford, Gerald, 3, 62, 87, 88
Ford administration, 75, 124; Angola and, 108, 114; Central Intelligence Agency and, 87–88, 108; Pinochet's Chile and, 79, 81
Foreign Agents Registration Act, 10, 84, 232n26
Freedom Corps, 41–42
Freedom Research Council, 185
Freedom Studies Center (American Security Council), 42–43
Free-market policies. *See* Neoliberalism
Free Pacific Association, 39. *See also* De Jaegher, Raymond
Frente Farabundo Martí Liberación Nacional (FMLN), 127, 135, 154. *See also* El Salvador
Frente Nacional de Libertação de Angola (FNLA), 108, 113, 116, 123. *See also* Angola
Friedman, Milton, 81
Friends of Rhodesian Independence (FORI), 49–50
Fuerza Democrática Nicaragüense (FDN), 118, 138, 144–45, 184; Singlaub and, 140. *See also* Nicaraguan Contras
Fuller, John Frederick Charles, 23

Gailani, Pir Sayyid Ahmed, 170–71, 173. *See also* National Islamic Front of Afghanistan

Garwood, Ellen, 141, 148
Gearhart, Daniel, 114–15
Germany. *See* East Germany; Nazi Germany; West Germany
Gibson, James William, 134, 151
Goldwater, Barry, 28–29, 31, 95, 153
Graham, Daniel O., 96; relationship to Singlaub, 96, 98, 121, 129; Strategic Defense Initiative and, 121
Gritz, James "Bo," 193–95, 203. *See also* POW/MIAs, Vietnam War
Guatemala, 24, 25, 29, 32, 35–36, 65, 101, 118, 128, 144, 157; Singlaub in, 98–99, 129; Movimiento Liberación Nacional in, 72–74, 121. *See also* Sandoval Alarcón, Mario
Guatemalan Freedom Foundation, 98
Guerrero, Raimundo, 62–63; founding of Confederación Anticomunista Latinoamericana and, 64–65. *See also* Federación Mexicana Anticomunista
Guerrilla warfare: anticommunism and, 1–2, 8, 156; gendered dimensions of, 10; leftist guerillas in Africa, 107–8; leftist guerrillas in Latin America, 66, 68, 69, 71, 72, 98, 127, 135, 136–37, 150, 154; leftist guerrillas in United States, 52, 97, 104–5; theories of, 23, 24, 33, 37, 39–40, 61, 75, 86, 92–94, 96–97, 101–3, 121–22, 129, 160–62, 167, 185, 214
Guevara, Ernesto "Che," 105, 122, 148, 181
Gulf Oil, 188
Gunrunners. *See* Arms trafficking
Guomindang, 13–15, 17, 19, 38, 56, 59, 73, 93

Hall, Sam, 153
Hampton, Fred, 104
Hargis, Billy James, 91
Harrigan, Anthony, 50
Hasenfus, Eugene, 197, 201
Hekmatyar, Gulbuddin, 170, 176, 298n107
Helms, Jesse, 60; Confederación Anticomunista Latinoamericana and, 77–78
Helms, Richard, 105

Heritage Foundation, 77, 158, 162, 176, 181, 185
Hezbollah, 125
Hoare, "Mad" Mike, 45–46, 110, 148
Ho Chi Minh, 38, 40, 93, 181
Ho Chi Minh Trail, 58, 93, 94, 143
Honduras, 25, 101; Civilian Military Assistance in, 152; Nicaraguan Contras and, 136, 137, 138, 147, 152; Singlaub and, 118, 140, 143, 144; *Soldier of Fortune* and, 118, 144
House Un-American Activities Committee, 43, 91, 97
Human rights, 8, 69, 70, 73, 79, 81, 82, 89, 90, 98, 99, 115, 126, 128, 135, 169, 182, 207
Humphrey, Gordon, 176
Hungarian Revolution, 13, 24, 32, 37
Hunt, E. Howard, 25, 30, 105
Hunt, Nelson Bunker, 141, 148
Huston, Tom Charles, 41–43
Huston Plan, 43

Insurrectional Movement for the Recovery of the Revolution, 34. *See also* Alpha 66; Bosch, Orlando; Brigade 2506; Cuban exiles
Inter-American Confederation for the Defense of the Continent (IACDC), 25. *See also* Prieto Laurens, Jorge
Inter-American Literacy Foundation, 36
International Freedom Foundation, 185–86
Inter-Services Intelligence (Pakistan), 164, 171, 175, 177
Iran, 100, 163, 178, 197
Iran-Contra scandal, 4, 196, 197–200; Singlaub in, 200–202, 204
Iraq, 208, 209, 210, 211
Irish Republican Army, 125
Islamic State, 211

Jamba, Angola, 184, 187; anticommunist conference in, 155, 184–86. *See also* Democratic International; Savimbi, Jonas; União Nacional para a Independência Total de Angola

Japan, 60, 169, 253n37
Jianrg Jieshi, 13–15, 17, 19, 23, 37, 58, 93, 120; founding of Asian Peoples' Anti-Communist League, 18
John Birch Society, 35, 40, 50, 78, 97
Johnson administration, 34, 38, 46, 75
Judd, Walter, 17, 18, 23, 41, 55, 57
Junta Coordinadora Revolucionaria (JCR), 69

Karen National Liberation Army, 123
Katanga, 44–47
Kearney, James, 104–5
Kennedy, John F., 31, 35, 105
Kennedy administration, 32, 35, 44, 75, 102
Khmer Peoples' National Liberation Front (KPNLF), 157, 160, 189, 190–91
Khmer Rouge, 189
Kilpatrick, James, 50
Kirkpatrick, Jeanne, 180, 181
Kissinger, Henry, 78, 79, 81, 88, 108
Koen, Albert, 121
Kohlberg, Alfred, 15
Kokalis, Peter, 131, 133
Kokusai Shokyo Rengo (International Federation for Victory over Communism), 59
Ku Chen Kang, 19, 120, 121
Ku Klux Klan, 52, 53, 78, 104, 151, 152, 194, 215
Kutner, Luis, 47, 115

Lamprecht, Nick, 109, 110
Lansdale, Edward, 19, 43, 135
Laos, 37, 55, 160, 161, 196, 199; anticommunist guerrillas in, 190, 191, 192–93, 195; Central Intelligence Agency in, 190; origins of Third Indochina War and, 189; *Soldier of Fortune* in, 195
Lao United Liberation Front, 195
LaPierre, Wayne, 214
La Técnica (Paraguay), 65
Leaderless resistance, 151
Lebanon, 150, 194, 197, 198
Lehman, Christopher, 183

Lehrman, Lewis, 184
Le Pen, Marine, 216
Letelier, Orlando, 82–83
Liberty Lobby, 50, 77, 113, 194
Liebman, Marvin, 2, 15–18, 199, 205; Aide Refugee Chinese Intellectuals and, 16; American-Chilean Council and, 79–84; American Committee to Aid Katangan Freedom Fighters and, 44–46; Asian Peoples' Anti-Communist League and, 12–13, 18, 55; Association of Former Intelligence Officers and, 103–4; Central Intelligence Agency and, 17; Committee of One Million and, 17–18; conversion to anticommunism, 16; Friends of Rhodesian Independence and, 49–50; relationship with Walter Judd, 17–18, 55; relationship with William F. Buckley, 30; Tshombe Emergency Committee and, 47–48; World Anti-Communist Congress for Freedom and Liberation and, 25–27, 42; World Anti-Communist League and, 55, 62; Young Americans for Freedom and, 41–42
Luce, Claire Booth, 104
Lumumba, Patrice, 44
Lundgren, Dolph, 186
Lyons, Daniel, 39–40, 50, 55, 56

Malcolm X, 52
Manafort, Paul, 183, 216
Manion, Clarence, 2, 28, 30–31, 32, 34–37; Cuban exiles and, 32, 34; *Manion Forum*, 31, 36; South Africa and Rhodesia and, 50
Manion, Marilyn, 35
*Manion Forum of Opinion*, 31, 36, 40, 50
Manrara, Luis V., 33–34, 50. *See also* Truth about Cuba Committee
Masculinity, 4, 10, 92, 94, 95, 105–6, 109, 123, 133, 139, 165, 182, 194, 201
Massoud, Ahmed Shah, 170, 298n115
Mataxis, Theodore, 167, 168, 177. *See also* Committee for a Free Afghanistan; McKay, Karen
McColl, Alex, 131, 132

Index | **345**

McDonald, Larry, 82; Western Goals and, 97–98
McFarlane, Robert C. "Bud," 134
McKay, Karen, 167–68, 169, 171, 172, 176; Jamba conference and, 304n213; relationship with Reagan administration, 168; travels to Afghanistan, 168. *See also* Committee for a Free Afghanistan
McNamara, Francis, 91
McVeigh, Timothy, 213–14
Mercenaries: in Angola, 113–14; in the Congo, 45–46; in Europe, 23; fantasies about, 134, 150, 151, 153; in Nicaragua, 139, 144–45; in Rhodesia, 108–13; U.S. investigations of, 114–15
Messing, Andy, 121, 129
Mexico, 25, 26, 30, 34, 35, 36, 57, 62–63, 64, 65, 66, 78, 128. *See also* Federación Mexicana Anticomunista
Military Professional Resources Incorporated, 208
Militia movement, United States, 4, 212–15; origins of, 151–52
Milliken, Roger, 98
*Missing in Action* films, 156, 194
Mobutu, Joseph, 44, 45, 46, 48, 187
Mojaddedi, Sibghatullah, 174. *See also* Afghan National Liberation Front
Montoneros, 72
Moore, Roger, 110
Moorer, Thomas, 121
Moser, Charles, 167, 305n225
Mosley, Sir Oswald, 23. *See also* British Union of Fascists
Movimiento Liberación Nacional (MLN), 72–74, 121
Movimento Popular de Libertação de Angola (MPLA), 108, 114–15, 116, 123, 179, 180, 183, 187, 188, 207. *See also* Angola
Mozambique, 53, 155, 161, 184, 214
Mugabe, Robert, 116, 178

National Committee for the Liberation of China, 40
National Islamic Front of Afghanistan, 170

National Liberation Front (Vietnam), 38, 40, 64
National Rifle Association, 214
Nazi Germany, 21, 22, 61, 63, 159; fugitives in Latin America, 69, 76
Neoliberalism, 4, 5, 6, 66, 69, 72, 74, 81, 83, 138, 179, 188, 205, 206
Neo-Nazis, 60, 78, 151, 152, 158, 159, 213, 215–16
Neutrality Act, 10
New World Order conspiracy theory, 215
Nguyen Cao Ky, 121, 192
Nicaragua, 4, 29, 35–36, 117, 122, 125, 155, 161, 166, 173, 190, 196, 197, 205; Anastasio Somoza Debayle in, 126; Carter administration and, 127; Luis Somoza Debayle in, 35, 126; *Manion Forum* and, 35–36; Reagan administration and, 127, 137, 138, 139, 140, 142, 145, 146, 147, 149, 152, 153; Sandinistas in, 126–27
Nicaraguan Contras, 118–19, 171, 172, 177, 184, 210; composition of, 137; goals of, 138; origins of, 136–38; outside business support for, 141–42; relationship with Singlaub, 140–44; *Soldier of Fortune* and, 144–45; U.S. congressional and popular antipathy toward, 138–39; U.S. humanitarian aid for, 146–47; U.S. mercenaries and, 144–45, 152–53. *See also* Boland Amendment; Fuerza Democrática Nicaragüense
Nidal, Abu, 125, 158
Nixon, Richard, 39, 43, 51, 57, 58, 59, 62, 78, 87; conflict with U.S. conservatives and anticommunist internationalists, 60–61
Nixon administration, 43, 58, 60, 75, 124
Non-governmental organizations (NGOs), 8
Norris, Chuck, 194
North, Oliver, 147, 153, 158; conflicts with Singlaub, 148–49, 198, 201
Iran-Contra and, 147–48, 197, 198–99

Oath Keepers, 215
Office of Strategic Services (OSS), 90, 92, 93, 103, 124, 149, 210

Oklahoma City bombing, 213–14
Operation Condor, 68, 70–72, 74–76, 81, 84–85, 158; assassination plots of, 70–71, 82–83; Confederación Anticomunista Latinoamericana and, 71–72; disappearances and, 71; expansion into Central America, 72–74, 130; expansion into Europe, 75–76; links to Croatian anticommunist groups, 76–77; links to Cuban anticommunist groups, 74–75; links to U.S. conservatives, 79, 82, 85; origins of, 68, 70. *See also* American-Chilean Council; Argentina; Chile; Paraguay
Order, The, 213
O'Reilly, Bill, 211–12
Organization of Solidarity with the People of Asia, Africa, and Latin America (Tri-Continental Conference), 64, 155
Organization of Ukrainian Nationalists (OUN), 20–21
Owen, Robert, 199

Pakistan, 17, 18; Afghan mujahedin and, 163, 164, 168, 171, 174, 177. *See also* Inter-Services Intelligence
Palestine Liberation Organization, 125
Paraguay, 55, 56, 65, 66, 77; military dictatorship in, 68; Operation Condor and, 70
Park Chung Hee, 55
Pastora, Eden, 140, 147
Pathet Lao, 99, 189, 193
Patton, George S., III., 98, 121
Pearson, Roger, 77–78, 121. *See also* Council on American Affairs
Penna Botto, Carlos, 25
Philippines, 18–20, 40, 59, 160; Asian Peoples' Anticommunist League and, 18–20; Edward Lansdale in, 20; Huks in, 20; Singlaub in, 197
Philips, Howard, 121, 181, 182
Pierce, Michael, 113
Pierce, William (pen name Andrew MacDonald), 78, 113, 116, 151, 213–14, 215
Pinochet, Augusto, 66, 67–68, 70, 75, 79, 80–84

Posey, Tom, 152–53. *See also* Civilian Military Assistance
POW/MIAs, Vietnam War, 193–95. *See also* Gritz, James "Bo"
Prats, Carlos, 70
Prieto Laurens, Jorge, 25, 26
Prince, Erik, 208–9. *See also* Blackwater
Private military firms (PMFs), 4, 11, 206; Cold War origins of, 117, 119, 130, 136, 143, 144, 146, 156–57, 160, 189, 206, 211; explanations for, 210–11; purported benefits of, 207; relationship to Iran-Contra, 209–10; relationship to states, 207–8, 209, 210. *See also* American International Security Corporation; Blackwater; DynCorp; Prince, Erik; Executive Outcomes; Military Professional Resources Incorporated

Race, 9, 25, 180, 182; apartheid and, 49; the Congo and, 48; Guatemalan Right and, 72; in southern Africa, 50–53; U.S. Right and, 9, 58, 52–53, 77, 116–17, 152, 194, 215–16; Vietnam War and, 40. *See also* White supremacy
*Rambo* films, 156, 194
Reagan, Ronald, 168, 179, 181; Afghan mujahedin and, 166, 177; Iran-Contra scandal and, 197–98; Jonas Savimbi and, 184, 187; Nicaraguan Contras and, 138; presidential campaign of, 117, 120; relationship with Singlaub, 120, 146; Sandinistas and, 127
Reagan administration, 1, 101, 119, 120, 121, 126; Afghanistan and, 163–64, 171, 173, 174; Angola and, 180, 181, 182, 183, 184, 187, 186, 188; Cambodia and, 190; El Salvador and, 126, 128–29, 132; Iran-Contra scandal and, 198–99, 200; Laos and, 190, 191; Nicaragua and, 127, 137, 138, 139, 140, 142, 145, 146, 147, 149, 152, 153; POW/MIAs and, 195; Singlaub and, 120, 124, 128; Vietnam and, 190, 192. *See also* Reagan Doctrine; Reagan, Ronald

Reagan Doctrine, 4, 125–26, 156, 160–62, 186, 190; as symbolism and public theater, 126, 187, 190; legacies of, 209, 211, 212
Red Army Faction (Germany), 75, 125
Red Brigades (Italy), 156
*Red Dawn*, 165
*Red Scorpion*, 186
Revolutionary United Front, 207
Rhodesia, 29; British mercenaries in, 111–12; as decolonization story, 48, demographics of, 48; in film, 110; *Soldier of Fortune* and, 109–10, 113, 115; U.S. conservatives and, 49–53; U.S. mercenaries in, 109–11, 112–13; war in, 107, 109–10; white supremacy and, 48–49, 50–51, 109
Robin, Corey, 6
Rodriguez, Felix, 148
Rodriguez, Rafael, 64, 75, 160
Romero, Oscar, 74, 127
Rusher, William, 30, 41, 57; on Chile, 81–82

Sanchez, Nestor, 129–30, 131
Sandinistas (FSLN), 126–28, 139, 140, 141, 143, 144, 145, 147, 153, 154, 197, 206; Carter administration and, 127; Reagan administration and, 136–38
Sandoval Alarcón, Mario, 72–74. *See also* Movimiento Liberación Nacional
Saudi Arabia, 177, 178, 183; financial support for World Anti-Communist League, 62
Savimbi, Jonas, 9, 155, 179–80, 184–86, 187; imagined bonds with Nicaraguan Contras and Afghan mujahedin, 181; Paul Manafort and, 183; physicality of, 182; South Africa and, 180, 181–82, 183; U.S. conservatives support for, 179–80, 181, 182, 183, 187–88; U.S. military aid to, 187–88. *See also* União Nacional para a Independência Total de Angola
Schlafly, Fred, 59–60; split with World Anti-Communist League, 60–62, 77. *See also* World Anti-Communist League
Schultz, George, 126

Schwarz, Fred, 57. *See also* Christian Anti-Communist Crusade
Secord, Richard, 147, 148, 149, 201, 203
Shackley, Theodore "Ted," 99–100; connections to Edwin Wilson, 100; Iran-Contra and, 147, 148, 203, 204; private sector work of, 101; views on anticommunist guerilla warfare, 101–3
Shatner, William, 194
Sierra Leone, 207
Singlaub, John, 1–2, 3, 9, 92, 117, 118–19, 124–26, 153, 154; Afghanistan and, 171, 172, 178; American Security Council and, 86, 96–97, 98; Angola and, 188; Anti-Bolshevik Bloc of Nations and, 121, 160; arms trafficking of, 142–43; Carter administration and, 95–97; Christic lawsuit against, 203–4; conservative movement and, 96, 120, 121; conspiracy theories about, 203–4; El Salvador and, 127, 128, 129–30, 135–36; Iran-Contra and, 147–48, 197–98, 202–4; Nicaragua and, 118, 139–44; POW/MIAs and, 194; Reagan Doctrine and, 125–26, 160–62; relationship with Adolfo Calero, 142; relationship with Oliver North, 148–49, 198, 201; relationship with Reagan administration, 124, 135–36, 140, 146; relationship with Robert K. Brown, 118–19, 130, 149–50; relationship with Ronald Reagan, 120; relationship with William Casey, 124–25, 140; Second World War service of, 92–93; Studies and Observation Group and, 93; United States Council for World Freedom and, 121, 146, 165, 181, 202; views on guerilla warfare and covert action, 86, 92–94, 96–97, 121–22, 129, 156, 160–62; views on Salvadoran death squads, 135; views on Vietnam Syndrome, 123, 129; Vietnam War service of, 93–94; Western Goals and, 97–98; World Anti-Communist League and, 1–2, 121, 123, 146, 155–56, 158–60, 171. *See also* Brown, Robert K.; Iran-Contra scandal; Nicaraguan

Contras; North, Oliver; *Soldier of Fortune*; Vietnam War; United States Council for World Freedom; and World Anti-Communist League

Smith, Ian, 49, 109, 112, 116

*Soldier of Fortune* magazine, 126, 139, 161, 180; as ad-hoc labor market, 109; Afghan mujahedin and, 165, 170, 172–75; conventions of, 150, 161, 173; founding of, 108–9; Jonas Savimbi and UNITA and, 182; Khmer Peoples' National Liberation Front and, 191; mercenaries in Angola and, 113–15; mercenaries in Rhodesia and, 109–11, 113, 115; Nicaraguan Contras and, 144–45; paramilitary culture and, 150–51, 152; POW/MIAs in Laos and, 195; as private military firm, 130–31, 144–45, 206; Salvadoran security services and, 131–33

Somoza Debayle, Anastasio, 72, 80, 138, 139, 140, 214; war against Sandinistas and collapse of regime, 126

Somoza Debayle, Luis, 35–37

Son Sann, 190

South Africa, 57, 78, 108, 143, 153; and Angola, 179, 180, 181, 182, 183, 184, 185–86; Executive Outcomes in, 207–8; Rhodesia and, 49–51, 111, 130; U.S. conservative movement and, 49, 51, 52

South African Defense Force, 186, 207

Southeast Asia Treaty Organization, 20

Southern Air Transport, 147

Southern Cone military dictatorships, 68–70; views of United States, 69–70. *See also* Confederación Anticomunista Latinoamericana; Operation Condor

South Korea, 19–20, 56, 59

South Vietnam, 12, 19, 38, 40–42, 55, 58, 59, 60, 69, 88, 59, 93–94, 106–7, 121

Soviet Union, 2, 3, 4, 9, 13, 18, 25, 26, 31, 116; Afghanistan and, 162–64, 167; collapse of, 4, 156, 200; the Congo and, 44; and Cuba, 32; détente with, 60, 61; Eastern Europe and, 21–22; El Salvador and, 127, 128; exile views of, 16; fears of Soviet espionage, 104, 124; fears of Soviet global expansion, 66, 120; fears of Soviet-sponsored racial subversion in United States, 52; global anticommunist guerrilla warfare against, 30, 61, 102, 122, 161, 184–85; Latin America's Southern Cone and, 69; Nicaragua and, 156, 157; southern Africa and, 53

Spencer, Richard, 216

Stallone, Sylvester, 194

Sterling, Claire: *The Terror Network*, 125

Stetsko, Yaroslav, 20–24, 26, 61–61; collaboration with Nazis, 21; ethnic views of, 22; guerrilla strategy of, 61, 122–23; travels of, 22–23

Strategic Defense Initiative, 121

Stroessner, Alfredo, 55, 65, 77, 226

Student protest, 36, 42, 87

Studies and Observation Group (Special Operations Group), 108, 114, 130, 131; Singlaub and, 93

Suarez Mason, Guillermo, 72

Taiwan (Republic of China), 13–17, 19, 37–39, 41, 42, 56, 57, 59, 160, 190; arms sales to Nicaraguan Contras, 142; China Lobby and, 15; Guomindang rule in, 13–14; links to Far Right in Central America, 73–74; U.S. relations with, 14–15, 120. *See also* Asian People's Anticommunist League; China Lobby; Jiang Jieshi; World Anti-Communist League

Tambs, Lewis, 199

Tecos (Mexico). *See* Federación Mexicana Anticomunista

Third Indochina War, 189

Thurmond, Strom, 60

Townley, Michael, 70, 76, 82

Truman, Harry S., 95, 103

Truman administration, 14, 15, 102

Trump, Donald J., 216

Truth about Cuba Committee, 33–34

Tshombe, Moïse, 29, 44–48; capture and execution, 46–47; execution of

Patrice Lumumba, 44; in exile, 46–47; U.S. conservatives and, 44; use of mercenaries, 45
Tshombe Emergency Committee, 46–47
Tupamaros, 72
Turner, Stansfield, 96, 102, 124, 166; Central Intelligence Agency and, 89–90; clashes with Ted Shackley, 100–101
*Turner Diaries*, 116, 151, 213, 214, 215. *See also* Pierce, William

Ukrainian Insurgent Army (UIA), 21, 122
União Nacional para a Independência Total de Angola (UNITA), 91, 108, 113, 116, 155, 157, 160, 179–84, 186, 187, 188, 207. *See also* Angola
Union Minière du Haut Katanga, 44
United Fruit Company, 35
United Nations (UN), 17, 44, 45, 46, 47, 49, 51, 80, 115, 180, 208
United States Council for World Freedom (USCWF), 146, 165, 181; founding of, 121; investigations of, 202
U.S. Department of Defense (Pentagon), 23, 71, 94, 124, 130, 131, 135, 168, 186, 209, 210
U.S. Department of State, 15, 17, 20, 23, 45, 65, 78, 103, 128, 134, 146, 168, 174, 187, 196, 202
Universidad Autónoma de Guadalajara, 62, 63
Uruguay, 69, 150; Confederación Anticomunista Latinoamericana and, 72; military dictatorship in, 68; Operation Condor and, 70, 71, 77

Van den Haag, Ernest, 46
Veterans and Volunteers for Vietnam, 106–7, 114
Vietnam, 161, 193–94; anticommunist guerrillas in, 192, 196; Third Indochina War and, 189–90. *See also* POWs/MIAs; South Vietnam; Vietnamese exiles; Vietnam War
Vietnamese exiles, 192

Vietnam Syndrome, 123, 129
Vietnam War, 3, 28, 38–41, 57–58; Central Intelligence Agency and, 93, 99; origins of, 38; protest movements against, 40, 42, 87; Robert K. Brown in, 108; Singlaub in, 93; Studies and Observation Group (SOG) in, 93. *See also* Vietnam Syndrome; Vietnam War veterans
Vietnam War veterans, 10, 106, 108–14, 118, 121, 130, 139, 144, 150, 151
Viguerie, Richard, 59, 196
Volunteer Freedom Corps, 23

Walker, William, 140
Walsh, Lawrence, 200
Walt, Lewis, 91, 121
Watergate, 62, 69, 87, 91, 96, 105, 106, 150, 181
Weaver, Randy, 213
Weinberger, Caspar, 168
WerBell, Mitchell IV, 149
Western Goals, 97–98
West Germany, 21, 22, 75–77, 111, 153, 160
Weyrich, Paul, 162, 176, 185. *See also* Eiva, Andrew; McKay, Karen
Wheeler, Jack, 184, 185, 188
White flight in Rhodesia, 48
White supremacy, 6, 29, 77, 78, 107; in Rhodesia and South Africa, 45–53, 107, 116, 180, 182; as a trans-Atlantic movement, 215–16; in the United States, 116, 121, 152, 194
Wilders, Geert, 216
*Wild Geese, The,* 110
Williams, L. H. "Mike," 113
Williams, Robert F., 53
Wills, Garry, 214
Wilson, Charlie, 164, 176
Wilson, Edwin, 144,
World Anti-Communist Congress for Freedom and Liberation, 25–27, 42
World Anti-Communist League (WACL), 1–2, 54, 55, 59, 78–79, 91, 120, 121, 171, 180, 190, 202; American Council for World Freedom and, 57–62; decline of, 205; founding, 55–56; Fred Schlafly as chair-

man of, 59; Iran-Contra scandal and, 202–3; Ku Chen Kang as chairman of, 19, 120; Singlaub and, 121, 146, 146, 155–56, 158–60, 171, 203; United States Council for World Freedom and, 121, 146, 165, 181, 121. *See also* Asian Peoples' Anticommunist League (APACL); Confederación Anticomunista Latinoamericana

World Youth Crusade for Freedom, 41–42

Ydígoras Fuentes, Miguel, 25, 35–37; on *Manion Forum*, 35–36

Yergan, Max, 45

Young Americans for Freedom (YAF), 56: origins and links to conservative movement, 41; World Youth Crusade for Freedom, 41–42

Yugoslavia, 76–77, 206, 216

Zimbabwe. *See* Rhodesia

Zimbabwe African National Union (ZANU), 107, 112, 116

Zimbabwe African Peoples' Union (ZAPU), 107, 112, 116